# PERSONALITY

## Determinants, Dynamics, and Potentials

*Personality: Determinants, Dynamics, and Potentials* is a comprehensive survey of contemporary research and theory in personality psychology. The book provides balanced coverage of biological, cognitive, affective, social, and interpersonal determinants of personality functioning and individual differences. The authors organize these factors within an over-arching theoretical framework that highlights the dynamic transactions between individuals and the sociocultural environment and the human capacities for self-reflection and self-regulation. The book's broad, integrative approach to the study of personality reveals how advances throughout the psychological sciences illuminate the classic questions of personality psychology. The volume is designed as a textbook for advanced-level courses and as a reference for professionals in psychology and related disciplines. The book meets personality psychology's need for an integrative analysis of the field that reviews recent advances, places them in their historical context, and identifies particularly promising avenues for the discipline's future development.

Gian Vittorio Caprara is Professor of Psychology at the University of Rome "La Sapienza," Rome, Italy. He is past president of the European Association of Personality Psychology. He has been a Fulbright scholar and a fellow at the Netherlands Institute for Advanced Study (NIAS). He is author or editor of twenty volumes.

Daniel Cervone is Associate Professor of Psychology at the University of Illinois at Chicago. He has been a fellow at the Center for Advanced Study in the Behavioral Sciences and is co-editor (with Yuichi Shoda) of *The Coherence of Personality* (Guilford Press).

# PERSONALITY

## Determinants, Dynamics, and Potentials

**GIAN VITTORIO CAPRARA**

*University of Rome "La Sapienza"*

**DANIEL CERVONE**

*University of Illinois at Chicago*

PUBLISHED BY THE PRESS SYNDICATE OF THE UNIVERSITY OF CAMBRIDGE
The Pitt Building, Trumpington Street, Cambridge, United Kingdom

CAMBRIDGE UNIVERSITY PRESS
The Edinburgh Building, Cambridge CB2 2RU, UK      http://www.cup.cam.ac.uk
40 West 20th Street, New York, NY 10011-4211, USA   http://www.cup.org
10 Stamford Road, Oakleigh, Melbourne 3166, Australia
Ruiz de Alarcón 13, 28014 Madrid, Spain

First published 2000

Printed in the United States of America

*Typeface* Aster 9/12    *System* QuarkXPress™   [HT]

*A catalog record for this book is available from the British Library*

*Library of Congress Cataloging-in-Publication Data is available*

ISBN   0 521 58310 1   hardback
ISBN   0 521 58748 4   paperback

*To Laura and Jenny*

# Contents

*cognitive appraisal of situation*

*disposition*

*negative affect*   *-ve -5*

*+ 5 +ve*   *positive affect*   *+ve*

*+10*

**PART TWO. DESCRIPTION AND EXPLANATION**

## Introduction: Description and Explanation                60

## 3   Individual Differences: Traits, Temperament, and Intelligence                                               62

# Preface

The goal of this volume is to provide a comprehensive review of the psychological study of personality. We explore personality psychology's recent theoretical and empirical advances and place them in their historical context. We critically evaluate the current state of the field with the aim of promoting its further development.

The book is intended for a range of audiences. A primary audience consists of students in graduate or advanced undergraduate courses in personality psychology. We have endeavored to meet their need for a volume that presents the contemporary field in depth. Another prospective audience consists of professionals in business, education, or health care who require an up-to-date overview of work on personality processes and individual differences. Finally, we address the volume to our colleagues in psychology. We present empirical reviews, conceptual discussions, and a theoretical framework which, we hope, will be stimulating even to the personality psychologist who already is fully familiar with the field.

Personality psychology must function as a cumulative science that contributes to individual and social welfare. This idea guides our coverage in a number of respects. Sciences seek to identify causal mechanisms that explain their phenomena of interest. We thus focus on the biological, psychological, and sociocultural factors that causally contribute to personality functioning; in other words, we focus on *determinants* of personality functioning. These determinants are not static forces that exert fixed effects on a simple, linear psychological system. Instead, they operate on, and within, a complex, dynamic system of psychological elements. We thus explore the cognitive and affective *dynamics* of personality. Finally, promoting personal welfare requires that one not be content merely with plotting what individuals tend to be like. One must also explore what individuals can become, that is, their *potentials*. We devote much attention to the psychological systems that enable people to regulate their experiences and actions and thus to contribute, as causal agents, to the development of their potentials.

Our work also was guided by the belief that the field of personality must develop as an integrative discipline. Personality psychology is defined by a unique set of phenomena. No other discipline so directly addresses the coherence of individual functioning and the differences among individuals. Many other disciplines do, however, provide ideas and scientific findings that illuminate these phenomena. Advances throughout the biological, cognitive, and social sciences, as well as philosophy, speak to personality psychology's core concerns. Throughout the text, we seek to draw on the insights of these other fields. Further, we note the potential value of personality psychology for the psychological and social sciences at large. Personality psychology can serve as a forum for integrating diverse and sometimes disconnected strands of knowledge about psychological functioning. It can be a setting in which to address the difficult task of relating relatively molecular physiological, affective, and cognitive processes to the more molar psychological events that make up the individual's life.

Personality psychology has changed rapidly in recent decades. It is likely to change even faster in the future. New findings and ideas are disseminated faster than in the past. New forms of research are possible. The internet, for example, facilitates cross-cultural research by enabling rapid communication across different parts of the globe. The results of such research often challenge the universality of Western conceptions of personality and thereby speed change in the field. This rapid pace of change has important implications for how one crafts a textbook. There is little point in merely compiling a list of current empirical findings. Such a volume would soon be out of date. Furthermore, it would fail to meet critical needs. Investigators need to place current efforts in historical context, if only to avoid recycling old ideas. They also must be able to locate research programs within an overall conception of individual personality functioning, so as to enable the discipline to advance in an organized manner and in meaningful directions. We strive to meet these needs by reviewing not only recent empirical findings, but also contemporary and classic conceptions of the person. We present the diversity of current work within an overall conception of personality that stresses the dynamic transactions between the individual and the sociocultural environment, as well as the human capacities for self-reflection and self-regulation.

On a more personal note, the authors of this text came to this project with different backgrounds. One difference is in nationality. Thanks to our respective European and American backgrounds, the text balances work from investigators on both sides of the Atlantic to a greater degree than is typical. Internationalism was not an explicit mission for the volume. Rather, it was a natural outgrowth of the fact that investigators in different areas of the world share common research agendas. Another difference is in scholarly background. GVC's research has included work on personality development, social adjustment, and assessment, and his training includes a background in political science. DC's work has focused on self-regulatory processes and personality coherence, and his training leads him to draw on cognitive and social psychological contributions to the field. We hope that these differences have proved to be complementary. Our joint interests in the role of social-cognitive and affective mechanisms in personality functioning provided a common ground that is evident throughout the volume.

The preparation of this book benefitted enormously from our experiences at two "sister" institutions: the Netherlands Institute for Advanced Study (GVC) and the Center for Advanced Study in the Behavioral Sciences (DC). Both authors are deeply grateful to the staffs of these two remarkable institutions for their invaluable assistance during our time in residence. Pilar Burgueno Van Breda, of the Netherlands Institute for Advanced Study, was of particular help in reconciling our linguistic idiosyncrasies and in serving as our "first referee."

We thank Nicole Schnopp-Wyatt for using a preliminary draft of this volume as a classroom text and providing us with valuable feedback, and Nilly Rafaeli-Mor for her many incisive and constructive comments on the manuscript. We are grateful to the many colleagues who sent us reprints of their work, clarified issues in discussion with us, and commented on various sections of the text.

Writing a book intrudes on one's personal life. We thank our students, friends, and family for putting up with these intrusions. GVC thanks Laura and Lorenzo for having shared all the enthusiasm and the turmoil of many days of writing. DC wishes to thank his wife, Jenny, for her support from the very outset of this enterprise, and his son, Nicholas, for joining in a short time later.

# PART ONE

# Introduction to Personality Psychology

# Personality Psychology as an Integrative Discipline

Psychology is as difficult as any other science. Its subject matter is of the greatest complexity. There are enormous practical and ethical constraints on research. Even an apparent advantage is a double-edged sword. People may have better intuitions about other people than about subatomic particles, cells, or stars, but by being both investigator and subject matter, those people who also are psychologists are prone to personal biases and subject to social pressures that are uncommon in other disciplines.

The study of personality is as difficult as any branch of psychology. Unlike colleagues in other parts of the field, the personality psychologist cannot be content with studying isolated aspects of psychological functioning (motivation, emotion, memory, etc.). The personality psychologist must tackle the entire beast. The subject matter is the whole person. The discipline addresses questions of reason and passion, human universals and cultural variability, idiosyncratic uniqueness and systematic individual differences. An astute observer of the field, after much reflection on the diverse, conflicting challenges it faces, aptly summed up the state of affairs: "Personality theory is hard" (Bem, 1983, p. 575).

To make matters worse, personality psychologists may have made things harder than they need to be. In 1957, Hall & Lindzey observed that "personality theory has never been deeply embedded in the mainstream of academic psychology" (p. 4). Psychoanalytic, phenomenological, and factor-analytic theories had made little contact with the rest of the field. Although Hall and Lindzey's statement does not apply as strongly today, it still contains a kernel of truth. The contemporary discipline has not fully capitalized on advances in the study of development, social structure, culture, and cognition. Improved solutions to the problems of personality psychology will require greater attention to the concepts, methods, and findings provided by other branches of psychology as well as by neighboring academic disciplines.

Conversely, other areas of psychology may benefit from attending to the issues confronted by the personality psychologist. Recent years have witnessed considerable advances in psychology's understanding of cognitive, affective, and motivational processes. Work in these areas, however, commonly lacks an integrative view of the psychological functioning of the whole person. Personality psychology can serve as a forum within which to integrate knowledge of the psychological functioning of the individual in a manner that benefits the entire discipline.

This volume addresses the unique set of scientific problems that defines the field of personality psychology. We review the empirical findings and theoretical perspectives that at present provide the best solutions to these problems. This primarily leads us to review the scientific literature in the discipline of personality psychology per se. However, we do cast a somewhat wider net. We freely draw on ideas and findings from throughout psychology and its neighboring disciplines that illuminate questions of personality functioning. In so doing, we hope to promote the growth of personality psychology as an integrative discipline.

## DETERMINANTS, DYNAMICS, AND POTENTIALS

### Determinants and Dynamics

Our net is wide in two other respects. Throughout much of its history, personality psychology has been concerned with individual differences in what might be termed "surface tendencies," that is, observable variations in styles of behavior, affect, and cognition. Investigators have posited trait or dispositional constructs to capture the consistent individual differences that are observed. They have sought to establish a universally applicable structure of observable, or "phenotypic," individual differences. We devote much coverage to this important research tradition. However, we do not limit ourselves to it. One ultimately must go beyond the mere mapping of surface-level tendencies; one must identify underlying causal processes. Much of our volume analyzes cognitive and affective mechanisms that causally contribute

to personality functioning. We explore the biological, interpersonal, and sociocultural factors that contribute to the development of these cognitive and affective systems. Our goal here is to direct the reader's attention to the fundamental scientific problem of identifying the determinants of both individual differences and intraindividual coherence in personality functioning.

Use of the terminology of determinants does not imply a deterministic view of human nature. Personality can be thought of as a complex, dynamic system of psychological elements that reciprocally interact with one another. The functioning of any such complex system cannot be fully understood through simple chains of cause and effect, and its development cannot be perfectly predicted from knowledge of its initial state. Personality psychology must seek determinants of personality functioning – i.e., factors that causally contribute to the psychological functioning and psychosocial adjustment of the individual – but it cannot embrace a deterministic scientific stance in which human actions are seen as the inevitable consequences of prior events and forces. Distinctions among alternative explanatory frameworks are considered in detail in Chapters 4 and 5.

Similarly, although we speak of psychological mechanisms throughout the text, the use of this term does not imply a mechanistic view of persons. People are more than a sum of their psychological parts. The specification of underlying mechanisms can explain complex human phenomena without explaining them away. Just as the study of biological mechanisms illuminates the wondrous complexity of the human organism, study of the psychological mechanisms of personality functioning illuminates the complex network of characteristics and capabilities that makes individuals unique. Dennett (1978) captures the spirit in which we use these terms when declaring that: "mechanism is here to stay, unlike determinism" (p. 233). He explains how an analysis of psychological mechanisms can coincide with the recognition that individuals are intentional, purposive agents with a capacity for self-control (Dennett, 1978, 1984). Relatedly, Searle (1998) explains that an understanding of human behavior requires an analysis of the intentions of actors. Such an analysis yields a causal explanation ("intentional causation"), yet this explanation is not deterministic in the sense in which an analysis of nonintentional physical systems may be deterministic, with causes following in an inevitable manner from effects.

The study of surface tendencies and of underlying determinants and mechanisms does not always converge. This critical point recurs throughout our volume. A variety of factors preclude a one-to-one mapping between surface profiles and underlying psychological systems. Different systems may give rise to superficially similar observable tendencies. People might fail to act in a "responsible" manner because they lack self-regulatory skills or because they are rebelling against authority. Further, a single psychological system may yield different behavioral tendencies in different contexts. People's goal of advancing within a competitive business organization might lead them to act submissively toward superiors and dominantly toward peers. Acts that seemingly should be grouped within the same behavioral category may actually arise from different underlying systems. People's "inhibited" behavior in response to novel objects versus social peers may be mediated by different physiological systems, which would explain why individuals who are inhibited in one context commonly are relatively uninhibited in another (Kagan, 1998b; Rubin, Hastings, Stewart, Henderson, & Chen, 1997). Such considerations force one to question whether global dispositional constructs are a sufficient basis for a science of personality (Cervone & Shoda, 1999a). If one wants to arrive at underlying causal systems, a map of global, surface-level tendencies might not get one there.

In discussing the determinants of personality functioning, we commonly speak of "dynamics." Personality factors function as elements of dynamic systems that develop over time. Specifically, the term dynamics highlights a number of issues that are critical to an understanding of personality. These include the within-person organization among the dynamically interacting elements that constitute personality; the ways in which these elements and their organization change over the course of development; the fact that such changes may be internally driven rather than externally imposed – dynamic systems have the capacity for internally generated change (Nowak & Vallacher, 1998); and, finally, the term calls attention to the motivational dynamics that guide thought, emotion, and action and that often involve conflicts between goals that are in opposition to one another.

### Potentials

People are not inert beings who are merely predisposed to react in a particular way when confronted with a particular stimulus. People select, interpret, and influence the situations they encounter. They are causal agents who contribute to the course of their development. Personality psychology, then, includes the study not only of habitual dispositions, but also of individual potentials (Caprara, 1999). Personality psychologists have the responsibility to address the personal and social processes that can contribute to the full expression of human capacities.

The inclusion of potentials in the domain of personality psychology has four implications. First, it expands on the discipline's traditional focus on personality dispositions. Although it is important to assess what people typically are like, it is of equal importance to explore what they can become. Society demands that personality psychology contribute not only to the assessment of individual differences but to the development of individual potentials. Boykin (1994) compellingly advances this point in discussing the educational attainments of African-American youth: "We must shift from a preoccupation with talent assessment . . . [to] a commitment to talent development . . . [This] will require a fundamental change in . . . how we conceptualize the individual" (p. 119). His point applies not only to the study of intellectual capacities but also to the study of the whole person.

Second, the study of human potentials contrasts with psychology's traditional focus on psychological vulnerabilities. It surely is true that some inherited characteristics, early life experiences, or socially learned cognitive tendencies make people vulnerable to psychological distress. However, as Bandura (1999), Kagan (1998b), and others recently have emphasized, a more striking feature of human nature is people's capacity to overcome adversities. Many individuals lead productive, well-adjusted lives despite profoundly traumatic experiences early in their development. The relatively positive life outcomes of children who were orphaned by World War II but later were adopted by middle-class families (Gardner, Hawkes, & Burchinal, 1961) attest to the "self-righting tendencies" (Werner & Smith, 1982) of psychological development. Research in developmental psychopathology and life-span development similarly speaks to the resilient qualities of the individual (Garmezy, 1991; Rutter, 1987; Staudinger, Marsiske, & Baltes, 1995). A great many of the elderly, for example, experience the demands and setbacks of aging without any loss of psychological well-being (Brandtstädter, Rothermund, & Schmitz, 1998). The capacities that enable people to overcome adversities and contribute productively to their development deserve personality psychology's utmost attention (see Seligman & Csikszentmihalyi, 2000).

Third, the notion of potentials draws attention to the fact that personal qualities develop and express themselves through dynamic interactions between persons and their sociocultural environment. People's psychological qualities cannot be gauged simply by counting up their typical behaviors in the settings they typically encounter. People may possess capacities that can only be realized within particular environments, which may or may not be part of their daily life. Kagan (1998b) provides an apt analogy. A rock lying at the bottom of a lake belongs to the category of potentially dangerous object. Its dangerousness is not an inherent, isolated property of the rock itself (as is its mass or hardness). Instead, dangerousness is a relational quality. It describes the relation between the rock and particular settings (e.g., being thrown indoors). Similarly, many psychological qualities are not inherent properties of isolated minds/brains. Instead, they are relational in that the expression of the quality requires a social setting that elicits, supports, or requires the quality in question. One cannot be "sociable" by oneself. Many readers of this text are potentially great parents, although that quality may not yet have expressed itself. These considerations naturally expand one's conception of personality psychology's goals. The field thus must explore a range of issues beyond the charting of typical behavioral tendencies.

Finally, potentials are inherent not only in persons, but in environments. Many environmental settings contain challenges, resources, and opportunities that foster personal growth. Choosing to attend college, get married, become a parent, change careers, or engage in programs of physical or spiritual development challenges one's abilities and forces one to develop new skills. People who make these choices encounter other individuals with shared goals who provide social support and model valuable coping skills. Meeting the challenges provides experiences of personal mastery, which can alter people's sense of self (e.g., Weitlauf, Smith, & Cervone, in press). The key point with respect to the notion of potentialities is that these experiences are chosen. The environments generally are not imposed on people (although there are significant exceptions). They are selected. People reflect on their values, goals, and abilities and choose the settings that comprise their personal and professional lives (Bandura, 1997; Snyder & Ickes, 1985). Prior to such choice, the environments – powerful though they may be – are mere potentialities. Indeed, even once one enters into a setting, many of its opportunities and resources will remain latent in the absence of active choice. College, for example, provides enormous opportunities for personal and intellectual growth and for the development of lasting friendships and professional networks. These opportunities, however, do not impose themselves on individuals but must be actively pursued. The expanded economic opportunities and greater access to information experienced in many nations of the world broaden the opportunities and resources available to individuals and thereby accentuate the role of personal choice in personality development.

The three points raised here – that personality psychology must be an integrative discipline that encompasses study of determinants and dynamics of personality functioning as well as of the development of human potential – are interlocking. Personality psychologists have long been interested in actualizing human potential. Maslow (1954) built his personality theory on a potentialist view of human nature. Murphy (1958) and Rogers (1961) similarly emphasized the human potential for self-directed change. Allport (1950) wrote of people's inherent potentialities for self-development. However, contemporary personality psychologists can draw upon bodies of knowledge in the behavioral, cognitive, and social sciences that are dramatically more extensive than those available in Maslow's, Murphy's, Rogers', and Allport's day. This is a critical advantage. The surest route to maximizing human potentials is first to understand the determinants and mechanisms of personal functioning. With this understanding, one can identify psychological processes that are subject to change and psychosocial factors that might change them for the betterment of individual welfare. Humanistic goals are best served by the scientific study of psychological mechanisms and the factors that shape them. The "hard" and "soft" sides of the discipline can proceed hand in hand.

## OVERVIEW OF THE VOLUME

This volume consists of five parts. Part One introduces the field of personality psychology. We discuss the aims of the field in Chapter 1 and review its history in Chapter 2. Recent developments in cultural psychology pose a challenge to many historically accepted views; these challenges also are addressed in our second chapter.

Part Two takes up the dual tasks of description and explanation. Personality psychology must characterize personal qualities and the differences among individuals and also must identify the causes of these qualities and variations. These tasks can be addressed in different ways. One strategy, discussed in Chapter 3, is to search for psychological dimensions that capture individual differences in psychological tendencies, or dispositions. These individual-difference dimensions then might serve as the basis both for describing persons and for explaining the psychological tendencies that are observed. A second strategy, discussed in Chapter 4, is to ground an explanation of personality functioning in the study of cognitive and affective mechanisms and of interactions between psychological mechanisms and the sociocultural environment. An analysis of affective and social-cognitive systems speaks to questions of individual differences while also directing one's attention to individual uniqueness and the within-person coherence of personality functioning.

Part Three of the text explores the development of personality. Our developmental coverage is somewhat broader in scope than is typical. We consider not only theoretical and metatheoretical models of development (Chapter 5), but also genetic influences and brain systems on development (Chapter 6), the role of interpersonal relations in the development of the individual (Chapter 7), and the socially and culturally constructed contexts in which persons develop across the life span (Chapter 8).

Part Four on "The Dynamics of Personality," explores knowledge structures (Chapter 9), affective experience (Chapter 10), unconscious and conscious processes (Chapter 11), and motivation and self-regulation (Chapter 12). The ideas discussed in these chapters are highly overlapping, and common themes emerge. As we will see, enduring knowledge about the world and the self contributes to people's interpretations of the world, affective states, conscious experiences, motivation, and capacity for self-regulation. Similar processes, then, come into play across these diverse phenomena. Another theme is that the study of cognitive–affective dynamics enhances our understanding of personality consistency and coherence. Cognitive mechanisms and cognition–emotion interactions contribute to stable individual differences and to the within-person consistency and variability of personality functioning. Finally, although we focus heavily on basic research, the work we review in this part of the text has applied implications. The cognitive structures of personality have social foundations. People acquire beliefs, competencies, and standards for self-evaluation through their interaction with others. An understanding of social-cognitive systems, then, can inform applied efforts to enhance people's capacity to control their actions and emotions in the service of their personal development.

Part V is an epilogue that looks ahead to the future of the field. Foresight is particularly important in personality psychology. The discipline has the potential to contribute mightily both to the sciences and to society at large. In the past, it has not always achieved this potential. Doing so in the future will require judicious choices among alternative scientific methods, research topics, and theoretical views of the person.

# CHAPTER ONE

# The Domain of Personality Psychology

**CONTENTS**

Personality psychology's history is a contentious one. In different eras, the merits of alternative world views, scientific methods, and psychological theories have been fiercely debated. To the present day, personality psychology can be profitably studied as a collection of competing theories, as the discipline's textbooks and college courses commonly attest.

Three factors in particular have fanned the flames of debate. The first is the diversity of philosophical traditions that are precursors to contemporary theory. Current psychological beliefs and practices have long, disparate philosophical roots. We consider the foundations of the contemporary field in detail in chapter 2.

The second factor is the difficulty of defining the field's object of study. Several ideas appear, alone and in combination, in the modern use of the word personality. These ideas include human being, person, the quality or fact of being a person, the quality or fact of being a particular person, individuality, patterns of habit, biophysical and mental activities that express themselves in qualities and habits, the sum of such qualities as they impress themselves on other persons, factors that make an individual conspicuously different from others, and attributes or dimensions according to which all individuals can be compared. Definitions, explicit and implicit, guide theory and inquiry. Divergent definitions foster debate. When the divergent definitions are acknowledged only implicitly, debate is particularly difficult to resolve. Progress can be slow when a field's "terminology alone is a mass of ambiguities" (Harré, 1998, p. 1).

A third source of contention throughout the field's history derives from the influence of sociohistorical and political factors on scientific inquiry. Scientific investigations must be understood in their historical context. Social trends draw scientists' attention to some topics and deflect it from others. For example, those who lament a breakdown of morality in contemporary society would not be surprised that personality psychologists currently devote less attention to questions of "character" than they have in the past. Further, political regimes often have suppressed forms of scientific inquiry that interfere with their aims. Both subtle and blatant influences may foster disagreement among scientists who live in different regions of the world or who are differentially influenced by the sway of social fashion or the rule of an authoritarian government.

Despite this diversity, today one can identify common themes in the discipline and common assumptions that guide the activities of most investigators. We begin this chapter by outlining these themes and assumptions. We then turn to an issue on which there is not commonality of opinion. In both its past and present, inquiry in personality psychology has not been guided by a single theoretical framework but by alternative conceptions of personality structure and functioning. We introduce the conceptual issues involved in this chapter and return to them at a number of subsequent points in the book. We close by briefly considering some methodological issues that the personality psychologist must confront.

## COMMON THEMES

Despite this history of debate over questions of theory, methods, and definitions, today one can identify significant agreement about the domain of investigation. Personality psychologists know where they want to go even if they do not all agree on how to get there or exactly how to describe the place. Phenomena examined by the contemporary field include:

Interindividual differences, that is, the habitual behavioral tendencies, dispositions, or traits that characterize the individual and distinguish people from one another

Intraindividual coherence, that is, how distinct psychological processes function as coherent systems, how people achieve a coherent sense of self, and how social and self-referent beliefs develop into an integrative system that expresses itself in the individual's distinctive patterns of experience and action

The interplay of biological and cultural factors that guides the course of personality development, setting constraints yet also providing opportunities for individual growth

The psychological process and mechanism that, across the course of life, interact with biological and social processes to sustain a continuous sense of personal identity and individuality

Interpersonal relations that provide a critical context for personality development and that mediate the influence of social structures on the individual

This is a vast territory, in which numerous issues converge, including the study of personality stability and change, developmental growth and decline, affect and cognition, well-being and suffering, intimate relationships, and bonds with one's community.

The breadth of phenomena that the field addresses should not be seen as a burden. Instead, it potentially gives the discipline an integrative character. Personality psychology stands at the crossroads of multiple disciplines in the social, behavioral, and biobehavioral sciences. It confronts questions of human nature that have often been the province of philosophy. This places the personality psychologist in a special position with regard to other sciences such as biology or anthropology. On the one hand, personality psychology cannot mature in ignorance of the developments in these domains of knowledge. On the other hand, because of its broad scope, the field may serve as an ambassador of psychological knowledge to other fields.

Personality psychologists must devote themselves not only to the accumulation of scientific knowledge but also to the solution of social problems. The application of knowledge is not a choice but an inevitability. Psychological theories guide social practices. Scientific conceptions determine whether societies view a given aspect of human nature as subject to change and whether they employ biological, psychological, or social factors to change it. The society-wide spread of psychological knowledge is accelerated by the growth of higher education and the dissemination of scientific information through the media and the Internet. Today, psychological theories reach far beyond the walls of the academy. This makes the critical evaluation of psychological theory more crucial than ever.

Among the pressing social problems of the day, personality psychology can speak with particular force to questions involving the recognition of human individuality and the actualization of human potentials. As but one example, consider questions about race and ethnicity (cf. Montagu, 1999; Rushton, 1995). The discipline can contribute to society's recognition that notions of race, as traditionally construed, no longer have reason to exist (Cavalli-Sforza, Menozzi, & Piazza, 1994). Owing to the interchange of genetic material between populations, which is accelerated by the contemporary breakdown of geographic barriers, races are mixtures rather than pure groups. "The concept of race at the human level," then, "has absolutely no meaning; it is merely a social construction" (Segall, Lonner, & Berry, 1998, p. 1107). Society's understanding of cross-cultural or ethnic differences in personal beliefs, attainments, and patterns of behavior, then, cannot be grounded in biology. Diversities reflect the influence of cultural systems and socioeconomic factors that are largely mediated, at the individual level, by the psychological systems we call personality.

A population's cultural history, then, partly resides in the minds of its individual members. After a period of dormancy that followed some promising beginnings (Kluckhohn, Murray, & Schneider, 1953), the study of personality and culture has reemerged as a common theme in personality psychology in recent years. It has become increasingly apparent that cultural meaning systems shape people's beliefs, decisions, and actions. Further, they partly determine the nature of the interpersonal relationships, family arrangements, and work experiences within which people develop. Culture provides not only static beliefs but also dynamic potentialities. Cultural knowledge and practices are tools that individuals can use to adapt to the physical and social world. Culture contributes to the individual's social knowledge and sense of self. These personal factors, in turn, give individuals the capacity for self-direction. Culture also can constrain individual development in that a cultural system may promote some developmental pathways and discourage others (Cervone & Rafaeli-Mor, 1999). Individuals often benefit from using the wisdom of their culture to realize their potential in a manner that is supported by the members of their society.

As nature and culture coevolve (Durham, 1991), technological innovations enhance our control over the conditions of life. These conditions, in turn, are destined to affect our very biological makeup. The study of personality contributes to our understanding of how individuals can seize the opportunities their culture makes available to them and how they establish stable personal identities in a rapidly changing world.

## DEFINITIONS, AIMS, AND ASSUMPTIONS

By personality, we refer to the complexity of psychological systems that contribute to unity and continuity in the individual's conduct and experience, both as it is expressed and as it is perceived by that individual and others.

As is apparent from this definition, the notion of personality can be viewed from different perspectives. From the perspective of the individual, one's own personality is the collection of one's attributes and inclinations. These enduring personal qualities convey a sense of identity (me), wholeness (thoughts, feelings, and behaviors are all part of me), and uniqueness (I am). From the perspective of the observer, personality is the set of psychological characteristics that distinguish individuals from one another. People observe others' behaviors and use these observations as data in forming impressions of them. They organize these impressions of personality into coherent belief systems. From this perspective, personality is a social construct involving systems of beliefs about the qualities of individuals. Finally, from the perspective of the scientist, personality is the psychological system that emerges from the interactions of the individual with the environment and that mediates intrapsychic functioning and person–environment transactions.

To the personality scientist, personality is both a construction and an agency. The psychological structures of personality develop gradually over the course of life. Although both cultural and biological factors contribute to this development, people are not passive vessels who merely store genetic endowments and absorb cultural meaning systems. People are active agents who causally contribute to their own development. Through their choices and actions, people significantly determine the nature of their experiences and the kinds of persons they become. They thus are causal agents who can play a role in the construction of their own personality.

Personality, then, is a self-regulating system with the capacity to serve individual development and well-being. The personality psychologist's domain of investigation must therefore include the capacities for self-reflection, forethought, and the construction of personal meaning, which enable people to function as self-regulating agents and to develop and maintain a stable sense of personal identity. Personality psychology thus encompasses the general psychological processes that enable people to regulate their personal and social experiences and the individual differences and unique individual qualities to which these psychological processes give rise.

Despite their different theoretical backgrounds, many investigators share some basic common assumptions about personality functioning. These beliefs provide a common

ground from which to evaluate specific theories of personality functioning (Bandura, 1986; Baltes, Lindenberger, & Staudinger, 1998; Magnusson and Stattin, 1998; Mischel & Shoda, 1998). These assumptions are not specific theoretical positions but broad metatheoretical assumptions that guide much of the research and theorizing that makes up the contemporary discipline. Thus, many investigators agree on the three general principles described below.

First, personality is a complex system of psychological structures and processes whose organization results from synergistic interactions among multiple subsystems. The different subsystems function with different degrees of independence versus interdependence. Inherited neurophysiological mechanisms, for example, are remote determinants of personality that are encoded in the genome, a system that functions relatively independently. In the course of ontogenesis, however, the exact development of neurological structures depends on both genetic programming and organismic experience (Kolb & Whishaw, 1998); development, in other words, involves interdependencies between the organism and the environment. In the overall course of personality development, multiple biological and psychological subsystems are restructured within the boundaries set by nature and society. As individuals develop competencies, personal standards, and aspirations, they play an increasingly proactive role in their own development.

Second, personality, as both an agency and a construction, develops and functions in an ongoing process of reciprocal interaction with the environment. Interactions with the social world lay the foundation for the development of agentic capabilities. As people develop, their enhanced personal capabilities give them greater control over their personal experiences. People thus contribute as causal agents to the development of their own capabilities.

Not only overt action but also internal mental life is governed by reciprocal influence processes. The internal beliefs and standards through which people regulate their behavior are shaped by external factors such as observations of others' behavior and feedback from the environment. The internal dialogues through which people reinterpret the past and contemplate the future are shaped by cultural meaning systems. The traditionally separate worlds of emotion and thinking can be brought together by recognizing that affective and cognitive processes reciprocally influence one another.

Many aspects of mental life occur outside of awareness and thus are difficult to control (Aarts & Dijksterhuis, 2000; Bargh & Chartrand, 1999; Uleman, 1989; Wegner & Wheatley, 1999). However, people do have a unique capacity for self-consciousness and self-directedness. Self-reflective capabilities grant people a degree of awareness and mastery over their experiences. By reflecting on past and ongoing experiences, people can identify settings, relationships, educational opportunities, and personal talents that can contribute to enhanced regulation of their social and emotional lives.

Interactions between persons and the sociocultural environment are the basis for constructing a coherent sense of self. By reflecting on their experiences and discussing these experience with others, people develop organized belief systems about their personal qualities as well as about the qualities of other people and of the environment. These belief systems are not static bits of knowledge. They are dynamic working models of the world that people draw upon to interpret events, select and change the environments they encounter, and chart courses of personal development. The study of life-span development vividly illustrates the interplay of cultural and biological factors in the formation of beliefs about the self. Different cultures prescribe different beliefs about the stages of life. Yet, in any culture, there are systematic developmental changes in people's beliefs about their capacities, since people of all societies must face common issues of physical decline in old age (Carstensen, Isaacowitz, & Charles, 1999; Heckhausen & Schulz, 1995).

Third, there is a coherence and continuity in personality, which can be fully appreciated only by considering the person as a whole and by examining the organization of personality across the life-span. Patterns of affect, cognition, and behavior rather than single acts reveal the underlying structure of the personality system. People's actions commonly are in the service of long-term goals, including the abstract yet important goal of maintaining a sense of personal identity and continuity.

Personal crises or normative life transitions that force people to move locations and adopt new social and professional roles can challenge the coherence of one's sense of self. Maintaining a coherent sense of identity may require psychological change. The capacity to change one's goals and strategies of goal pursuit is critical to effective personality functioning (e.g., Sanderson & Cantor, 1999). The adaptive individual is capable of changing goals and plans to take advantage of novel opportunities as well as of reconciling competing demands for consistency and diversity, stability and change, adaptation and self-direction. Even when life goals change, people are able to maintain a continuous sense of identity by developing and updating narratives about the course of their development (Bruner, 1990; McAdams, 1996).

These basic principles are shared by many researchers. Nonetheless, consensus should not be overstated. Contemporary personality psychology is not guided by a single conceptual paradigm. There still exist deep, albeit subtle, differences in the theories and metatheoretical assumptions embraced by different investigators. We thus turn to questions of theory and scientific explanation in personality psychology. We return to these questions at a number of points throughout our text.

## THEORIES AND EXPLANATIONS

Personality psychology contains a rich set of theoretical conceptions. Some of these overlap and some conflict. The field also contains a diversity of research, only some of which is directly related to a particular personality theory. The task of organizing the field's theory and research thus is challenging. Two organizational schemes present themselves – the discipline can be organized according to theories or according to phenomena. A textbook presentation, in other words, could be arranged according to the theories that personality psychologists have developed or the phenomena that they have explored. Both approaches have virtues and limitations.

Organizing the field around a series of competing theories (e.g., Hall & Lindzey, 1957) has an important pedagogical advantage. Developing adequate theory is a fundamental task for personality psychology, as for any discipline. A theory-based organization provides detailed coverage of psychologists' best efforts at theory construction. This may stimulate readers to improve on existing efforts. However, the limitations of theory-based organization are twofold. Exposure to a series of competing theories may lead readers to overemphasize theoretical differences and underestimate commonalities. This is especially likely when different theories use different terms to refer to common psychological processes. Second, a theory-based organization may not fully capture the field's accumulated knowledge about a given phenomenon. Different research paradigms that are associated with different theories may provide converging evidence on a question of general interest. This fact may be missed when research is organized by theory.

The alternative is to organize the field around research topics. One could review a series of phenomena that have received the personality psychologist's empirical attention. This overcomes the limitations of a theory-based organization but raises new problems that are at least as serious. The difficulty is in deciding which phenomena to present. Should one begin by discussing achievement? Aggression? Agreeableness? Attachment? Altruism? Which phenomena are fundamental? Answering this question requires theory. From some theoretical perspectives, agreeableness, for example, is a fundamental structure of personality. From others, it is an arbitrary social construction that bears no necessary relation to any structures in the person. The phenomena one judges to be fundamental are determined by the theory one holds; indeed, a key function of a scientific theory is to identify the problems that are most worthy of empirical attention. A theory-free presentation of empirical facts is thus impossible. Organizing the field exclusively around selected research topics begs the question of how we select the topics.

Theory, then, cannot be brushed aside; important theoretical differences do still exist in the contemporary field. Yet, we have not organized our text around a series of competing theories. One can gain an understanding of the most important theoretical differences in the contemporary field without necessarily working one's way through the entire panoply of "grand theories" of the past. Contemporary investigation is not guided by a large number of separate theories but by a small number of broad theoretical frameworks (Cervone, 1991). The conceptual task, then, is to identify these frameworks. What issues bring subsets of investigators together and what issues continue to divide the field?

## Distinguishing Among Theoretical Approaches

It is not a simple task to distinguish among theoretical approaches. A number of well-known conceptual distinctions no longer accurately characterize the field. Cronbach (1957) recognized that the discipline was once divided along methodological lines. One subdiscipline embraced experimental research strategies, whereas another adopted correlational techniques. As Cronbach himself suggested (1975), this distinction is no longer adequate to describe the field. Innumerable investigators share the belief that progress requires a judicious combination of experimental and correlational techniques but do not share more fundamental beliefs about how to build a personality theory.

Another well-known distinction separates the field into *person* and *situation* theorists.

This division suggests that the former group studies personality attributes that express themselves in a consistent way irrespective of social context, whereas situationists are interested in environmental influences and uninterested in personal factors. Commentators have continued to divide the field in this way despite the fact that it would be nearly impossible to identify any investigators in the past quarter-century of the discipline who would accept either label as an accurate characterization of their beliefs.

One also can differentiate between *structure* and *process* theories. The former are said to investigate enduring attributes that individuals possess, whereas the latter address dynamic processing that varies from moment to moment. Although this distinction may be more useful than the previous two distinctions, it also is not adequate. Processes rest on structures, and structures are inert in the absence of dynamic processing. Thus, few theorists confine their work to the analysis of structures or processes in isolation.

The theoretical differences that exist in the contemporary field no longer involve methodological preferences, extremist person versus situation beliefs, or an exclusive focus on process versus structure. Instead, the differences are more subtle. They involve metatheoretical assumptions about how one should build a personality theory and, once the theory is in hand, how one should explain personality functioning. We consider these issues briefly here and return to them in detail in chapter 3 and again in the closing chapter of our book.

## What is a Personality Theory to Do?

The first step in evaluating similarities and differences among personality theories is to inquire about the function of the theories themselves. What is a personality theory supposed to do? The simplest answer is that, as a theory in the sciences, a personality theory should provide a scientific explanation of phenomena in its domain of investigation. The purpose of scientific investigation is to explain phenomena (Salmon, 1989). Descriptive stud-

ies are of value, of course. In the study of personality, they may identify recurrent behavioral tendencies that require explanation, but the ultimate goal of the personality theorist is to provide the explanation itself.

If scientific explanation is the goal, then two questions arise: What are the phenomena we need to explain? How do we provide an explanation?

As this book will make evident, personality psychologists address an extremely wide range of phenomena. In each case, they seek to explain the phenomenon under study. Therefore, in some respects identifying the core phenomena that are the targets of explanation, or the "explicanda" (Salmon, 1989), is no different from listing the field's topics of study. The list is particularly large both because of the complexity of the target (persons) and because different theoretical approaches call attention to different phenomena.

Despite this diversity, one can identify an overarching mission for the field. Most investigators would agree that a central phenomenon for the field to explain is the integrated, coherent quality of personality functioning. Founders of the field, such as Stern (1935) and Allport (1937), recognized that explaining the coherence of personality is the central charge of the field. Writers as different as Jung and Rogers posited that people have a basic motivation to attain a coherent sense of self. A review by McAdams (1997) of the disparate grand theories of the mid-20th century (e.g., Allport, 1937; Cattell, 1950; Lewin, 1935; Murray, 1938; Murphy, 1947) noted that all of these theories "emphasize the consistency and coherence of normal personality and view the individual organism as an organized and complexly structured whole" (p. 12). Vigorous interest in the coherent, holistic functioning of the individual continues to the present day (Cervone & Shoda, 1999b; Magnusson, 1999).

The phenomenon of personality coherence can be seen to incorporate three closely interrelated issues (Cervone & Shoda, 1999a, c). The first is the interrelation among distinct psychological processes in personality functioning. Personality processes function not as independent entities but as integrated systems. The personality psychologist hopes to explain the coherent, system-level integration of personality processes. The second issue is coherence in overt psychological response. Across both time and place, people exhibit patterns of behavior that are interconnected, or that *cohere*. The search for coherence in social behavior has been a major point of interest, and contention, throughout much of the field's history, as we review in chapter 2. Finally, personality coherence involves continuity in phenomenological experience. People generally experience a coherent sense of self. Even in the face of life transitions and conflicting social roles, the individual experiences himself or herself as a whole, continuous being. A personality psychology that explained how psychological, biological, and social systems contribute to these three aspects of personality coherence would be quite a success.

In addition to the coherence of personality functioning, the personality psychologist wishes to explain how individuals differ from one another. The two core topics of personality coherence and individual differences go hand in hand to some degree. The individual differences one wants to explain are differences not in isolated acts but in interconnected patterns of affect, cognition, and behavior. A deeper question, though, is the relation between individual-difference analyses, on the one hand, and the identification of psychological mechanisms that underlie the coherent functioning of the individual, on the other. Is the study of individual differences in observable, surface-level dispositions a reliable route to discovering underlying personality structure? On this question, one finds serious disagreement.

## Dispositions as Phenotypes and Genotypes

Many investigators judge that a first step in explaining personality functioning is to identify the primary ways in which individuals differ from one another. Specifically, researchers survey a large set of potential person-to-person variations and employ statistical techniques that are designed to identify a small set of dimensions that explain much of the variability. The resulting dimensions are commonly construed as "phenotypic" dispositions, the implication being that subsequent study might identify underlying "genotypic" structures that explain the surface variations. Although some investigators search for brain systems that correspond to the dimensions that are found (see chapter 6), others treat the dispositions as hypothetical constructs.

The identification of individual-difference structures, then, may serve two possible functions in theory development. First, the dimensions can be seen as an empirical fact that needs to be explained. Once a robust set of dimensions is established, one might search for psychological mechanisms that explain why an individual's experiences and actions cohere with respect to each dispositional category. The second possibility takes this idea one step further. The dispositional constructs might be not only descriptive facts but causal explanations. The dispositions identified in the analysis of surface-level tendencies, in other words, may correspond to psychological structures with causal force. In this view, dispositions are both phenotypes and genotypes. The existence of a robust set of individual-difference dimensions is explained by hypothesizing that all persons possess underlying structures that correspond to each dimension, with different people possessing different amounts, or levels, of each structure. Just as the intercorrelation among test items that call for intelligent reasoning can be explained by positing a psychological structure of general intelligence, the intercorrelation among test items that tap neurotic or conscientious tendencies can be explained by positing that people possess psychological structures of neuroticism or conscientiousness.

Consider how this dispositional strategy of explanation works in a particular case. Suppose an analysis of individual differences has identified conscientiousness as a basic dispositional tendency. A cluster of more specific tendencies, such as the tendency to be motivated, diligent, reliable, and punctual, might all correlate with the higher-order factor of conscientiousness. Now suppose we observe a particular individual, Bob, who consistently works diligently to fulfill obligations and pursue his goals. One might explain Bob's behavior by positing that he possesses a relatively high amount of conscientiousness and inferring, based on the previous analysis, that conscientious people work hard and are committed to their pursuits. The trait of conscientiousness thus explains Bob's consistent pattern of behavior.

This strategy of explanation defines one predominant theoretical perspective in the contemporary field. Many investigators base the study of personality on the analysis of individual differences in psychological dispositions or traits. Their goal is to identify a universal set of trait dimensions. Once this is done, the personality functioning of any individual can, in principle, be understood by determining the person's location within the established dimensional system, that is, finding the trait on which the individual's standing determines the consistent forms of behavior exhibited by that person. A variety of theories of personality advance this general perspective; we review them in detail in chapter 3.

■ *Limitations of Dispositional Constructs.* If only because of their popularity and influence in the field, the way in which dispositional approaches explain personality functioning deserves careful scrutiny. Consider, again, three elements of the explanation of Bob's behavior. First, the observed acts (fulfilling obligations and working hard in pursuit of goals) were seen as indicators of a high-level personality disposition (conscientiousness). The acts and the disposition, then, are related hierarchically, in that working hard and fulfilling obligations are ways of being conscientious. Second, the high-level personality disposition was seen as a universal quality. Although it may originally have been identified in the study of individual differences in the population, it is assumed to apply at the level of the individual person. Third, the high-level, universal disposition then served to

explain consistency in the person's actions. The individual's acts, in other words, are explained by positing that the person has some amount of the high-level disposition (the disposition is a basic, essential quality of the individual) and that the disposition has causal power. The disposition is ultimately responsible for the consistencies in action that are defining for the individual's personality.

A number of writers have scrutinized this strategy of explanation and found it to be severely wanting. One of the first of these was Kurt Lewin (1931, 1935), who distinguished between Aristotelian and Galilean explanatory concepts in psychology. An Aristotelian model, as Lewin (1935) explained, considers "abstractly defined classes as the essential nature of [an] object and hence as the explanation of its behavior" (p. 15). These classes are defined irrespective of situations; they are essential qualities, which are inherent to the object being explained and which may then express across any of a variety of settings. Lewin called on psychologists to do what physicists had done centuries before: abandon Aristotelian essentialism and embrace Galilean forms of explanation. In the latter approach, one explains phenomena by specifying the dynamic processes through which they come about. The Galilean perspective does not look for abstract essences that are invariant across contexts (also see Kagan, 1988). Instead, as Lewin emphasized, it explains action by reference to both individual characteristics and the environmental context in which action occurs.

The dispositional explanation outlined above can be seen as a modern version of Aristotelian thinking. Bob's behavior was explained by reference to an abstract, essential quality of Bob, his conscientiousness. This quality served as an explanation despite the fact that the causal dynamics linking it to the observed behavior were unknown. In Lewin's view, this explanation is scientifically inadequate because it treats the disposition as an endogenous causal variable when, in fact, Bob's personality disposition is not a cause but the phenomenon that needs to be explained by reference to underlying causal processes.

A similar point comes from the work of the philosopher Harré (1998), who has articulated the problems inherent in claiming that high-level personality dispositions explain a person's behavior. Harré notes the distinction between classification and explanation. Some scientific constructs are merely classificatory. They organize entities in a useful manner but do not provide a scientific explanation. For example, although chimpanzees can rightly be classified as primates, "to say that a chimpanzee is a primate does not explain anything about its characteristics" (pp. 80–81). Primate is a taxonomic classification, not an explanation. In this analysis, then, the claim that dispositions are explanations is simply a mistake. High-level dispositions "are of the wrong logical type" (Harré, 1998, p. 80) to serve as explanations. In psychology or any science, dispositions are observable properties, which must be explained by reference to specified structures and properties with causal power. To view dispositions as explanations, then, "is to confuse dispositions (traits) with powers and liabilities" (Harré, 1998, p. 79). "Dispositions could not be unobservable, explanatory properties of anything . . . the only explanatory concept that could be imported to explain personal dispositions would be personal powers" (Harré, 1998, p. 79). Dispositions such as the tendency to work hard and meet obligations must be "explained by causal powers, not by more higher-order dispositions" (p. 80).

A further problem with treating individual-difference variables as causes is that it mixes levels of analysis. A personality theory must provide causal explanations that apply at the level of the individual person. Dispositions, however, generally are identified in the analysis of populations. There is no guarantee that the population-level constructs will apply at the level of the individual. If one computes the average height in a population, the result may not correspond to the height of any individual person. Similarly, if one factor analyzes the dispositional tendencies of a population, the resulting factors may not correspond to the individual tendencies of any particular person in the group. Aggregation of data "over individuals who [may be] qualitatively different from each other," can "[distort] the aggregate into an entity that has no parallel in the group" (Nesselroade & Molenaar, 1999, p. 224).

■ *Social-Cognitive and Affective Systems.* Arguments such as those of Lewin and Harré suggest an alternative route for building a scientific explanation of personality functioning. One could explore the dynamic processes that underlie consistency and coherence in personality functioning. Rather than searching for abstract essential qualities, one would examine how interactions among specific psychological mechanisms and between psychological mechanisms and social contexts give rise to the psychological characteristics that we call personality. As Harré instructs, one would explore the personal capabilities that power experience and action.

A variety of theorists reject the notion that people can be understood by fitting them into a fixed set of dispositional tendencies. Instead, they study psychological mechanisms that give rise to individual differences, as well as patterns of intraindividual variability and coherence in personality functioning. These approaches include the social-cognitive theories of personality (see Cervone & Shoda, 1999b), which we introduce more formally in chapter 3. Social-cognitive approaches explore the psychological mechanisms that enable people to acquire social competencies, adapt to the environment, plan and execute courses of action, and attain personal meaning in their lives. They address the reciprocal interactions between these personality structures and the sociocultural environment. Personality is conceptualized, not as a set of endogenous essential qualities that are present from birth, but as a set of psychological processes and structures that emerge in the course of development and gradually coalesce into coherent psychological systems. Explanation does not rely on abstract classification but on the identification of specific cognitive and affective mechanisms that give rise to the psychological phenomena being explained (Bandura, 1999). The notion of dispositions is not confined to average behavioral tendencies but includes characteristic variations in behavior that people exhibit across time and place (Mischel & Shoda, 1995, 1998). Finally, the notion of individual differences is not confined to differences in surface-level features but includes differences in the basic mechanisms of personality functioning. This approach to explanation defines a second major theoretical perspective in the contemporary field.

Readers may be wondering if the two approaches outlined here – the trait/disposition and social-cognitive – converge. Should the studies of dynamic social-cognitive mechanisms and surface-level individual-difference tendencies not map on to one another? The answer here may be no. Different underlying mechanisms may give rise to similar surface-level dispositions. Bob may be consistently diligent and responsible because he finds his daily activities personally fulfilling or because he wishes to avoid the social censure that may result from his failure to meet obligations. A single social-cognitive mechanism may give rise to actions that are aspects of different dispositional individual-difference categories. Bob's beliefs about conscientiousness may incorporate the opinion that one should conscientiously strive to be interpersonally sociable and agreeable. In general, there may be no one-to-one correspondence between surface-level individual-difference constructs and underlying causal systems that function at the level of the individual (cf. Kagan, 1994b). This theme recurs throughout our book. In chapter 3, we devote particular attention to the question of alternative strategies of explanation in personality psychology. We suggest that a distinction in the philosophy of science between top-down and bottom-up strategies of explanation (Salmon, 1989) is a valuable heuristic approach for understanding how different personality theories approach the tasks of description and explanation (Cervone, 1997, 1999).

In summary, all personality psychologists agree on the importance of understanding the phenotypic patterns of behavior, thought, and action that is, the surface-level dispositions, that distinguish people from one another. Disagreement is found on the questions of how to describe and explain these dispositional qualities. The focus on individual-difference dimensions, which capture consistent behavioral tendencies, versus social-cognitive and affective mechanisms, which might explain both consistency and variability in the individual's psychological functioning, defines two distinct theoretical approaches in the contemporary field.

### Related Metatheoretical Issues

The different approaches to explanation and theory construction outlined here are closely related to two broad conceptual issues, which are of relevance to personality theorists of any viewpoint. One is a metatheoretical framework for analyzing causality in complex systems. The other is a question about how one interprets multiple measures of a person, each of which may be seen to relate to a common personality construct.

■ *Complex Systems.* Many sciences have been influenced by the study of complexity in nonlinear, dynamic systems (Bak & Chen, 1991; Gell-Mann, 1994; Nicolis and Prigogine, 1987). Research on nonlinear dynamics indicates that the behavior of a complex system can be understood in terms of interactions among its elements. The interactions among elements of a system may be simple and regular at one level but not at another. Chaotic subsystems may give rise to a relatively stable macrosystem, yet even small perturbations to the subsystem may have large, unpredictable effects. The macrolevel system, in other words, may exhibit properties that cannot be anticipated by analyzing its individual components.

The behavior of complex systems often is nonlinear. Rather than developing in a gradual, step-by-step manner, the system may shift suddenly from one state to another. In psychology, a common example is the perception of a Necker cube, which shifts from one spatial appearance to another without passing linearly through intermediate states.

A key feature of complex systems is that they tend to self-organize (Bak & Chen, 1991). The systems tend to take on patterns that are highly ordered and stable, but they do not do so because a high-level organizer preordains that the system will take on this form. Instead, the system's organization is a product of the interactions among its many elements. Low-level interactions give rise to the high-level order and structure that the system eventually acquires. Striking illustrations of self-organization come from the study of simple cellular automata, systems that contain a large collection of units that do nothing other than to take on a small number of internal states and influence the state of immediately adjacent units. Even these exceedingly simple systems display complex, organized patterns of behavior (Waldrop, 1992). The system as a whole may cluster into a number of stable subgroups or may alternate systematically among a fixed set of different states, even though the clustering and alternations were not in any way programmed into the individual cells. Their system's complex, organized behavior, then, is an *emergent property* of interactions among its simple elements. A relevant social science example is the behavior of a macroeconomic market system, which may act as if an invisible hand were stabilizing prices, supplies, and consumer demand.

Psychologists have come to recognize the importance of nonlinear dynamics for their field (Barton, 1994; Carver & Scheier, 1998; Fogel, Lyra, & Valsiner, 1997; Nowak & Vallacher, 1998; Vallacher & Nowak, 1994, 1997). Personality can be perceived as a complex system of interacting elements. As in other complex systems, these elements tend to achieve stable patterns of organization, which may be achieved "without prespecification" (Lewis, 1997). In other words, no a priori, fixed structure exerts its influence throughout the course of development. No preexisting structure determines the exact final form of the system. Instead, organization and stability

are achieved gradually, and the systems attain mature forms that are not entirely predictable. A complex-systems view of psychological development, for example, views distinct cognitive and affective processes as reciprocally interacting elements, which gradually become linked to one another. "Processes develop over time into more complex and stable organizations" (Caprara, 1996, p. 18). The psychological system thus self-organizes. This self-organization can, for the individual, take on any of a large variety of final forms. "Developmental self-organization [tends] to dig its own idiosyncratic trenches" (Lewis, 1997, p. 196).

Branches of psychology outside of personality provide many examples of psychological phenomena that arise from interactions among a complex system's multiple elements, no one of which directly corresponds to the phenomenon to be explained. In connectionist models (Rumelhart, McClelland, & PDP Research Group, 1986), one form of a complex systems analysis, the phenomenon of word detection is explained through interactions among simple units, no one of which is a word detector. In the neurosciences, the phenomenon of long-term episodic memory can be understood by reference to interconnected neural systems, no one of which independently stores a complete episodic memory (Schacter, 1996). The research of Latané and colleagues on group dynamics provides a vivid illustration of complex self-organization in the social domain. Individuals with similar attitudes tend to be found clustered near one another in social space. This can be explained by reference to low-level dynamic interactions among individuals. In other words, the group contains attitudinally consistent spatial clusters, even though no individual member of the group had the goal or intention of forming clusters (Latané & L'Herrou, 1996).

Inside of personality psychology, computer simulations by Shoda and Mischel (Mischel & Shoda, 1995; Shoda & Mischel, 1998) speaking directly to this issue. These authors were seek to understand how the tendency to exhibit a characteristic, mean level of response with respect to a dispositional category (i.e., to display a stable personality trait) may arise from interactions among multiple cognitive and affective processes. The trait, then, is an emergent property of a complex system. Their simulations indeed suggest that stable dispositions can be understood in terms of interactions among elements of a complex cognitive-affective system. The key point is that none of these cognitive-affective elements – no individual unit in the psychological system – corresponds directly to a tendency to display a stable, mean level of response. There is no causal trait that corresponds to the observed stable disposition. Stable levels of response, instead, are one emergent property of interactions among low-level causal elements of the system.

Nowak, Vallacher, and associates (reviewed in Nowak & Vallacher, 1998) similarly have employed computer simulations to model the dynamics and organization of the self-system. They developed a cellular automata model containing large numbers of elements each representing an aspect of self. Initially, each element was set to be evaluatively positive or negative, and the positive and negative elements were ordered randomly. In the course of the simulation, each element influenced neighboring aspects of self. Despite the fact that the system's initial configuration was random, it quickly became highly organized and stable. The organization was not in any way prespecified. Instead, the simulated self-system became "organized in a fairly efficient manner . . . due to [the system's] intrinsic dynamics alone" (Nowak & Vallacher, 1998, p. 164).

Research on how "marginal deviations" influence the course of personality development illustrates the nonlinearity of personality processes (Caprara & Zimbardo, 1996). Adolescents exhibit substantial individual differences in problem behavior. These variations are predictable from differences that are observable much earlier in life. However, the early-life predictors do not correspond in size to the large variations in prosocial and dysfunctional conduct observed later. Instead, they are often small, subtle variations, whose impact aggregates over time. Individuals who differ slightly from the norm in the early years may differ markedly from the norm later on. Their marginal early-life deviation serves as one factor in a complex, cyclically interacting network of self-referent beliefs, social reputations, and interpersonal interactions. In the reciprocal interplay between persons and social environments, then, marginal liabilities can evolve into significant deviancy.

■ *Data from Different Response Systems: Indicators of a Common Construct or Distinct Yet Functionally Interrelated Systems.* In the concluding section of this chapter, we will briefly consider the range of research methods that are employed by the contemporary personality psychologist. Before turning to this issue, however, we first address here an issue that, on the surface, also appears to be a methodological question. However, it actually is a question that has deep metatheoretical implications for the conception of personality variables and is an issue that divides alternative theoretical approaches. It is the question of how to interpret psychological measures that index different response systems (e.g., affective systems, conscious cognition, nonconscious cognition).

Suppose one is studying anxiety. Measures of interest might include participants' self-reports of their mental states, physiological measures of their levels of arousal, and behavioral measures such as whether they confront or avoid a setting that makes them anxious. All investigators agree on the usefulness of collecting these multiple measures. However, they do not necessarily agree on how to interpret them and relate them to one another.

One possibility is to interpret the different measures as functionally equivalent indicators of a common individual-difference construct, anxiety. Investigators of personality traits since Cattell (1957) have recognized that any given trait can be assessed via multiple sources of data. Self-reports, physiological measures, behavioral measures, and the reports of informants could all be combined into a common index of a person's level of anxiety. Statistical techniques such as structural equation modeling (Bollen, 1989) are designed to combine multiple indicators of a construct. Convergence among these multiple indicators generally gives one greater confidence in the assessment of the given construct.

Although combining measures of multiple response systems is a reasonable practice for many purposes, it does have a significant drawback. It forestalls questions about the possible functional relations among the systems. In the case of anxiety, it might be that behavioral avoidance and physiological arousal are functionally related, with arousal causally influencing performance. Alternatively, both behavior and physiological arousal may be functionally related to self-referent beliefs (which are best tapped by the self-reports), with low beliefs triggering both greater avoidance and greater anticipatory arousal. These and other possibilities can only be explored if "response classes [are] given independent conceptual statuses from one another and analyzed separately" (Bem, 1972, p. 54). This point is of both theoretical and practical importance. Dissecting the functional relationships among the systems may be critical to the design of interventions, since interventions must target causally influential systems. In the case of anxiety, research on functional relations among thought, anxious arousal, and behavior (e.g., Bandura, Reese, & Adams, 1982) suggests that self-referent beliefs indeed influence levels of avoidance behavior and anticipatory arousal. Behavior-change interventions that target this influential belief system prove more effective than those that merely calm a client's physiology (Bandura, 1997; Williams & Cervone, 1998).

Kagan (1988) has emphasized a related point. He criticizes psychologists' "tendency to use the same term for . . . different classes of data, as if the theoretical meaning of a term was unaffected by the form of its evidence" (p. 615). The difficulty is that the meaning of a construct depends, in part, on what it refers to (its referential meaning). The truth value of a proposition about a construct may depend on the way it is made operational. This is not only because different operationalizations are more or less statistically reliable but because different operationalizations change the meaning of the construct. Adapting an example from Kagan (1988), the validity of the statement "expensive harps are more beautiful than less expensive ones" may depend entirely on whether one's measure of beauty indexes the harp's appearance or its sound. Both can be beautiful, but the different measures change the meaning of the term beauty. Even if the measures are correlated .99 in a group of harps, one obviously would not want to combine them statistically as indicators of the hypothetical construct beauty. Similarly, the question of whether people with high self-esteem are more anxious than people with low self-esteem may depend entirely on whether self-esteem is measured with explicit or implicit measures and whether anxiety is indexed by self-report or by physiological arousal (Spalding & Hardin, 1999). Combining data from different response systems by statistically aggregating the two self-esteem measures and the two anxiety measures might indeed yield a more reliable index of the hypothesized constructs. On conceptual grounds, however, it might be a mistake because the different measures tap into different things, that is, they index different psychological response systems.

The question of how one treats measures from different response systems is related to the distinction between explanatory strategies noted above. If personality is being explained in terms of a small number of high-level dispositional tendencies, then one is naturally inclined to combine disparate measures into an aggregate index. The high-level disposition serves the conceptual function of organizing the various measures, each of which is seen as an indication of the dispositional tendency. In contrast, if personality functioning is explained by reference to a system of interacting cognitive and affective mechanisms, one naturally is inclined to separate measures of different response systems. The question of how different systems influence one another becomes a target of investigation. This can only be answered by keeping measures of separate response systems separate.

## METHODOLOGICAL ISSUES

In introducing the study of personality psychology, we primarily have focused on problems to be solved and theoretical strategies for solving them. However, personality psychology also is distinguished by its research methods. Here, we consider some very general issues regarding research strategies in the field. Specific methodologies are exemplified, of course, throughout the subsequent chapters of our text.

Theoretical conceptions determine one's preferred research methods. Disagreements about theory thus have fostered disputes about methods throughout the field's history (see Allport, 1962; Bruner, 1990; Holt, 1958, 1962; Gergen, 1994; Meehl, 1954; Polkinghorne, 1988). Debate has centered on a number of different points. One is the use of *idiographic* versus *nomothetic* methods. Some contend that research should examine the personality structure of the potentially idiosyncratic individual. Others seek universal structures and laws (the word nomothetic derives from the Greek word for law, *nomos*) that are applicable to all persons. A second issue is the scope of investigations. Some researchers seek to test specific, limited causal hypotheses as unambiguously as is possible. Others employ research methods that are designed to yield a comprehensive portrait of the person. A third issue is the criterion through which one evaluates results. Historically, psychologists have employed the criterion of statistical significance: Do results exceed what would be expected by chance? Many have questioned the usefulness of this standard. Some recommend that findings be evaluated according to their clinical significance, that is, whether the findings are relevant enough and generalizable enough to orient practice outside the laboratory. Others suggest that the hypothesis-testing procedures of the sciences are insufficient to capture the nature of human experience. They reason that science seeks objective, universal laws, whereas human lives involve subjective meaning processes that are historically and socioculturally situated. They thus advocate narrative methods for capturing these situated meaning processes. Interest in each of these alternatives has waxed and waned throughout the field's history. Disagreement on some points endures to the present day. Nonetheless, the contemporary field features much more agreement about research strategies than was present in the past.

Almost all investigators today recognize the advantages of employing multiple methods. Converging evidence from multiple sources enhances confidence in one's conclusions. In the past, some investigators tied theories to a single form of evidence (e.g., psychoanalysis and the free association technique, behaviorism and the operant conditioning paradigm). Today, personality psychology's research methods include experimental, correlational, and observational strategies; multiple sources of information about persons; a variety of experimental, cross-sectional, and longitudinal research designs; and a spectrum of data analysis techniques. Some investigators study people for brief periods in research designed to examine the functioning of particular psychological mechanisms. Others study persons in multiple contexts and over extended periods to detect patterns of experience and actions that illuminate the individuals' characteristic tendencies and that additionally provide insight into their private worlds of experience. Ideally, experimental and correlational techniques are combined to evaluate theoretical models.

Past debate that denigrated one versus another type of evidence now seems misguided. Indeed, philosophers of science encourage us to be more creative and innovative (Feyerabend, 1975). Innovation, we must recall, should be applied to the two missions of the scientist: to pursue knowledge and to challenge with all possible means one's existing knowledge (Popper, 1959, 1969). A hypothesis should be held only as long as it is falsifiable, has not yet been falsified, and is contributing to the advancement of knowledge.

Empirical findings are always interpreted in the light of preexisting hypotheses and beliefs. This lends a subjective quality to the scientific enterprise. Nonetheless, it does not turn scientific research into mere subjectivity. Some empirical conclusions rest on findings that are obtained reliably and consensually and that thus can be considered more solid than others. Such findings often speak not only to the confirmation of existing theories, but to their refutation.

The day of "one science, one method" is past. A given research method should not be understood as being superior to another but as being potentially more suitable to the particular problem at hand, at a particular level of analysis, and in light of practical constraints. Houts, Cook, and Shadish's (1986) *critical multiplism* speaks directly to this point. These authors suggest that investigators employ multiple techniques to study a common problem, while recognizing that no single method will provide an unambiguous critical test of a hypothesis. Their framework is a useful heuristic approach as long as one remains attentive to the possibility that different techniques may yield results that differ meaningfully from one another. Note also that multiplism does not imply complete eclecticism, in which one is indifferent to the validity of alternative research methods. Rather, it implies a commitment to a practice of discovery and a set of scientific standards, which, beyond being consensually legitimated, derive their authority from their capacity to solve problems and to expand knowledge.

## SUMMING UP

Historically, the discipline of personality psychology has been known for its competing theories and research traditions. The discussions throughout this chapter, however, reveal that although the contemporary field continues to harbor some conceptual disagreements, it also features substantial points of consensus. Personality scientists aim to understand the psychological processes and structures that contribute to the distinctive functioning of the individual. In pursuing this goal, a great many investigators share basic assumptions. As we have seen, these include the beliefs that personality is a complex system whose overall organization results from synergistic interactions among biological and psychological subsystems; that people have the capacity to contribute proactively to their experiences and development; and that there is a coherence and continuity to personality that can best be appreciated by considering the person as a whole and examining the development of the individual across the life span.

A small set of broad theoretical frameworks organizes much of the field's ongoing scientific activity. These include trait-theoretic frameworks that highlight interindividual differences in psychological tendencies, and social-cognitive perspectives that explore psychological mechanisms underlying people's capacity to interpret the world and to regulate their feelings and actions. Investigators working within both of these frameworks, as well as the field's other guiding theoretical conceptions, tackle a broad range of scientific problems by drawing upon a diverse and ever-expanding array of methodological tools.

The diversity of methods and itineraries in the contemporary field is a minor price for personality psychology to pay for its growth. The convergence of findings is a challenging goal to reach, as the field tries to expand its base of accumulated knowledge. In this regard, greater awareness of the strengths and limitations of past efforts may better enable one to assess current research options. The next chapter therefore delves into the field's past.

# CHAPTER TWO

# Origins, History, and Progress

Personality psychology sometimes seems doomed to repeat its past. Purportedly novel developments elicit a sense of déjà vú (Bem & Allen, 1974; Mischel & Peake, 1982). Theories that seem to have succumbed to empirical scrutiny reappear like the phoenix. The discipline's most common subtitle for theoretical critiques is surely "Old wine with new labels."

If the dictum about history is right, knowledge of the field's past may spare us from reliving it. This chapter charts the history of personality psychology. We take a long and broad view. We do not confine our coverage to the 20th century academic discipline because doing so begs the question of that discipline's origins and more seriously, it restricts the history of speculation about personality to Western concepts. These appear increasingly limited in light of contemporary knowledge about cross-cultural variations in psychological functioning and concepts of the person. We consider below the challenges posed by cross-cultural data as a prelude to our detailed coverage of personality psychology's origins, history, and progress.

## THE ORIGINS OF PERSONALITY PSYCHOLOGY WITHIN THE HISTORY OF IDEAS

Personality psychology as we know it today developed within the traditions of Western civilization, where philosophical analysis has long turned to questions of human nature and the properties of human nature that make it possible for people to ask questions about themselves.

Although inquiry into human nature has long been a part of the Western tradition, the current use of the term *"personality"* is a more recent development. Its current meaning was approximated in the past by terms such as reason, psyche, or human being. Regarding its origins, the term personality has no obvious equivalent in ancient poetic or philosophical Greece (Gill, 1996). Its etymological origin is the Latin word *persona,* which referred to the masks worn by actors and actresses in theatrical performances. Each mask was associated with a character in a play and served as a means of preparing the audience for the states of mind and actions that character was to portray. It was not until the Middle Ages that persona became synonymous with a human individual and began to be used in a manner similar to the modern notion.

Much time elapsed between the development of the modern conception of personality and the birth of a scientific personality psychology. For centuries, questions about mind, behavior, the emotions, and individuality were the province of philosophy. The establishment of a science of personality required a series of steps. Psychology had to free itself from philosophy as well as from reductionistic physiological theorizing. Personality psychology then had to find its own identity within the various subfields of psychological inquiry. It is not surprising, then, that psychology in general and personality psychology in particular developed as distinct scientific disciplines much later than did physics, chemistry, and biology. It took time not only to establish a body of theory and findings but to establish first that the topic of study was open to scientific investigation. The road to contemporary conceptions of humankind as part of nature and thus as a potential object of scientific investigation was a long one (Burnham, 1968).

Philosophical traditions, sociopolitical world views, and social structures have shaped developments in personality psychology to a far greater extent than most other disciplines (Caprara and Van Heck, 1992). A history of the field therefore must include a history of the cultural traditions that are the precursors of the contemporary discipline and of the social contexts within which the contemporary field developed.

### Problems and Perspectives in the History of Psychology

Western conceptions about mind, personality functioning, and the uniqueness of the individual are based on Greek-Jewish-Christian traditions. This is true despite the potential impact of other belief systems. Religious and philosophical systems such as those of Buddha and Confucius preceded or were contemporary with those of Plato and Aristotle. Great civilizations were developed prior to, or progressed independently of, Greek-Roman civilization. We must acknowledge the wisdom contained in other world views. Confining the history of a discipline within the framework of any particular civilization may seriously limit progress in that discipline by excluding the acquired knowledge of other cultures. The history of science should reveal links that connect problems and solutions over time and across different contexts rather than consisting merely of a chronology of events in one context.

In examining the history of people's questioning of themselves, one must explain why some problems have taken precedence, some epistemological strategies have been promoted over others, and some conjectures have been vigorously pursued while others remain unnoticed. One should determine whether particular questions and forms of inquiry are found in only some cultures, whereas other questions about human nature are asked universally. Unfortunately, the history of psychology has not addressed this question adequately. Histories of psychology have tended to be ethnocentric. They commonly review a limited range of ideas, namely, Western philosophical and psychological conceptions. These view the person as a "bounded, unique, more or less integrated motivational and cognitive universe, a dynamic center of awareness, emotion, judgment and action organized into a distinctive whole and set contrastively against other such wholes and against a social and natural background" (Geertz, 1975, p. 48).

**The Challenge of Cultural Diversity**

The limitations of this viewpoint have become increasingly apparent to personality psychologists thanks to the efforts of investigators in cultural psychology (Berry, Poortinga, Segall, & Dasen, 1992; Boesch, 1991; Cole, 1996; Fiske, Kitayama, Markus, & Nisbett, 1998; Miller, 1999; Segall et al., 1998; Shweder, 1991; Triandis, 1994). This work is supplemented by new understandings of how biological and cultural processes are linked and coevolve (Durham, 1991). These advances, plus the promise of new vistas of knowledge that this field will open, cast a shadow of doubt on any prior conceptions of the person that cannot address the challenges posed by cultural diversities.

Although culture has often been overlooked, it is to the person as water is to the fish. Culture is the medium through which one experiences the world (Jahoda, 1993; Lillard, 1998). The opportunities and constraints within which one constructs a sense of individuality are embedded in the culture. Cultures tell their members how to behave and tell their scholars how to think about the causes of behavior. At different cultural latitudes, people not only eat different foods, wear different clothing, use different utensils, and speak different languages. They act within different social roles, hold different beliefs about religion and the nature of the universe, use different constructs to think about personal and social problems, and embrace different expectations and beliefs about the mind and the self. Although we acknowledge that many empirical results in personality psychology are obtained cross-culturally, it nonetheless would be foolhardy for the field to disregard the role of culture in the development of the individual. Cultures provide the settings and the explicit and implicit meaning systems within which people construct a sense of personal being. This sense of self dynamically influences all aspects of personality functioning.

The various ways of defining culture all acknowledge the role that culture plays in defining personhood and furnishing a background context for personal development. Among the various definitions, the one proposed by Geertz (1973) has been widely adopted by anthropologists and is particularly suitable to personality psychology: Culture is a set of control mechanisms, plans, recipes, rules, and instructions for the governing of behavior.

Scientists through this century have explored the role culture plays in shaping personality (Benedict, 1934; Erikson, 1950; Kardiner and Linton, 1939; Kluckhohn et al., 1953; Vygotsky, 1934; Whiting & Child, 1953). Only recently, however, have Western psychologists directly challenged the generality of research findings and the universal applicability of the methods of inquiry that generate them. Thanks to these efforts, we now recognize that what are assumed to be psychological universals may turn into culturally relative patterns when the cross-cultural data come in (Berry et al., 1992; Choi, Nisbett, & Norenzayam, 1999; Lillard, 1998; Shweder, 1991; Triandis, 1990). Kitayama and Markus (1999) review a number of such findings. The correspondence bias (Jones & Davis, 1965) or the fundamental attribution error (Ross, 1977), that is, the tendency to overattribute the causes of action to personal rather than situational factors, is weaker in Japan, India, and China (Kitayama & Masuda, 1997; Miller, 1984; Morris & Peng, 1994). Choi et al. (1999) have noted that as compared with Westerners, East Asians believe that dispositions are relatively malleable and view other people as holistically embedded within sociocultural contexts. The link between self-criticism and depression found commonly in the West is not found among Japanese (Kitayama, Markus, Matsumoto, & Norasakkunit, 1997). Cognitive dissonance effects, a robust phenomenon in Western cultures, are less likely to be observed in Eastern cultures, apparently because an internal inconsistency among attitudes or actions is less threatening to one's sense of self in the East (Heine & Lehman, 1997). Chinese may be persuaded by argument structures that violate Western norms of internal logical consistency (Peng & Nisbett, 1999). Attitudes are relatively stronger predictors of behavior than are social norms in the West, whereas social norms are relatively more important predictors in the East (Triandis, 1995). Even the need for positive self-regard, which many have assumed to be universal, appears to be less prevalent in the East (Heine, Lehman, Markus, Kitayama, 1999).

Culture, then, is more than a medium for transmitting knowledge and beliefs. The conceptual systems of a culture operate as a set of socially transmitted instructions that pervade virtually every aspect of human experience. A culture's conceptual system should be understood not as a static set of symbols but as a dynamic collection of tools used to interpret oneself and the world. It "is not a catalogue of signs, it is a system in *use*" (Harré, 1998, pp. 24–25). This places the meaning systems of a culture at the root of emotions and patterns of thinking and action.

The evolution of human cultures and human biology are intertwined. Both genetic and cultural factors guide the evolution of human diversity. Both contribute to the differences observed in human populations that have developed in geographically separated regions. Durham (1991) documents the striking interrelations of cultural and biological differences. Over the course of millennia, the struggle for survival in different environments fostered different economic systems. These, in turn, led to the diffusion of diverse habits and specialized skills. This sociocultural diversity, in turn, influenced biology via the selection and genetic transmission of characteristics that proved to fit with social contingencies. Genetic diversities and cultural diversities thus co-evolved.

Variations in different human populations in a biological characteristic, tolerance to milk (lactose absorption), illustrate this process. Different human populations display strikingly different levels of toleration to lactose. The biological mechanisms involved in lactose absorption and variations in the ability to process lactose are well understood. The question is why different populations would have differentially evolved the ability to process this milk product. Research strongly suggests that cultural practices played a significant role in the evolution of the biological mechanisms (Durham, 1991). Higher percentages of lactose-tolerant humans are found in populations that traditionally have been involved in dairying and that contain cultural beliefs that encourage milk consumption. These cultural practices thus constitute a selection pressure for lactose tolerance. The cultural practices did not arise in a vacuum; instead, they are most prevalent in northern climates, where vitamin D is typically deficient, with lactose absorption compensating for this deficiency (Durham, 1991), Cultural practices involving milk and dairying and genes for lactose absorption thus have "coevolved as a function of latitude" (Durham, 1991, p. 282). Over the generations, this coevolutionary process yielded today's differential prevalences of the biological characteristic.

The core idea of cultural psychology is that "individuals and traditions, psyches and cultures, make each other up, and that the processes of consciousness (self-maintenance processes, learning processes, reasoning processes, emotional feeling processes) may not be uniform across the cultural regions of the world" (Shweder, 1991). This thesis is substantiated by a variety of findings, which force a revision of much traditional thinking.

A particularly impressive body of information derives from the last two decades' research on individualism and collectivism (Triandis, 1990). The psychology with which we are familiar has developed within an individualistic culture, which promotes the welfare of the individual over the group. However, most of the world's population think and behave according to principles of collectivism, which promote the group (the family, the lineage) over the individual. These alternative world views, individualism and collectivism, have dramatically different implications for conceptions of the person. Indeed, the very notion of personality acquires different meaning in the different contexts. In individualistic Western civilizations, persons consist of self-contained attributes. The isolated individual is an object with inherent rights, dignity, and worth. In Indian and Chinese civilizations, the individual is part of a whole. Persons are the expression of a network of relations. They are the link in a chain of generations. In Western cultures, the realization of personal potential entails autonomous personal growth. In the East, it involves an integration of the individual into the collective units that structure the social order. People are distinguished by traits, abilities, and goals in the West. In the East, people are more attuned to social roles and obligations.

Cultural variations are also found in the people's global ratings of themselves and their life. A survey of life satisfaction conducted in 61 nations (Suh, Diener, Oishi, & Triandis,

1998) reveals that in individualistic cultures, the pleasantness of everyday emotional experiences strongly predicts life satisfaction. In collectivist contexts, in contrast, emotional experience is a less strong predictor, and perceptions of social norms regarding the appropriate level of personal satisfaction with one's life gain greater importance. Life satisfaction is also differentially linked to ratings of self-esteem in the different cultural contexts, with self-esteem and life satisfaction being more strongly related among individualists (Diener & Diener, 1995).

Even analyses of broad-band personality inventories such as the NEO-PI-R (Costa & McCrae, 1992) reveal the influence of acculturation factors. McCrae, Yik, Trapnell, Bond, and Paulhus (1998) explored the possibility that cultural factors account for the finding that Chinese obtain lower scores on extroversion, vulnerability (a facet of neuroticism), and competence (a facet of conscientiousness). To test the role of culture, McCrae et al. (1998, study 2) studied ethnic Chinese students at a Canadian university who varied systematically in their degree of exposure to European and/or North American society. These included groups who were born in Canada, who immigrated prior to 1986, and who immigrated after 1986; data were collected during the 1992–1993 academic year. Greater exposure to the Canadian culture systematically lessened the differences between Chinese scores and European/North American norms (McCrae et al., 1998). The critical implication here is that differences that might have been attributed to inherent, biologically based variations between ethnic groups primarily reflect differences in culture. Different cultural systems support different construals of the self (Kitayama & Markus, 1999).

These cultural views affect not only persons at large but the psychologists who study them. Cultural beliefs have shaped formal definitions of personality and determined which hypotheses about personality functioning have been tested. Research topics such as the self, volition, morality, the emotions, and altruism are inevitably viewed through a scientific lens that is culturally grounded.

The field of cultural psychology calls our attention to the possibility of multiple end points of personality development, multiple ways of construing the same psychological phenomenon, and multiple forms of evidence that may shed light on questions of personality functioning. Findings alert us to the possibility that our standard questions about personality may be egocentrically biased. They challenge the fundamental premise of many that personality coherence can be explained in terms of global personality traits, that is, characteristics that exist in a stable form that is independent of the particular features of the sociocultural environment (cf. Allport, 1937; Shweder & Sullivan, 1990). In Eastern conceptions, persons are not envisioned as collections of stable essences but as fluid beings. Personality does not express itself as consistency but as a balance between inconsistent, opposed forces, a yin and yang (Kitayama & Markus, 1999).

Traditional analyses of culture today face novel, unforeseen problems. These challenges arise from the "hybridization" and "deterritorialization" of culture (Hermans & Kempen, 1998). Thanks to the influence of the media and the Internet, as well as the mobility of populations, cultures are no longer tied to geographic regions or territories. "Hybrid phenomena result from the transformation of existing cultural practices into new ones . . . leading to the creation of . . . such multiple identities as Mexican schoolgirls dressed in Greek togas dancing in the style of Isadora Duncan . . . Thai boxing by Moroccan girls in Amsterdam, and Native Americans celebrating Mardi Gras in the United States" (Hermans & Kempen, 1998). While people in different regions of the world may substantially share habits and values, subgroups within a region may vary as much as do groups that are geographically remote.

Hermans and Kempen (1998) further note that global forces influence local cultural practices. In these "glocalization" processes, distinctive qualities of the local culture may be promoted as a way of protecting against globalizing forces (e.g., CNN, McDonalds). Simply dichotomizing cultures or regions of the world deflects attention from this dynamic interaction between global and local forces (Hermans & Kempen, 1998).

Despite globalizing forces, diversities between groups still do matter, as indicated by the continued existence of ethnic conflicts on the world scene. Diversities, however, are less likely today to involve divergences in overt preferences and behavioral styles. Instead, they increasingly operate at a more invisible level than in the past, further requiring deep cultural insights (Geertz, 1996).

## The Construction of Histories

Histories of psychology and of personality psychology may be limited not only by being confined to Western traditions but by the absence of a thorough historiographic analysis. History is not a simple chronicling of events. To construct a history, one must select sources and interpret events. These are subjective, personal activities, which are socially and historically situated. Different histories should be compared to shed light on the implicit conceptions and goals of the historians no less than on the conditions of life and the ideological pressures operating on historians at that time. Such historiographic activity has been rare in our field.

It is commonly related that Western psychology has its roots in the classical tradition of Greek thinkers, that it gradually was emancipated from philosophical thought between the 17th and 18th centuries, and that it established itself as an autonomous scientific discipline in the second half of the 19th century (Boring, 1950). Although this account contains much truth, the journey from Democritus, Plato, and Aristotle to the Enlightenment and then to the turn of the 20th century is probably not as direct and linear as this narrative suggests. In the following, we address the historical influence of the Roman world, the Christian Middle Ages, the Renaissance, the Reformation and Counter-Reformation, and then Enlightenment thinking. We consider social, political, and economic changes that have variously promoted or hindered progress in understanding persons. We note the relation between personality psychology and other disciplines, including the vexing question of why psychology in general, and personality psychology in particular, developed as scientific disciplines so much later than other sciences.

When considering historically influential thinkers, one should ask not only about what they thought but about why their thoughts, as opposed to those of others, attained such prominence. The intuitions of Locke, Descartes, and Kant today receive more attention than those of Machiavelli, Hobbes, and Rousseau. The former group surely deserves recognition. Various contemporary ideas can be traced back to their contributions (e.g., interactionism to Descartes, elements of cognitivism to Locke and Kant). Nonetheless, one easily could argue that the contributions of Machiavelli, Hobbes, and Rousseau are no less important to the contemporary scene. The ideas of this latter group may be viewed as precursors of 20th century research on power, aggressiveness, and altruism (Caprara & Gennaro, 1994).

Having said this, we also note that tracing current activities to earlier thought is a risky endeavor. Hilgard (1980) recommends that one proceed cautiously when linking the moderns and the ancients. Although similar ideas may appear to be expressed in different eras, the meaning of psychological terminology may have changed over time. The terms reason, power, and authority may have had subtly different meanings for 16th and 17th century philosophers than for today's psychologists. The often cited interactionism of Descartes has relatively little in common with the modern sense of the term. One thus should question the degree of continuity between current psychological theory and the ideas of great thinkers of the past.

### The Matrices of Western Thought

The history of ideas in Western civilization begins with the great thinkers of classical antiquity. Starting in the 5th century B.C., these thinkers formulated beliefs about the world and our place in it that dominated Western intellectual inquiry into the 17th century (e.g., Geymonat, 1970; Gusdford, 1960). This period, more than two millennia, is enormous in relation to the individual life-span yet not in relation to the life of our species (over 100,000 years) or the 10,000-year period of civilization beginning with the origins of agriculture and concomitant social organizations (Cavalli-Sforza, Menozzi, & Piazza, 1994).

The drama of classical antiquity unfolded on a stage formed by the various coasts of the Mediterranean Sea. The action took place primarily along the coastline, barely reaching the inland areas of the three continents surrounding this sea's borders. Two cities were the major protagonists: first Athens and then Rome.

### Conceptions of the Person in Ancient Greece

The *polis*, the Greek city-state, came into being between the 7th and 6th centuries BC. It fostered a sociopolitical order that profoundly transformed both the relations among social groups and people's conceptions of themselves, society, and the cosmos.

Some aspects of Greek civilization probably were present in advanced forms in the civilizations of Mesopotamia and Egypt. It is impossible to determine exactly how much Greek civilization owes to other cultures. Still, intellectual activity flourished uniquely in Greece. Greek thinkers determined the subsequent course of inquiry into the nature of being (ontology), moral conduct (ethics), and the cosmos (cosmology).

A theme that ran through much of Greek thought was the search for equilibrium. The task of moral thinking is to achieve an equilibrium between reason and passions in the individual and a wider equilibrium among individuals, to be achieved in accordance with the harmony regulating the universe. This theme is evident in Plato's and Aristotle's search for perfection, a pursuit deriving from the conviction that there is an orderly plan for the cosmos. Everybody can participate in this plan through a process of revelation guided by reason. The task of philosophy is to recognize the elements that constitute the basic nature of all things. The philosopher tries to grasp the essence of objects and to indicate the ends toward which they naturally tend.

The prevailing notion of *human being* in ancient Greece differed somewhat from the contemporary Western concept (Gill, 1996). The Greek concept was less individual-centered than the Western concept that developed by the time of Descartes and Kant. The Greeks emphasized participation in interpersonal and communal relationships. To be a human being was to act on the basis of reason and to honor the obligations of membership in a community.

Greek speculation about human nature was guided by two primary assumptions: essentialism, or the belief in inherent, unchanging qualities of an object; and finalism, the belief that reasons for action lay in the end state toward which objects tend. Essentialism guided the search for the elements at the basis of mental activity ("ideas" for Plato and the "soul" for Aristotle). Finalism guided analyses of reasons for behavior and for individual existence. These assumptions were destined to influence psychological explanation across the ages. The recurrent belief that individuals possess fixed, inherent personality characteristics, which simply unfold over time but are basically unchanged across the life course, continues the essentialistic thinking of the ancients. Other Greek thinkers were less inclined to make reference to transcendental entities or final causes. Democritus was concerned with the search for equilibrium and wisdom but sought an understanding in terms of natural laws that did not separate body and mind or soul.

Among the early contributors to the description of personality was Theophrastus, a disciple of Aristotle. He sketched characters (the liar, the adulterer, etc.) who were defined according to their moral attributes. His character sketches are enlightening portrayals of common types in Greek society.

However, before Theophrastus, a more systematic approach to personality and the underlying causes of individual differences was provided by Hippocrates. The *Corpus Hippocraticum* was a collection of medical knowledge that attested to the advances in Greek medicine, which achieved emancipation from the magical and superstitious thought of the past. This work sought laws governing the functioning of the organism and the development of illness. It embraced a unitary conception of the organism. Illness was caused by an alteration of a global equilibrium rather than by a dysfunction in one or more discrete, separable parts. This vision of a whole organism that is connected to an environment that promotes or inhibits its development anticipates aspects of contemporary thinking (e.g., Bronfenbrenner, 1992; Gottlieb, 1998).

Hippocrates introduced the notion of temperament. The four humors (blood, phlegm, yellow bile, and black bile), alone and in combination, determined one's predominant psychological temperament (sanguine, melancholic, choleric, or phlegmatic). This idea opened the door to work on the relation between physical constitution and behavioral dispositions. It also introduced a unitary conception of mind and body, with common elements being at the root of both physical and psychic health. The Hippocratic typology was developed further by Galen in the 2nd century AD. It became fashionable during the Renaissance and was systematically explored in more recent eras, as is reviewed in the next chapter.

**Roman Thought**

The Greek *polis* declined and Roman power emerged between the 3rd and the 2nd century BC. In this era, epicurean and stoic philosophers contemplated the question of what conditions of life would best promote happiness and peace among citizens. Such reflections were more congenial to the Roman ethos. Rome, although deeply indebted to Greek civilization, was more concerned with everyday reality than with the metaphysical issues that attracted Greek thinkers. In modern terms, the Romans were pragmatists and functionalists. *Homo faber* (the doer) replaced *homo cogitans* (the thinker). Law, with its practical implications, became the highest expression of this culture. Good government meant creating conditions for the extension of power and the compliance of the dominated. Ethics was a repertoire of practical wisdom, which drew its inspiration from common good sense and experience. Moral education consisted of recommendations for reconciling the needs of society with people's natural inclination to pursue pleasure.

These more practical concerns made Roman thought particularly relevant to topics that were to engage personality psychologists many centuries later. However, two millennia separate us from ancient Rome. Thus, we can only indirectly grasp the exact sense of the writings that have come down to us. Yet one can not help but be surprised by the contemporary relevance of influential Roman thinkers such as Cicero and Seneca. Their analyses of conflicts between reason and passion and of the roles of education and experience in shaping the habits of individuals seem cogent to the present day.

In Roman thought, the essentialistic and finalistic concerns of the Greek tradition were replaced by more practical concerns. People were the arbiters of their own destiny. An important responsibility for the wise individual was to pursue conditions of life that would promote happiness and peace with others.

Unlike the Greeks, who lived in a mosaic of self-centered separate cities, the Romans did not remain isolated from the peoples and cultures of the tribes and nations they conquered. Although this may have sustained the empire at its height (Gibbon, 1776), the plurality of peoples probably combined with the pressure of the "barbarians" to induce a sort of implosion, which marked the Roman world's decline.

For centuries, the memory of ancient Greek and Roman cultural traditions seemed threatened. The Roman Catholic Church, however, guarded this knowledge and established a continuity with classical traditions. The church recovered ancient works, the monks transcribed them, and the clergy interpreted them. This was not a simple, direct translation, however, since the church's work was carried out within its spiritual view, which, for the entire medieval period, aimed at removing the human being from all forms of knowledge that were not imbued with revelation and faith. Eight centuries separated Saint Augustine from Saint Thomas Aquinas, but these motives remained constant. Through their teachings and the rich production of the Scholastics, the relevance of Platonic and, even more, Aristotelian thought was renewed, but in forms congenial to the defense and promotion of the faith. *Homo faber* was thus replaced by the *homo religiosus*, while much of continental Europe remained silent in the absence of any written tradition outside the monasteries. The intellectual contributions of the Far East or of the Arab world, such as the 11th- and 12th-century interpretations of Aristotelian thought provided by great thinkers such as Avicenna and Averoës, were hardly noticed.

## The Birth of the Sciences

■ *The Renaissance and the Enlightenment.* The Renaissance brought about a revolution in people's thinking about their relation to nature. The new thinking introduced remarkable new opportunities for individual initiative and creativity. Profound changes occurred at economic, social, and political levels. The expansion of markets, stimulated in part by new geographic discoveries, fostered considerable growth in technical and commercial activities. Broader social mobility was possible than in the past. The secularization of the state led to a strengthening of governmental organizations and to a nationalization of politics. The Reformation and Counter-Reformation testified to a turmoil in which religious inspiration was interwoven with social demands and national aspirations. The taste for discovery, interest in life, and reliance on individual abilities led, over the course of two centuries, to a process of secularization of the entire society, which culminated in the 1700s, the century of the Enlightenment.

The Enlightenment celebrated the importance of the individual and reaffirmed the primacy of the *logos*, or reason. A transformation from philosophical speculation to logical, scientific reasoning took place in a series of disciplines: first physics, then chemistry, then biology, and only later the social sciences. The contributions of philosophers such as Descartes, Locke, Hume, and Kant to these trends, particularly as they relate to psychology, have been duly noted (Boring, 1950; Hunt, 1993). Descartes and Kant were particularly influential in placing a high value on individuality and uniqueness; this oriented most of subsequent Western psychological thought to questions of individualism and subjectivism (Gill, 1996). During this era, empiricism (the idea that sensory experience is the only true source of knowledge) and rationalism (the idea that intellect rather than sensory experience is the true source of knowledge) represented the two banks between which reasoning on psychological matters flowed. According to the prevalence of one or the other, interest oscillated between issues of mind and body, cognition and emotion, nature and culture, individual and environment.

During the Enlightenment, philosophical speculation about the properties of mind and differences between individuals anticipated many of the concerns of the contemporary personality psychologist. In this regard, scholars now recognize Kant's *Anthropology from a Pragmatic Point of View* (1798) as a singularly important contribution. Kant differentiated temperament from moral character. Temperament originates primarily in the body and is similar to the "types" described by Hippocrates and Galen. Moral character corresponds to what individuals are able to make of themselves. The modern notions of self-regulation and personal agency capture what Kant referred to as character.

■ *Faculty Psychology.* Contemporary personality psychology has been influenced not only by the philosophy of this era but by its biology. The progress of medicine contributed to greater knowledge of anatomy and physiology. Armed with this knowledge, scientists began to investigate the biological bases of psychological functioning. They inquired about the relation between mental phenomena and physical stimuli and connections between physical constitution and personal attributes. The *organology* of Franz Joseph Gall and the *phrenology* of Johann Caspar Spurzheim are particularly noteworthy. Both these thinkers attempted to anchor the mental faculties to physical properties of the brain. The unique feature of this work was that, rather then seeking generic biological mechanisms that differentiated people from one another, they sought biological bases for a large number of mental faculties, each of which is possessed in varying degrees by all persons. Prior faculty psychology had speculated about general properties of the mind, such as memory, intelligence, imagination, and will. In contrast, Gall and Spurzheim viewed the brain as composed of as many particular organs as there are faculties, tendencies, and feelings expressed by the individual. Different mental functions – love for offspring, attachment, the instinct for self-defense, the sense of propriety, educability, pride, vanity, religious belief – were localized in different regions of the brain.

Although the limitations of these contributions is today apparent, their original appeal was surprisingly enduring (Lombardo & Duichin, 1997; Zola-Morgan, 1995). Contemporary neuroscience reveals the limitations of their conceptions, while also recognizing the originality of their intuitions (Damasio, 1994).

■ *Evolution.* Psychological investigation was significantly reoriented by the ideas about evolution initiated by Jean Baptiste de Lamarck and fully developed by Charles Darwin (Jacob, 1970). Darwin, in particular, explained that species had not been separately created. Instead, natural selection, through the preservation of favorable variations, had gradually created distinct species. The darwinian message influenced psychology immeasurably. It provided a rationale for various instinct and drive theories and opened the door to psychological research with lower species since these species were recognized as being similar to humans in many important respects. Darwin's thinking immediately influenced Francis Galton's studies of heredity and intelligence, also had an impact on the work of James and Freud, and in many ways helped to establish psychology as a science. As Bowlby (1990) has noted, "not only did Darwin change the course of biological science, but he changed forever how philosophers and theologians conceive man's place in nature" (p. 1).

Notions of variation and natural selection undermined beliefs about preordered principles that determine the value and status of a given species. They overthrew the religious doctrine that the nature of species was preordained, replacing it with the idea that any given species reflected a history of transactions between organisms and the environment. In a sense, then, Darwinism supported both innatism and environmentalism. More specifically, it demonstrated that the innate and the learned could not be dissociated, since evolution is driven by exchanges between biolological organisms and the environments to which they adapt.

### Social Science and Social Change

Finally, a further impulse toward the establishment of psychology and its subfields as scientific disciplines came from developments in other social sciences. Social and political factors spurred these developments. The Industrial Revolution and expansion of markets transformed social institutions and political orders. The emergence of new social groups and the need for new forms of government drew scholars' attention to the dynamics of social context. This favored the development of sociology, economics, and political science. When questions about social interaction shifted to questions of the individual and the possibility of modifying the individual's behavior, it was unavoidable that the discourse shifted to the field of what later was to become psychology.

Although speculative, the psychological intuitions of Durkeim, Tarde, Weber, Mill,

Spencer, and Marx had a long-lasting impact on psychology's study of social processes in personality development and functioning (Sills, 1968). Psychoanalysis, behavioral and social learning theories, interactionist perspectives, and more recent social-cognitive viewpoints have been variously influenced by Emile Durkheim's analysis of collective conscience and of suicide (and, in this context, his ideas on egoism, altruism, anomia, and fatalism); Gabriele Tarde's ideas on innovation, imitation and conflict; Max Weber's work on types of authority and the Protestant ethic; J.S. Mill's speculations on the motivation toward pleasure; Herbert Spencer's confidence in the merits of individualism and liberalism; and Karl Marx's conception of the essence of man.

### THE FOUNDING OF PERSONALITY PSYCHOLOGY

As we have seen in the preceding sections, the activities of personality psychology began long before the discipline was formally established. In the following, we address the conceptual developments and historical events that contributed to the official establishment of the field.

Although we are closer in time to the founding of the scientific discipline than to its philosophical roots, it nonetheless is difficult to provide a brief account of the start of the discipline that adequately recognizes the contributions of all relevant scholars. In the early days of psychology, investigators' interests were more eclectic than today. People commonly explored various subfields, moving, for example, from the study of perception and memory to more global phenomena such as intelligence or character. Thus, numerous psychologists who may not be formally identified with the personality contributed to the development of the discipline. The pressure of multiple unsolved problems, together with the absence of highly specialized research technologies combined to foster eclecticism in the early years.

In constructing a history of the field, choices must inevitably be made from among alternative ways of organizing its developments. For example, one could adopt chronological or geographic criteria, with the discipline being organized around year-to-year developments or around progress in separate regions of the world. Alternatively, one could organize a history around separate research topics, tracing the development of work on one versus another problem. Such schemes, however, may overlook important themes that guided research across time, regions, and research problems.

In the following, we consider three issues around which scientific activities were organized in the early days of the discipline and which sometimes divided the field into competing camps. The first is an epistemological concern that cut across various specific areas of investigation – specifically, different investigators embraced *structuralist* versus *functionalist* assumptions The second organizing principle concerns paradigms of personality, that is, different broad conceptions of personality that were shared by different sets of investigators. Third, from its early days the field was organized around alternative research traditions, that is, conceptually linked bodies of research, which in their entirety, constituted a coherent trend in scientific inquiry. Different research traditions can be assessed according to an "economic" criterion, in which one determines the productive payoff deriving from a linked set of contributions.

## Structuralism and Functionalism

Structuralism and functionalism were the two guiding metatheoretical principles that oriented research in psychology in its early years. Since these terms can take on various meanings, as has often been discussed, we will specify the meaning we attribute to them. Structuralism refers to the study of basic elements of mind. Structuralists assume that psychological experience can be understood as the combination of simple discrete elements. They aim to identify the basic ele-

ments, or components, of mental systems. In personality psychology, this prompts questions such as: What are the stable, universal, constituent elements of personality? Functionalism focuses on the processes through which people adapt to the environment. The functionalism that dominated American psychology in its early days studied the "mind in use" (Boring, 1950, p. 506) as the individual struggled to adapt to environmental contingencies. This leads to personality-related questions such as: What is personality for? What does personality do? Today, psychologists might study structures such as dispositions, beliefs, and motives and functions such as learning or self-regulation. The foremost advocates of structuralism and functionalism, respectively, were Wilhelm Wundt and William James, giants of the field, who shaped psychological theorizing for decades.

Wundt's (1896) structuralist orientation was evident in his work on temperament. Wundt studied emotion by searching for its basic elements. He first distinguished three kinds of feelings: pleasure – displeasure, tension – relief, and excitation – calmness. He then drew upon the Kantian revision of the Hippocratic-Galenic temperaments to develop a system of four temperaments, which resulted from combining two main axes, strength of emotions and changeability of feelings. Persons of choleric or melancholic temperament show strong affect, whereas those of sanguine or phlegmatic temperament are affectively weak. Regarding changeability, those who are choleric or sanguine change rapidly in response to new stimuli and ideas, whereas melancholic and phlegmatic persons are slower to change. These ideas guided later work. Eysenck (1947, 1970) drew upon Wundt's contributions in distinguishing extraversion from neuroticism and in proposing that the Hippocratic-Galenic temperaments could be understood in terms of a system of two temperament dimensions, emotional – unemotional and changeable – unchangeable.

James (1890) epitomized American psychology's interest in the functions served by mental processes. For example, in analyzing emotions, James did not work toward a taxonomy of basic elements. Instead, he sketched the dynamic functional relations between physiological activation and phenomenological experience. In studying consciousness, he emphasized not basic elements but the flow of experience. Finally, his elaboration of functionally distinct aspects of the self later became a point of reference for personality psychologists striving to understand the processes underlying the differentiation and the unity of individual experience.

In the past, an emphasis on structure versus process differentiated scientists from one another. Some primarily investigated structural concepts such as temperamental features, constitutional types, or dispositions. Others addressed dynamic processes that operate within the mind or in person – environment transactions. As we noted in chapter 1, however, today the distinction between process and structure perspectives is no longer adequate to capture differences among theoretical perspectives. Even extreme structural views speculate about processes that link stable structures to behavioral dynamics (McCrae & Costa, 1996). Process perspectives contend that processes organize themselves into stable configurations, which constitute enduring structural properties of the person (Mischel & Shoda, 1995). Contemporary personality psychologists thus recognize that structures and functional processes are interdependent. Both are essential for understanding what personality is and how it functions. All psychological processes rest on psychological structures and all structures result from processes (Caprara, 1996). Establishing how structures and processes act on one another is only possible through a diachronic analysis, that is, through an analysis of the reciprocal causation among structures and processes over the course of life.

## Paradigms

Two main research paradigms marked the study of personality in the first phase of its development. One of these conceptualized personality as a hierarchical organization in which broad, basic characteristics (dispositions or temperamental features) were superordinate to narrower behavioral tendencies. The narrowed characteristics were seen as relatively more modifiable by experience. Within this conception of the person, the primary research task was to identify and classify the high-level characteristics. Methods were devised to establish a universal set of characteristics and to investigate how they explained the individual's phenotypic qualities. In personality psychology, this conception fostered the study of "high-level" individual-difference factors, traits and supertraits.

A second line of inquiry conceived of personality as a system that develops in ontogenesis under the push of competing internal and external pressures. These pressures activate psychological processes. In so doing, they pose the conditions for the development of mental structures that mediate an individual's relationship with the environment. Investigators who adopted this approach first tried to identify the basic mechanisms involved in the functioning of the personality system. They then addressed the types of interpersonal or social events that influence the developing organization of personality. Theoretical development within this paradigm was intertwined with clinical practice. Individual cases were the scientist's laboratory, and the treatment of mental disorders provided the elements for understanding personality on the assumption that there is no strict division between normal and abnormal personality functioning.

## Research Traditions

A third organizational feature in the early days of personality psychology was the existence of coherent research traditions. Two broad research traditions were evident; in other words, investigators recognized two broad sets of empirical problems to be solved. One was the classification of interindividual differences; the other was the explorations of the internal dynamics of personality. These empirical concerns, of course, were linked to the conceptual paradigms just discussed.

The tradition of classifying individual differences can be traced to the taxonomy of Wundt noted above, the work of Galton (1869), and the often neglected work of Heymans and Wiersma (1906–1909). As Eysenck (1992b) noted, the work of Heymans and Wiersma contains the foundations for what later became the systematic study of temperament and personality. They built a personality structure on a strong foundation of empirical evidence by conducting both a study of families that included more than 2,000 individuals and a biographical investigation of 110 historical figures. From this evidence, they identified a large number of traits and reduced the list to the three basic temperamental dimensions, namely, activity, emotivity, and resonance. These dimensions foreshadow systems, proposed decades later by Buss and Plomin (1975) and Strelau (1983), which are discussed in chapter 3). Note that Heymans and Wiersma obtained this structure despite not yet having access to factor analysis, the standard tool for identifying trait dimensions in subsequent eras. Combinations of the dimensions yielded a taxonomy of eight psychological types.

The dynamic tradition began with the work of Pierre Janet and Sigmund Freud, who investigated the interactions among and dissociations between multiple internal psychic mechanisms. We review the work of Janet in the following section on progress in the field, and we consider consider the Freudian tradition in detail in the final section of this chapter.

In using the term *tradition*, we are indebted to Laudan (1977), who has treated research traditions as sets of general assumptions regarding the problems to be handled and the appropriate methods to be used in a domain of study. A focus on traditions highlights the continuity of discourse that transcends the research methods of a particular generation.

Research traditions transcend the talents of individual investigators. To assess their ultimate value, then, one must ask whether the combined efforts of a tradition's multiple investigators have increased knowledge and whether the accumulated knowledge has been transmitted across generations of researchers. One must consider whether the tradition has opened new areas of investigation and whether scientific efforts have significantly changed the conditions of people's lives. One must bear in mind, in other words, the criterion of *value added*, that is, the unique long-term contribution of a tradition. This consideration is particularly important in personality psychology, which has sometimes seemed dominated by fads that come and go, leaving little lasting trace of their passing (Meehl, 1978).

## Continuities and Discontinuities in the Progress of the Discipline

The long-term heuristic value of a research tradition derives in part from its ability to stimulate interest in important research questions. This criterion is key to appreciating the true value of early 20th-century efforts. Contemporary psychologists may rightly question whether the details of these early studies are still of value. However, it would be difficult to question the value of the overall traditions, which clearly raised important questions and thereby prompted research. There is much continuity between early efforts and later developments. If only for this reason, the traditions established early in the century were crucial to the growth of the discipline.

Acknowledging continuities should not cause one to lose sight of theoretical breaks, diasporas, and innovations. For example, despite continuity in the trait approaches, there are significant differences between early differential psychology and the trait psychology of Allport (1937), who placed lesser stock in interindividual methods. Significant discontinuities mark the transition from Freudian psychoanalysis to subsequent dynamic approaches, which emphasized social motives (Fromm, 1955; Horney, 1939) and object relations (Winnicott, 1958). Other contemporary perspectives cannot be traced to the early traditions. The history of social-cognitive approaches owes little to the trait and dynamic traditions, other than that these traditions served as a counterpoint to the social-cognitivists' theoretical themes (Bandura, 1986; Mischel, 1973). It is thus surprising that social-cognitive theory today addresses the same questions about personality dynamics that psychoanalysis did (Westen, 1991).

In retrospect, a range of problems was inaccessible to the early investigators because they lacked knowledge and technologies that have come to psychology via other disciplines (e.g., the neurosciences, computer science). Despite any such limitations, these two traditions provided an impetus for the discipline's efforts to grasp what is universal and unique in individual personality. Their impact on society, education, work organizations, medical practice, and literature has survived beyond their heuristic value for guiding research.

## THE PROGRESS OF PERSONALITY PSYCHOLOGY

Developments in 20th-century personality psychology generally have been organized according to competing schools of thought. Most students have been introduced to the field by theory comparisons. The foundation for this approach to the discipline was established by Hall and Lindzey (1957) in their famed undergraduate textbook. Their volume was so widely used and so widely imitated that it constitutes a rare example of an undergraduate textbook that was of historical importance to a discipline. Not only did it shape the teaching of personality psychology but in retrospect, its various editions serve as a barometer of trends in the field.

In their first edition in 1957, Hall and Lindzey presented twelve theories, each of which had one or more protagonists. The dynamic psychologies of Sigmund Freud, of Carl Jung, and of Alfred Adler and of the neo-Freudians, including Erich Fromm, Harry Stack Sullivan, and Karen Horney, took up a quarter of the volume. The psychology of indi-

vidual differences, which took up less than half the space of the dynamic tradition, clustered theorists who promoted biological-constitution and factor-analytic approaches. Some space was dedicated to learning theory. The rest of the volume covered theorists whose work, in a broad sense, could be traced to common holistic-dynamic inspirations. These theorists included Andras Angyal, Gordon Allport, Kurt Goldstein, Kurt Lewin, Gardner Murphy, Abraham Maslow, Henry Murray, and Carl Rogers.

By the time of the third edition in 1978, substantial changes were evident. The volume was organized differently, with clinically oriented theories grouped together in the first half, experimental and quantitative theories in the second half. The first half now included Erik Erikson's contributions to psychoanalysis and the European existential-phenomenologist approach of Medard Boss and Ludwig Binswanger. The latter half discussed Allport, Cattell, and Skinner. Between the halves, a new chapter presented Eastern personality theories and their influence on Western psychology. It is somewhat surprising that even at the end of the 1970s, there was little mention of the cognitive revolution or the field's pending person – situation debate and relatively little discussion of contemporary theorists such as Albert Bandura and Hans Eysenck. Indeed, these two investigators only received separate chapter coverage in a fourth edition (Hall, Lindzey, & Campbell, 1998), after their ideas had already shaped the field for some time. The Hall and Lindzey text, then, did not always update the reader on contemporary developments. However, it thereby did avoid passing fads. In general, the text masterfully presented well-established theoretical contributions while indirectly attesting to the difficulty of bringing them together into a cumulative science of personality.

### Freedom, Resources, and Critical Mass

In the early days of the discipline, most investigators were from the old continent. Social transformations in 18th and 19th century Europe accelerated scientific progress in all fields. Things changed in the 20th century. New opportunities for science abounded in the United States. The United States offered new university chairs and laboratories and applied opportunities not found elsewhere. This reflected not only the growing economic power of the United States but the congeniality of the discipline to the ideology of the New World. In Europe, particularly after the First World War, sociopolitical forces opposed psychology. Of the dominant schools of thought, idealism was not sympathetic to psychology and positivism and logical positivism were, at best, ambivalent. Various political regimes viewed psychology with suspicion. The discipline was easily overwhelmed in the ideological clashes that accompanied geopolitical and socioeconomic change. Nazism in Austria and Germany and Fascism in Italy silenced at least two generations of psychologists, forcing some into exile. Psychology took part in the "brain drain" across the Atlantic between the world wars. Over half of the personality theorists discussed in the third edition of Hall and Lindzey were originally from continental Europe, but the majority of these persons later emigrated to the United States to avoid racial persecution. In the Soviet Union, a regime of different ideology but with methods of government similar to the authoritarian regimes of Germany and Italy disallowed ideas that conflicted with the collective goals of state socialism.

In both authoritarian and democratic nations, insufficient material resources and difficulties in communication discouraged the formation of critical masses of interacting scientists. Nevertheless, by the 1920s and 1930s the field had produced a range of seminal ideas, which profoundly influenced the future of personality psychology. These included, in particular, the dynamic psychology of Pierre Janet, the field theory of Kurt Lewin, the personalism of William Stern, and the historical-cultural approach of Lev Vygotsky.

Janet began work on psychopathology in the late 19th century. He was initially interested in the loss of personality cohesion that results when psychological functions became automatic and dissociated from the whole person. He subsequently investigated two forms of neurosis, namely hysteria and psychasthenia, and arrived at a dynamic theory, which conceived of every form of conduct as the result of the combination of psychic force and psychic tension. Whereas the former concerns the quantity of psychic energy supporting the various activities, the latter concerns their level of organization and synthesis. Janet subsequently became more interested in the social determinants of personality. Although behavior may result from the complex organization of dynamic tendencies, this organization, he reasoned, largely depends on interpersonal and social factors (Janet, 1889, 1929).

Kurt Lewin's novel conceptions anticipated many contemporary cognitive and interactionist ideas. As we noted in chapter 1, Lewin wished to overcome the essentialism implicit in psychology's efforts to explain behavior. Rather than explaining behavior by reference to a taxonomy of essential personal qualities, he sought to identify dynamic psychological and social forces that contribute to behavior.

Lewin's field theory took mathematical topology as a model. Every behavior (B) was a function (F) of the person (P) and of the environment (E), formalized in the equation $B = F(P,E)$. Within this framework, Lewin emphasized the perceptions (today one might say construals) that individuals have of themselves and the environment. The perceptions of self (needs, abilities, goals) and of the physical and social environment (opportunities, pressures, obstacles) are the elements that count as explanations of personal action. Lewin examined these factors as forces (needs and goals) operating in the psychological field (what is present in the individual mind at a certain moment). This implied that the person should be examined in the concrete situation, to derive the reasons for his or her behavior from the totality of facts that are psychologically relevant to that person (Lewin, 1935, 1936, 1951).

William Stern used the term *personalistics* to refer to the science that studies the human person in totality. The current notion of personality is often traced back to Stern, whose theorizing placed particular emphasis on the characteristics of unity, indivisibility, and purposiveness that mark the person. Personality was conceived as a whole rather than an aggregation of parts, an *unitas multiplex*, which is neither entirely determined by dispositions nor entirely determined by the environment. Whereas traits represented the basic and stable elements of individuality upon which the various dispositions are rooted, dispositions were viewed as goal-directed, malleable entities, whose outcomes depended on the person's propensity to chart his or her own life course. Ultimately, people's intentions and values were seen as decisive in shaping the environment and their own experiences (Stern, 1935).

Vygotsky has recently been rediscovered, primarily for his contributions to the developmental psychology of thought and language. However, he also played a very important role in personality psychology. Vygotsky established the premises of what later was to become the historical-cultural approach (Leont'ev, 1975). This approach represented the only real alternative to Pavlovism in personality psychology in the countries of the former Soviet Union and its satellites.

As a loyal Marxist, Vygotsky accepted Marx's notion that the essence of human beings could be traced back to their social relationships. He developed the theory that all higher psychic functions resulted from the internalization of social relations. Social relations were transformed into internalized strategies and rules, which in turn function as structures that underlie psychological functioning. The individual transforms tools and symbols in the social environment into cognitive capabilities. A person's abilities thus reflect the opportunities available in the concrete conditions of his or her life. Social circumstances govern potentialities and shape personality.

To Vygotsky, the development of language is key to the overall development of the psychological functions. Language first carries an interpersonal function of communication but then adds an intrapsychic function of self-regulation. Interpersonal processes, then, become intrapsychic ones. Individuals thus are defined by a set of mental strategies, which ultimately derives from their social relations. Once internally represented, social relations orient personality in its relationships with the world, and taking action in the world turns potentialities into realized capabilities (Vygotsky, 1934).

## Developments in the United States

As we noted, working conditions for psychologists in the United States differed from those in Europe. From its early days, U.S. psychology was able to meet important social needs in education, work, and health. Psychologists' efforts were congruent with society's aims of assimilating different populations and making the most efficient use of human resources. Psychologists applied scientific management principles to work organizations, tested military recruits, assessed students' intelligence, and evaluated social attitudes. The expansion of public education, as well as the pressing need for solutions to social problems involving race relations, enlarged psychologists' opportunities to influence society in the 20th century's first four decades. During the Second World War, researchers in individual-difference testing and attitude change could channel their efforts to the defense of democracy.

Psychology appealed to university administrators, intellectuals, and the American public at large. Its strong functionalist orientation made possibilities for application readily apparent. Its unconstrained optimism about the possibility of making psychology a scientific discipline in the mold of the natural sciences helped to establish its role in the university. By the early 1930s, the field achieved the "critical mass" needed to maintain a vibrant discipline, which could be organized according to various specialized subfields.

Our subfield of interest acquired the status of an autonomous domain in part through the efforts of Gordon Allport (1937) and Henry Murray (1938). They both developed theoretical frameworks aimed at explaining what is universal and what is distinctive about each person. Their common goal was a unified discipline that would reconcile the depth of clinical insights with rigorous research, and in achieving this goal, they moved beyond the theoretical traditions of the past (psychoanalysis and the psychology of individual differences). Allport's and Murray's contributions continue to be points of reference for contemporary scientists.

Three elements of Allport's theory either anticipated or directly shaped developments many years later. The first was his definition of personality *traits*. In one of the best-known passages in the history of the discipline, Allport defined traits as "neuropsychic structures . . . with the capacity to render many stimuli functionally equivalent, and to initiate and guide consistent forms of adaptive and expressive behavior" (Allport, 1937, p. 295). This definition guided subsequent theory on traits and prompted empirical research by both proponents and opponents of the trait concept on the relative consistency versus inconsistency of social behavior. Depending on their generality across individuals, traits were classified by Allport as either universal or *common* traits, or as *individual* traits that could not be assessed in populations but only in individual persons. Depending on their pervasiveness across a person's behavior, traits were further classified into cardinal traits, which influence almost all of the person's actions; central traits, which are highly distinctive of the person; and secondary traits, which are relatively narrow in focus and less distinctive of the individual.

Second, Allport's (1937) postulate of the *functional autonomy of motives* was an important step in the history of the psychology of motivation. The idea was that an activity that originally was engaged in for one reason (e.g., to obtain resources that meet basic biological needs) may become an end in itself. The activity then is engaged in for its own sake; the behavior is independent of the original motive. To Allport, then, all actions could not rightfully be traced back to any small set of primitive instincts or drives. The principle of functional autonomy explained the variety and indefinite growth of motives. Rejecting the tension-reduction models of both psychoanalysis and behaviorism was one of Allport's best insights.

Third, Allport's notion of the *proprium* (Allport, 1961) anticipated subsequent developments in the psychology of the self. The proprium refers to the collection of self-perceptions and self-referent beliefs. Allport saw the proprium as being at the core of personal identity. The proprium developed over time, increasingly contributing to the coherence of personality functioning.

Contemporary debate still echoes Allport's concern with methodological pluralism and with idiographic (later morphogenic) methods. In striving to capture uniqueness without renouncing the search for general regularities, Allport unhesitatingly combined idiographic methods, such as the study of personal documents, with nomothetic methods, such as scales and questionnaires. His wise eclecticism was quite original.

As with other early contributions, the wisdom of hindsight enables us to see shortcomings in Allport's work. The notion of functional autonomy was not grounded in analyses of mind and brain, as such a theory would have to be today. Speculation about the nature of the proprium and of various traits was not anchored in precise analysis of the structures and processes that supported their functioning. His methodological pluralism left open the question of how to integrate alternative methods and levels of analysis on which personality can be analyzed. Although Allport's ideas no longer may guide contemporary research activity, they remain of historical importance if only because they set the stage for so much of what was to follow.

Murray's impact was similar to Allport's, although his theoretical inspiration was different. Whereas Allport was influenced by Stern and was firmly committed to a teleological view, Murray was influenced by Freud and was sympathetic to a mechanistic view of mental functioning. To Murray, personality was an organizing and governing agent, and a function located in the brain.

To describe personality and explain its functioning, Murray proposed a triad of constructs, namely, need, press and theme. *Needs* were internal forces that organize experience. A need organized perceptions, motivation, and action, thereby giving the organism a particular directional tendency. *Presses* were forces in the environment. They were environmental pressures that interacted with a person's strivings, making particular pursuits more or less difficult. *Beta press* referred to opportunities and impediments as perceived, whereas alpha press referred to objectively existing facilitators or obstacles. *Thema* were more molar units of analysis. Thema include a need and a press, and thus are person-and-situation units that capture both a personal striving and the situation in which the person operates in goal pursuit.

Murray's theorizing enduringly influenced multiple areas of psychological inquiry. His notion of a need for achievement stimulated a major approach to the study of motivation (see chapter 12). His projective test for assessing motives, the Thematic Apperception Test (TAT), is still used in the present day by innumerable motivation and clinical psychologists. Murray's construct of thema is echoed in recent work on personal concerns, personal strivings, and personal narratives (see chapters 9 and 12). More generally, his work gave impetus to systematic methods in clinical psychology, particularly the use of diagnostic councils, or case conferences, in which many observers come together to bring different perspectives on a given client. He helped to inspire an entire tradition of research on biographies and life narratives and, indirectly, on life course development. Like Allport, then, Murray's historical impact is far broader than might be suggested by a simple cataloguing of contemporary references to his work. The breadth of his impact reflected the breadth of his thinking. Murray collaborated with sociologists and with anthropologists. He also delved deeply into the analysis of literary cases. Murray, for example, was a Melville

scholar, providing a penetrating analysis of *Moby Dick*, in which Ahab represents the forces of the id unleashed against the repressive, godlike superego that is the white whale (Murray, 1951).

Also as with Allport, the contemporary psychologist can detect the limitations inherent in Murray's conception of personality. He embraced a tension reduction model of mental functioning, which now is generally recognized as inadequate. His attempt to explain motivation via a universal motive taxonomy seems dated in light of contemporary knowledge of cross-cultural variations in motivational processes and of the processes through which interrelated affective and self-regulatory processes contribute to motivation and personality coherence. Still, there can be no doubt of the creativity, originality, and value of his contributions.

Personality psychology can not boast of discoveries that unequivocally moved us from states of ignorance to knowledge. The field seems instead to have experienced stops and starts. Unequivocal progress is only apparent when one takes a broad view, examining advances across the years in the methods by which problems are conceptualized and studied, as well as the aggregate knowledge that is thus gained. From this broad perspective, Allport's and Murray's contributions undoubtedly have been critical to the advance of the field.

## A Period of Transition

During the years 1930 to 1950, personality psychology firmly established itself as a unique, organized discipline. Efforts were made to integrate clinical, correlational, and experimental research contributions. Personality psychologists rejected the perceived reductionism of other branches of the field, focusing instead on the unity, totality, and complexity of the person. This was an era of great promise. Scholars from other disciplines, such as anthropology and social philosophy, became attracted to the study of personality (Adorno, Frenkel-Brunswik, Levinson, & Sanford, 1951; Kluckhohn,

Murray, & Schneider, 1953). The discipline was the place where diverse ideas from psychoanalysis, behaviorism, the study of traits, and the study of cultures were integrated. The threat of fascism, the Second World War, and the reestablishment of peace in a world still devastated and divided by war were testing grounds on which the discipline was directly called to the defense of democracy. By the beginning of the postwar era, the critical developments in psychology began to take place in the United States, where the axis of the discipline had shifted.

The period of the early to mid 1950s was one in which the discipline reached a peak of creative activity. Sears (1950) helped to give direction to this growth by identifying the field with respect to three key areas of investigation: structure, dynamics, and the development of traits and motives. The discipline was charged with explaining the structures of personality, the dynamic processes that sustain and orient behavior in a coherent fashion, and the development of a personality system in which different components become integrated. A number of novel ideas spoke to this challenge. The "new look" emphasized the impact of motivational and personality factors on basic processes of perception, thought, and memory (Bruner 1957a, b). This development promised for personality psychology an important role in integrating diverse branches of the psychological enterprise. Dollard and Miller's (1950) attempt to reconcile psychoanalysis and learning theories similarly seemed a harbinger of broadly integrated knowledge of the person.

Unfortunately, it soon became clear that these promises of an integrative personality psychology could not be fulfilled. On the one hand, personality psychologists did not find in the rest of the field the knowledge required to address precisely the questions of their discipline. Necessary progress in developmental, cognitive, and social psychology, behavioral genetics, and the neurosciences only came years later. The seminal *personal construct theory* of George Kelly (1955) illustrates the point. Kelly conceived of behavior as guided by the anticipation of events, where the anticipations reflected the constructs through which people viewed their relation to the world. This cognitively grounded theory was ahead of its time. Kelly, surrounded by behaviorism, had no formal models of knowledge representation on which to draw. It was not until years later that his contributions were fully appreciated and expanded on, thanks to psychology's increased knowledge of information-processing mechanisms (Cantor & Kihlstrom, 1987; Higgins, 1990; Mischel, 1973).

On the other hand, even by the 1950s experimental psychology was easily advanced enough to expose the methodological limits of personality psychology, in which experiments generally were precluded by ethical considerations and the difficulty of representing complex phenomena in the laboratory. This fostered a separation between personality psychology and the broader base of psychological knowledge. First, psychoanalysis became divorced from scientifically oriented personality psychology. It later became difficult to reconcile the experimental tradition with clinically oriented approaches such as those of Maslow (1954) and Rogers (1961). The hegemony of behaviorism imposed a severe toll on a discipline whose object of investigation posed great obstacles to experimentation. The 1950s closed with less promise than they began.

The period between the middle and late 1950s and the late 1960s was a difficult and controversial one. Grand theories were replaced by microtheories. Great hopes about even these narrower theories were often followed by disillusionment (Caprara & Van Heck, 1992; Pervin, 1990). Levinson (1981) has observed that, in contrast with the vitality and innovation of previous decades, the new era featured pedestrian conformity and lesser imagination. A concern with methods and measurement narrowed investigators' scope of activity and indirectly deflected attention from the field's original aims. With rare exception (e.g., Block, 1961), investigators appeared to be more interested in individual differences with respect to single variables (e.g., aggression, extroversion, trait anxiety, locus of control) than in the coherent integration of personality variables within the whole person.

It is likely that the narrowing of interests was a by-product of investigators' efforts to achieve legitimacy within the prevailing ideology of science. Researchers perceived a need to test well-defined ideas in a rigorous manner. Rigor eventually was combined with theoretical breadth in the work of a set of investigators who had a lasting impact on the field. Norman (1963, 1967) advanced the psycholexical approach by expanding on and refining the seminal work of Allport and Odbert (1936) and Cattell (1946). His identification of five individual-difference factors was a critical step in the historical development of the five-dimensional individual-differences model that was destined to become the leading framework for describing personality in later decades (John, 1990). Cattell (1965) and Eysenck (1970) refined factor analytic techniques, and Eysenck's (1967) laboratory research began to identify biological correlates of personality traits. Although Eysenck's initial hypotheses about the biological bases of personality were not firmly supported (Eysenck, 1990; see also chapter 6), his efforts nonetheless were a valuable step in an enduringly important research tradition.

The study of motivation also progressed in this era. This subfield freed itself from the dominance of instinct theories, drive theories, and need taxonomies. Investigators addressed affective and cognitive processes regulating the initiation and direction of behavior (Atkinson, 1964; McClelland, 1961), as well as people's motivation to achieve not only external rewards, but personal competence (White, 1959). The systematic study of the achievement motive and then of power and affiliative motives was critical to subsequent progress of research on the dynamics of action and the relations between personality and motivation (Atkinson & Birch, 1970; Heckhausen, 1991; McClelland, 1985; Weiner, 1992; also see chapter 12).

Finally, early social learning theories (Bandura and Walters, 1963; Rotter, 1954,

1966; Sears, 1951; Sears, Rau & Alpert, 1965) also paved the way to the modern cognitive and social-cognitive perspectives. Work by Sears and colleagues on identification and socialization processes illustrated the importance of interpersonal relations and social interactions in the formation of personality patterns. Rotter's (1966) study of general expectancies of locus of control prompted subsequent developments of attribution theory. The dimension of internal-external locus of control could be viewed, from an attributional perspective, as one of a number of attribution dimensions that are critical to the regulation of emotional and motivational states (Weiner, 1985, 1986). Finally, Bandura's research on modeling in the early 1960s alerted all of psychology to the power of influence of vicarious experience–a particularly timely alert given the rapid expansion of television. Research on modeling also hastened the development of cognitive models of social behavior. Behavioristic analyses could not adequately explain the fact that people who observed a novel, skilled act at one point in time could perform that action later and could do so even in the absence of reinforcement (Bandura, 1965). Such findings could only be explained by reference to a system of attentional, memory, and production processes that enable people to acquire skills by observation (Bandura, 1977b). Bandura's theoretical contributions are reviewed in more detail in chapter 4.

Even in retrospect, one cannot confidently assess whether the main contributions to progress have been the grand theories, which pointed the way, or theories of more limited scope, which sometimes succeeded in taking valuable, irreversible steps down the path. Scholars have criticized the track taken by personality psychology in the 1960s, contending that the era had lost sight of the person (Carlson, 1971; also see White, 1981). Still, it is difficult to imagine what the field would look like today if it lacked the foundations laid in the 1960s in the areas of personality description, construct definition, assessment methods, social learning processes, and psychological mechanisms of motivation, belief, attributions, expectancies, and behavior.

## Substantive Challenges, Rhetoric, and Debate in the Advancement of Knowledge

In the 1960s, the field was shaken by a series of volumes that questioned the core assumptions of the discipline (Peterson, 1968; Vernon, 1964). The most impactful of these was Mischel's (1968) *Personality and Assessment*. Mischel's book, which originally was conceived as a simple review of the field, turned into a penetrating critique. His survey of the empirical literature revealed that in the study of objectively measured social behavior, the internal states identified by psychodynamic and trait formulations and operationalized through projective methods and questionnaires rarely predicted more than 10% of the variance in overt behavior. Personality correlations failed to exceed .30. The infamous value .30 came to symbolize the limitations of the discipline.

It is ironic that, in citing .30, Mischel inadvertently may have led readers to underestimate the magnitude of his critique. The value .30 became so well known that commentators mistakenly interpreted it as a typical validity coefficient obtained when one uses personality constructs to predict behavior. In Mischel's review, though, .30 was not a modal value but was an upper limit; typical validity coefficients were in the .10 to .15 range. These discouraging values were obtained in two predictive contexts: predicting specific acts from scores on global personality questionnaires and predicting cross-situational consistency in behavior, that is, predicting an act in one social context from an act in another context, when both acts are indicators of a common dispositional category. People with high scores on an extraversion scale were not necessarily more extraverted than others when observed in a specific social context (Newcomb, 1929). Children who cheated on tests were not necessarily more dishonest than others in playground games (Hartshorn & May, 1928). A body of such results led Mischel to conclude

that the validity coefficients typically obtained when using projective techniques and questionnaire methods were so low that these assessments had almost no value other than as rough screening devices.

The gist of Mischel's critique, though, did not involve merely the practical question of behavioral prediction; it involved fundamental issues of theory. Mischel pointed out that if we had known of the poor predictive value of psychodynamic and trait constructs at the beginnings of the discipline, we would never have embraced these constructs in the first place. Why adopt, as core units of analysis for a psychology of persons, variables that forfeit more than 90% of the between-person variability in human action?

Mischel (1968) highlighted the shortcomings of the extant empirical literature in order to promote novel theoretical developments. He argued that the empirical failures of psychodynamic and trait formulations argued for the development of new units of analysis for conceptualizing personality. In this regard, he advanced two key points. First, the new units should account not only for individual differences in average behavioral tendencies but also for within-person differences in behavior from one context to another. Second, the new units of analysis, whatever they prove to be, should be grounded in psychology's overall knowledge of cognitive and social learning processes (Mischel, 1968). Mischel was arguing for an integrated discipline, that is, a personality psychology that brought together diverse strands of psychological knowledge into a comprehensive portrait of the individual.

In 1968, Mischel was not able to present an adequate set of alternative units for conceptualizing persons. Much of the second half of *Personality and Assessment* was devoted to a behavioristic analysis of social behavior that Mischel himself saw as inadequate within only a few years. In 1973, Mischel presented a set of cognitive-social *person variables*. These units of analysis placed at the center of personality theory the processes through which people acquire and organize information about themselves and the environment. In 1973 Mischel proposed variables of cognitive and behavioral construction competencies, encoding strategies and personal constructs, behavior–outcome and stimulus–outcome expectancies, subjective stimulus values, and self-regulatory systems and plans. These variables constituted a new lexicon with which to talk about persons and individual differences. This "reconceptualization" of personality reflected a number of influences. These included the seminal ideas of Mischel's mentors, George Kelly and Julian Rotter; developments in the study of observational learning and cognitive mechanisms of behavior change spearheaded by the work of Bandura (1969), and Bandura and Walters (1963); the information-based model of behavior proposed by Miller, Galanter, and Pribram (1960); and the cognitive psychology of Neisser (1967) and later Lindsay and Norman (1972). Mischel's viewpoint was greatly expanded and updated in subsequent years. In collaboration with Yuichi Shoda, he developed a theory of how interacting cognitive and affective systems give rise to stable personality dispositions (Mischel & Shoda, 1995, 1999).

■ *The Rhetoric of Debate: Persons Versus Situations.* It is worth recalling that in 1968 Mischel was criticizing both trait theories and psychodynamic theories, the two dominant approaches to the study of personality at the time. The criticisms were made on rather different grounds. Psychodynamic approaches were promising theoretically but lacking methodologically. In principle, psychodynamic units might be capable of capturing both the stability and the dynamic variability in action that characterize the individual. Unfortunately, the theories were formulated in a way that made them largely untestable, and the associated interview and projective assessment methods were so unreliable as to make accurate prediction impossible. In contrast, trait approaches were, in some respects, strong methodologically, yet they were lacking conceptually. Questionnaire methods might display perfectly adequate internal reliability

and test–retest stability. Mischel was well aware that people's descriptions of themselves are quite consistent and stable over time. However, trait constructs failed, in his view, because they were too static, global, and essentialistic. Universal dispositional categories failed to identify underlying causal processes and failed to do justice to the uniqueness of the individual.

Mischel, then, was not questioning the existence of personality and meaningful individual differences. He was questioning the existence of adequate personality theory and was criticizing the way in which individual differences were conceptualized and assessed. He was trying, ultimately, not to destroy the discipline of personality psychology but to revitalize it.

Mischel quickly realized that he had been widely misunderstood. These misunderstandings are an object lesson in the rhetoric of debate. Mischel's critique (1968), though carefully phrased, had the effect of exaggerating perceived differences between his approach and others. Mischel himself contributed to this state of affairs by placing so much emphasis in 1968 on the situational control of behavior, as opposed to the person-based mediators of behavior outlined a few years later (Mischel, 1973), and relatively little emphasis on the ways in which trait and psychodynamic theorists might confront the issues he raised. Stating an extreme version of an opponent's position as a way of promoting one's own is a common rhetorical device. In this instance, it might not have been the optimal strategy. Mischel soon came to be known as a "situationist," who did not believe in personality. Trait and psychodynamic theories became known as person approaches, which were uninterested in the role of situations. Neither view was accurate. Nonetheless, these exaggerated positions became the terms of a prolonged person–situation debate, which dominated the field throughout the 1970s and early 1980s (e.g., Alker, 1972; Bem, 1972; Bem & Allen, 1974; Bem & Funder, 1978; Block, 1977; Epstein, 1979; Jackson & Paunonen, 1985; Mischel & Peake, 1982); for reviews see

Kenrick & Funder, 1988 and Schmitt & Borkenau, 1992.

The way in which different theoretical camps responded to Mischel during the person–situation debate further illuminates the advantages and disadvantages of alternative rhetorical strategies. Psychoanalysts did not respond at all. Mischel's compelling critique of psychoanalytic theory and methods seemingly went unheard. His arguments thus had little impact among dynamically oriented scientists and practitioners. Trait psychologists, in contrast, responded forcefully. In so doing, they brought greater attention to the conceptual and empirical limitations of the trait approaches of the time. In essence, they drew greater attention to Mischel's critique of trait theory.

Though the original terms of person–situation debate may have been unfortunate, the debate itself yielded a number of valuable theoretical and empirical advances. Three contributions are of particular note. Bem and Allen (1974) revived the moderator variable strategy propagated earlier by Ghiselli (1963) and Saunders (1956). Rather than assessing the degree to which people, in general, were consistent with respect to a trait, they proposed that people vary in their consistency with respect to a trait category. Evidence for the traitlike consistency of behavior may be found among people who explicitly describe themselves as cross-situationally consistent with respect to a given disposition. Self-reported consistency, in other words, might moderate the strength of relations among trait indicators, including the behaviors sampled across different situations. Unfortunately, the methods of these authors were somewhat flawed, their findings were mixed, and subsequent investigations generally failed to replicate their results (e.g., Chaplin & Goldberg, 1983; Mischel & Peake, 1982). Despite this, Bem and Allen's work (1974) did reactivate interest in the moderator–variable strategy. Rather than examining self-perceived consistency with respect to a particular trait, other scientists explored global moderators, that is, personality factors that might influence a person's overall degree of behavioral consistency. Snyder (1974, 1987) suggested the construct of self-monitoring, and Fenigstein, Scheier, and Buss (1975) explored the role of self-consciousness.

A second methodological solution came from Epstein (1979), who reminded the field of the critical need to aggregate data across multiple observations (cf. Block, 1977). Single, unaggregated behavioral acts may be so laden with statistical error that accurate prediction is impossible. Consistency studies may fail in the domain of behavioral prediction, then, simply because the difficult-to-obtain behavioral measures are few in number and hence unreliable. Epstein (1979) demonstrated the predictive gains to be made by aggregation; however, by aggregating diverse acts, and across diverse contexts, his results spoke more to the question of temporal stability of behavior than to the central issue of coherence in action across contexts.

Mischel and Peake (1982) demonstrated that even highly aggregated acts may yield little evidence of cross-situational consistency. Their detailed observations of "conscientious" acts exhibited among students at a liberal arts college revealed considerable temporal stability in behavior but quite low cross-situational consistency (in the $r = .13$ range). Low consistency coefficients were obtained even when aggregated, statistically reliable behavioral measures were employed. Mischel and Peake also took a major step in resolving the so-called consistency paradox, that is, the fact that our intuitions suggest that a person's social behavior is consistent, whereas our scientific data do not. Mischel and Peake found that people who judged themselves to be cross-situationally consistent with respect to a trait were, in fact, no more cross-situationally consistent than others. However, they were more temporally stable with respect to that trait. People who judged themselves to be cross-situationally conscientious displayed high temporal stability with respect to a few key behaviors that were prototypic of the act category conscientious (Mischel & Peake, 1982).

Mischel and Peake's work elicited much debate and counterdebate. One noteworthy contribution was that of Jackson and Paunonen (1985), who demonstrated that substantial cross-situational consistency – exceeding the famed .30 – could be obtained through psychometric techniques. Within Mischel and Peake's original set of 17 behavioral indicators of conscientiousness, they identified a cluster of five situations across which individual differences were quite consistent. However, like Epstein's contribution, Jackson and Paunonen's was methodologically sound but only indirectly relevant to Mischel's theoretical critique. Mischel had contended that consistency could not be obtained with respect to broad trait categories such as conscientiousness. Jackson and Paunonen obtained consistency across a narrow set of five circumstances which, by any account, could not be interpreted as an adequate indicator of the original, broad trait category. By psychometrically whittling away at the original trait indicators, the construct of conscientiousness was lost.

■ *Interactionism.* Debate of this sort did not lead to a dead end. Unnecessary controversy eventually ceased and wisdom was acquired. Beginning in the 1970s, interactionism, an old idea with new clothes, took the floor (Ekehammar, 1974; Endler & Magnusson, 1976). Soon, virtually all investigators posited that behavior should not be explained in terms of person factors or situation factors alone but rather some interactive combination of the two. This position became so popular that the only point of debate was the question: Who was more interactionist than the others? A volume edited by Magnusson and Endler in 1977 brought different positions under a common umbrella, while calling everyone's attention to the "crossroads" at which personality psychology had arrived thanks to the person–situation debate.

In addition to its theoretical substance, the nationalities of the scientists involved in this volume (Magnusson & Endler, 1977) are of note. The editors were Swedish and Canadian, the contributors North Americans and a broad representation of Europeans. This diversity was novel to the field. After decades of silence, the 1970s brought Europeans back on the scene. Their importance was destined to grow during the 1980s and 1990s, together with that of scientists from other continents who had previously not participated in research in this area.

### Facing the Present and Looking to the Future

As our history moves to the 1980s and 1990s, it begins to overlap with the substantive coverage that comprises the rest of this text. Thus, we will be brief here. The 1980s witnessed a renewed vitality in personality psychology, which continued through the close of the century. A number of trends contributed to this sense of renewal. Curiously, these trends did not necessarily converge, despite what one might expect given the general state of optimism.

One development was an expansion of the field's understanding of interactionism. Early interactionist studies had shown that, whereas the percentage of variability accounted for by dispositions and situation factors are often similar and modest in size, the variability accounted for by the interaction of person and situations is superior to either alone. Once this point was established, it gradually became clear that this analysis of variance approach was inadequate to capture the dynamics of person–situation transactions. The statistical model is too static to capture the ways in which persons and situations influence each other dynamically over time (Endler, 1984; Magnusson & Stattin, 1998). Further, its underlying formula, Behavior = $f$(person X situations) (behavior is a function of the interaction of person and situation factors) overlooks the influence of behavior on persons and situations. Actions affect environments and beliefs about the self, a point emphasized by Bandura (1986) in his principle of *triadic reciprocal determinism*. Some even began to question whether it was sensible to posit separate person and situation factors, since the meaning of situations derives from the people who are involved in them, and the processes through which people create meaning are shaped by their sociocultural environment (Shweder & Sullivan, 1990). These alternative forms of interactionism are considered in detail in chapter 4.

The recognition of reciprocal influence processes helped to trigger a second trend. The 1980s and 1990s witnessed renewed interest in self-regulation, control beliefs, and personal agency. This reflected a greater acknowledgment of the proactive qualities of mind. Not only do individuals respond differently to the same environment, a point highlighted by the interactionism of the 1970s, but they actively construct and transform environments. In creating and reflecting on their experiences, people develop a sense of their own identity and individuality. The study of self-referent processes was gradually broadened in the last quarter of the 20th century. Investigators considered not only people's beliefs about their personal attributes (or their self-concept), but also the dynamic self-regulatory mechanisms through which they exert causal agency over the events of their lives. This trend expands the notion of personality. Personality includes not just static tendencies and beliefs but dynamic potentialities. Personality functioning is purposive. The field gained much greater understanding of goal-directed action and self-regulatory capabilities in the latter part of the 20th century, as subsequent chapters of this volume attest.

The field also received a sense of renewal from longitudinal research. The seminal contributions of Block (1971, 1993), Elder (1974, 1985), Magnusson (1988), and others demonstrated the importance of studying lives through time and of invoking sociohistorical factors in interpreting longitudinal findings. It became clear to all that not only is there significant stability in personality across time but that there are also dynamic interactions between persons and the social environment, which contribute to both stability and meaningful patterns of change. Part 3 of our text examine these advances.

A fourth development is that the field of psychology at large began to address topics that historically were of interest to personality psychology but that had not received adequate scientific study in previous eras. Two topics stand out, emotions and unconscious processes. Personality, social, and cognitive psychologists as well as neuroscientists turned to these phenomena. We address these topics in chapters 8 and 9.

Another development, which had particular impact in personality psychology in the United States, was the growth of evolutionary psychology (e.g., Buss, 1999a). Writers suggested that a Darwinian analysis of psychological processes forces one to rethink standard beliefs about the architecture of the mind, with significant implications for the study of individual differences and personality functioning. Rather than domain-general psychological mechanisms (e.g., global traits or an ever-present ego), evolutionary psychologists sought to explain behavior in terms of domain-specific mental mechanisms, each of which evolved to solve a particular adaptive problem (Pinker, 1997; Tooby & Cosmides, 1990). We review the ideas of evolutionary psychology at multiple junctures in the chapters that follow.

Perhaps the single most influential development of this period was the resurgence of the trait and dispositional models of personality structure criticized by Mischel (1968). In the early 1970s, a common criticism of Mischel was that the strong trait position he criticized was also one he created. In other words, Mischel purportedly had created the fictitious "straw man" position that personality consists of a fixed set of endogenous, global traits, which are unaffected by the social environment. To the surprise of many, in the 1980s and 1990s this straw man came to life. Investigators enthusiastically endorsed strong trait positions that would have seemed absolutely untenable 15 to 20 years earlier (e.g., McCrae & Costa, 1996).

Three factors contributed to the resurgence of the trait approach. One was ephemeral but two were substantive. The ephemeral one was a natural outgrowth of the belief that Mischel had argued against the existence of personality. Investigators tended to interpret any evidence of behavioral consistency across place or time as an argument against Mischel and by extension, for traits. Since behavior in not patterned randomly, almost any bit of behavioral coherence was interpreted as evidence in favor of trait models of personality structure. The obvious flaw in this argument is that virtually every conceivable psychological theory predicts that behavior is coherently structured. Evidence of consistency coefficients greater than zero thus does not uniquely support trait theories.

The two substantive points are as follows. First, behavior genetic findings added substance to trait approaches. The significant influence of inherited factors on personality development could not be denied by even the most ardent proponent of socialization processes. Second, trait researchers achieved remarkable success on a key empirical problem. This did not happen to be the problem that Mischel cited, namely, the problem of behavioral prediction. Instead, it was the problem of establishing an adequate taxonomy of individual differences. The "big five," or five-factor model (Digman, 1990; Goldberg, 1993; Hofstee & De Raad, 1992; John, 1990; McCrae & Costa, 1996; Ostendorf & Angleitner, 1992) emerged as a remarkably robust trait structure. The factors could be obtained in the analysis of trait adjectives and psychological inventories, in self-ratings and observer ratings, and across languages and cultures (see chapter 3).

A final development of note was a set of advances in social-cognitive analyses of personality structure and functioning. Throughout the 1980s and 1990s, investigators in this area became increasingly able to apply knowledge of cognitive and affective mechanisms to the classic questions of personality psychology (e.g., Cantor & Kihlstrom, 1987; Dweck & Leggett, 1988; Higgins, 1990). Issues of motivation, emotion, self-control, and personality coherence could be addressed within a relatively unified social-cognitive framework (Cervone & Shoda, 1999c). As both Bandura (1999) and Mischel (1999b) emphasized, by the end of the century social-cognitive theories could speak powerfully to the question of personality dispositions, the traditional concern of the trait theories.

The developments we have just outlined clearly do not converge. Advances in evolutionary psychology are difficult to reconcile with the developments in cultural psychology that we reviewed earlier in the chapter. Trait-based explanations of personality structure are difficult to reconcile with social-cognitive theory (Cervone, 1991, 1999a). Glossing over these differences would be a mistake. Part 2 of this text explores alternative conceptual models for explaining personality development and functioning.

## THE CASE OF PSYCHOANALYSIS

Psychoanalysis figures prominently in contemporary thinking. The media convey the notion that personality psychology is equated with, or subsumed under, psychoanalytic thinking. Laypersons know something of the unconscious, the id, the pleasure principle, symbols, dreams, slips of the tongue, and the defense mechanisms. In the academy, undergraduate personality texts generally devote substantial coverage to psychoanalysis.

However, very little psychoanalysis is to be found in contemporary personality psychology. Personality psychology and psychoanalysis began to take different routes some decades ago. Different scientific societies, journals, and lexicons attest to a separation that is regrettable yet difficult to reverse.

The discussion in this volume will only occasionally return to the topic of psychoanalysis. However, before proceeding, we think it is appropriate to look at psychoanalysis, not only to pay tribute to a movement that is part of our cultural heritage (Jervis, 1999) but to make readers aware of psychoanalysis as a pending issue. Although psychoanalysis is not thriving, it is not dead (e.g., Westen, 1998). Indeed, psychology's renewed interest in unconscious processes, interpersonal relations, and the control of emotions raises anew the intriguing question of what contemporary investigators should do with answers already provided by psychoanalysis. Throwing away the baby with the bathwater brings two risks. One may waste time on issues that previously have been appropriately rejected by psychoanalysts, or may overlook phenomena that actually are relevant.

Many distinguished scholars have produced sound appraisals of psychoanalytic theory and its clinical applications (e.g., Eagle, 1984; Ellenberger, 1970; Erdelyi, 1985; Greenberg & Mitchell, 1983; Gill, 1994 Grunbaum, 1984; Holt, 1989; Luborsky, 1984; Thomä & Kächele, 1985). We thus limit ourselves to the distinctive characteristics of the Freudian conceptual model and the general theory that is Freud's metapsychology. We then discuss the primary divisions, or secessions, that took place within the psychoanalytic movement. We will conclude with some thoughts on the status of psychoanalysis in the contemporary field.

## Freud's Metapsychology

Psychoanalysis originally was the name given to a treatment for a particular type of nervous disorder or psychoneurosis. Gradually, psychoanalysis broadened. It became a scientific and cultural movement that influenced the beliefs and practices of an academic discipline and the way of thinking of an era.

The psychoanalytic method is fundamentally a historic-clinical technique. It aims to uncover the principles regulating psychic functioning by exploring and reconstructing the past. Regression and self-reflection make previously repressed material accessible. This enables one to locate the source of conflict and affect and to discover the personal meanings of events that may have troubled individuals for a lifetime.

The psychoanalytic inspiration was notably rationalistic, namely, to bring back into the sphere of consciousness – that is, a sphere of responsibility and personal control – long forgotten mental content that otherwise may have governed behavior and experience outside of the individual's awareness. This inspi-

ration was in harmony with the spirit of the times.

Psychoanalytic conceptions of the operation of psychic systems similarly reflected the scientific beliefs of the day. Physics provided a basis for conceiving of the mental apparatus as a mechanistic tension reduction system. This system functioned to maintain a stable internal equilibrium by regulating relations between the organism and the environment in a manner that satisfied the demands of both. All psychological functioning was thought to rely on psychic energy that accumulates as a result of internal and external requests and that seeks discharge in order to preserve the equilibrium of the organism at the lowest level of tension.

Avoiding the displeasure of psychic tension that results from competing pressures is the basic notion from which two principles of mental functioning derive, the pleasure principle and the reality principle. Whereas the pleasure principle governs activity in accord with the total and immediate fulfillment of any internal pressures, the reality principle pursues the search for pleasure in harmony with environmental constraints and opportunities (Freud, 1911).

Freud (1915) placed the notion of *Trieb* (drive) at the cornerstone of his theoretical construction. Drives are the ultimate determinant of all psychic activity. They are psychic representations of endosomatic stimuli and thus bridge the mind and the body. Drives provide the energy that powers the psychic apparatus, flowing among the mental structures and determining their relative strengths as they confront one another. Drives express themselves in the wide variety of exchanges that take place between the organism and the environment.

It should therefore be obvious that the notion of *Trieb* corresponds to something other than instinct, to which it has been frequently and erroneously assimilated in the past. The Freudian conception of *Trieb* is in fact a propulsive power whose sources and possible outcomes are relatively undetermined. The notion of instinct, in contrast, is generally associated with specific states of appetite and consummation. The vicissitudes of drives are open to multiple outlets, whereas those of the instincts are relatively fixed. As noted by Laplanche and Pontalis (1967), use of the term *instinct* as a synonym for *Trieb* is a mistake in translation, which has resulted in misinterpretations and confusion. Equating *Trieb* with instinct distracted people from the flexibility of Freud's construct, causing psychology to underestimate its heuristic potential.

Among the properties characterizing a drive, Freud listed the source (in the body), the intensity, the end (the action that leads to satisfaction), and the object (the target, often the person, who elicits the drive to whom the action is directed and who ultimately mediates the satisfaction). Of these, the last was the most important in determining the course of personality development. Personality dynamics consists primarily of individuals' investing energy in one versus another object. It is the object of the drive that mediates the transactions between the individual and the environment. In this regard, psychoanalysis provides an interactional perspective on personality.

Psychoanalysis posited alternative ways of thinking, known as primary and secondary process thought. These alternative modes reflect the different forms of organization of the psychic apparatus, relating to its various functions in handling the pressures of competing drives. Primary process thought is illogical and timeless. It operates through processes of symbolization (replacement of one image by another), displacement (a shift of focus from one mental content to another), and condensation (fusion of two or more ideas or images). In primary process thought, reality is barely distinguishable from fantasy, as experienced in dreams and hallucinations. Primary process thinking involves a search for immediate and global satisfaction of the drives, in accordance with the pleasure principle. Secondary thinking, in contrast, obeys the reality principle. It operates according to the rules of logical thinking. Reality and fantasy

are distinguished, contradictions are avoided, and thinking is oriented in time. Drive satisfaction is pursued by delaying gratifications and planning long-term goals. Over the course of life, secondary processes gradually take greater precedence, as the individual develops psychological structures that are capable of redirecting blind urges and affects into socialized aims.

In his earlier works, Freud described the psychic apparatus as a system including three subsystems, namely, the unconscious, the preconscious, and the conscious. The subsystems were distinguished by the degree to which their contents were accessible to consciousness (Freud, 1900). In later works, a developmental and structural view replaced this descriptive-topological one. Freud (1923) presented a new version of his theory in which the id, ego, and superego were hypothetical structures that lay at the base of psychological functioning. These three structures were not distinguished from one another by their accessibility to consciousness but by their functions and modes of operation. The id was conceived as the reservoir of all psychic energy. It is the most archaic structure of psychic functioning, operating unconsciously and according to the pleasure principle. The ego is derived from the id. It serves the id's pursuit of pleasure and tension reduction, but in accordance with the reality principle; the ego, in other words, seeks objects in the world of reality that will satisfy the needs of the id. The ego was seen to operate both consciously and unconsciously, primarily through the defense mechanisms. The superego, the last structure to develop, results from the internalization of social norms and values that are presented primarily by the parents. The superego derives its energy from both the id and ego, and operates unconsciously either as ally or antagonist of one or the other (Freud, 1923).

Intrapsychic conflict – between pleasure and reality, between drives, and between structures – rests at the core of the theory. The person is ultimately conceived of as a system struggling between the opposite obligations imposed by nature and culture (Freud, 1930).

## Secessions and New Directions of Research

Freud's work developed over a period of nearly fifty years, during which important changes took place in his thinking. As Freud's thinking developed, so did that of other scientists who initially were his followers. Secessions in the psychoanalytic movement became unavoidable. New directions of research attested to the vitality of the movement.

The two secessions that proved most important to clinical practice and to the study of personality were Alfred Adler's development of his *individual psychology* and, a few years later, the *analytical psychology* of Carl Gustav Jung (Ellenberger, 1970). Adler (1920, 1927) insightfully explicated the role of family relations and social interactions in the formation of character and the development of psychological well-being. His work anticipated themes found later in the work of scholars such as Karen Horney (1939), Erich Fromm (1955), and Willhelm Reich (1945), who embraced psychoanalytic insights while attending more carefully than Freud to the world of social relations. Jung elaborated on Freud's model of the unconscious. He proposed that, in addition to the personal unconscious of Freud, there exists a collective unconscious that is a universal product of human evolution. He also posited a novel personality typology. People were said to differ according to two basic orientations toward life, extroversion and introversion. These orientations involved opposing tendencies with regard to thinking versus feeling and sensing versus intuiting. Jung's work also was unique in that he unhesitatingly explored the domains of religion, myth, alchemy, and astrology in an effort to gain insight into psychic functioning.

Jung's (1917, 1921, 1928) complex theoretical construction inspired many followers and broadly influenced modern thought (Samuels, 1985). Yet, little trace of his work can be found in the contemporary science of personality.

His discussion of the collective unconscious and its components, the *archetypes,* remains fascinating. However, these conceptions were not translatable into systematic research that might have sustained psychologists' interest. It may appear that Jung's thinking is echoed by contemporary evolutionary psychologists who, like Jung, posit that mental contents have evolutionary origins. However, contemporary evolutionary psychology actually owes little to Jung's thinking. The evolutionary psychologist sees mental elements as having evolved to solve highly specific adaptive problems (Barkow et al., 1992). Jung posited archetypes that were broader in scope and whose adaptive function was not always clear. Similarly, although investigators today are keenly interested in differences between extroverts and introverts, contemporary theorizing has moved very far from the Jungian premises.

Within orthodox psychoanalysis, two main trends developed, psychoanalytic ego psychology and the psychoanalysis of object relations. The works of Anna Freud (1936, 1965), Heinz Hartmann (1939), and David Rapaport (1960) belong to the first of these directions. They acknowledged autonomous functions of the ego. Some ego functions, in other words, were seen to be conflict-free and independent of the id. Psychoanalytic ego psychology viewed psychoanalysis as a general developmental psychology, which should be grounded in systematic scientific research as well as clinical practice. Ego psychologists were particularly concerned with linking the progress of psychoanalysis to advances in other branches of scientific psychology.

The second main trend, object relations, is represented by the works of Ronald Fairbairn (1952), Melanie Klein (1932, 1957), and Donald Winnicott (1958). These theorists investigated people's relations with objects, that is, significant persons in one's social environment. Their therapeutic experiences and observations of young children led them to focus on early relations between the child and the caregiver. The mother generally represents the object who provides resources necessary for survival, mental development, and coping with vulnerabilities. Mother – child exchanges lay a foundation for personality development. Thoughts and feelings associated with the mother gradually are internalized, becoming enduring mental representations, which form a basis of one's own autonomous identity.

Psychoanalytic ego psychology and the psychoanalysis of object relations developed between the late 1930s and the 1960s, with little intellectual exchange between them. Ego psychology developed primarily on the American continent, whereas object relations theory was a European phenomenon, with England as its focal point. These divisions partly dissipated in the 1970s, when object relations became central to the work of American psychoanalysts such as Kernberg (1976, 1980) and Kohut (1971, 1977).

## Is There Still a Place for Psychoanalysis in Personality Psychology?

Over time, the influence of the Freudian conceptual model gradually declined. Scientific psychology and psychoanalytical practice separated. Scientific criticism of psychoanalysis mounted. A number of factors contributed to these trends. Although psychoanalysts in clinical practice were the first to become aware of the limitations of Freud's theoretical constructions, they often did little to rectify them. Nonpsychoanalysts studying personality dynamics had little communication with the psychoanalytic world. Psychoanalytic clinical discourse was obscure to nonanalysts, and analysts rarely tracked developments in personality psychology at large. This created a nearly unbreachable gulf between psychoanalysts and other personality scientists.

When the scientific legitimacy of psychoanalysis came under fire, psychoanalysts were not fully prepared to counteract the criticism. They commonly distinguished general psychoanalytic theory and metatheory from clinical theory, and claimed that the latter was valid even if the former was not. This, however, failed to convince skeptics, especially

since the evidence supporting clinical theory rarely met traditional scientific standards.

There were, however, notable exceptions to the splitting of psychoanalytic thinking and scientific practice. Bowlby's (1969, 1973, 1980) attachment theory was rooted in psychoanalytic thinking but interacted fruitful with the world of scientific inquiry. One also should note the research of Shevrin (1988), Silverman's (1983) studies of subliminal psychodynamic activation, and the perceptgenetic strategy of the School of Lund (Westerlundh & Sjoback, 1986), as well as the work of Blatt and Lerner (1983) and of Holt (1978), who used projective techniques to investigate psychoanalytical assumptions about thought processes, conflicts, defenses, and object relations. Finally, Stern's (1977, 1985) efforts to link clinical observations to research on affect, cognition, and the development of the self created a bridge between clinicians and developmental psychologists.

■ *Westen on the Scientific Legacy of Freud.* A particularly valiant effort to resurrect the psychoanalytic tradition within psychological science is that of Westen (1998). Being equipped with expertise in psychodynamic theory, social-cognitive psychology (Westen, 1991), and contemporary cognitive science, Westen is particularly able to identify points of intersection between Freudian and non-Freudian psychodynamic thought and the contemporary science of psychology.

Westen posits that contemporary psychodynamic theory rests on five fundamental postulates, and that each postulate has received substantial empirical support. We outline the postulates, but not the support, here, since relevant empirical findings are reviewed in many subsequent chapters of our text (especially chapters 9 and 11). The fundamentals of psychodynamic theory, to Westen, are that (1) much mental life is unconscious, which implies that people commonly are unaware of the causes of their emotions and motivations; (2) multiple mental events can occur in parallel, which inherently gives rise to intrapsychic conflict; (3) childhood experiences play a significant role in shaping adult personality characteristics, especially in the domain of inter-personal relations; (4) social behavior is guided by mental representations of the self, significant others, and interpersonal relation-ships; and (5) successful personality develop-ment involves a gradual evolution of the capacity to form and maintain mature inter-personal relationships. Critics readily might argue that the first four points are so much a part and parcel of contemporary psychology that they lend no unique support to psychody-namic formulations. This argument applies less readily to the fifth point. Even in a con-temporary light, psychodynamic formulations are relatively unique in their focusing on the individual's increasing capacity to develop meaningful, intimate relations with others. Westen's own research documents that chil-dren's capacity to care about others' needs expands systematically across the grade-school years (Westen et al., 1991).

Westen (1998) also contends that develop-ments in cognitive science are congruent with the psychoanalytic model of mind. Freud's belief that multiple mental units can process information at the same time, or in parallel, indeed is congruent with the basic postulates of contemporary parallel-distributed process-ing models of human cognition (Rumelhart et al., 1986), as Westen notes. However, cognitive science is not monolithic. One can easily cite developments that seem to discredit basic psychodynamic premises. Some branches of contemporary cognitive science attribute reasoning to a large number of domain-spe-cific mental structures (Pinker, 1997). Psychoanalysis attributes reasoning exhibited across a virtually infinite range of activities to a domain-general ego. Developmental cogni-tive science finds that, at any one point in development, the child may function at differ-ent mental levels (or be at different stages) in different cognitive and social domains (R. Gelman & Williams, 1998; Wellman & S. Gelman, 1998). In psychoanalysis, the child progresses through a series of domain-general stages. Cognitive neuroscience suggests that perceptual mechanisms are directly involved in high-level reasoning processes, including

moral reasoning (Lakoff & Johnson, 1999). It seems difficult to reconcile this possibility and its implications with the traditional psychoan-alytic model of mind, which leaves little room for perceptual mechanisms to become directly involved in ego or superego functions, rather than serving merely as inputs to those processes.

An additional consideration, which bears on the value of psychoanalysis as a framework for analyzing psychological development and interpersonal relations, is the difficulty of rec-onciling Freudian analyses of child develop-ment with contemporary theory and research inspired by Darwinian analyses of evolved psychological tendencies and the nature of family dynamics. Sulloway (1996) presents numerous analyses indicating that child-child conflicts are more important than suggested by Freud, who focused primarily on parent-child conflict. Further, taking issue with Freud's postulated Oedipal complex, Sulloway suggests that "owing to natural selection, Freudian genes coding for patricidal wishes would soon vanish from any population" (1996, p. 123).

With respect to its bearing on psychoana-lytic postulates, the empirical literature is like a projective test. It can yield multiple interpre-tations, which may reflect the goals of the interpreter. Continuities in personality from childhood to adulthood may be seen to sup-port psychodynamic theory (Westen, 1998). Children's ability to overcome deprivations experienced during the purportedly formative early years of life (Kagan, 1996) may be seen to make psychoanalysis a fundamental mis-leading framework, which grossly underesti-mates the human potentiality for resilient psychological development.

■ *Conclusions.* Today, it is difficult to deter-mine whether psychoanalysis is a vital compo-nent of personality psychology or just a chapter in its history. Psychoanalysis did much in its time. It met an otherwise unfilled social demand for a psychological account of personal development and the integrated functioning of the individual. It gave voice, within the rationalistic and anthropocentric

Western tradition, to the psychic problems of the contemporary person. It recognized intrapsychic conflict as a core element of individuality, while also giving people some confidence in mastering warring aspects of the self. The psychoanalytic technique gave patients insight into the meaning of their experiences, emotions, and fantasies. Psychoanalytic theory also fulfilled a critical scientific task, namely, identifying problems requiring systematic investigation. Psychoanalytic thinking, for example, paved the way to contemporary advances in attachment processes and defensive information processing. In this regard, the contemporary field undoubtedly is indebted to psychoanalysis.

The controversial issue is whether psychoanalysis can still play an active role in the investigation of issues that once seemed so firmly within its domain, for example, unconscious thought and affect; motivated cognition; interpersonal relations in the development of internal representation of the social world; and the construction and representation of self (see Dazzi & De Coro, 1992; Horowitz, 1991b; Kihlstrom; 1999; Lichtenberg, 1989; Westerlundh & Smith, 1992). Many recent advances in these areas owe little to psychoanalytic theory or method. Theories can best meet the goal of fostering novel research when they are stated in a manner that makes than testable. Many psychoanalysts, however, would claim that the criterion of testability leads to an impoverishment of theory and a neglect of clinical evidence. Such divisions between psychoanalysis and psychological science are difficult to reconcile. Reconciliation requires movement on both sides, but apparently very few are inclined to make such moves.

## FORECASTING THE FUTURE

The growth of journals, professional conferences, and handbooks (Hogan, Johnson, & Briggs, 1997; Pervin, 1990; Pervin & John, 1999) in the 1990s indicates that personality psychology has attained a new lease of life. The decline of geographic and linguistic barri-

ers, among investigators from different nations and between investigators and research participants from different cultures, suggests that personality psychology's future life may be less encumbered by cultural limitations than was its past. Advances in information technologies should prove increasingly important in this regard. Electronic communication enables the collection of large, varied samples of data that previously were unthinkable. The Internet enables investigators who have never met to share research instruments and thus to contribute jointly to data collection (Goldberg, 1999). Access to larger populations, with both groups and individuals studied in depth and throughout the course of life, may prove to redefine completely issues of personality stability, change, transition, and well-being. These developments also raise new challenges. The decline of traditional geographic and cultural barriers raises our awareness of cultural diversity and the range of pathways that human development may take.

Disciplinary barriers also are beginning to decline. Much progress in the study of personality now comes from outside the field itself. Neuroscientists and molecular biologists illuminate biological bases of individual differences. Sociological and anthropological inquiry informs us about the interdependences between persons and their sociohistorical and cultural contexts. The further breakdown of professional barriers cannot help but put personality psychology and related disciplines on a firmer footing.

Despite this, obstacles to progress remain. Some appear no less formidable than they did a decade or more ago. There exist deep, significant differences among personality scientists with regard to the priorities of the discipline. Some theoretical positions remain quite distant from one another. Most seriously, some paradigms remain relatively disconnected from the rest of the psychological enterprise, just as Hall and Lindzey (1957) observed many decades ago. The very status of the discipline is threatened if colleagues in the rest of the field fail to appreciate the contributions of personality psychologists and if we fail to appreciate theirs. Personality psychology has a unique charge: to explore the integrated psychological systems that lend coherence to our experiences, actions, and `sense of self, that differentiate individuals from one another, and that enable people to contribute agentially to their actions, experiences, and personal development. No other branch of psychology takes up this challenge. But the uniqueness of the charge is no license for insularity in theory and methods. Personality psychologists cannot succeed without capitalizing on and consolidating knowledge from the various corners of the psychological enterprise, as well as the neighboring biological, social, and behavioral sciences. The field of personality psychology can only succeed as an integrative discipline.

In this volume, we are both reviewing and taking part in the field's ongoing discussions and debate. The following chapters aim to convey an up-to-date picture of the field. Like most pictures, ours undoubtedly reflects the qualities of both the subject and the picture taker.

## SUMMING UP

Our aim in this chapter has been to encourage the reader to think critically about the history and nature of the field. We hope that awareness of personality psychology's history, including the strengths and limitations of its various schools of thought, will best enable the reader to confront developments in the contemporary field.

It has been a long journey from today's field back to the beginnings of personality psychology's history as a discipline and further back to its ancient origins. What has been said more generally can also apply to personality psychology: One can refer to a long past, but to a recent history. Rethinking our field's past may help to avoid repetition. Yet, we know that the recurrence of ideas is unavoidably part of history (Vico, 1725). Perhaps the greatest advantage of historical review is that it better enables one to evaluate alternative pathways for the field's future development.

Today personality psychology would appear to be in relatively good health. It has great ambitions that are pursued by numerous scholars in multiple nations. They take part in what is, in total, a vast scientific enterprise. However, good auspices have often been followed by unexpected disappointments in the past. It thus is wise not to underestimate the obstacles, seen and unseen, that may block the road to true progress. We return to considerations of our field's state of health in the epilogue that concludes this volume. For now, we note that awareness of our field's history best prepares investigators for the path ahead, as personality psychologists work toward making the field the integrative discipline it can be.

# Description and Explanation

# Description and Explanation

Since at least the time of Francis Bacon, 400 years ago, scientists have recognized that they face two tasks. They must describe the phenomena in their purview, and they must explain the phenomena they observe. When stated this way, science seems straightforward. First one collects and systematizes a large number of descriptions and then one induces explanatory principles.

If only things were so easy. The tasks of description and explanation generally cannot be disjoined and taken up one at a time. Description and explanation go hand in hand. It is hard to determine what constitutes a meaningful description without some sense of explanatory principles. As Russell (1945) explained, in commenting on Bacon, "usually some hypothesis is a necessary preliminary to the collection of facts, since the selection of facts demands some way of determining relevance. Without something of this kind, the mere multiplicity of facts is baffling" (p. 545).

The standard difficulties are compounded in personality psychology. Throughout most of its history, the field has harbored multiple theories. Different theories admit different types of description as meaningful. The question of whether to describe personality through objective tests, projective tests, narratives, behavioral observations, or physiological recordings has divided personality psychologists over the years (see, e.g., Craik, 1986).

The intermingling of description and explanation, however, cuts far deeper than merely to the question of measurement technique. Different theories implicitly pursue different types of explanation. Different explanatory frameworks suggest different things to describe. Much of chapter 3 is devoted to theoretical frameworks that explain the individual's emotional and cognitive functioning by locating that person within a system of interindividual-difference dimensions. People's standing on the various dimensions explains their consistent psychological qualities. The descriptive goal, in this view, is to identify an $n$-dimensional system of basic individual differences, where $n$ is large enough that the system is comprehensive but small enough that it is of practical value.

Chapter 4 reviews theory and research that embraces a somewhat different approach to description and explanation. Three beliefs about explanation characterize this work. First, many investigators judge that personal functioning should be explained by reference to underlying cognitive and affective mechanisms; these mechanisms are seen to function as a complex, interacting system. Second, they believe that the cognitive–affective system develops and functions through transactions with the environment. An explanation of personal functioning, then, must address the social foundations of personality by exploring situations and person–situation interactions. Third, many of these investigators believe that a psychology of personality must explain not only individual differences but the coherent psychological functioning of the unique individual. These three beliefs suggest that individual-difference dimensions may be inadequate to describe and explain the complex patterns of consistency, variability, stability, and change that distinguish people from one another. The descriptive and explanatory strategies of interactionist and social-cognitive theories of personality, then, are outlined in chapter 4.

# CHAPTER THREE

# Individual Differences

## *Traits, Temperament, and Intelligence*

**CONTENTS**

To many scientists, the most striking aspect of people is how similar they are. Geneticists report that the human genome overlaps enormously across individuals and groups. Anthropologists find that significant aspects of social life are experienced universally (Brown, 1991). To the layperson, however, the most striking aspect of people is how much they differ. The language we naturally use to talk about people is primarily a language of individual differences (Goldberg, 1981). Many cultures explain social behavior by reference to psychological attributes that differentiate people from one another (Fiske & Taylor, 1991). Individual differences are a staple of everyday social discourse.

Personality psychologists recognize universals. However, like laypersons, they revel in the differences. In this chapter, we review personality psychologists' various strategies for describing and explaining individual differences in personality functioning. We begin by exploring the intercorrelated patterns of affect, cognition, and behavior, which under the names of *dispositions* or *traits* have been a primary focus of personality psychology's research enterprise. We review efforts to identify a comprehensive structure of dispositions and the achievement of a consensus on five individual-difference factors. We then turn to questions of human temperament and the parallel efforts to identify the structure of temperamental qualities. Our final section explores intelligence and alternative models of human intellectual capabilities.

As we will see, many investigators in these areas use factor analysis to identify the structure of individual differences in psychological tendencies. Their goal is to find a simple, overarching set of factors that can organize the myriad ways in which individuals might differ from one another in their typical behaviors or psychological experiences. The factor-analytic approach generally yields a set of broad, high-level dispositions (e.g., global personal traits or general intelligence), which describe primary dimensions of variation in the population.

To some investigators, the dimensions that derive from factor analyses of individual differences are of interest because they are not only descriptive but explanatory. In principle, the factors might correspond to underlying psychological structures with causal force. Factor analysis would then be a route to identifying the mechanisms that explain consistency in personality functioning. Individuals' tendencies could be explained by determining how much of each individual-difference factor they possess.

Throughout this chapter, we strive not only to review empirical findings but to address conceptual issues in the description and explanation of how people differ from one another. Commentators commonly have lamented that empirical advances in the study of personality traits have not been accompanied by conceptual advances in our understanding of what traits are, that is, in our understanding of the ontological status of trait constructs. The commentators are right. The conceptual status of individual-difference constructs and their role in the development of personality theory deserve greater attention. No one questions the enormous practical importance of identifying a comprehensive set of individual-difference constructs and developing tools for their assessment. However, many question whether such constructs can serve as the foundation for a theory of personality, that is, for a scientific theory that can explain intraindividual coherence and interindividual differences in personality functioning.

In this chapter and the next, we again suggest that investigators adopt a broad, integrative approach to their topic of study. Personality psychology is the intellectual home base for the study of dispositions and individual differences. Yet the investigation of dispositions can not be conducted by the personality psychologist alone. The study of dispositions is where the personality theorist meets the differential psychologist, the behavioral geneticist, and the molecular geneticist. It is a point of convergence for efforts in personality, developmental, and social psychology. Statistical tools are required to map and simplify the variety of individual differences. Biological and social developmental research are necessary for understanding their origins. Social psychological analyses illuminate how and why people infer that others possess stable dispositional qualities (see chapter 9). Ideally, a synthesis of knowledge from these areas of study would yield a broad portrait of the nature of individual differences as they are expressed by the social actor and construed by the social perceiver.

## DISPOSITIONS: DEBATE AND UNRESOLVED ISSUES

This ideal, however, has rarely been realized. Rather than serving as a context for the synthesis of knowledge, the study of personality dispositions more often has been a context for debate, as we noted in chapter 2. In some respects, the person–situation debate of the 1970s and 1980s ended constructively. Today, no one contends that people fail to exhibit stable personality characteristics, and no one questions whether social contexts shape affect, cognition, and action. At a deeper level, however, the debate concluded without truly being resolved. Disagreement on core issues thus continues to the present day. In historical retrospect, the reasons for lingering debate and conceptual unease are clear. The person–situation debate primarily addressed methodological issues. Since people questioned the magnitude of correlation coefficients obtained in personality-based prediction (e.g., Mischel, 1968), investigators sought the "coin of the realm: bigger correlation coefficients" (Bem & Allen, 1974, p. 512). By aggregating data across persons, situations, and methods, significant personality stability was demonstrated (e.g., Epstein, 1979). The issues of the person–situation debate, however, were not solely empirical but conceptual. The questions that were, and are, in contention are not whether people have enduring, distinctive dispositional tendencies, but how to conceptualize and explain these tendencies. What was needed was not just statistical tinkering but conceptual analysis of the psychological processes that contribute to coherence in psychological response. During the person–situation debate, surprisingly little attention was devoted to the psychological mechanisms that contribute to coherence in response.

Despite points of agreement (Kenrick & Funder, 1988), the person–situation debate failed to yield consensus on the following three questions: (1) Can the individual's psychological tendencies be captured by universal psychological dimensions or are tendencies uniquely and idiosyncratically organized? (2) Do the psychological tendencies that distinguish individuals from one another consist solely of average tendencies to perform one versus another class of response?

Or do they also encompass distinctive variability in response patterns, such that people with the same "average" tendencies actually may differ from one another in meaningful respects? (3) In seeking to explain dispositional tendencies, should one invoke biological mechanisms, hypothetical constructs that correspond to consistent response tendencies, or affective and cognitive self-regulatory systems that give rise to both consistency and variability in response?

In the contemporary field, different traditions embrace different answers to these questions. The tradition to which most of this chapter is devoted sees the structure of personality as consisting of response tendencies that are organized hierarchically (e.g., Eysenck, 1947, 1970; Hampson, John, & Goldberg, 1986; Paunonen, 1998). Broad, high-level traits (e.g., extraversion) reside at the highest levels of the hierarchy. The high-level constructs organize lower-level tendencies (e.g., sociability), which in turn supervise lower-level behavioral habits (e.g., the tendency to organize social gatherings). Constructs at the highest and middle levels correspond to chronic, average tendencies to perform a given class of response; "stability, consistency, repeated occurrence of actions" (Eysenck, 1970), define constructs at these levels. The highest level of the hierarchy, which encompasses the broadest response tendencies, is interpreted as the basic structure of personality. It is widely assumed that this basic structure is universal. The research goal, then, is to identify the universal set of highest-level constructs. As we will review, significant consensus has been achieved on the constructs that are necessary and sufficient to include at this level (see De Raad, 1998; Goldberg, 1993; McCrae & Costa, 1996).

Note that this research tradition embraces a particular pair of answers to the first two questions above. It assumes that the dispositional tendencies of interest in a psychology of personality (1) can be captured by a universal set of dimensions (e.g, extraversion, conscientiousness) and (2) correspond to average response tendencies, with variability in response (e.g., variable high–low extroversion or conscientiousness in different contexts) not being of fundamental importance to the identification of personality structure. These assumptions are common to nomothetic dispositional approaches, or *trait theories* of personality. Different theorists within this tradition embrace different answers to our third question, the issue of how one should explain dispositional tendencies.

## ON THE VARIETIES OF TRAIT THEORY

The first thing to say about trait theory is that there is no such thing as "trait theory" in the singular (Goldberg, 1994; Goldberg & Saucier, 1995). Different adherents of a trait approach adopt different conceptual strategies. However, commonalities among the approaches can be identified.

People exhibit consistent, stable patterns of experience and action that distinguish them from one another. At least since Allport (1937), most personality psychologists have explained this phenomenon by positing psychological constructs that correspond to average tendencies to exhibit one versus another class of response. These psychological constructs are known as trait variables, or *dispositional* variables, since they capture a person's average tendency, or disposition, to exhibit a particular type of response. People who are high and low on a trait of *conscientiousness* are people who, on average, are disposed to exhibit more or fewer acts that count as indicators of the trait.

Trait variables are decontextualized, that is, they are defined as global tendencies to exhibit one versus another class of response (e.g., Funder, 1991). Trait constructs thus directly refer to consistencies in behavior that people may exhibit across different situations. Trait theorists of course recognize that different traits are differentially relevant to different settings. No one expects that people will act in a way that is insensitive to social contexts. However, the trait approach does choose to study personality through units of analysis

that are domain-general rather than domain-specific. Basic trait constructs might include "agreeable" and "anxiety," not "agreeable toward superiors" or "anxious with women."

There are a number of options in constructing a trait theory. One choice is whether to adopt an idiographic or a nomothetic approach. Idiographic strategies recognize that the individual person may possess a unique set of uniquely organized traits (Allport, 1937). Nomothetic approaches seek a taxonomy of traits that applies to all persons. Nomothetic conceptions dominate the field. Investigators recognize the usefulness of having a single, overarching taxonomy of individual differences.

A further differentiation among trait theories concerns the ontological status of traits. Some conceive of traits merely as surface tendencies, or phenotypes, with no causal power (Buss & Craik, 1983; Robins, John, & Caspi, 1994; Saucier & Goldberg, 1996). Saying that a person has a trait is merely to describe that person's typical, average behavior. Others see traits as causal genotypes (e.g., Funder, 1991; McCrae & Costa, 1996). In the latter view, persons may act, on average, in a conscientious or dominant manner because they *have* dominance or conscientiousness. The traits are thought to be psychological systems that directly correspond to broad behavioral tendencies. At the extreme side of this position, "personality traits are postulated to be endogenous dispositions whose origin and development are independent of environment influence" (Costa & McCrae, in press).

A third differentiation among the trait theories hinges on the status of biological mechanisms (see Revelle, 1995). Some theorists equate trait structures with specific biological systems (Cloninger, 1987; Eysenck, 1990; Gray, 1987). Dimensions of personality correspond to linear variations in underlying physiological or biochemical mechanisms. Others, in contrast, eschew biological theorizing, preferring instead to treat traits as hypothetical constructs (McCrae & Costa, 1996). Despite advances in the study of biological mechanisms of personality (e.g., Zuckerman, 1991,

1995), much empirical research reflects the hypothetical construct view. Investigators commonly employ multivariate statistical techniques to identify traits structures without positing associated biological mechanisms.

Further distinctions are possible. People might be described in terms not of trait dimensions, but of personality types (Block, 1971; John, Pals, & Westenberg, 1998; Robins, John, Caspi, Moffitt, & Stouthamer-Loeber, 1996). One might, for example, identify distinct subgroups of individuals who share similar profiles across a set of nomothetic personality dimensions. In principle, the types one observes might correspond to underlying genotypes that are categorical in nature; people's inherited biological structures of personality might vary categorically (Kagan, 1998b). The existence of discrete types can be confirmed through psychometric techniques (e.g., Gangestad & Snyder, 1985; Meehl, 1992).

John and Srivastava (1999) review findings from eight studies that appear to converge on the existence of three reliable personality types: resilient individuals who display high levels of psychological adjustment; "overcontrollers," who appear agreeable but socially inhibited; and "undercontrollers" who are relatively disagreeable, unconscientious, and neurotic. This convergence of findings is a promising sign for future work, as is the fact that individuals classified into different personality types display significantly different developmental outcomes (Hart, Hofmann, Edelstein, & Keller, 1997). An issue for future investigation in this area is to explore further the degree of homogeneity versus heterogeneity within each categorical type. Are the individuals who fall within each type so homogeneous that one can reasonably search for underlying psychological structures that are common to the group? Or do these broad, decontextualized categories mask significant within-category variation that might be revealed in a more fine-grained analysis of the contexts in which individuals reveal resilient, overcontrolled, and undercontrolled tendencies?

Despite the promise of typological research, historically it has received relatively little attention. Most investigators have pursued dimensional systems, using factor-analytic techniques to identify basic dimensions of personality (e.g., Cattell, 1965). From this perspective, then, the question is how to identify the basic dimensions.

## DESCRIBING INDIVIDUAL DIFFERENCES: LEXICAL APPROACHES, QUESTIONNAIRE APPROACHES, AND THE FIVE-FACTOR MODEL

Scholars long have searched for a universal lexicon to describe personality. The biological sciences benefit from a universal taxonomy, which organizes the various plant and animal species. It is reasoned that, in a similar manner, the science of personality might benefit from a taxonomy of variation within the human species.

Among the many questions that arise in constructing a personality taxonomy, two stand out. The first is the question of where to start. What database should be mined to create the taxonomy? One option is to draw on the wisdom of the natural language. People have evolved a rich, detailed language for describing one another. This language may inform us about the underlying structure of personality. Admittedly, the natural language contains many terms of questionable merit. People used to call others witches. Today, they call each other Scorpios, Leos, and Geminis. When talking about the physical world, people erroneously explain the movement of objects by attributing impetus to them. As Kagan (1994b) has noted, "No other natural science decided on its major concepts by going to the dictionary" (p. 43). Nonetheless, many investigators have banked on the possibility that our natural language of persons might provide a useful basis for a scientific taxonomy of individual differences.

The second option is to draw on the wisdom of the professional psychologist. Personality and clinical psychologists constructed innumerable individual-difference measures throughout the past century. It might be reasoned that, although these instruments are a disorganized lot, in total they are comprehensive. It is unlikely that the panoply of questionnaire measures has completely missed an individual difference of great significance. Under this reasoning, a systematic analysis of existing individual-difference measures might yield an overall portrait of the main ways that people differ from one another.

Whether one starts with the lexicon or psychologist's questionnaires, one must narrow the enormous list of individual-difference descriptors. For this task, almost all investigators view factor analysis as the tool of choice. Those who have pursued a universal structure of individual differences have factor-analyzed the personality ratings of populations of individuals. The resulting factors, which summarize intercorrelations among responses, are widely interpreted as "the structure of personality."

We put "the structure of personality" in quotes because this phrase has multiple meanings and must therefore be interpreted cautiously. Three questions of interpretation stand out. The first, noted in chapter 1, is whether the structure is classificatory or explanatory (Harré, 1998). Does a factor-analytic structure of individual differences merely organize observable variations, in which case it serves a useful assessment function, or does it also correspond to underlying causal elements, in which case it serves as the basis for personality theory? A second question, considered later in this chapter, is whether the structure is a "population" structure or a "person" structure (see John & Srivastava, 1999). The structure of psychological tendencies identified in the analysis of a population may not replicate itself in the tendencies of each individual. If the factor structure is only applicable at the level of the population, then calling it the structure of personality is a somewhat odd choice of words. A biologist would not call the Linnean classification of plant and animal species the structure of any organism.

Even if one were to assume that the structure of individual differences applies at the level of the individual (i.e., that each individual has, or possesses, some level of each of the individual-difference constructs), a third interpretive issue arises. This is the question of whether the phenotypic individual-difference structure can reasonably be interpreted as the structure "of personality." Consider a biological analogy. Suppose one factor analyzed anatomical individual differences. One might obtain factors such as height and weight. It would be safe to assume that each individual indeed possesses a certain amount of height and weight. But it would seem quite unreasonable to refer to height and weight as the structure of the body. One could not locate anatomical structures, or even know what structures to look for, if one's map of the body only indicated variations in height and weight. The dimensions leave out far too much information to be interpreted as a structural map. Analogously, a map of phenotypic individual differences may leave out so much information about the structures that underlie personality functioning that "the structure of personality" is a misnomer.

This point is underscored by the finding that the individual-difference structure obtained when studying humans overlaps enormously with the structure obtained when studying nonhuman animals. Work in the oxymoronically titled subfield of animal personality reveals that most dimensions of the five-factor model are found in organisms such as monkeys, hyenas, and octopuses (Gosling & John, 1999). If future work were to establish that the same mechanisms underlie individual-difference dimensions in human and nonhuman species, then this finding would be a remarkable demonstration of the preservation of psychologically relevant biological structures across species. However, it still would require considerable poetic license to call the cross-species structures the structure of personality. With all due respect to our eight-legged friends, we bipeds possess psychological mechanisms that are not found in octopuses but that are crucial structures of our personalities and that contribute to the differences among us.

## Five Basic Factors

There is no guarantee that factor analyses of the natural-language lexicon and of psychologists' questionnaires will converge. A key finding is that they generally do. Factor analyses of both data sources suggest that individual differences can be organized according to a five-factor structure. The dimensions of extraversion (or surgency, energy), agreeableness (or friendliness), conscientiousness, emotional stability (or neuroticism), and intellect (or openness to experience, or culture) emerge robustly.

The robustness of the five-factor model across observers, methods, and even some languages and cultures (McCrae & Costa, 1987, 1997, 1999) fostered a widespread movement in the field in the 1980s and 1990s. Advocates of the *big five* (Goldberg, 1993; John, 1990) and *five-factor model* (McCrae & Costa, 1996) suggested that the most fundamental fact of personality psychology is that dispositional tendencies can be well described by this set of five linear dimensions. Throughout the 1980s and 1990s, the five-factor movement gained such momentum that enthusiasts came to see it as a common ground on which to reconcile diverse theories and findings and to build a cumulative personality science (e.g., Digman, 1990; Wiggins, 1996).

As suggested by our discussion of the varieties of trait theories, one must distinguish two types of five-factor approaches. Big Five advocates conservatively construe the factors as a descriptive structure, that is, as a summary of phenotypic tendencies (Goldberg, 1993; John & Srivastava, 1999). Advocates of the five-factor model boldly reify the factors, treating them as inferred hypothetical constructs that are causally responsible for the individual's dispositional tendencies (McCrae & Costa, 1995, 1996, 1999). In this view, the factors are psychological structures and the five-factor model is a personality theory that explains coherence in cognition, affect, and action.

In the following, we review the history of the lexical and questionnaire traditions, so that the reader may gain an understanding of the basis of the five-factor approach. We then evaluate the claim that the five-factor model can serve as a foundation for personality theory.

## Lexical Studies

The idea that the terms of the natural language might be a useful lexicon for the psychological scientist dates back to Sir Francis Galton. Galton (1884) tried to identify the most salient aspects of character by scanning a dictionary. He located about a thousand personality descriptors and classified them into groups, thereby bringing order to what otherwise would be a disparate mass of terms. In the early 20th century, scholars, including Partridge in 1910 and Perkins in 1926 in the United States (both cited by Allport and Odbert, 1936) and Klages (1926) and Baumgarten (1933) in Germany similarly turned to the lexicon to identify the bases of personality structure. However, these efforts had little lasting impact as compared with the subsequent work of Allport and Odbert (1936).

Allport and Odbert viewed lexical trait terms as socially conceived symbols. Society's natural interest in psychological and ethical issues gives rise to a set of linguistic symbols for discussing and evaluating human qualities. Turning to the 400,000 entries of Webster's New International Dictionary, Allport and Odbert extracted the longest list of person-related terms examined to that point, 17,953 terms. They grouped these into four categories. The category of main interest contained terms signifying stable personality traits, with traits being defined as generalized personal tendencies (e.g., aggressive, sociable). The other three categories included terms related to temporary moods and mental states (e.g., abashed, frantic), social evaluations of character (insignificant, worthy), and a miscellaneous collection of allegorical terms and words relating to physical qualities and abilities. Allport and Odbert's list proved of great value to subsequent investigators.

Cattell extended and legitimized the psycholexical approach via his *"sedimentation hypothesis,"* which suggested that most relevant individual differences are encoded as single words in the natural language. Empirically, he narrowed Allport and Odbert's list through a rational process of eliminating and selecting trait terms. This yielded 171 clusters of terms, which through statistical reduction he reduced to 35 clusters, all but two of which involved bipolar trait forms. Factor analysis yielded 12 factors, which served as the original foundation for his personality theory and measurement system (Cattell, 1943; 1945a, b; 1946; 1947).

In the early 1960s, while most investigators were working with multitrait questionnaires, Warren Norman turned again to the dictionary. He supplemented the original Allport and Odbert list of traits, employed factor analysis to identify a simple structure, and in so doing revitalized the lexical approach. Norman (1963), much like Fiske (1949) and Tupes and Christal (1961) before him, obtained a five-factor structure in self-ratings and other ratings. Factors of surgency, agreeableness, conscientiousness, emotional stability, and culture emerged as the main dimensions of individual difference.

Norman's work, including his enumeration of 2,797 stable traits terms (1967), provided a foundation for the subsequent contributions of Goldberg and Peabody. Using various factorial analytic techniques, they replicated Norman's five-factor structure across different sets of trait terms, different samples, different types of ratings (self, peer), and different types of target persons (pleasant vs. unpleasant). They provided a broad taxonomy of English trait terms and identified adjectives that were strong markers (i.e., that had high loading on only one factor) of each factor of the Big Five (Goldberg 1981; 1982; 1990a; Peabody, 1987; Peabody and Goldberg, 1989).

A subsequent development in the psycholexical tradition was the Abridged Big Five Circumplex (AB5C) model (Hofstee, De Raad & Goldberg, 1992), which provides a means of tapping personality dimensions that correspond to blends of the five principal factors. This method examines the ten bipolar spaces

(or circumplexes) that result from pairwise crossings of the five factors (extraversion vs. agreeableness, extroversion vs. conscientiousness, etc.). In the AB5C model, each circumplex space is further divided into 12 segments or "slices" positioned at 30-degree angles from each other. These subdivisions thus are configured to identify 90 possible personality types, corresponding to 80 different bidimensional blends of aspects of the Big Five plus the 10 "pure" poles of the same five factors. The circumplex space resulting from pairing extraversion and agreeableness, for example, shows pure markers of each dimension located near the two principal axes that generate the bipolar space, with blends of extraversion and agreeableness located in the eight slices between the principal axes.

This approach circumvents the problem of "fuzzy" boundaries between factors and simultaneously provides a more finely grained description of personality, which captures aspects of personality functioning that might be lost in simpler factorial structures.

## The Questionnaire Tradition

The analysis of personality structure in professionally constructed questionnaires provided a major impulse behind the five-factor model in the 1980s and 1990s. McCrae & Costa, at the Gerontology Research Center of the U.S. National Institutes of Health, began their analysis of personality structure by examining responses on the 16 Personality Factor questionnaire of Cattell (Costa & McCrae, 1976; see McCrae & Costa, 1990). Drawing also on the insights of Eysenck and of Goldberg and Peabody, they gradually identified five robust personality factors and developed an instrument for measuring them, the NEO Personality Index (NEO-PI) (Costa & McCrae, 1985, 1989). Its revision, the NEO-PI-R (Costa & McCrae, 1992), assesses extraversion, agreeableness, conscientiousness, neuroticism, and openness to experience, as well as six lower-level traits (or facets) for each main dimension.

In their empirical research, McCrae and Costa analyzed the personality tendencies of a large population of individuals of various ages over years of time. This enabled them to establish two critical facts about the five factors. First, the factors can be obtained in both self-ratings and observer ratings, and the two data sources significantly correlate with one another (e.g., McCrae & Costa, 1987). Despite this convergence, McCrae and Costa (1997) are critical of the lexical approach, suggesting that some traits (e.g., need for novelty) simply are not represented in the language as single words. Second, the factors are highly stable over time, at least among adults (McCrae & Costa, 1990). Five-factor ratings are stable in two senses. In populations of individuals, the temporal stability of the factor scores is very high. Cross-sectionally, there are only small differences in mean factor scores among different age groups. This stability has led Costa & McCrae to suggest that personality characteristics are "set like plaster" (Costa & McCrae, 1994) once the individual reaches early adulthood.

McCrae and Costa also contributed to the question of how the five-factor structure related to the gamut of previously existing assessment devices. They reconciled the five-factor model with the previous taxonomies of Cattell, Eysenck, Guilford, & Comrey. Specifically, they found that one can locate previously existing structures within the five-factor space. A wide range of personality dimensions, developed within a range of theoretical traditions and identified by a variety of assessment procedures, can all be related to the five factors (see McCrae & Costa, 1996). The ability of the five-factor model to represent constructs identified previously in alternative personality theories led McCrae and Costa (1996) to conclude that the five-factor model itself can serve as a theoretical foundation for personality psychology. We now consider some alternative dimensional structures and their relation to the five factors.

## Comprehensive Individual-Difference Structures

In developing the NEO-PI, Costa and McCrae were taking part in one of the great research traditions of personality psychol-

ogy, namely, the development of comprehensive psychometric measures of human individual differences. Work in this tradition began early in the 20th century. Researchers extended to the study of personality the factor-analytic techniques that originally were employed in the study of intelligence in Great Britain (Burt, 1937; Webb, 1915). Cattell, Eysenck, Guilford, and Comrey made lasting contributions.

Cattell factor-analyzed multiple sources of data, including self-ratings, observer ratings, and behavioral manifestations of personality traits. He retained 16 oblique primary traits and incorporated them into the Sixteen Personality Factor Questionnaire (16 PF) (Cattell, 1957; Cattell, Eber & Tatsuoka, 1970). Cattell's primary traits were defined as follows: A. Warmth outgoing–reserved); B. Intelligence (bright–dull); C. Emotional Stability (emotionally stable–affected by feelings); E. Dominance (assertive–humble); F. Enthusiasm (happy-go-lucky–sober); G. Conscientiousness (conscientious–expedient); H. Boldness (venturesome–shy); I. Tender-mindedness (Tender-minded–tough-minded); L. Suspiciousness (suspicious–trusting); M. Imagination (imaginative–practical); N. Shrewdness (shrewd–forthright); O. Apprehensiveness (apprehensive–placid); Q1. Experimenting (experimenting–conservative); Q2. Self-sufficiency (self-sufficient–group-dependent); Q3. Self-sentiment (compulsive–uncontrolled); Q4. Tension (tense–relaxed).

Eysenck developed a model of personality structure that was a paragon of clarity and simplicity. Rather than dealing with a relatively large number of traits that were moderately intercorrelated, as did Cattell, Eysenck sought a simple system of orthogonal factors. To obtain these, he relied on secondary factor analysis, that is, a factor analysis that examines structure in a set of intercorrelated dimensions, which themselves were identified through factor analytic techniques. Through this method, he initially obtained his well-known pair of second-order factors, or *superfactors:* extraversion and neuroticism. He subsequently added to his theoretical system a third factor, psychoticism. These three factors were at the peak of his hierarchical organization of personality (Eysenck, 1947, 1959, 1970, 1982a), in which each broad superfactor (e.g., extraversion) subsumes a set of more specific traits (e.g., beneath extraversion one may find sociability, impulsiveness, activity, liveliness, and excitability) which in turn subsume habitual response patterns (e.g., entertaining people), which organize a variety of specific behaviors at the lowest level of the hierarchy (e.g., telling jokes). This theoretical organization also formed the basis for Eysenck's efforts at psychological measurement, which over the years led to the development of the Maudsley Personality Inventory (Eysenck, 1959), the Eysenck Personality Inventory (Eysenck & Eysenck, 1964), the Eysenck Personality Questionnaire (Eysenck & Eysenck, 1964, 1975), and the Eysenck Personality Questionnaire-Revised (Eysenck, Eysenck & Barrett, 1985).

An alternative assessment scheme was presented by Guilford, who initially identified 13 primary factors, which were subsequently reduced into a 10-dimension assessment system. These dimensions include: general activity versus slowness and lack of energy; restraint and seriousness versus rhathymia (lightheartedness) and impulsiveness; ascendance and social boldness versus submissiveness and timidity; sociability and social interest versus seclusiveness and shyness; emotional stability and optimism versus instability and depression; objectivity versus subjectivity and hypersensitivity; friendliness and agreeableness versus hostility and belligerence; thoughtfulness or reflectiveness versus unreflectiveness; good personal relations and cooperativeness versus criticalness and intolerance; and masculinity of interests and emotion versus femininity (Guilford, 1959; 1975). Guilford provided assessment batteries including the Inventory of Factors STDCR (Guilford, 1940), the Guilford-Martin Inventory of Factors (Guilford & Martin, 1943a), the Personnel Inventory (Guilford & Martin, 1943b), and the Guilford-Zimmerman Temperament Survey (Guilford & Zimmerman, 1949, 1956).

Subsequently, Comrey, a student of Guilford, presented a new taxonomy and assessment instrument, the Comrey Personality Scales (CPS) (Comrey, 1970, 1980, 1995). Like other investigators, Comrey sought to identify the most important dimensions of variation in normal human personality and pursued this goal by seeking a parsimonious, hierarchical model in which traits at one hierarchical level organized groups of lower-level traits. The traits at the lowest level in the hierarchy were developed through the factor analysis of personality test items. Clusters of similar items define the low-level traits, which in the CPS system are called Factored Homogeneous Item Dimensions (FHIDs); they are homogeneous in that, to constitute an FHID, the items must have been written specifically to measure the same defined trait and must have emerged with substantial loadings on the same factor in a factor analysis of items. The low-level traits measured by FHIDs are numerous and can be created virtually at will starting with almost any defined personality characteristic. These FHID variables provide the raw material to identify by means of factor analysis the more comprehensive, less numerous, and potentially more theoretically meaningful traits at the next level in the factor hierarchy. Comrey's CPS assesses eight broad dimensions, each of which is indexed by five FHIDs. The dimensions are trust versus defensiveness; orderliness versus lack of compulsion; social conformity versus rebelliousness; activity versus lack of energy; emotional stability versus neuroticism; extroversion versus introversion; masculinity versus femininity; mental toughness versus sensitivity; and empathy versus egocentrism.

The main problem with this set of taxonomies is their lack of consensus. Despite the adoption of similar theoretical premises and statistical techniques, investigators come to different conclusions about the core components of personality structure. It is here that the five-factor model is of such value. These alternative assessment schemes can each be represented within the five-factor framework, which, then, provides a unifying view able to reconcile differences among alternative models. For example, the three superfactors of Eysenck can be reconciled with the five-factor model by splitting psychoticism into low ends of agreeableness and conscientiousness. The 16 factors of Cattell, 10 of Guilford, and 8 of Comrey can be statistically subsumed within the Big Five dimensions. In addition, the five factors can represent dimensions contained in other major assessment systems, such as the 18 rationally constructed scales of the California Psychological Inventory (Gough, 1987), the Jungian Myers-Briggs Type Indicator (Myers & McCaulley, 1985), and Jackson's Personality Research Form (1984), which is based on Murray's taxonomy of needs (e.g., Amelang & Borkenau, 1982; Barbaranelli & Caprara, 1996; McCrae, 1989; McCrae & Costa, 1985; McCrae & John, 1992; Noller, Law & Comrey, 1987; Ostendorf & Angleitner, 1992). Further, it is noteworthy that temperament dimensions, such as activity and sociability, and variations in affective experience, such as positive and negative affectivity, can be retrieved under the five-factor dimensions of extraversion, agreeableness, and emotional stability (see our discussion of temperament, below and in chapter 8). Elements of variation in intelligence are probably also reflected in the five-factor dimension of openness.

It is not surprising, then, that individual-difference researchers have flocked to the five-factor model. Although different investigators may define and label the factors in slightly different manners, most agree that a five-factor system provides a comprehensive, economical, comprehensible, and reasonably sufficient framework for organizing individual differences in personality dispositions. In so doing, the model reconciles these and other taxonomies and research traditions. It thereby may contribute to a coherent, accumulating body of knowledge. After many years of dispute among scientists aiming to discover the structure of individual differences through factor analytic techniques, the Big Five taxonomy promises to end the theoretical controversies that in the past have severely jeopardized the credibility of the discipline. However, as we will see, contentious issues remain.

## Generalizability of the Five-Factor Structure Across Languages and Cultures

Advocates claim that the five-factor model provides a structure of personality that is universal. This term has two meanings. Universal may mean applying to all individuals. One may claim that the factors are personality structures possessed by every individual. We evaluate this claim below. Universal also may mean pancultural. The five-dimensional structure of individual differences might capture personality variations in all languages and cultures. We examine the evidence for this claim now.

Claims of pancultural universality are partly based on behavior genetic (see chapter 5) and longitudinal data (mentioned earlier). If the factors are found to be inherited, stable personality characteristics in one culture, this would suggest that they are universal since there is so little genetic variability across regions of the world. This, however, is a rather indirect argument. More direct evidence of universality comes from cross-cultural studies.

Both routes to the development of the five-factor model, the lexical and the questionnaire, began in the West and in the English language. Research participants initially were relatively homogeneous with respect to educational levels, income, and related factors. This raises the possibility that the structure is specific to a narrow subset of the world's population. In recent years, much attention has been devoted to this question.

There are two ways of investigating cross-cultural generalizability, "emic" and imposed "etic" approaches (see Berry, 1969). Imposed etic studies import a list of personality questionnaires or lexical terms describing personality from one language to another. Emic studies start directly from the target culture. Indigenous sources such as interviews, spontaneous descriptions of personality in conversation, media descriptions of persons, or lists of terms from the dictionary of the native language serve as the database for analysis in emic approaches.

Imposed etic studies generally have replicated or at least approximated the five-factor structure. This conclusion holds across Western and non-Western cultures, Indo-European and non-Indo-European languages, college-educated and working-class populations, and test items consisting of trait adjectives and questionnaire items (e.g., Benet-Martínez & John, 1998; Caprara, Barbaranelli, Bermudez, Maslach & Ruch, in press; McCrae & Costa, 1997). Despite these results, one must draw conclusions cautiously, since the invariance of personality structure may partly reflect the method used (e.g., Church, Katigbak, & Reyes, 1996), the still restricted number of cultures examined, and the nonrepresentiveness of samples (participants commonly are college students).

A number of researchers have adopted the emic strategy of analyzing personality descriptors in the dictionaries of different languages. Factor analysis is used to identify latent constructs in the adjectives, nouns, and verbs that different languages use to describe personality (e.g., Angleitner, Ostendorf, & John, 1990; Brokken, 1978; Caprara & Perugini, 1994; Church, Katigback, & Reyes, 1996; De Raad, 1992; De Raad & Hoskens, 1990; De Raad, Mulder, Kloosterman, & Hofstee, 1988; DiBlas & Forzi, 1998; Hrebickova, 1995; John, Angleitner, & Ostendorf, 1988; Shmelyov & Pokhil'ko, 1993; Szarota, 1996; Szirmak & De Raad, 1994). Investigators select dictionary terms according to criteria of appropriateness, clarity, and frequency of use in personality description. Original lists of thousands of terms are reduced to several hundred. Factor analysis is used to identify main individual-difference factors and the markers of each factor.

Results employing this emic strategy are not as consistent as are findings from the imposed etic approach. When emic studies have not included a large number of adjectives that are explicitly evaluative, a five-factor structure resembling that of Norman (1967) is often retrieved. However, there are significant exceptions, and even when five factors are obtained, they may differ in significant ways from the standard factor solution obtained in English. Among noteworthy exceptions, the five-factor solution was not replicated in Hungarian, a non-Indo-European language, where the fifth factor did not emerge (Szirmak & De Raad, 1994). In Italian language studies, three factors were the preferable solution (Di Blas & Forzi, 1998, 1999). Even when the structure of nouns or adjectives yields the five-factor model, the analysis of verbs may differ, yielding only two main dimensions (De Raad, 1992). Even when a five-factor structure is retrieved, the order of extraction of factors may change across languages, expected markers may load on more than one factor, and a given term may be located under different factors in different languages.

Research in Asian cultures illustrates these issues. Yang and Bond (1990) compared emic and etic structures obtained in Chinese in ratings made by university students in Taiwan. Although indigenous emic descriptors yielded five factors, these did not map directly on to the imposed etic dimensions, which resembled the canonical Big Five. A given emic Chinese factor (e.g., competence) might be a combination of separate etic dimensions (e.g., emotional stability and culture). Further, the canonical conscientiousness dimension did not emerge among the Chinese. Triandis (1997), commenting on this result, has speculated that the Chinese culture's emphasis on reliable behavior socializes people "to be conscientious to such an extent that individual differences on this variable do not stand out." In contrast, Church, Katigbak, and their colleagues report somewhat greater success in obtaining the standard five-factor structure through emic procedures, for example, in a study of written personality descriptions in the Filipino language Tagalog (Church & Katigbak, 1988). However, the degree to which Filipino dimensions and American dimensions overlap depends on the particular method of factor analysis employed (Katigbak, Church, & Akamine, 1996). Further, even when Filipino and American dimensions do overlap, there is no perfect, one-to-one relation between the two indigenous systems. The American dimension neuroticism does correlate highly with the Filipino dimension affective well-being, in support of the universality of these dimensions. However, Katigbak et al. (1996) report that, within their Filipino sample, neuroticism also correlates significantly with *every other* Filipino dimension, including responsibility, social potency, emotional control, concern for others, and broad-mindedness. Finally Hahn, Lee, and Ashton (1999) succeeded in recovering four of the five factors (extraversion, agreeableness, conscientiousness, and neuroticism) in a study of Korean trait adjectives.

A further limitation is that most studies have restricted their item pools to adjectives that are not highly evaluative. Evaluative terms such as "marvelous" and "awful" (and their translations) are commonly excluded from the pool of descriptors. This decision can be questioned, in that personality appraisal is an inherently evaluative enterprise. Years ago, analyses by Rosenberg and colleagues indicated that "good–bad" was an important dimension of implicit personality theory, with a term such as "popular" being a marker of the dimension (Rosenberg, Nelson, & Vivekananthan, 1968). More recently, when investigators have systematically included evaluative adjectives in adjective pools, a seven-factor solution often results. Dimensions of positive valence (represented by terms such as "outstanding" and "special") and negative valence ("deceitful," "immoral") emerge in addition to the canonical five dimensions (Almagor, Tellegen, & Waller, 1995; Benet & Waller, 1995, 1997). Additionally, dimensions such as "religiousness" and "humor" are either independent of or only approximately traceable to Big Five dimensions (Saucier & Goldberg, 1998).

Cultures may be differentially sensitive to certain classes of affect and action and thus employ more words in their description.

Another variation on the standard five-factor model, then, is that certain dimensions may be more salient in some languages than others, and the boundaries between dimensions such as extraversion, agreeableness, and emotional stability may be difficult to distinguish in some cultures. Caprara and Perugini (1994) and Di Blas and Forzi (1998, 1999), for example, find that the stereotype of sociable Italians is confirmed by the dominance of interpersonal dimensions in the Italian personality descriptive language. Also, terms that load on more than one factor may shift from one factor to another in different cultures. For instance, "sociable," while loading in extraversion and agreeableness, ultimately may be recovered under one versus the other factor in different cultures.

Some cultures may describe individuals with terms that have no direct, single-word equivalent in English (e.g., filial piety) or obvious location within the five-factor space (e.g., karma). Despite recent efforts, the field still knows relatively little about personality description in non-Indo-European languages and in populations that have been little influenced by the European–American world. Studies that have been conducted in non-Western cultures often have employed university students as research participants; this population may be highly exposed to Western culture despite residing elsewhere.

Finally, one must bear in mind that cross-cultural research on the five-factor model possesses whatever within-culture limits the model possesses. The structured questionnaire methods generally give participants little opportunity to indicate whether an item is relevant to the target or whether other descriptors not in the questionnaires might provide a better portrait. The statistical methods generally analyze populations as a whole and thus are insensitive to the possibility that a culture contains subgroups of individuals who are not describable within the five-factor structure. Studies that restrict personality descriptors to terms describing dispositional tendencies are insensitive to the possibility that a culture may describe individuals primarily in a nondispositional language, for example, a language of goals, social roles, or position within a family structure (see Shweder, 1991).

Despite all these considerations, within the boundaries of its theoretical assumptions and methodological practices the five-factor model has fulfilled its promise to bring order to a potential Babel of taxonomies and instruments. Awareness of the model's limits may, in the long run, facilitate an accurate map of the personality descriptors used at different cultural latitudes.

### Five-Factor Instruments

The successes of the five-factor framework have prompted the development, in various languages, of psychometric instruments whose properties parallel those of the NEO-PI-R.

Caprara and colleagues have drawn on lexical analyses of Italian personality adjectives to produce the Big Five Questionnaire (BFQ). This instrument assesses dimensions of energy, friendliness, conscientiousness, emotional stability, and openness in both adults and children (Barbaranelli & Caprara, 1998; Barbaranelli, Caprara, & Rabasca, 1998; Caprara, Barbaranelli, Borgogni, & Perugini, 1993). Although the number of items and of facets (two for each main dimension) of the BFQ adult version is smaller than the NEO-PI-R, its validity and generality across languages has proved to be similar (Caprara, Barbaranelli, Bermudez, Maslach & Ruch, in press). Similarly, the Big Five Observer (BFO) instrument, which consists of polar opposite adjective markers rather than the BFQ's questionnaire statements, indexes each of the big five factors (Caprara, Barbaranelli, & Borgogni, 1994).

Van Heck and colleagues have produced a contextualized Big Five questionnaire, called TinSit, for traits-in-situations (Van Heck, Perugini, Caprara, & Froger, 1994). They employ generalizability theory (Cronbach, Gleser, Nanda & Rajaratnam, 1972) to analyze not only the five dispositional tendencies, but their expression across a taxonomy of ten situ-

ations. The situation taxonomy, developed previously by Van Heck (1984, 1989), includes situations involving (1) interpersonal conflict; (2) joint working, exchange of thoughts, ideas, and knowledge; (3) intimacy and interpersonal relations; (4) recreation; (5) traveling; (6) rituals; (7) sport; (8) excesses; (9) serving; and (10) trading. Within this framework, generalizability theory enables one to assess functional equivalences among persons, situations, and response modes of trait indicators. It provides an estimate of multiple source of systematic variation and error of measurement. The resulting Tin-Sit thus is a particularly valuable tool for investigating the relative importance of persons, situations, and response modes.

Another Big Five questionnaire is the Five-Factor Personality Inventory (FFPI), (Hendriks, Hofstee, & De Raad, 1999), developed in conjunction with the AB5C approach to personality description described earlier (Hofstee, De Raad, & Goldberg, 1992). This instrument is available in three languages, Dutch, English, and German. Starting from a set of 1,311 Dutch personality descriptors, the questionnaire has been reduced to 100 items, each of which is a brief, concrete statement written in the third person singular. The most significant difference between the FFPI and Big Five structures is that the FFPI's fifth factor is autonomy, which includes the tendency to maintain an independent opinion and not to be socially influenced.

Other well-known assessment systems also are compatible with the Big Five framework. The Hogan Personality Inventory contains six dimensions, namely, ambition, sociability, friendliness, prudence, adaptation, and intellect. The first two dimensions correspond to different aspects of extraversion, and the others map onto agreeableness, conscientiousness, emotional stability, and openness to experience (Hogan, 1986). The Multidimensional Personality Questionnaire (MPQ) (Tellegen, 1982, 1985; also Church & Burke, 1994) operationalizes a higher-order personality structure of four dimensions: agentic positive emotionality (defined by social closeness, well-being, and social potency), communal positive emotionality (defined by well-being, social potency, achievement, and absorption), negative emotionality (defined by absorption, stress reaction, alienation, and aggression), and constraint (defined by control, harm avoidance and traditionalism). Extensive research on this model has been done by Church and colleagues (Church & Burke, 1994; Katigbak et al., 1996). Caprara and colleagues (Caprara, Barbaranelli, & Incatasciato, 1995) related the MPQ to the five-factor model assessed by the BFQ and found that agentic positive emotionality correlated with energy-extroversion ($r = .62$), communal positive emotionality with friendliness ($r = .49$), negative emotionality with emotional stability ($r = -.46$), and constraint with conscientiousness ($r = .59$).

One five-dimensional model does differ significantly from the standard five-factor model. This structure, proposed by Zuckerman, is assessed via the Zuckerman-Kuhlman Personality Questionnaire (ZKPQ). Although Zuckerman identified his proposed dimensions through the standard statistical analyses of questionnaire scales, the dimensions have the advantage that they can be linked to biological characteristics in a more direct way than can the dimensions of the Big Five. The ZKPQ dimensions are impulsive sensation seeking, neuroticism-anxiety, aggression-hostility, activity, and sociability (Zuckerman, Kuhlman, Joireman, Teta, & Kraft, 1993). Research suggests that despite their differences in origin, the structural model of Zuckerman significantly converges with the five-factor model and with the three-factor model of Eysenck, especially with respect to the dimensions of neuroticism and extroversion–sociability (Zuckerman et al. 1993).

Although these instruments do not provide a fine-grained assessment of psychological dispositions, they have proved to correlate with behavioral outcomes to a statistically significant degree. The positive pole of extraversion, including venturesomeness, energy, and positive affectivity, predicts the capacity to master various daily life activities and to be engaged in multiple rewarding activities (Watson & Clark, 1997). Agreeableness relates to prosocial behavior, altruism, and interpersonal adjustment (Graziano & Eisenberg, 1997). Emotional stability, in combination with a lack of agreeableness, is related to personality disorders (Costa & Widiger, 1994). Conscientiousness has been shown to be a valid predictor of job performance (Barrick & Mount, 1991; Hogan & Ones, 1997), and of length of life (Friedman et al., 1995). Openness to experience is associated with divergent, creative thinking as well as liberal attitudes (McCrae, 1996; McCrae & Costa, 1997).

## Merits and Limits of the Five-Factor Model

There can be no question of the five-factor model's practical value. Its synthesis of psychology's multiple individual-difference measures clearly benefits the practicing psychologist who needs a simple, comprehensive way to assess variations (Caprara, Barbaranelli, & Livi, 1994) in dispositional tendencies in the population. Managers, educators, and others who must describe and evaluate assessments of large numbers of individuals benefit from the fact that assessments can be made in a simple manner. The factor system also is of use in studying sociopolitical issues. For example, the Big Five predicts political preferences more strongly than standard predictors such as sex, age, and education (Caprara, Barbaranelli, & Zimbardo, 1999).

If the five-factor model were construed solely as a description of individual differences in the population in surface-level tendencies, there would be little controversy. However, much stronger claims are made. The five-factor framework is viewed as a contribution not only to psychological assessment but to personality theory (see Wiggins, 1996).

As we have noted, in assessing claims about the five-factor structure one must distinguish two views. Big Five advocates prudently view the factors as a useful descriptive organization of observable individual differences, leaving questions of genotypic explanation for another day (e.g., De Raad, 1998; Saucier & Goldberg, 1996). The five factors are judged to "provide a well founded set of basic concepts with which traits of persons can be described at an abstract level" (De Raad, 1998, p. 119).

Five-factor model advocates make a stronger claim, which has broad theoretical implications. They assign causal status to the factors (McCrae & Costa, 1995). Their reasoning is straightforward. If individual differences are captured by a five-factor structure, a simple explanation is that all individuals possess each of the factors at varying levels. The factors thus constitute "the universal raw material of personality" (McCrae & Costa, 1996), where "universal" means not only pan-cultural but applicable to all individuals. The factors purportedly are the core of human nature and are ultimately responsible for the coherent patterns of thought, affect, and action displayed by each and every individual (McCrae & Costa, 1996). Once the five dispositions are granted causal force, they "follow their own intrinsic course of development" (Costa & McCrae, in press); the five-factor model becomes a personality theory, that is, a theory that offers a scientific explanation of all other aspects of personality functioning, such as self-concept, attitudes, and personal strivings.

The popularity of the five-factor approach makes it imperative that these claims be evaluated carefully. The notion that all individuals possess the factors and that the factors constitute the basic structure of personality (McCrae & Costa, 1996) rests on two assumptions that commonly receive little attention from five-factor advocates. The first is that the five-factor model applies at the level of the individual. The second is that the structure of personality corresponds to experiential and behavioral consistency. Both assumptions can be severely questioned on both conceptual and empirical grounds.

■ *Does Anybody Have the Five Factors?* Personality psychologists may disagree on many points. However, everyone must agree that, for a set of ideas to be called a personality theory, they must apply at the level of the individual person. Obvious as this point may be, it is worth stating for the following reason. Many valid ideas about people are only valid at the level of the population. Drawing on an example from Rorer (1990), consider the following two claims: (1) Native Americans are a proud people; (2) Native Americans are disappearing. The former notion applies at the level of the individual; in principle, all Native Americans may be proud of their ethnic heritage. The latter applies only at the level of the population. The population may be disappearing in the sense that its size and influence diminished greatly during the course of the 19th and 20th centuries, but no matter how long one looked at an individual Native American, the person would not disappear. Rorer (1990) notes that to assume that population-level constructs apply at the level of the individual is to commit an error of logic.

This point is relevant to five-factor theory in the following way. In viewing the factors as "universal raw material" (p. 66) that "define[s] the individual's potential and direction," McCrae & Costa (1996) claim that the factors are universally applicable at the level of the individual person. But the five-factor structure was not identified in analysis of individual persons. Investigators did not find that, one after another, the dispositional tendencies of each and every individual were organized around each of the factors. Indeed, in the development of the five-factor structure, no investigator found that the dispositional tendencies of any individual were organized in this manner. Such a finding is required, however, if one is to claim that the model applies at the level of the individual, a claim that is clearly implied by the contention that the psychological factors are akin to features such as the circulatory system (Costa & McCrae, 1998, p. 114) in physiology. If we examine the physiology of each and every individual, we will find a circulatory system. To support the psychological claim, one must be able to examine the psychology of each and every individual and find the factors.

This issue has received remarkably little empirical attention. Investigators have worked at the level of the population, not the level of the individual. The obvious limitation is that population-level constructs simply may not apply at the level of the individual, a point that has become more widely recognized in recent years (Lamiell, 1997; Revelle, 1995). The assumption that one can pool a large aggregate of persons and end up with a structure that describes all of the individual cases simply is not warranted. Nesselroade and Molenaar (1999) provide a relevant empirical demonstration. As part of their intensive time-series analyses of individual cases, they developed a technique for formally assessing the assumption that one can characterize a population of individuals via a single factor-analytic structure. In other words, they assessed the appropriateness of pooling data from individuals into a common structure. After analyzing covariance functions computed on each of 31 research participants, they found that only 10 individuals' functions met the criterion for pooling. Ten participants, in other words, were similar enough to be describable by an aggregate population-level statistic. This means, of course, that the large majority of persons could not easily be fitted into any aggregate model. As they point out, this finding is "troubling to researchers who pool information across multiple subjects with no apparent concern about its appropriateness or no way to muster statistical support for their actions" (Nesselroade & Molenaar, 1999).

At the time of this writing, only a small number of studies speak to the question of whether the five-factor model applies at the level of the individual. Both Borkenau & Ostendorf (1998) and Fleeson (1998) have examined whether intraindividual variations in personality tendencies across time fit the five-factor structure. Their work tests five-factor theory in the following way. In the five-factor model (Costa & McCrae, 1992), high-level structures organize lower-level tendencies. For example, extraversion is responsible for the tendencies to be warm, to be assertive, and to experience positive emotions, whereas neu-

roticism organizes tendencies such as anxiety, self-consciousness, and impulsiveness. If the factors exist at the level of the individual, then these sets of lower-level tendencies should go together and also should form separate factors at the level of the individual case. The five-factor structure should be recoverable through *P-technique* factor analyses (Cattell, 1946), in which one studies a given individual who is observed on a large number of occasions (rather than the typical approach of studying a large number of individuals on one occasion).

Results do not provide strong support for the hypothesis that the five-factor structure can be recovered at the level of the individual case. Borkenau and Ostendorf (1998) evaluated the degree of fit between individual-level structures and the standard population-level structure; this was done by determining whether the degree of match exceeds a conventionally accepted criterion for concluding that two factor structures match (specifically, a .90 criterion). They found that the individual-level structures matched the population-level structure in less than 10% of the cases identified. An individual case illustrates how a particular person may vary from five-factor expectations. In the case reported, the adjective "calm" had only a low loading on neuroticism, and "industrious" and "responsible" loaded highly on extraversion but not on conscientiousness. "Domineering," which has little to do with the canonical definition of conscientiousness, was the third highest-loading conscientiousness adjective (Borkenau & Ostendorf, 1998). In a similar analysis, Fleeson (1998) obtained the standard five-factor model in analyses of the population but found that the structure fitted *none* of his individual participants. No individual's structure exceeded standard goodness-of-fit criteria. Analyses of individual cases reveal that for some individuals, elements of the purportedly independent factors become blended; for example, an individual's disposition to experience positive emotions (an extraversion facet) might be linked to that person's being low in self-consciousness (a neuroticism factor). Another person might be impulsive (a facet of neuroticism) when experiencing warmth (a facet of extraversion). Within-person structures, then, differed from one person to another, and differed from the between-person five-factor structure (Fleeson, 1998). Further, Fleeson (1998) reports that the difference between within-person and five-factor structures is particularly large with respect to factors that are more important to an individual; in other words, the more within-person variance in an individual's self-ratings that the factor explains, the more it tends to deviate from the structure of a five-factor dimension.

A different type of challenge to the universality of the five-factor model comes from the findings of Caprara, Barbaranelli, and Zimbardo (1997). They examined the possibility that the structure might not be found among particular targets of personality description. The structure of personality, in other words, may differ when different personalities are evaluated. Differences may be found in the number of factors extracted and their order of extraction. In this work (Caprara et al., 1997), participants used adjective markers of the Big Five to rate the personalities of politicians (Clinton and Dole in the United States, Prodi and Berlusconi in Italy). Only two factors could be extracted; one was a blend of extraversion and openness and the other a blend of agreeableness, conscientiousness, and emotional stability. The five-factor solution was, in contrast, confirmed in self-ratings and partially supported in ratings of nonpolitical celebrities.

As a general rule, the use of personality terms can be highly idiosyncratic and dependent on the relation between the rater and the target. With emotionally or ideologically charged targets, dominant characteristics may spread over less central ones, yielding a simpler structure than is generally found. Thus, the consideration of individual differences in affect and cognition further expands the range of variation in personality perception that one should expect.

Further research is needed to determine the range of structures that may be found in lexical ratings of the observable tendencies of individual persons. The findings we have reviewed clearly indicate that personality descriptors do not necessarily retain a constant meaning and structure across different people in different situations. People use words flexibly. The lexical items people use to describe personality can not be treated as if they are fixed elements of a periodic table.

■ *Dispositions: Why Study Only the Average?*
The second assumption of five-factor theory is logically independent of the first. Suppose, hypothetically, that the factors did routinely apply at the level of the individual. In other words, suppose that each individual's average behavioral tendencies could be captured by assigning to that individual a set of five-factor scores. The factor scores would still capture only one thing, the person's average tendencies. Dispositional qualities other than averages would be missed. The general point here is that, by their very nature, global dispositional constructs sacrifice information about variation in behavior across circumstances. This is acceptable if such variations are merely statistical noise (i.e., random error). However, if variability in action is not random – if it is a stable characteristic that distinguishes people from one another – then not only average tendencies but also patterns of behavioral variability must be included in the definition of personality dispositions.

The extensive research of Mischel, Shoda, and Wright (Wright & Mischel, 1987; Mischel, 1999b; Mischel & Shoda, 1995, 1999; Shoda, 1999) severely questions the practice of equating dispositions with average tendencies. Although these investigators recognize that charting mean-level tendencies is of interest, they essentially ask: Why study only the average? Why should one sacrifice all information other than mean tendencies when describing an individual's personality dispositions? Characterizing people solely in terms of their average tendencies, aggregated across contexts (e.g., an average tendency to be extraverted or agreeable), sacrifices potentially valuable information about the distinctive ways in which their characteristic behavioral styles vary from one context to another (Mischel & Shoda, 1995).

This point gains enormous power from the finding that variations around the average are not statistical error. Instead, patterns of variability are temporally stable; they constitute part of an individual's distinctive, enduring "behavioral signature" (Mischel & Shoda, 1995). In their research, Mischel and Shoda examine the behavior of individuals as they confront the varying challenges of their day-to-day lives (e.g., Shoda, 1999). They chart the person's tendency to display behaviors indicative of a single dispositional category (e.g., aggressive acts) and plot "if . . . then" profiles that display the individual's tendencies in each of the situations studied. The key finding is that the overall shape of the profile (the pattern of highs and lows) is not random error but is temporally stable. People's deviations around the mean are a reliable marker of their personalities.

Other recent contributions reach similar conclusions. The *triple typology model* of Vansteelandt and Mechelen (1998) strives to identify equivalence classes of persons, of situations, and of behaviors (cf. Bem, 1983). Individual differences, from this perspective, involve not only mean-level tendencies but also person-to-person variations in situation–behavior profiles. Through hierarchical classification analyses, one can formulate a taxonomy of person types, in which individuals within each type share a similar profile of situation to situation variations in behavior (Vansteelandt and Mechelen, 1998). Research on the level of agreement between personality ratings made by oneself and by others reveals that higher agreement is found when individuals display temporally stable patterns of response across different facets of a given high-level personality trait descriptor (Biesanz, West, & Graziano, 1998; cf. Mischel & Peake, 1982; Shoda et al., 1994).

A critical implication of these approaches is that different people who have the same average-level tendencies may possess different underlying personality dynamics. In the study of aggressive children, one child may be found to behave aggressively when threatened by peers but not when confronted by authoritative adults, whereas another child may display exactly the opposite pattern. By studying these variable patterns rather than aggregating them together into total aggressiveness scores, the "if . . . then" profile method permits differentiation between two people who may be psychologically different even though they happen to obtain the same mean score on a global trait dimension. Mischel & Shoda's findings, then, indicate that global trait scores are insufficient to describe people's behavioral tendencies. As stated elsewhere, the shortcoming of dispositional constructs is not that people fail to exhibit mean behavioral tendencies but that "individuals exhibit complex patterns of coherence that would be missed if personality functioning were viewed solely through the filter of nomothetic trait categories" (Cervone & Shoda, 1999b, p. 11).

The implication of Mischel and Shoda's findings for theoretical explanation is plain. The observed patterns of variation clearly require explanation. Equally clearly, trait variables cannot provide this explanation because trait constructs describe mean tendencies and treat variability around the mean as noise (Mischel & Shoda, 1995). Thus, alternative units of analysis are required to explain people's distinctive dispositional tendencies. This reasoning motivates Mischel and Shoda's cognitive-affective processing system approach, described earlier.

In conclusion, the identification of a robust five-factor structure clearly helps to organize the assessment of individual differences in surface profiles and may aid in the prediction of behavior in some domains. However, their identification and assessment can not replace the investigation of affective and cognitive mechanisms that contribute to the overt dispositional tendencies. In part, this is because the psychologist's goal is not only to describe tendencies but also to promote capabilities and desirable forms of behavior. In the area of achievement, one hopes not only to describe but to promote conscientiousness. This requires that one identify the psychological processes involved in making and meeting commitments, setting goals and persisting in their pursuit, and being orderly, punctual, and reliable. Similarly, in studying dispositional tendencies to be aggressive, one ultimately hopes to capture the mechanisms that turn negative affect into aggressive intentions and that lead people to perceive that the exploitation of others is a legitimate instrument for pursuing one's own goals. The practical usefulness of aggregating differing forms of conduct into global traits may distract one from searching for the multiple psychological mechanisms that lie behind the behavioral expressions.

## FACTOR ANALYSIS IN THE STUDY OF PERSONALITY

Psychology's study of individual differences is built almost entirely on the statistical technique of factor analysis. Factor analysis is to the individual-difference researcher what the telescope is to the astronomer – the means of sighting the structures that are the targets of one's investigation. The telescope, however, is a considerably more direct method of observation. Factors are not direct observations but statistical abstractions. They merely summarize interrelations among sets of variables, and these summaries are computed under particular sets of mathematical assumptions. The technique may yield misleading results if these assumptions do not hold, as writers have emphasized for many years (Armstrong, 1967). The method and its results must be cautiously evaluated.

Since the days of Spearman (1927) and Thurstone (1934, 1935, 1947), investigators have extended the factor-analytic techniques developed in the study of mental abilities to the study of personality, values, and beliefs. Webb (1915), a student of Spearman, undertook protofactorial studies of temperament and obtained factors that would be recognized much later as conscientiousness and emotional stability–instability (see Deary, 1996; Eysenck, 1970). Burt (1937) subsequently iden-

tified temperament factors that anticipated Eysenck's extraversion and neuroticism. Thurstone (1934) factor-analyzed personality descriptors, with results that anticipated the dimensions of the five-factor model. Cattell, Eysenck, Guilford, and Comrey, discussed earlier, all rooted their personality theories in factor analysis. They shared the belief that the technique could identify latent dimensions that were responsible for covariance among observed variables.

Among contemporary investigators, the method is employed almost universally in work on interindividual differences, where it is used not only to summarize data but also to generate and confirm hypotheses about underlying structures. Technological advances have made factor analysis a technique that is widely available, efficient, and therefore popular (Comrey & Lee, 1992; Harman, 1976).

### The Technique

Factor analysis is a multivariate statistical technique that reduces the interrelations among numerous observed (or manifest) variables to a small number of hypothetical latent constructs. The constructs, or factors, capture some proportion of the overall pattern of covariation among the observations. The greater the covariation among observed variables, the greater the variance that can be accounted for by the latent constructs.

The starting point of factor analysis, then, is a covariance or correlation matrix that summarizes the relationships among the manifest variables. The end point is a matrix that represents the association among all observed variables plus the resulting latent constructs. *Loading coefficients* represent the strength of association between observed variables and latent factors. Also, the method calculates the percentage of total observed variance that each factor explains.

Thus far, the technique may seem as straightforward as computing a mean. However, it is not. The factor analyst must make a number of decisions about how the analysis is conducted. The choices made greatly influence the resulting factor structure and cannot be based solely on objective, quantitative grounds. They involve subjective judgments about how the analysis should best proceed. For example, many methods have been developed to identify latent factors (e.g., principal components, common factors, maximum likelihood, minimum residuals). Not infrequently, they yield different results.

Other critical decisions concern how many factors to retain and how to rotate the factors to enhance their interpretability. Among the various methods for establishing the number of latent dimensions to retain (e.g., Everett, 1983), the most widely used is the scree test of eigenvalues (Cattell & Vogelmann, 1977). Among rotation methods, the most popular include the orthogonal varimax rotation (which identifies uncorrelated latent factors), the oblique oblimin rotation (which identifies correlated latent factors), and the promax rotation (which combines the advantages of the oblique and orthogonal approaches). All three seek a "simple structure" (see Thurstone, 1947) in which each variable loads only one factor. The factors should be highly correlated with a few observed variables and uncorrelated with others. In this ideal, the factors are easily interpretable. They unambiguously reduce the complexity of interrelations in the original data set under the assumptions of the linear model.

In practice, simple structure is often violated. Variables load on more than one factor. This has led some investigators to represent individual differences via circumplex models (Hofstee, De Raad, & Goldberg, 1992; Wiggins, 1979; Wiggins, Steiger, & Gaelik, 1981). Two main circumplex dimensions define a circular psychological space. Although some variables load onto the main axes and are located at the poles, others are represented as blends of factors and thus take positions somewhere along the arc of the circle defined by the axes. Since many personality descriptors correlate substantially with more than one primary factor, a circumplex structure is well suited to their representation.

■ *Exploratory Factor Analysis.* Factor analyses are often "exploratory" in nature. Investigators may have no a priori theory about how variables go together. Instead, they strive to obtain a data-driven rather than a theory-driven depiction of how variables interrelate. However, even exploratory analyses are never theory-free, since theory guides the choice of options in the analysis and the decision to use factor analysis in the first place.

■ *Confirmatory Factor Analysis.* An alternative to exploratory methods is to test, or "confirm," a theory about the pattern of interrelations among observed variables. Confirmatory factor analysis generally employs structural equation modeling. This technique evaluates how well a specified model of the relationships among a set of variables actually fits observed covariances among those variables (Loehlin, 1992). One first specifies the number of latent variables in the model and the relations among latent variables and observed variables. Then one computes the goodness of fit of the model, that is, how well it fits the observed data (see Bollen, 1989).

Confirmatory factor analysis also is useful in the study of construct validity. To assess construct validity (i.e., the extent to which an operationalization measures the concept it is supposed to measure), Campbell and Fiske (1959) proposed a multitrait-multimethod (MTMM) design in which indicators of two or more traits are measured by two or more methods. An MTMM matrix, then, consists of the correlations of more than one trait measured by more than one method. This combination of traits and methods allows for an examination of variance that is due to traits, variance that is due to methods, and unique or error variance. Two aspects of construct validity are considered: convergent validity, the degree of agreement among multiple measures of the same concept; and discriminant validity, the degree to which measures of different concepts differ. Given the importance of both method error and construct validity in personality assessment, a method that enables the decomposition of sources of variance is obviously of great benefit (Bagozzi, 1993; Fiske, 1987; Ozer, 1989). Confirmatory factor analysis is particularly appropriate to MTMM requirements in that it allows the total variability in observed variables to be decomposed into a linear combination of latent trait and method variables plus error. One can compute how much variability is due to traits, to systematic method effects, and to random error (Bagozzi, 1994; Kenny & Kashy, 1992). Work by Borkenau and Ostendorf (1990) and by Barbaranelli and Caprara (2000) illustrates how confirmatory techniques can be used to test theoretical models of the structure of dispositional tendencies.

The advantages of confirmatory factor analysis are clear. The evaluation of a theoretical model is generally superior to a theory-free exploration. However, confirmatory factor analysis cannot always be applied. For example, although evaluating the goodness of fit of the five-factor model is an obvious application, problems arise here. It is difficult to specify on theoretical grounds the complete pattern of loadings that link observed variables to latent constructs, and the statistical requirements of confirmatory factor analysis may be too stringent or "oversensitive" to permit a fair evaluation of the model (Borkenau & Ostendorf, 1990; Church & Burke, 1994; Katigbak et al., 1996; McCrae, Zonderman, Costa, Bond & Paunonen, 1996). For this reason, procrustes rotation has been considered a viable alternative to evaluate the NEO-PI structure (McCrae et al., 1996).

**Interpreting the Method**

Factor analysis has contributed greatly to psychology's understanding of the primary dimensions of variation in psychological tendencies. Yet, as with any other statistical technique, factor analysis cannot replace theory development. Theory is needed to determine the meaning of the factors and the meaningfulness of using the approach to solve any given problem. Proper interpretation requires that one weigh a number of considerations, particularly involving the nature of the data being analyzed. Factor structures are affected by the characteristics of the samples considered, the nature and the distribution of the selected variables, and, indirectly, the theoretical premises that have guided the choice of variables and populations (Briggs & Cheek, 1986; Comrey, 1978; Comrey & Lee, 1992; Kline, 1987; Lykken, 1971). Block (1995), for example, suggests that the high replicability of the five-factor model partially reflects the fact that the model in some studies is an almost inevitable product of the highly preselected clusters of items that were factor-analyzed. The factors, in other words, may have been prestructured (Block, 1995) in the initial data set.

Further, a number of writers contend that the analysis of individual differences, through any technique, may not be a reliable route to discovering underlying causal structure. They advance this point by considering well-understood domains (e.g., Cervone, 1999; Epstein, 1994; Mischel & Shoda, 1994). Suppose one were to factor-analyze differences among automobiles. One might obtain robust factors of maximum speed and reliability, but these factors would shed little light on the causal components under the hood (Epstein, 1994). The factor analytic results would not cause a mechanic to search for a structure of reliability; indeed, if a mechanic said that your car broke down "because of its low reliability," you would seek a new mechanic. The problem, which we noted in other contexts, is that the unitary statistical factor does not have unitary underlying causes. The car's maximum speed is affected by engine horsepower and torque, the car's weight, its tires, design, etc. An understanding of these distinct mechanisms is required if one wants to maximize the performance of one's car. We return to this theme in our epilogue (part 5).

In light of the many statistical assumptions and subjective decisions that are part of the technique, the notion that factor analysis can yield the "real" structure of personality seems naive. The factor analysis of phenotypic tendencies may yield important clues to human nature, but this is a far cry from saying that the factors constitute components of human nature itself. In summary, the technique must be used with caution, and in any case, findings cannot substitute for the responsibility of scientists in choosing data, selecting analyses, and interpretation.

## TEMPERAMENT AND PERSONALITY

Personality should not be disembodied. Although psychological attributes cannot be reduced to biological processes, they are emergent properties of a biological being. Inquiry in personality psychology thus must be informed by knowledge of the organism that sets the initial conditions for personality functioning. Knowledge of inherited biological structures and processes converges with the analysis of psychological characteristics in the study of temperament.

The notion of temperament is an ancient one. The idea that people, from birth, possess biological factors that are responsible for psychological characteristics is found in the medical theories of the Hippocratic school of the 5th century B.C. As we noted in chapter 2, the Greek notion endured, being visible in the work of Kant and Wundt. It influenced popular literature and everyday language through the ages.

### Early 20th-Century Contributions

Temperament began to figure prominently in psychology's study of individual differences by the early 20th century. The contributions of Heymans and Wiersna (1906 through 1909), who organized traits according to three basic dimensions of temperament, were critical (see chapter 2). However, their work primarily investigated phenotypic behavioral differences. It thus failed to capitalize on the possibility that temperament research could identify and directly study specific physiological mechanisms that underlie observable behavioral variation. Advances in this regard derived from the work of Pavlov (1935 through 1955) and his students, who explored relations between nervous system functioning and behavior (Berlyne, 1968; Gray, 1964; Strelau, 1983, 1997; also see chapter 5).

In his research on classical conditioning, Pavlov recognized significant individual differences in the speed and accuracy with which conditioning takes place. These differences manifested themselves in excitatory and inhibitory conditioning processes. Three attributes of the nervous system were postulated, namely, strength, balance, and mobility. Strength, or the working capacity of cortical cells, expressed itself in both excitatory and inhibitory processes. Balance referred to the relationship between excitation and inhibition. Mobility referred to the organism's ability to adapt to a changing environment by alternating between excitation and inhibition (Pavlov, 1951–1952). Nowadays, this conception seems dated because it searches for overall qualities of the entire nervous system. Pavlov had no access to contemporary knowledge of multiple and partially independent neural systems and thus gave little consideration to the possibility that different subsystems within the same individual may have different properties.

One other early contribution of note is that of Sheldon and Stevens (1942). They explored the relation between temperament and physical constitution, linking three temperament clusters (viscerotonia, somatotonia, and cerebrotonia) to corresponding bodily characteristics (endomorphy, mesomorphy, and ectomorphy). The absence of strong empirical support caused this approach to have little lasting impact.

### Defining Temperament

The founders of modern personality psychology generally conceived of temperament as one element of the individual's overall attributes. Personality, the enduring organization of a person's character, included moral and volitional components, the cognitive component of intelligence, and the emotional component of temperament. Allport (1937) defined temperament as individuals' characteristic "emotional nature," including their speed of response and typical mood. He viewed temperament as based in biology and largely inherited. Similarly, Eysenck regarded temperament as the "affective sector" (1947, p. 25) or "the more or less stable and enduring system of affective behaviour" (1970, p. 2).

In later scientific writings, personality and temperament were used interchangeably, as they commonly are by the layperson. Students of individual differences in activity, emotionality, and impulsivity tend to equate the terms (e.g., Cloninger, 1987; Cloninger, Svrakic & Przybeck, 1993; Gray, 1987; Zuckerman, 1991). Some consider temperament as the aspect of personality that is expressed earliest in life and is most strongly inherited (Buss & Plomin, 1975, 1984). Finally, although some contend that "there is no useful distinction between personality and temperament since the two are equivalent" (Costa and McCrae, in press), others warn against confounding the terms or subsuming one under the other (Strelau, 1987). These warnings are quite reasonable; regardless of one's view of the nature and importance of temperament, it should be apparent that the notion of personality encompasses capacities and functions that go beyond inherited affective predispositions.

Even the contemporary field contains "no consensus on basic terms, measurement procedures, or robust generalizations" (Kagan, 1998a, p. 178). Of four fundamental issues of disagreement among contemporary temperament investigators noted by Kagan (1998a), three involve questions so fundamental that they bear on the very definition of the term: (1) Do temperamental qualities vary dimensionally or categorically? (2) Should one search for a small, overarching system of temperamental qualities or remain open to the possibility of large numbers of context-specific temperaments? (3) Is temperament an "essence," that is, an unchanging structure, or do temperamental qualities emerge, develop, and potentially change over the course of childhood? The fourth issue concerns sources of evidence, particularly whether parental reports validly indicate the temperamental qualities of their children. Historically, most investigators have employed parental reports and searched for a simple, dimensional system of essential temperamental qualities.

They have done this despite the repeated admonitions of Kagan (e.g., 1994b, 1998a), who believes that investigators should look beyond simple, essentialistic explanations and should consider alternatives to dimensional models. The dimensional approaches, he contends, reflect a potentially unwarranted importation of the models of physics into psychology. They are then reinforced by psychologists' nearly exclusive training in linear statistical methods.

One might be suspicious of an area of study that has failed to establish agreement on such fundamental issues. However, despite conceptual controversies, the study of temperament has flourished in recent decades. Ideas about inherited qualities that were widely criticized a quarter-century ago are now a part of the standard belief system of the personality psychologist. Virtually all investigators recognize temperament as a critical concept for relating biological structures to affective and behavioral dispositions. The growth of research on temperament makes a truly comprehensive review impossible here (but see Kohnstamm, Bates, & Rothbart, 1989; Rothbart & Bates, 1998; Strelau, 1998; Strelau & Angleitner, 1991; Wachs & Kohnstamm, in press; Watson, 2000). We limit ourselves to a review of empirical and theoretical contributions that have been particularly influential in establishing an overall system of temperamental qualities.

**Dimensions of Temperament**

In common usage, the term *personality traits* largely refers to characteristic tendencies to perform particular types of action that can be defined according to their content or goals. A five-factor dimension such as conscientiousness, for example, captures individual differences in behavior that possesses specific social content ("conscientious" acts). Temperament, in contrast, refers to stylistic qualities that involve affect, energy, or attention and that do not pertain to a particular class of social actions. Temperament, then, mostly concerns the formal and stylistic features of behavior, such as the individual's sensitivity and responsivity to environmental demands.

One can conceptualize temperament characteristics at different levels of analysis: observed behavior, patterns of neurophysiological events, constellation of genes, and patterns of gene-environment interactions. These different conceptual levels have different operationalizations and methods. Temperamental qualities are studied through a variety of physiological and psychological data sources, including observed behavior, peer or parent ratings, neurophysiological recordings, and genetic analyses (Bates, 1989). Work over the years has yielded a number of models of the structure of temperamental qualities. In the following, we review four prominent models.

Thomas and Chess (1977, 1980, 1986) defined temperament as the stylistic characteristics of behavior, or the "how" of behavior. Based on interviews with the parents of infants, they identified nine temperament dimensions that differ qualitatively although they may not be statistically independent. These are activity level, which involves the motor component of activities such as eating, playing etc.; rhythmicity, or the regularity and predictability of biological functions such as sleep, nourishment, and evacuation; approach versus withdrawal in reaction to novel stimuli; adaptability, or ease of change in response to altered situations; threshold of responsiveness to subtle stimulation; intensity, or energy level of reactions; positive versus negative mood; distractibility; and attention span and persistence.

Principally on the basis of clinical observations, Thomas and Chess identified dimensional profiles that defined three temperamental types: easy, difficult, and slow. Easy children have regular rhythms in the biological functions, display positive reactions to new stimuli, adapt easily to change, and express a moderately intense positive mood. Difficult children have irregular biological rhythms, withdraw from novelty, are resistant to change, and show intense and negative emotional reactions. Slow children display fairly good regularity in their vital functions. Although they adapt slowly, they can attain quite normal reactions if they receive appropriate supports from the environment.

Thomas and Chess recognized that the outcomes experienced by children with a particular standing on an easy–difficult continuum could not be predicted or understood by examining the child's qualities in isolation. Temperamental characteristics inevitably encounter environments that either support or oppose them. One must consider goodness of fit, that is, the consonance or dissonance between the temperamental characteristics of the child and the expectations, demands, and opportunities of the environment (particularly as represented by the parents). Thomas and Chess contended that to understand the link from early temperament to later personality outcomes, one must attend not only to temperamental qualities but to patterns of interaction between children and their social environment.

Strelau (1983, 1997, 1998) similarly regards temperament as the formal aspects of behavior and personality. However, his contributions developed quite independently of clinical and developmental traditions such as that of Thomas and Chess. Strelau's work is grounded in the Pavlovian tradition. It also incorporates Hebb's (1955) concepts about optimal levels of arousal and the regulation of stimulation. It thus parallels biologically oriented theories such as those of Eysenck (1970) and Gray (1987) (see chapter 5). In Strelau's regulative theory of temperament (RTT), temperament is a set of stable features determined by configurations of neurological (central and autonomic nervous system) and endocrine mechanisms (Strelau, 1983; Strelau & Plomin, 1992). These mechanisms are present from birth and are subjected to slow changes due to maturation and environmental influences.

Despite these biological premises, Strelau's research program has not directly investigated neural systems in the Pavlovian tradition. Instead, he has identified temperament dimensions via questionnaire studies, generally conducted with adult populations (e.g., Strelau, Angleitner, Bantelmann, & Ruch,

1990; Strelau, Angleitner, & Ruch, 1990). His early research led to a distinction between the energetic and temporal aspects of temperament. Energetic components refer to reactivity and activity levels, whereas temporal features refer to qualities such as the speed and persistence of response. In his subsequent work, temperament consists of seven dimensions. Three concern the energetic characteristics of behavior, namely, sensory sensitivity, endurance, and activity; three concern temporal characteristics, namely, mobility, perseverance, and liveliness; and the seventh factor, emotional reactivity, is affective (Strelau, 1983). Strelau and Zawadzki (1995) revised this conception in a temperament inventory composed of six scales: briskness (the tendency to react quickly, maintain a high tempo of activity and shift response easily when surrounding activities change); perseverance; sensory sensitivity; emotional reactivity; endurance; and activity. These revisions attest to the difficulty of confirming temperament constructs psychometrically.

Most of Strelau's empirical work has examined emotional reactivity and activity. Reactivity is manifested in the intensity of reactions to stimuli. High reactives prefer low levels of stimulation. They avoid intense external stimulation because it would arouse them beyond their optimal level of physiological activation. Low reactives, conversely, prefer activity of high stimulative value. They need external stimulation to maintain an optimal level of activation. Reactivity of temperament influences the regulation of behavior by determining the individual's sensitivity threshold and by determining individual capacity to work (endurance). Activity is revealed in the amount and range of actions the individual undertakes. Reactivity and activity are related in that individuals' degree of need for stimulation predisposes them toward actions that, in turn, have a stimulative value.

Buss and Plomin have investigated the inherited bases of temperament. They suggest that inherited factors contribute to three temperament dimensions that emerge early in life, namely, emotionality, activity, and sociability (EAS) (Buss & Plomin 1975, 1984; also see Strelau & Plomin, 1992). Emotionality is the proclivity to become affectively arousable and to experience distressful emotions such as fear and anger. Activity levels reflect the individual's optimal level of stimulation. Activity manifests itself in strength and speed of movements. Sociability concerns affiliative tendencies, such as interacting with others and seeking social rewards.

The research of Rothbart (1989) indicates two fundamental dimensions of temperament. One is reactivity, defined as the ease with which motor, affective, autonomic, and endocrine systems become aroused. The idea that reactivity is part of the individual's biological constitution is supported by findings that even fetal levels of activity are positively related to postnatal levels (Madison, Madison, & Adubato, 1986). The other is self-regulation, which refers to attentional and behavioral processes through which the individual seeks to adjust or govern aversive arousal. These processes can include cognitive and behavioral approach toward, or withdrawal from, aversive stimuli. The idea that there is an enduring inherited contribution to the ability to control emotional states is consistent with the finding that individual differences in impulse control are identifiable early in life and are highly stable (see chapter 5).

Although it is possible to find significant commonalities among the four models reviewed here, diversities are no less relevant, attesting to the difficulty of arriving at a common taxonomy and of grounding the various dimensions on knowledge of specific processes.

## Context and Categories

The dimensional models we have reviewed have the goal of identifying a small number of temperament qualities, each of which comes into play across a broad range of stimuli and contexts. Indeed, commentators commonly equate biological temperament with context-free personality characteristics; the "genetic component" of personality "accompanies the individual wherever he or she goes" (Harris,

1995, p. 463). Although this is true in a trivial sense, inherited biological mechanisms may be more contextualized than this position implies.

The idea that temperament consists solely of broad, context-free tendencies is not an empirical finding but an assumption. The decision to factor-analyze parental ratings of children's overall behavioral tendencies biases one toward finding a small number of broad, context-free dimensions; the identification of such dimensions is the very purpose of factor analytic techniques. The work of Kagan (1994b, 1998a, b) challenges this approach by indicating that temperamental qualities may be neither small in number, context-free, nor dimensional.

Kagan (1994b) reviews dimensional models of temperament and draws a general conclusion that is congruent with arguments we have made elsewhere in our text. "One problem with all of these approaches is that they are top down. Their creators begin with a theoretical ambition to keep the number of constructs at a minimum, without a persuasive rationale for that choice" (p. 48). As Kagan emphasizes, the strategy of analyzing phenotypic tendencies to identify a simple, high-level system of temperaments has three drawbacks. First, the search for a small number of constructs may lead one erroneously to equate children who actually differ. "Children with similar surface profiles can belong to different groups"; they may have "different histories and [be] in possession of different physiologies" (Kagan, 1994b, p. 122). Second, the search for generalized temperament qualities obscures the possibility that inherited temperament mechanisms may be highly context-specific rather than context-free. This is an important possibility to consider, since many biological mechanisms are activated only by specific external inputs. Finally, the search for dimensions overlooks the possibility that temperamental qualities are categorical. Particular temperamental qualities may be possessed by qualitatively distinct subgroups of the population. If so, temperament would vary from one individual to another, not linearly but categorically. This would be missed by correlational and factor analytic methods, which, by their mathematical design, yield linear results.

In their research, Kagan and colleagues identify subgroups of infants who are hypothesized to possess inhibited and uninhibited temperaments. They study these children across childhood to explore stability and variability in temperamental tendencies. When children are only 4 months of age, they are presented with a range of novel visual and auditory stimuli. Infants are classified as "high reactive" and "low reactive" based on the combination of two criteria, amount of limb activity and amount of distress and crying when the stimuli are presented. These categorizations are based on theorizing about the underlying physiology of inhibition; these ideas focus on the role that neural circuits involving the amygdala play in the processing of unfamiliar events (Kagan, 1998a). At 14 months of age, the children are observed as they are exposed to novel stimuli (e.g., a toy robot). At 4.5 years, they are observed in social settings, including interactions with unfamiliar children and an interview with a woman who is unfamiliar to them. Infant profiles predict later behavior. High reactive infants, based on the classification at 4 months of age, react more fearfully to novel stimuli at 14 and 21 months, and are less outgoing and sociable with other children and more subdued toward the interviewer at age 4.5 (Kagan, 1994b, 1998a). Note that the temperament profile is preserved across time but expresses itself in different ways at different ages; 4.5-year-olds do not simply kick their legs as they did in infancy. Instead, the temperamental qualities cohere over time. They are meaningfully related in an age-appropriate manner to the underlying physiology of inhibition.

Two other notes about Kagan's findings are, first, that context matters. One can not simply group together, for example, all children who tend to cry. Instead, the stimulus that evokes crying is important. At 4 months of age, some children cry when they hear a tape-recorded voice that is not accompanied by normal motor movements in a displayed face. Others cry when a mobile is presented but not when they hear the incongruous voice or face. These two groups of cryers differ behaviorally at age 2 (Kagan, 1994b). Similarly, infants who cry in reaction to physical restraints differ from those who cry in response to auditory stimulation (Kagan, 1998a, p. 220).

The second point is that the variations between children appear to be categorical. Degrees of crying and limb activity at 4 months are not linearly related to later fear reactions. Instead, as would be expected if underlying systems are categorical, "once an infant attains a value for motor activity and crying that places him or her into the high-reactive group, more crying or motor arousal has minimal consequences for later fear behavior" (Kagan, 1998).

Before drawing firm conclusions about the potential categorical nature of temperament qualities, one would wish to have more evidence (see Meehl, 1992), including evidence involving qualities beyond inhibitedness or uninhibitedness. Nonetheless, the possibility that the structure of temperament consists of a potentially large number of context-specific qualities, which are possessed by discrete subsets of the population, has far-reaching implications. It suggests that the application of factor-analytic techniques to the study of temperament is severely limited if not misguided. Further, the continued application of factor-analytic techniques will never reveal its limitations. Suppose, for the moment, that Kagan is correct that a subgroup of 20 to 25% of the population contains an inhibited profile and another categorical subgroup is uninhibited. If one were to combine these two categorical groups with the rest of the population and subject the responses of the totality to factor analysis, one may well find a linear factor of inhibitedness (or reactivity). One would interpret this result as indicating that individuals vary along a linear continuum of uninhibitedness–inhibitedness. But if Kagan is right, this conclusion is wrong. The dimension is a statistical artifact of the extreme, highly intercorrelated scores of the two subgroups. Since much of personality psychology's enterprise of

analyzi[...]
built o[...]
argume[...]

Fina[...]
temper[...]
change[...]
not de[...]
ject to [...]
1999, p[...]
numbe[...]
files ch[...]
mothers make appropriate demands [...] children rather than continually protecting them from stress, their children are more likely to overcome extreme reactivity and inhibition (Arcus, 1991; cited in Kagan, 1998).

## General Conclusions

Research on temperament features enough consensus to inspire optimism but enough discrepancies and open questions to suggest that our understanding of the phenomenon may still be rudimentary. Extant work conveys a sense of the complexity of human temperamental qualities but does not allow firm conclusions about their nature. On the one hand, factor-analytic studies generally indicate that dimensions such as positive and negative affectivity, attention span, persistence, activity level, and social inhibition represent individual differences that are grounded in biological constitution. Behavior genetic studies further support the biological underpinning of these variations. There can be no doubt that human beings inherit qualities of psychological significance that are detectable early in life and that may have enduring consequences for psychological development.

On the other hand, the view that temperamental qualities consist of a small number of linear, context-free dimensions is far from confirmed. Temperamental qualities often appear to be context-specific, with global constructs such as reactivity or emotionality encompassing more than one physiological system or psychological quality. The understanding of temperament may be enhanced by a somewhat greater reliance on physiological evidence and on contextualized constructs that can be

...y to biological mecha-
...ultiple sources of evidence
...portant in this area in light of
...uestions that have been raised
...alidity of parental reports and the
...allenges that remain in relating tem-
...mental features to later personality char-
...teristics (Halverson, Kohnstamm, & Martin,
1994; Kagan, 1994b, 1998b; Kohnstamm,
Bates, & Rothbart, 1989; Rothbart & Bates,
1998; Strelau & Angleitner, 1991).

Progress in the neurosciences is likely to deepen our understanding of the nature, development, and modifiability of temperament mechanisms. Future years should bring more detailed evidence of how neurological and neurochemical systems contribute to specific psychological processes (e.g., attention, exploration, motor execution, behavioral and emotional control) in specific environments (e.g., involving novelty, threat, reward, social bonds). Biological and traditional psychological research may provide converging evidence regarding aspects of temperament that are stable versus those that are modifiable (see Rothbart & Bates, 1998). Still, it is important to bear in mind that, whatever the advances, research on inherited neural systems cannot provide a complete picture of emotion and personality functioning. As the individual develops, cognitive factors become increasingly important to motivation and affective experience. The knowledge and skills that enable people to regulate behavior and affect largely derive from socially and culturally grounded learning experiences. Individuals play an active role in acquiring these experiences and thus in developing their own capacity for "emotional intelligence" (Salovey & Mayer, 1990). We consider this possibility below, as we turn to the general question of intellectual capabilities.

## THE INTELLIGENCES: GENERAL, PRACTICAL, SOCIAL, AND EMOTIONAL

Through the history of psychology, the study of personality has often been intertwined with the study of intelligence. The two fields have met in the areas of differential, developmental, and clinical psychology and in applications in education, work, and psychological adjustment.

The personality psychologist's concern with intellectual capacities can be traced at least as far back as psychoanalytical theory, which provided an account not only of emotions and drives but also of cognitive development and functioning (Gill, 1967; Rapaport, 1960). Conversely, the influence of intelligence research on personality originates in factor-analytic studies of mental abilities, which served as a prototype for the study of personality dispositions. Piaget (1947) influenced personality psychology indirectly in that his stage-model approach to intellectual functioning was later imported into the domains of moral reasoning and personality functioning (Kohlberg, 1964; Loevinger, 1966). Studies of cognitive style, begun at the onset of the cognitive revolution, bridged personality and intelligence by pursuing individual differences in thinking and problem solving and relating them to individual differences in motivation and interpersonal relations (Gardner, Jackson and Messick, 1960; Klein, 1970; Witkin and Goodenough, 1981).

Personality trait theorists have taken differing views of the role of intelligence in personality structure. Intelligence is a factor in Cattell's personality theory (see above). Eysenck (1947) at first conceived of intelligence as a cognitive dimension of personality. Later, after positing his three-dimensional (extraversion, neuroticism, and psychoticism) personality trait model, he used the term intelligence to refer to three different orders of phenomena – biological intelligence, psychometric intelligence, and social intelligence (Eysenck, 1994) – and explored relations between these forms of intelligence and personality traits.

Over time, research specialization in the respective domains of intelligence and personality caused the traditions to separate. Personality psychologists increasingly explored social behavior and affect, whereas intelligence researchers focused on cognitive capabilities of the sort expressed in academic problem solving (e.g., verbal, logical, spatial, and mathematical reasoning). These separations probably reflected practical convenience more than epistemological convictions. A comprehensive theory of personality cannot completely avoid questions of cognitive capabilities, since these capabilities contribute to the coherence and continuity of personal functioning that is of such interest to the field. The study of cognitive performance cannot be disjoined from the study of personality processes, since factors not involving ability but involving motivation and self-referent beliefs partly determine the levels of performance people achieve. Ideally, investigators would examine how cognitive capabilities and self-referent beliefs interrelate and jointly contribute to people's efforts to realize their potentials.

In the late 1980s and the 1990s, cognitive, developmental, personality, and social psychologists began to integrate the field's study of personality and intelligence (see Cantor & Kihlstrom, 1987; Sternberg & Grigorenko, 1997; Sternberg & Ruzgis, 1994). Investigators came to realize not only that intellectual capacities influence personality functioning and others' impression of one's personality but that intelligence research also provides an important lesson for how one conceptualizes personality structure. The key developments in the study of intelligence highlighted three aspects of skillful cognitive performance, which typically had been slighted in traditional IQ formulations: expertise, context, and pragmatics (Cantor & Kihlstrom, 1987). People do not simply inherit a fixed amount of mental ability; they gradually acquire knowledge, which gives them the expertise needed to solve problems. Regarding context, investigators recognized that intelligence cannot be fully described apart from the contexts and intellectual challenges that make up the person's day-to-day life. Intelligence develops and expresses itself in real-world contexts, and the actions that are intelligent in one sociocultural setting may not be intelligent in another.

Finally, the notion of pragmatics highlights the goal-directed qualities of the behavior we call intelligent. One cannot determine whether an individual is acting intelligently without considering the aims toward which the person is directing his or her behavior. Since people can set their own goals and can partly determine the contexts they experience, these considerations draw attention to the role of human agency in the development of intellectual capacities, as Bidell & Fischer (1997) emphasize. In the course of development, "the active construction of new cognitive skills by the developing person weaves biological and sociocultural systems into new patterns of relations, creating new context-specific forms of intellectual abilities" (Bidell & Fischer, 1997, p. 206). We consider contextualized analyses of intelligence and attempts to integrate the study of intelligence and personality below, after first reviewing psychometric work on the components of intellectual capabilities.

## Components and Expressions of Intelligence

The systematic study of intelligence is greatly indebted to the psychometric tradition. Factor analysis brought order to the field by yielding a $g$ factor, which was interpreted as an inherited generalized mental ability. Despite cogent attacks on this concept (e.g. Gould, 1981; Kamin, 1974; Sternberg, 1999), the notion that individual differences in intelligence derive from a common generalized factor remained popular in many quarters (Jensen, 1998). Spearman (1927) identified a general intelligence factor, which operated in combination with factors that influenced more specific aspects of intellectual performances ($s$ factors). Thurstone (1938) identified seven primary abilities. Cattell (1963, 1971) distinguished two different expressions of general intelligence: fluid intelligence, the culture-free ability to see complex relationships and to implement new ways of thinking in solving problems, and crystallized intelligence, or the use of previously acquired skills, knowledge, and ways of thinking.

The search for general intelligence has invoked not only psychometric evidence but biological findings. Both psychophysiological and behavior-genetic evidence have been brought to bear on the explanation of individual differences in global IQ, as assessed by tests such as the Wechsler Adult Intelligence Scale (Wechsler, 1981). Psychophysiological work using electroencephalographic measures has yielded clear associations between brain electrical activity and intelligence scores (e.g., Jensen, 1998; Vernon, 1993). Both electrophysiological and chronometric evidence supports the hypothesis that individual differences in intellectual ability reflect variations in speed of mental processing (Deary & Caryl, 1993; Eysenck, 1994). New imaging technologies, such as magnetic resonance imaging (MRI) and positron emission tomography (PET), promise novel advances in this area. Still, most research is correlational, so results are not entirely convincing. The fact that a particular biological factor covaries with IQ scores clearly does not imply that the factor *is* intelligence. Further, how mental speed relates to practical intelligence, wisdom, or other intellectual qualities important to personality functioning remains unclear.

Turning to behavioral genetic research, numerous findings indicate that the variation in IQ scores within any given population is substantially inherited. Within the assumptions of the standard behavior genetic method (see chapter 5), genetic factors are found to account for the majority (often 70% or more) of the population variance in *g* (Bouchard, 1993; Brody, 1992; Jensen, 1998). Identical twins obtain relatively similar IQ scores even if they are separated in infancy and reared apart (Bouchard, Lykken, McGue, Segal, & Tellegen, 1990).

Despite the consistency of evidence from twin studies, the idea that humans possess a unitary quality of intelligence at a level that is primarily inherited remains highly controversial (see Sternberg & Grigorenko, 1997). Some evidence directly contradicts the notion that IQ scores index a biological feature of the human mind (brain). The "Flynn effect"

(Flynn, 1999) is a striking example. The Flynn effect is that IQ scores of a wide variety of human populations have risen during the past decades, often by an extremely large margin. For example, if one scales IQ scores among citizens of Great Britain such that the mean IQ score in the year 1992 is 100, one finds that the mean IQ score in 1942 was less than 75. This logically raises two possibilities, the first of which – that citizens of Britain became innately more intelligent to a dramatically large degree, in the span of two to three generations – is implausible. The other, far more plausible, possibility is that IQ scores are not a direct index of biologically based intelligence and thus cannot be used to compare the levels of intelligence of different groups. Although the causes of population-level gains in IQ test scores are not fully understood, it is clear that the test score gains are not the result of enormous leaps in true human intellectual capacity during the 20th century (Flynn, 1999). Note that the gains could reflect relatively trivial factors; for example, contemporary citizens may be more familiar with the sort of multiple-choice test items used in most IQ tests than were people earlier in the century.

When evaluating twin-study evidence that genetic factors explain much of the population variance in IQ scores, it is important to inquire carefully about two things; namely, the nature of genetic factors and the nature and meaning of IQ scores. Consider first the genetic factors. Behavior geneticists can survey the population and produce a singular estimate of heritability. This, however, does not imply that there exists a singular biological factor that correspondingly explains the variability in scores. A large heritability coefficient merely means that identical twins were more similar to one another than were dizygotic twins. From one twin pair to another, the similarity may be due to different biological factors, as Kagan (1998a) has noted. One twin pair may share a hearing impairment, which interferes with their ability to acquire language skills. Another may share an inherited deficit in attentional abilities, which interferes with their learning at school. The list obviously could go on. The biological factors that contribute to the singular heritability estimate may be multifaceted, and many factors may have little to do in a direct way with the cognitive capacities we call intelligence. A similar argument can be made regarding twin-study evidence of the heritability of personality characteristics.

Turning to the test scores, the notion of IQ has at least two big drawbacks. The scores tell us little about how people acquire knowledge and put it into practice or how they may acquire new knowledge that enhances their intellectual capacities. The IQ says little about the proactive properties of mind, which over the course of development enable people to contribute to their own levels of capability (Bidell & Fischer, 1997). Individuals who are fortunate enough to have inherited superior information-processing capacities are unlikely to develop into successful members of their community who are perceived as intelligent unless they muster the effort required to develop knowledge and thinking skills. Einstein said it more succinctly: Genius is 99% perspiration. The second limitation is that human intelligence may be far too multifaceted to be captured by a single linear dimenson. Many investigators reject the factor-analytic approach and the associated search for biological correlates of *g*. They study human intelligence without any reference to constructs such as generalized intelligence (see Neisser et al., 1996). Instead, they examine specific information-processing mechanisms that underlie the individual's capacity for intelligent action (e.g., Gardner, 1983; Sternberg, 1985). Just as personality psychology harbors two traditions, one focused on the psychometric analysis of global individual differences and the other on dynamic, contextualized cognitive and affective processes (Cervone, 1991), the study of intelligence harbors two traditions, one focused on individual differences measured via standardized tests and the other on the cognitive processes that underlie intellectual performance and that may vary from one problem-solving domain to another (Ohlsson, 1998). The cognitive processing tradition indicates that the mental abilities involved in skill acquisition, problem solving, and creativity are more multifaceted than suggested by the psychometric tradition. In the following, we briefly review some main contributions to this tradition.

Hunt (1983) has identified three sets of processes in which individuals may differ. Variations may be found in the ways people (1) mentally represent problems, (2) manipulate mental representations (by encoding, information transfer, etc.), and (3) implement the various information processing steps required to reach desired outcomes. Failure to achieve an objective, then, may be rooted in any one of these processes.

Other contributions suggest that the cognitive mechanisms underlying intelligent behavior are domain-specific. Different mental subsystems may be specialized to solve different sorts of problems, that is, problems in different content domains. Gardner's (1983) theory of multiple intelligences proposes seven components of mental ability: linguistic, logic-mathematical, spatial, musical, bodily-kinesthetic, interpersonal (the ability to understand others), and intrapersonal (the ability to understand one's own affective life) intelligence. Gardner marshals converging sources of evidence to support his view that intelligences are specialized rather than generalized. Child prodigies commonly display prodigious talent in one domain but ordinary ability in others. As a child, the artistically gifted Picasso struggled to learn reading, writing, and arithmetic (Gardner, 1993). Sufferers of brain damage frequently lose one component of mental functioning while others are left intact. Adults commonly display wide variation in cognitive functioning across domains. The domain specificity of exceptional performance often renders questions about general intelligence nearly meaningless. The answer to "Who was smarter, Mohandas Gandhi or Miles Davis?" is "This is not a good question." They both were geniuses in particular domains of functioning.

In Gardner's view, the various intelligences are not completely separated from one another, as would be suggested by accounts of mental functioning in which the mind consists of separate mental modules that do not communicate with one another (see Fodor, 1983). Instead, people may bring different aspects of intelligence to bear on common problems. As one example, creative musical composition may employ mathematical logic, as in the work of Bach (Hofstadter, 1979).

The intelligences that are most valued in any given society may vary across cultures and historical periods. In recent eras, Western cultures have particularly valued linguistic and logical–mathematical forms of intelligence. This is reflected in the widespread use of intelligence tests that tap quantitative reasoning and verbal abilities. However, other intelligences may have greater adaptive and survival value in other settings, and other cultures may define intelligence very differently from the Western psychometrician. In traditional Tibetan psychology, intelligence is primarily conceived as a mental function that accurately recognizes positive acts and protects the mind from inaccurate perceptions of the world, largely by "not falling prey to the emotions" (Guenther & Kawamura, 1975, p. 54). Intelligence in this view blends Gardner's intrapersonal intelligence with capacities that Western psychologists would call self-regulation. It is closer to what we might call emotional intelligence than to IQ. Even in the West, the layperson's intuitive conception of intelligence is both more detailed and more contextualized than the concept of global IQ (Sternberg, Conway, Keton, & Bernstein, 1981).

Sternberg's "triarchic" theory (Sternberg, 1985, 1988) posits three interdependent components of intelligent behavior: analytical, practical-contextual, and creative-synthetic intelligence. Analytic processes are involved in abstract reasoning and the evaluation of ideas; this form of intelligence is particularly important in academic pursuits. The practical application of knowledge and expertise is important to solve real-world problems. Creative intelligence involves the development of novel, inventive concepts, which often

comes about through unique combinations of preexisting ideas.

In Sternberg's view, intelligence is not a quality that resides in a static manner in one's head. Instead, it is a capability with which one solves problems. Intelligence is adaptive. It involves "the purposive adaptation to, selection of, and shaping of real world environments relevant to one's life and abilities" (Sternberg, 1988, p. 65). Intelligence expresses itself not just in IQ tests but in shaping and solving the problems of everyday life.

Sternberg's distinction between academic intelligence, which is measured by IQ tests, and practical intelligence, which expresses itself in specific contexts, is important to the practical matter of predicting individual differences in success on tasks. Although a measure similar to an IQ test, the Graduate Record Examination (GRE), is used to select applicants for graduate study in U.S. universities, the work of Sternberg & Williams (1997) suggests that the correlation between GRE scores and graduate school success may be quite low, at least among applicants admitted to highly competitive psychology programs. Professional success requires a range of qualities not tapped by the GRE. To cite a well-known example from another discipline, James Watson, Nobel Prize winning codiscoverer of the double-helical structure of DNA, obtained only modest IQ scores. Tacit knowledge, the ability to learn from and to capitalize on experience, distinguishes experts from novices and greatly determines success. Successful performance commonly requires the capacity to manage oneself, tasks, and others. These capacities, in turn, require the ability to reflect accurately on one's capabilities, to organize knowledge and skills, and to solve interpersonal problems (Wagner & Sternberg, 1985; Sternberg & Wagner, 1986).

Sternberg has made a second contribution to bridging the gap between personality and intelligence. His work on thinking styles incorporates the important influence of proximal contexts such as family, school, and culture (Sternberg, 1994, 1997b). Thinking styles do not refer to absolute levels of cognitive capability but to preferred styles of cognition. Different people of similar ability may be more comfortable engaging in different forms of thinking; for example, one person may prefer structured tasks with clear objectives whereas another's style is to engage in unstructured tasks that require creativity. To illuminate the range of possible styles, Sternberg employs a governmental metaphor. Governmental functions (legislative, executive, judicial), forms (monarchic, hierarchic, oligarchic, and anarchic), levels of action (national, local), and the scope of social government (internal/domestic vs. external/foreign affairs) capture the multiplicity of individual differences in patterns of thinking. People may, for example, prefer to plan, execute, or evaluate problem-solving procedures; to work on one structured task rather than an anarchic collection of unstructured problems; and to think about global problems rather than specific concerns. The individual's style is a combination of these different aspects, reflecting his or her experiences as well as the effectiveness of each style in meeting contextual demands and challenges.

## Social Intelligence, Emotional Intelligence, and Wisdom

Both Gardner's and Sternberg's contributions suggest that there are social and personal aspects to intelligence. Intelligences reveal themselves contextually, as people interact with others and attempt to solve real-world problems. Similar reasoning is found in work on social intelligence (Cantor & Kihlstrom, 1987), emotional intelligence (Goleman, 1995; Salovey & Mayer 1990, 1994), and wisdom (Baltes & Smith, 1990; Baltes & Staudinger, 1998; Maciel, Heckhausen, & Baltes, 1994). Each of these constructs is located at the intersection of emotion, cognition, and motivation. Each illuminates the agentic properties of personality.

■ *Social Intelligence.* Although previous investigators had examined issues of social intelligence, conceived as a person's perceptiveness in social interactions (Walker & Foley, 1973), Cantor and Kihlstrom (1987)

substantially advanced the area by expanding our understanding of both the concept itself and the determinants of socially intelligent behavior. To Cantor and Kihlstrom, social intelligence consists of expertise that people can bring to bear on life's problems. People differ in their domain-specific areas of expertise; some might have a rich store of knowledge about interpersonal relations at work, others about how best to care for their children, etc. Social intelligence, then, cannot be captured by a global "social IQ" score. Instead, social intelligence involves the application of knowledge to real-world problems. In their theory, Cantor and Kihlstrom explore the self-schemas, social knowledge, and problem-solving strategies that people employ in solving life tasks, that is, personally significant goals that organize cognition and action over significant periods of time (see chapter 12). Schemas about the self, others, and social contexts enable people to interpret events efficiently and learn quickly. Well-developed problem-solving strategies enable people to respond flexibly to demands and changes in life circumstances. Life tasks are a setting in which people integrate the knowledge and strategies in pursuit of goals; life tasks "connect the individual to his or her daily life contexts, and the person's preferred strategies are evoked in turn in these task-context conditions" (Cantor & Harlow, 1994, p. 145). In this view, social intelligence is reflected in people's ability to adjust their behavior flexibly to take advantage of circumstances in the pursuit of their goals.

■ *Emotional Intelligence.* In the last decade, the notion of emotional intelligence has attracted considerable scientific and popular attention. Emotional intelligence generally refers to the capacity to manage affect and interpersonal relations; in other words, it is the "ability to monitor one's own and others' feelings and emotions, to discriminate among them, and to use this information to guide one's thinking and actions" (Salovey & Mayer, 1994, p. 312). Salovey and Mayer (1990) (also Salovey, Hsee, & Mayer, 1993) helped to launch study in this area by providing a comprehensive theoretical framework in which emotional intelligence consists of three primary domains with five components: the accurate recognition of emotions in oneself and others; the regulation of emotions in both self and others; and the strategic use of emotions for purposes of motivation and problem solving. Goleman (1995) brought widespread public attention to the topic in a book that proposed seven aspects of emotionally intelligent behavior: self-awareness, self-motivation, persistence in the presence of adversities, impulse control, mood regulation, empathy, and optimism.

A particularly valuable feature of the emotional intelligence framework is that it highlights the dynamic, functional role of emotions in self-regulation. People's feelings are not an epiphenomenal accompaniment to motivated action; instead, they are a determinant of behavior (see chapter 12). People act to achieve positive feelings about the self and to avoid guilt and self-censure. For example, when people engage in altruistic behaviors that bring personal costs, they appear to be motivated by the long-term goal of "being able to look back on their actions and experience pride and great satisfaction" (Salovey et al., 1993; also see Salovey, Mayer, & Rosenhan, 1991).

Note that the relations between affect and altruism are reciprocal. Helping others engenders positive mood in oneself (Salovey et al., 1991). Once one knows this – that is, once one has emotional intelligence with respect to the influence of altruism on affect – one can agentically shape one's own emotional experience by using the behavior of helping as a strategy for fostering positive mood.

A difficulty in the study of emotional intelligence concerns the measurement of the construct. Some measures of emotional intelligence have proved to have low reliability, whereas others lack divergent validity in that they significantly overlap with preexisting measures of behavioral dispositions and affective tendencies (Davies, Stankov, & Roberts, 1998). More psychometric work is required, then, to establish the unique boudaries of the emotional intelligence construct. Despite the

difficulties here, the construct continues to have great promise. Rather than merely describing affective tendencies, the emotional intelligence framework draws our attention to the cognitive and self-regulatory capabilities that contribute to emotional experience and that potentially can be enhanced to improve the individual's emotional life.

■ *Wisdom.* Another aspect of human intelligence that has attracted scientific attention in the last decade is wisdom (Sternberg, 1990). A particularly prolific line of theory and research on wisdom is that of Baltes and his colleagues (Baltes & Smith, 1990; Baltes & Staudinger, 1998); Maciel, Heckhausen, & Baltes, 1994; Staudinger & Baltes, 1996). Wisdom, in their view, is cognitive expertise in matters concerning the meaning and pragmatics of life. It entails knowledge about essential features of human nature and its development, the relation of the individual to the social and spiritual (broadly defined) world, and the achievement of meaningful goals and styles of life.

Baltes and colleagues present an expertise model of wisdom. As in other areas of cognitive performance, people can only achieve expertise in wisdom-related domains if they possess both declarative and procedural knowledge about the fundamental conditions of life. To be wise, in other words, one must possess both factual knowledge about human nature and strategies for putting that knowledge to use (e.g., strategies for resolving conflicts or giving advice to others; Baltes & Staudinger, 1998). This knowledge is gradually acquired through experience. Baltes and Staudinger (1998) suggest that factors such as interactions with a wise mentor and mastery of experiences in critical life circumstances contribute to the development of wisdom. They further emphasize that these experiences, and therefore the exact nature of wisdom, must be understood in cultural context: "Wisdom is fundamentally a cultural and collective product in which individuals participate" (p. 13).

Wisdom is not only "cold" cognition. Wisdom combines knowledge and virtue. To be wise, one must be sensitive to values and priorities in life and, Baltes and Staudinger (1998) suggest, to others' rights to hold values that are different from one's own.

Unlike many other intellectual qualities, wisdom seems to increase with advanced age. To explain how wisdom can grow even if other aspects of intelligence decline, Baltes and associates have drawn on earlier conceptualizations of fluid and crystallized intelligence (Cattell, 1971; Horn 1982) and on Hebb's (1949) distinction between intellectual power and intellectual products. They distinguish between intelligence as basic information processes (the mechanics of cognition, such as information processing rate and working memory capacity) and intelligence as cultural knowledge (the pragmatics of cognition, including the declarative and procedural knowledge conveyed by one's culture). Although processing capacities may decline with advanced age, increased cultural knowledge readily compensates. Wisdom, then, corresponds to expertise in culturally specific pragmatics. The enhanced wisdom of old age can enable the elderly to navigate the challenges and adversities of the later years in an optimal manner by selecting supportive activities and relationships and compensating for diminished capacities.

This work on wisdom is part of the more general theory of life-span development of Baltes and colleagues. This approach, plus research on the question of how wisdom can be enhanced through communicative interactions with others, is addressed in part 3 of our text.

## SUMMING UP

Most of this chapter has been devoted to personality psychology's study of global individual-difference dimensions. In each of the areas we have covered, the traditional form of investigation was to identify a small set of generalized tendencies that capture the ways in which people consistently differ from one another. In adult personality, these differences were global dispositions or traits. In the study of temperament, they primarily were dimensions of affective experience. In the study of intellectual functioning, the main dimension was general intelligence.

These global dimensions generally were identified through factor analysis. High-level factors provided a descriptive organization of the myriad surface-level variations that were observed. The factors sometimes were interpreted as psychological structures that were causally responsible for consistency in personality functioning.

In each area of study, however, subgroups of investigators have questioned this mode of investigation. Some personality psychologists have suggested that the personality dispositions of the individuals cannot be adequately represented by population-level individual-difference constructs because people display idiosyncratic dispositional tendencies that involve patterns of both consistency and variability. Some temperament researchers have suggested that global temperament dimensions might not illuminate underlying biological mechanisms, since temperament mechanisms may consist of multiple, distinct physiological systems, which are activated in particular contexts and that bear no 1:1 relation to surface profiles (Kagan, 1998b). Many intelligence researchers have suggested that a global $g$ factor fails to capture the distinct psychological mechanisms underlying different domain-specific forms of intelligence (Gardner, 1983) and that it depicts intelligence as an entity that resides statically in one's head, thus obscuring the fact that intelligence involves dynamic psychological systems, which enable purposive problem solving in real-world environments (Sternberg, 1994).

These arguments lead to a very general point with broad implications for the study of personality. Despite their appeal and applied usefulness, taxonomies of global individual-difference tendencies have their limits. They may be adequate to describe salient dimensions of individual difference in surface-level characteristics. In so doing, they may enable statistically significant prediction of important life outcomes. However, this does not imply that global trait dimensions can describe the unique psychological tendencies of the individual or provide an explanation of these surface-level expressions. Global individual-difference constructs, whatever their merit, may fail to capture the complex ways in which psychological systems interact with social environments to give rise to the unique tendencies of the individual person.

The issue in contention is not the relevance of individual differences but their origins and operationalizations in building a theory of personality. Many investigators doubt that a theory of personality should be grounded on any set of individual-difference dimensions (Bandura, 1986, 1999; Lamiell, 1997; Mischel, 1990). They do not question the importance of interindividual differences but instead judge personality to be of such complexity that no universal system of trait dimensions can do it justice. Further, they judge that personal factors are intertwined with situational factors to such a degree that explanations of personality functioning must be grounded in an analysis of interactions between persons and environments (Hettema, 1979; Magnusson & Stattin, 1998). We consider these viewpoints in our next chapter.

# CHAPTER FOUR

# Personality Coherence and Individual Uniqueness

## Interactionism and Social-Cognitive Systems

### CONTENTS

This chapter continues the discussion we began in chapter 3. We maintain our focus on questions of description and explanation but now view these issues through the lens of personality theories that differ from the dimensional, factor-analytic approaches to which much of the previous chapter was devoted. Here, we first review *interactionist* approaches to personality. Since interactionism highlights the interplay between personal characteristics and situational factors, we next consider psychological analyses of situations. Third, we outline a particular interactional theory of personality, namely, social-cognitive theory.

The final sections of the chapter address the relation between social-cognitive and trait theories of personality. Given the prominence of these two approaches, exploring this relation is one of personalty psychology's most compelling theoretical tasks, as others have noted (McCrae & Costa, 1996). The theme we develop is that the differences between these approaches is not superficial but deep, in that they embrace different strategies of scientific explanation. Much of our discussion, then, is devoted to reviewing alternative strategies for explaining the consistency and coherence of personality functioning.

## INTERACTIONISM

The simplest form of a person-based explanation of behavior would be to posit that people possess personal qualities that influence their behavior globally, in other words, in a relatively consistent manner across diverse circumstances. Personal attributes might be seen to exert a unidirectional causal effect on behavior. However, few personality psychologists explain behavior in this manner; instead, most are interactionists. They see behavior and experiences as arising from the interactive effects of personal and situational factors (Ekehammar, 1974; Magnusson & Endler, 1977; Magnusson & Stattin, 1998).

A variety of viewpoints fit the rather general definition of interactionism given in the preceding sentence. A key distinction among these interactionist views distinguishes between statistical and dynamic interactionism. In a statistical approach, one might assess separate person and situation factors and determine whether the statistical interaction term *person × situation* predicts as much as or more variance in behavior as the person or situation factors alone. The interaction term indeed does account for the lion's share of the variance in many circumstances (e.g., Endler & Magnusson, 1976; Sarason, Smith, & Diener, 1975). Dynamic interactionism moves beyond the mere description of interactions to address underlying processes. Behavior is seen to result from "a continuous process of multidirectional feedback between the individual and the situations he or she encounters," and the person is seen as "an active agent in this interaction process" (Magnusson & Endler, 1977, p. 4).

Hettema and Kenrick (1992) have distinguished six different types of interaction identified by interactionist theorists. Behavior may be influenced by the fit or "mesh" between person and situation factors, by individuals' choices of the environments they encounter, or by environmental factors that essentially "choose persons" through entrance requirements. Behavior also is influenced by people's transformation of environments, by the transformation of people by environments, and by transactions between persons and environments, in other words, by "mutual changes in persons and environments over time" (Hettema & Kenrick, 1992, p. 404). The reader should note that the discussion of alternative forms of interaction recur throughout subsequent chapters, especially in our coverage of development (see chapter 5) and of the contextual activation of cognitive and affective processes (part 4).

Magnusson recently has emphasized that person and environment factors are not separate elements, which simply happen to bump into one another from time to time. Instead, persons and environments can be viewed more holistically (Magnusson, 1999; Magnusson & Törestad, 1993). One can conceive of a "person–environment system," which functions as a "totality" (Magnusson & Stattin, 1998, p. 698). Although such holistic thinking might once have sounded vaguely unscientific, the scientific analysis of complex systems (see chapter 1) has given psychologists a better appreciation of how holistic functioning can take place within any system that has large numbers of interacting elements.

### Theoretical Models and Research Strategies

■ *Magnusson.* In the theoretical perspective proposed by Magnusson, the individual develops through "a continuous reciprocal interplay between mental and biological factors" (Magnusson, 1992, p. 120). Development is not only intrapsychic, but social. Mental and biological factors develop through interactions between individuals and their environments (Magnusson, 1992). Magnusson emphasizes that this reciprocity among biological, psychological, and social determinants should discourage investigators from examining one or another personality variable in isolation. One must consider the within-person patterning of multiple variables that characterize the individual.

This theoretical view has major implications for research (Magnusson, 1999). A proper study of personality development, from this perspective, not only should be longitudinal, to chart the developmental course of the individual. It also should be multidimensional, that is, it should include measures of the person's biological makeup, psychological characteristics, and socializing environment. Further, it should include a population large enough that one can identify subsets of persons who may possess rare yet important patterns of characteristics that have unique developmental implications. Such large databases also enable one to study individuals who face rare, personally significant adversities early in life; as Magnusson (1992) notes, such persons commonly overcome adversities, and it is critical to identify the factors that contribute to such resiliency. Much to his credit, Magnusson has taken on the daunting task of conducting this sort of research in his individual development and adjustment study (Magnusson, 1988, 1992).

In this work, Magnusson and colleagues tracked the development of a primary participant group of approximately 1,400 individuals in central Sweden. Participants were studied from age 10 through adulthood. In the grade school years, through the 12th grade, measures included a battery of self-reports and observer reports of personality, indices of biological functioning, and parental and sociodemographic data. Data beyond the 12th grade included questionnaire reports of educational, employment, and interpersonal outcomes, as well as measures of maladjustment such as criminal behaviors, psychiatric care, or problems with alcohol.

Although we cannot review here the range of findings derived from this extensive program of research, we will report selected results that illustrate some of Magnusson's main theoretical themes. The importance of considering holistic patterns of personality variables is illustrated by data on predictors of criminality and alcohol use among boys. The value of Magnusson's approach is perhaps best illustrated by first contrasting it with a standard individual-difference viewpoint. It is often observed that early aggressiveness is correlated with later criminality; Magnusson (1992) observes such a correlation in his data. However, he emphasizes that this correlation does not imply that, in the population at large, higher levels of early-life aggression predispose one to later life criminality. Two considerations caution against such a conclusion. First, the population-level correlation may reflect the influence of "a small number of people" (Magnusson, 1992, p. 129). Second, these people may not only be extreme scorers on a dimension of early-life aggressiveness, but they may also possess a cluster of characteristics that are jointly necessary for the prediction of later criminality. Only the patterning of multiple variables, in other words, may predispose one to the later-life outcome. If one overlooks this patterning and conducts a single-variable individual-difference study, one will draw erroneous conclusions.

In the data that illustrate this point, six potential early-life predictors of criminality and alcohol abuse were assessed in a group of 296 boys: aggressiveness, motor restlessness, poor concentration, poor school interest, underachievement, and poor peer relations. Magnusson found that boys with one or two early-life predictors were no more prone to criminality and alcohol abuse than were boys with no indicators of problem behavior; there was no simple, linear relation between number of indicators and later adjustment problems. In particular, children who were aggressive but showed no other early-life predictors were no more prone to criminality than were unaggressive youth. Later criminality and alcohol abuse were only observed among subgroups of boys who, early in life, displayed a pattern of multiple predictors.

Children who evidenced five of the six predictors were substantially more prone to antisocial behavior later in life. When this subgroup was eliminated statistically, "the correlation between early aggressiveness and subsequent criminality and alcohol problems dropped to a purely random level" (Magnusson, 1992), despite the fact that the remaining sample was large enough to detect a relation if it had been there.

Data on the psychosocial development of girls provides interesting evidence of the interplay of biological and social factors in development, and of the way in which people may overcome problems of adolescence once they enter adulthood. Magnusson and colleagues compared the developmental courses of girls who experienced early versus late biological maturation. These groups differed substantially at age 15. Early-maturing girls were more likely to have been caught for cheating in school, to have been truant, and to have tried marijuana. Compared to late-maturing girls, they were nearly 6 times more likely to have reported multiple episodes of drunkenness. In accord with Magnusson's biosocial approach, the relation between menarchal age and norm violations was mediated by peer affiliations. Early-maturing girls who reported having older friends engaged in more risky behaviors.

Did the adolescent problems of early-maturers continue into adulthood? In a word, no. "In adulthood, there were very few differences in with respect to social adaptation and social relationships" (Magnusson, 1992, p. 126). Early- and late-maturerers did not even differ in self-reported alcohol use, where they had so differed earlier. Early-maturers, then, did not possess an enduring character flaw. They merely experienced a period during which they differed biologically from chronological peers. These biological differences fostered peer relations that contributed to risky behavior. This period in life naturally passed, and the girl's long-term psychosocial outcomes were generally good.

■ *Endler.* The work of Endler (1984) represents a second major contribution to interactional psychology. Endler has succeeded in developing assessment instruments that directly tap the interaction of personal qualities and situational factors. His multidimensional anxiety scales (Endler, Edwards, Vitelli, & Parker, 1989) measure self-reports of anxiety in each of four types of situations: social evaluation, physical danger, ambiguous circumstances, and daily routines. Assessing trait anxiety in this multidimensional manner allows for fine-grain, person × situation predictions. In other words, one does not need to make a simple global prediction, such as: People who are high in trait anxiety will, on average, tend to be more anxious than others. Instead, Endler and colleagues are able to make the more specific prediction that a person's state of anxiety will reflect the match between features of the situation and the particular dimension of anxiety that is most important to the individual.

Results support Endler's interactional model. Factor analyses reveal that trait anxiety is multidimensional (Endler, Parker, Bagby, & Cox, 1991). Numerous laboratory and field studies demonstrate that situational factors and aspects of trait anxiety interact in the prediction of state anxiety (Endler, 1984). For example, Canadian university students who were particularly high in trait anxiety in ambiguous situations experienced greater state anxiety prior to an ambiguous circumstance of national significance, namely, a referendum on the separation of Quebec from Canada (Flett, Endler, & Fairlie, 1999).

■ *Hettema.* Hettema (1979) has provided a comprehensive model of person–situation interactions, which explicitly aims to incorporate both biological and cognitive aspects of personality functioning. His *open-systems adaptation model* conceptualizes personality functioning at three levels. A *cognitive-symbolic* level mentally represents situations, goals, and strategies for goal attainment. This level, then, contains a system of socially learned strategies for goal attainment. A *sensorimotor-operational* level enacts people's attempts to accomplish their goals by modifying the environment. This level, then, manifests itself in overt behavior. Finally, between these two levels is a *control level*, which is able to alter functioning at either of the other two levels. If the individual senses a loss of control over the flow of events in the environment, operations at the control level might influence either the sensorimotor-operational level, leading the person to attempt different action to influence the environment, or the cognitive-symbolic level, leading the person to engage in thinking designed to conform to the environment (e.g., the person might cognitively redefine the situation). Note that, by contrasting efforts to alter the environment with efforts to conform one's intrapsychic events to reality, Hettema captures a distinction made also by Lazarus and Folkman (1984), who distinguish problem-focused and emotion-focused coping, and Heckhausen & Schulz (1995), who contrast primary and secondary control efforts (see chapter 12).

Cognitive social-learning factors and biological factors interact in Hettema's theoretical system in the following way. A person can gain control in one of two ways, namely, through transformations or equilibrium. *Transformations* are strategic attempts at control that are socially learned and regulated at the cognitive-symbolic level. *Equilibrium* is a state of balance between cognitions and behavior; people's efforts to maintain equilibrium are posited to occur through a *tactical subsystem*, which is part of the individual's inherited biological capacities (Hettema, 1979; Hettema & Kenrick, 1992). A person's preference for various alternative tactics (e.g., the tactic of reflecting on a situation versus persisting with one's current strategy) is thought to be influenced by inherited temperament mechanisms.

We note that two aspects of Hettema's theoretical system are particularly compatible with our call for bottom-up strategies of explanation (see chapter 1 and below). First, in Hettema's approach to the study of personality functioning, person-situation interactions receive primary consideration (Hettema & Kenrick, 1992). Rather than beginning with a broad conception of personality types, which

is hard to relate to the more molecular details of person–situation transactions, Hettema first conceptualizes the detailed interactions that occur at the interface of persons and situations. Second, Hettema's work is extremely sensitive to the fact that surface-level behaviors cannot be mapped directly onto underlying mechanisms. Different mechanisms and processes may generate superficially identical behaviors. Any given social act could be a spontaneous output of the tactical system or a more deliberate product of the strategic cognitive system, and from the outside, it may not be apparent which system is involved (Hettema & Kenrick, 1992). These two points enable Hettema to construct an understanding of personality functioning on a a firm foundation of knowledge about biological, cognitive, and social processes.

Recently, Hettema, Leidelmeijer, and Geenen (2000) have emphasized that information processing may be a key link from biological bases of personality to social behavior. Inherited biology may contribute to consistent information processing tendencies that mediate action. To address this issue, Hettema et al. (2000) draw on a conceptual system proposed by Pribram and McGuiness (1975), which differentiates three aspects of information processing, namely, the processing of inputs, the preparation of motor outputs, and the coordination of the input and output systems. By measuring relevant physiological systems as people were exposed to films of diverse interpersonal content, they established that individual differences associated with each of these three systems are evident in a consistent manner across diverse stimuli. Thus, patterns of physiological response, rather than merely patterns of overt behavior, were shown to differentiate people from one another.

### Beyond Separate Person and Situation Factors

Most interactional positions in personality psychology are predicted on the assumption that it is reasonable to speak of separate person and situation factors. Individuals possess a set of qualities that are distinct from the environment (e.g., trait anxiety of some form) and situations contain elements that are distinct from the persons who inhabit them (e.g., physical or social threats). One then examines how these separate person and situation forces combine to produce social behavior.

Some question this separation of persons from the social environment, and of the environment from the persons who inhabit it. Shweder and Sullivan (1990) argue that an analysis of individual functioning should focus on the ways in which people construct meaning out of the situations they are in. People draw inferences about the meaning of their life circumstances by employing conceptual schemes, which to a significant degree reflect the conceptual belief systems of their surrounding community and culture (also see Kitayama & Markus, 1999; Valsiner, 1998). In this view, person and situation factors are not distinct but intertwined. People's conceptual schemes reflect their sociocultural environments, and social environments only take on meaning as a result of being interpreted by persons. Shweder and Sullivan (1990) are critical, then, of interactionists who "continue to talk about persons as though they were vessels for autonomous mental states, such as shyness, hostility, or dependency" and who appeal to these autonomous dispositions as causes of behavior. Dispositions are labels that outside observers apply to the actor's behavior, and "what people are disposed to do as viewed from the outside (e.g., to be honest...) is not a causal explanation for why they do it" (Shweder & Sullivan, 1990, p. 408).

As Shweder and Sullivan note, their critique of the separation of persons from situations overlaps not only with other arguments in psychology and the social sciences (Geertz, 1973; Mischel, 1968), but with a broader postmodern analysis of the meaning of symbols, or "texts." They cite the work of Fish (1980), who argues that the meaning of any text lies not in the independent symbol itself, but in the active interpretations of the perceiver. Cognitive processes, in this view, do not medi-

ate the influence of environmental factors that exist apart from the interpretations of the perceiver because "there is no such thing as a raw stimulus situation that exists independently of someone's interpretive assumptions" (Shweder & Sullivan, 1990). In Fish's analysis, the reader creates the meaning of a text through his or her interpretive activities. The individual's interpretive activities, in turn, reflect the beliefs and cognitive styles of the broader community of which the person is a part. Once one recognizes this interdependence of reader, text, and the community, "the dilemma that [gives] rise to the debate [in literary theory] between the champions of the text and the champions of the reader is dissolved because the competing entities are no longer perceived as independent" (Fish, 1980, p. 14). Substituting "situation" for "text" and "person" for "reader" makes it plain that Fish's analysis resolves personality psychology's person versus situation dilemma, too. It leads one to seek the causes of behavior not in traits, which are defined independently of the social environment, but in individuals' socioculturally grounded interpretations of the world. "It is not Allport's trait but rather Fish's stimulus situation – a stimulus situation *already* saturated with our consciousness – 'that is the crucial determinant in behavior that expresses personality'" (Allport, 1960, p. 132) (Shweder & Sullivan, 1990, p. 411).

This analysis of interpretive processes suggests that the study of personality functioning should be centered on the individual's cognitive strategies and the ways in which people develop cognitive capabilities through interaction with their community and culture. This is precisely the tack taken by social-cognitive theories of personality, reviewed below. Before turning to these theories, we first review psychological analyses of situations. Although these situational analyses are not grounded in the deconstruction of separate person and situation factors that we have just outlined, many investigators do recognize that the study of situations cannot proceed apart from the study of the mental activities of the individuals who populate them.

## SITUATIONS

The traditional interactionist argument that behavior reflects a dynamic interplay among distinct person and situation factors inherently requires a psychology of situations. One should be able to delineate different types of situations and explain how they contribute to the determination of behavior in interaction with qualities of the person.

The most common thing to say about situations in reviews of the psychological literature is that they have received insufficient study. There are innumerable studies of the qualities of people, but relatively few systematic investigations of the situations in which they live. This common criticism is not without merit. However, one should recognize that many investigators have systematically explored the nature of situations and attempted to develop situation taxonomies. Although outnumbered by personologists, their efforts are significant.

Before considering some contemporary efforts to incorporate an analysis of situations into the psychology of personality, we first briefly note some classic contributions, which are reviewed in detail in other sources (e.g., Argyle, Furnham, & Graham, 1981; Forgas & Van Heck, 1992). Symbolic interactionism contended that people actively construct the definition of the situations they encounter (Mead, 1934). Situations thus do not have a direct physical effect. Instead, their effects are mediated by the active, symbolic cognitive processing of the inhabitants of the social setting. Barker's ecological psychology (1968) promoted the study of behavior in its environmental context, providing detailed analyses of the *behavior settings* that make up the life of a community. Behavior settings (e.g., lecture halls, grocery stores, churches) include physical features and typical patterns of action, which shape the behavior of individuals and groups who enter that setting. Somewhat more generally, the field of environmental psychology explores psychological reactions to natural and artificial (man-made) physical environments. Although some work in this field is criticized for overemphasizing the

direct causal impact of objective physical features of the environment (Argyle et al., 1981), Stokols (1987) has explained how environmental psychology can be understood as a contextual approach, which examines transactions between persons and social settings. The field highlights molar features of everyday social settings, which might be overlooked by experimental approaches that explore only molecular stimuli that can be manipulated in the laboratory.

Of particular historical note in psychology's study of situations is the work of Brunswick (1956). He called psychologists' attention to the need for representative research design, that is, research that systematically samples life situations that are representative of individuals' normal day-to-day lives. Although Brunswick's work did not have a large, immediate impact, its influence is present in a number of the lines of research noted above and described in detail below.

### A Functional Analysis of Situations

A systematic analysis of the features of social settings has been provided by Argyle et al. (1981), who present a functional theory of situations. In this approach, particular situations exist in the particular form that they do because of the functions the situation serves for a society. The purposes of some situational contexts (e.g., stores) are explicitly known to the members of society, whereas others (e.g., rituals surrounding a religious or patriotic holiday) serve more implicit, latent functions.

A functionalist approach inherently highlights particular features of social situations. Rather than superficial situational qualities (e.g., the number of people present in the situation), it calls attention to qualities that are relevant to the execution of purposive, functional behaviors. Specifically, Argyle et al. analyze situational goals, rules, and roles. Different situations facilitate the accomplishment of different goals. It is the fulfillment of these goals that generally draws people to the given situation. Rules determine the types of behavior that are and are not permitted in any given setting. In this regard, Argyle et al. view human behavior as regulated heavily by social rules rather than by individual instincts or drives (also see Harré & Secord, 1972). Groups discover routes to the accomplishment of group goals. They institutionalize, as rules for behavior, prescriptions for action and prohibitions against activities that interfere with group puposes. Rules, then, "are created and changed in order that situational goals can be attained" (Argyle et al., 1981, p. 133).

A third important feature of situations are roles. Any given situation has different positions that individuals fill. The various positions entail different expectations and rules for behavior. The particular role one fills can strongly influence one's actions. For example, research by Langer & Benevento (1978) demonstrated that people who are assigned to an inferior social role may perform more poorly on cognitive tasks, even when the role assignment occurs purely by chance.

A particularly advantageous feature of the work of Argyle et al. (1981) is that situations and persons are analyzed through a common language. This facilitates an understanding of person–situation interactions. One can explore the relation between an individual's goals, internal standards, and competencies, and the goals, rules, and role requirements of particular situations. Read and Miller (1989) have presented an account of personality and interpersonal behavior along similar lines.

## A Lexical Analaysis of Situations

Van Heck (1984, 1989; Forgas & Van Heck, 1992) has adopted a lexical approach to the analysis of situations. He reasoned that the most important situational characteristics would be found in the natural language dictionary. A search of the dictionary produced a pool of situation terms, which included 263 items after deletion of synonyms and archaic words. After generating this list, Van Heck asked a large group of research participants to generate free-response descriptions of the fundamental characteristics of each situation term; analyses of the response protocols yielded a large set of situational attributes, which were organized into eight content cate-

gories (physical environment, actions and activities, etc.). A second group of participants rated the situation concepts and the large set of attributes, factor analysis being used to identify dimensions of variation in situation concepts. This yielded the situation taxonomy described in chapter 3, in which situations vary along dimensions such as interpersonal conflict or the presence of interpersonal intimacy (Van Heck, 1989).

## Mental Representations of Social Episodes

Another approach to studying situations is to focus on people's mental representations of situations. Implicit beliefs about situations may by idiosyncratic or may be widely shared by members of a group. Numerous investigators have contributed to an understanding of people's cognitive representations of social situations (e.g., Cantor, Mischel, & Schwartz, 1982; Hettema, 1979; Schank & Abelson, 1977; Van Heck, 1984, 1989), and this general topic is addressed at a number of subsequent points in our text. At present, we focus on a particular line of research that explores implicit dimensions underlying people's situational beliefs.

Forgas and colleagues have used multidimensional scaling techniques to represent people's knowledge of the situations of their lives (reviewed in Forgas & Van Heck, 1992). Participants rate the similarity of each of a wide variety of circumstances, and multidimensional scaling reveals the implicit dimensions underlying these ratings. Three findings are of note. First, the primary dimensions revealed in this method are not physical dimensions (e.g., hot versus cold environments) but dimensions of psychological meaning. Situations are differentiated primarily according to dimensions such as the pleasantness or friendliness of the setting. Second, different subgroups may hold differential representations of the same situations. University faculty members were found to evaluate university settings according to whether they were boring or interesting, whereas advanced students tended to evaluate whether situations were social or work-related, and low-status staff members focused on whether situations were anxiety-provoking (Forgas & Van Heck, 1992). Finally, different individuals within the same group differentially represent social situations. In their beliefs about social episodes, confident, socially skilled individuals tend to weight the episodes' degree of interest to them, whereas individuals lacking in confidence and skills distinguish among situations in terms of the degree of anxiety they provoke (Forgas & Van Heck, 1992). A key function of high versus low self-efficacy beliefs may be to change the very meaning of the situations the individual encounters.

## Situation Cognition and Personality Coherence

The role of situational beliefs in the coherence of personality functioning has been explored in detail by Krahé (1990). Her research program constitutes an individual-centered approach to the study of situational beliefs and personality coherence. The content of individuals' representations of social situations is studied idiographically to capture features of personality functioning that may be scientifically lawful, yet idiosyncratic. Krahé's fundamental hypothesis is that cross-situational coherence in personality functioning reflects situational beliefs that overlap from one objectively distinct circumstance to another. "Intraindividual correlations between similarity profiles in the perception of and behavior in [different] situations" (Krahé, 1990, p. 118) should predict cross-situational coherence.

In her research, Krahé (1990) has studied beliefs about anxiety-provoking situations. She employs a *situation grid* technique that was inspired by the contributions of Kelly (1955) (see chapter 8). The grid consists of two rating dimensions, namely, the situations people encounter and the constructs they use to represent the situation. This technique yields an idiographic depiction of individuals' situational beliefs and enables one to plot the degree to which beliefs about different situations overlap. Her work yields preliminary

support for the hypothesis that responses cohere across situations according to the perceived similarity of the situations (Krahé, 1990). Somewhat earlier, Klirs and Revelle (1986) also provided evidence that perceived situational similarity underlies behavioral variability versus consistency in response.

## Universal Forms?

Before leaving the topic of social situations, one perspective that differs substantially from the work cited above deserves mention. This is Alan Fiske's analysis (1991, 1992) of four basic forms of social relations. Fiske proposes that social life is organized around relationships that consist of four fundamental types. Each type, or each domain of social life, evokes different belief structures, and cognition and behavior in the different domains proceed according to different principles. The differences may be so large that socially meaningful actions in one domain may be meaningless in another.

The four domains involve different interconnections among the members of human groups. *Communal sharing* relationships occur when members of a group are treated as equals. Commonalities of interest among group members are emphasized, and resources are shared. In *authority ranking* relationships, certain individuals have higher or lower rank than others. One's relative rank governs relations with others. *Equality matching* relationships are based on a balanced exchange of resources among members. The provision of goods or services entails the reciprocal provision of equally worthy goods or services. People owe each other reciprocal favors or goods, or may even owe "eye for an eye" revenge. Finally, *market pricing* relationships are ones in which obligations are computed according to a common metric (e.g., money). Unlike the other relationship forms, in market pricing relations people recognize ratios (e.g., they may be part owners of a venture) and weigh proportional risks and benefits.

Fiske (1992) provides a novel conceptual analysis, which extends these fundamental forms to numerous aspects of social life, including work, motivation, social identity, and moral judgments. He further speculates that these forms are universally basic because they are evolved, endogenous products of the human mind. Different cultures may determine how the forms are realized, but the basic forms should appear cross-culturally. Fiske's field work in a village in Burkina Faso leads him to conclude that social life in this West African nation indeed is marked by the four different forms but that the forms come into play in different settings and to different relative degrees than they do in the United States (Fiske, 1991, 1992).

Although the work on interactionism and situations that we have reviewed is highly informative, in a sense it leaves personality psychology's most critical question unanswered. The work tells us that person and situation factors interact. It tells us about the nature of the situation factors: different settings facilitate different goals, and situational beliefs structure much social activity. But what about the person factors? In our interactional model of persons and situations, how are we to conceptualize persons? What units shall we use? (cf. Allport, 1937). The global trait units discussed earlier in this chapter seem insufficient to the task, if only because they fail to capture the dynamic transactions between individuals and sociocultural environments that are highlighted by all of the various interactional psychologists whose work we have reviewed.

We now turn to a contemporary perspective on personality, which offers an alternative set of "person variables." This alternative is designed to capture the dynamic psychological processes underlying personal development and functioning and the reciprocal interactions that occur between the developing person and the sociocultural environment. We review the family of approaches known as the social-cognitive theories of personality (Cervone & Shoda, 1999b) and devote particular attention to the highly comprehensive social cognitive theory of personality of Bandura (1986, 1999).

## SOCIAL-COGNITIVE THEORIES OF PERSONALITY STRUCTURE, PROCESS, AND FUNCTIONING

Social-cognitive theories play a significant role in the contemporary field. Observers characterize them as "the current favorite among academic personality psychologists" (Pervin & John, 1997). Proponents of social-cognitive theory are among the most influential psychologists in the discipline (Mayer & Carlsmith, 1997). Proponents of alternative approaches acknowledge the need to reconcile their work with the social-cognitive tradition (McCrae & Costa, 1996). It is not uncommon to find edited volumes of personality theory in which a social-cognitive theorist, such as Bandura, is the only contemporary writer represented alongside historical figures such as Freud and Jung (e.g., Frick, 1995). We therefore consider the approach in detail here.

### A Brief History

A review of the history of social-cognitive theories (see Cervone & Shoda, 1999c) reveals three contributions of particular historical importance. Two of these were noted in chapter 2. The research of Bandura and colleagues on observational learning (Bandura, 1965; Bandura & Walters, 1963) expanded psychology's conception of the learning process and simultaneously called personality psychologists' attention to the diverse ways in which social experiences contribute to personality development. Bandura's (1969) analysis of cognitive mechanisms that mediate therapeutic behavioral change directed attention away from the behavioristic conceptions that had dominated the field; his efforts here shaped the activities of a generation of clinicians and clinical researchers (Meichenbaum, 1990).

Mischel's critique (1968) of trait and psychodynamic theories and his later positing of a set of cognitive-social person variables (Mischel, 1973) formed a second pillar in the construction of a social-cognitive approach to personality. His theorizing and his research on self-control processes (Mischel, 1974, 1979) showed how an analysis of basic cognitive processes could illuminate the classic problems of personality psychology (e.g., Mischel, 1974, 1979; see also chapter 11).

A third development came from cognitive social psychology. Here, the advance of most importance to personality psychology is that researchers identified not only general psychological processes in social thinking but also enduring individual differences in the cognitive structures that underlie judgment, affect, motivation, and socially intelligent action (Anderson & Weiner, 1992; Cantor & Kihlstrom, 1987; Dweck & Leggett, 1988; Higgins, 1990; Kruglanski, 1996; Markus, 1977). Social psychological research thus became far more than an analysis of situational influences. The social psychology laboratory yielded information about stable psychological structures that contribute to stable cognitive, affective, and motivational tendencies.

These developments did not lead to a single monolithic theory but to a set of coherently interrelated social-cognitive perspectives (Cervone & Shoda, 1999a). These perspectives can be seen to constitute an integrative theoretical framework for analyzing personality. Three features define the social-cognitive approach.

## Defining Features of Social-Cognitive Theory

■ *Units of Analysis.* Social-cognitive theories are most clearly defined by the units of analysis through which they conceptualize personality functioning and the differences among individuals. Personality is understood by reference to basic cognitive and affective processes, which develop in social settings and are activated by elements of the social environment. They therefore are termed social-cognitive.

In social-cognitive theories, psychological mechanisms are seen to operate in concert as coherent psychological systems. Social-cognitive mechanisms, then, are not a set of independent forces but instead consist of a set of functionally distinct systems, which interact with one another in the flow of experience and

behavior. The coherence of personality functioning is viewed as an emergent property of interactions among multiple psychological mechanisms (Cervone & Shoda, 1999b).

Social-cognitive theory views cognitive and affective systems as being tightly and reciprocally interrelated. In advancing a social-cognitive perspective, Mischel and Shoda suggest that these interrelations are so strong that personality is best viewed as a "cognitive-affective system" (Mischel, 1999b; Mischel & Shoda, 1995, 1998b). In this system, it is the stable organization of cognitive and affective elements that characterizes the individual and constitutes the structure of his or her personality. Different people develop different interrelations among cognitive and affective elements. This organization in the cognitive-affective network underlies the behavioral expressions that distinguish individuals from one another (Shoda, 1999). Interrelations among cognition and affect are reviewed in chapters 9 and 10.

The personality variables of social-cognitive theory are contextualized. Social-cognitive units of analysis are person-in-context variables. People's competencies, goals, and standards for performance, expectations about the world, and appraisals of their ability to cope with it are conceptualized and assessed with respect to the circumstances and life tasks that make up the individual's life (e.g., Cantor & Kihlstrom, 1987). As we note at many points in this volume, numerous advances throughout psychology and the cognitive sciences highlight the fact that mental systems function in a domain-linked manner. Various cognitive architectures point to the domain specificity of knowledge and skills (Linville & Clark, 1989). The situative perspective (Greeno, 1998) on cognition, which posits that cognitive processes function in reciprocal interaction with environmental constraints and affordances, reveals the interconnections between thinking and social settings. Findings in cognition and cognitive development illustrate domain specificity by showing that rates of learning and cognitive skills often display little transfer from one domain or context to another (Detterman & Sternberg, 1993; Gelman & Williams, 1998). Even analyses of inherited affective systems suggest that emotional systems do not function in a global, domain-free manner (Kagan, 1996). The biggest challenge to the belief that personality consists of a set of global traits is that virtually every branch of psychological science outside of personality psychology reveals that mental systems are not global but domain-linked. Bandura (1999, p. 192) sees it as "ironic that, at a time when other subfields of psychology are becoming contextualized and discarding global personal structures for more particularized ones, much of the field of personality is seeking the personal causes of human behavior in omnibus conglomerate traits."

Before moving on to the other two defining features of social-cognitive theory, we first must confront a potential misreading of the approach. The social-cognitivists' embrace of contextualized personality variables implies neither that contexts are "in control" of behavior nor that social behavior will show no generality from one context to another. We consider these points in turn.

As we noted in chapter 1, commentators often have characterized personality psychology as having two traditions, a person and a situation tradition. Person theorists purportedly keep the field afloat while situationists aim to sink it. This dramatic plot line fails to describe the actual state of the field. There simply are no longer any situationists, although they did exist at an earlier era in our field's history. Behaviorists tried to explain personal functioning in terms of environmental causes, with some indeed looking forward to a day when personality theories would be "regarded as historical curiosities" (Farber, 1964). However, by the start of the 1970s, behaviorists were as scarce in personality psychology as everywhere else, and all personality psychologists were "person" theorists.

We make this point because social-cognitive theory continues to be misconstrued, in some reviews of the field, as a "situationist" model of personality, that is, an approach in which situational forces are seen to govern behavior. These construals undoubtedly are triggered by the social-cognitivists' rejection of global trait constructs. We emphasize here that whatever one thinks of the social-cognitive approach, the situationist label is a complete misreading of contemporary social-cognitive theory. An analogy may be useful here. In the study of intelligence, many investigators reject the utility of the global IQ construct (e.g., Gardner, 1993; Sternberg, 1985). No one would claim that these intelligence researchers are situationists. They clearly do not reject global IQ because they think situations are in control of intellectual functioning. Instead, they believe that the mechanisms underlying intelligent human behavior are too varied, complex, and flexible to be captured adequately by the global construct. Social-cognitive theory holds precisely the same position with respect to personality functioning.

With regard to the generality of behavior, social-cognitive theory treats the issue of cross-situational consistency versus variability in social behavior as an empirical question. The degree of generality in action may vary from person to person, and the domains in which consistency is found similarly may vary from one person to the next. The empirical task, then, is to identify and explain the patterns of cross-situational coherence that characterize the individual. In principle, a number of social-cognitive mechanisms may contribute to cross-situational coherence in personality functioning. As we noted above, people may respond in a relatively consistent manner across circumstances that they subjectively categorize together as an equivalence class (see also Champagne & Pervin, 1987; Lord, 1982). When people acquire new coping skills in valued life domains, they may experience a boost in beliefs in their capabilities, which generalizes across domains (Smith, 1989; Weitlauf et al., in press). People's enduring goals may underlie not only behavioral specificity but also patterns of coherence that are evident across interpersonal or achievement domains (Grant & Dweck, 1999). A social-cognitive strategy for identifying and explaining cross-situational coherence (Cervone, 1997, 1999a) is presented in detail below.

■ *Common Language.* A second defining feature of social-cognitive theories is their goal of developing a common language for understanding both consistency and variability in social behavior (e.g., Grant & Dweck, 1999; Higgins, 1990, 1999). As Higgins has emphasized, one need not develop two distinct conceptual systems to explain personality consistency versus situational variability in people's experiences and actions. Instead, one could identify general principles of psychological functioning and then explain both interindividual differences and situational influences in terms of this common set of principles.

This common language perspective has interesting implications for the study of person–situation interactions. In interactionism, one need not define persons in a way that removes them from the contexts of their lives and situations in a way that makes no reference to the persons who inhabit them. Instead, persons and situations can be construed in a way that highlights the common set of processes through which both individuals and contexts contribute to behavior. "Both persons and situations can be sources of variability in the same principle," so one should explore "how 'situation' and 'person' sources of variability work together" (Higgins, 1999, p. 85). Higgins' own research on principles of knowledge activation concretely illustrates this approach (see chapter 9). Recognition that personality consists in part of a system of knowledge and beliefs opens the door to analyzing personal and situational factors that jointly activate elements of the belief systems (Higgins, 1990, 1996).

■ *Correlational and Experimental Methods.* Social-cognitive theories also are marked by their methodological strategies. Social-cognitivists commonly bring both correlational and experimental methods to bear on questions of personality functioning.

The social-cognitive approach goes beyond the common approach of using laboratory techniques to identify cognitive and physiological markers of stable individual differences. Instead, laboratory methods are used to experimentally manipulate psychological structures that underlie phenotypic individual differences. Strong tests of theoretical hypotheses are obtained by studying social-cognitive processes correlationally, to relate chronic levels of a given variable to a target outcome, and experimentally, to clarify causal relations among personality processes and outcomes (e.g., Caprara, 1987, 1996).

## Bandura's Social Cognitive Theory

A remarkably comprehensive analysis of social and cognitive factors in personality functioning is that provided by Bandura (1986, 1997, 1999). His social cognitive theory is built on two central principles. The first is an overarching framework for explaining personality functioning; the second addresses the type of variables (the units of analysis) on which one should center a personality theory.

The explanatory principle is triadic reciprocal determinism (Bandura, 1978, 1986). This principle states that personal functioning arises from interactions among three interlocking factors: the physical and social environment; the cognitive and affective systems that constitute the person; and the individual's behavior. Each of these factors causally influences the others; the three elements, then, "reciprocally determine" one another, with different influences occurring in different contexts.

In this analysis of reciprocal influence processes, Bandura uses the word determinism "to signify the production of effects by events" (Bandura, 1978, p. 345). In this use, the term does not imply that a person's actions arise from simple, predictable chains of cause and effect. Instead, "events produce effects probabilistically" (Bandura, 1978, p. 345). Probabilism is underscored by Bandura's analysis of chance encounters in human development. Discontinuities in life paths often arise from events that are fundamentally unpredictable random occurrences (Bandura, 1982).

As we have noted, most personality psychologists are interactionists, Bandura among them. Perhaps the most unique feature of Bandura's interactionist system is its treatment of behavior. In social-cognitive theory, unlike many theoretical frameworks, action is as much an input into the personality system as it is an output. People's actions, and their effects, shape the person's competencies, feelings, and self-beliefs.

■ *Personal Determinants.* The second key feature of Bandura's social cognitive theory is the set of variables it uses to conceptualize the person. Bandura's choice of variables reflects what may be the most striking feature of human life – people's adaptive capabilities. People are capable of living in physical environments ranging from rain forests to frozen tundras, in social environments ranging from the urban to the nomadic, and under an extraordinarily diverse range of marital arrangements, socioeconomic organizations, and spiritual belief systems. People display virtually universal competence in domains that are cultural inventions, and where the given competence thus cannot be a wired-in product of evolution (e.g., reading and writing). People have a striking ability to adapt their behavior to physical, interpersonal, and social circumstances; to alter the circumstances they encounter to fit their requirements; and to maintain personally valued courses of action in the relative absence of tangible or social support. An analysis of personal functioning, then, must specify the psychological mechanisms that give rise to these capacities.

In this light, Bandura (1986) builds his social cognitive theory on cognitive mechanisms that enable people to learn about the world and themselves and to use that knowledge to regulate their behavior and psychological experiences. Specifically, Bandura proposes a set of five basic capabilities. *Symbolizing capability* refers to people's ability to represent knowledge symbolically. Language, of course, is the most pervasive example of the human ability to reason using symbols. This symbolizing capability is, in a sense, the most fundamental of human capacities, in that it is necessary for the others. *Vicarious capability* is the capacity to acquire knowledge, skills, and affective tendencies by observation or through modeling. Bandura's analysis of vicarious processes in skill acquisition makes his theoretical system unusually comprehensive; many psychological systems analyze the regulation of action while devoting little attention to how people acquire the knowledge and skills that enable them to act effectively. *Forethought capability*, or the capacity to anticipate future contingencies, is central to both motivation and emotional life. Much psychological distress, for example, arises not from people's actual experiences but from dread of experiences that they anticipate in the future. *Self-regulatory capability* is the capacity to set goals, to evaluate one's actions in relation to internal standards of performance. *Self-reflective capability* is the uniquely human capacity for conscious thought about oneself. Reflections on one's capacity to execute courses of thought and action or reflections on self-efficacy (Bandura, 1997) figure prominently in social cognitive theory, as we explain below.

These distinct capabilities commonly work in concert. In particular, the capacities for forethought, self-reflection, and self-regulation combine to function as a *self-system*, which constitutes the core of personality (Bandura, 1999). Persons regulate their emotional and social lives through an interacting system of self-referent processes. Thanks to the human capacities to set goals and monitor behavior in relation to personal standards, to react self-evaluatively to actions, and to reflect on one's capability for coping with future challenges, people causally contribute to their actions, experiences, and personal development. The analysis of the self-system is reviewed in detail in chapter 11.

■ *Perceived Self-Efficacy.* Although personality functioning rests on a complex system of affective and cognitive elements, research in social-cognitive theory suggests that one element of the self-system plays a particularly large role in personality functioning. This is perceived self-efficacy (Bandura, 1977a, 1997), which refers to people's appraisals of their capabilities to execute courses of action and thereby to achieve designated types or levels of performance.

Perceived self-efficacy plays a prominent role in social cognitive theory because of the pervasive role of self-efficacy judgments in human affairs. In both achievement and interpersonal domains, people's decisions about how to act are regulated in large part by their judgments of how effectively they can act. Appraisals of the relation between one's skills and the demands of the environment, then, are a key proximal determinant of the courses of action that we see as revealing of the individual's personality.

Efficacy beliefs are important not only to overt behavior but also to internal psychological life. People with a robust perception of their efficacy envision more positive futures, experience fewer distressing emotions, and are better able to organize the complex cognitive skills required to cope with demanding environments (Bandura, 1997; Cervone & Scott, 1995).

Although the role of self-efficacy beliefs in personality development and functioning is discussed at a number of different points in this text, we consider the role of control beliefs and efficacy appraisals in particular detail in chapter 12.

■ *Personal Determinants Versus Individual Differences and Dispositions.* The basic capabilities of social cognitive theory differ in three ways from the units of analysis adopted in dispositional theories of personality (Bandura, 1999). First, they are not individual-difference variables in the traditional sense of this term. Bandura emphasizes that an individual-difference analysis may obscure important capabilities possessed by the individual. This would occur either if the capability is rare (and as a result is undetected in a factor analysis, which searches for a small number of primary dimensions of variation) or if it is common but possessed to a similar high level by all individuals. The fact that virtually everyone possesses a given capacity (e.g., the ability to use symbols, the capacity

for reflective self-consciousness) makes the capacity no less important to personality functioning, even though it may not emerge as a primary dimension of individual difference.

Second, Bandura's set of cognitive capabilities does not merely speak to the question of average behavioral tendencies, as is the case for dispositional variables. Instead, the capacities for self-reflection and self-regulation contribute to both consistency and variability in action. As Mischel & Shoda (1995) also emphasize, people's goals, preferences, and cognitive capabilities are revealed in the way that their actions vary across circumstances as they manage the diverse conditions of their lives. This point has important implications for the task of personality description. It suggests that dispositional taxonomies are inadequate to the task of description because they capture only mean-level tendencies (average levels of extraverted, conscientious, etc., behavior) and sacrifice valuable information about behavioral variability. A further descriptive point, discussed below, is that the individual's social-cognitive system may contribute to unique patterns of behavior that violate the descriptive categories that are included in standard individual-difference categories.

Third, in social cognitive theory the definition of personality structure and the explanation of how personality factors contribute to social behavior differ fundamentally from a dispositional approach. In social-cognitive theory, dispositional tendencies are not viewed as personality structures, as in the five-factor theory of McCrae & Costa (1996). Instead, personality structures consist of affective and cognitive systems, which causally contribute to the patterns of behavior that are the individual's dispositional tendencies. Dispositions, then, are effects, not causes. To Bandura (1999), "the proponents of taxonomies founded on behavioral descriptors locate the personality structure in the wrong place" (p. 200). In social-cognitive theory, standard dispositional taxonomies thus are seen as inadequate for fully describing the individual or for explaining his or her personality functioning (also see Wright & Mischel, 1987).

This social-cognitive analysis of psychological mechanisms and dispositional tendencies speaks not only to the issues of description and explanation. It also relates to the question of theory integration. The issue of concern here is the relation between the explanation of personality functioning provided by dispositional analyses of individual differences (e.g., McCrae & Costa, 1995) and that provided by an individual-centered analysis of social-cognitive and affective systems. Since, by many accounts these are the two predominant theoretical perspectives in the contemporary field, the question of how they relate to one another is of pressing importance.

Some suggest that the dispositional and social-cognitive approaches can be easily married (McCrae & Costa, 1996). The thesis we develop below is that they cannot, because they embrace different strategies of scientific explanation (Cervone, 1997, 1999). To develop this point, we address the issue of strategies of explanation in the study of personality and social behavior and draw upon literature in the philosophy of science to help articulate the alternative strategies embraced by personality psychologists.

## ALTERNATIVE STRATEGIES OF EXPLANATION

### Trait and Dispositional Constructs as Causes

All personality psychologists recognize that a personality theory must explain the consistency and coherence of individual functioning. A point that has been less widely recognized is that there is more than one way of explaining this phenomenon. One strategy of explanation is embodied in dispositional, or trait theories.

In trait (dispositional) approaches, the consistency of psychological response is explained via psychological constructs that correspond to consistent patterns of behavior. The dispositional constructs, in other words, refer simultaneously to a consistent pattern of action that one has observed and to an inferred psychological system that is the cause of the consistency. In an idiographic trait approach of the sort promoted by Allport (1937), trait constructs "refer to two things at the same time: (a) a complex pattern of behavior from which the trait is inferred, and (b) the psychological structures and processes that are the source of the pattern" (Funder, 1991, p. 32). In a nomothetic trait approach such as five-factor theory, traits are "dimensions of individual differences in tendencies to show consistent patterns of thoughts, feelings, and actions . . . (and) also . . . a property of an individual that accounts for his or her placement along this trait dimension" (McCrae and Costa, 1995, p. 235). In both the idiographic and the nomothetic perspective, then, trait constructs refer to both a surface-level tendency and a corresponding causal structure. The trait structure embodies the observed tendency and hence explains it. People consistently act in a conscientious manner, for example, because of their conscientious*ness*.

Although this form of explanation has been quite popular in personality psychology, it unfortunately violates a basic principle of scientific explanation. The principle is that the scientific constructs used to explain a given property or attribute should not themselves contain that attribute. "A fundamental explanation of [a] property . . . will not refer to other things with that very same property; the possession and functioning of that property is what is to be explained" (Nozick, 1981, p. 632). "What requires explanation cannot itself figure in the explanation" (Hanson, 1961, p. 120). Hanson (1961) provides an illustration in the physical sciences: "If the colors of objects are to be explained by atoms, then atoms cannot be colored" (p. 121). Nozick (1981) provides an illustration in the behavioral sciences: "If there is to be an explanation of" "free choice, creativity, or love," it must be in terms of "components which don't themselves make free choices," "aren't themselves creative," and "aren't themselves 'in love.'"

By extension, then, in a science of personality the explanation of a person's consistent pattern of response should be in terms of variables that do not themselves correspond to the consistent pattern of response. The pattern of response is the thing to be explained; it therefore should not figure in the explanation. Paraphrasing Nozick, if there is to be an explanation of agreeable or conscientious tendencies, it should be in terms of psychological variables that are not themselves agreeable and conscientious. In other words, it should be in terms of variables that are *not* agreeable*ness* and conscientious*ness*. The adjective might do a good job of describing the pattern of response, but turning the adjective into a noun does not yield a good scientific explanation. A related critique of the use of dispositional constructs as causes has been made by Harré (1998), as we reviewed in chapter 1.

## Social-Cognitive and Affective Systems as Causes

Social-cognitive theory can be seen as an attempt to explain the coherence of personality functioning while adhering to these principles of scientific explanation. In social-cognitive theory, personality functioning is explained by reference to interactions among multiple underlying psychological processes. No one of these social-cognitive mechanisms directly corresponds to broad patterns of response; instead, multiple interacting systems contribute to any given response tendency. A person's characteristic level of conscientious behavior, for example, would not be attributed to "conscientiousness," but to the system of goals, preferences, and self-regulatory capabilities that motivate and enable the person to act in the manner that we call conscientious.

This approach to explanation in personality psychology naturally reorients one's scientific goals. In social-cognitive theory, the primary goal is to understand the functioning of the social-cognitive system, in other words, to understand how social-cognitive and affective mechanisms contribute to the individual's actions and experiences. A second aim is to understand how the social-cognitive system develops across the life-span as the individual interacts with the social environment. A third goal is to identify social conditions and psychological experiences that have the power to alter the social-cognitive personality system. Achieving this goal can have great practical benefits. Therapeutic programs can be designed around basic knowledge of how psychosocial conditions alter personal and social beliefs; for example, basic research on how experiences of behavioral mastery boost self-efficacy beliefs has proved to have enormous applied benefits (Bandura, 1997). Finally, the goal of developing a taxonomy of individual differences has a lower priority in social-cognitive theory than it does it trait approaches. Social-cognitive investigators wish to explain individual differences by exploring underlying determinants of the individual's behavior, not by fitting the individual into a fixed taxonomy of person types. This point is expanded on below.

Although social-cognitive investigators reject the notion that dispositional constructs are adequate to explain personality, this is not in any way a rejection of the fact that inherited neuroanatomical and neurochemical factors contribute to coherence in personality functioning, as Mischel (1999b) has emphasized. The question is not whether biological factors are contributing factors, but how to conceptualize their role in personality structure and coherence. Acknowledging the importance of biological temperament is not at all equivalent to adopting a trait model of personality structure. This point is underscored by the fact that scholars who study biological temperament are among the five-factor model's severest critics (Kagan, 1994b).

A variety of social-cognitive investigators have explored interactions between affective systems and social-cognitive processing (see Cervone & Shoda, 1999b). Metcalfe and Mischel (1999) view inherited affective tendencies as part of a "hot system" of personality, which influences the development of the "cool" cognitive system. The hot system, in turn, comes under the control of the cool system as the individual gains metacognitive knowledge over the course of development. Other discussions of affective and social-cognitive interactions are found, for example, in the work of Bandura (1997), who views affective arousal as one of a number of factors that individuals appraise in forming judgments of self-efficacy (also see chapter 11), and of Dodge (1996; in press), who presents a model of the development of conduct disorder that illustrates how biological factors can be incorporated into a dynamic social-cognitive system. The general theme in all this work is that an inherited affective mechanism does not create or directly correspond to a broad dispositional tendency. Instead, inherited qualities are conceptualized as inputs into a complex system of social-cognitive and affective processes that jointly contribute to the individual's distinctive patterns of experience and action. The biological factors, cognitive mechanisms, and social experiences reciprocally interact; much work indicates, for example, that social experiences influence biological mechanisms (see chapter 6).

## Top-Down and Bottom-Up Strategies of Explanation

As we have seen, social-cognitive theory constitutes an approach to personality psychology that differs significantly from a traditional dispositional approach. In part, the differences are found in personality psychology's enduring question of what units of analysis are optimal in constructing a scientific theory of personality (Allport, 1937). Unlike the trait approach, social-cognitive theory grounds the study of personality in cognitive and affective systems and views thoughts and feelings about the self as prime personal determinants of personality functioning.

Cervone (1997, 1999a), however, suggests that the differences between social-cognitive and trait-dispositional approaches should be understood in a broader context. The approaches are similar in that they both seek to explain the consistency and coherence of individual functioning. They differ in the nature of the explanations that they present. These two personality models exemplify two different strategies of scientific explanation – strategies recognized in the philosophy of science as "top-down" and "bottom-up" explanatory strategies.[1]

In top-down explanatory strategies, one seeks to establish a highly general theoretical system, which organizes information about the world (Kitcher, 1985). Particular facts are explained by fitting them into the overarching organizational framework. This framework provides a preexisting system within which new facts can be anticipated and understood. By organizing and anticipating facts, the high-level framework can be seen to have a form of explanatory power (Kitcher, 1985). Top-down explanations have the advantage of relieving investigators from grappling with large numbers of explanatory principles and numerous details about individual instances. Instead, individual cases simply are "fit within"

---

[1] All words are open to multiple meanings, and "top-down" and "bottom-up" are no exceptions. In the philosophy of science, the terms are used as we use them here, to signify alternative strategies of scientific explanation. However, there are at least two other senses in which terms may be used, and we do not imply either meaning here: (1) Within the context of information-processing models of thought, the terms refer to theory-driven versus stimulus-driven information processing; (2) in the analysis of how scientific theories develop (and in questions of epistemology more generally), they may refer to the development of ideas via conceptual reasoning versus empirical observation; in the extremes, one might develop a personality theory via "armchair speculation" or "dust-bowl empiricism." If the terms are used in either of these latter two senses, there is an interplay between top-down and bottom-up processes; theory informs observation and vice versa. However, the philosophical literature we cite is a literature about *explanation;* once one has developed a theory, and whether or not the theory has anything to do with information-processing models of thought, a question that can be asked is: What sort of explanation does the theory provide? Here, two explanatory forms are a top-down strategy of identifying a simple, overarching system of variables that captures regularities in the phenomena observed; and the bottom-up strategy of explaining phenomena in terms of an interacting system of causal elements, where that system might be capable of capturing both regularities and idiosyncratic instances.

(Salmon, 1989, p. 182) an overarching system, which "[reduces] the number of independent phenomena we have to accept as ultimate or given" (Friedman, 1974, cited in Wylie, 1995, p. 1).

An interesting feature of top-down explanatory systems is that they can be formulated in the absence of knowledge about underlying causal mechanisms (Salmon, 1989). In principle, one could posit laws or taxonomic categories of broad scope without necessarily being able to identify the processes underlying one's basic principles. Even without this knowledge, the top-down scheme can explain events by subsuming them "under some kind of lawful regularity" (Salmon, 1989).

In contrast, bottom-up explanatory strategies seek to uncover "the underlying mechanisms . . . that produce the phenomena we want to explain" (Salmon, 1989). The goal is not to formulate overarching principles that correspond to recurring trends in data but to identify specific underlying mechanisms that actually come into play in particular instances. One seeks to identify "the internal workings . . . the hidden mechanisms" (Salmon, 1989) that give rise to observed phenomena. Bottom-up causal analyses are designed to account not only for recurring trends but for individual instances that may violate statistical norms (Salmon, 1989).

Although simplicity is a valuable aspect of any causal model, simplicity is not the overriding consideration in a bottom-up approach. The fundamental goal is to identify the causal mechanisms that truly "are operative in our world" (Salmon, 1989). A seemingly parsimonious explanatory framework that fails to correspond to facts about underlying causal processes would, of course, be rejected.

Wylie (1995) provides an example in the social sciences that illustrates the strengths and weaknesses of these alternative explanatory forms in these disciplines. She considers a problem in archeology. Many archeologists seek to explain the spread of the family of Indo-European languages from areas near the Black Sea to regions as remote as northern Europe during a roughly 1,500-year period

(Renfrew, 1989). One available explanation is a prototypically top-down principle. The overarching principle involves agriculture-induced population growth (Renfrew, 1989, 1992). When inhabitants of Black Sea areas adopted agriculture, their population grew. The larger population required more land to sustain its growth. When a farming population acquires new land, it takes its language with it. It is estimated that agriculture-induced growth forces a population to spread at about 1 km per year (Ammerman & Cavalli-Sforza, 1984). At this rate, it would take about 1,500 years to get from the Black Sea to northern Europe, which corresponds to the historical evidence (Renfrew, 1989).

Despite the seeming comprehensiveness and parsimony of this explanation, other archeologists pursue a completely different approach. They begin their work by exploring the potential multiplicity of specific causal processes that could contribute to linguistic spread in any particular time and place. They study "the process and context of the transition to farming" and "[model] the social processes" (Barker, 1988) that produce linguistic change. In this approach, one seeks to develop specific causal models only after a relatively firm understanding of these underlying processes is obtained. As proponents of this bottom-up strategy readily admit, it yields an explanation that is not nearly "as neat and tidy" (Barker, 1988) as the top-down explanation cited above.

Why would one pursue this messy bottom-up approach when a simple system of high-level variables is available? The top-down model may fail to apply at the level of the individual case. The model accounts for linguistic spread in the aggregate, specifically, it accounts for data that are aggregated across languages and across time. There is no guarantee that the aggregate, population-based description and explanation will apply to individual languages and particular historical periods. Indeed, in numerous particular instances languages appear to have spread more quickly than expected from the top-down model or more slowly, or in the absence of marked population growth (Barker, 1988). The top-down model, then, can "be held accountable, *not* to individual instances, but to aggregate outcomes characterized in appropriately general terms" (Wylie, 1995, p. 17).

This, of course, is exactly the problem noted earlier with respect to the five-factor model. Five-factor theory (McCrae & Costa, 1995, 1996) offers a top-down strategy of explanation. High-level dispositions summarizes recurring trends in lower-level psychological processes and observable tendencies. The high-level dispositional variables have causal status. The individual's behavior is explained by fitting him or her within a fixed set of high-level variables. A shortcoming of the system, though, is that the model is based on analysis of the population at large. It thus may fail to capture the within-person organizations of psychological structures and overt dispositional tendencies found at the level of the individual.

Social-cognitive theory, in contrast, offers a prototypically bottom-up strategy of explanation in personality psychology. The individual is understood by reference to underlying psychological structures and processes. This underlying system of affective and social-cognitive processes gives rise to coherent patterns in personality functioning. These dispositional patterns may, but sometimes may not, happen to fit the structure of high-level individual-difference categories. The social-cognitivist thus is attempting to specify the psychological mechanisms that account not only for common psychological patterns but also for idiosyncratic tendencies expressed by potentially unique individuals.

Shaffer (1996) has analyzed contemporary developments in personality psychology, including the alternative theoretical paradigms discussed here. Shaffer highlights the implicit goals and assumptions that drive theoretical approaches. She concludes that the goal of factor-analytic trait research (e.g., Goldberg, 1993) "is not to give the causal foundations of observable behavior; it is to find *predictors* of specific behaviors which meet administrative needs in applied settings" (p. S95). Social-cognitive theory, in contrast, assumes that "the goal of . . .

research is to give causal models which are empirically adequate to behavior across contexts" (Shaffer, 1996, p. S94).

The theoretical distinction between top-down and bottom-up explanatory strategies can be further understood by considering how these different approaches treat a classic issue in personality psychology, namely, cross-situational consistency in response.

## A Bottom-Up, Social-Cognitive Analysis of Cross-Situational Coherence

The study of cross-situational consistency in psychological response has been dominated by top-down strategies of investigation. From the early days of the 20th century through the era of the person–situation debate (see chapter 2), researchers have approached this issue by gauging the degree to which a group of individuals behaves consistently with respect to a high-level dispositional category. Little attention has been devoted to identifying and assessing the exact psychological mechanisms that might cause psychological responses to generalize in a consistent manner across diverse contexts.

Whatever its merits, a top-down approach to the study of cross-situational consistency has two drawbacks. First, it may overlook cross-situational coherence that does not happen to correspond to the investigator's definition of the given trait construct. An individual's responses may, in principle, cohere across idiosyncratic sets of circumstances that do not match a generic, high-level category. Second, it yields little information about the underlying causal mechanisms responsible for any cross-situational consistency that is observed.

In a bottom-up approach, one would begin an investigation by asking about psychological mechanisms that may cause responses to cohere. A theoretical analysis of underlying causal mechanisms would guide the methodological search for consistency. In principle, the theoretical model might predict patterns of consistency that vary from person to person and thus cannot be captured by fixed, high-level trait categories.

Research on cross-situational coherence in perceived self-efficacy illustrates this approach

(Cervone, 1997). The study of perceived self-efficacy is concerned with people's appraisals of their capabilities for performance (see chapter 12). Since these self-appraisals may vary considerably across situations and behavioral domains, perceived self-efficacy is defined and assessed contextually. Self-efficacy measures tap people's confidence in their capabilities to perform specified actions in designated settings (Bandura, 1977a, 1997). These contextualized assessments often prove to be highly predictive of subsequent behavior.

The question, then, is whether people display consistently high or low perceptions of self-efficacy across different situations. If so, how should one describe and explain this phenomenon? In a top-down approach, one might begin by positing a high-level variable such as generalized self-efficacy (Sherer, Maddux, Mercandante, Prentice-Dunn, & Rogers, 1982; Tipton & Worthington, 1984), that is, an overall tendency to be confident, or not, of one's capabilities. Next, one would specify a set of lower-level situations and responses that are valid indicators of the global construct. By aggregating across this set of specific responses, one could assign to each individual a single score, which might be interpreted as indicating how much generalized self-efficacy that individual has.

Although this strategy is useful for some purposes, it has significant shortcomings. By focusing on high-level dispositional variables, it deflects attention from questions about the underlying psychological mechanisms that may produce cross-situational generalization in self-efficacy appraisals. By describing individuals via an aggregate score, it disregards the potentially unique patterns of high and low efficacy beliefs that distinctively characterize the individual. Indeed, by aggregating, it begs the question of whether each individual actually displays a generalized tendency toward high versus low self-efficacy beliefs.

The alternative strategy is to begin by focusing directly on these underlying mechanisms. Why may people's appraisals of their coping capabilities in different situations meaningfully

interrelate, or cohere? Cervone (1997) suggests that two psychological mechanisms contribute to cross-situational coherence, self-schemas and situational construals. Salient, schematic beliefs about the self (Markus, 1977) might come to mind in a number of different situations and foster consistent patterns of self-appraisal. A belief that one is prone to becoming anxious, for example, may come to mind and lower self-efficacy appraisals in various academic, work, or social activities. Second, situational construals may determine the exact settings in which these aspects of self-knowledge come to mind and influence self-efficacy appraisals. Some persons who see themselves as sociable may believe that this attribute is only relevant to their social life, whereas other people may see it as also influencing their success at school or work.

In research that explored this possibility (Cervone, 1997), participants first were asked to identify their most important, self-defining personality characteristics (i.e., their "schematic" attributes). They then indicated the situations that they believed were relevant to these characteristics; in other words, they indicated what they felt were the best indicators of each of their schematic attributes. Finally, they later completed a multidomain self-efficacy questionnaire, which assessed their confidence in being able to perform a variety of designated acts in designated settings. Information about people's self-schemas and situational beliefs was used to identify clusters of schema-relevant situations in which people were predicted to display consistently high or consistently low self-efficacy perceptions.

Two findings are of note. First, people's self-schemas and associated situational beliefs were highly idiosyncratic and often had a structure that bore little relation to standard individual-difference categories. For example, one individual reported that she was determined and that her determination manifested itself in her ability to (1) earn good grades and lose weight (tendencies that might generally be linked to conscientiousness); (2) give people orders if they are not working hard enough (an assertive act, which might be related to low agreeableness in a five-factor approach); and (3) cheer up a depressed friend (a warm, altruistic act, which might be linked to extraversion or *high* agreeableness in a five-factor approach). For this individual, fragments of a number of independent individual-difference dimensions were grouped together into a single equivalence class. Another person's schematic attributes included his being both shy and skilled at public relations. This individual's beliefs, then, split apart circumstances that traditionally would go together as part of a single individual-difference category. He believed that some "extraverted" acts were linked to his shyness, whereas other "extraverted" acts were linked, in an opposite manner, to his public relations skills (Fig. 1). This individual's ten-

dencies, then, could not be adequately captured by assigning him to any single location on an introversion–extraversion dimension.

The second finding indicates that these variable self-descriptions are not just meaningless "cognitive noise." Instead, self-beliefs and situational beliefs significantly predict cross-situational consistency in response. People expressed consistently high confidence in their coping capabilities across situations that were relevant to their self-identified positive personality characteristics. They displayed a low sense of efficacy across situations that were relevant to their negative personality characteristics (Cervone, 1997). Similar results were not obtained when analyzing common personality attributes that were not of particular relevance to individuals.

These findings relate to our discussion of strategies of explanation in the following way. In this work, cross-situational coherence did not derive from any single psychological mechanism. Individuals did not display consistently high or low self-efficacy perceptions. Instead, both high and low self-appraisals were identified for each person. Coherence

Figure 1. One research participant's schematic personal strength and personal weakness, and a subset of situations that the individual judged as relevant to the two characteristics. The figure illustrates how circumstances that typically are grouped together in nomothetic analyses of a high-level personality trait (extraversion) became split apart in analyses with this individual. From Cervone, 1999.

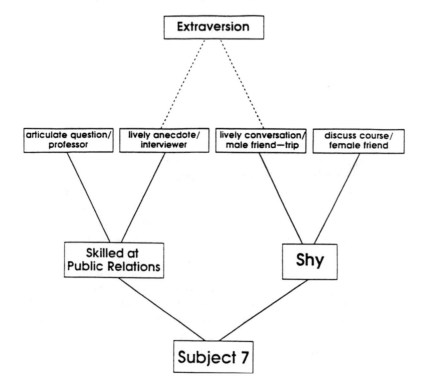

was not predictable from assessments of self-schemas or situational beliefs alone. Instead, one needed to consider how these aspects of knowledge interact. Cross-situational coherence, then, was understood in the manner of bottom-up explanatory strategies. Coherence reflected interactions among processes in an underlying system that gave rise to cross-situational consistency patterns that often were highly idiosyncratic. Much of consistency in response might have been missed if unique individuals had been forced into a universal template of personality dispositions.

In a similar spirit, Shadel, Niaura, & Abrams (in press) provide a bottom-up analysis of individual differences in smoking cessation and relapse. Whether people succeed in abstaining from cigarettes is partly affected by social-cognitive factors, including subjective beliefs about their present smoking status and the possibility of becoming nonsmokers. Shadel et al. (in press) specify a set of self-schemas and self-regulatory processes that contribute to individual differences in smoking, smoking-related affect, and relapse efforts. They assess these cognitive mechanisms idiographically to capture the potentially idiosyncratic ways in which people relate self-knowledge to the social circumstances that might trigger relapse. They find that relations among cognitive structures and social situations are highly idiosyncratic, but that once one takes this idiosyncrasy into account, one can predict abstention versus relapse. Thus, their work reveals a link between personality factors and clinical outcomes that would have been obscured by a top-down, nomothetic assessment scheme.

## SUMMING UP

People differ from one another in ways that are stable, meaningful, and consequential. This fact, however, does not imply that a sci-ence of personality can rest exclusively, or even primarily, on the study of intraindividual differences in psychological tendencies. The description of personality must go beyond global dispositional terms of the sort that, in social discourse, one uses only to describe people one knows superficially (McAdams, 1992, 1994b). The explanation of personality functioning must go beyond between-person differences to include the study of within-person psychological dynamics and organization (Pervin, 1994). A thorough understanding of how people differ from one another "requires an integrated conceptual scheme that classifies not only behaviors, but specifies their determinants and key mechanisms through which they operate" (Bandura, 1999, p. 200). This understanding of personality dynamics is necessary both for the development of personality theory, and for the development of interventions that might benefit individuals and society at large (Bermudez, 1999).

Psychology is called on to assist people in their efforts to develop meaningful lives that maximize their individual potentials. Meeting this goal does not require that one abandon the study of intraindividual-difference dimensions, but it does require one to move beyond it. The individual's "potential and direction" (McCrae & Costa, 1996, p. 68), is not defined by a set of endogenous tendencies but by his or her skills, goals, beliefs, and self-regulatory competencies and by the sociocultural environments that facilitate the development of some potentials while standing in the way of others (Caprara, 1996, 1999). These intraindividual mechanisms and person–situation transactions cannot be understood simply by locating the individual within a system of linear dimensions. They require study of the biological and social dynamics of development and of the cognitive and affective processes that contribute to human emotion, motivation, and self-regulation. It is to these topics that we devote the following sections of this text.

# The Development of Personality

# The Development of Personality

Part 3 of our text explores the development of personality over the life-span. In chapter 5, we review theoretical models of life-span development. Chapter 6 examines biological mechanisms in personality functioning; we consider both genetic influences and specific brain systems underlying individual differences. Chapter 7 explores the role of interpersonal relations in the development of personality, and Chapter 8 reviews the broader social systems within which personality develops.

This part of our text builds on our earlier discussions. We have defined personality as the complex system of psychological structures and processes through which people regulate their actions and experiences. This system conveys to the individual and to observers a sense of the person's identity, continuity, and uniqueness. Personality is constructed through interactions between the organism and the social environment. As we have emphasized, people do not passively absorb environmental influences but actively shape and interpret them. It is from this perspective that we now address the development of the individual's capacities, preferences, and tendencies.

Our coverage includes a wide-ranging and somewhat complex set of determinants of personality development. Such complexity is necessary because development is not a simple matter. It "involves multidimensional and multidirectional elements in constant states of organization and reorganization" (Hartup & van Lieshout, 1995, p. 659). Due to this complexity, development can proceed in a number of different directions from any given initial state and, conversely, different development routes can lead to similar outcomes (Baltes et al., 1998). A critical aspect of this multidirectional complexity involves the mutual influence of biology and experience on one another. Inherited biological mechanisms, of course, contribute greatly to the individual's psychological qualities, but biological mechanisms and the activation of genetic influences are affected by behavioral experience (Gottlieb, 1998; Nelson, 1999). Neural systems display relatively greater plasticity at the early stages of development. Nonetheless, even the mature brain exhibits substantial plasticity in the face of changed inputs (Garraghty, Churchill, & Banks, 1998).

Though our goal is to provide a comprehensive framework for thinking about biological, interpersonal, and social determinants of development, we note at the outset that comprehensiveness cannot be ensured because so much of the existing research has been conducted in European-American societies. The portrait of development that this work yields may not be complete. Different cultures may promote different developmental processes and outcomes. Cultures may differentially influence the development of identity, beliefs about the nature of mind and the causes of social behavior, and the role of language and communication in regulating thought and action. Students of personality must capitalize on knowledge of both universals and diversities in their search for the bases of personal uniqueness. This search may benefit from a map of the terrain, which is what we aim to provide here.

## Development and Interactionism

The belief that biological and sociocultural factors interact in development is adhered to by theorists of diverse persuasion (cf. Bandura, 1999; Buss, 1995b; Hettema & Kenrick, 1992; Magnusson & Stattin, 1998). Indeed, the acceptance of interactionism is so broad that it may deflect attention from the significant differences among interactional perspectives. Some of these were discussed in our last chapter. Others arise in our coverage of development.

A theoretical perspective with a unique view of person–situation interactions is evolutionary psychology (e.g., Buss, 1997a, 1999a). The evolutionary perspective is interactional in that overt behavior reflects a combination of two factors: evolved psychological mechanisms and environmental inputs to one versus another evolved module. However, it is not as fully interactional as the perspectives discussed earlier (e.g., Bandura, 1986; Magnusson & Stattin, 1998). In evolutionary psychology, behavioral experiences do not change the basic functioning of evolved mechanisms, although they may alter the threshold at which various mechanisms and their biologically programmed strategies come into play (Buss, 1995; Buss & Kenrick, 1998; Tooby & Cosmides, 1996). Buss, Haselton, Shackelford, Bleske, & Wakefield (1999), for example, question the entire notion of biological plasticity. They argue, by way of example, that "no amount of higher education will cause a human brain to suddenly develop the echolocation abilities of bats" (p. 444). We consider evolutionary psychology in more detail when reviewing research on sex differences in chapter 6.

Conceptions of person–situation interaction are not a matter for isolated debate among personality psychologists. Other disciplines speak to this question directly. Models of cognitive development demonstrate how behavioral experiences shape mental structures and their interconnections (Karmiloff-Smith, 1992, 1994; Rogoff, 1990, 1998). Findings in the neurosciences document the extraordinary plasticity of the brain in the face of new behavioral experiences (Gottlieb, 1998; Kolb & Whishaw, 1998; Nelson, 1999) (also see chapter 5). If persons are beings who think by using their brains, then personality psychologists cannot disregard findings from the cognitive sciences and neurosciences in their study of personality development. These findings commonly illustrate that psychological structures and their biological underpinnings are partly a product of the organism's experiences.

## Agency and the Course of Development

Three main sources of causation contribute to the course of development: nature, nurture, and the agentic person. Inherited factors shape the biological brain whose functioning gives rise to mental processing. Experiences with the physical and social world influence the development of the brain and mind. The developing person constructs a personal identity, which causally influences his or her experiences and actions. The human mind is generative, selective, proactive, and self-reflective, not just reactive and adaptive, and this makes the person an active agent in development.

Acknowledging the role of personal agency in development expands one's view of human nature. People do not consist merely of a set of tendencies that progress in a predetermined sequence toward inevitable end states. Development across the life-span also involves potentialities whose realization requires supportive social environments. In many cases, people must actively take steps to expose themselves to environmental settings that can contribute to the development of their potential. Recognizing these points further highlights the interplay among personal and situational determinants of development. Different social contexts promote the development of different competencies and beliefs. These psychological processes gradually develop into stable psychological structures, which in turn supervise subsequent social-cognitive processing. Studying these dynamics enables one to understand how personality develops as a stable system consisting not only of affective and behavioral tendencies but of self-referent knowledge, which lends coherence and continuity to the individual's experiences despite shifting environmental conditions (Cervone & Shoda, 1999b). These considerations expand the agenda for research on personality development.

Progress in the study of development is sometimes stalled by a failure of findings to generalize across contexts and cultures. Sometimes this reflects investigators' reliance on limited samples that lack representativeness. Other times the failure to generalize is more meaningful, in that a particular psychological construct may be a social construction that simply does not exist in all cultures. Yet another factor, however, is that investigators have sometimes neglected the influence of personal determinants of personality development. A given temperament factor may have different developmental implications in different sociocultural settings. Some cultures may promote skills that compensate for weaknesses and allow people to capitalize on their strengths. A rebellious youth could turn into a social outcast in some societies and a valuable social critic in others, depending on whether the society provides avenues for developing and expressing that person's capacities.

# CHAPTER FIVE

# Personality Development Across the Course of Life

It is tempting to begin a discussion of personality development by asking simple questions and seeking simple answers. Do people change? Do early-life events determine later-life personality? What percent of personality is due to nature and what percent to nurture?

Rather than succumbing to this temptation, we begin with questions of theory, metatheory, and epistemology. This is where one has to start. These conceptual considerations reveal that many simple questions can only be answered by making risky theoretical assumptions. Further, they suggest that some questions are not very good ones in the first place. Consider the question: Does the experience of parental divorce affect children's personality later in life? Though this question seems reasonable enough, no yes or no answer will suffice. Neither will in-between answers such as: divorce versus intact parental marriage accounts for X% of the variance in adult personality. Any such formulations raise two problems. First, answers may vary dramatically from one context to another. The influence of divorce may vary as a function of culture (e.g., do predominant religious beliefs condemn or allow for divorce?) and demographic factors that change from one society and historical period to another (e.g., what percentage of families in the given society experience divorce?). These contexts surely affect children's interpretations of the meaning of the divorce and the degree of support they receive from adults and peers as they cope with its ramifications.

The second problem is that the very structure of the question implicitly reflects a particular view of development. It suggests that development proceeds in a continuous, lawful manner, with events affecting one another in sequence. This then implies that later events (e.g., maladjustment in adulthood) can be logically traced back to earlier ones (divorce). Under this assumption, one can ask whether the tracing, or path, from the early to the later event is significant. However, other perspectives on development – other metatheories – question this assumption. If, for example, development entails qualitative changes from one period to another, with fundamentally new psychological properties emerging at new stages of development, then later outcomes cannot be traced in a deterministic manner to early-life precursors. Early and later developmental events may not be linked in a simple, mechanical manner (Lerner, 1998). This latter possibility suggests that many simple questions must be reformulated before reasonable answers can be achieved.

## ASSUMPTIONS IN THE STUDY OF DEVELOPMENT

The echoes of epistemological debates on goals, methods, and standards of evidence in scientific inquiry (Feyerabend, 1975; Kuhn, 1962; Lakatos, 1978; Laudan, 1977; Popper, 1959, 1969) have led many psychologists to question the foundations and legitimacy of their discipline. Particularly cogent discussion of these issues is found in developmental psychology.

Overton and Reese (1973), Overton (1984), and Ford and Lerner (1992) reject the notion that human development can be understood via a simple accumulation of empirical findings. The problem is that theory not only follows from evidence, but precedes it. Research design and interpretation inevitably reflect a priori theoretical assumptions. Investigators' theoretical beliefs determine the types of empirical evidence they seek. This raises the question of whether any finding can provide independent evidence in support of a theory. It also raises questions about the legitimacy of aggregating results from different laboratories. Since data are not theory-free, the compatibility of research procedures and the conceptual paradigms from which they arise must be assessed carefully.

Research is shaped not only by specific psychological theories but by broad metatheoretical assumptions. Overton and Reese outline two world views that guide much inquiry, *mechanistic* and *organismic* perspectives. The metaphors of a machine and a living organism capture the gist of these alternative approaches (Table 5.1).

### Mechanistic Perspectives

Mechanistic perspectives explain human behavior through chains of causation. The human organism is seen to consist of parts, each of which is an assemblage of basic biochemical components. Each of these components follows the basic laws of chemistry and physics. A fixed set of scientific laws, then, suffices to explain the full range of physicochemical, biological, and psychological phenomena. Lerner

**TABLE 1    Organ and Nature of Scientific Research Programs**

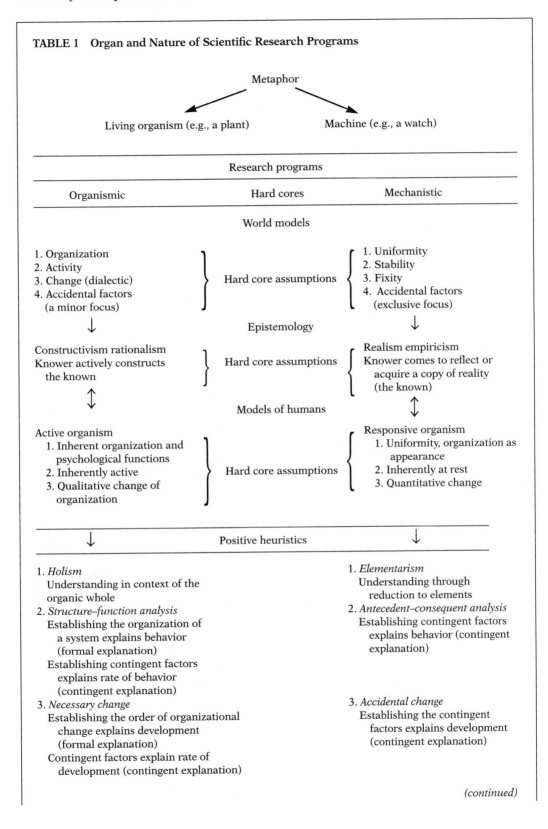

Metaphor

Living organism (e.g., a plant)          Machine (e.g., a watch)

Research programs

| Organismic | Hard cores | Mechanistic |
|---|---|---|

World models

| 1. Organization<br>2. Activity<br>3. Change (dialectic)<br>4. Accidental factors<br>(a minor focus) | Hard core assumptions | 1. Uniformity<br>2. Stability<br>3. Fixity<br>4. Accidental factors<br>(exclusive focus) |

↓                    Epistemology                    ↓

| Constructivism rationalism<br>Knower actively constructs<br>the known | Hard core assumptions | Realism empiricism<br>Knower comes to reflect or<br>acquire a copy of reality<br>(the known) |

↕                  Models of humans                  ↑↓

| Active organism<br>    1. Inherent organization and<br>    psychological functions<br>    2. Inherently active<br>    3. Qualitative change of<br>    organization | Hard core assumptions | Responsive organism<br>    1. Uniformity, organization as<br>    appearance<br>    2. Inherently at rest<br>    3. Quantitative change |

↓                  Positive heuristics                  ↓

| | |
|---|---|
| 1. *Holism*<br>Understanding in context of the<br>organic whole<br>2. *Structure–function analysis*<br>Establishing the organization of<br>a system explains behavior<br>(formal explanation)<br>Establishing contingent factors<br>explains rate of behavior<br>(contingent explanation)<br>3. *Necessary change*<br>Establishing the order of organizational<br>change explains development<br>(formal explanation)<br>Contingent factors explain rate of<br>development (contingent explanation) | 1. *Elementarism*<br>Understanding through<br>reduction to elements<br>2. *Antecedent–consequent analysis*<br>Establishing contingent factors<br>explains behavior (contingent<br>explanation)<br><br><br><br>3. *Accidental change*<br>Establishing the contingent<br>factors explains development<br>(contingent explanation) |

*(continued)*

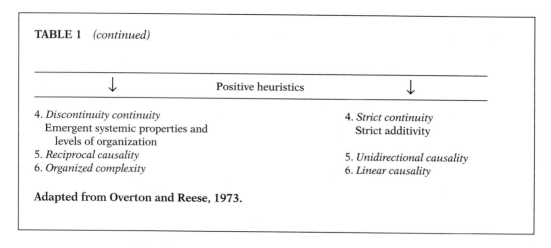

TABLE 1   *(continued)*

| ↓ | Positive heuristics | ↓ |
|---|---|---|
| 4. *Discontinuity continuity*<br>   Emergent systemic properties and<br>   levels of organization | | 4. *Strict continuity*<br>   Strict additivity |
| 5. *Reciprocal causality* | | 5. *Unidirectional causality* |
| 6. *Organized complexity* | | 6. *Linear causality* |

Adapted from Overton and Reese, 1973.

---

(1986) and Overton and Reese (1973) describe but do not embrace this perspective.

In the mechanistic view, different entities do not differ qualitatively but only quantitatively. Different entities merely vary in their level of complexity. An automobile is not a unique entity, but just a big internal combustion engine with wheels. Its functioning can be understood through the same physical principles that explain the functioning of little engines and other less complex machines.

The mechanistic approach generally implies reductionism or "elementarism." A large, complex entity is explained in terms of scientific laws that govern its simple, elementary components. It is reduced to a collection of simple elements. In the extreme, psychological elements might be reduced to their biological components, which in turn are reduced to their chemical and physical constituents. This reduction enables one to apply the same set of physicochemical scientific laws to both living systems and nonliving entities.

From a mechanistic perspective, personality development is generally construed as a gradual accumulation of psychological qualities. People acquire more psychological parts or more interconnections among the parts over the course of development. From time 1 to time 2, then, the psychological system simply changes in its level of complexity. Development involves the emergence of new capabilities due to the expression of capabilities that existed

initially. In 20th century psychology, behaviorism is the paradigm case. Development is construed as a continual increase in stimulus–response connections. At time 2 the organism has a larger "behavioral repertoire" than at time 1. The same laws of learning apply throughout the course of development and apply to the development of all organisms. In this view, a person is not just a laboratory rat, but is a really complex laboratory rat.

As in the case of behaviorism, mechanistic viewpoints generally depict a passive organism. Development is shaped primarily by external forces. Just as one's car does not decide to acquire a new engine, the developing psychological system is not endowed with properties of personal agency that enable it to shape the course of its development. In this view, it is not reasonable to speak of the potentials of the organism, since organisms do not have any fundamental capabilities other than the ability to be shaped by the environment.

## Organismic Perspectives

The organismic perspective recognizes that living systems cannot be explained merely by reference to their physical and chemical components. Biology is not just applied physics (Mayr, 1988), and psychology in turn is not just an application of any of these more "molecular" disciplines. Just as the wetness of water cannot be explained by the isolated properties of hydrogen and oxygen, the complex psychological qualities of human beings cannot be explained by the physical and chemical properties of isolated neurons or neurotransmitters. As one moves to higher levels of organization, one observes complex properties, which simply are not present at the lower levels. The complexity of organisms gives rise to emergent properties, which cannot be reduced to simple elements (Lerner, 1986; Overton & Reese, 1973).

The organismic view, then, lacks the reductionism of mechanistic perspectives. The philosopher Harré has noted that we have no "physics of chairs." Chairs have both molecular physical components and molar functional features (comfort, esthetics, etc.), but the molar features cannot be reduced to, or explained in terms of, the chair's molecular components.

The organismic view recognizes that people may change qualitatively across the course of development. At different stages, different capacities emerge. The later organism does not simply have more of what the earlier one had. Instead, it has qualitatively different properties. The psychological determinants of the mature organism's behavior, then, may differ fundamentally from the determinants of the less mature one. If we observe a child across time, we may observe that she is inhibited with strangers at ages 1, 4, and 12. This surface-level continuity, however, may mask underlying changes. At age 1, the behavior may reflect inhibitory mechanisms in the limbic system. At age 4, social behavior may be controlled by internalized speech (e.g., internalization of parental dictates to "watch out for strangers"). At age 12 the child may be inhibited due to self-consciousness about her appearance and how it is evaluated by others. The same behavior has different meaning at different times (Kagan, 1998b). The later stages of development witness the emergence of psychological functions that simply were not there previously. The 1-, 4-, and 12-year-olds differ qualitatively.

The organismic perspective entails an *epigenetic* viewpoint (see, e.g., Lerner, 1986). In this view, the causes of behavior at one point in development cannot be traced directly to events or tendencies at an earlier point. The 12-year-old's social self-consciousness is not just a reenactment of her inhibitedness at age 1 (although her biological propensity may have been one contributing factor in her later development of self-conscious tendencies). Erikson's (1950) expansion of the Freudian model of developmental stages, reviewed below, is an epigenetic view. Conflicts of adolescence and adulthood are not mere repetitions of childhood conflicts. Instead, qualitatively different concerns arise at the later ages.

Unlike the mechanistic perspective, organismic views leave open the possibility that people actively contribute to their development (Lerner & Busch-Rossnagel, 1981). The external world does not shape psychological characteristics in the way that physical forces might, for example, shape the structure of a rock formation. Instead, in the organismic view, "people are *constructors* of their world rather than passive responders to it" (Lerner, 1986, p. 55). People assign meaning to events and select activities to pursue and competencies to develop, thereby contributing to the course of their development.

Finally, the organismic view recognizes that personality functioning involves interactions among a complex system of biological and psychological components. The elements of the system reciprocally interact with one another, and the system as a whole develops and organizes itself in reciprocal interaction with the social environment. System-level functioning enables continual developmental reorganizations, which may take place in a manner that is largely independent of external circumstances. In this world view, behavior can be understood only within the context of the whole system of which it is a part.

## Developmental Contextualism

Even the organismic view is seen by some as overly deterministic. By focusing on the emergence of properties within the organism, it may underestimate the degree to which behavior is not a function merely of the organism, but of person–situation transactions

(Lerner, 1986). The organismic view may, then, be seen to underestimate the role of social context. Because of the role of context, organisms may show different patterns of growth or decline.

These considerations have prompted the development of a third metamodel, developmental contextualism (Lerner, 1986; Ford & Lerner, 1992). Developmental contextualism constitutes a system-epigenetic view of development (Ford & Lerner, 1992). It recognizes that novel properties emerge in the course of development (i.e., the principle of epigenesis) but also that human beings are open systems, that is, systems that develop through a series of reciprocal exchanges with their surrounding context. Development, then, does not involve merely an unfolding of psychological events within the person. Instead, it involves a set of transactions between persons and environments. Developmental organization emerges and gains complexity gradually. As in any complex system, the exact developmental path of the psychological system is not entirely predictable. The individual's distinctive developmental pathways can be traced only probabilistically to common determinants, end states, and patterns of change. As in the organismic view, later forms of organization cannot be reduced to earlier ones. Developmental contextualism "looks for organized patterns of person–context variables operating to influence one another and leading to different developmental pathways depending on the nature of the variables and their dynamic interaction" (Ford & Lerner, 1992, p. 15).

**Superordinate Assumptions**

Although the frameworks of Overton and Reese and Ford and Lerner have great value, even these sophisticated views should be interpreted cautiously. These metatheoretical frameworks commonly are used as taxonomies with which one can classify specific existing theories. Such classifications entail two risks. They may overstate the similarity among theories that are classified together and overstate the differences between theories

that are categorized separately. Further, classifying theories (e.g., as mechanistic versus organismic) may deflect attention from the fact that common ideas can be found in theories that fall into different categories. To cite two cases, contemporary attachment theory differs fundamentally from the mechanistic perspectives embedded in early psychoanalysis, yet it contains ideas that have persisted from its psychoanalytic past. Contemporary social-cognitive theory shows traces of its earlier social learning traditions, although it now embraces an agentic view of personality functioning that differs fundamentally from the mechanism of its learning theory past. Placing these theories into one versus another metatheoretical slot may obscure the ways in which theorists have combined the virtues of different traditions.

One should recall that ideas about the nature of human psychological development did not begin in the 20th century. Contemporary theories and metatheoretical principles reflect even more general assumptions that have shaped people's beliefs about human nature throughout the ages. We briefly consider two superordinate assumptions here, teleology and determinism.

The teleological or finalistic viewpoint ("finalism") implies the idea of a superordinate design or purpose governing the cosmos. This purpose leads persons toward particular final ends. This assumption is traceable to the thinking of Plato and Aristotle and is profoundly rooted in the Christian philosophy of the Middle Ages. It dominated Western thought until the 16th century. Finalism survived in personality psychology in that a finalistic inspiration can be found in the works of Allport, Jung, and Stern (see chapter 2).

Deterministic assumptions view natural phenomena as the necessary result of chains of causation. These views, which are traceable to the thinking of Democritus (fourth century B.C.E.), were the core of the 17th century's scientific revolution. Deterministic views freed scientific disciplines from philosophical and religious speculation. They still guide most scientific enterprises. In psychology, determinism implies a sequential order of causes and effects, which regularly recur in determining behavior. Assumptions of linearity and reversibility among events lie at the basis of deterministic explanations. Frameworks as diverse as psychoanalysis and behaviorism were explicitly committed to a deterministic view of psychological functioning.

Progress in physics, chemistry, and biology has raised doubts about the ultimate utility of determinism. One often cannot explain complex phenomena in terms of linear and reversible chains of causation. When systems contain large numbers of interacting elements, their resulting complexity can make it impossible to predict events precisely or to separate causal mechanisms into distinct elements. In physics, the strict determinism of classical mechanics has been replaced by quantum theory, which recognizes that some predictions can only be made probabilistically. In biology, where causal processes involve numerous interdependent and constantly changing components, determinism also appears inadequate (Mayr, 1988).

In this light, probabilism emerged as a third framework for confronting the complexity of reality. Probabilistic theories claim that governing laws do not produce phenomena invariantly or inevitably. Instead, they create likelihoods or tendencies for a phenomenon to occur. Probabilism is particularly appealing in the analysis of living systems. In living systems, wholes are not reducible to parts and systems are not stable but in continuous state of change. There is equifinality (the same effects may result from different causes), equipotentiality (the same causes may have different effects), and irreversibility (the effects of some causes cannot be undone). Further, the objects of study influence the external conditions in which they function. These considerations clearly imply the inadequacy of simple, linear models of causality. Probabilism seems to be the shore on which most personality psychologists are landing in their attempts to understand human development.

Although these brief considerations do not do justice to the history of the debate regarding these assumptions – a history that itself has not followed a linear, continuous pathway – they do suggest a more comprehensive framework in which to evaluate the various models of development. We share Overton and Reese's and Ford and Lerner's concern with preconceptions that shape scientific inquiry. However, we are more indulgent toward pragmatic compromises among frameworks. Different metatheoretical assumptions may be useful in different contexts. Nothing prevents one from being a teleological determinist in the church, a cosmological determinist when studying learning in a laboratory, and a probabilist when exploring well-being along the course of life. What matters is awareness of how these assumptions guide one's theorizing and research. Such awareness is particularly important for personality psychology, in which opposing teleological and deterministic assumptions have been extremely influential.

Teleology (the belief in a final cause) does not, in principle, exclude the validity of deterministic explanations (the search for efficient and proximal causes). However, theological determinism, that is the belief in predestination, does oppose cosmological determinism, according to which all natural occurrences take place in accordance with natural regularities. Thus, it would be naive to conceive the modern form of probabilism as being antagonistic to the best known form of determinism, the cosmological. Modern probabilism derives its aims largely from determinism. Both aim to pursue and protect knowledge from the attacks of nihilism and relativism expressed in postmodern thinking (Gergen, 1994; Giddens, 1991; Kvale, 1992; cf. Smith, 1994).

The mechanistic model reflects deterministic assumptions. However, it is not necessarily incompatible with a teleological view, as suggested by the ancient distinction between efficient causes, which directly produce an effect or result, and final causes, which invoke the purpose for which something is designed. A mechanistic view could cite teleological final causes.

The question of whether the organismic model originated in deterministic or teleological assumptions is less clear, especially since the organismic view emerges gradually during periods in which scientific beliefs shifted. In the history of biology, mechanistic viewpoints were once opposed by vitalists, who contended that life is sustained by a vital force, or life force, which cannot be explained in terms of chemical and physical principles (Cimino & Duchesneau, 1997). The vitalism of the 18th and 19th centuries may be considered a precursor of the organismic view. In was not until Darwin that biology could explain how complex organisms could arise nonteleologically, that is, in the absence of a predetermined design or designer (Dennett, 1995; Jacob, 1970).

During periods of the 19th century, then, teleology remained a dominant assumption in philosophy and parts of biology, whereas determinism was the predominant assumption in the physical sciences. One way for early psychologists to cope with these clashing assumptions was to adhere to *parallelism.* or the idea that the study of mind and of brain should be treated as separate areas of investigation that proceed in parallel. Criticism of classic determinism in the sciences did not fully developed until the 20th century. It is not surprising, then, that 19th and early 20th century psychologists (e.g., Freud) were determinists committed to a mechanistic model or that when dealing with the purposiveness of human action, they often used deterministic models in the service of teleological inspirations (e.g., Allport, 1937).

**Contemporary Views of Development**

Today, most students of personality development embrace an organismic model. Distinguished investigators such as Baltes (Baltes et al., 1998), Magnusson (1992, 1996, 1999), and Lewis (1990) emphasize activity, plasticity, organized complexity, multiple levels of reciprocal causality, and nonlinearity. Their thinking reveals the influence of general systems theory (von Bertalanffy, 1968) and the epistemology of complexity (Gell-Mann, 1994;

Gleik, 1987; Maturana & Varela, 1980; Morin, 1977, 1982, 1986; Nicolis & Prigogine, 1987). Theorizing that is based on a complex systems approach has stimulated the development of computational models, which reveal how developmental phenomena can be understood as emergent properties of interactions among psychological mechanisms and environmental inputs (Van Geert, 1998). The organismic and complex systems perspective in psychology, then, reflects the overall progress of scientific knowledge.

Today's developmentalists recognize that the way biological and psychological subsystems function and interact with one another is affected by the context in which the individual is operating. Since people influence their environments, personality factors contribute to the contexts, which in turn feed back to affect personality. Further, any given environment is typically shared by others, whose personalities also contribute to the environmental influences one experiences.

An investigator who has done much to advance this perspective is Bronfenbrenner. His ecological system theory of individual development (1992) emphasizes the contextual embeddedness of human development. "Any human quality is inextricably embedded and finds both its meaning and its fullest expression in particular environmental settings"; there is such interplay between the psychological characteristics of the person and of a specific environment that "the one cannot be defined without reference to the other" (p. 225).

Bronfenbrenner provides a taxonomy of developmental contexts in which he identifies a hierarchically ordered set of systems. He distinguishes a microsystem, mesosystem, ecosystem, and macrosystem. The microsystem of development refers to recurring social contexts in which social activities and roles are carried out within a well-defined physical setting and with particular people. Examples of microsystem contexts are home, school, peer groups, and the workplace. The mesosystem involves links among two or more settings that the individual encounters, such as the link between work and family life. The mesosystem, then, is a system of microsystems. The ecosystem is broader in that it encompasses settings that are relevant to the developing individual but that may not contain him or her directly. The links among the parent's various activities, for example, may be part of the developmental context of the child. The macrosystem is the overarching pattern of micro-, meso-, and ecosystems that are characteristic of a given culture, subculture, or coherent subset of society. It includes beliefs, behavioral styles, interpersonal patterns, and opportunities that may pervade each of the lower-level systems.

As Bronfenbrenner's discussion makes clear, critical developmental contexts are shared by multiple persons. Further, contexts are defined primarily in terms of interpersonal features, which predominate over physical characteristics of the environment. This means not that physical characteristics are irrelevant but that they are relevant as they are socially defined and personally acknowledged.

Incorporating the influence of culture into the study of personality development inherently highlights the complex interactions among biological, psychological, and social factors and the attendant need for a probabilistic perspective. Probabilism, then, appears to be an ultimately valuable framework within which to explore developmental pathways and potentialities.

That said, the contemporary epistemology of complexity still has a lot of difficult work to accomplish in psychology. Awareness of the complexity of living systems is no license for endorsing a simple rhetoric of complexity that cannot go beyond the restatements of well-known problems. In developing the perspective, it would be inappropriate to deny the contributions that determinism has made in advancing psychology or to dismiss programs of research derived from determinism that still are effectual. As noted by Thelen (1992, p. 192), "dynamic systems, although complex and nonlinear, are nonrandom. Even those systems deemed 'chaotic' are globally deterministic. This global determinism is a product of the internal and external

boundaries of the system, its components and energetic status."

Current work conducted from a dynamic-systems perspective rests on knowledge acquired previously by deterministic endeavors. One still can benefit from traditional research paradigms that illuminate how single mechanisms function within an overall complex system. This consideration further argues for methodological pluralism.

In sum, one need not select, as ultimately superior, one versus another metatheoretical assumption (organismic vs. deterministic vs. probabilistic). Instead, there is value in an integrative perspective in which one chooses methods that are most appropriate to the problem and level of analysis under consideration. An awareness of the limitations of each position can foster a broader integration of research programs that are potentially complementary. As an example, the person-centered perspective on personality and development advocated by Magnusson (1996), on the same premises adopted by Allport (1937), Murray (1938), and Block (1971), is not, in principle, incompatible with a variable-centered approach. Variable-centered approaches examine a specific aspect or dimension of personality across individuals. Person-centered approaches explore the organized patterning of variables within the individual as it develops over time. These approaches can be complementary, as long as the variable-centered approach does not lose sight of the whole person. Methods designed to isolate single variables across a population cannot provide a portrait of the complex, integrated, within-person patterns of affect and cognition experienced by the individual. However, they can explain how single psychological mechanisms operate under changing conditions.

## THE DOMAIN OF DEVELOPMENTAL INQUIRY

In addressing issues of personality development, a common starting place is to distinguish between biological and cultural determinants. This distinction is defensible as long as one recognizes that it primarily is a distinction of pedagogical convenience. In reality, interactions over the course of millennia have led biology and culture to influence one another mutually, or to coevolve (Durham, 1991). One thus cannot reasonably speak about the separate influences of heredity versus environment. Nature and nurture are not opposing forces. The study of personality development requires a more sophisticated conception of how biological and environmental factors coact synergistically.

Phenotypes are the result of both genetic influences and events that occur in the course of development. The coaction of biology and experience is critical to development. The various components of the organism interact not only among each other, but with the physical and social environment (Gottlieb, 1992). The biological structures that result are best characterized as emergent properties of the system of coacting elements. Exchanges between the organism and the environment determine the sequence of developmental change. Gottlieb (1998) provides illustrations of how environmental and experiential factors influence gene expressions and thus the basic biology of the organism.

Advances in the understanding of biological systems indicate that the person's selection of environmental settings and experiences can influence biological potentialities (Edelman, 1987, 1992; Karli, 1996; Thelen & Smith, 1994). Developing individuals take action to capitalize on opportunities made available by the environment. Children are not passive recipients of environmental influences, as previously thought, but active creators of their own environment from the beginning of life. Children influence their development through the reactions they elicit and the social interactions they promote (Fogel, 1993; Nadel & Camaioni, 1993; Scarr, 1992). Later in life, people continue to have a hand in their development. Research on aging informs us that active development proceeds throughout the life course, even if various forms of personal decline are unavoidable (Baltes & Baltes, 1990; Birren &

Schaie, 1996). Agentic personality development, then, starts earlier and lasts longer than was previously thought.

Development cannot be treated as synonymous with physical growth or maturation. Growth is increase in size of the body. Maturation is the progressive differentiation and integration of biological structures and functions that derive from the interaction of genetic processes and environmental conditions. Processes of both growth and maturation toward prototypical end states are important components of development. However, neither biological growth nor maturation is synonymous with development, since development also involves agentic processes through which people may define their own developmental end states and chart unique paths for reaching them.

Another consideration that falls within the domain of developmental inquiry is that development is embedded within larger historical and cultural contexts. As we will see, the effects of a given personality factor on long-term outcomes often can only be understood by considering the sociohistorical context in which the individual lives (Elder, 1999).

In summary, development involves continuous interactions between persons and the interpersonal and sociocultural contexts in which they develop. Although these developmental dynamics feature much continuity across time, they also can give rise to change. People experience greater functional capacities and more complex organization among personality characteristics, and these developmental changes endure (Ford & Lerner, 1992). A further point is that such developmental changes may involve qualitative shifts from one period of life to another. One of psychology's most pervasive notions is that psychological development entails not only continuous age-related changes, but movement across discrete psychological stages.

## AGES AND STAGES

Does chronological age structure personality development? Do changes across the years consist of transitions from one distinct stage to another, each characterized by unique concerns, capacities, and challenges? Do life stages unfold in a fixed, universal sequence? Or does the notion of stages arbitrarily partition what actually is a continuous process of growth? Such questions have preoccupied personality psychologists since the field's outset. Although development was once viewed as a sequence of predetermined steps dictated by nature or early life experiences, psychologists have increasingly come to recognize that development is a lifelong process in which individuals play an active, agentic role.

Laypersons often endorse the idea that individual development can be divided into a series of discrete stages. Our contemporary society commonly identifies childhood, adolescence, adulthood, and old age as distinct stages of life. We recognize the beginning of formal education, the transition from school to work, and the transition from work to retirement as significant moves from one phase of life to another. The different phases are viewed as so fundamental that they are accompanied by change in social status and civic obligations. However, these apparently unambiguous categories have not always been used by human societies to slice up the life course. In Western civilization, the contemporary notion of childhood did not exist before the 17th century and there was no adolescence before the 1800s (Aries, 1960). Children were viewed as miniature adults prior to the Enlightenment. Contemporary ideas of childhood are the result of relatively recent moral philosophies about human rights and social justice, as well as advances in scientific knowledge about maturation and socialization processes. The notion of adolescence reflects a differentiation of the life course that was linked to economic and political changes associated with industrialization and the establishment of compulsory mass education. The ideas that children need care and protection to reach their potential and that adolescents need encouragement and support to develop into productive adults began with the upper middle class, or bourgeoisie, and only became pervasive in all Western societies in the 20th century.

Cultural diversities are no less important than historical ones. Contemporary Japanese culture embraces the same distinctions among childhood, adolescence, adulthood, and old age as the West. However, the terms young and old had different meanings in the two societies until the 19th century. The cultures differentially valued different stages of life. Different values reflected deeper religious beliefs about life and death. The Japanese saying "Before seven, among the gods" attests to the high consideration children were granted in traditional Japan. This, however, did not prevent infanticide, among the possible justifications for which one cannot exclude the belief in a future better life following the miserable conditions of the present. Aging began at the age of 40, and longevity was highly valued. While most females entered adult life on marrying before age 20, males did not attain a socially independent adult status until marriage 10 to 15 years later, prolonging their young adult conditions of life (Kojima, 1986, 1998).

Current distinctions among stages of the life course, traceable to given ages, guide our legal systems, social policies, and civic responsibilities and opportunities. Age determines when one may drive, vote, leave school to take a permanent job, be sentenced in the penal system, and retire. However, despite the importance of chronological age as a signpost in the life-span, it is insufficient to capture all the sequences and transitions that characterize the cycle of life. Thus, in addition to chronological age, new constructs have been suggested to partition the course of life.

## Developmental Tasks and the Seasons of the Life Cycle

The notion of developmental task originates with scholars of the early 1940s, who addressed the problems that the developing individual faces in adjusting to his or her environment (Havighurst, 1973). The term came to refer to problems that are associated with a given period in life, that bear on emotional well-being and social acceptance, and that contribute to success or failure in later life activities (Havighurst, 1972). We consider here two prominent theoretical models of developmental tasks, namely those of Erikson and Levinson.

Erikson's (1963) broad-based contributions drew on ideas from psychoanalysis, analyzed the impact of social and cultural institutions, and included psychohistorical studies of well-known individuals. Psychoanalysis was his conceptual starting place. Erikson revised Freud's theory of psychosexual development to include not just the vicissitudes of biological drives but also social needs and conflicts that change across development. Based on analyses of clinical cases, cultural influences, and the course of individual lives, Erikson posited eight psychosocial stages, each defined by a central life task. The tasks reflected the interplay of biological propensities and social influences: "the human life cycle and man's institutions have evolved together" (Erikson, 1963, p. 250).

In Erikson's view, personality is shaped by the way the individual confronts the tasks of each stage. The life tasks challenge one's sense of self. Enduring attitudes toward self and society are determined by efforts to meet the challenges and by society's responses to one's efforts. Specifically, each stage features two alternative basic attitudes, which result from a positive or negative resolution to the problem faced at the given stage. These problems inherently change from one stage to the next. In infancy, the child's relations with caregivers are critical to growth. The task the infant has to master is to trust, particularly to trust that the caregiver will return from absences. Trust versus mistrust are potential resolutions of this stage. Toddlers must master motor control, communication, and the control of emotions and actions as required by society. Autonomy versus shame (from a loss of self-control) are opposing outcomes. Subsequent childhood stages involve initiative, versus guilt from socially inappropriate goals, and industry, versus inferiority or a sense of incompetence. Adolescents and young adults face the challenge of achieving identity (ver-

sus identity diffusion) and experiencing love and intimacy (versus isolation). In adulthood, when establishing family and career and assuming civic duties each represent substantial life challenges, the primary psychosocial crisis involves the production of offspring, products, and ideas. Generativity versus stagnation are the two potential outcomes here. Finally, the elderly face the task of maintaining psychological integrity versus experiencing despair. Integrity represents the achievement of full personality growth at the end point of development.

Erikson's model is highly functional. It organizes the primary challenges and transitions that mark the life of individuals in Western society. It valuably highlights processes of emotional and social development. It is flexible, in that it recognizes that any given challenge may present itself again later in development. Erikson also recognizes that different challenges will vary in importance in different societies; nonetheless, in all societies optimal development involves harmonizing nature and culture in the service of personal growth.

Similar themes are found in the work of Levinson (1978). The primary database for his theory was an interview study of 40 American men of varying age and social class background (Levinson, 1978). In this population, Levinson identified four major "seasons" of the life cycle: childhood and adolescence, early adulthood, middle adulthood, and late adulthood. Each corresponds to qualitatively different periods of individual development and serves to contextualize the "concrete process" of everyday life and the main changes that occur throughout life owing to biological, personality, and career development. Each season lasts approximately 25 years, "partially overlapping with periods of transition" (p. 18) from one season to another, each of which encompasses 4 to 5 years. Each season, to Levinson, has "its own distinctive and unifying qualities, which have to do with the character of living" (p. 18).

At any given point in time, the individual's life may be understood in terms of a life structure, which represents "the basic pattern or design of a person's life" (p. 42) at that time point. The person's life structure can be viewed from three perspectives: "the individual's sociocultural world as it impinges upon him. . .; the self, [which] includes a complex patterning of wishes, conflicts, anxieties, and ways of resolving or controlling them; [and] the man's participation in the world" (p. 44). Although recognizing the unique features of each life, Levinson identified some common features of importance to the development of all men in his study. These include, in particular, issues of work and of marriage and family, which are common features of human life. Levinson addressed the choices and challenges these life tasks presented to the men at different life transitions. For example, at the transition to early adulthood, the men faced challenges involving the formation of mentor relationships; of an occupation; of love relationships, marriage, and family; and of a "life dream" (an idealized aim), which is given an appropriate place in the life structure. The transition to middle adulthood featured reappraisals of the past, modification of the dream, and embarking on paths of decline versus further expansion and creation.

Levinson's conceptualization is insightful, and his warnings against any reification of stages and his awareness of humans' extraordinary potentialities for development are of great value. However, one might question whether the conclusions one may trace from his study are generalizable to other cultures, to the other sex, and even to American males 20 years later. Developments in the study of sex differences and of culture reviewed elsewhere in this volume illustrate the enormous risks of basing general psychological models on limited, culture-specific samples.

## Stages of Ego Development

During the period that Erikson developed his approach, an alternative route to understanding personality development was taken by Loevinger. She divided development into "four main streams or channels: physical, psychosexual, ego, and intellectual" (Loevinger, 1966,

p. 195), and focused her empirical research on the development of the ego. Loevinger (1966) recognized that "ego development is an abstraction, a juncture of a developmental sequence and a characterology" (p. 204). Nonetheless, she judged that the construct captured "what is common to a certain developmental sequence and a certain characterology that applies almost independently of age level" (p. 106).

Loevinger (1966, 1976, 1997) proposed that the ego develops in a sequence of stages. As in Piaget's (1932, 1947) analysis of cognitive development and Kohlberg's (1964) model of moral reasoning, the stages are said to occur in an invariant, hierarchical order. The individual progresses from one stage to another, with a given stage having to be mastered before the next can be achieved. Reciprocal interactions between internal maturation and external forces drive the person's progression through the stages. Individuals differ in the number of stages through which they progress, the highest stages being reached by very few persons (Loevinger, 1997). Although Loevinger hesitates to say that the highest stages are the best, the more advanced stages do encompass previous achievements of the ego while progressively allowing for a more coherent sense of self.

In Loevinger's model, the first stage of ego development is an impulsive one. The child has a sense of self but is unable to inhibit desires. In subsequent self-protective, conformist, self-aware, and conscientious stages, the child progresses from a preoccupation with self-interest to a respect for social rules and then to an awareness that there may be allowable exceptions to those rules. In a later individualistic stage, the person takes a broad view of his or her own psychological development and develops tolerance and respect for others. An autonomous stage features greater awareness of the complexity and inherent contradictions of life and of the ways in which one's life and the lives of others are interdependent. Finally, in the rarely achieved integrated stage, the person is able to transcend personal concerns and to focus instead on the well-being of the wider human society. Loevinger's development of the Sentence Completion Test (Loevinger & Wessler, 1970), a quantitative assessment of an individual's stage of ego functioning, spurred empirical research relating ego development to other variables such as intelligence, moral development, and the use of defense mechanisms.

Loevinger's model has the considerable merit of calling attention to individual differences in people's ability to reason about themselves and the world around them. However, one must note that the model also has been subjected to empirical and theoretical criticism. Some decades ago, Hauser (1976) reviewed the empirical evidence and concluded that "there was meager support for two critical assumptions made by Loevinger: (a) The sequence of ego development stages has an invariant order and (b) The stages correspond to a range of character types, each with structural coherence of diverse personality dimensions" (p. 952). The idea that development progresses through a set of stages that is fixed and universal has been questioned by students of cognitive and moral development (Bandura, 1991a; Flavell, 1992). The idea that a single psychological entity, the ego, is responsible for the enormous diversity of psychological functions that Loevinger considers fails to accord with a major trend in the study of development, namely, the recognition that reasoning about the physical and social world involves a variety of different knowledge structures that function in domain-specific manner (R. Gelman & Williams, 1998; Wellman & S. Gelman, 1998).

Vaillant provides an alternative and more flexible model of ego development. Working from psychoanalytical premises similar to those of Erikson, Vaillant conceives of ego as "the adaptive and executive aspects of human brain: the ability of the mind to integrate, master, and make sense of inner and outer reality . . . the capacity of the integrated mind to accommodate and assimilate the world" (1993, p. 3). His theorizing rests primarily on data from three longitudinal studies that involve interviews and life histories. A prelim-

inary study, the Grant study, was a longitudinal investigation of 95 men who were Harvard sophomores when the study began in 1938. The work subsequently was expanded to include data from a second longitudinal study started in 1940 among men from Boston inner city schools (the "Core City" sample). Finally, Vaillant's work included 90 women from Lewis Terman's study of gifted individuals in the California public schools (Vaillant, 1977, 1993).

From this empirical base, Vaillant proposes two development stages in addition to those posited by Erikson. After confronting the Eriksonian question of intimacy versus isolation, individuals are said to confront the issue of career consolidation versus self-absorption. Career consolidation involves the development of work competence and commitment to work and brings with it contentment and compensation. After generativity versus stagnation, one confronts the issue of "keeper of the meaning," which involves the capacity to put one's own experience and capacities at the disposal of the community and society.

Vaillant also is similar to Levinson in many ways. Both explore the adult life cycle and maintain that intimacy and career issues are crucial challenges for the people of our time. Both view midlife as a critical fork in the road leading to paths of stagnation or regeneration. Both recognize that development involves the challenge of realizing one's potential, often in the face of adversities and the need to recover from detrimental early experiences.

Although it proves a valuable framework for addressing life changes, Vaillant's work is limited by its restricted body of empirical evidence. Further, as with Loevinger, the broad conception of ego seems incompatible with recent progress in cognitive development, which highlights the importance of domain specificity. Findings generally suggest that the developing mind consists of multiple domain-specific subsystems and that different systems may develop at different rates. At the same point in time, an individual may be functioning at one stage in one domain of reasoning and another stage in another domain. This raises problems for any development model that is built on the analysis of domain-general life stages. In the study of ego, these problems are compounded. The ego is involved in self-regulation. Research on self-regulation, however, suggests that self-regulatory functions are multifaceted. People regulate their actions and emotions via a complex system of distinct mental processes, not a single monolithic ego (e.g., Kuhl, 1996; see chapter 11). The traditional notion of ego may serve as a metaphor for capturing the agency and resiliency of the person, but it appears insufficient to capture the multifaceted nature of self-control processes and their development. Stages based on ego development, then, may serve only as broad metaphors for partitioning the life cycle into gross segments.

## THE DEVELOPMENT OF THE SELF SYSTEM

The previous section reviewed broad conceptions of development that were important to the field throughout the last third of the 20th century. In this section, we focus on contemporary advances in personality and developmental psychology that provide insight into the development of the "self."

We put "self" in quotes to remind readers that the self is not a unitary, bounded entity like the heart or the pineal gland. A wide variety of psychological processes are, in various ways, self-referent and thus part of the "self." The field's classic distinction between self-processes comes from William James (1890). He distinguished the "I," the active subject who experiences the world, from the "Me," which is one of the things that the "I" experiences. The Me, in other words, includes people's conscious knowledge and beliefs about the self. It is a tribute to James that investigators continue to find this distinction to be heuristic more than a century after it was proposed.

As summarized by Hart and Yates (1997), James fundamentally distinguished between two aspects of thinking about the self, self-

awareness and self-understanding, both of which contain distinct components. Self-awareness, they suggest, consists of two components, a dispassionate focus on the self and a more emotional identification with one's qualities. Self-understanding consists of three aspects of knowledge (Hart & Yates, 1997): (1) personal memories; (2) cognitive representations of one's attributes, where these representations may be functionally independent of personal memories (i.e., people may develop abstract beliefs about the self that are not directly tied to remembered personal experiences); and (3) theories of self, which can function to integrate multiple personal memories and representations.

The content of the third facet of self-understanding, theories of self, appears to vary systematically across development (Damon & Hart, 1988; Hart & Yates, 1997). From about age 10 to late adolescence, personal theories may shift from a concern with ability and effort (e.g., "I'm good at basketball because I work hard practicing") to social acceptance, which is a particularly key aspect of early adolescence ("If I were taller, I'd have more friends and dates"). Later, theories shift to a greater focus on personal values and goals ("I want to help people by using my intelligence to become a doctor"). Earlier in childhood, children lack integrative self-theories. Instead, starting around age 2, children tend to think about themselves using only simple categories that heavily involve a moral sense of "good" and "bad" (Kagan, 1998b).

It is beyond our scope to provide complete coverage of advances in the study of self-concept in personality, cognitive, and developmental psychology. Instead, we provide readers with a "map" of this domain in the form of a brief overview of work on the development of five self-referent psychological phenomena: representations of personal qualities attributes, evaluations of one's worth or self-esteem, perceptions of self-efficacy, metacognitive knowledge of self-control strategies, and standards for evaluating one's behavior. Although these psychological processes are conceptually distinct, one should recognize that they commonly work in concert as a coherent system. They constitute an integrated self-system, through which people regulate their experiences and actions (Bandura, 1999). As just noted, this integration partly derives from theories of self (Damon & Hart, 1988), which interrelate multiple aspects of self-knowledge. Higgins (1996b) similarly has proposed that people develop a "self-digest," which organizes knowledge about the relation between oneself and the environment. As these cognitive self-systems develop, children become better able to control their emotions, organize courses of action, and thereby contribute to their development.

## Mental Representations of Personal Attributes

People's mental representations of their personal qualities shift across the life course, in accord with change in cognitive capacities and shifting forms of social interaction (e.g., Damon & Hart, 1988; Harter, 1998). As reviewed by Harter (1998, 1999), toddlers think of themselves in terms of simple categories, which they are not able to integrate with one another, partly because of their limited working memory capacity. Children of this age hold unrealistically positive views of themselves. This is due, at least in part, to their inability to distinguish desired from actual capabilities or, more generally, reality from imagination.

In middle childhood, children develop the capacity to relate personal qualities to one another. Qualities may be organized around the categories of good and bad, which function as bipolar opposites that tend to trigger extreme, all-or-none evaluations. In late childhood, there is greater integration of the various features that one recognizes in oneself. Children use more abstract concepts, such as personality trait categories, to organize knowledge of their personal qualities. Social comparison gains importance, as children acquire the ability to rank their abilities in relation to those of others. During the course of adolescence, then, children become increasingly able to recognize abstract qualities of the

self and to relate these abstract qualities to one another (Harter, 1998).

## Feelings of Self-Worth

Children develop not only beliefs about the attributes they possess, but feelings about the worth of those attributes. They also may develop an overall sense of their worth as a person, or a global sense of self-esteem. The seemingly subtle distinction between feelings of self-worth and a singular sense of "self-esteem" may be an important one. All students of the self since James (1890) recognize that people develop feelings of self-worth that are based, at least in part, on how they compare their actual attributes or achievements with idealized standards or goals. However, many question the utility of the construct self-esteem, with some judging it to have "minimal theoretical value" (Kagan, 1998, p. 178). A primary concern is that the practice of assigning to people a single self-esteem score may fail to do justice to the individual's potentially diverse collection of self-views; self-evaluations may have to be represented in terms of a multidomain profile (Harter, 1986). A somewhat different concern is that even if a single self-esteem score adequately summarizes a person's self-views, this does not provide grounds for treating self-esteem as a unitary causal entity. Harré (1998) contends that self-esteem scores may simply summarize the way in which people talk about themselves when asked to describe their attributes. These discourse summaries, he argues, should not be reifyed and granted causal status.

Even if one accepts self-esteem as a useful construct, it is difficult to answer questions about the development of self-esteem without first establishing exactly what self-esteem is. The field currently harbors alternative theories about its nature (Brown, 1998). Affective models view self-esteem as primarily involving feeling states. Affect centers around feelings of acceptance and mastery. Cognitive models view self-esteem as more dependent on conscious reasoning processes. People essentially compute their self-esteem by adding up their strengths and weaknesses and perhaps weighting these qualities according to dimensions such as personal importance (James, 1890). Although some evidence does support this later, Jamesian view (Harter, 1998; Pelham, 1995; Rosenberg, 1979), Brown (1998) has criticized cognitive modesl as presenting "too rational a portrait of self-esteem" and has defended an affective perspective. The affective view would suggest that the field should attend more carefully to the relation between self-esteem and temperamental qualities involving affect.

Putting the conceptual points aside, empirical research has documented some systematic relations among developmental periods, psychosocial factors, and evaluations of self-worth (reviewed, for example, in Harter, 1998). Older children's self-appraisals are more accurate than those of younger ones, and they therefore experience more realistic, lower self-evaluations as a result of recognizing discrepancies between real and ideal self-images. Regarding social determinants, objective external factors such as income level or social status do not directly affect appraisals of self-worth. Instead, self-evaluations are influenced more strongly by subjective social comparison processes (Brown, 1998; Wood, 1989). This role of social comparisons is particularly important in the domain of physical attractiveness. Many studies document a strong relation between self-perceived physical attractiveness and self-esteem; this relation holds for both boys and girls (Harter, 1998). Given the consistency of this link between perceived attractiveness and a stable personality factor, self-esteem, is it somewhat surprising that physical attractiveness has not received more attention in the behavior genetic literature (see chapter 6). In principle, identical twins' shared physical appearance may contribute to their similarity in self-reported personality characteristics.

## Self-Efficacy Beliefs

Questions about the development of self-esteem and the development of self-efficacy beliefs are distinct because these psychological constructs are distinct. Perceived self-efficacy does not refer to feelings of self-worth, as does self-esteem, but to beliefs about one's ability to execute courses of action. The initial emergence of these beliefs is contingent on children's recognizing the link between their actions and effects in the environment. Efficacy beliefs, then, are fundamentally grounded in experiences of behavioral mastery (Bandura, 1997).

Since we address the reciprocal relations between behavioral experience and self-efficacy perception at many junctures of this volume, at present we will confine ourselves to noting, as Bandura (1997) has, that relatively little research has been done on the initial emergence of efficacy beliefs. Research in this area faces methodological difficulties. Beginning in middle childhood, self-efficacy beliefs can be tapped through self-reports. Early in childhood, however, children's limited linguistic skills obviously interfere with such assessments. Bandura (1997) suggests that children's choices of activities and actions to pursue might provide a reasonable indirect index of the emergence of efficacy beliefs in young children.

## Metacognitive Knowledge of Self-Control Strategies

With greater age, children gain greater control over their emotions and behavioral impulses. Psychodynamic formulations attribute this development to the growth of the ego. A somewhat different formulation is that children gradually develop greater metacognitive knowledge, that is, greater knowledge of their own thinking processes and the factors that influence their behavior. The advantages of a metacognitive as opposed to an ego framework are threefold. A metacognitive analysis is more amenable to test, since one can tap metacognitive knowledge far more directly than one can assess the functioning of a hypothesized ego. It is better able to account for instances in which a person displays different levels of functioning in different life domains, since there is no assumption that individuals possess a single, generalized level of ego development. Finally, it facilitates the design of interventions to promote self-control. The development of metacognitive knowledge and thinking skills can become a target for clinical intervention. Meichenbaum's (1977) cognitive–behavioral technique for teaching thinking skills illustrates this advantage. In this method children are taught to engage in self-guiding speech in which they verbalize strategies for coping with challenges.

Research by Mischel and colleagues shows how a metacognitive analysis can uncover developmental trends in knowledge and self-control competencies. Children of different ages are found to vary in their understanding of the social cues and thinking strategies that facilitate delay of gratification, that is, the ability to avoid immediate temptations in favor of greater rewards in the future. Four-year-olds were found to prefer delay strategies that were known to backfire, whereas only children at the end of their fifth year consistently selected strategies that reduce frustration and enhance delay abilities (Mischel & Mischel, 1983). Metcalfe and Mischel (1999) discuss these results in terms of separate "hot" and "cool" psychological systems. The cool system, which contains knowledge and self-control strategies, is seen to develop more slowly than the impulsive hot system. As the cool system develops, children are better able to control emotions and impulses.

## Standards for Self-Evaluation

A pervasive feature of psychological life is the human tendency to evaluate whether our actions are praiseworthy. People rarely observe their actions in a cool, emotionally detached manner. Instead, they react with feelings of self-satisfaction and pride, or with dissatisfaction, shame, and guilt.

The human capacity for evaluating the worthiness of actions develops early. By the second year of life, children develop a moral sense (Kagan, 1998b). They recognize that some actions will bring parental approval, whereas others violate social norms and bring disapproval. They react emotionally to the "good" or "bad" acts. Kagan (1998b) notes that these self-evaluations are relatively complex cognitive processes, which require the integration of multiple component abilities. One must be self-aware, aware of others' thoughts and feelings, able to apply evaluative categories to oneself, able to reflect on one's past actions, and able to recognize that an action could have been avoided or that alternative actions could have been taken. Since other species lack this combination of capacities, motivational systems involving self-approval and self-punishment are uniquely human capabilities (Bandura, 1986; Kagan, 1998b). During the course of development, social standards become internalized and people react evaluatively to self-standards, that is, personal criteria for judging the worthiness of actions.

Although all people may be predisposed to self-evaluation of their behavior, the exact content of self-evaluative standards is heavily determined by social factors. When children observe psychological models who exhibit stringent standards for evaluating their performance, they readily internalize the standards as a basis for self-evaluation (Bandura & Kupers, 1964; Bandura & Mischel, 1965; Lepper, Sagotsky, & Mailer, 1975).

Children develop not only standards for discrete activities, but also more global orientations toward self-evaluation and goal setting. Dweck and colleagues (e.g., Grant & Dweck, 1999) suggest that children differ in whether their self-evaluative standards involve the mastery of new personal attributes or the validation of attributes that they already may possess. Higgins and colleagues highlight variations in whether children's developing self-regulatory standards involve positive outcomes that one may attain or negative outcomes that one should avoid. Preliminary results suggest that different styles of child–caretaker interaction promote different self-regulatory orientations in the child (Higgins & Silberman, 1998). Questions of self-regulation are considered in detail in chapter 12.

## STABILITY, CONTINUITY, AND CHANGE

A developmental perspective on personality raises fundamental questions about stability and change. To what degree is personality stable? What aspects are stable? What are the sources of stability? Conversely, when, how, and why might personality change?

These questions intersect with others addressed throughout this volume. Do "phenotypic" expressions of personality reflect a small number of endogenous "genotypic" entities that are stable across time? Or should the links from past to present be understood in terms of dynamic processes that tend to promote personality stability but that might also produce change? How do these conceptual alternatives bear on the empirical question of whether early-life personality assessments can predict later outcomes and pathways?

As we have discussed, answers to such questions partly rest on metatheoretical assumptions about causation. These assumptions guide the direction and interpretation of research. Structuralist assumptions direct one toward identifying stable basic elements or entities, as well as invariant orderings of developmental phenomena. Functionalism orients investigators toward processes of transformation and adaptation. Mechanism highlights the possibility of predictable chains of causation. Organicism suggests the existence of unpredictable, emergent properties. Either mechanists or organicists may, in principle, endorse either structuralist or functionalistic propositions. In the history of psychology, Freud illustrates a confluence of mechanism and functionalism. Piaget combines organicism and structuralism. We recognize that such distinctions risk oversimplifying complex positions. Nonetheless, the risk seems acceptable here because of the great importance of recognizing the role of metatheoretical assumptions in this domain. It is impossible to gauge levels of personality stability, continuity, and change without first making assumptions about what personality is.

Kagan (1980) reminds us of metatheoretical assumptions commonly embraced by the "Western mind" which "seems inimical to the apparent lawlessness of the emergent form and insists on inventing invisible essences that provide a continuity between the present and the succeeding phenomena" (p. 26). "Western scholars have favored the notions of stability of structure, continuity of process, and derivative change . . . with . . . a faith in connectedness" (p. 44), which lead us to "view psychological development as consisting of a series of stages of increasing complexity that proceed in an invariant order, with each stage containing some of the structures and processes evolved in the preceding stages" (p. 52). Indeed, many Western scientists, as we have noted, view personality development as a sequence of invariant stages. Psychoanalysts have maintained that later experiences add very little to essential qualities formed early in life. Some trait theorists conceive of traits as "endogenous basic tendencies," which are broad in scope and barely shaped by any experiences whatsoever.

The point is that these popular essentialistic viewpoints reflect not only cold empirical findings but broad assumptions that direct the course of research and the meaning of stability and continuity in personality. If personality is thought to consist of a small set of unchanging structures, then stability and continuity go hand in hand; the temporal stability of personality is revealed in the repetition of acts that arise from the stable essential structure. If personality is viewed as a dynamic cognitive–affective system that interacts with the social environment, then stability and continuity are far from equivalent. Continuity in personality functioning may be revealed in *in*stability of overt action; for example, enduring goals and competencies may produce unstable patterns of behavior if individuals experience a sudden transition in environmental circumstances and resources that forces them to attempt novel strategies of goal pursuit (Sanderson & Cantor, 1999).

## Stability

Since the field has not achieved a final consensus on the differences between stability and continuity, distinctions cannot be other than arbitrary and provisional. Yet such distinctions must be considered to avoid the confusion that could result from inadvertently using the same terms with different understanding. One possibility is "to use stability to refer to persistence of structures and behaviors and continuity to refer to maintenance of psychological processes or functions" (Kagan, 1980, p. 31). However, this distinction unavoidably leads into turbulent waters, since the distinction between structures and processes is highly inferential; investigators may not share beliefs about what structure and process might mean in different theoretical contexts (see discussions in Bandura, 1999; Caprara, 1996a).

Longitudinal stability in interindividual differences has been clearly demonstrated in self-report characteristics. A relatively unambiguous definition of stability is psychometric. Scores on tests designed to assess individual differences in personality dispositions may be consistent over time, or temporally stable.

Psychometric analyses differentiate among a number of different aspects of temporal stability. One distinction is absolute versus relative stability. Absolute stability refers to maintenance of a given amount of an attribute over time (assessed via a score, frequency, rating, etc.). Relative stability refers to the maintenance of one's *standing* in relation to others, that is, to the stability of interindividual differences. Another distinction contrasts structural and ipsative stability. Both refer to the persistence of correlational patterns among variables, but the former refers to correlations within a population, the latter to patterns within single individuals.

Although all aspects of temporal stability have been explored, a particularly large body of work has explored relative stability. The question most commonly asked is whether individual differences in self-reports of personality characteristics are stable over time. Do people with relatively high (low) scores at time 1 also obtain scores that are high (low) relative to others at time 2? The answer here is unambiguously yes. People's relative standing on self-report measures often is remarkably stable over long periods of time. Costa and McCrae (1997; also see McCrae and Costa, 1999) review a large body of longitudinal stud-

ies on this issue. Even when the test–retest interval exceeds 10 years, the correlation coefficient between adults' self-reports at the different assessment periods commonly exceeds .5, and sometimes exceeds .7. Note that these correlations are not corrected for attenuation due to unreliability of measures, in other words, they are not corrected for the fact that, owing to errors of measurement, the correlation between scores obtained from one day to the next is less than perfect. When corrected for attenuation, stability coefficients commonly exceed .9 (Costa & McCrae, 1997; also see Schmitt & Borkenau, 1992). The relative stability of adults' self-reports is one of the most robust findings in the personality psychology literature.

It is possible that behavior and self-reports do not correspond to one another. Self-reports of dispositional tendencies may be insentive to actual changes in behavior, perhaps because people are biased to maintain a stable self-concept. Findings on the temporal stability of observer-report measures argue against this possibility. Work on both individual differences (McCrae & Costa, 1990) and ipsative, within-person structures (Block, 1971) indicate that observer ratings of personality also are significantly stable across extended periods.

Finally, stability is found not only in correlational patterns but in mean levels of trait self-reports (Costa & McCrae, 1997). Cross-sectional studies find little evidence that scores on the dimensions of the five-factor model vary from one age of life to another. One important consideration here is that people may compare themselves with age cohorts when making self-ratings. As a result, self-reports may underestimate actual change. Hypothetically, mean levels of self-rated healthiness may underestimate objective changes in health status because less healthy elderly individuals compare themselves with equally unhealthy members of their age group when making self-judgments. Fleeson and Heckhausen (1997) find that directly asking people whether their attributes have changed over the years yields greater evidence of developmental change in personality than does simply charting mean levels on self-report scales (also see Krueger & Heckhausen, 1993).

These psychometric findings say little about the developmental course of specific psychological mechanisms. People could be stably conscientious across time, for example, because they carry in their heads a stable psychological structure, which enduringly determines their level of conscientiousness. However, at least two alternatives present themselves. First, people's dispositional qualities may be stable owing at least in part to social factors. The stability of scores on a measure of openness to experience, for example, might partly reflect the influence of family and social factors that consistently promote or discourage unconventional attitudes. The second possibility is that different people are consistent for different reasons. In principle, one person might obtain consistently low conscientiousness scores because he or she lacks self-regulatory skills. Another might obtain consistently high scores because of fear of authority figures who might punish transgression of social norms for responsible behavior. Multiple psychological mechanisms may each be stable over time and contribute to consistent conscientiousness scores, although no individual mechanism corresponds to the global construct conscientiousness (Cervone, 1999).

## Continuity

Continuity refers to correspondences among psychological tendencies observed at different periods in life. Unlike the notion of stability, which implies an absence of change, the idea of continuity recognizes that people may develop dynamically across time periods. Despite these developmental changes, certain psychology qualities may continue to be evident. Block (1993), who has contributed mightily to our understanding of the preservation of qualities across time, emphasizes that "individuals may change and indeed do change . . . they [are] not 'stable'" (p. 32). People's relative standing on interindividual differences may be consistent from childhood

to adulthood, but this implies the presence of continuities and coherence, not stability (Block, 1993). Even when interindividual differences are preserved, the personality structure of individual persons may have changed significantly.

One difficulty in the study of personality continuities is determining whether a given empirical finding is evidence of continuity or change. Any complex expression of personality is multidetermined, and change is continuous in development. Deciding whether a given degree of connectedness in a phenotypic tendency is indicative of psychological continuity or discontinuity, then, is partly a matter of convention. A standard convention is to use the term continuity to refer not only to absolute consistency but also to changes that are expected theoretically. Links from early shyness to later social inhibition or early impulsivity to later antisocial behavior may be taken as evidence of continuity, even though the former and latter outcomes are not identical.

Discontinuity, then, would refer to an unexpected change in the level or quality of psychological functioning, particularly when that change shifts one's sense of self-worth or the way one is evaluated by others. Discontinuities are violations of expected functioning in highly self-relevant domains (Zimbardo, 1999).

In evaluating the literature, then, one must consider the criteria that investigators adopt and their theoretical assumptions about what qualifies as evidence of continuity or discontinuity. At least two approaches to the question of continuity can be identified. One relates an interindividual difference variable at time 1 to the same, or a conceptually related, interindividual difference at time 2. The other relates clusters of within-person characteristics to later outcomes experienced by the individual. The former is a dimensional or variable-centered approach, whereas the latter is a typological or person-centered strategy (Block, 1971; Magnusson, 1998).

■ *Emotional Reactivity and Control.* The challenges faced by the student of personality development are well illustrated by research on emotional and motor reactivity, that is, the arousability of affective and motor systems (Rothbart, Ahadi, & Hershey, 1994). Phenotypic levels of reactivity are not determined by a single underlying psychological mechanism. Instead, they reflect different factors at different points in development. At first, reactivity is governed by emotionally based systems, such as those involving fear. Later, cognitive self-regulative systems, which involve factors such as attentional control and self-soothing, develop and affect the levels of reactivity one observes. As Rothbart and Bates (1998, p. 128) explain, "Early reactive systems of emotionality and approach become overlain by the development of at least two temperamentally linked control systems. The first, behavioral inhibition of action and emotional expression, is linked to the development of fearfulness late in the first year. The second, effortful attentional control, develops across the preschool period and likely beyond."

These facts pose a significant challenge. Charting the developmental course of a particular psychological mechanism requires disentangling interactions among multiple affective and cognitive systems. Simply plotting interindividual differences in overall success at emotional control runs the risk of equating children who are quite different psychologically – in other words, children who are equally successful but for different reasons. Different children may fail at self-regulatory tasks because of highly reactive affective systems, a lack of cognitive self-regulatory skills, or stressful life circumstances, which in turn affect their physiological reactivity.

Despite these challenges, some findings have achieved a degree of consistency that allows for confident conclusions. Early inhibition is connected to later internalizing and depression, and early unmanageability is related to later problems of externalization such as aggression (Rothbart & Bates, 1998). Early negative affectivity is related to both outcomes; however, findings also raise the possibility that negative affectivity is too

broad a construct to capture the relations between affective temperament and personality characteristics. Different negative affects relate to different characteristics. Irritable negative affects, such as anger, relate positively to antisocial characteristics in childhood. In contrast, passive, low-arousal negative affects, such as sadness, are positively related to prosocial characteristics such as empathy (Rothbart and Bates, 1998).

Longitudinal findings indicate that undercontrol (i.e., early unmanageability) at age 3 predicts high negative emotionality and low constraint at age 18. Personality characteristics at age 18, in turn, mediate the link between early undercontrol and health behavior at age 21 (Caspi & Silva, 1995; Caspi et al., 1997) However, the different routes and underlying mechanisms, biological and social, remain equivocal. Although the relations between temperamental dimensions such as activity level and reactivity, and personality dimensions such as emotionality and extraversion may appear striking, the isomorphism between these variables may be more apparent than real (Hartup & van Lieshout, 1995).

Since both temperament and personality develop over time, it is difficult, conceptually and empirically, to establish how they overlap or whether personality truly is a continuation of temperament. The fact that scientists of different orientations adopt different theoretical assumptions and research methods results in further ambiguities in the literature.

■ *Relation of Temperament to Broad Behavioral Outcomes.* The situation becomes, if anything, more problematic when one asks about continuities between temperament and broad behavioral outcomes or syndromes such as depression, delinquency, or criminality, where the impact of multiple biological and environmental factors must be considered (Cicchetti & Toth, 1998; Frombonne, 1995; Loeber & Stouthamer- Loeber, 1998; Maughan & Rutter, in press). Clearly the identification of temperament-based predictors would be of great benefit to the design of interventions to prevent maladjustment and promote social adjustment. Unfortunately, at the moment one should count only on modest correlations in this domain, whose underlying nature still remains unclear.

After reviewing much of the available literature, Kagan and Zentner (1996) concluded that "children have a natural tendency to grow toward health" (p. 347), even children who have individual liabilities and live in adverse circumstances. Analogous conclusions are suggested by the fact that the majority of people pass through life successfully in spite of multiple liabilities and adversities (Rutter & Rutter, 1993; Werner & Smith, 1992). The field's tendency to focus retrospectively on the links between current undesired outcomes and earlier vulnerabilities has highlighted those continuities that do exist between early-life adversities and later-life maladjustment. However, since early vulnerability often fails to predict poor social outcomes later in life, a more prospective viewpoint would highlight the capabilities that enable people to overcome adversity and improve their lives.

In spite of much evidence attesting to the practical value of assessing traits, it is unlikely that work on global dimensions will illuminate the mechanisms of continuity and discontinuity. Why do certain early liabilities dissipate over development while others foster maladjustment? Which social pathways foster a rewarding adulthood and which jeopardize the course of development? Why do different individuals with similar early-life experiences attain different adult outcomes? It is likely that answering such questions requires not just a dimensional approach, but also person-centered, typological approaches, which chart development longitudinally. Such a strategy allows one to identify coherent patterns of dispositions, strategies, and behaviors and chart these patterns over the course of life, and thereby to understand how they change and to which outcomes they lead. Since the seminal contributions of Block (Block, 1971; Block & Block, 1980), this person-centered approach has been revitalized. Ego control and ego resiliency have become popular constructs for examining patterns of dispositions and behav-

iors associa...
refers to the...
affective in...
"the dynan...
modify a cl...
either dire...
characteris...
so as to pr...
tion" (Blo...
the years, ...
that have assessed different personality dimensions (activity level, delay of gratification, emotionality, impulsivity, aggression, shyness) through different methods (Q-Sort, self-reports, ratings) have converged to identify similar patterns and types that are relatively stable over time and are associated with psychosocial adjustment (Block, 1993; Caspi and Silva, 1995; Magnusson, 1988; Pulkkinen, 1996). Although the number of distinct typological categories that are identified may vary from one study to another, findings substantially confirm three types – undercontrolled, inhibited, and well adjusted. All studies identified defects of impulse control as a risk factor for later maladjustment, particularly in males.

It is likely that more detailed knowledge of the different itineraries of lives in their sociohistorical settings will shed more light on the mechanisms that determine whether temperamental factors turn into desirable or undesirable outcomes.

## Developmental Continuities and Discontinuities in Their Sociohistorical Context

A complete understanding of how childhood personality factors are linked to long-term outcomes requires that one attend to the sociohistorical context in which personality development takes place. In this regard, the life course approach of Elder and colleagues is exemplary (Elder, 1974, 1985, 1999; Caspi, 1998). Their work reveals how social adversities arising in particular sociohistorical contexts interact with personality factors to determine life outcomes. As Elder (1999) explains, life course theory examines how human lives become organized over the

ment as individuals relate to
...ay change substantially across
...ical forces shape the trajectories
... school, and work, which in turn
...ce behavior and particular lines of
...lopment" (Elder, 1999, p. 309). Individuals
...rtly construct their own life courses
through their choices and actions, which must
be understood within the constraints posed by
their current social circumstances.

Elder (1999) has explored life course
development by charting the educational,
professional, and social experiences of the
children of the Great Depression, who were
born in the United States in the late 1920s
and thus entered the work force in the late
1940s. A number of historical factors are of
note in considering the life trajectories of this
group. The work force they entered was
increasingly white collar, and thus increasingly required social skills rather than the
ability to engage in hard manual labor. The
work force was dominated by men; thus,
even women with high potential may not
have reached high levels of achievement.
After service in World War II, many men benefited from the GI bill for continuing education. As a result, the level of education one
achieved was determined less by socioeconomic factors (e.g., a family's ability to pay
for college) and more by personal determinants (e.g., intellectual and self-regulatory
capabilities). Research on the developmental
course of individuals who were identified as
ill-tempered early in life (Caspi, Elder, &
Bem, 1987) illustrates the interplay of personal factors and historical forces.

Caspi et al. (1987) traced the development of
children of the Depression who frequently
exhibited severe temper tantrums that included
physical assaults or verbal abuse. Among men
of middle-class origins, they identified two
pathways from childhood temperament to
adult professional outcomes. First, the tendency to exhibit outbursts of temper directly
affected men's workplace stability. Ill-tempered
boys became men who changed jobs often.
Second, ill-temperedness was linked to adult
occupational status indirectly. Ill-tempered

boys achieved lower levels of education, which
in turn caused them to have attained lower
occupational status at midlife. Ill-temperedness
and occupational status were not linked
directly; that is, the pathway from ill-temperedness to occupational status flowed entirely
through the mediating effects of education. The
effects of ill-temperedness on education, then,
appear to have accumulated over time. Ill-tempered boys repeatedly got into trouble in
school and gradually fell behind educationally.
Caspi, Bem, & Elder (1989) use the term
"cumulative continuity" to describe cases in
which a personal factor influences the course
of development through its recurring effects on
sociocultural factors. In contrast, "interactional
continuity" refers to cases in which individuals
carry with them a social-interactional style that
manifests itself in a similar manner across the
life course. Ill-temperedness was linked to occupational instability in this manner.

Interestingly, these paths from temperament to professional outcomes were not
found among men of lower-class origins. Ill-
temperedness did not further lower their
already low economic status. These pathways
also were not found among women, who
rarely entered the workplace. However, ill-
temperedness did affect women's social outcomes. Ill-tempered women tended to marry
men of relatively low socioeconomic status
and to experience somewhat higher rates of
divorce (Caspi et al., 1989), a life event that
further erodes economic welfare.

Analyses of parental well-being and adolescent adjustment similarly yield evidence of
sequential links among social and interpersonal conditions and personality development
(Conger et al., 1992). Among boys living in the
rural United States in the late 1980s, economic hardship indirectly influenced adolescents' adjustment (operationalized as their
self-confidence, school performance, and positivity of peer relations). Economic pressures
lowered the psychological well-being of parents. This, in turn, fostered marital conflict
and less nurturant parenting. Less skilled parenting, in turn, predicted greater adjustment
problems among adolescents.

This body of findings illustrates that correlation coefficients may be inadequate to account for the various interactions that take place among personal and social factors at a given historical time. A correlation, for example, between childhood and adult attributes does not imply that individuals carried around in their heads a stable psychological structure that was essentially unchanged across the life course. The work of Elder and colleagues shows that personality continuity and discontinuity arise from psychological and social processes that may attenuate or magnify individual differences that are detectable early in life (Caspi, 1998).

## OPTIMAL DEVELOPMENT THROUGH SELECTION AND COMPENSATION

Developmental potentials are not unlimited. It is important to investigate conditions that constrain development and strategies through which people may maximize their potential across the life course.

Strategies for optimal development must be understood within the overall time frame of life. As life progresses, a basic fact is that one has less time left to cultivate competencies (e.g., Carstensen et al., 1999). Time for personal accomplishments is set by three different clocks: a biological clock, which reflects the constraints of nature; a social clock, which reflects the norms and obligations of society, and a psychological clock, which is set according to our own plans and expectations. One measure of the effectiveness of personal functioning is the ability to set goals and develop strategies that maintain well-being within these temporal constraints.

The work of Baltes and his colleagues (Baltes & Baltes, 1990; Baltes, 1997; Baltes et al., 1998; Baltes et al., 1999) provides great insight into the processes that foster successful development. Their functionalist and contextualist perspective views development as consisting of changes in personal and social resources. Various personal competencies (e.g., intellectual and physical skills) tend to increase and then decline across the life course, primarily according to the dictates of biology. Various external resources (e.g., education) are more readily available at some points in life than others, partly in accordance with social norms. Successful development, then, involves the maximization and minimization of positive and negative outcomes, respectively, within this set of temporally bound opportunities and constraints.

Successful development can be achieved through a balancing of three factors: selection, optimization, and compensation. People must select life goals that are manageable within the constraints of biology and culture. They must optimize their allocation of personal and social resources in goal pursuit; this may require focusing on one domain of life while lessening attention to others. Finally, they must develop strategies to compensate for losses of personal and social resources that they may experience in a domain of functioning. Baltes (1997) illustrates these selective optimization with compensation (SOC) processes with the case of Arthur Rubinstein. The pianist maintained exceptional performance late in life by selecting a small repertoire to perform publicly, practicing the works extensively to optimize performance, and, to compensate for inevitable age-related declines in motor speed, playing certain passages more slowly than in his youth to heighten the contrast between slow and fast material. Sports fans may recognize similar SOC processes at play in the career of basketball player Michael Jordan, who maintained extraordinary athletic effectiveness late in his career by selecting key moments of games in which to concentrate his energies, by optimizing his fitness through physical strength and conditioning programs, and by compensating for minor physical declines by developing novel techniques for scoring that required less exertion than those he employed in his youth.

The ways in which people balance selection, optimization, and compensation vary across the life-span. Early in life, resources primarily are directed toward growth and the development of competencies. In middle adulthood, people seek to use their personal and social resources to maximize gains. In old age, as resources decline, people must compensate for declines to avoid substantial negative outcomes. Although biological declines are inevitable in the later years, a decline in social resources is not. Drawing on social ties and cultural resources, then, has the potential to offset the losses in well-being that might otherwise accompany old age.

Research by Freund and Baltes (1998) illustrates the role of SOC processes in successful aging. A sample of elderly residents of Berlin completed a self-report measure of SOC processes. The measure tapped their ability to select a small number of significant life goals on which to focus, to concentrate their energies on a goal until it is achieved, and to compensate for setbacks by developing novel strategies or drawing on social resources. People who reported using SOC strategies also reported higher levels of subjective well-being and more positive affective and interpersonal experiences. The relationships between SOC variables and well-being were maintained even after controlling for the effects of Big Five constructs and beliefs in the internal versus external controllability of life events.

An interesting possibility is that the employment of SOC strategies may influence not only psychological well-being, but physical health. Those who successfully compensate for biological declines may maintain lifestyles that enhance fitness and length of life. Data on this question are sparse and merely suggestive at present (Baltes & Freund, 1999). The potential relation between SOC processes and physical well-being, then, clearly is deserving of further study.

Although developed in the study of successful aging, the SOC model is a valuable general framework for investigating personality development throughout the whole course of life. From the beginning, people face tasks of selection, optimization, and compensation as they attempt to cope with age-specific life tasks. The success of development and adaptation ultimately depends on the effectiveness of strategies implemented to enhance, maintain, and manage the loss of an individual's assets. The SOC model is applicable whether one's developmental criterion of interest is general well-being or a specific component of functioning, such as school or job performance, success in cognitive or interpersonal tasks, or success in managing emotional experiences. The model makes it possible to capture how different personality processes develop over time and how different behaviors may be implemented to achieve the same outcomes. It also captures interactions among biological and psychological subsystems in personality functioning; through the psychological system, people can develop strategies to enhance biological competence and fitness and to compensate for biological decline. Finally, the SOC model provides a framework for understanding how multiple biological and social determinants of personality functioning converge on the individual, and how the individual can retain the capacity to function as an active agent who contributes to his or her own destiny.

## PSYCHOSOCIAL TRANSITIONS AND PERSONAL DETERMINANTS OF LIFE TRAJECTORIES

As we have seen, development is in many respects a continuous process. Opportunities, constraints, competencies, preferences, and beliefs shift gradually across the life course. Nonetheless, discontinuities can be found. Discrete change often occurs when people face life transitions, that is, changes in personal circumstances that may compel them to develop novel strategies for meeting social demands and to reassess their sense of self, their role in family and social life, their personal goals, and the standards through which they evaluate their actions (e.g., Baltes et al., 1998; Cantor & Kihlstrom, 1987).

Transitions can be triggered by either biological or social factors, and the relative import of biology and society is not the same for all transitions. Hormonal changes, not social changes, trigger the transition from latency to the beginnings of sexual attraction (McClintock & Herdt, 1996; chapter 5). Social norms, not biological determinants, create cultural and historical variation in the modal age at which people undergo transitions such as the move from single to married life or the beginning of parenthood.

Among the circumstances that trigger life transitions, some are normative and predictable whereas others are fortuitous. Opportunities for personal or professional development may be found in chance encounters with individuals who may prove crucial to one's development. Disruptions to development occur when individuals confront unpredictable illnesses, accidents, or changes in sociopolitical circumstances. In discussing the role of fortuity in personal development, Bandura (1982, 1997) has emphasized that, despite the uncontrollability of the chance event, personal agency is still of importance to development. People often must draw on personal resources to capitalize on chance opportunities or to minimize the effects of random setbacks.

In many cultures, the primary psychosocial transitions include beginning school, starting a career, forming a family, and retiring. When considering these transitions, one should recall that their social meaning has changed historically, with the changes being particularly rapid in the past century. Sociocultural changes have been driven, in part, by demographic factors such as changes in birth rates, life expectancy, normative educational levels, and the roles played by males and females in society. As compared with contemporary society, people of earlier centuries became involved in jobs at an earlier age, received less education, and had different social rights and duties. The last century has seen a fall in the average age at which people reach puberty, a rise in the age at which people complete their education, a massive entrance of women into the work force, a rise in the age of marriage, delays in retirement, and prolonged expectancy of life. As norms change, the meaning of any given transition changes.

Marrying in one's teens is now exceptional in many regions where it used to be common. Continuing one's education into adulthood is common, although it used to be exceptional. These changes in social contexts and practices may profoundly affect life-course trajectories (Hurrelmann, 1988).

## PSYCHOSOCIAL TRANSITIONS AND PERSONAL AGENCY

The question for personality psychology is how to conceptualize the role of personality factors in people's efforts to cope with psychosocial transitions. An obvious point is that a given transition may have different effects on different people. A deeper point is that personality factors are not passive moderators of transitions. It is not merely the case that people with different dispositional styles may respond differently when confronted with a given transition. Instead, self-regulatory factors may determine whether the person experiences the transition in the first place or has the resources needed to cope with a transition once it occurs. People can partly determine whether a transition ultimately serves as a disruption to development or an opportunity for personal growth.

This point is illustrated in the study of unemployment. Dropping out of the job market is a highly significant transition, which can substantially impair physical and mental health. An important task for personality psychology, then, is not only to chart individual differences in the tendency to remain employed or to be vulnerable to the deleterious effects of unemployment. One also should explore the proactive steps people can take to enhance their ability to reenter the job market, and the personality mechanisms that mediate these effects. Research by Vinokur, Van Ryn, Gramlich, and Price (1991) has taken up this task. These investigators enrolled large numbers of unemployed American adults in a relatively brief training program (consisting of eight 3-hour sessions), which taught skills for identifying and pursuing new employment. As compared with people in a control condition who did not receive this training, the trained individuals had higher levels of employment and higher earnings at a follow-up assessment $2^{1}/_{2}$ years after the intervention (Vinokur et al., 1991). Mediational analyses indicate that the intervention had its effects largely through its influence on perceived self-efficacy (Van Ryn & Vinokur, 1993; also see Vinokur & Schul, 1997). Perceived self-efficacy influenced the behaviors involved in seeking reemployment both directly and indirectly, through its effects on job search attitudes. By focusing on agentic capabilities rather than static vulnerabilities, these investigators were able to demonstrate how a brief intervention can enhance people's potential to bring about significant, long-term improvements in their course of development.

The role of efficacy beliefs in employment deserves greater attention in nations outside the United States. In many countries, educational systems fail to prepare individuals for competition in the global economy. Many youths thus risk passing from unemployment to retirement without ever holding a permanent job. These conditions inevitably erode competencies, self-esteem, and perceptions of personal efficacy. Yet, even in such difficult circumstances, a great many young people do persevere enough to attain economic self-sufficiency, a fact that attests to the human capacity to overcome difficult circumstances. A related issue is the set of long-term implications of leaving school prematurely to enter the labor force. Dropping out not only leads to jobs of low economic status but also may markedly affect personal development, especially in an age in which higher education has become increasingly important to finding and maintaining a socially valued occupation (Hogan and Lichter, 1995; Leffert & Petersen; 1995; Smith, 1995).

Another key personal transition is forming a family. This remains an important goal for most men and women, despite significant changes in the Western family in the recent era (Hess, 1995; Scabini, 1995). Nowadays,

people generally marry later and have fewer children than in the past. Marriage rates have declined in most Europeans countries and in the United States (Monnier and Guibert-Lantoine, 1996). Young independent living (i.e., living neither with one's parents nor a spouse) has increased in the United States, but decreased in southern European countries and remained relatively stable in most countries of northern and central Europe (Cherlyn, Scabini and Rossi, 1997). Being an unmarried single or a stepparent is more common than it used to be. Separations and divorce have increased. These changes in many ways have altered parents' and children's social and economic opportunities, as well as their values and attitudes about the family. Conjectures about how these changes will affect the function and future of contemporary family (e.g., Donati, 1998) must take account of the proactive role of individual decisions and actions in the maintenance of the family unit.

People's belief in their efficacy to fulfill family roles may be a significant personal determinant of the well-being of family members. Self-efficacy for parenting skills is an important factor here (Coleman & Karraker, 1997). Parents who lack social support and have temperamentally difficult children have lower perceptions of their efficacy for parenting and, in turn, more postpartum depression (Cutrona & Troutman, 1986). As we note in our discussion of family life in chapter 8, the modeling of parenting skills can enhance parents' efficacy perceptions (Gross, Fogg, & Tucker, 1995).

Education is another domain in which social and personal factors combine to determine individual achievement. Despite improvements in educational access, quality of education remains highly linked to students' socioeconomic background in many parts of the world. Higher socioeconomic status still predicts higher educational achievement, with social class being positively related to career achievements even after controlling for educational attainment (Erikson and Johnson, 1996; Fisher et al., 1996; Shavit & Blossfeld, 1993). The effects of socioeconomic status, though, are heavily mediated by individual self-regulatory processes. Higher economic status influences children's academic achievement largely through its effects on parental efficacy beliefs and aspirations, which in turn influence the beliefs and goals of their children. Investigators increasingly have come to recognize that educational aspirations and success rest heavily on self-regulatory capacities, which in turn are a product of social experiences in society, the home, and school (Bandura et al., in press; Schunk & Zimmerman, 1994).

Finally, old age is the site of what may be the most profound of changes in the human experience. In most industrialized countries, life expectancy increased by about 10 years in the last half-century and 25 years in the last full century. The population's age distribution used to have a pyramidal shape, with a thick base and narrow apex. Now, the base and apex are of similar width. The percentage of the population above age 65 actually exceeds that below 18 in some countries. Medical progress has dramatically improved quality of life among the elderly. Economic conditions and social policies in many Western nations have made the elderly wealthier than in the past. Many elderly have access to family support and social structures that enable them to sustain strategies that can attenuate or compensate for unavoidable losses due to aging (Baltes, 1997).

As we have just noted in our review of the SOC model, the psychology of aging is yet another domain in which people are found to be capable of proactively influencing the nature of their experiences. Well being depends not just on the availability of medical technologies and favorable socioeconomic conditions but on people's employment of psychological strategies that enable them to maximize the opportunities and minimize the psychological losses of the advanced years (Baltes, 1997).

## SUMMING UP

Our review of personality development across the course of life has highlighted two main themes. One is the sheer complexity of the theoretical and empirical issues in this domain of inquiry. It is not possible to gain a full understanding of work on personality development unless one makes explicit the diverse theoretical and meta-theoretical assumptions that have guided investigation in the area. With respect to empirical findings, it has become clear not only that there are substantial continuities in human personality across the life course, but also that these continuities cannot be understood via simple analyses that examine only personal qualities of individuals. One must address the dynamic person–situation transactions that contribute to the continuity of personality, and the cultural and historical contexts in which these transactions occur. Traditional notions of age-linked or stage-based development also have proven inadequate. People do not develop according to fixed schedules. Instead, they develop along life trajectories that are influenced by sociohistorical and cultural pressures and opportunities.

A second main theme is that individuals have the potential to contribute in an agentic manner to their development. With increasing age, cognitive capability, and life experience, people develop greater capacities for self-regulation. They become able to control their emotional states, reflect upon themselves, and plan courses of action. They develop strategies for optimizing their development in the face of gains and losses which may occur due to biological change and social events. We continue to explore this capacity for self-direction in the chapters ahead.

# CHAPTER SIX

# Genetics, Brain Systems, and Personality

This chapter examines the contribution of genes to the potentialities of the individual and reviews biological systems that support personality development and functioning. We quite intentionally cast the scientific problems to be solved in terms of contributions, potentialities, and support. We hope at the outset to bypass outmoded dichotomies and to avoid simple statements about how genes determine behavior. The field must move beyond formulations that pit nature against nurture or maturation against learning. Such formulas falsely dichotomize factors that actually work together. They deflect psychology's attention from scientific advances in understanding the processes through which biology and culture coact. Extraordinary progress in the fields of molecular genetics and neuroscience in the past 20 years has revealed a subtle interplay of genetic and experiential processes (Gottlieb, 1998). As we consider the role of genetic factors and biological systems in personality, we can do so from the basis of a firm consensus that the biological organism dynamically interacts with the environment throughout the life course.

An understanding of biological potentialities and constraints is important not just for its own sake but because it may enable one to exploit environmental opportunities for personal growth. The recognition that biology and experience influence one another raises new questions about how behavioral experiences can compensate for inherited liabilities (Brown, 1999; Nelson, 1999). It also bears on classic questions. To what extent are organisms born with behavioral capacities built in? If capacities are built in, then the environment could be seen to select from among a range of potentialities (as seems to be the case with immune system capacities, for example, in which antibodies are selected from an existing pool of antibodies that are part of the organisms' genetic makeup; Edelman, 1992). Alternatively, to what extent are environmental challenges and opportunities decisive for the genesis of organismic capabilities?

## THE ROLE OF GENETICS IN PERSONALITY DEVELOPMENT

In recent decades, psychologists increasingly have come to recognize that psychological experience cannot be understood without also understanding the biological features of the experiencing organism. Even students of sociocultural factors in personality development recognize that in order to understand the influence exerted by the environment on the person, one must also recognize that biological factors shape one's experience of the environment and that biology imposes constraints on the individual, society, and culture. A natural place to begin the study of biology and personality is with an analysis of the genetic mechanisms that transmit biological propensities across the generations.

We begin by considering some conceptual issues in the study of the biological bases of behavior. We next review basic mechanisms involved in the transmission and expression of genetic information. The chapter then explores

recent progress in behavior genetic analyses of individual differences. Subsequent sections review the neural mechanisms that ultimately must mediate any influence of genetics on personality; genetic influences on personality and social behavior ultimately must be understood not only in terms of heritability coefficients but in terms of underlying biological architecture. Within this section of the chapter, we review one of the great research traditions in the history of personality psychology, namely, the search for individual differences in neural systems that underlie affective and behavioral tendencies. The chapter concludes by addressing biological mechanisms in the most noticeable of human variations, biological sex differences. Throughout this chapter, we often will find that our current state of knowledge raises important scientific questions that the field is not yet able to solve.

### The Long Road from Genes to Behavior

In earlier eras, behavioral genetics was commonly associated with conservative, if not authoritarian, social agendas. Ideological struggles were so severe that in some circles it was considered inappropriate even to discuss the possibility that genetic factors play a role in social behavior. Times, however, have changed. Most investigators now acknowledge a role for genetic mechanisms in personality development and functioning.

The widespread acknowledgment of genetic influences does not imply that there is consensus on the crucial question of how genes influence individuals' affective, cognitive, and behavioral tendencies. Genes code for proteins, not actions. There is a long road from genetic material to phenotypic behavior and investigators do not all agree on the nature of this path. Some conceive of the genes as the primary instruction system that governs the growth of the biological mechanisms that underlie psychological dispositions. Findings in support of this view document that population variance in surface-level traits is partly, and sometimes primarily, explained by genetic factors rather than purely by environmental ones. Rather than being impressed by the consistency of such findings, other commentators question the basic assumptions of the behavioral genetic paradigm on which they are based. The separation of psychological traits into their genetic and environmental components fails to capture the facts of coaction among genetic and environmental factors (e.g., Lerner, 1995). Genes and environmental factors influence one another. Specifically, gene expression is influenced by environmental factors and behavioral experiences that affect both hormone levels and the cytoplasm of cells, where DNA is located (Gottlieb, 1998). As Gottlieb (1998) emphasizes, the genes thus are not a separate, encapsulated system that provides a blueprint for the developmental course of the organism. Instead, genes are one element of a continuously developing biological system. Like other elements, they are subject to influence by behavioral and environmental factors. "Natural selection has preserved (favored) organisms that are adaptively responsive both behaviorally and physiologically to their developmental conditions" (Gottlieb, 1998, p. 796). This fact becomes particularly apparent in the human case when one considers phenotypic variations across cultural settings, while recognizing that cultural changes take place much faster than the length of time over which natural selection operates. If the essential question is how genes and environment coact (Plomin, 1994), we must seek answers in paradigms that go beyond a simple partitioning of environmental versus genetic variance (Plomin, DeFries, McClearn, & Rutter, 1997).

**Strong and Weak Biologism**

Behavior genetic findings commonly violate both one's intuitions and one's ethical sense. Genetic factors seem to influence not only phenotypes that reflect basic biological systems (e.g., arousal and affective reactions) but others that would appear to be entirely sociocultural in nature (e.g., criminality, religious beliefs, political attitudes). How could we have genes for phenotypic categories that are contemporary social constructions?

Turkheimer (1998) provides a way out of this conceptual conundrum by distinguishing between strong and weak biological explanations of behavior. A strong explanation is one in which a high-level (i.e., surface-level) tendency can be explained in terms of a specific "structurally or functionally localized" (Turkheimer, 1998, p. 783) biological mechanism. To use an example from Turkheimer, if a mute individual is found to have stroke-induced damage in Broca's area, the brain mechanism provides a strong biological explanation of his muteness.

A weak biological explanation is one that simply posits the existence of some biological material that contributes to a surface-level characteristic. A weak explanation asserts that the explanation of the surface-level characteristic is to be found somewhere in the brain and body. Suppose another mute individual is found to have enrolled in a religious order that enforces muteness among its members. In principle, his muteness could be explained on biological grounds (e.g., in terms of biological mechanisms that might contribute to decision making, to individual-difference characteristics that are predictive of joining religious orders, etc.). One might garner support for this weak biological explanation by finding that identical twins show relatively high concordance in decisions as to whether to join religious orders.

The point, of course, is that no matter what the twin concordance data, these two explanations are different in type. The strong explanation links the surface characteristic to a specific underlying biological system. The weak explanation simply says that there must be some biological systems in the body, somewhere, that contribute to the surface-level characteristic. Turkheimer points out that in any materialist philosophy, the weak explanation is true essentially by definition. "There is no need to conduct empirical science to locate thoughts, feelings, and beliefs in the body and brain" (Turkheimer, 1998, p. 783). For complex psychological phenomena (such as making a decision to join a religious order), simply demonstrating that genetic-biological factors contribute in some way to surface-level characteristics is thus almost completely uninformative.

As Turkheimer analogizes, suppose one's computer system crashes owing to a "bug" in a software program one is running. One would not search the computer hardware in the hope of eventually locating an electronic structure that explains the crash. True, the hardware may function a bit differently when running programs that do or do not contain the software bug, but there is no specific, dedicated electronic structure that determines the crash. Instead, the crash is determined by the high-level software program. Similarly, suppose one wants to explains a complex psychological phenomenon. One would not often search the brain in the hopes of locating "the neurological structures that determine it, because there are no neurological structures that determine it" (Turkheimer, 1998, p. 784). Just as there is no "electronics of software crashes," or no "physics of carpets" (Harré, Clarke, & DeCarlo, 1985), there is no "neurology of religious beliefs" or "biology of political attitudes" because there are no single biological systems dedicated to these complex, multiply determined, socioculturally located phenomena.

Many complex psychological and sociocultural phenomena simply are not open to strong biological explanations. Criminality, happiness, proneness to divorce, the joining of religious orders, etc., certainly may be heritable in the weak sense that at birth, people differ in the likelihood with which they will experience one versus another outcome. But this in no way implies that the outcomes are biological in the strong sense that there are specific biological mechanisms that subserve each of the high-level tendencies (Turkheimer, 1998). As we emphasize throughout this text, it is risky and often foolhardy to explain a surface-level tendency by searching for a single biological or psychological system that is its cause. Multiple systems may contribute to any complex, molar, surface-level tendency. Different underlying systems may contribute to the same high-level tendency for different individuals.

## Definitional Issues in the Study of Genetics and Personality

Given the complexities in discussing the path from genes to personality structure and behavioral expression, it is best to begin with some clear definitions. Once terms are made explicit, one can address difficult issues with less risk of misunderstanding.

*Biological heredity* refers to the full set of biological processes through which characteristics are transmitted from parents to offspring. *Phenotype* refers to the observable characteristics of organisms in body structures and physiological and psychological functions, whereas *genotype* is the genetic contribution of an organism, that is, its inherited genetic elements. Multiple variations in genotypes occur depending on how inherited material is transmitted and assembled. As a consequence, offspring do not exactly replicate the genotypes of their parents and no two offspring (except identical twins) have exactly the same genotype. This variation yields extraordinary opportunities for natural selection.

A genotype consists of pairs of *genes*, each pair being composed of two *alleles*, which correspond to the alternative forms of a gene that may exist in a population and that a person inherits from each parent.

Genes are the functional units transmitted from parents to offspring. Genes have the double function of transmission of heritable information and diversification of traits across generations and among individuals. The entire collection of genes possessed by an organism is referred to as the *genome*.

Many genes contribute to phenotypic variations in a trait, a phenomenon referred to as *polygenic inheritance*. If the multiple genes each contribute a small amount to the phenotype, their effect is referred to as *additive*. Interactions among alleles may yield genetic influences that do not simply add up, or *nonadditive* genetic effects. Nonadditive effects may derive from the interaction of alleles at the same locus (dominance) or at different loci (epistasis). Particular genes may influence more than one phenotype, a phenomenon referred to as *pleiotropy*.

In organisms that reproduce sexually, allelic genes segregate and pass to different sex cells, or gametes, with each gamete receiving one allele. When gametes unite in fertilization the double dose of hereditary material is restored and a new individual is created. The new individual resembles his or her parents but of course is far from being a replication of them. Independent assortment and recombination of genes create great diversity between parents and offspring and among the different offspring of the same parents. In the reproduction process, alleles recombine into new pairs, which show different degrees of dominance due to the independent assortment of alleles. Some are dominant and others recessive, with the former masking the action of the latter. Since many genes are represented by multiple allele forms within a population (e.g., three codominant alleles govern the various blood groups) and many individual traits are affected by more than one gene, the number of increased allelic combinations adds to the interactions among genes in further expanding the diversity of genetic outcomes.

It is valuable also to consider genetic processes at a more specific level. In human beings, a process of cell division called meiosis ends in the formation of gametes. Each gamete has a nucleus containing one set of 23 chromosomes, which are brought together into 46 chromosomes (23 from each parent) when the egg and the sperm nuclei fuse together to create a new individual. Along each chromosome in the nucleus are thousands of genes, while around the nucleus in the cytoplasm and also in the membrane other chemicals join the action exerted by the genes. Chromosomes are thus the repository and the carriers of genes. *Loci* are the locations of genes on a chromosome. The alternate forms of alleles of a gene at a given locus determine its full range of variation at a given moment in a specified population.

Chromosomes consist of deoxyribonucleic acid (DNA), ribonucleic acid (RNA), and a variety of proteins. DNA is the chemical basis of heredity and the repository of genetic information. It contains, in specific subunits called *nucleotides*, a detailed set of chemical instructions for the activation and control of the biochemical process of life. Each nucleotide contains one of four organic bases: adenine (A), thymine (T), cytosine (C), and guanine (G). The total arrangement in orderly linear sequence of these bases (e.g., CAG TTCG...) along the DNA constitutes the individual's genotype, which conveys instructions that contribute to the assembling of his or her phenotype.

Since Watson and Crick's (1953a, b) famous contribution, DNA has been recognized as a double helix, consisting of "two helical chains both coiled round the same axis" (1953a, p. 737). The chains are linked by hydrogen bonds between the bases joined together in pairs in which the As and the Cs of one chain are respectively linked to the Ts and Gs of the other. "The precise sequence of the bases are the code which carries the genetical information" (1953b, p. 965).

Along the DNA genes are the chemical units that carry hereditary information. Chainlike molecules of nucleic acids encode instructions for producing the proteins that are largely responsible for the structure, development, and functioning of the organism.

DNA never leaves the cell nucleus. RNA transcribes and translates the genetic code into the cytoplasm, where protein synthesis takes place. Genes operate under the control of DNA, switching on and off at appropriate times in development. Some genes are directly involved in the production of proteins; others regulate, repair, or compensate for the activity of other genes, yielding remarkable organismic plasticity.

The transcription and translation from the DNA to the RNA is not a unidirectional process. Reverse effects, from RNA to DNA, have also been established (Gottlieb, 1998). Multicausality also reigns in that, as noted above, multiple factors affect the cellular environment in which genes become active and protein synthesis takes place. The existence of billions of nucleotide pairs and thousands of genes at each of the 23 pairs of chromosomes, of multiple interactions among genetic material and spontaneous or environmentally triggered mutations, and of interactions between DNA and RNA contribute to the incredible complexity of the human fabric.

Although genetic processes direct the production of proteins and proteins are the basic building blocks of the organism, genes do not completely determine the exact form of physiological structures. The environment contributes significantly to the unfolding and expression of the genotype. The action of genes is mediated by a number of biochemical and anatomical transformations. Proteins lead to cells and cells in their turn, by division, migration, adhesion, and differentiation, lead to tissues and bodily morphology. Variation is the rule at each step of this chain. Finally, resulting physiological structures merely set the potentialities for behavior. Thus, when we refer to genetic influence on personality, we actually are referring to a complex path involving genes and a variety of other biological systems that ultimately end in structures and processes supporting behavior.

Along this path from genes to behavior, there are reciprocal influences between biological processes and behavior. Development is "the result of regulatory processes that involve a dialogue between genes and the intracellular and extracellular environment" (Plomin, 1994 p. 16). The probabilistic epigenesis model of Gottlieb (1992, 1998) illustrates the interacting roles of genes and behavior at a number of different levels. As a general schematic diagram (which is a simplification of a somewhat more complex depiction of genetic and behavioral processes in Gottlieb, 1998)[1]:

Internal and external environment →

DNA ↔ RNA ↔ protein

Genetic expression is affected by activity in the cytoplasm of cells and by hormones enter-

ing the cell. The environmental influence on DNA can be represented as follows:

External environment ⟶ cytoplasm

Behavior/psychological
    function/experience ⟶ hormones

It is this interplay among biological mechanisms and between biology and experience that enables any given genome to yield a wide range of phenotypic expressions (Gottlieb, 1998).

## Behavior Genetic Analyses of Individual Differences

Behavior geneticists have worked to estimate the degree to which genetic and environmental factors and their interaction account for variability in the population in phenotypic characteristics. Thus, although ultimately interested in biological processes of heredity, investigators actually explore *heritability*, that is, the proportion of phenotypic variance accounted for by genetic differences among individuals (Plomin et al., 1997). Specifically, heritability estimates indicate the proportion of *observed variance* in individual-difference scores that can be attributed to genetic factors in the particular population studied. They do not, then, indicate the degree to which a given trait reflects the influence of heredity for an individual. Further, they say nothing about whether the expression of a trait may change in response to environmental modification or why a particular individual does or does not possess a given trait. Finally, no matter what the heritability of a phenotype, environmental considerations may still be crucial to understanding it. Although sociopolitical attitudes maybe heritable (Eaves, Eysenck & Martin, 1989), no one would hold conservative or radical views in the absence of a sociopolitical environment.

With this caveat in mind, one may fully appreciate the important contributions of quantitative behavior genetics. This field has overcome the problems posed by ethical and methodological limitations on human genetic research. One cannot manipulate human

---

[1] The influence of protein on RNA is a theoretical possibility specified in probabilistic epigenesis (Gottlieb, 1998).

genetic material through inbred strains of selective breeding, as is done routinely in studying animals. Instead, one must capitalize on experiments of nature and of culture. Twin designs compare individuals whose genetic relatedness varies systematically. Adoption designs distinguish genetic and environmental sources of variability by comparing biological relatives raised apart with unrelated individuals raised together. Family designs assess the resemblance between family members as a function of their relatedness.

■ *Twin Method.* Twin studies are the dominant behavior genetic paradigm. One compares monozygotic (MZ) twins, who are genetically identical, with dizygotic (DZ) twins, who share 50% of their genetic material on average. Arithmetic models estimate the degree of heritability of any given phenotype.

The simplest such model works as follows (Plomin & Daniels, 1987). In populations of MZ twins and of DZ twins, one measures the phenotypic trait of interest (via questionnaire, observer rating, or observable performance) and computes the correlation between each individual and his or her twin. Correlations are computed separately for MZ and DZ twins. The population variance due to heritability is estimated to be twice the difference between the MZ and DZ correlations [$H^2$(heritability)= $2(r_{MZ} - r_{DZ})$]; note that the difference is doubled because one is interested in the total genetic effect (100% versus 0% genetic overlap) but the data source involves only half the overall effect (100% versus DZ twins' 50% overlap).

The behavior genetic model estimates not only genetic effects, but also environmental influences. Whenever heritability coefficients are less than 100% (or further below 100% than one would expect based on considerations of measurement error), the model indicates that environmental factors influence the phenotype. Environmental variance can be partitioned into two components. *Shared* environmental effects make twins more similar than one would expect based on genetics alone. *Nonshared* effects are those that make even twins raised in the same household dif-

ferent from one another. Whereas shared environmental effects (income, housing, etc.) impinge equally on all members of a given family, nonshared environmental effects (accidents, differential parental treatment or perception of parenting, different peer groups) impinge differentially on family members (Plomin & Daniels, 1987). Since children may be treated differently, environmental factors may also impinge differently on MZ twins and DZ twins owing to assimilation mechanisms, which amplify diversities, and contrast mechanism, which decrease similarities. For example, the interactions between siblings may either exaggerate or reduce the initial differences between children in a given family (Rutter et al., 1997).

Subsequent years witnessed an expansion of the original equation and increased sophistication in data analysis (Eaves et al., 1989; Falconer, 1989; Plomin et al., 1997). Genetic variance is decomposed into additive and nonadditive components. Genetic–environment interactions are estimated. Phenotypic variance can be viewed as a linear composite of multiple terms:

$S^2$phenotypic = $S^2$ total genetic ($S^2$ additive + $S^2$ nonadditive) + $S^2$ total environment ($S^2$shared + $S^2$nonshared) + $S^2$ (genetic × environment) + $S^2$ error.

The above model is descriptive. Among recent developments is another modeling approach, which instead of conducting multiple group comparisons, enables the simultaneous estimate of multiple sources of influence from a single data set. The researcher first builds a mathematic model of anticipated causal relations and then estimates how well the model fits the empirical data. In the last two decades, access to larger populations, the assessment of twins reared together and apart, and analyses of whole extended families, including biological and nonbiological parents and half-siblings, have greatly expanded the information available and the possibility of decomposing the various sources of variance.

Despite these advances, caution in interpreting results is warranted. For example, the models employed assume that questions about genetics and personality structure can be answered nomothetically. Everyone typically is analyzed via the same model. A single population-wide estimate of heritability is computed. The approach thus is not sensitive to the possibility that standing with respect to a given trait may be determined primarily by genetics for some individuals but by environmental factors for others. Eley, Lichtenstein, & Stevenson (1999) have recently explored this issue in the study of antisocial behavior. In each of two large, independent samples from Sweden and Britain, genetics were found to differentially influence nonaggressive antisocial behavior in men versus women. Genetic factors strongly accounted for individual differences in antisocial behavior among women, whereas shared environmental factors were a major determinant among men. As the authors note, one possible explanation for this result is that men's level of exposure to shared factors that promote nonaggressive antisocial behavior is greater than women's (Eley et al., 1999). The possibility that heritability of a given characteristic will vary from one group to another is also implied by the idea that distinct subsets of the population inherit particular temperament profiles (Kagan, 1998a). Among subsets of people who inherit inhibited and uninhibited profiles, genetic factors may account for a substantial share of the variance in phenotypic profiles. In principle, among everyone else, interindividual variations may be primarily environmental in origin.

■ *Estimating Genetic and Environmental Effects.* Although there is controversy about the method, there is great agreement regarding the findings it yields. There is broad consensus of heritability over 70% (mostly additive) for general cognitive ability or IQ (McGue, Bouchard, Jacono & Lykken, 1993). There is much agreement on an average heritability of 50% (about 30% of which is additive) for each of the Big Five Personality dimensions, when measured either through self-reports or observer ratings (Loehlin, 1992; Riemann, Angleitner & Strelau, 1997). Similar figures are reported for traits of other taxonomies, such as the Eysenckian three-factor model (Eaves, Eysenck & Martin, 1989) or the eleven primary first-order factors and the three higher-order factors of Tellegen (Finkel & McGue, 1997; Tellegen et al., 1988; McGue, Bacon & Lykken, 1993).

Whereas resemblances between identical twins reflect both additive and nonadditive effects, resemblances between other genetically related individuals reflect mostly nonadditive effects. Lykken, McGue, Tellegen, and Bouchard (1992) have suggested that nonadditive genetic effects are particularly important in personality development since personality traits may be an "emergent property of a configuration of more basic traits that are themselves partly genetic in origin" (p. 1569). The term *emergenic* is proposed for this phenomenon. Extraversion, ego control, leadership, and creativity are among the emergenic traits produced by interacting polymorphic genes and "by configurations of polymorphic genes interacting with the environment both embryologically and during subsequent development" (Lykken et al., 1992, p. 1575).

Considerable heritability has also been found in childhood temperamental dimensions such as negative affectivity, activity level, and emotional regulation. Relevant evidence includes work employing multiple instruments, different samples of children, and admirably large samples (Goldsmith, Buss & Lemery, 1997; Saudino, McGuire, Reiss, Hetherington, & Plomin, 1995). Note that in this domain it is difficult to disentangle variation due to children's personality from that due to parents' personality, especially when temperament is assessed by parental reports (Goldsmith, Losoya, Bradshaw & Campos, 1994).

Genetic effects vary with age and sometimes in a manner that violates one's intuitions. Intuitively, one might expect genetic influences to diminish across the life course owing to the accumulation of environmental experiences. Surprisingly, genetic influences account for greater variance in IQ as age increases (McGue, Bouchard, Iacono, & Lykken, 1993). Longitudinal studies of personality dimensions yield findings that are closer to one's intuitions. With increasing age, genetics account for less variation in personality and environment accounts for more. A meta-analysis of twin studies from 1967 through 1985 shows that, as children grow up, they grow further apart in activity and impulsivity (McCartney, Harris & Bernieri, 1990).

Viken, Rose, Kaprio, and Koskenvuo (1994) analyzed nearly 15,000 twins who were studied over a 6-year time span and who represented cohorts varying in age from their late teens to their late 50s. Heritability coefficients for both extroversion and neuroticism were found to decrease with age. Accumulating nonshared effects apparently contributed to variation on personality dimensions over time. This finding accords with the general conclusion that nonshared environmental influences account for the lion's share of environmental variability in that nonshared factors outside the home become more prevalent over the course of social development. An important related issue is the role of genetic and environmental factors in personality stability and change. McGue, Bacon, and Lykken (1993) suggest that personality stability mostly results from genetic factors, whereas personality change depends on environmental influences.

In the findings involving both IQ and personality traits, genetic factors are shown to account for variance in broad, high-level individual-difference dimensions. These dimensions probably involve aggregates of multiple subdimensions. When lower-level dimensions are examined, genetic effects may diminish; this lessening occurs for cognitive abilities (Fulker, Cherny, & Cardon, 1993) but is equivocal for personality. Unlike intelligence, inheritance of personality may involve large numbers of factors that are relevant to particular subtraits (Finkel & McGue, 1997). As noted by Loehlin (1982), the examination of broad personality dimensions may mask significant differences in heritability of lower-order personality traits.

One's intuitions also are violated by findings regarding environmental influences. Intuitively, shared environmental effects such as social class, culture, or parental rearing style would seem to shape personality structure. In one of the most surprising findings in the personality literature, behavior genetic studies suggest that such shared effects are negligible (Plomin & Daniels, 1987). Rearing MZ twins together appears not to make them more similar on broad-band personality measures than rearing them apart (Bouchard et al., 1990). This counterintuitive finding does not, however, imply that environmental influences are irrelevant. The correlation between scores of identical twins reared in the same household is only about .50; identical twins raised in the same culture and household differ substantially (e.g., Bouchard et al., 1990; Plomin & Daniels, 1987). This implies a major role for the nonshared environment. Nonshared environmental effects reliably account for nearly 50% of the variation in people's standing on personality dimensions.

The fact that unique environmental experiences of a family member appear to predominate over shared, within-family influences suggests that those family processes that are influential do not involve sociostructural parameters (family income, education etc.). Instead, they may involve the family relational system and the microenvironments that develop within families. This conclusion calls attention to the long tradition of studies on family relations and the unique network of interpersonal relationships in which individuals' lives unfold (Bateson, 1972; Minuchin, 1974).

On the other hand, the notion that nonshared environmental effects predominate and shared effects are negligible cannot be assumed to hold universally. With respect to methods, estimates of nonshared environmental variance include variance due to measurement error; this may cause nonshared effects to be overestimated. With regard to results, exceptions to the rule can be found. Waller and Shaver (1994) studied self-reported experiences and attitudes about romantic relationships in MZ and DZ twins. Genetic factors accounted for little variance on dimensions of romantic beliefs, whereas shared environmental factors accounted for 20 to 30% of the variance on some dimensions. Although criminality has been shown to have a genetic component, clear shared environmental factors are observed across studies. Shared environmental factors such as peer pressure and home difficulties contribute to juvenile delinquency (Di Lalla & Gottesman, 1989; Lyons et al., 1995; Maughan & Rutter, 1997; Rowe, Rodgers & Meseck-Bushey, 1992). Relatedly, the work of Eley et al. (1999), noted above, documents that shared environmental factors significantly influence levels of nonaggressive antisocial behavior (whereas genetic factors strongly influence levels of aggressive conduct). Further, specific, discrete shared experiences may impinge significantly, and in a common manner, on that subset of siblings who happen to encounter them. Parental loss has been reported to be an environmental factor that raises siblings' (pairs of female twins in this study) risk for depression and anxiety (Kendler, Neale, Kessler, Heath, & Eaves, 1992).

Behavior genetic data also suggest that the influence of heredity extends far beyond IQ and the Big Five, although there is less consensus in other domains. Variation in social attitudes, such as conservatism and radicalism (Eaves et al., 1989), risk of divorce (McGue & Lykken, 1991), and child rearing styles and socioeconomic status (Rowe, 1994) is claimed to have a genetic basis. These are precisely those domains in which biological explanations are, of necessity, "weak" ones (Turkheimer, 1998), as discussed above.

■ *Genetics and the Environment.* Behavioral geneticists emphasize that the child's genetic constitution influences the environment he or she experiences. Genetic propensities play a role in eliciting, selecting, and modifying the child's environment. Genetic factors thus may influence environmental variables such as parental warmth, peer acceptance, and social

support (Plomin and Bergeman 1991; Plomin, 1994). When traditional measures of the environment, such as children's and parents' perceptions of family environments, are treated as phenotypes in genetic analyses, significant genetic influences are found. As Plomin (1994) reports, genetic contributions consistently emerge in children's perceptions of parents' and siblings' behavior toward them. Although further research is needed in this area, thus far perceived acceptance, rejection, warmth, and affection have repeatedly shown significant genetic effects. Genetic effects also appear to influence a wide range of extrafamilial environmental factors involving peers and teachers and including events such as accidents, television viewing, and exposure to drugs (Plomin, 1994).

Genetic influences account for a smaller percentage of variance in environmental measures than in indices of intelligence and personality dispositions. Nonetheless, the former findings deserve the personality psychologist's careful consideration. They constrain claims of environmental influences on personality. When relating an environmental factor to a concurrently measured personality characteristic, one must consider the possibility that inherited qualities shaped the environment. Ultimately, one must understand the processes through which heredity operates on and coacts with social contexts.

One technique for addressing this complex issue and disentangling the multiplicity of reciprocal interactions comes from work on genotype–environment (GE) correlations. This work follows on Plomin, De Fries and Loehlin's (1977) distinction between passive, reactive (or evocative), and active correlations (Loehlin and Rowe, 1992; Plomin, 1994; Scarr, 1992). "GE correlations represent a restricted set of gene-environment transactions, a subset defined by a statistical association between environmental and genetic effects. When there is a tendency for an individual with an above-average genotype to be exposed to an above-average environment, and vice versa, a GE correlation is present" (Loehlin and Rowe, 1992, p. 363). Taking the examples provided by

Plomin: "passive GE (genotype-environment) correlation occurs because children share heredity as well as environmental influences with members of their family . . . for example, if musical ability is heritable (and this is not known), musically gifted children are likely to have musically gifted parents who provide them with both genes and environment conducive to the development of musical ability. Reactive, or evocative GE correlation refers to the experiences of the child derived from reactions of other people to the child's genetic propensities. For example, musically talented children might be picked out at school and given special opportunities. Active GE correlation occurs when individuals select or create environments that are correlated to their genetic propensities. For example, even if no one does anything about a child's musical talent, the child might gravitate toward musical environments" (Plomin, 1994, pp. 106–107). In this way, genes affect personality development early in life by predisposing the individual to experience a congenial environment; then over the course of development, genes predispose the individual to engage in certain activities or relations that elicit several environmental responses and to shape his or her own environment, within the family and outside.

## Assessing the Traditional Behavior Genetic Paradigm

Multivariate genetic analyses conducted within a variety of nonadoptive and adoptive family designs have provided a wealth of information about the degree to which interacting genetic and environmental factors contribute to individual differences. The findings are consistent and often surprising. They open promising directions for research on the mediators of genetic influences.

Much remains to be done, however, before drawing broad generalizations. The limitations of measures, the restricted size of populations, and the difficulty of controlling the multiple and conflicting influences exerted by both the genotype and the environment suggest caution. One may conservatively state that behavioral genetic analyses supply devel-

opmental and personality psychologists with new information about sources of variance in individual differences and the existence of interactions between nature and nurture. However, the mechanisms through which genetic influences act – in different environments, at different points in time, and especially at the level of the individual – require considerable clarification. Acknowledging the importance of genes does not warrant an infinite regression to genetic determinism. Such a move sidesteps the most critical issues regarding the processes, structures, and mechanisms that govern personality functioning over time and at any given point in time. The role of inherited factors in personality development cannot be fully understood without exploring the ways in which environmental experiences affect the expression of genetic potentialities (Gottlieb, 1998).

Population statistics of the sort provided by behavior genetic paradigms provide, at best, only gross indications of the mechanism that operates at the level of individual experience. Thus, it is not surprising to find severe criticism of this literature from various quarters (e.g., Shweder & Sullivan, 1990). Those who emphasize the plasticity of psychological and biological mechanisms and a systems view of development are particularly critical. To such investigators, behavior genetic research rests on a conception of genetic influence that is "counterfactual" (Lerner, 1995, p. 146). Behavior genetic methods estimate the degree to which distinct genetic versus environmental factors influence a trait. It is the premise that there are such things as distinct genetic versus environmental factors that comes under attack. As we stressed above, the environment and genetic material coact. To cite an example from Gottlieb (1991), environmental events can influence hormonal levels; hormones, in turn, enter cell nuclei and activate DNA, which in its turn triggers protein production. Attributing independent causality to genetic mechanisms in the production of broad personality characteristics is, then, seen to be an error. Lerner (1995) argues that this error has pernicious social consequences. By promoting the scientifically unwarranted perspective that genetics *cause* traits and behaviors, the behavior genetic view may deflect attention from the broad scope of environmental interventions that can beneficially shape the conditions of people's lives.

The social and behavioral sciences must avoid a repetition of past divisions and sterile controversies. The positions of behavioral geneticists such as Plomin and systems developmentalists such as Lerner do differ in a fundamental way. Yet it may be possible to express these differences in a manner that capitalizes on similarities and integrates known findings. Both positions do share a probabilistic assumption regarding the multiple outcomes of personality development, in light of their recognition of the complexity of the multiple interacting systems that regulate development and functioning. Both positions recognize plasticity and potentialities of the genetic system. Both reject the notion that heritability coefficients imply predetermination of phenotypic characteristics. Both behavioral geneticists and developmental psychologists share the goal of improving people's quality of life, and both advocate environmental changes to maximize human potential. One wonders, then, where the sources of the divergent opinions lie.

In this regard, one should recall that the language of scientific debate is not only a means of conveying investigators' thoughts. It also is an interface, which mediates others' inferences about the investigators' thoughts and intentions. The language of debate in behavioral genetics, like all language, is open to multiple inferences. It illustrates the multiple interpretations that are possible in scientific language and the concomitant difficulty of specifying scientific positions unequivocally. Discussions sometimes appear to overlook the critical distinction between estimates of variation and of causation. The existence of significant variation due to genetics does imply some manner of inherited influence. However, heritability estimates do not yield, or even directly point to, the sort of causation generally sought in the sciences, in which one

seeks to identify specific underlying mechanisms and processes that produce a phenomenon of interest (Salmon, 1989).

There can be no doubt that genes play a role in shaping psychological phenotypes. However, it is unlikely that we inherit personality traits or behaviors as such. Rather, we inherit "chemical templates that produce and regulate proteins involved in building the structures of nervous systems and the neurotransmitters, enzymes and hormones that regulate them" (Zuckerman, 1995, p. 331). The rich and varied interplay between persons and their environments undoubtedly interacts with these biological processes; however, the causal mechanisms involved are not particulary well understood as noted by Rutter et al. (1997). Studies of pathology illustrate how genes drive experience (as in the case of phenylketonuria) and how experience (radiation) may influence genes. Analogous findings are rare in the study of "normal" human behavior and "healthy" personality functioning; evidence that examination related stress modulates gene expression involved in immune system response among medical students is a rare exception (Glaser et al., 1990).

## Moving the Behavior Genetic Paradigm Forward

Although physical appearance (height, weight) is strongly genetically determined, it is the environment that decides to treat differently the taller from the shorter, the fat from the thin, the dark-skinned from the light-skinned. An important new direction for research on genetics and personality is to examine environmental mechanisms that are essential to the link from genes to behavioral expressions and social outcomes. In this regard, Bronfenbrenner and Ceci (1994) highlight the *proximal processes* through which the genetic potential for effective psychological functioning is achieved. Proximal processes refer to reciprocal interactions between an acting, evolving biopsychological human organism and the persons, objects, and symbols in the immediate environment. They call attention to the material conditions in which these interactions take place and the cognitive processes and affective investments these interactions involve. Such a research direction necessitates expansion of not just the quantity but also the type and quality of data one acquires in studying personality development. Rather than relying exclusively on retrospective self-reports of generic behavioral tendencies, one must obtain more careful measures of both personal attributes and features of the social environment.

■ *Molecular Genetics.* A second promising development is the use of molecular genetic methods. Rather than plotting twin concordances in ignorance of specific genetic mechanisms responsible for similarities in twin pairs, investigators focus on the genetic mechanisms themselves. In so doing, they begin to provide an account of the processes leading from genes to action, which behavior genetic methods simply cannot provide.

A key recognition in molecular genetic research on personality is that no single gene is likely to control a personality phenotype. Instead, a multitude of genes may contribute to a global affective or behavioral tendency. The label *quantitative trait loci* (QTL) (Plomin & Caspi, 1998; Plomin, Owen, & McGuffin, 1994) has been given to chromosomal regions associated with detectable effects on a phenotype. A quantitative trait locus is a segment of DNA that may contain a gene affecting a continuous trait but may also contain other DNA of closely linked genes that may not play any coding function. Under the assumption that genetic effects are additive, the effects of a large number of different QTLs may add up to explain jointly the genetic variance in a trait.

Molecular genetic research on personality characteristics is quite new, the first reports having appeared in 1996 (Lesch et al.). We briefly convey the nature of the work here, partly drawing on a review by Plomin & Caspi (1998). We recognize that any summary of research in this burgeoning field of study will soon be out of date.

The largest body of studies has examined the potential link between novelty seeking (see Cloninger Adolffsson, & Svrakic, 1996, and

coverage later in this chapter) and a gene that codes for the production of a dopamine receptor (dopamine D4, DRD4), which exists in both short and long allelic forms. The short forms code for a dopamine receptor that is more efficient in binding dopamine than are the long forms. Thus, people who possess the short forms should have higher levels of dopamine and therefore have less need to seek novelty to stimulate additional dopamine release. People with the long form should be low in dopamine and therefore should be novelty seekers.

Two initial findings provided encouraging support for this hypothesis (Ebstein et al., 1996; Benjamin et al., 1996). The DRD4 variation, assessed via blood samples from research participants, accounted for 4 to 6% of the variance in self-reports of novelty seeking. Subsequent findings, however, were quite mixed. The next 10 research reports on this phenomenon revealed as many failures as successes in finding a relation between DRD4 variations and novelty seeking (Plomin & Caspi, 1998). Although methodological issues, such as limited sample sizes, could account for some failures to replicate (Plomin & Caspi, 1998), it remains a fact that the link from DRD4 to novelty seeking is not a robust result.

Other traits have been explored. Lesch et al. (1996) related neuroticism to variations in an allele involved in the production of a protein that influences levels of serotoninergic activity in cortical and limbic regions of the brain. The presence versus absence of a particular amino acid sequence yields long versus short versions of this allele. Lesch et al. (1996) reported that this genetic variation accounts for 3 to 4% of the variance in self-reports of neuroticism.

It is important to recognize that even if one does identify a QTL that is reliably related to a personality trait, this does not imply that the QTL relates to that trait uniquely. The QTL, in other words, may not be dedicated to the specific trait that the investigator happened to choose to study. DRD4 variations for example, have been related to phenotypes as diverse as hyperactivity, drug dependence, panic disorder, and depression (Plomin & Caspi, 1998). Such diffuse effects of a single QTL underscore the fact that the simple identification of a relation between a QTL and a self-reported dispositional tendency leaves unanswered many questions about the mechanisms underlying the variation in self-reports.

Separate genes or groups of genes may control different components of a broad phenotype. It may be valuable, then, to explore how different genetic influences relate to different aspects of the same phenotypic behavioral category. This approach is well illustrated by research on dyslexia by Grigorenko et al. (1997). Their results indicate that two different chromosomal regions are linked to two quite distinct phenotypes involving phonological awareness versus single word reading.

The same genes can yield different phenotypes depending on whether they are inherited from the mother or from the father. Skuse et al. (1997) have studied females with Turner's syndrome, which is caused by the possession of only one complete X chromosome. Females with a paternally derived X chromosome proved to have much better social skills than those with a maternally derived X chromosome.

■ *Genetics and Personality: Final Caveats.* Research in both traditional behavior genetics and more recent molecular approaches display great sophistication and care in its handling of potential genetic influences on phenotypes. However, one cannot help but be disappointed that equal care has not been devoted to conceptualizing and measuring the phenotypes themselves. The phenotypes under consideration generally involve behavioral preferences and affective tendencies. However, investigators rarely have assessed affect or behavior. Instead, they have assessed beliefs; the phenotypic measures of personality in these studies generally are self-reports. Self-reports surely are statistically related to behavioral and affective mechanisms to a significant degree. However, they are not identical to these mechanisms. The difficulty of linking self-reports of neuroticism to physio-

logical markers of the trait (see Eysenck, 1990; plus discussion below and in chapter 11) is but one illustration of this point. Further, the individual-difference constructs themselves may be conceptually limited. Focusing on highly global constructs may obscure the existence of qualitatively different subcategories of the phenotype. For example, IQ is a frequently examined phenotype in behavior genetic studies, yet the constructs raise problems among cognitive psychologists who recognize the diversity of mental abilities and differentiate among distinct components of intelligence (Gardner, 1993; Sternberg, 1985, 1997).

Investigations have yet to be made of the role of genetic influences in complex processes such as self-perception and social perception, causal attribution, decision making, motivation, volition, self-regulation, efficacy beliefs, and moral reasoning. From a life-span perspective, it would be crucial to establish the combined role of genes and the environment in sustaining tactics and strategies related to the maintenance of well-being, regulation of loss, and optimization of functioning through compensation (chapter 5). In such domains, it may be expected that genes and environment will impinge on personality differently at different times. Personality differences in juveniles may have quite different causes from personality diversities in adults. Genes may be responsible for specific behaviors at one time, whereas environments are responsible at another time.

Before drawing any conclusions about the role of the environment in these or any other psychological constructs, one must recognize that the restrictions of range in the environments represented in extant data limit any conclusions about heredity versus environment that one may draw. Heritability coefficients increase with uniform environments and decrease with highly diversified, impactful environments. The arguments in favor of genetic influences on personality undoubtedly have benefited from the study of populations whose development and functioning have basically taken place within the same cultural environment, with similar material conditions of life.

The fact that only a fraction of our world's citizens and environmental conditions are represented in psychological research unavoidably limits claims about the generalizability of findings. Populations who suffer from poverty, malnourishment, genocide, or displacement due to war remain underrepresented in research. The consideration of such harsh environmental conditions presents perhaps the greatest challenge to the conclusion that shared environmental factors play little role in shaping the developing individual. We also note that studies in non-Western cultures are rare in this literature.

In conclusion, great progress has been made in defining a domain of inquiry, setting the general coordinates for locating the effects of various sources of variation, refining a lexicon and a set of methods, and charting a general course for the study of individual personality development. However, much remains to be done, and progress will require not only enhanced quantitative and molecular evidence but firmer conceptions of the psychological variables that are meaningful targets of genetic investigation. It is clear that researchers who either ignore genetic effects or ignore environmental influences do so at their peril (Rutter et al., 1997). It is also clear that genetically sensitive designs (twin, adoptee, and blended family studies) will benefit by being complemented by longitudinal designs that are sensitive to how specific environments and interindividuals trajectories unfold over time and how individuals play a role in selecting and shaping their environments and thus charting their own pathways.

## BRAIN SYSTEMS AT THE BASIS OF PERSONALITY DEVELOPMENT AND FUNCTIONING

To appreciate how genes influence personality, one must understand the neurophysiological systems through which their effects are mediated. Therefore, we now consider the main

brain systems that sustain the development and functioning of personality. Although we cannot provide thorough coverage of the enormous literature in this brief section of our chapter, we will outline the main neural and biochemical systems involved. We recognize that future years are sure to expand greatly our knowledge of how the nervous system, endocrine system, and immune system coact on personality and are in turn influenced by the individual's own experiences and actions.

## Conceptualizations of Brain and Personality

Our understanding of the biological foundations of individuality and the person's capacity for self-regulation is still quite incomplete. Personality psychologists have devoted far greater attention to findings in behavior genetics than to research on biological systems that subserve personality functioning. Textbook coverage commonly reflects this fact. In principle, one might have expected personality psychologists to focus initially on specific biological systems and processes and then to inquire about genetic bases of these mechanisms. In practice, however, it seems to have been easier for the field to handle behavior genetic data than to deal with findings emanating from psychoneuroimmunology, neuropsychology, and psychophysiology.

Although advances in the neurosciences have been complex and diverse, they point to a simple conclusion. Multiple neural systems act in concert to produce complex psychological phenomena. Most phenomena of interest to the personality psychologist reflect numerous subsystems, which are reciprocally interconnected. This interconnectedness suggests that some traditional research paradigms must be interpreted with caution. Much research has been "locationist." Investigators seek a specific biological locus (i.e., a distinct brain region) that underlies a particular dispositional difference among individuals. In animal research, this locationist strategy is associated with experimentation in which a specific brain site is lesioned. In work on biological dimensions of personality (Eysenck,

1990; Gray, 1987; Gruzelier and Mecacci, 1992), investigators seek biological systems that underlie an observed behavioral tendency. Although the locationist strategy may be of great value, one must always recall that psychological experience is likely to reflect multiple systems and paths of causation. These inevitably include, in the human, reasoning processes through which people strive to regulate their physiology, emotions, and well-being.

In studying brain and personality, one must attend to the interrelations among three factors: biological mechanisms, psychological capabilities, and the social environment. The metaphor of a dialogue is useful here. Communications occur among three teams, each of which contains different actors who play different parts. There is the biological organism with its physical and chemical constituents, the mind as a self-regulating agency, and the environment with its social and physical features. Drawing on the work of Karli (1995, 1996), one can say that the person is a kind of *human trinity* made up of three major facets: a "biological individual, a social actor, and a reflecting and deliberating subject." Each "progressively emerges, coexists and closely interacts" with the others. Each facet carries on a dialogue with an environment of its own, namely, the biological organism's material environment, the actor's social milieu, and the self-reflective subject's inner world. These dialogues serve different aims, process different information, and are governed by different rules, although they coexist within the same being. Each represents a distinct level of organization within the person.

Significant changes in the paradigms that guide research in this area should be noted. Investigation used to rest on a tension-reductive model of the organism. Psychological functioning was viewed primarily as a reactive process in which organisms responded to internal drives and external stimuli. Today, this model is recognized to be inadequate. It fails to explain the full range of potentialities of the organism, including individuals' agentic capacity to influence the environmental stimuli and the organism–environment transactions that they experience. Another change is in the conception of universal versus unique psychological qualities. Traditionally, a tacit assumption has been that inherited mechanisms underlie qualities that are common across individuals, whereas environmental factors explain unique, idiosyncratic psychological features. Today, in contrast, many investigators seek the origins of both similarity and uniqueness in the interactions among biological mechanisms and sociocultural experiences.

Another broad development in conceptualizations of brain functioning and personality is the recognition that the brain is not an encapsulated system. Brain functioning depends heavily on the activity of other biological systems. The science fiction notion of a disembodied brain that can maintain its normal psychological functions is just that – fiction. The functioning of the central nervous system is directly related to that of the endocrine system and indirectly linked to that of the immune system. An understanding of brain systems and personality development thus requires a broader understanding of how these systems interact over time (Kolb & Whishaw, 1990).

Finally, perhaps the greatest change in the study of brain from a generation ago is a change in research technologies. In the past, investigators were forced to rely primarily on animal models or human cases of brain injury. Today, imaging techniques enable one to explore the brain bases of normal human psychological functioning.

In the following sections, we provide an overview of brain structures and then of brain functions. We then review conceptual models of brain and personality.

## Brain Structures and Processes

The brain itself is made up of populations of cells. Several billion neurons are devoted to the task of transmitting information between the periphery and the center and connecting the various structures of the brain. The existence of multiple neural pathways provides for the complexity and flexibility of behavior. Impulses are transmitted from one nerve to another through a variety of media. These include neurotransmitters (such as acetylcholine, norepinephrine, and dopamine), neuroregulators (among them enzymes such as monoamine oxidase and endogenous morphinelike peptides such as endorphins), and hormones (among them cortisol, androgens and estrogens). This brain chemistry regulates the excitation level of neurons and shapes the multiple connections among them (Zuckerman, 1991, 1994).

The brain is linked to the rest of the body both neurally and chemically. Nerve cells throughout the peripheral nervous system bring impulses from brain to body and from body to brain. Chemical communications occur through substances released via the bloodstream, such as hormones and peptides. Chemical substances produced by the body's activities reach the brain via the blood, and the brain acts on the body by manufacturing or modulating the chemical substances released into the blood. The endocrine glands release into the bloodstream chemical substances that influence psychological functioning by propagating neural information, maintaining metabolic functions, and alerting and protecting the organism against noxious agents and stimulations. Brain and body thus are indissociably integrated by biochemical and neural connections.

Brain growth, although genetically programmed, is sensitive to the environments in which it takes place and to the information the brain is currently processing. Over the course of development, as the individual's life history progresses and experiences accumulate, there occurs a progressive bringing into play of "higher" anatomical and functional levels, which are characterized by an increasing plasticity. Higher functions subordinate more elementary functions so that "bottom-up" causality becomes combined with a "top-down" causality, which ensures coherence (Karli, 1996). The processes of forming new connections in the service of

neural regulation take place throughout the life-span.

Considering three gross divisions of the brain helps to clarify its morphological architecture. These divisions are the telencephalon, the brainstem, and the cerebellum. The telencephalon includes the two hemispheres, which include the cerebral cortex's so-called gray matter of the brain (i.e., regions of brain that contain primarily neural cell bodies that are gray in color). Each hemisphere is conventionally divided into six so-called lobes: frontal, parietal, temporal, occipital, central, and limbic. Underneath the cortical gray matter is the white matter of the brain, which contains mostly cell axons that connect to other brain regions and neural structures. In addition, there are the ventricles and, deep within the cerebral hemispheres, large masses of gray matter called nuclei. Among these are the caudate nucleus, the putamen, the globus pallidus, and deep temporal structures (the amygdala and hippocampus). The brainstem, from which all cranial nerves emerge, includes the diencephalon (which itself includes the thalamus and the hypothalamus), the mesencephalon, and the rhombencephalon (including the pons, the medulla oblongata, and the reticular formation). Finally, the cerebellum is connected to the pons and fills the greater part of the posterior fossa of the skull.

Much evidence suggests that the brain has evolved through a series of organizational stages, with later-evolving systems showing greater complexity and modifiability. MacLean's (1977, 1990) classic notion of a *triune brain* distinguishes among three systems, each with its own organization and functions: a reptilian brain, which regulates vital bodily functions; a paleomammalian brain, represented in the limbic system[2]; and the neomammalian brain,

---

[2] The notion of a limbic system has somewhat fallen out of favor in light of knowledge about functional subsystems within the traditional limbic brain. Nonetheless, the concept continues to deserve mention, if only because it has been of such historical importance to the study of neural substrates of emotion.

consisting of the cerebral cortex, which covers the more ancient reptilian and paleomammalian structures. Interconnections among the structures yields a coherent brain system that is composed of interdependent parts. MacLean views these three systems as so radically different in structure and functioning that they essentially consititute three distinct mentalities, or three hierarchically organized brains in one. The integrative role that the cerebral cortex plays in coordiniating psychological experience leads MacLean to call the cortical hemispheres the psychencephalon (MacLean, 1990).

Different brain regions are interconnected through a set of subcortical structures. The thalamus serves as a relay station for neural pathways conveying sensory information from the periphery to the cortex. The hypothalamus plays a major role in controlling and coordinating the activities of the sympathetic and parasympathetic autonomic nervous systems. It also regulates the endocrine glands that secrete hormones – among them the pituitary, the thyroid, the adrenal, and the reproductive organs – and also is involved in immune system functioning. Other subcortical structures, such as the hippocampus, the septum, the cingulum, and the amygdala extending from the telencephalon to the diencephalon, are heavily involved in modulating emotional, motivational, and exploratory behaviors. The reticular formation is involved in regulating levels of alertness and excitation.

Through the autonomic nervous system and the endocrine system, then, the brain extends its connections and actions to the extreme periphery of the organism. Even systems such as the immune system that seem unconnected to the "psychological" features of the brain are now known to interact continuously with the brain (Maier, Watkins, & Fleshner, 1994).

## Brain Functions

One method of understanding the complexity of the brain is to distinguish among brain structures, as we have done above. Another is to distinguish among brain functions and the systems that serve those functions.

As Damasio (1994) notes, "the overall function of the brain is to be well informed about what goes on in the rest of the body, the body proper; about what goes on in itself; and about the environment surrounding the organism, so that suitable, survivable accommodations can be achieved between organism and environment" (p. 90). One may further distinguish among systems such as the ascending reticular system, whose primary function is to supply the activation needed for implementing mental activity; systems such as the limbic system, which are involved in directing behavior to avoid pain and search for pleasure, maintaining in this way the minimal conditions for surviving and coping effectively with life-challenging circumstances; and systems such as the cortex of the two hemispheres, whose primary function is to assimilate and integrate experience so as to purposively direct one's own behavior.

A first level of organization, which mostly concerns the satisfaction of primary biological needs, is subserved by mesencephalic and diencephalic structures through the mechanism of approach and avoidance and through systems supervising the experience of reward and punishment. At this level, the hypothalamus has an essential role in the regulation of approach and avoidance behavior. In particular, two neuronal systems contribute to the individual's basic attitude and overt behavior: a lateral system underlies approach and reward, and a medial periventricular system underlies aversion, flight, and defense. A second level of organization, concerning the temporal continuity and affective connotation of experience, is chiefly achieved by a number of structures of the temporal lobe at this level. The hippocampal formation is a nodal component of memory circuits, which allows the brain to play its role of history-produced and history-producing dynamic entity. The hippocampal formation closely interacts with the amygdala, which has an essential part in the interplay of appetitive and aversive responses and in the regulation of social behavior. A superior level of organization is finally achieved by the structures of the prefrontal cortex, which supervise the internal representation of experience and the individual's active projection into the world (Karli, 1995). The prefrontal cortex with its privileged development in the human brain, its great plasticity, and its reciprocal connections plays an important role in the planning, control, and adaptation of intentional behavior. At all levels, top-down and bottom-up interconnections are critical.

Research on the biological foundations of normal personality rarely has focused on the complex interactions among higher-level and lower-level neural systems. Instead, work has primarily examined subcortical structures, such as the ascending reticular activating system (ARAS) and the limbic system and their relation to the autonomic nervous system, as well as on various biochemical secretions of the glands. Recent years, however, have seen greater attention paid to the role of the two hemispheres and to multiple neurotransmitters. This new attention is supported by the progress of noninvasive techniques (not only electroencephalography and evoked potentials but new methods of imaging the brain's activity such as positron emission tomography and a variety of techniques for assessing hormonal variations in body liquids) to study how the different areas of the brain work and how different biochemicals may affect its functioning and behavior.

## BRAIN SYSTEMS AND PERSONALITY

### The Seminal Contributions of Pavlov

Much work on brain systems in personality functioning can be traced back to the contributions of Pavlov. On the basis of his classic research on conditioning, Pavlov (1927) reformulated the four Hippocratic temperaments. He did so by distinguishing between inhibitory and excitatory processes. Pavlov posited that choleric individuals are high in excitation, whereas melancholics are high in inhibition. Sanguine and phlegmatic individuals were both seen to be in a state of equilibrium, although with the former more inclined to excitation and the latter to inhibition.

Subsequently Pavlov (1935) distinguished three different characteristics of the nervous system: strength, related to the working capacity of neural cells (whether in excitatory or inhibitory processes); equilibrium or balance, related to the ratio between strength of inhibition and strength of excitation; and mobility, related to the capacity to change and alternate excitation and inhibition in meeting continuously changing environmental demands.

Later, Teplov (1972) and Nebylitsin (1972) implemented an important program of neurophysiological research on the properties of the nervous system. It led to distinctions among strength, or the capacity to tolerate continuous stimulation; dynamism, the organism's facility in generating neural processes; and mobility, or the speed of starting and ending a neural process. Both Teplov and Nebylitsin were convinced that the properties of the nervous system did not reveal themselves in the content of behavior but in its stylistic and dynamic aspects. Nebylitsin identified general activity (mental, motor, and social) and emotionality (including sensitivity, impulsivity, and emotional weakness) as the two main dimensions of temperament. He posited that the cortical-reticular system was responsible for regulating activity, and that the limbic system was responsible for regulating emotionality. Although this program of research concluded with the death of Teplov and Nebylitsin, their ideas continued to inspire contemporary work on temperament by, among others, Strelau (1983, 1998) and Rusalov (1979, 1989; see also Bodunov, 1993; Mangan, 1982; Strelau, 1997).

### Contemporary Models of Brain Systems and Individual Differences

■ *Eysenck.* The work of the Pavlovian school remained relatively unknown in Western personality psychology until Eysenck and Gray bridged the research traditions. Eysenck's main contribution was to explore the role of the ascending reticular activating system (ARAS) in introversion–extroversion and the role of the limbic system in neuroticism.

Regarding introversion–extraversion, Eysenck based his theorizing on ARAS research by Moruzzi and Magoun (1949) and on the notions of optimal level of arousal proposed by Hebb (1957). The ARAS had been found to project to multiple cerebral cortical sites and to regulate levels of activation in the cortex. The reticular formation thus was implicated in the initiation and maintenance of a wide variety of psychological functions, including emotion, cognition, and conditioning. Hebb's notion of optimal arousal suggested that organisms aim to achieve level of arousal that are ideal (i.e., neither too high nor too low) for them. The exact level of arousal that is optimal may vary from one individual organism to another. Combining these notions, Eysenck originally hypothesized that introverts are characterized by relatively high levels of activity in the corticoreticular loop. They are, then, chronically more cortically aroused than extroverts. As a result, they have little need to seek additional stimulation from the environment. High levels of environmental stimulation produce levels of arousal that are higher than optimal for them. In contrast, extroverts naturally possess low levels of arousal and therefore seem to need environmental stimulation. Functional relations among ARAS activity, cortical arousal, and stimulation seeking, then, explain why introverts tend to avoid stimulating social situations that extroverts seek.

Regarding neuroticism, Eysenck hypothesized that individual differences in psychological functioning reflect levels of arousal produced by the limbic system. People high in neuroticism were posited to possess a limbic system that is particularly responsive to threat or stress. Eysenck's theory, then, placed arousal at the base of both of the main dimensions of individual difference; the arousal levels of two independent neural systems underpinned two independent dimensions. Note that, to distinguish autonomic arousal resulting from limbic activity from the general arousal produced by the ARAS, Eysenck labeled the autonomic arousal *activation*.

Eysenck's work left an enduring legacy to the field. His conceptual strategy of grounding individual-difference dimensions in specific physiological systems is particularly admirable. It circumvents the limitations that arise if one treats dispositions merely as hypothetical constructs, without inquiring into their psychological or physiological basis (Eysenck, 1992a) (see also chapter 3).

Eysenck's theory also served the valuable function of fostering research. Thousands of studies have been inspired by the Eysenckian hypotheses outlined above. This included work by Eysenck himself supporting the link between introversion–extraversion and baseline levels of arousal. Classic findings showed that introverts and extraverts are differentially sensitive to conditioning stimuli in learning experiments. As the original theory predicted, introverts and extraverts were found to undergo conditioning more readily in circumstances that present low versus high levels of stimulation, respectively (Eysenck, 1967; also see Levey & Martin, 1981). Subsequent work suggests that introverts and extraverts do not differ in baseline arousal as strongly as they differ in arousability, that is, changes in arousal when a stimulus is presented. Particularly informative here is work employing cortical evoked response measures that assess changes in brain waves in response to a stimulus (Geen, 1997). Introverts display larger brain wave amplitude changes than extraverts (Stelmack & Achorn-Michaud, 1985; Daruna, Karrer, & Rosen, 1985).

Despite a wealth of research and many promising findings, there were "many anomalies [and] failures to replicate" (Eysenck, 1990, p. 270). Research on the proposed physiological basis of neuroticism was particularly disappointing. Although work on introversion–extraversion was more encouraging, as we just noted, even here "the results have been mixed" (Geen, 1997, p. 393). Other developments forced a number of modifications in the original thinking (Eysenck, 1990; Geen, 1997). Findings indicate that the corticoreticular and the limbic systems are only two of the various arousal systems. Further, these two systems do not operate independently from one another. It also has become clear that the search for the biological determinants of introversion–extroversion, neuroticism, and psychoticism (a third Eysenckian individual-difference dimension; see, e.g., Eysenck, 1990) can not be confined to the ARAS or to the limbic system. Multiple neurotransmitters and the endocrinic system and their reciprocal relations are significantly involved in these dimensions (Eysenck, 1990; Zuckerman, 1991, 1994).

■ *Gray.* Following a parallel road to that of Eysenck, Gray (1987, 1990) proposed a theory of personality centered on two primary dimensions. Gray's dimensions, though, are anxiety and impulsivity. Psychometrically, these may be conceived as a rotation of the Eysenckian dimensions of extroversion and neuroticism[3] (see Figure 2). Whereas anxiety goes from the pole of stable extroversion to neurotic introversion, impulsivity goes from stable introversion to neurotic extroversion.

Although Gray's dimensions are, psychometrically, a simple rotation away from Eysenck's, their proposed underlying biological basis is significantly different. Gray proposes that different physiological systems process signals of punishment and nonreward, on the one hand, and reward and nonpunishment, on the other. Punishment and nonreward are processed by a behavioral inhibition system, which activates fear and anxiety and suppresses behavior. Reward and nonpunishment are processed by a behavioral approach system, which activates approach behavior. These two systems, then, respond to signals of reward and punishment. A third sys-

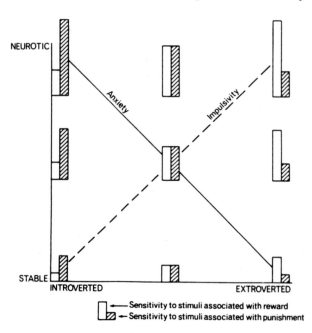

Figure 2. Personality dimensions (anxiety and impulsivity) proposed by Gray, and their relations to the dimensions (extraversion and neuroticism) proposed by Eysenck. From Gray, 1991.

tem, the fight–flight system, responds to unconditioned negative stimuli. The fight–flight system activates either escape or aggressive behavior.

The three systems are interconnected and jointly contribute to behavior. Their actions and interactions are modulated not only by energy supplied by arousal mechanisms but also by decision mechanisms; since the different systems impel different sorts of action, a decision mechanism must be involved so that motor systems receive commands that do not conflict (Gray, 1987). In addition to the decision mechanism, Gray posits a comparator, which compares actual consequences with expected ones.

The proposed systems, their functions, and their interrelations are based primarily on research with animals. Lesion and drug studies enable experimental tests of the model (Gray, 1987).

Most of Gray's efforts have been devoted to clarifying the nature of the behavioral inhibition system and the emotions of fear and anx-

[3] Although the Eysenck-to-Gray rotation is commonly thought to be one of 45 degrees, Matthews and Gilliland (1999) note that the proper rotation is closer to 30 degrees, with Gray's dimension of anxiety being closer to neuroticism and his impulsivity dimension being closer to extroversion.

iety, which are elicited by stimuli associated with either punishment or frustration. Gray proposes that the behavioral inhibition system, and therefore the septohippocampal system, is the first place to look "for differences between people with characteristically high or low levels of susceptibility to anxiety" (Gray, 1987, pp. 332–333). Highly anxious people are particularly susceptible to signals and reinforcements of punishment, and highly impulsive people are particularly susceptible to signals and reinforcements of rewards.

Following the above reasoning, Gray treats individual differences in anxiety as due to differences in the reactivity of the behavioral inhibition system. Individual differences in impulsivity are due to differences in the reactivity of the behavioral approach system. Turning to the Eysenckian dimensions, Gray treats introversion–extraversion as a derived dimension reflecting the "balance" between the reactivities of the behavioral inhibition and approach systems, and neuroticism as a derived dimension reflecting the "summation" of the approach and inhibition systems reactivities. Gray (1989) has speculated that the third dimension posited by Eysenck, psychoticism, may reflect individual differences in the reactivity of the fight–flight system; however, given the interactions among systems, he acknowledges that the whole matter requires further examination and prefers to abstain from "playing what is still at present an amusing game" (p. 192) of theory comparison.

With regard to self-report assessments of individual differences in the behavioral inhibition and behavioral approach systems, much work on Gray's theory has employed instruments that initially were developed to explore other theories but that could be adapted to test Gray's formulations. As Carver and White (1994) note, this is not an optimal way of testing Gray's theoretical scheme, since such scales often contain items that are not truly relevant to Gray's theories. After reviewing and critiquing existing instruments that were designed to test the theory, including the questionnaire of Gray and Wilson (Wilson, Barrett, & Gray, 1989; Wilson, Gray, & Barrett, 1990),

Carver and White (1994) presented brief self-report behavioral inhibition and behavioral approach scales that exhibited acceptable psychometric properties.

■ *Evaluating the Eysenck and Gray Models.* Ideally, the field of personality psychology would have developed a firm database with which one could evaluate the relative merits of the Eysenck and Gray models of individual differences. Unfortunately, this is not the case, as is made evident in a comprehensive review of neural systems and individual differences by Matthews and Gilliland (1999). At least three problems conspire to make comparisons difficult. The first is methodological. It often is impossible to obtain precise measures of the activation levels of the exact neural systems posited by the theories to mediate particular responses. The second problem is conceptual. In many domains, it is difficult to derive unambiguous predictions from either theory. The theories often fail to specify the exact neural systems and the associated mediating and moderating factors that link individual differences to behavior; as a result, there is considerable "scope for post hoc rationalization" (Matthews & Gilliland, 1999, p. 620). The third problem is empirical. When proper methods can be found and predictions can be derived, findings often fail to support either theory. In studies of attention, memory, and response rate, "at best, neither theory seems likely to account for more than a subset of observed personality effects on performance" (Matthews & Gilliland, 1999, p. 615).

Matthews and Gilliland's probing review raises issues that go far beyond the question of how Eysenck's model compares with Gray's. Matthews and Gilliland note fundamental difficulties faced by any neural model of personality, that is, any model that tries to ground an understanding of personality functioning and individual differences in a small number of biological systems. "The difficulties which both theories have experienced in explaining the human performance data challenge the centrality of neural explanations" (p. 620). Instead of explaining personality at the level of neural systems, Matthews and Gilliland's review leads them to suggest that the field turn to the level of human thought: "Cognitive constructs may be more appropriate than biological ones for explaining the majority of behaviors" (p. 620). "Cognitive and social-cognitive models," then, "may provide viable alternatives" (p. 620) to the neurally grounded personality theories of Eysenck and Gray. We wholeheartedly agree, and devote part 4 of our text to advances in the study of cognitive factors that contribute to emotion, motivation, and performance. For now, though, we consider a third neurobiological model of individual differences, while bearing in mind that the issues raised in reviewing the Eysenck and Gray models are currently relevant to any neural model of personality.

■ *Cloninger.* A further contribution to the study of brain mechanisms in personality functioning and development is the biosocial theory of Cloninger (1987; Cloninger, Svrakic & Przybeck, 1993; Stallings, Hewitt, Cloninger, Heath & Eaves, 1996). An early version of the theory (Cloninger, 1987) presented three primary personality dimensions of genetic variability in temperament: novelty seeking, harm avoidance, and reward dependence. These dimensions were associated with three genetically independent neurobiological systems. An interesting feature of the theory is that, although the genotypic variation is independent, surface-level features may be correlated. Phenotypic correlations among genetically independent factors arise from environmental influences that may act in a common manner on more than one temperament characteristic and from interactions among different aspects of temperament. As an example of such interactions, high levels of harm avoidance would tend to temper phenotypical levels of novelty seeking.

Cloninger's theory has been subsequently revised by Cloninger and colleagues into a temperament and character model. The revision incorporates four dimensions of temperament; persistence, which previously was included under reward dependence, was added as an independent dimension. The model also includes three dimensions of developing character: self-directedness, cooperativeness, and self-transcendence. Whereas the temperament dimensions are hypothesized to be mostly biologically determined and to manifest themselves early in development, the character dimensions are associated with the development of self-concept as a process of social learning. "Heritable temperament factors initially motivate insight learning and the development of self-concepts, which then modify the significance and salience of perceived stimuli to which the person responds" (Stallings et al., 1996).

Cloninger sees the regulation of temperament as primarily involving three brain systems: the incentive, or behavioral activation system; the punishment, or behavioral inhibition system; and the reward, or behavioral maintenance system. The various brain systems are interdependent and operate in concert; personality functioning is marked by "complex non-linear dynamics" and "self-organization" (Cloninger et al., 1996). Nonetheless, variation in each temperament dimension can be primarily related to the activity of specific monoaminergic pathways. Dopaminergic activity is seen to play a major role in the regulation of novelty seeking, as does serotoninergic activity in the regulation of harm avoidance and noradrenergic activity in the regulation of reward dependence.

With respect to novelty seeking or behavioral activation, dopaminergic cell bodies in the midbrain function as "the final pathway for the behavioral activation system" (Cloninger, 1987, p. 575) by receiving information from multiple neural systems and projecting this information to the forebrain. Individuals who are higher than average in novelty seeking and average with respect to the other dimensions are characterized as impulsive, quick-tempered, and exploratory. Dopaminergic agonists (such as amphetamines and cocaine) facilitate dopaminergic transmission and thus behavioral activation.

The harm avoidance or behavioral inhibition system involves variations in punishment systems in the brain. These include "the septohippocampal system, serotoninergic projections from the raphe nuclei in the brainstem, and cholinergic projections to the frontal neocortex from the ventral tegmental area and the basal nucleus of Meynert" (Cloninger, 1987, p. 576). Regions of the frontal cortex ultimately act to inhibit behavioral activity. Individuals high in harm avoidance are said to be pessimistic and beset by tension and worry.

Norepinephrine is posited as the major neuromodulator for the reward-maintenance, RD system. Variations in this system give rise to individual differences in signals of reward and approval from others. Individuals who are high on reward dependence and average on the other dimensions are emotionally dependent on others, socially sensitive, industrious, and sentimental, and they strive to please others (Cloninger, 1987). The underlying biological systems involve a small number of noradrenergic neurons that project to a large number of brain regions. "Ascending noradrenergic pathways arise from the locus ceruleus in the pons and project to the hypothalamus and limbic structures, including the amygdala, septum and hippocampal formation, and then branch throughout the entire neocortex" (Cloninger, 1987, p. 577).

Cloninger's model seems to overlap somewhat with Gray's, as well as with other models of temperament that happen to embrace different theoretical premises and to be less committed to specific biological underpinnings. Novelty seeking resembles Eysenck's extroversion, factor 1 of the five-factor model (energy, surgency, extraversion), positive affect (Tellegen, 1985; Watson & Clark, 1997), activity (Buss & Plomin, 1984), and sensation seeking (Zuckerman, 1984). Harm avoidance resembles the neuroticism factor of Eysenck and the five factor model negative emotionality, or negative affect (Tellegen, 1985; Watson, 2000; Watson & Clark, 1984), emotionality (Buss & Plomin, 1984), reactivity (Strelau, 1983), and shyness (Kagan, Reznick, & Snidman, 1988). Reward dependence appears related to factors 2 and 3 of the fight–flight model, constraint and sociability (Buss &

Plomin, 1984; Zuckerman, Kuhlman, Thornquist & Kiers, 1991).

The contributions of Eysenck, Gray, and Cloninger illustrate the considerable progress that has been made in our understanding of brain mechanisms in personality functioning but also illustrate the difficulties one confronts when trying to relate personality dispositions and determinants to complex, interacting brain systems.

## SEX DIFFERENCES

Males and females are biologically different. Although anatomy and physiology are not destiny, it is likely that these biological differences affect male and female psychology. Discounting biological sex differences would disembody personality and deprive individuals of a significant component of their own identity. Thus, we consider in this section of our text biological factors in human sex differences. The role of social and cultural factors in how the sexes develop is addressed later.

When examining the question of biological sex differences, one must bear in mind that the biological person develops in a social environment. The meaning of biological maleness and femaleness is socially and culturally determined. Biological differences are completely intertwined and confounded with social and psychological sex. Masculinity and femininity must be seen as products of biology and socialization working in concert. A biopsychosocial perspective is required to understand links from biological sex differences to behavior, the construction of sex as a biologically based social category, and the sense all persons have of their own maleness or femaleness (Ehrhardt, 1984; Hood, Draper, Crockett & Petersen, 1987). In particular, sexual identity is the culmination of multiple processes ranging "from prenatal to pubertal hormones, from body morphology to body image, and from prenatal hormonalization of the brain to postnatal assimilation of cultural stereotypes of male and female" (Money, 1987, p. 16).

## Sex Differentiation and Development

Biological sex differentiation starts at conception, based on the fate of the 23rd pair of 46 chromosomes contained by each cell. Females receive from both parents an X chromosome, whereas males carry a X chromosome from the mother and a Y chromosome from the father. A person's genetic sex, then, is determined by the father. One should not forget, though, that the same genes may act differently when transmitted from each parent to their offspring, whether male or female, as previously noted in reporting the work of Skuse et al. (1997) on females with Turner's syndrome.

Sex chromosomes determine whether male (testes) or female (ovaries) reproductive glands develop from the undifferentiated gonadal tissues present in both sexes. The Y chromosome promotes the synthesis of a protein called the H-Y antigen, which among other things, helps the primitive gonads to differentiate into embryonic tests. Genetic sex also is responsible for the development of a sex-differentiated endocrine system, including the gonads, the mammary glands, the pituitary gland, and specific brain areas in the hypothalamus.

Biological differentiation continues through several stages of fetal development. Key developmental steps include the differentiation of the gonads, their secretion of sex hormones, and the differentiation of internal reproductive organs and external genitalia. Gonadal hormones organize these physical and neural developments. Hormones – testosterone and other androgens in males, and estrogen and progesterone in females – determine and accompany the differentiation of internal reproductive organs and of external genitalia. Whereas prenatal development of female sexual structures is primarily under genetic regulation, androgen secretion is determinant for male development. Both males and females produce androgens and estrogens, but their different concentrations and the ratio of androgen to estrogen is critical for sex differences.

Hormones play a critical role in brain development. Areas of the hypothalamus, for example, are particularly sensitive to the action of sex hormones. Morphological differences between males and females have been found in the preoptic area of the hypothalamus, where males show more neurons than females. However, the effects of these differences on mental functioning and behavior are not clear (Swaab & Fliers, 1985). Hormones also affect the lateralization of brain function. It has been reported that females show less brain lateralization than do males, with possible effects on cognitive functioning (Halpern, 1992; Molfese & Segalowitz, 1988). However, findings are still controversial; the timing, mechanisms, and complete extent of hormonal influences are not yet fully understood.

Much of the knowledge we do have about hormonal influences and biological sex derives from the study of clinical populations exposed prenatally or postnatally to hormonal imbalance. Most studies have examined females who suffer a prenatal excess release of androgens (adrenogenital syndrome) or whose mothers had been treated with excessive amounts of androgens during pregnancy. High levels of prenatal androgens result in high physical energy expenditure in outdoor play and a long-term tomboyish behavior pattern (Money & Erhrhardt, 1972). However, these effects did not preclude the formation of a female sexual identity. Boys exposed prenatally to excessive progesterone and estrogens showed no problem maintaining a male sexual identity. In contrast, consider the case of genetic males carrying a disorder that made them androgen-insensitive. Their sexual differentiation of external genitalia took place along females lines, they were reared as girls, and they developed a sexual identity concordant with their sex of rearing, not their genetic sex. Thus, sex of rearing appears to be the critical determinant of sexual identity (Money & Erhrhardt, 1972). Although prenatal hormone imbalance may influence subsequent development in various ways, it is likely that it will only determine individuals' sexual identity in rare extreme cases (Ehrhardt, 1987; Hood, Draper, Crockett, & Petersen, 1987).

Other findings suggest that not even sex of rearing can be considered the ultimate cause of sexual identity. Males suffering from a metabolic disorder (5-alpha-reductase deficiency), which prevents the development of male-type genitalia, have been raised in childhood as girls. In puberty, they developed into boys when the development of secondary sexual characteristics was no longer impeded (Imperato, McGinley-Peterson, Gautier, & Sturla, 1979).

Over the course of childhood development, both androgens and estrogens can be produced in the ovaries and testes. Both hormones influence brain functioning and ultimately, behavior. Their role becomes mostly activational, rather than organizational as in prenatal and neonatal stages. Various factors make it difficult to determine the exact role of hormonal influences in any sex-linked personality characteristic; these include reciprocal interactions among hormones, hormone sensitivity to environmental conditions (e.g., stressors), individual variations in the level of circulating sex hormones, and the existence of different thresholds for hormonal activity (Feder, 1984; Goy & McEwen, 1980; Money & Ehrhardt, 1972).

At puberty, hormones trigger further sexual differentiation in morphology and physiology, leading to the development of secondary sex characteristics. Increased levels of androgens stimulate the growth of pubic and underarm hair in both sexes and produce voice deepening, facial hair growth, and further genital development in boys. Increased levels of estrogens produce breast development and hip widening (relative to the shoulders) in girls (Petersen & Taylor, 1980). Boys reach puberty about two years later than girls, which leaves them two extra years to grow taller and stronger and probably to complete the organization of their brain, although hypothetical differences in hemispheric specialization remain conjectural.

In the adult years, events such as the menstrual cycle, pregnancy, and menopause in females attest to the differential influence of hormones in both sexes. Although these are biological events, we emphasize that their psychological effects cannot be fully understood apart from the sociocultural contexts and meaning systems that surround them.

Hormonal sex differences have also been implicated in male–female differences in intellectual performance. Research on intelligence and cognitive performance yields few if any sex differences in global IQ or in the use of complex cognitive skills. Differences are found, though, on tests of cognitive subskills (Neisser et al., 1996). Men often obtain superior scores on tests of spatial and mathematical ability, whereas women obtain higher scores on some verbal tasks. As reviewed by Neisser et al. (1996), hormonal differences could contribute to these effects; women exposed to high levels of androgens in utero have been found to obtain higher spatial ability scores as adults (Resnick, Berenbaum, Gottesman, & Bouchard, 1986). However, Neisser et al. (1996) also note that these, and all other documented group differences in intellectual performance, "are well within the range of effect sizes that can be produced by environmental factors" (p. 94). At present it is nearly impossible to disentangle the effects of inherited biology from those of behavioral experiences that may affect brain development. Further, it is not clear whether the obtained sex differences are widely generalizable, since most studies have been conducted in the United States.

There is no doubt, then, that hormonal influences contribute to psychological differences between the sexes. Establishing the exact link from hormones to social behavior, however, is an arduous task. Although some findings may suggest a link between androgens and activity level, dominance, or aggression, it seems unlikely that complex behavior patterns can be traced to hormonal factors in a direct manner. It is a long way from a mere disposition toward physically energetic outdoor play behavior (which may correlate with testosterone concentration) to dominant attitudes toward others or physically harmful patterns of behavior. Androgens and other hormones interact with other biological and psychosocial factors in setting the conditions that may facilitate or repress the unfolding of chains of events that eventually turn into specific patterns of behavior (Parsons, 1980; Hood et al., 1987; Ehrhardt, 1985). Different interactions, leading to opposite effects, may account for highly conflicting results in research aiming at clarifying the hormonal basis of male–female differences in behaviors such as aggression. In childhood and early adolescence, male hormones predict aggression for girls but not for boys. In late adolescence and adulthood, instead, male hormones are markedly related to aggressive and antisocial conduct for males but not for females (Buchanan, Eccles, & Becker, 1992; Dabbs & Morris, 1990; Olweus, Mattison, Schalling, & Low, 1988; Susman et al., 1987).

Homosexuals, lesbians, and transsexuals pose a further challenge to our understanding of the mystery of sex, the plasticity of the human organism, and the versatility of human personality. In this regard, we find Money's statement (1987) apt: "The difference between male and female is something that everybody knows and nobody knows" (p. 14). Even the most commonly accepted beliefs about sex differences and the development of sexuality have come into question. It has generally been thought that the development of sexual attraction takes place at puberty, which occurs, on average, at ages 12 and 14 for girls and boys, respectively. This belief is reflected in the notion that ages 6 to puberty constitute a latency period. A review by McClintock and Herdt (1996) notes that this belief is contradicted by two facts. There are no sex differences in self-reported first age of sexual attraction, despite the sex differences in age of onset of puberty. Second, self-reported age of first sexual attraction is 10, which is years before puberty begins for either sex. These findings hold for both heterosexual individuals and for homosexuals and lesbians (McClintock & Herdt, 1996). The findings suggest that sexual attraction, rather than being triggered by physiological changes at puberty, may arise from the maturation, at age 10, of the adrenal glands, which

produce sex steroids (McClintock & Herdt, 1996).

When contemplating the role of hormonal factors in sex differences, one must recall that biological sex is a much weaker determinant of one's destiny today than in the past. Enduring female and male roles that once appeared as immutable qualities of the sexes have changed dramatically with changing social and economic conditions. Particularly profound changes have occurred in the workplace, a situation we now address.

Social experience has been found to bring about changes in the "biology of sex differences." A profound change in contemporary social life is women's widespread entry into the work force. This change has brought both opportunity and stress. Women commonly must confront not only the stresses of the workplace but the tradeoff between obligations of work and parenting. A social discourse that is uninformed by the findings of personality psychology might question whether women are "inherently fit" for such roles and seek answers in biological sex differences that might make men "naturally" more inclined to compete in a stressful workplace. Research findings, however, undercut the very logic of this discourse. Seemingly inherent biological sex differences actually vary as social conditions change. The study of psychophysiological reactions at the workplace is a paradigm case in which changing social conditions alter biological factors that at first may appear to be immutable aspects of human nature.

As reviewed by Frankenhauser (1991, 1994), laboratory research on stress reactions conducted during the 1970s revealed consistent sex differences in physiological reactions to stress. When engaged in challenging achievement tasks, men experienced a greater rise in the release of catecholamines, particularly epinephrine. These differences might be interpreted as indicating that men, by virtue of their inherent male biology, are more responsive to the sort of stressors encountered at the workplace. However, subsequent research by Frankenhaeuser and colleagues called this conclusion into question. Swedish women who had acquired experience in occupations that traditionally had been filled by men (bus driver, lawyer) were found to exhibit the same levels of epinephrine release in response to achievement challenges as men did. Further, when the particular challenge that was presented to research participants was switched from a cognitive task to a task demanding social skills, women experienced a greater rise in epinephrine levels than men Frankenhaeuser (1994).

As Frankenhaeuser emphasizes, cognitive appraisals trigger stress. Changing life experiences and social expectations alter women's views of self and their resulting cognitive appraisals and stress reactions. "When men and women become more alike in their value judgments and attitudes, their physiological stress reactions, too, will become more similar" (Frankenhaeuser, 1991, p. 199).

## Evolutionary Psychology and Sex Differences

Another approach to understanding biological mechanisms and sex differences is grounded in evolutionary considerations. Men and women have different "investments" in parenting (Trivers, 1972). Men can father many children at once, whereas women usually carry only one child at a time and do so for a lengthy period of pregnancy. It is possible that over the course of evolution, males and females have evolved different psychological mechanisms to meet these different reproductive pressures. This simple notion carries with it a broad implication, namely, that there exist distinct psychological mechanisms that have evolved to carry out very specific tasks that promote the survival and reproduction of the organism. This is the core idea of evolutionary psychology (Barkow, Cosmides, & Tooby, 1992). In the following, we first review the basic tenets of the evolutionary approach and then examine how they apply to the analysis of sex differences.

Evolutionary psychology (see Barkow, Cosmides & Tooby, 1992; Buss, 1995a, 1996a, 1999a, b; Buss & Kenrick, 1998; Pinker, 1997)

is, in essence, a theory about the architecture of the mind. The approach has considerable implications for the study of personality because the proposed architecture speaks to questions about personality structure and the nature of individual differences. Evolutionary psychology posits that the mind consists of a large number of "modules" (Fodor, 1983) or "mental organs" (Pinker, 1997), each of which evolved through natural selection to solve a distinct adaptive problem (Barkow et al., 1992). Each module, then, is an adaptive computational system (Pinker, 1997), that is, a set of procedures that has proved, over the course of evolution, to promote survival and reproduction by solving a particular adaptive problem. The mechanisms do not necessarily solve a problem that is directly related to sexual reproduction. Instead, they have evolved to solve problems that in the long run promote the reproductive fitness of the organism. Indeed, this point holds for both biological and psychological evolved mechanisms. Just as the biological mechanism of callus formation solves a particular physical problem that is linked to reproductive success in only the most indirect way, evolved psychological mechanisms may have evolved to solve social problems that are only indirectly linked to survival and reproduction (Buss, 1991).

The feature that markedly distinguishes evolutionary psychology from other psychological frameworks is the following. Adaptive psychological mechanisms are seen to perform computations on only a particular class of inputs and to generate solutions that have been evolutionarily effective in solving the problem presented by the particular given input. This type of mental architecture is a rather obvious fact if one is considering, for example, perceptual information-processing systems. Ears and eyes perform computations only on sound and light. The intriguing part of evolutionary psychology is that it extends this reasoning to psychological mechanisms that solve social problems. A problem involving the care of one's child activates mental mechanisms that have evolved to solve problems of child rearing. One involving the negotiated price of an object to be purchased activates mechanisms that have evolved to solve problems of social exchange (Cosmides, 1989). Child rearing and social exchange mechanisms are as specialized and as distinct from one another as are eyes and ears. This view differs profoundly from most prior conceptions of the architecture of mind, which have posited general-purpose or so-called domain-general reasoning processes. In the domain-general view, a common mechanism of logical reasoning might handle issues of child rearing, social exchange, or any of a diversity of other problems. The evolutionary psychologist dismisses this domain-general view as part of at outmoded "standard social science model" of mind (Tooby & Cosmides, 1992).

This model of mind has direct implications for our very conception of human nature. The "standard social science" view is that biology provides capacities and constraints. Culture and socialization processes provide direction. People can become almost anything, within the wide latitudes of their biological makeup, and socialization determines what they become. The evolutionary psychology view is very different. Evolved psychological mechanisms not only process particular inputs but also generate particular strategies, namely, strategies that have proved to be effective in the course of evolution. The implication is that biology provides not only capacities and constraints but also directional tendencies. To the evolutionary psychologist, women's preferences for wealthy men and men's preferences for young, buxom women (Buss, 1988; Sprecher, Sullivan, & Hatfield, 1994) are no more products of socialization than are people's preferences to eat sweet foods, stay warm in winter, or sleep at night. We do each of these things because our ancestors did them, or more specifically, because the people who did them in the past were more reproductively successful and thus became our ancestors. Each of these tendencies is the output from a particular evolved mechanism.

A variety of processes might explain individual differences with an evolutionary framework (Buss, 1991). Many adaptive problems have more than one solution. The problem of mating, for example, can be solved via short-term or long-term strategies, that is, strategies that differ in their focus on brief versus long-lasting relationships (Buss & Schmitt, 1993). A variety of factors may predispose individuals to invoke one versus another strategy; these include inherited individual differences in the tendency to adopt a given strategy, or social experiences that "calibrate" the evolved mechanism in a different manner for different people (Buss, 1991). Some evidence, for example, suggests that absence of the father during childhood predisposes people toward more promiscuous mating relationships later in life (Belsky, Steinberg, & Draper, 1991).

Turning specifically to sex differences, females and males contribute differently to reproduction, with women giving birth to children and breastfeeding offspring. Women are limited in the number of potential offspring they can produce as a result of their large contribution to each one, whereas men can contribute to many more offspring, but until very recently, they have never been in the position to be sure of their paternity: *Mater semper certa, pater numquam* (the mother is always certain, the father never). Females and males also differently experience the pleasure of sex, women being potentially able to have more orgasms within a short period of time than males. Both reproductive and sexual experiences may significantly shape personality.

Sociobiologists and evolutionary psychologists have claimed that different reproductive interests have, in the course of evolution, selected for biological mechanisms that are responsible for men's and women's differential strategies for attracting mates. To maximize fitness (i.e., gene frequency in subsequent generations), women must be more discriminating and caring to obtain and hold a man with good genes, resources, and parental skills. Men, in contrast, may maximize fitness by seeking to mate with many women by competing with other men, and by exerting close control over the sexual behavior of the mother of their own children (Archer, 1996; Buss, 1994; 1995a,b; Smuts, 1995; Trivers, 1972). In the eyes of the man, female youth and physical fitness are important indicators of potential reproductive success. In the eyes of the woman, the man's ability to provide resources for the child is important. The recurrence of these themes throughout evolution is seen to be responsible for contemporary differences in mating behavior.

These arguments are provocative and the associated findings are suggestive, although not unequivocal. Self-report data indicate that, when trying to attract members of the opposite sex, men do spend relatively greater effort in displaying financial resources, whereas women expend greater effort in making themselves look physically fit and attractive (Buss, 1988). Men have reported more casual and frequent sexual activity than females. This, of course, is a puzzle, in as much as the man requires a partner to have heterosexual relations and men and women exist in about the same proportion in the population. It may be that a few statistically exceptional females satisfy multiple men. It is likely that men's and women's self-reports may be distorted by over- and underestimation. On the other hand, whereas fear of pregnancy may interfere with the free experience of sexuality in women, prostitution in most countries does provide more of an outlet to male than to female desire (Symons, 1979).

Jealousy seems to be experienced in different ways in men and women. Men are more concerned with their own partner being sexually intimate with another man, which puts them at risk of supporting another's offspring. Women are more concerned with their partner's emotional involvement with another woman, which thus risks a diversion of resources to another's offspring (Daly, Wilson & Weghorst, 1982; Buss, Larsen, Westen & Semmelroth, 1992).

The scenarios depicted by sociobiologists and evolutionary psychologists must be viewed with caution. Although some aspects of evolutionary psychology currently can be tested (Buss, 1996a), others cannot (Cervone, 2000). Hood et al. (1987) note the obstacles in verifying an evolutionary basis of sex differ-

ences: "First, the finding of sex differences may be epiphenomenal . . . an accidental outcome of some other factor (with) no relationship to reproductive advantage. Second, the original evolutionary contexts in which the sex differences were consolidated are no longer available for inspection. Therefore it is not possible to determine empirically what selective advantage is provided by a particular trait or behavior" (p. 68). Caporael (1997) similarly notes that the "psychological mechanisms contributing to sexual jealousy may not have evolved as a direct result of paternity uncertainty" (p. 283). This is likely to be the case among populations (e.g., the Wari of the Amazon basin) that believe that the baby results not from fertilization at one point in time but from an accretion of semen and maternal blood through multiple sexual encounters. "If a woman has multiple partners, it means that the baby has multiple fathers" (Caporael, 1997, p. 283) Further, sexual dominance, mate preference, and jealousy are often dictated by cultural values and are related to a socioeconomic system's forms of accumulation and distribution of wealth and organization of labor.

The recognition that biology has coevolved with culture (see Archer, 1996; Durham, 1991) further cautions against attributing patterns of social behavior solely to evolved biological mechanisms. The study of contemporary behavioral patterns cannot resolve the question of how biological and cultural factors may have interacted over multiple generations to yield the patterns we observe today.

Evolutionary biologists valuably remind us that evolutionary processes select not just for fixed behavioral patterns but for the capacity to vary one's behavior flexibly to meet the challenges of diverse habitats. Natural selection shapes for proximate utility and relies on potentialities and variability rather than on fixedness and purposiveness (Dobzhansky, 1972; Gould, 1987). Although evolutionary psychologists stress that one should ground an explanation of behavior in underlying mechanisms, not surface-level actions (Buss, 1991), research rarely identifies the mechanisms.

Instead, investigators search for universalities in surface-level tendencies. A greater empirical focus on psychological mechanisms might illuminate evolved mechanisms that contribute not only to fixed patterns of action but also to behavioral flexibility.

Rather than attributing sexual differences primarily to primeval evolutionary causes, it may be possible to explain observed variability in terms of contemporary social conditions. Some contemporary conditions present contingencies that differ markedly from those that were present during the course of evolution. For example, contraceptive devices have disjoined sex from reproductivity, as Bussey and Bandura (1999) have noted. It is difficult to reconcile the sudden behavioral changes that may accompany sociocultural change with the slow pace of nature.

Eagly and Wood (1999) have contrasted explanations of sexual differences that are grounded in evolutionary versus social structural theory. Social structural accounts locate the origins of sexual differences in the differential social positions held by men and women; despite the many changes on the world scene, women continue to hold fewer positions of power and to earn less money than men. Differential economic power rather than evolutionary pressures may explain women's greater preference for a wealthy mate. To test this idea, Eagly and Wood reanalyzed Buss' (1989) multicultural study of male and female mate preferences. They found that a primary determinant of mate preferences is a culture's degree of economic and political sex equality. In support of the social structural position, greater equality was associated with lesser sex differences. For example, in cultures with greater sex equality, women showed less preference for older men, and men displayed less preference for younger women (Eagly & Wood, 1999). Sociocultural theories of the differences between men and women are reviewed again in chapter 8, when we discuss the social construction of sex.

Whatever the differences between the sexes in personality functioning, they generally are overwhelmed by individual variations within each sex. This suggests a greater empirical attention to the distinctive qualities of individuals rather than to average tendencies of groups of men and women. Personality psychologists must consider the continuous, multiple influences that biological sex exerts on the individual and how the individual interprets these influences in potentially idiosyncratic ways. The study of sexual differences is a uniquely valuable forum for understanding how biology and culture work in concert to influence personality functioning. The field of personality can uniquely contribute to an understanding of the intertwining of sex as a biological endowment, and sex role as a social construction over the life course.

## SUMMING UP

Recent years have witnessed enormous progress in our understanding of the genetic factors that function as distal influences on personality, and of the brain systems that are more proximal determinants of psychological functioning. A particularly intriguing feature of research findings in this area is that they highlight the influence not only of biology, but of environmental experience. Biological factors and environmental experiences are found to influence each other reciprocally. Brain systems exhibit much plasticity in response to recurrent environmental events. Genetic factors influence psychological tendencies, whereas behavioral experiences partly determine the activation of genetic mechanisms and thus the nature of the biological person. These facts make it obvious that it is no longer appropriate to pit nature versus nurture in explanations of personality development. Instead, a question to address is "the nurture of nature," that is, the ways in which nurturing experiences can facilitate individuals' achievement of their biological potentials. Our genetic endowment equips us with a vast array of potentialities. These potentials are realized through experiences with the world. Since people often select their experiences and influence the situations they encounter, they causally contribute to their personal development.

# CHAPTER SEVEN

# Interpersonal Relations

In our previous two chapters we have construed personality development as a lifelong, dynamic process. A person's psychological qualities reflect a continual process of interaction among three elements: the biological being whose genetic endowment partly determines his or her preferences and capacities; the sociocultural environment, whose conceptual systems and environmental settings facilitate some developmental pathways while inhibiting others; and the agentic individual, who causally contributes to the course of his or her development through the human capacities for forethought and self-regulation.

In the present chapter, we consider how personality development is shaped and sustained by interpersonal factors. Although interpersonal settings at first sound as if they are merely an aspect of the sociocultural environment, in reality their nature and influence reflects all three of the factors noted above. Biological endowment influences interpersonal interactions in that different temperaments elicit different reactions from others (Plomin et al., 1997). Cognitive, agentic factors are important in that people strategically influence the course of interactions and, with increasing age, select the interpersonal relations that constitute their social life. Finally, interpersonal relations achieve meaning within social and cultural contexts; indeed, they are a primary vehicle through which the sociocultural environment influences the individual.

The metaphor of a dialogue is frequently employed to capture relations among the biological, cultural, and personal determinants of development. As in a dialogue, developmental factors influence one another reciprocally and evolve continually over time. In the case of personality, dialogue actually is more than a metaphor. Interpersonal dialogues mediate people's relationships among one another. Internal dialogues contribute to the formation of personal identity. The former are needed for the development of the latter (Hermans, Kempen, & Van Loon, 1992). Interpersonal experiences provide interpretive frameworks through which individuals construct enduring beliefs about the self. The belief systems and normative standards that make up the self-system, then, largely evolve out of interpersonal relationships; in contemporary society, these include the symbolic relationships people form with figures whom they encounter only through the media and other forms of electronic communication.

We begin this chapter with a brief historical review of influential theoretical contributions to the study of interpersonal relations. We then review work on child–caretaker interactions that is guided by attachment theory. Since interpersonal relations are primarily a setting for communication among individuals, we next review the role of language and communicative exchanges in development. Finally, we explore how peer relationships and friendships contribute to the development of the individual.

## INTERPERSONAL RELATIONS: THEORETICAL FRAMEWORKS

The list of scholars who have contributed to the understanding of interpersonal relations in personality development is long. Traditionally, textbooks divide these scholars into alternative theoretical camps. Such classifications should be made cautiously, however, since diversities within a camp often equal the variation between various approaches.

In personality psychology, the importance, depth, and enduring nature of the impact of interpersonal relations on personality development was first discerned by psychoanalysts. Interest in interpersonal experiences is common to all psychoanalytic scholars. However, the question of exactly how interpersonal relations should be treated theoretically has been a controversial point, which has fostered divisions in the psychoanalytic movement. Some psychoanalysts contended that early relationships mold the urges and vicissitudes of drives (Freud, 1965; Klein, 1932; Winnicott, 1958). Others abandoned the theory of drives and instead placed interpersonal relations at the very core of personality development (Fairbairn, 1952). This more explicit focus on interpersonal relations led to a substantial revision of psychoanalytic constructs, resulting in new theories of personality, among which those of Sullivan (1953) and Bowlby (1969, 1973, 1980) are noteworthy. Sullivan's work primarily influenced clinical practice, whereas Bowlby, as we shall see, exerted a tremendous influence on research in personality development. Other recent psychoanalytical developments highlight early parent–child relations, including the mother's role in emotional and cognitive development and the formation of the self (Kernberg, 1976; Kohut, 1971; 1977; Stern, 1985).

Existentialist and phenomenological traditions, while focusing primarily on private experiences, have also called attention to interpersonal factors in development. The internal world revealed in phenomenological therapies commonly indicates that interpersonal relations and expectations about oneself of persons important in one's life contribute to the formation of self-concept and to intrapsychic conflict (Laing, 1965; Rogers, 1961). Longitudinal research supports this therapeutic insight by showing that some early-life interpersonal factors identified by phenomenological theorists predict later-life outcomes. Children who experience "Rogerian" parenting (i.e., parents who are relatively noncritical and encourage independent exploration of the world) develop into more creative adolescents (Harrington, Block, & Block, 1987).

Relational systemic approaches, while mostly focusing on intrafamily relations, also highlight interpersonal relations that occur outside the family. Individual development and functioning is seen to occur within multiple interpersonal networks. These networks involve reciprocal obligations, demands, and constraints (Bateson, 1972; Minuchin, 1974, 1985).

All these approaches have emphasized the impact of interpersonal relations on the development of affect, feelings of interpersonal trust, and confidence in oneself. Various social-cognitive and cognitive-developmental theories indicate that interpersonal relations also are a vehicle of socialization, which contributes to the development of thought processes and cognitive competence. Mead (1934) and Vygotsky (1934) both made seminal contributions here, albeit of somewhat different natures. Mead's work revealed how interactions and shared meanings contribute to the construal of self and others. In the process of socialization, the role of interpersonal and social relations in self-development is fundamental in as much as people develop a sense of self by viewing themselves from the perspective of other members of society (the *generalized other*), and by behaving in accordance with their expectations. Vygotsky explored the influence of interpersonal experiences on intrapsychic organization and thus on the development of thought and abilities (chapter 2; also see Rogoff, 1998; Van Geert, 1998).

Social learning approaches originally focused on mechanisms of identification, modeling, and reinforcement that take place primarily within the family (Bandura & Walters, 1963; Patterson, 1982; Sears, Rau & Alpert, 1965). Subsequent social-cognitive approaches have emphasized how internal standards and self-regulatory capabilities express themselves in interpersonal settings. Parents, peers, and teachers among others provide the occasions for actualizing one's own potentialities, developing one's standards, challenging one's capacities, and validating self-beliefs (Bandura, 1986, 1997).

Finally, social exchange theory provides a framework for understanding interpersonal and close relationships. It elucidates cognitive and motivational mechanisms that underlie interdependence among individuals (Kelley & Thibaut, 1978; Kelley, 1979).

This list does not exhaust the array of theoretical contributions in this area. These and other perspectives, within and outside of psychology, have converged in stressing that interpersonal relations are a basis of cognitive and emotional development and personality functioning. These valuable traditions have remained somewhat isolated from one another. Despite this fragmentation in the field, significant progress has been made (Bersheid, 1994; Hinde, 1997), as we will see in the following sections focusing on attachment, communication, and peer relations.

## ATTACHMENT

Work on attachment stems from the seminal contributions of Bowlby and Ainsworth (Ainsworth, 1967; Ainsworth, Blehar, Walters & Wall, 1978; Ainsworth & Bowlby, 1991; Bowlby, 1969; 1973; 1980; 1988). The impact of their work, which has only increased in recent years, exceeds that of perhaps any other contribution to our understanding of interpersonal factors in personality development.

Bowlby himself was a clinician. He drew from not only scientific findings but also from clinical practice with children, mothers, and families. His intuitions developed from the object-relation traditions in psychoanalysis, to which he added concepts from evolution theory, ethology, system theory, and cognitive psychology. Ainsworth's contributions were crucial in providing a solid empirical basis to those intuitions and in building a bridge between clinical practice and systematic research.

As Bowlby writes, "Attachment theory regards the propensity to make intimate emotional bonds with particular individuals as a basic component of human nature, already present in germinal form in the neonate and continuing through adult life into old age" (1988, pp. 120–121). For their survival and growth, human children are dependent on others for prolonged periods. Basic biological functions thus require a stable relationship between child and caregiver, generally the mother. The very survival of the species depends on the child's being equipped with a stable behavioral system, which seeks to acquire protection from the caregiver, and the caregiver being equipped to protect the vulnerable child. This relationship, then, is a two-way street; attachment behavior and maternal behavior form an interlocking behavioral system. It is this intimate, reciprocal, biologically rooted bond that Bowlby views as a "basic component of human nature."

This social bond leaves a lasting psychological legacy. It provides the basis for enduring mental representations of interpersonal relations. Mental representations of parental interactions function as effective *working models* (Bowlby, 1969), which are the foundation for the more general representations of relationships with other people that children form as they move into the wider world. These working models incorporate knowledge of the relation between the individual's potentialities and environmental affordances.

Children's mental models, then, reflect their treatment by the parents and, in turn, shape their views not only of the parents but of others. "The patterns of interaction to which models lead have become habitual, generalized, and largely unconscious, [they] persist in a more or less uncorrected and unchanged state even when the individual in later life is dealing with persons who treat him in ways entirely unlike those that his parents adopted when he was a child" (Bowlby, 1988; p. 130). Thus, attachment experiences are ultimately internalized into beliefs and expectations about others and about the self as worthy of love – beliefs that are destined to influence personality throughout life.

## Attachment Styles

Based on extensive interviews with mothers and observations of mother–child interactions in villages in Uganda, Ainsworth identified three main clusters of individual differences corresponding to distinct styles of attachment: secure, insecure-resistant, and insecure-avoidant (Ainsworth, 1967; Ainsworth et al., 1978). Secure infants have harmonious relationships with their mother, who provides a secure base from which to move into the world. They are cooperative, relatively unconflicted, and relatively willing to comply with the mother's requests. Insecure-avoidant infants are unable to use the mother as a secure base. They are chronically anxious and ambivalent in relations with her. Insecure-resistant infants tend to be angry and detached because of the frustration experienced in relations with the mother.

These three patterns have been identified through naturalistic observation, longitudinal studies, and laboratory research. Laboratory work generally employs the "strange situation" paradigm (Ainsworth et al., 1978; Bowlby, 1988; Sroufe, 1988; Van Ijzendoorn & Kroonenberg, 1988). Children are observed as they face stressful situations, including an unfamiliar environment, a stranger, and short separations from the mother. Specifically, eight episodes are presented in a standard order. First, mother and child are introduced by an observer to an unfamiliar environment (an experimental room with two chairs and some toys on the ground). One observes how readily the child moves away from the mother to explore the surrounding space in the absence of contact with the mother. Next, with the mother present, a stranger enters and slowly approaches the child. The mother subsequently leaves the room to return after a few minutes. Then the stranger leaves; the mother leaves again (with the child remaining alone in the unfamiliar environment); the stranger returns; the mother finally comes back; and the stranger leaves. The child's reactions to separation and reunion with the mother are coded in terms of six behavioral variables: proximity and contact seeking, contact maintaining, resistance, avoidance, search, and distance of interaction. These are the elements for assessing the three different patterns of attachment.

Findings reveal that infants generally become attached to their mothers by age 1 year (Ainsworth et al., 1978). However, patterns of attachment vary. Secure infants seek proximity to the mother on reunion, communicate their feelings of stress, but then return to exploration. Insecure-resistant infants combine proximity seeking with contact resistance. They respond to separation with intense stress and are long unsoothable. Insecure-avoidant infants evade proximity, show little distress during separation, and remain distant from the mother or ignore her when reunited with her.

These different patterns of child attachment are thought to reflect different styles on the part of the mother. The most important feature here is not the total amount of time that the mother spends with the child but the quality of the attachment, that is, whether the mother provides a secure base and is sensitive to the child's signals of need for protection and comfort. Such sensitivity is critical to the development of secure patterns of attachment. On the child's side, the key marker that discriminates among attachment groups is not crying, per se, but recovery from distress after reunion with the mother. Mothers who provide a secure base enable children to explore, knowing that the mother will remain available to provide physical and emotional support, reassurance, and protection.

A key feature of attachment theory is that it predicts that individuals will reproduce, later in life, patterns of attachment that they acquire in early parent–child interactions. Differential attachments lead some people to be confident, open to experience, and resilient in the face of separations; others become anxious and worry about potential neglect, rejection, or abandonment; yet others lack confidence in other persons and become self-sufficient, isolated, and hostile.

Bowlby believes that the human tendencies to seek attachment and to support the child who is seeking it have biological roots. Yet his theory is not strictly deterministic. Rejecting notions of developmental stages, he emphasizes the great potentialities associated with human diversity and the multiple developmental pathways that individuals may traverse. Some children are more resilient than others, some parents more responsive than others, and the sequelae of some encounters more protective than others. Although one's attachment style tends to stabilize over time and to express itself as a stable personality trait or cognitive-emotional style, new experiences may alter one's style. In this regard, interventions to change parental insensitivity are likely to be more effective than attempts to change children's attachment insecurity, and preventive interventions are likely to be more effective than therapeutic interventions intended to change attachment patterns that have crystallized across a variety of intimate relationships (Van Ijzendoorn, Juffer, & Duyvestyn, 1995).

Attachment theory is flexible and open to development. This contributes to its attractiveness among scholars of diverse orientations. Among clinicians, attachment theory has influenced both psychoanalysts (Dazzi & De Coro, 1992) and cognitively oriented therapists (Guidano & Liotti, 1983; Guidano, 1987). In developmental psychology, attachment theory and the study of emotional and cognitive development have become intertwined (Sroufe, 1996). In personality psychology, three promising lines of research, to which we now turn, explore (1) personal characteristics of the mother and of the child at the onset of attachment, (2) cultural differences, and (3) stability and pervasiveness of attachment patterns across the life course and across generations.

## Temperament of the Child and Sensitivity of the Mother

The child's attachment style is affected not only by qualities of the mother but by those of the child. Some children's biological predispositions may make them relatively vulnerable to insecure attachment. Temperament can have direct or indirect effects. An inherited predisposition to be anxious and inhibited in the presence of novel situations may directly influence attachment classification in the "strange situation," since the situation is a novel circumstance. Alternatively, a child's temperament may influence parental reactions, which in turn influence attachment outcomes.

Some evidence does support the contention that children's temperamental tendencies to be inhibited, which can be identified early in life (14 months), contribute to attachment classification later in childhood (Calkins & Fox, 1992). However, at present, there is insufficient evidence to disentangle the effects of the caregiver's personality from the temperament of the child or to establish which temperamental features are protective and which are sources of risk (Fox, 1995; Goldsmith & Alansky, 1987).

Multiple findings attest to the influence of mothers' sensitivity on attachment outcomes. Mothers who are responsive to their children tend to produce securely attached offspring. Those who are inconsistently responsive tend to produce ambivalently attached children. A neglecting or rejecting parental style fosters avoidant attachment (Ainsworth et al., 1978; Belsky, Rovine & Taylor, 1984; Grossmann, Grossman, Spangler, Suess & Uzner, 1985; Isabella, 1993). A meta-analysis by DeWolff & Van Ijzendoorn (1997) documents a modest association between sensitivity and attachment.

Parental style should be viewed not as the sole determinant of attachment outcomes but as an important element in a sequence of events that tends to produce enduring personality patterns. Parental styles interact with children's temperaments. Reviews suggest that parental qualities are particularly influential among children who inherit a vulnerability to insecure attachment. Specifically, mothers who are flexible in allowing their children to explore and to face risks more often have securely attached children (Kagan, 1998a).

Experiential factors such as physical handicaps, childhood illnesses, traumas, and severe material deprivation may further impair attachment bonds. Unfortunately, extreme cases of these factors may be relatively inaccessible to researchers, with the factors therefore not being adequately reported in the scientific literature.

## Cultural Differences and Social Networks

Cultural differences are revealed in meta-analysis of the strange situation conducted by Van Ijzendoorn & Kroonenberg (1988). Although secure attachment predominates (55–65%) over insecure-resistant and insecure-avoidant patterns in all cultures that have been examined, variations across cultures are found. Secure attachment is relatively prevalent in the United States, resistance to attachment is more frequent in Israel and Japan, and avoidance is more prevalent in Western European countries. No less important than cross-cultural differences are intracultural variations, which account for 1.5 times the variation accounted for by cross-cultural differences (Van Ijzendoorn & Kroonenber, 1988). Preliminary findings also suggest that secure parent–child attachment patterns are preferred by parents.

Further cross-cultural research is necessary to verify these conclusions and to identify the processes underlying the observed patterns. Wider social networks also are important to development. Siblings, peers, and caretakers other than the mother may provide a secure base for children (Van Ijzendoorn & Sagi, 1999). This realization expands the traditional dyadic perspective on attachment processes.

## Stability and Pervasiveness Across Generations

Research on attachment style has not rested solely on the original paradigms (Ainsworth, 1967). Investigators have developed novel methods to assess interpersonal styles. This has promoted research on the stability and pervasiveness of early patterns of attachments, on their transmission across generations, and on the diagnostic and predictive value of attachment patterns for health outcomes and social adjustment (Armsden &

Greenberg, 1987, Bartholomew & Horowitz, 1991; Feeney, Noller & Hanrahan, 1994; George, Kaplan & Main, 1985; Hazan and Shaver, 1993; Klohnen & Bera, 1998; Van Ijzendoorn, 1995).

Among these novel methods is the Adult Attachment Interview, which taps parents' mental representations and evaluations of their own childhood attachment experiences. It is assumed that these recollections reflect a "state of mind" (Main, Kaplan & Cassidy, 1985) that is derived from these experiences and that influences parents' sensitivity and capacity to provide a secure base for the child. In coding interview responses, the emphasis is not on the veracity of autobiographical memories but on their organization and reconstruction. What matters is the coherence of the discourse; the degree of idealizations, dissociations, contradictions, and repressions; and the capacity to acknowledge and express positive and negative experiences in a complete, focused, and orderly way.

Coding of the Adult Attachment Interview leads to three main classifications: autonomous, preoccupied, and dismissing. These parallel the secure, resistant-ambivalent, and avoidant classifications in children. Autonomous persons are characterized by open and critical reflections on their attachment experiences. Preoccupied individuals are anxious and concerned about their relations with parents. Dismissing persons deny or minimize the influence of earlier attachment experiences.

Preliminary estimates of the distribution of the three adult attachment patterns among normal populations are similar to those of the strange situation. The autonomous style predominates, comprising about 60% of the population, with approximately 20% of the population falling in each of the other groups.

Findings indicate that attachment patterns identified by the Adult Attachment Interview are relatively stable over the life course, although stability is significantly moderated by parental responsiveness and by life events that disrupt, aggravate, or compensate for earlier attachment experiences. There is evidence of systematic convergence of attachment pat-terns in mating, with autonomous women often marrying autonomous men. Attachment patterns thus are pervasive in that they are part of a more general strategy for interaction with others. There also is growing evidence that attachment patterns are stable across generations. Secure infants are more frequently the offspring of autonomous and responsive parents. Whereas autonomous persons generally are better adjusted than the preoccupied, who are overrepresented among clinical or at-risk populations, findings linking Adult Attachment Interview patterns to psychopathological syndromes are still inconclusive (Van Ijzendoorn, 1995; Van Ijzendoorn & Barkemans-Kranenburg, 1997).

Stability of attachment styles and their influence on adult relationships should not be taken to imply that individuals cannot change. People often overcome the potentially deleterious effects of poor attachments early in life (Kagan, 1998b).

**Interpersonal Orientations**

Are mental models of early relationships revised and modified over the course of development? Do issues of trust and security constitute a core of relationship beliefs that are basically stable, despite life transitions? Is the notion of a person's possessing one general interpersonal orientation compatible with the considerable variability in behavior that people exhibit in different types of relationships? One of the great contributions of Bowlby's theory is that is has spurred empirical research on these difficult questions. This work explores adult interpersonal orientations in a manner that is highly informed by original attachment theory reasoning. The work of Hazan and Shaver (1987) and Bartholomew (1990) is particularly noteworthy here.

Hazan and Shaver have proposed that romantic love is an attachment process. The three attachment types – secure, avoidant, and anxious-ambivalent – color adults' experience of romantic love (Hazan & Shaver, 1987; Shaver & Hazan, 1993). The link between attachment styles and adult romantic relationships is evident in people's characterizations of themselves in relationships. Secure adults endorse self-descriptors such as "I find it relatively easy to get close to others and am comfortable depending on them" or "I don't often worry about being abandoned or about someone getting too close to me." Avoidant adults endorse statements such as "I am somewhat uncomfortable being close to others," "I find it difficult to trust them completely, difficult to allow myself to depend on them," or "I am nervous when anyone gets too close, and often, love partners want me to be more intimate than I feel comfortable being." Anxious-ambivalent adults state that "I find that others are reluctant to get as close as I would like," or "I often worry that my partner doesn't really love me or want to stay with me." Secure adults are found to be more likely to trust their lovers, whereas avoidant partners are least likely to accept their partner's faults and anxious-ambivalent adults show too much intense longing. Furthermore, different attachment styles predict different beliefs about love and different memories about earlier relationships in a manner consistent with attachment theory (Hazan & Shaver, 1987; Shaver & Hazan, 1993).

As reviewed by Shaver & Hazan (1993), research supports the notion that people possess a predominant interpersonal orientation, which pervasively impinges on their affective experiences and relationship satisfaction. An avoidant style fosters denial of attachment needs, a failure to focus on feelings, an inability to self-disclose, and reluctance in emotional commitment; these factors interfere with the enjoyment of intimacy and the benefits of others' support in stressful circumstances. An anxious-ambivalent style involves a preoccupation with potential losses and frequent expressions of anger, fear, jealousy, and overdependency. The secure style fosters experiences that are the opposite of the insecure tendencies described above; people with a secure style tend to gain self-worth from their relationships. As expected by attachment theory, the expression of secure versus insecure interpersonal styles is quite stable longitudinally, even when interpersonal styles are

assessed across long time periods and through both self-report and observer-report methods (e.g., Klohnen & Bera, 1998). Insecure styles are meaningfully related to early-life events that interfere with the development of parental relationships. For example, avoidant adult women are more likely than secure adults to have lost a parent early in life or to have grown up with few siblings. As compared with avoidant women, securely attached women are more satisfied with their relationships, more self-confident and trustful, less defensive, and less vulnerable to stress.

Research by Bartholomew also has explored the Bowlby-inspired hypothesis that one's predominant attachment style has broad implications for interpersonal relationships. Bartholomew suggests that individual differences in attachment style reflect two distinct kinds of working models related, respectively, to self and others. People's views both of themselves and of others may range from positive to negative (Bartholomew, 1990; 1993; Bartholomew & Horowitz, 1991). Rather than a three-category scheme, as suggested by other investigators, Bartholomew's work indicates a four-category taxonomy of adult attachment orientations defined by the 2 × 2 matrix of positive versus negative self-regard and positive versus negative regard of others. Two kinds of avoidant individuals have been distinguished: *fearful* (afraid of intimacy, owing to a negative view of self and others) and *dismissing* (a detached, self-protective style resulting from the combination of positive self-views and negative views of others. *Secure* individuals (positive view of self and others) tend toward intimate relationships that maintain personal autonomy, whereas *preoccupied* individuals (negative view of self, positive view of others) are similar to those characterized by the earlier notion of *ambivalent*, a style involving worry about acceptance from others. This fourfold scheme can be understood in terms of two dimensions that have been identified empirically: security and preoccupation. Secure and fearful types lie at the opposite end of the security dimension. Anxious-ambivalent and dismissing types define opposite ends of the preoccupation dimension. Bartholomew and Horowitz's (1991) Relationship Questionnaire (adapted from the previous work of Hazan & Shaver, 1987) assesses attachment styles by asking people to indicate the degree to which they resemble prototypic descriptions of each of the four types. It is unusual to find individual people who cleanly fit any one of the attachment prototypes; individuals often show elements of more than one style and vary their style across contexts. Nonetheless, analyses of self-reported individual differences do support the distinctiveness of the four styles for capturing variations in the population (Bartholomew, 1990; Bartholomew & Horowitz, 1991; Diehl, Elnick, Bourbeau, & Labouvie-Vief, 1998).

Since the seminal work of Hazan and Shaver (1987) and Bartholomew (1990), studies of adult attachment have multiplied, and new measures have been provided to assess the various styles (see Fraley, Waller, & Brennan, 2000). Styles have been conceptualized both categorically, with people classifying themselves into a typology (as if the various attachment styles are mutually exclusive), and dimensionally, with participants completing questionnaires that tap dimensions of variation (Brennan & Shaver, 1995; Collins & Read, 1994; Feeney, Noller & Hanrahan, 1994; Griffin & Bartholomew, 1994). These advances have enabled investigators to relate attachment patterns to a number of personality, experiential, and sociodemographic variables.

In light of the popularity of the five-factor model of individual difference structure, Shaver and Brennan (1992) explored the relation between the five NEO Personality Index (NEO-PI) factors and the three attachment styles (secure, insecure-ambivalent, insecure-avoidant). Attachment was assessed in two ways: by a categorical measure, which asked people to indicate what type they are; and by a dimensional method, which asked how characteristic (on a 7-point scale) each style was of the individual. Extroversion, agreeableness, and conscientiousness were positively, yet weakly, or related with security. Secure sub-

jects were less neurotic and more extroverted than insecure subjects and more agreeable than avoidant subjects. Similar findings have been obtained by Carver (1997) in a study that conceived of attachment styles via a four-category model, which was similar to Bartholomew's (1990) but which used different measures of attachment and of the five-factor model. Securely attached people were found to be more extroverted, agreeable, and conscientious. Preoccupied and fearful people were more neurotic and introverted. People with dismissing tendencies were less agreeable.

Mickelson, Kessler, and Shaver (1997) have examined the relation of secure, avoidant, and anxious attachment patterns to sociodemographics (e.g., sex, age, education, race, income, marital status), personality, psychopathology, childhood adversities, and parental representations. This work involved a large, nationally representative sample of American adults. The distribution of adult attachment styles was 59% secure, 25% avoidant, and 11% anxious. The securely attached were relatively more likely to be female, older, married, white, well-educated, and financially well off. Levels of self-esteem, internal locus of control, extroversion, and openness were related positively to the secure pattern and negatively to the two insecure patterns. In contrast, mood, anxiety, and conduct disorders were related positively to both the insecure patterns and negatively to the secure pattern. Most childhood adversities (including parental discord, neglect, and abuse) were negatively related to secure attachment and positively related to anxious and avoidant patterns. Parental warmth positively predicted secure attachment and negatively related to both insecure patterns.

Viewing personality as a purposive, self-regulatory system rather than merely a collection of global dispositional tendencies highlights potential relations between attachment patterns and specific affective, cognitive, and motivational mechanisms. Attachment patterns include cognitive-emotional and behavioral strategies. These strategies should be seen as part of the mechanisms involved in coordinating the whole functioning of a personality system. Thus, we expect that early in life, attachment patterns would contribute to the development of self-regulatory structures. Over the course of life, these self-regulatory capabilities should contribute to one's choice of relationship experiences and to success in managing relationships and personal stress. Indeed, evidence suggests that the relation between women's mental models of attachment and their adjustment to a stressful life event, abortion, is partly mediated by perceptions of self-efficacy for coping with the event (Cozzarelli, Sumer, & Major, 1998). Attachment experiences, then, may be seen to involve the same processes (attention, emotion regulation and expression, attributions of meaning, symbolic communication, self-appraisal, etc.) through which individuals manage other aspects of their life. The enduring cognitive and affective structures that result from the organization of these processes should mediate the impact of early attachment experiences on a variety of interpersonal relations.

Similarly, efforts to promote healthier relations between children and parents in the promotion of well-being should be complemented by sounder knowledge of how attachment patterns are related to specific psychological structures. Particularly noteworthy is the relationship between the elements of the self-system and attachment. Consider the evidence of a positive relation between security and global perceptions of self-worth. This empirical relation may encompass an impact of attachment experiences on a number of different components of the self-system, not just feelings of esteem. Mikulincer (1995) assessed attachment styles in accord with Hazan and Shaver's (1987) prototypical descriptions of attachment and found that secure adolescents have more balanced, complex, and coherent self-structures than the insecure (either avoidant or anxious-ambivalent). Brennan and Morris (1997) distinguished self-liking from self-competence when assessing attachment styles in accord with the Bartholomew (1990) fourfold

model. They found that both secure and dismissing individuals scored higher than the preoccupied and fearful in both self-liking and self-competence. However, whereas the secure style was associated more strongly with self-liking than self-competence, the dismissing style showed the reverse pattern. Fearfulness and preoccupation were associated more strongly with low self-liking than with low self-competence.

To explore how attachment working models influence knowledge structures that filter and color interpersonal experience, Mikulincer (1997, 1998a) has related attachment styles to memory accessibility, information processing strategies, and affect regulation. In a first study, securely attached individuals were found to report relatively low levels of anxiety and to exhibit moderate levels of defensiveness. Unpleasant memories were more accessible to them than to avoidant individuals. Unlike others, the securely attached tended not to experience a spreading of emotional tone from a dominant negative emotion to nondominant emotions. In contrast, anxious-ambivalent people reported relatively high anxiety and low defensiveness and showed the shortest retrieval times for negative memories. These memories were linked to highly intense negative emotions. Avoidant individuals expressed different cognitive–affective patterns. They reported moderately high levels of anxiety and high levels of defensiveness, showed the longest retrieval times for negative memories, and exhibited the lowest emotional intensity linked to these memories (Mikulincer & Orbach, 1995).

In a second study, two aspect of information processing, information search and integration within cognitive structures, were found to relate positively to the secure attachment pattern. "Security in attachment," then, "has a cognitive facet, consisting of active information search, openness to new information, and flexibility of cognitive structure, which seems to improve coping with, and adjustment to, a changing and complex world" (Mikulincer, 1997, p, 1226). In further work, secure persons, in comparison with the insecure (avoidant and ambivalent), showed better capacities to handle anger and hostility in a functional manner. Secure persons experienced anger in a reasonable, instrumental way. They attributed less hostile intent to others, endorsed more constructive goals regarding the preservation of relationships with individuals who instigated anger, and anticipated more positive interpersonal outcomes (Mikulincer, 1998a). Attachment styles also were found to relate significantly to self-appraisals (Mikulincer, 1998b) and perceived similarity to others (Mikulincer, Orbach, & Iavnieli, 1998), where both self-appraisals and perceived similarity have been viewed as strategic variations of affect regulation. Secure persons held a stable, positive self-view and showed more accurate evaluations of their similarity to others. Avoidant and ambivalent persons had less stable appraisals of themselves and of their similarity to others. Avoidants tended to display a compensatory positive self-view and to underestimate their similarity to others, whereas ambivalents tended to show a negative self-view and to overestimating their other-similarity.

Collins and Read (1994) conceive of attachment patterns as part of a broader system of cognitive and motivational processes that influence experiences and actions in relationships. They view attachment working models as highly accessible cognitive constructs, which are automatically activated in response to attachment-relevant events. Once activated, these knowledge structures influence information processing (attention, memory, attribution) and emotional response patterns. These cognitive structures come into play specifically within relevant interpersonal settings. Collins (1996) finds that working models of attachment are poor predictors of social cognition in the case of attachment-irrelevant situations, such as when research participants envision a fictional dating partner and hypothetical interpersonal events. In contrast, they predict social thinking within scenarios involving an actual individual with whom one was engaged in a romantic relationship.

Secure subjects made more benign explanations and attributions and were less likely to predict conflict than either of the insecure groups (avoidant and preoccupied).

Baldwin (1992, 1999) has further extended the analysis of mental representations underlying attachment phenomena. He distinguished between knowledge availability and accessibility, that is, whether people possess a certain type of knowledge versus the salience of that knowledge (see chapter 9). Any given individual may possess knowledge representative of two or three different attachment styles, although one knowledge structure may predominate or may be most "chronically accessible" (Higgins, 1997). A critical prediction from this view is that cognitively priming one versus another cognitive representation may shift an individual's attachment style. Baldwin and colleagues primed representations by asking research participants to visualize an acquaintance with whom they have either a secure, an avoidant, or an anxious-ambivalent relationship. In a purportedly separate study, participants rated the attractiveness of potential dating partners whose characteristics represented each of the three styles. Priming a secure relationship increased participants' attraction toward secure dating partners. This social-cognitive viewpoint contradicts the assumption that all individuals can be characterized as stably possessing a single orientation toward interpersonal relationships resulting from their possession of a single type of mental representation. Instead, people may possess knowledge of varying sorts, held at varying levels of accessibility, with a resultant "variability in relationship-specific attachment orientations" (Baldwin, Keelen, Fehr, Enns, & Koh-Rangarajoo, 1996, p. 107). Change in attachment is more than an exception as attested by the 30 to 40% rates of attachment style change reported by longitudinal studies (Baldwin & Fehr, 1995; Kirkpatrick & Hazan, 1994).

Flexibility in attachment style may itself be an important individual difference, with some individuals being more prone to attachment style change than others. Attachment style fluctuations may be associated with attachment insecurity as well as other vulnerability factors, as suggested by a 2-year longitudinal study of young women, in which 30% of women with a previous history of psychopathology were particularly prone to attachment style instability (Davila, Burge, and Hammen, 1997). However, it is likely that changes in attachment also strongly reflect changes in external contingencies. Different styles are more consonant with specific contexts, tasks, and predominant encounters.

These studies, which attest to the fruitfulness of Bowlby's original contributions, also are valuable reminders that interpersonal styles can change across the life-span. The findings force an expansion of the original formulation to incorporate the facts that attachment patterns are cognitive systems that may change across time and context. We noted this human potentiality for change in chapter 1, where we cited examples (also reviewed in Kagan, 1998b) in which individuals and groups who experienced poor early-life attachments subsequently had the benefit of skilled adult care. The human potentiality for change and growth is illustrated by the normal personality outcomes achieved by these individuals despite their poor early-life attachment experiences.

At present, no evidence speaks to the possibility that specific brain systems govern attachment seeking in the child and caring by the mother. Attachment styles have not been convincingly related to any specific genetic sources of variability. There are, then, no "strong biological" explanations of attachment behavior (Turkheimer, 1998). The findings that attachment patterns may change through life and across relational contexts and that individuals other than the mother may provide a secure basis instead speak to the human potential for adaptability in the face of varying social circumstances. These recent advances in attachment research prompt one to consider future directions that should be pursued.

A better understanding is needed of how cultural and intracultural differences influence the phenotypic expressions of attachment and its continuity throughout life and across generations. Other contributions should examine whether trust and security orientations with friends, family members, and other acquaintances can be traced to attachment styles or constitute independent interpersonal dimensions. It would be valuable to establish more firmly whether interpersonal styles (assessed via interview or self-report) partly reflect current personal states or interpersonal relationships.

Finally, links between attachment experiences and other aspects of knowledge and behavior that have proved important to social development and adaptation deserve greater attention. Prosocial behavior is a good candidate (Graziano & Eisenberg, 1997). Preliminary findings support the link between prosociality and security. Prosocial subjects show more secure attachments than do individualists and competitors (Van Lange, Otten, De Bruin, & Joireman, 1997). As suggested above, perceived efficacy beliefs are other good candidates (cf. Cozzarelli et al., 1998) insofar as they are signficant determinants of prosocial behavior and of rewarding interpersonal relations (Bandura, 1997).

## COMMUNICATION

Many decades ago, Vygotsky (1934) contended that a key to the development of personality was the development of language (see chapter 2). Children regulate their actions by internalizing communications that initially were interpersonal. The intrapsychic speech contributes to the child's capacity for self-regulation.

Research on early communication in the 1990s (Adamson, 1995; Fogel, 1993; Nadel & Camaioni, 1993) came to recognize the seminal contributions of Vygotsky. Investigators emphasized that languages are not just abstract symbol systems. Language use is social behavior. Language is the most common medium for our most common social act, communicating with others. As Vygotsky suggested, language first serves as a medium to communicate with the external world and then as a medium to communicate with oneself. This makes the study of language a part of the study of interpersonal behavior and personality development. Interpersonal relations provide the context for developing interpersonal and intrapersonal dialogues. These dialogues, in turn, contribute to the critical personality task of self-regulation. The development of language, then, contributes to the child's capacity to function as an interacting causal agent in social affairs. Social contexts spur the full development of this human potential. Language development, then, is not a mere unfolding of a genetic blueprint but a contextualized growth process.

The greater recognition of these points fostered a reconceptualization of the communication process. Rather than "the emit/receive/answer telegraphist model of communication" that was suggested by information theory analyses of language, the new conceptualization treated communication as a "context bound process . . . which undergoes general processes of change and variations . . . and whose outcomes vary according to differences in the social contexts in which it occurs" (Nadel & Camaioni, 1993, p. 2). "Context" does not refer merely to the physical and sociocultural environment, but to interpersonal factors such as "shared meanings . . . conventionalized acts (and) symmetrical/asymetrical role relations" (Nadel & Camaioni, 1993, pp. 3–4). Nadel and Camaioni propose an "orchestra" metaphor to capture the holistic, dynamic, and contextual properties of communicative exchanges. Contexts and individual attributes contribute to decisions about what to perform and to the harmonic quality of the performance.

Even at a young age, children actively contribute to the flow of communication. They bring their own intentionality, individuality, and theory of mind into relationships. They thereby partially shape the encounters that in turn contribute to the construction of their personality.

Over the course of development, children establish social meanings, goals, and a sense of identity through communicative exchanges with others. These reciprocal negotiations of meaning rest, of course, on both linguistic communication and nonverbal expression. Thus, both cognitive and affective individual differences shape the exchanges that take place.

Early in life, communication is rudimentary. Simple signals between infant and caregiver primarily exchange information about basic affective states (pain, pleasure, relaxation, excitement, curiosity). Yet even these simple exchanges are influenced by the caregiver's quality of response to the child's needs. The infant's crying, smiling, looking, and clinging are calls for communication. They provide information not only for the mother but for the child in turn – the mother's voice, her tone and cadence, her eye contact, and her touch and physical affection. The development of symbolic language enormously expands the possibility for communications about affective states and thus can strengthen the child's relations with others. Thus, although language fosters the development of thought and self-reflection, its capacity to strengthen interpersonal relations is also fundamental.

Communication includes more than linguistic exchanges. It involves multiple processes such as imitation, symbolization, social comparison, nonverbal emotional expression, and behavior. As Watzlavick, Bavelas, & Jackson (1967) note, when at least two people are together, it is impossible not to communicate. Talking, looking, not talking, and looking away are all forms of communication. They all may serve as signals that affect the behavior and internal psychological states of the individuals in the relationship.

People's specific communicative maneuvers reflect the repertoire they have developed from past interactions and their own internal dialogues. Communication thus reflects the history of one's relationships, one's personality and conceptions of oneself and others, expectations about the possibilities of the given relationship, and social rules that govern conversation. Children learn quickly to coordinate their moves, tune their feelings and thoughts, and negotiate their goals in accordance with others. These techniques develop into a capacity to communicate as a distinctive aspect of one's personality.

According to Fogel, two key features of any communication are coregulation and framing. *Coregulation* refers to the social process "by which individuals dynamically alter their actions with respect to the ongoing and anticipated actions of their partners" (1993, p. 34). *Framing* refers to the scope and the limits of the discourse: its location, its setting, "the actions that are to be taken as communicative . . . the main focus or topic . . . the background understanding of events" (1993, p. 18). Consensual framing is critical for satisfactory communication. The necessity of a consensual frame becomes particularly evident when one enters an unfamiliar culture, in which unknown rules may disrupt the normal coregulation of communication. Under these circumstances, improved communication often requires that individuals explicitly confront their conflicting frames for meaning and the associated expectations that they have brought into an encounter. The capacity to "metacommunicate" (Watzlavick et al., 1967) is necessary to establish normal interpersonal relations. *Metacommunication* requires knowing the implicit rules and meanings that underpin discourse and how they contribute to the maintenance of a relationship.

Communicative capacities thus exert pervasive influences on personality development and functioning. Mastery of communicative and metacommunicative skills is required to establish rewarding relationships, to meet the mutual obligations that relationships entail, and thus to collaborate effectively with others. These collaborative relationships, in turn, contribute to self-development by promoting the socioemotional skills that are required to establish and maintain intimate relationships (Brehm, 1992).

The capacity to communicate openly with parents has proved to be a protective factor among early adolescents (Caprara et al., 1998; Caprara, Scabini, Barbaranelli, Pastorelli, & Regalia, 1999). Adolescents who report having more open communications with their parents are found to be less likely to engage in antisocial actions, including alcohol use, drug use, theft, and the destruction of property and less likely to experience depression. Open communication with parents, then, is a source of support that protects against adolescent risks. When parents openly discuss emotions and emotional problem solving, children develop greater emotion regulation skills, which in turn promote their personal adjustment (Parke and Buriel, 1998).

Baltes and Staudinger's (1996) concept of *interactive minds* is a particularly promising conceptual development in the study of interpersonal relations, communication, and personality development. These investigators recognize that most personal capabilities are fundamentally social in origin. People develop the ability to think constructively about themselves and the social world through their communications with others (cf. Mead, 1934; Vygotsky, 1934). Interpersonal settings, then, constitute the place where cognitive competencies develop and express themselves. The "reciprocal influences between minds" (Staudinger & Baltes, 1996, p. 746) contribute to the individual's full realization of his or her cognitive capacities.

The role of interactive minds in individual personality functioning is well illustrated by work (Staudinger & Baltes, 1996) that applied an interactive minds framework to the study of wisdom, that is, the expression of cognitive expertise in matters concerning the meaning and pragmatics of life (Baltes & Staudinger, 1998) (see chapter 3). Staudinger and Baltes reasoned that wisdom is not merely a personal matter, but a social interactive one. People's capacity for wisely contemplating personal matters develops through communicative interactions with others. Settings that enable people to engage in dialogues about interpersonal problems, then, should enhance the capacity for wisdom.

To test this possibility, Staudinger and Baltes (1996) assessed wisdom-related performance by asking individuals to generate solutions to interpersonal problems and crises (e.g., participants were asked what one should do if confronted by a friend who is contemplating suicide); the solutions were scored according to a set of predefined wisdom-related criteria. Participants generated these solutions after first experiencing one of five conditions. Two conditions particularly promoted the interaction of minds: a dialogue with a companion followed by time to contemplate the dialogue, and a period of thinking in which participants were encouraged to engage in internal dialogues in which they considered what other persons would say about the problem at hand. The results revealed that these two conditions enhanced wisdom-related performance more than did the other three groups, in which participants were not prompted to dwell on dialogues they had with others. After contemplating interpersonal dialogues, participants were more capable of generating solutions that appropriately recognized the vagaries and complexities of life.

This work reveals that the capacity for wisdom is not a fixed property of isolated minds. Instead, the human potential for wisdom is cultivated in social contexts that enable interpersonal communication. "Any performance setting that ignores the interactive-minds aspect of wisdom clearly underestimates wisdom-related performance capacity" (Staudinger & Baltes, 1996, p. 758). The insights of the interactive-minds framework, combined with other perspectives on the social foundations of social-cognitive capabilities (Bandura, 1986; Levine, Resnick & Higgins, 1993), then, speak eloquently to the way in which interpersonal processes contribute to the development of the individual.

As noted, the study of social foundations of thought, self-awareness, and identity construction has a long history (Mead, 1934; Vygotsky, 1934). Contemporary work explores how the presence of others results in mental representations of the others that function to organize one's own experience. It examines how mental representations of one's own relations become associated to internal interactions or inner dialogues leading to the formation of the self and how the internal interactions between one's self and other representations determine one's actual relations with them, leading to new experiences and promoting development.

When inquiring into the social foundations and interactive components of linguistic knowledge, thought, memory, moral judgment, and motivation, emphasis is placed on the processes that unfold over time and on the interpersonal relations that foster these processes and turn them into mental structures that organize experience. The first questions one addresses about the earlier stages of personality development deal with when and how internalization of others takes place, an internal dialogue starts, and the capacity to engage in collaborative exchanges develops. Then the question one addresses is how transactions influence the course of development in setting beliefs, goals, and standards, that is, in promoting knowledge structures that guide actions toward multiple pursuits.

Other questions concern those other persons who are most influential at different times. Whereas the above arguments on attachment and earlier communication highlighted the impact of the caregiver in the early stages of development, it is evident that the influence the caregiver exerts on the development of the child cannot take place in isolation. Other sources of interpersonal influence are involved. A mother's feelings and behaviors toward her child are largely influenced by her own transactions with others (partner, other children, relatives, friends). Furthermore, it is clear that other socializing agents join the influence of parents and gradually replace it over the course of development, although the extent to which earlier family relationships influence relations with others outside the family remains a point of debate. Concerning this issue, the role of peers and friends in the development of personality has received considerable attention in recent years.

## PEER RELATIONS AND FRIENDSHIPS

People's identity, confidence in themselves, and personal goals in life strongly derive from interactions with others. Early in life, these interactions primarily involve parents, caretakers, and siblings. Gradually, however, peer relations take on greater importance as social determinants of personality.

Peer relations quickly develop from simple to complex. As described by Hartup (1983), they change "from loosely coordinated exchanges to coordinated interaction, and from primitive awareness of the needs of others to reciprocities based on complex attributions and the utilization of multiple sources of information" (p. 120). As peer relations develop, then, they require greater social skills and cognitive capabilities. Effective functioning necessitates social skills, such as the capacity to achieve reciprocal understanding with others and to negotiate mutually satisfactory social exchanges. These, in turn, require cognitive capabilities, including imitation, social comparison, and behavior and affect regulation.

The development of these skills brings personal benefit. They enable one to participate in peer exchanges that provide emotional support and access to social resources through basic interpersonal transactions involving friendship, cooperation, and acceptance. A rapidly growing literature on friendship attests to its importance in socioemotional and cognitive development (Azmitia, 1996; Bukowski, Newcomb & Hartup, 1996; Hartup, 1992, 1996; Hartup & Stevens, 1997, 1999; Youniss, 1980; Youniss & Smollar, 1985). Furthermore, friendship networks may be important to physical well-being. Friends contribute to actual and perceived levels of social support. Higher levels of social support often predict higher levels of physical health (Adler & Matthews, 1994; Stroebe & Stroebe, 1996).

Peer relations provide not only support, but challenges. Individuals experience pressure to conform to group norms and rejection if they fail to do so. They face conflicts, which they must learn to negotiate. Learning how to resolve conflicts and to create alliances is important, not just to the day-to-day life of children but to their later adjustment. Conflicts are inevitable in social life. The development of skills to resolve them fosters social acceptance and friendship (Ross & Conant, 1992; Hartup, 1992; Putallaz & Sheppard, 1992).

Interestingly, then, social conflicts play both negative and positive roles in personality development. Excessive conflicts among adolescents are associated with antisocial behaviors such as aggression and victimization (Aboud, 1992; Perry, Perry & Kennedy, 1992). Yet conflicts can be valuable developmental experiences. Fully developing one's potential for socially skilled conflict resolution requires that one occasionally confront conflicts. Challenges to one's point of view prompt individuals to develop their skills for resolving disagreements and maintaining close relationships despite differences of opinion (Hartup, 1992; Collins & Larsen, 1992).

### Peer Relations in Younger and Older Childhood

Friendships begin relatively early in life. Children prefer interacting with particular peers, whom they refer to as their "friends," by age 3 to 4 (Hartup & Stevens, 1999). Even at this young age, one already may notice early evidence of the more complex interpersonal relations that develop later in life. These include patterns of intimacy and prosocial behavior that are a prelude to stable friendships. Imitation and more complex forms of observational learning are probably the most powerful mechanisms for spurring the development of these interpersonal patterns. By observing others, children incorporate complex rules of social behavior involving the coordination of efforts, sharing of emotions, and understanding of feelings (Rosenthal & Zimmerman, 1978).

In middle childhood, children spend more time with friends than they do during the early years. They become increasingly able to initiate, maintain, and repair peer relationships. These capacities reflect an improved capacity to empathize and to regulate affect and behavior in accord with norms of reciprocity. This fosters more enduring relationships, which can survive occasional conflicts (Eisenberg & Fabes, 1991, 1992; Eisenberg & Mussen, 1989; Radke-Yarrow, Zahn-Waxler & Chapman, 1983). Enduring relationships enable the child to experience social bonds of intimacy, loyalty, and caring.

Children continue to spend a significant percentage of their time in the company of friends during adolescence. In the middle childhood and adolescent years, it is estimated that on average, people spend almost one third of their waking hours with friends; this proportion then drops substantially in adulthood (Hartup & Stevens, 1999).

At all ages, friendship is characterized by reciprocity. Friends are people who can count on one another to exchange support and resources. Although reciprocity is a constant feature of friendship, the nature of reciprocal exchange varies across development. Early childhood friendships are marked by participation in common play activities. In adolescence, in contrast, intimacy and self-disclosure move to the center of the reciprocal exchanges. Issues of confidence, trust, and support that develop in adolescence remain important into adulthood. The behavioral activities of friendship, then, change considerably across the life course, whereas the meaning of friendship may remain relatively constant. In this regard, Hartup and Stevens' (1997) distinction between the deep structure and surface structure of friendships is useful. The former refers to the enduring social meaning of a relationship, whereas the latter refers to the particular social exchanges among friends that take place at any given moment in any given situation.

## Early Friendships and Prosocial Capabilities and Later Psychosocial Outcomes

A question that naturally arises in the study of friendship and personality is whether having friends enhances psychological well-being. Establishing the causal impact of friendship is particularly difficult, since people who are psychologically well adjusted may be better able to establish friendships. However, longitudinal research does suggest that having friends enhances self-esteem; even when controlling for early childhood levels of self-esteem, people who have many friends in childhood are found to have higher self-esteem in young adulthood (Bagwell, Newcomb, & Bukowski, 1998).

A related question involves prosocial competence and its relation to psychosocial or achievement outcomes. In principle, "a repertoire of friendly, prosocial and competent social behaviors" may foster "social acceptance, while devious, aversive reactions to other children enhance one's chances of social rejection" (Hartup, 1983, p. 135). However, once again, firmly establishing the unique causal influence of prosocial skills is difficult, since they are embedded in a network of interacting factors such as temperament and parenting style (see Hartup & van Lieshout, 1995).

Recent findings do, however, provide evidence of a long-term impact of prosocial capabilities. In longitudinal research conducted in a school system in Italy, children's prosocial behavior at age 7 to 8 was found strongly to predict their academic achievement and social acceptance 5 years later (Caprara, Barbaranelli & Pastorelli, in press; Caprara, Barbaranelli, Pastorelli, Bandura, & Zimbardo, in press). A number of processes may contribute to the link from prosocial abilities to academic achievement. Prosocial behavior opens opportunities for help and collaboration, elicits reactions of sympathy, and counteracts depression and problem behavior that can interfere with the educational process (Bandura, Barbaronelli, Caprara, & Pastorelli, 1996a,b; Bandura, Pastorelli, Barbaranelli, & Caprara, 1999). Interpersonal processes, then, can help children to maximize their intellectual potential. This underscores the fact that not only teachers but one's peer groups contributes to both social and intellectual development.

Other findings from this research program identify additional personal determinants of

adjustment. These include perceived interpersonal and social self-efficacy and moral
standards for behavior. The perceived capacity to advance one's own point of view, to
resist group pressures, and to persuade others fosters peer acceptance and social adjustment. The tendency to disengage moral
standards, in contrast, fosters hazardous
behaviors and the develoment of relationships with socially deviant peers (Bandura et
al., 1996a,b).

## Peer Relations and the Development of Self-Concept

In adolescence, peer relationships contribute
greatly to self-knowledge and self-evaluations. Peers provide social comparison information and social support. Egalitarian
friendships featuring acceptance and trust
enable individuals to disclose emotional
experiences to others, which promotes inner
dialogues and self-understanding. Boys and
girls are differentially likely to experience
such relationships. Girls experience intimate
conversations more frequently than boys in
childhood, which leaves them with greater
skills and higher expectations for intimate
friendships in adolescence (Golombok &
Fivush, 1994).

Both close friends and one's wider peer
group influence evaluations of the self. Their
impact, however, is not equivalent. Across age
groups, self-esteem is linked more closely to
peer approval than to approval from one's
friends (reviewed in Harter, 1998). It appears
that individuals generally view peer approval
in public domains of social life as more credi-
ble information about the self than supportive
personal statements from intimates.

A meta-analytic review (Newcomb and
Bagwell, 1995) reveals significant differences
between friendships and relations with non-
friends. Friendships involve more intense
social activity and more frequent conflict resolution. Friendship prevents diversities and
divergences from turning into hostilities that
jeopardize relationships. A greater concern for
fairness and equity enhances attention to others' feelings and fosters interpersonal commu-

nications that serve one's own and other's self-
worth.

## Friendships and Maladjustment

Not all friendships are good. Rather, the
friends one keeps and the way people face
friendships are an indicator of adjustment.
Making and maintaining friends requires a
person to be other-oriented as well as self-ori-
ented. The number and identity of friends and
the affective character of friendship (closeness, supportiveness, conflict) thus partly
reflect individual social and self-regulatory
skills. Children who lack self-control skills and
are impulsively aggressive, for example, tend
to be rejected by peers (Coie & Dodge, 1998).

The quality of friendships is not only an
indicator but a determinant of adjustment.
The tendency of aggressive youth to associate
with deviant peer groups contributes to their
likelihood of their dropping out of school
(Cairns, Cairns, & Neckerman, 1989; Cairns &
Cairns, 1994). Work by Magnusson (e.g.,
Magnusson, 1992) further reveals a role for
peer group relations in antisocial behavior. As
we noted in chapter 4, early-maturing girls
tend to engage in more antisocial activities
than do late-maturing girls during adolescence. Results suggest that peer relations
partly mediate this effect. Early-maturing girls
develop peer relations with other girls who are
early-maturing and spend more of their time
with older members of the opposite sex. It is
these interpersonal contacts that shape self-
image and behavior (Magnusson, 1992). Thus,
the biological factor (early versus late matur-
ing) does not produce the antisocial behavior
directly. Instead, it contributes to a complex
system of determinants.

Friendships, then, can be assets or liabilities depending on who one's friends are and
the quality of one's relationships with them.
Hartup and Stevens (1997) suggest that supportive and intimate relationships between
socially skilled individuals can be developmental advantages, whereas supportive
friendships of behaviorally disturbed persons
are deleterious. The quality of friends is ultimately of greatest importance. Friendships

can serve as either protective or risk factors, depending the environmental opportunities and the individual's capacity to select good friends. Predicting the developmental impact of friendships, then, requires evaluating qualitative features of particular relationships, as well as the social context in which the friendship develops and the functions it serves

## Group Influences

Similar considerations hold with respect to the influence of peer groups. Peer groups operate as reinforcers, models, tutors, and sources of social support. Group processes define and reinforce reciprocal obligations and set limits on individuals' behaviors and aspirations. In groups, individuals learn to experience well-defined roles and to endorse group values. As Gecas (1990) notes, peer groups are an arena for exercising independence from adult control. Children's experiences in peer groups affect the development of self-concept and social competencies, as children must learn to adopt social roles and manage the impression they create in others.

Harris (1995, 1998) has stressed the impact of peer group processes in socialization. Indeed, she claims that the major interpersonal processes in personality development occur in peer groups, not within the family. The main group processes that modify the child's innate psychological tendencies are assimilation and differentiation. "Assimilation transmits cultural norms, smooths off rough edges of personality, and makes children more like their peers. Differentiation exaggerates individual differences and increases variability" (Harris, 1995, p. 482). Harris's arguments about the dearth of within-family influences clearly challenge many traditional views of socialization and personality development.

Harris's conclusion that "parental behaviors have no effects" (1990, p. 459) surely may understate the role of parents and caretakers. The evidence underlying Harris's conclusion often involves data that are aggregated across large populations and that involve global dispositional tendencies. Such evidence may obscure within-family effects that involve more

contextualized or more idiosyncratic aspects of personality functioning. Nonetheless, Harris does valuably highlight social influences that may be overlooked in traditional focuses on temperament and the family. Peer groups challenge one's personal resources in a manner that goes beyond the role of the family, and that constitute a prelude to adult challenges.

Peer influences probably contribute to personality development in conjunction with other aspects of the social and cultural environment, including the family, schools, and, more than in the past, the media (Bandura, 1986; Wartella, 1995). Children and adolescents spend a substantial portion of their waking hours watching television, although the amounts of time significantly vary from one culture to another. The screen provides numerous, recurring models of group relations (see chapter 8).

## Peers, Parents, and Adolescent Storm and Stress

Throughout the 20th century, social scientists devoted much attention to the possibility that adolescence is a period of "storm and stress," as Hall (1904) termed this life period in his early review. Intuitively, it appears that adolescence is a time of rebellion for many youths, with boys in particular engaging in high levels of antisocial conduct.

This phenomenon may, in principle, involve the full range of personality determinants discussed in this and previous chapters. Biological factors that develop at puberty might predispose the adolescent to rebellious conduct. Parental relations might be involved, with parents seeking to maintain control over children who are developing a greater sense of independence. The interaction between parental relations and peer group settings also may be key. As children age, family surveillance decreases. Peer groups become settings in which children can act independently of parental oversight. Children who experiment with risky activities such as drinking and smoking commonly do so in peer group settings. Furthermore, joining organized, deviant groups may seriously jeopardize self-development and physical health by inducing people to participate in detrimental activities (Jessor, 1998). Social organizations and subcultures that exist within civil society strongly contribute to the endorsement of antisocial norms and to delinquent activities (Caprara & Rutter, 1995; Smith, 1995).

A recent review suggests that the storm-and-stress phenomenon can be subdivided into three components: parental conflict, negativity of mood, and risky and antisocial behavior (Arnett, 1999). In all three domains, evidence verifies the reality of storm and stress, yet also indicates that adolescent disruptions are not an inevitable feature of development. Regarding the first two domains, narrative and meta-analytic reviews reveal that child–parent conflict is more frequent during early adolescence than during previous or subsequent developmental periods (Laursen, Coy, & Collins, 1998; Paikoff & Brooks-Gunn, 1991). Research employing experience-sampling methods to measure mood (participants carry a beeper, which signals them intermittently throughout the day to record their affective state) confirms that adolescents experience more negative moods and greater mood swings (e.g., Larson & Ham, 1993). These mood effects may reflect cognitive development, with adolescents' greater recognition of social pressures and threats contributing to more negative emotional experiences (Larson & Richards, 1994).

The third feature of storm and stress, risky and antisocial behavior, has been the subject of particular attention. Hall (1904) saw engagement in antisocial behavior as a normal feature of boys' development (see Arnett, 1998). Work by Moffitt (1993) reaches similar conclusions. Her analysis reveals that a large percentage of males adopt antisocial behavior patterns in adolescence that are abandoned in adulthood. Moffitt's theory of "adolescence limited antisocial behavior" suggests that the reduction of aggression and antisocial activity in adulthood can be understood through a cost–benefit analysis. In adulthood, the negative consequences of breaking the law outweigh the excitement of antisocial behavior.

Moffitt's (1993) analysis, as well as work by Magnusson (1992), suggests that adolescent boys who engage in frequent antisocial acts actually consist of two distinct subgroups. One group, just noted, is antisocial only during adolescence. Their antisocial behavior may best be understood in terms of peer group effects. The other subgroup is aggressive across the life course; its members display antisocial behavior as children, adolescents, and adults. Personal factors or family influences may better explain this group's behavior.

Research exploring biological factors in antisocial behavior confirms the existence of two distinct subgroups of antisocial male adolescents. Persistently antisocial males display lower levels of epinephrine secretion in stressful situations than do males who either do not engage in antisocial acts or engage in antisocial behavior only in the teen years (Magnusson, 1992). As Magnusson notes, this finding contradicts the notion that there is a fixed link between antisocial conduct and low biological reactivity to stress in the adrenal system. The biological functioning of males who are antisocial only during adolescence appears no different from that of males who completely refrain from antisocial conduct during all periods of development. A further point is that the existence of two subgroups of antisocial male youth illustrates the difficulty of using surface-level behavioral tendencies to identify underlying causal mechanisms. At the level of surface behaviors, the two subgroups are similar if not identical; they would be equated, for example, in an analysis of the frequency with which individuals perform aggressive acts. Nonetheless, the underlying determinants of their action differ.

Findings, then, support the belief that greater storm-and-stress is found in adolescence than during other life periods. However, considerable individual differences and cultural variations are found here, too. Arnett's (1999) review suggests that adolescent storm-and-stress is more common in Western industrialized nations than in preindustrialized nations, which place greater emphasis on family coherence than on the independence of the child. Further, even in industrialized nations, a great many youths avoid lapsing into a stormy and stressful period, as Bandura (1997) has emphasized. Many adolescents continue to regulate their actions according to family values and standards of conduct and develop peer networks that reinforce traditional beliefs rather than breeding conflict. These cultural and individual variations indicate that storm-and-stress is not an inevitable feature of human life. Although universal biological factors such as hormonal changes indeed play a role in this phenomenon, "the hormonal contribution to adolescent mood disruptions appears to be small and tends to exist only in interaction with other factors" (Arnett, 1999, p. 322).

Work on storm-and-stress illustrates the general point that an array of multiple interacting causes may contribute to any developmental outcome. Hormonal factors, parental relations, peer influences, and internal cognitive factors combine to determine the emotional life and behavioral tendencies of the adolescent. Furthermore, individual peer and peer group effects do not operate in a historical vacuum. People bring into peer relations their own socioculturally acquired and historically situated values, beliefs, and norms. Peers influences thus must be examined as part of a sequence of events that constitute a dialogue between the individual and the environment. Peer relations, as well as earlier family relationships, offer a double-sided lens to the personality psychologist. Conceived as effects, they enable one to see how early-life experiences and individual characteristics predispose the individual toward certain peers and groups. Conceived as causes, they focus attention on how personality functioning may be affected by particular types of peer and group relationships.

## SUMMING UP

From the beginnings of life, an essential feature of the human condition is the interpersonal relationships between the individual and his or her network of family members and peers. Psychological theory and research have begun to illuminate the role of these interpersonal relations in personality development. Bonds of attachment between mother and child appear broadly to influence the development of individuals' views of self, affective experiences, and orientations toward the world. The quality of relationships with peers is found both to reflect individuals' level of social and emotional skills and to contribute to their psychosocial adjustment. Work on interpersonal relations has implications for psychological science as a whole, in that it shows how individual minds develop through reciprocal interactions with others.

Interpersonal relationships are rooted in broader sociocultural systems that significantly determine the nature of the relationships that take place and their meaning for the individual. Our next chapter, then, moves from the interpersonal to the social world, and considers the socially-derived categories that individuals use to make sense of themselves and their experiences.

# CHAPTER EIGHT

# Social Contexts and Social Constructions

## Work, Education, Family, Gender, and Values

To understand the determinants of personality development, one must address the social contexts in which development takes place. The interpersonal interactions that contribute to development (see chapter 7) occur within family systems, work organizations, educational systems, and legal and sociopolitical frameworks. These social contexts partly determine the meaning of any interaction and its contribution to personal development. A period of parent–child separation has a different meaning within a traditional nuclear family system than it does on a kibbutz. An awareness that one's professional competencies are superior to one's peers has different personal implications in economic systems that encourage versus those that limit independent advancement.

In this chapter, then, we consider the social contexts of work, education, and family life, in that order. Since individuals are born into families, attend school, and then enter the work force, it might seem as if we have gotten something backwards. However, the family's work and socioeconomic status can so strongly influence educational opportunities and family conditions that we address the world of work first.

In chapter 6, we reviewed work on biological sex differences. This yielded only a limited view of the differences between women and men. Beliefs about masculinity and femininity are constructed within cultural and sociopolitical contexts that prescribe the meaning of the sexes. In the second half of this chapter, then, we review theory and research on the social construction of gender, and gender differences in personality development.

This chapter's analyses shift our focus from the level of the individual to the group. Such shifts may entail new explanatory principles. Insights may come from looking beyond any single discipline. In theory, one could study the role of social contexts in personality development by integrating the insights of multiple psychological and social sciences. In practice, however, such integration is difficult to achieve. The specialization of academic disciplines, as reflected in their unique professional training, journals, and associations, both attests to and contributes to a separation of activities that would be puzzling to those outside of the academy. Nonetheless, we do attempt in this chapter to bring an interdisciplinary perspective to bear on questions of personal development.

Our primary goal in this chapter is not merely to review studies that simply correlate an isolated aspect of the social environment with an equally isolated individual-difference variable. Instead, we seek to introduce the complexity of social systems and the reciprocal interactions between individuals and these social structures. Personality psychologists must devote careful attention to the macro social systems in which individuals develop. Too often, personality psychologists claim to be contextualists, yet operate as if individuals develop outside of socioeconomic contexts. Contextual factors prescribe obligations and set limits on potentialities. People must adjust their personal and interpersonal lives to fit the demands of social structures. One cannot ask well-informed questions about personality and social context without having a well-informed view of contextual variables. For example, a question such as "How do work experiences influence women's personality development" is not meaningful without further inquiry into factors such as the percentage of women in the labor force, the percentage of employment and unemployment in the society, women's typical roles in the economic system, and social beliefs about the sexes.

Not only can personality psychology be informed by the study of social structures, but the study of society can be informed by personality psychology. Societies today are more open and mobile than in the past. Social norms no longer prescribe roles or determine life paths. With this lessening of constraints on individual development, personal determinants of behavior influence the individual's life outcomes to an ever larger degree. In many nations, a person's educational level, economic status, and family life are determined by personal competencies and preferences rather than being dictated by ascribed roles and social expectations.

In the study of social contexts and personality development, a basic question to confront is how society preserves and reproduces its organization from generation to generation through the socialization of individuals. How does social stratification influence the day-to-day lives of individuals? How do differential job attainments or access to consumer goods and services affect the person? How does society, through its labor organizations, educational systems, and family structures, constrain or facilitate personal development? Research on these questions is sometimes sparse or equivocal. Firm answers cannot always be offered. In this chapter, then, we do not merely review a series of research findings but also raise questions that are in need of further research in the future.

## WORK

### Marxist Analyses

Karl Marx (1844) stated with greater conviction than any previous thinker that the essence of humans is their social relations. Social relations of particular importance occur in the context of work. In the Marxist view, personality depends for its development and functioning on an individual's position in the organization of labor. Primary considerations involve ownership of the means of production and the division of labor. People's degree of control over the means of production determines their position in the division of labor and consequently their access to a variety of growth opportunities.

Marx pervasively influenced modern thought. He alerted investigators to the role of social classes and stratification in personal development. Specifically, he highlighted the fact that different classes make social resources differentially available to their members. Underprivileged classes have less access to resources, which precludes opportunities for personal growth (Séve, 1975). For example, lower family social position provides less access to education, fewer role models of educational success, and lower educational expectations. Family socioeconomic status can function, then, as a gatekeeper regarding educational and professional opportunities.

Despite their value, Marxist historic-materialistic analyses have proved unable fully to capture the dynamics of contemporary societies. The Marxist division of society according to classes' control over the means of production may have fitted the early stages of industrialization. Today, however, this scheme is problematic. Contemporary society, with its global markets, features a growing diffusion and anonymity of ownership. One's position in the division of labor is more precarious in today's fluid societies than in the past. "The classic bourgeoisie-proletariat distinction," then, is "insufficient as a depiction of the class structure of modern capitalist society" (Kohn and Slomczynski 1990, p. 32). Even the basic distinction between capital and labor does not easily fit new economic organizations, in which capital and labor exert control over one another. Traditional distinctions between manual labor and intellectual work, or among autonomous, semiautonomous, and nonautonomous work, do not fit all societies equally well. Kohn and colleagues find that distinctions among six U.S. social classes (owners, petty bourgeoisie, managers, supervisors, manual workers whose work is predominantly nonmanual, and proper manual workers) differ from distinctions among classes in Poland before the fall of the Berlin wall. These latter distinctions fail to capture the structure of the new democratic Poland.

Instead of the capital–labor distinction, a better framework for studying social organization and personal development may be the notion of social stratification, which refers to the hierarchical ordering of members of society in terms of power, privilege, and prestige. Members of different strata have different access to goods and services and differential control over their lives. Work organization and social stratification are related in that occupational status determines an individual's value and power in a society. Occupational status indicates an individual's expected accomplishments. These expectations often reflect implicit beliefs about the person's competence, which in turn may determine the individual's potential mobility from one occupational position to another.

## Social Status, Action, and the Development of Capacities

The key question, then, is how occupational settings affect personality development. In Marx's view, work organizations and family structures set the conditions for reproducing in the minds of people the same relationships of power and control that hold at the level of the distribution of wealth. Both work and family systems contain positions of differential status. Authoritarian family relations mirror the differential power relationships of the workplace, and the occupational status of the family provider determines the social expectations of the children (Horkeimer, 1936). Through family relations, then, lower-class children expect to maintain the family's traditional social status. Some authors have not hesitated to view the individual's character, then, as functioning to reproduce social stratifications. Individual character carries society's values and preserves its organization (Fromm, 1947; Reich, 1945).

■ *Séve.* In this regard, the contributions of Séve (1975) are probably the most brilliant application of the Marxist intellectual tradition to the issues of personality psychology. Séve contends that workers in capitalistic societies are excluded from the possibility of exerting control over the conditions and products of their jobs. They thus are systematically deprived of opportunities to express their own personal potential. Séve considers four variables in this process; namely, time, needs, acts, and capacities. To satisfy elementary needs, alienated workers must invest all of their time in simple repetitive actions. The limited scope of action precludes the development of new capacities and the emergence of more advanced needs.

The primary shortcoming of Séve's work is one shared by most Marxian psychophiloso-phers. No empirical evidence confirms the correctness of the principles. Research in countries where true socialism has been attempted is lacking.

The seminal ideas of Vygotsky (1925, 1929, 1934) and the later developments of the his-torical-cultural approach (Leont'ev, 1959, 1975) pursued a similar analysis. Cognitive and personality development were linked to social activities and relations that were conceived as culturally and socially situated. Unfortunately, these contributions failed to yield systematic research on the mechanisms through which social organizations prescribe activities that in turn influence personality throughout the course of life.

The exact processes through which occupational status and work activities in contemporary society influence individual beliefs, standards, and aspirations remain to be fully established. The Marxist emphasis on actions performed at work is potentially limited today, in light of the mobility of workers across occupations and their involvement in multiple activities in and beyond the workplace. Greater social freedoms allow people to select and diversify their own activities. Thus, parental occupational status and work activities may not have any simple, direct impact on self-esteem, values, and social competencies of children (see Coopersmith, 1967). Instead, parental influences may be largely mediated by personal interpretive processes and by the growing importance of socializing agents external to the traditional family (e.g., teachers, peers, and media).

■ *Kohn.* Among extant contributions to our understanding of social stratification, work, and personality, those of Kohn and colleagues (Kohn & Schooler 1983; Kohn & Slomczynski, 1990) are particularly noteworthy. Their work is remarkable for its systematic attempt to link the complexity of these contextual factors to personality functioning.

Kohn studies the processes through which social structures are reproduced from one generation to the next. He focuses on how occupational status influences self-direction, that is, people's sense of freedom and autonomy in what they are doing. Kohn posits that "the higher their social stratification positions, the more value men place on self-direction and the more confident they are that self-direction is both possible and efficacious" (Kohn & Schooler, 1983, p. 32). The basic idea is that "doing self-directed work . . . affects off-the-job psychological functioning" (Kohn & Slomczynski, 1990, p. 235). The effects of occupational experiences, then, are seen to extend from people's views of the workplace to their beliefs about the world and the self. By influencing self-views and values of workers who become parents, the effects of social structures are maintained across generations (Kohn & Slomczynski, 1990).

Kohn posits that the primary job-related variables influencing self-direction are the substantive complexity of work, freedom from close supervision, and variety in job activities. Occupations with less self-direction erode people's sense of self-direction outside of the workplace, including child rearing. Job conditions, then, affect adult personality "mainly though a direct process of learning from the job and generalizing what has been learned to other realms of life" (Kohn & Slomczynski, 1990, p. 6).

Longitudinal research that spans more than 20 years and that draws on both U.S. samples and cross-national data has explored this thesis (Kohn & Slomczynski, 1990). In this work, structured interviews are used to assess participants' occupations, career paths, education, values, and orientations toward self, children, and society. Questionnaires tap stylistic and cognitive individual differences, including beliefs about the self. As reviewed by Kohn, empirical findings substantially confirm the hypothesized links: "Social structural position affects parental occupational self-direction; occupational self-direction affects parental values; parental values affect children's values" (1990, p. 201). A more conservative reading of the data would acknowledge the clear correlational relations among sociostructural positions and individuals' values and orientations toward self and society. As always, disentangling causal influences in a

system of reciprocally interacting variables is difficult. It does appear, however, that people who are in a position to control their activities generally show a more positive orientation toward themselves and society and that self-direction mediates the impact of occupational position on aspirations.

Kohn emphasizes the role of educational experiences in the process of intergenerational transmission of values and aspirations. Educational experiences partly mediate the influence of family occupational position. They also have an effect that is distinct from parental influences; "adolescents' and young adults' educational self-direction affects their values, just as parental occupational self-direction affects parental values" (Kohn & Slomczynski, 1990, p. 201). The independent effects of educational experiences may eventually overshadow parental influences.

Kohn does caution that further research is required to substantiate his conclusions and establish their generalizability. Ideally, future research would improve the psychological measures used and include a finer-grained analysis of jobs. A further consideration in assessing Kohn's work is to acknowledge the impact of theoretical premises on empirical findings. As is generally the case, theoretical beliefs here significantly determine the data that are collected and the conclusions drawn from analyses. Finally, the learning generalization model on which Kohn's analysis rests seems quite limited in light of contemporary psychological knowledge. The generalization process is passive and thus does not adequately capture people's proactive capabilities.

Acknowledging the influence of social status and work activities should not foster a deterministic view of personality development. As noted by House (1990), first, one must adequately understand the multiple aspects, dimensions, and components of social structure; second, one must understand how the influences of broad and complex systems are translated, via proximate structures and interpersonal relations, into effects that impinge directly on individual experiences;

and finally, one must understand when, how, and to what extent macrosocial phenomena and proximal microsocial phenomena affect individual personality. In this regard, the Marxist premises that underpin Kohn's analysis could be updated to account better for the organization of modern industrial society and its effects on individual functioning and intergenerational transmission. Occupational status remains a key contextual feature that shapes interpersonal relations and the development of values and norms. However, as we have noted, the major changes witnessed in contemporary society lessen the impact of family-linked social norms. It thus is difficult to relate earlier findings on work and personality development to the contemporary scene. Automation, the contraction of manufacturing positions, and growth of services alter the nature of work for large percentages of the population. Furthermore, organizational cultures and climates significantly moderate the meanings people attribute to their job and their resulting expectations and commitments (Erez & Early, 1993; Schein, 1985).

Personality may be more severely affected by a lack of work than by work experiences. Unemployment precludes the development of personal capacities and excludes one from social relations. Unemployment rates commonly reach 10% within industrial societies (20% among youth), which raises questions about how lack of work, job insecurity, part-time work, changes of occupation, and prolonged exclusion from productivity affect behavior and well-being. Such effects may be moderated by social policies and family supports, so that the same percentage of unemployment has different meanings in different contexts. For example, in southern Italy unemployment rates are high among youth. This does not entail a social crisis, probably because families support unemployed family members. The effects of the same unemployment rate would probably be markedly different in the United States, where family support for adult offspring is less normative. Elder (1999) reports on how occupational status differentially relates to psychological well-being

and development in different sociohistorical contexts.

Work influences do not operate in a vacuum. Among other relevant social and personal factors, union activism moderates the influence of occupational position on alienation and authoritarianism toward the family (Caprara & Vinci, 1978; Caprara, De Vincenti, & Funaro, 1981). Activism can increase beliefs in one's capacity to play an active role in society. Such beliefs may moderate the influence of occupational position on values and life orientations. Family relations, group affiliations, and active participation in community life may provide alternative challenges, which attenuate the influence of occupational position on individual behavior and the influence of world views transmitted to offspring.

Work may influence personality differently at different points in the life cycle. Autonomy, supervision, and variation in activities may have differential effects at the beginning versus the end of one's career, as different incentives and concerns become salient and strategies of selection and compensation differentially affect well-being (Baltes et al., 1998; chapter 5). For example, Carstensen's theory of socioemotional selectivity would suggest that the same job promotion would have greater effects in middle adulthood than in the later years since, with the passing of time, people's goals increasingly center on family life rather than on the development of professional opportunities (Carstensen, 1993, 1995; Carstensen et al., 1999).

Unfortunately, there is a paucity of lifespan research on work and personality across the course of adult development. Much research has related personality traits, motives, and attitudes to work performance, leadership, and morale with the aim of predicting career attainments and improving organizational efficiency (Bray, Campbell and Grant, 1974; Bray, 1982). Individual differences in achievement and power motivation (McClelland, 1985) and more recently, conscientiousness (Hogan & Ones, 1997), have received much attention. However, few studies have explored the effects of work experiences on personality across the life-span. Research by Roberts (1997) is a valuable exception to this rule. An analysis of American women who reached adulthood in the 1960s found that women who worked between the ages of 27 and 43 became more agentic, that is, they experienced stronger feelings of personal assertiveness, confidence, and independence (cf. Kohn & Schooler, 1983). These women also appeared to adhere more closely to social norms as a result of their work experiences (Roberts, 1997). Given the substantial entrance of women into the work force and their associated change in life aspirations (Helson, Pals, & Solomon, 1997), the impact of work experiences on women deserves continued research attention. The assessment of dynamic, socioculturally situated personal determinants of motivation and action, such as self and collective efficacy beliefs, personal standards, and goals (see chapter 11), may valuably contribute to such efforts.

## EDUCATION

Psychologists deal with few questions as emotionally charged and socially important as that of individual differences in educational attainment. Academia and society at large witness recurring debates about whether inherited variations in cognitive ability constrain the individual's capacity to achieve. These debates may only intensify as the breakdown of socially imposed barriers to success heightens the impact of personal determinants of achievement. Those who claim that genes predetermine social attainment and opponents who plead for social programs to develop the full potential of individuals share the belief that personal factors can greatly contribute to success but diverge on the nature and malleability of these factors and the resultant potential for education to produce social equality.

Focusing on how personality influences educational attainment should not deflect attention from the role of educational settings as a context for development. Educational

effects on personality development accumulate over time (Caspi et al., 1987; Kohn & Slomczynski, 1990). Educational opportunities thus profoundly affect personal capabilities and social mobility; this, of course, is why educational policies are a battleground in public policy debates.

Education is key to social and governmental policies to actualize individual potential (or, in economic terms, to optimize human capital). Sociologists generally agree that the extension of obligatory education is essential, although not sufficient, to reduce inequality, and that educational attainment will only become more important for social attainment in the years ahead, at least in industrialized societies. However, there is no consensus on two issues of enduring importance: What prevents lower-class children from attaining the same level of academic success as middle-class children of the same IQ? and What prevents lower-class children from reaching the same socioeconomic level as middle-class children with similar educational attainment? (Erikson & Johnson, 1996).

Adequate answers to these questions probably cannot be reached unless one addresses both contextual factors and personality characteristics other than IQ; IQ only partly affects educational attainment, and educational attainment only partly determines professional achievement. Links from IQ to long-term achievement and well-being are relatively weak (Neisser et al., 1996). These facts force one to consider determinants of achievement other than ability (Sternberg, 1996) that may be shaped by the educational system. School affects student self-concept, expectations, and goals.

School can be understood as a microcosm of the broader social world. Children and adolescents face challenges to their capacity to interact effectively with others, which mirror the challenges to be faced later in society. They learn social roles that go beyond those of the family and that foreshadow those experienced later in life. They learn to conform to adult and peer expectations and to assert their independence. These experiences are the context for the child's development of social knowledge and self-regulatory skills.

Many theories of personality have explored relations among personality functioning and educational processes. Trait theories have examined stable dispositions (e.g., conscientiousness or perseverance) that may promote scholastic achievement (DeRaad & Schouwenburg, 1996). Cognitively oriented dispositional theories highlight thinking styles such as field independence versus field dependence, cognitive complexity versus simplicity, leveling versus sharpening, and reflection versus impulsivity (Messick, 1996). Much other work explores student motives and goals and implicit beliefs that orient students toward particular goals (Ames, 1992; Covington, 1992; de Charms, 1976; Deci & Ryan, 1985; Dweck and Leggett, 1988; McClelland, 1985) (also see chapter 11). Social cognitive theory particularly emphasizes self-regulatory mechanisms and self-regulated learning strategies (Bandura, 1997; Schunk, 1989, 1995; Schunk & Zimmerman, 1998) and thereby shifts "the focus of educational analyses from students' learning ability and environments as 'fixed' entities to . . . personally initiated processes" (Zimmerman, 1990, p. 4).

Whatever one's personality theory, the effects of personality variables cannot be examined in isolation from the social and interpersonal contexts within which they are embedded. The same personality processes may have differential effects in different educational contexts. Work by the community psychologist Kelly (1971) has revealed how different schools may hold different social norms, with the result that the same personality factor differentially predicts attainment in one school versus another.

In certain cases, the school primarily corresponds to a set of "prescriptions" to which the child conforms. Grades not only index competence but reward conformity to social beliefs and values (Gecas, 1990). In other cases, the school represents a variety of opportunities that children may capitalize on depending on what they contribute and the relations they establish. Children bring their personality,

beliefs, and expectations into school, and their family-based beliefs may lead to different perceptions of school as they may be differentially valued in different contexts (Minuchin & Shapiro, 1983).

## Social and Cognitive Processes in Educational Attainment

Much effort has been devoted to understanding social and cognitive processes in educational attainment. A particularly important set of processes involves the potential stereotypes and expectations of teachers. Teachers' expectations about their students' capabilities may cause them to treat the students differently, yielding a "self-fulfilling prophecy" effect in which student outcomes match teacher expectations (Jones, 1977; Rosenthal, 1978). Work on the so-called *Pygmalion effect* called great attention to this possibility (Rosenthal & Jacobson, 1968). However, disentangling the self-fulfilling processes operating in the classroom has proved difficult, and the magnitude of self-fulfilling prophecies in educational settings has proved to be smaller than initially thought (Jussim, 1991; Jussim & Eccles, 1995). Nonetheless, teachers may, through both explicit and subtle nonverbal cues, create educational climates that differ in warmth, challenge, and opportunity for achievement and rewards (Rosenthal, 1994).

A more reliable set of findings in the study of social-cognitive processes and education involves attributional processes. Teachers' evaluations can influence students' attributions for their success and failure. Attributions, in turn, affect motivation and achievement. Attributing success to effort promotes motivation more than attributing it to chance (Weiner, 1992). Attributional feedback that credits the causal impact of students can promote perceived self-efficacy (Bandura, 1997; Schunk, 1995).

Teachers' evaluations of their students may exert both direct and indirect influences on children's self-judgments. In addition to the obvious direct effect, teacher expectations may contribute to peers' beliefs about a given student. Longitudinal findings document the reciprocal influence of teacher and peer evaluations on children's self-reported aggression and thus illustrate how attributions and reputation contribute to the construction of stable dispositions (Caprara, 1996a). Since teachers, like most others, are susceptible to the fundamental attribution error (Ross, 1977) in which causality is overattributed to stable dispositions, they may quickly conclude that a student's classroom behavior is indicative of enduring personal qualities. The internalization of teacher beliefs affects children's self-definition and esteem, and the aggregation of reciprocal effects between children's behavior and others' reactions become crystallized over time into stable expectations and behavior patterns, which may either promote or endanger scholastic achievement and personal adjustment.

Depending on the broader sociocultural context, a factor that may greatly influence educational beliefs is race or ethnicity. Some racial effects may, of course, involve blatant stigmatization, discrimination, and prejudice. Others may be more subtle. Steele and Aronson (1995) caution that stigmatized groups (e.g., African-Americans) may underperform scholastically owing to group stereotypes. Specifically, their concern with the possibility of confirming a group stereotype may interfere with their performance. Furthermore, students of a minority racial group may feel that they do not 'fit' in school. A resultant reduction of interest in school and rejection of the school environment may create poor performance, which further increases the student's sense of intellectual inferiority.

Although educational feedback is objective (i.e., people receive scores and grades on objective scales), the meaning people assign to educational outcomes is largely determined by social comparison processes. A low grade is not as demoralizing if most other people did even worse. In educational processes, multiple types of social comparison may be available. Students might compare their achievements with national norms or with the achievements of their friends. Research suggests that social comparisons most commonly involve "local"

norms and standards; that is, people compare themselves with reference groups that make up their immediate social context. Students who perform equally well with respect to national norms may form different self-appraisals, depend on whether their day-to-day peer group is performing below, at, or above their level (Miller & Prentice, 1996).

Self-efficacy beliefs, self-regulatory capacities, and educational success have all been affected by three of the most striking features of education today as compared with the past. These are (1) the greater range of educational options available (students do not simply progress through a structured classical education); (2) the increased availability of self-instructional technologies (which accompanies the greater availability of personal computers); and (3) the increased need to continue education beyond the traditional school years (to cope with technological innovations and the obsolescence of earlier training). All three of these social-contextual factors heighten the impact of personal choice and self-efficacy processes on educational and professional success. Novel, challenging, fluctuating circumstances force people to reappraise their educational efficacy as they consider their educational options (Bandura, 1997; Pajares, 1996; Schunk & Zimmerman, 1998).

Research on the multifaceted impact of self-efficacy beliefs on academic achievement illustrates how self-efficacy beliefs can influence school performance (Bandura, Barbaranelli, Caprara, & Pastorelli, 1996a). Children's beliefs in their ability to regulate their learning and academic attainments were found to contribute to achievement both independently and by promoting high academic aspirations, prosocial behavior, and less vulnerability to feelings of futility and depression. Children's perceived social efficacy (particularly to manage social pressure for detrimental conduct) also contributed to academic attainments by raising aspiration levels and lowering depressive tendencies. Perceived self-regulatory efficacy (i.e., appraisal of one's capability to resist peer pressure for risky activities) influenced academic achievement both directly and through adherence to moral self-sanctions against detrimental conduct and problem behavior. Efficacy beliefs and aspiration levels of parents also contributed to children's academic aspirations, efficacy, and achievement. Socioeconomic status only affected academic achievement indirectly, mostly through its impact on parental academic aspirations (see Figure 3). In general, then, the findings highlight the role of self-referent thinking in mediating the educational impact of social position.

## Rectifying Educational Inequalities?

Despite promising social trends, educational inequalities between advantaged and disadvantaged groups are still substantial. Poverty, segregation, and stigmatization contribute so strongly to the poor intellectual and scholastic performance of disadvantaged groups that their lower achievements seem almost to have come about "by design" (Fisher et al., 1996). Thus, focusing on individual processes will not explain enduring differences among social strata and ethnic groups.

A promising development in rectifying inequalities is the development of national and international programs to promote individual capacities to resist adversities and to navigate

Figure 3. Multifaceted paths of influence through which parental and child efficacy beliefs influence academic achievement. From Bandura et al., 1996a.

life challenges. The World Health Organization (WHO) sponsors a worldwide program of life skills education for children and adolescents. Skills of decision making, problem solving, creative thinking, communication, interpersonal relationship development, self-awareness, empathy, and coping are stressed (WHO, 1993). It is recognized that personal achievement requires not only intellectual skills but social, emotional, and practical intelligence as well. Although these programs will not eliminate inequality, they promise to better equip young people to cope with challenges to their well-being and that of their community. Schools thus may contribute not only to scholastic learning but to social welfare and peace (Deutsch, 1993). Such contributions generally require parental involvement in school activities. Parents are important in encouraging students' initiative and autonomy and providing optimal conditions to foster personal development (Mortimore, 1995).

## FAMILY

Our frequent reference to family influences on personality development suggests that one carefully attend to the nature of the family system. To many investigators, the family remains a cornerstone of our understanding of personality development and social relations. The family deservedly has received the attention of many academic disciplines.

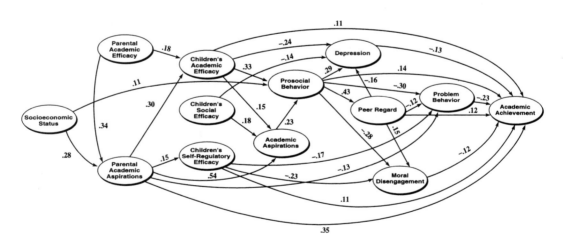

We cannot here review the entire vast domain of interdisciplinary knowledge about family dynamics. Such a task is beyond the scope of personality psychology. Although families consist of individual persons, levels of analysis beyond the individual are required to understand family functioning. Here, we limit ourselves to considering the family as a context for socialization. We aim to provide a general frame of reference from which to understand family processes in personality development. We confine our attention to the Western family, while acknowledging the possibility of cultural differences that have yet to be uncovered. We highlight the main social functions provided by the family and changes in family structure in recent years.

## The Contemporary Western Family

The family serves functions that extend far beyond the mere reproduction of the species. The family can be understood as a social institution, which functions to reproduce a society and to promote psychosocial development across the life-span (Gecas, 1990; Hess, 1995). The family carries out these functions by transmitting social values and norms and by supporting the next generation's development. There are, then, two family functions, social control and individual promotion. These are intertwined. Family members trade obligations and limitations on personal freedom for the support and care of family members. Family support, in turn, contributes to the achievements of the individual and the society.

In some respects, each family is a unique system that provides its members with a unique environment. However, since families operate within sociocultural boundaries, certain family structures are common within a society or social structure. Family structure in industrialized societies may show only part of the same structure as the family in a society based predominantly on an agricultural economy. The society's dominant family structure inevitably guides the ways that particular families shape individual development.

Debate on the history of the Western family continues among historians and sociologists

(Hess, 1995; Laslet & Wall, 1972). Yet, as a general rule, historical change in Western societies has involved a shift from a multigenerational family, which prevailed in the past, to a modern nuclear family, usually composed of father, mother, and a few children. Recent years have seen larger numbers of single-parent households. Other major changes in recent decades include greater balances of power between husbands and wives; new management of sexuality as a result of changed values and the use of contraceptive devices; challenges to parental authority and a greater recognition of children's rights; more equal treatment of men and women with respect to obligations, emotional support, and economic and educational opportunities; higher divorce rates; greater maternal employment; and somewhat enhanced parental involvement with children (e.g., Golombok & Fivush, 1994).

At any given point in history, significant cross-cultural variations in family life are found. Individual roles within the family and relations between the nuclear family and extended relatives vary considerably across countries, economic conditions, social and legal systems, and cultural traditions (EUROSTAT, 1997; Hess, 1995; McLanahan & Casper, 1995; Smith, 1995). Different regions of the world have experienced somewhat different paths of change in family life. In northern Europe, traditional marital relations are often replaced by cohabitation, and almost half of the children are born to unmarried parents. In Italy and Spain, young adults live for extended periods with parents, and the number of children born to unmarried parents remains relatively modest (EUROSTAT, 1997). The prolonged cohabitation of young adults with parents raises new questions about the relationships among generations. This trend is a concern when it reflects an inability of adult children to become financially self-sufficient.

Sociohistorical changes not only have altered the family, but have brought entirely new family forms. The existence of homosexual and lesbian parenting (Lamb, 1998; Patterson, 1997) illustrates this point.

Research comparing children raised in lesbian households with those raised by a single heterosexual mother suggests that children's gender identity does not differ in the two family forms (reviewed in Golombok & Fivush, 1994). Such a result argues against a social stereotype that a nuclear family is necessary for proper development, while also providing evidence that challenges the view that gender development is grounded in parental relations.

Changes in family life must be understood in conjunction with sociodemographic changes such as prolonged life expectancy, delays in age of marriage and retirement, and the prolonged education of men and women. Marital partners' greater tendency to pursue both family and professional goals may reflect not only family dynamics, but greater life expectancy, which widens the latitude for goal pursuit (Carstensen et al., 1999). Women's greater financial contributions to the family may reflect not only family-specific processes, but activities before the family was formed. Women today commonly achieve high levels of education and professional advancement prior to marriage. Children may become somewhat more economically dependent on their parents than in the past, but this may not reflect changes in parent–child dynamics. Instead, economic dependence can reflect the need to extend education beyond the college years to compete in today's marketplace. Nature and culture likely have coacted in creating today's diversification of family forms.

The postponement of marriage and parenthood has particularly noteworthy social and personal implications. It serves to reduce family size. Fertility is at replacement level (approximately two children per woman) in some countries (e.g., Holland, France) and below replacement level in others (e.g., Italy, Germany) (EUROSTAT, 1997). This, of course, is a matter of social concern, especially when combined with lower marriage rates and the increased decision to marry without procreation (although, at the same time, unwanted pregnancies are a large concern, especially in the United States and the United Kingdom and among the teens of disadvantaged minorities). On the personal level, postponement of marriage may yield wiser choices and prolonged unions, yet less passion and more reluctance to renegotiate one's own habits and life goals. Postponement of parenthood may bring more attention to child care and involvement from both parents, yet less parental energy and more parental concern about their ability to accompany the child into adulthood.

The changes in family size brought about, in part, by the postponement of marriage may alter the dynamics of family relations. Large families may raise concerns about children's intellectual development because of their limited interactions with verbally fluent parents (see Zajonc, 1976, and below). Today, many children have no siblings, which raises concerns about social development. Concerns about intellectual development may persist if both parents work, as is increasingly common. Smaller family size also reduces the broader kinship network. This, in turn, erodes traditional social support systems.

### The Family System

Historically, most psychological literature on the family has explored the influence of parents on children. Families, however, are interactive systems. From childhood through adulthood, all family members influence one another. In the past decade, investigators increasingly have embraced a systems view of family socialization processes in which the family is seen to consist of multiple interlocking relationships (Belsky, Rovine & Fish, 1989; Cox & Paley, 1997; Lerner, 1989; Parke, 1988; Parke & Buriel, 1998; Scabini, 1995). "The family" is treated "as a social system in which the full range of subsystems including parent-child, marital, and sibling systems are recognized" (Parke & Buriel, 1998, pp. 463–464). It is further recognized that each of these subsystems may possess its own developmental trajectory.

A systems perspective is informative, yet a bit abstract. Ideally, one would be able not only to describe the general system-level functioning of the family but to identify specific psychological mechanisms that are a product of family interactions and that, in turn, contribute to developmental outcomes. Parke and Buriel (1998) suggest a conceptual scheme to accomplish this task. Family interactions are posited to influence two mediational systems: an emotional system, which governs the interpretation and expression of emotional displays, and a system of mental representations that guide and regulate social behavior (Figure 4). As we noted in our discussion of communication in chapter 6, when parents discuss emotions and emotion management with children, children appear to gain greater competence in encoding emotional experiences and regulating their own emotional life. Regarding the cognitive system, family interactions underpin the expectations, goals, and efficacy beliefs through which children plan and regulate their interactions with peers. Research examining parents' and children's proposed solutions to interpersonal problems reveals that the interpersonal goals and problem-solving strategies possessed by both mothers and fathers influence the goals and strategies possessed by their children (Spitzer & Parke, 1994).

Figure 4. Schematic diagram of the affective and cognitive processes linking family and peer systems. From Parke & Buriel, 1998.

The diversity of family subsystems naturally implies that family life features a diversity of relationship forms. However, one can identify a common theme across subsystems, namely, the theme of reciprocal interpersonal support. Parents support children and children care for aged parents. All family members support one another in times of need. These supportive relationships are based not only on emotional ties but on values and norms that are transmitted across generations. The links among generations, especially the reciprocal obligations among younger and older family members, distinguish families from other social institutions.

■ *Family Subsystems and Their Developmental Trajectories.* The mother–child dyad constitutes a system characterized by its own developmental trajectory, as we have seen when discussing attachment and early communication (chapter 7). The more the mother is committed to pursuing her own professional career and the more she contributes to the economic support of the family, the more she expands on the traditional role of affect supplier. This expansion of social roles may create uncertainty about balancing the opposing demands of caregiver and provider.

The father–child subsystem historically has received less attention from psychologists than the mother–child system. It was not until the last two decades of the 20th century that

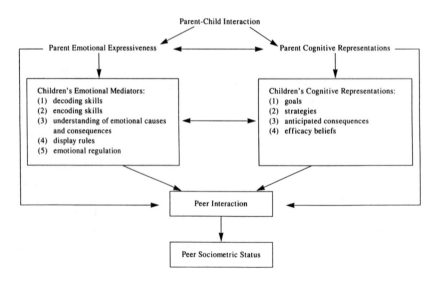

investigators systematically began exploring the impact of fathers on children's personality development and adjustment (Rohner, 1998). Evidence suggests that children's cognitive capabilities and feelings of control can be enhanced by greater participation of fathers in child rearing (Golombok & Fivush, 1994; also see Lamb, 1998). Fathers who are more emotionally accepting of their children appear to promote children's sense of well-being and to reduce their likelihood of maladjustment; father effects commonly predict these psychosocial outcomes over and above the effects of mothers (Rohner, 1998). Thus, although mother–child and father–child interactions may differ, both contribute to psychological growth (Maccoby & Martin, 1983).

A common social recommendation, and one supported by these findings, is that fathers should become more actively engaged in child care. Implementing this recommendation can be difficult for families. Sociostructural factors such as income, employment, and professional constraints and the availability of institutional and extended-family support determine the allocation of time and the actual behavior of parents despite their attitudes and intentions (Bronfenbrenner, 1986; Parke, 1988; Scabini, 1995).

Psychologists have increasingly recognized the effects of children on parents. Since Bell's (1968) seminal review of these effects, various research traditions have emphasized reciprocal parent–child influences. Transactional models conceive of development as a continual interplay between a changing organism and a changing environment, with child characteristics influencing parental practices, which in turn affect children's behavior, which affects parental behavior (Sameroff & Chandler, 1975; Halverson & Wampler, 1997). Behavior genetic findings on the influence of non-shared effects on personality (see chapter 5) directed attention to the unique environment of each child within the family and to the question of how each person contributes to others and to his or her own environment (Scarr, 1992; Scarr & McCartney, 1983; Plomin & Daniels, 1987). Whereas genetic

endowment entails a range of potentialities, which delimit the niches one may fill, the exact course of development partly depends on resources made available within the family.

Social cognitive theorists have emphasized how developing individuals directly (as agents) and indirectly (as targets of others' reactions and expectations) influence their own development and the family itself. Different children react differently to the parent, make different demands, pose different challenges, and by virtue of their gender or talents, represent different future possibilities in the parents' minds (Bell & Harper, 1977; Maccoby & Martin, 1983). Depending on one's society, the child's gender may trigger different concerns and aspirations for the child's future. Such gender-triggered concerns may influence not only the behavior of the parents but also that of relatives and friends. Children also influence parents through their social and academic pursuits. Children's achievements increase parental pride and self-esteem, and their struggles with physical or cognitive limitations are a source of strain.

Investigators recognize that siblings are important to the developing child (Brody, 1998; Dunn & Kenrick, 1982; Dunn & Plomin, 1990; Lamb & Sutton-Smith, 1982) and that their influence may extend into adulthood and old age (Scabini, 1995). However, as with other factors, empirically it is difficult to disentangle sibling effects from other factors (e.g., birth order, age). In trying to assess sibling effects, it is important to recognize that siblings may play different roles at different stages in life. They may serve as competitors, supporters, models, stress, buffers, substitute parents, and partners in old age. The unique family environment of siblings is a product of the level of parental investment in each child, the treatment they receive by parents and other relatives, and various idiosyncratic experiences (illness, separation from family, etc.) (Hoffman, 1991).

The husband–wife dyad is another system whose functioning changes over time. For example, parenthood changes the social-cognitive and motivational tendencies of the married couple (Ruble, 1994). Longitudinal evidence involving middle-class families in the United States and Canada suggests that women become more dissatisfied with some aspects of their marital relationship after childbirth when their prebirth expectations about their husband's contributions to housework and child care are violated (Ruble, Fleming, Hackel, & Stangor, 1988). Parenthood thus may not have a direct and inevitable effect on the marriage but instead appears to exert its influence through subjective social-cognitive processing. The variety of changes in the functioning of the couple only increases when one considers relations between the married couple and other relatives over the course of life.

Thus, understanding the effects of the family system on individuals requires an appreciation of multiple sources of influence that interact reciprocally, with effects partly mediated by subjective norms and expectations. Multiple subsystems operate, coact, and change in parallel with the life course of individuals.

■ *Siblings and Intellectual Development.* When one contemplates the influence of family systems on children's development, one usually thinks of how families might affect the child's emotional life or social behavior. However, the structure of the family system also can affect children's intellectual growth. Children with fewer siblings may experience greater intellectual development by virtue of their greater contact with adults who model a sophisticated vocabulary and abstract thinking skills. Zajonc's (1976, 1983) *confluence model* predicts that firstborns will experience a boost in IQ as a result of their interaction with mature adults. Each successive child should experience successively lower IQ, because he or she spends relatively more time with siblings, who are less cognitively sophisticated than parents. Firstborns also benefit from acting as parental surrogates in tutoring siblings.

Findings support Zajonc's confluence model. The strength of support, however, depends on the nature of the data one examines (Zajonc & Mullally, 1997). Birth order

accounts for only a small percentage of the overall variance in IQ. Inherited factors and demographic influences such as socioeconomic status are far more important. However, if one gauges birth order effects while controlling for these biological and social factors, clear evidence of birth order effects emerges. Across different tests and different countries, the numbers of siblings one has correlates negatively with scores on intellectual ability tests (Zajonc & Mullally, 1997). This finding supports the confluence model and, more generally, indicates that IQ is not just a product of inherited biology, with intellectual capabilities developing partly through interpersonal interactions.

There are theoretical alternatives to the confluence model. Taubman & Behrman's (1986) *depletion theory* focuses on the division of family resources. Material and intellectual resources in the family are fixed (or nearly so). With increasing numbers of siblings, the division of resources leaves a decreasing portion for each child. Later children thus are relatively deprived as compared with firstborns.

Theoretically, not only IQ but personality factors may be influenced by family size and birth order. Children of different birth orders may develop systematically different strategies to to gain family attention, acceptance, and resources. One survey of a large body of worldwide evidence, however, brought meager support for this hypothesis and raised questions about the magnitude of birth order effects on IQ and achievement. Ernst & Angst (1983) report that, in their survey, sibship showed "a very slight independent negative influence on school achievement" and that firstborns only "achieve slightly more at school" (p. 284). Neither sibship nor birth order affected personality when social background variables were controlled. These findings were not based on the data aggregation procedures endorsed by Zajonc and Mullally (1997), which yield stronger birth order effects, as we noted.

Establishing the long-term effects of family configurations on personality, intellectual development, and achievement is difficult, especially when one considers the variations that may occur across economic and cultural contexts. Future work may benefit from expansion of the traditional paradigms. Since socialization effects may be partly driven by parental expectations, birth order variations in parental beliefs and behavior could be explored. Historical analyses also can be revealing. Sulloway's (1996) extensive analysis of birth order and achievement in domains such as science, politics, and religion led him to conclude that, among great historical figures, firstborns tend to be more conservative and conscientious than later siblings, who are more liberal and open to experience and innovation.

### The Life Cycle of the Family

Family life can be viewed in terms of a life cycle consisting of a sequence of transitions across distinct developmental periods, each of which is characterized by its main tasks.

■ *Forming a Couple.* Family life begins with the formation of the marital union, a process involving both emotional intimacy and mutual commitment between partners. Marriage implies commitments to provide emotional support and adjust personal habits and goals in accord with the needs of one's spouse and the new extended family members. The influence of spouses on one another draws attention to choice of marital partner in personality development and continuity. One's choice of spouse may sustain personal qualities one already possesses or may lead one to develop new personal attributes.

Research on spousal choice indicates that people tend to choose partners who are similar to them. There is positive *assortative mating* (or assortative marriage) in intellectual capability, values, and dispositions, where the term assortative mating simply means that the pairing of individuals deviates systematically from a chance pairing (Gruber-Baldini, Schaie, & Willis, 1996). The similarity hypothesis (birds of a feather flock together), then, receives more support than the complementarity hypothesis (opposites attract). Effects,

however, are moderate and variable depending on the trait, value, or interest dimension examined (Bentler & Newcomb, 1978; Caspi & Herbener, 1990; Karney & Bradbury, 1995). Spousal similarity can reflect both social and personal factors. People tend to have greater access to individuals who are similar to them, owing to influences of family, educational level, economic status, or chosen profession. Personal beliefs, goals, internalized norms, and preferences can further drive similarity. People seek similar others and seek in others what they value in themselves (Klohnen & Mendelsohn, 1998).

An important implication for the study of personality development is that the choice of a marriage partner may influence levels of personality continuity over time. Two possible influences present themselves. One involves the relation between the personality of the two spouses. Longitudinal findings indicate that although spouses do not become more similar in personality characteristics over time, their shared experiences maintain their initial level of similarity over long periods; "in the absence of shared experiences [they] would grow increasingly different" (Caspi, Herbener, & Ozer, 1992, p. 289). This evidence of a shared environmental experience on personality dispositions of course conflicts with the contention that shared environmental factors are not influential in personality development (see Chapter 6; also see Rose & Kaprio, 1988). The second possibility involves the within-person organization of personality variables. Findings suggest that choosing a marital partner similar to oneself promotes the intraindividual consistency of one's personality attributes. Caspi and Herbener (1990) found that Q-sort personality ratings are more stable across time among persons with spouses who are similar to themselves, where similarity was gauged by a comparison of husband and wife Q-sort descriptions. This finding raises the interesting possibility that people can agentically determine long-term consistency or change in their personality by choosing spouses who are similar or who are different from themselves.

Couples do appear to become more similar over time in intellectual functioning and cognitive style (Gruber-Baldini et al., 1996). This result naturally follows from the fact that couples create a shared environment, which in turn shapes their thinking patterns.

The precise causal links among marital choice, marital satisfaction, and marital stability are difficult to establish. The privacy of the feelings and behaviors involved adds to the more common obstacles to research. Thus, most findings are merely suggestive. Intimacy, commitment, congruency of reciprocal perceptions and attributions, and orientation towards common values are found to predict long-lasting and rewarding unions (Laver & Laver, 1986; Scabini, 1995). Findings on personality characteristics and marital success are less conclusive. Despite efforts that trace back to Terman's (1938) work on spouse personality traits and marital happiness, much remains unknown about whether and how personality affects the course of a marriage across life. Neuroticism may be a source of marital instability (Kelly & Conley, 1987; Wilson, 1997). Yet traits of one spouse do not affect marital happiness independently from traits of the other, and traits work in conjunction with social attitudes, gender role orientation, needs, and values. Furthermore, same personality characteristics may differentially affect marital choice, union, and dissolution, depending on the contingencies of life. Both attachment patterns (Hazan & Shaver, 1994) and self-efficacy beliefs regarding the management of emotions and intimate relations (Bandura, 1997) seem to be important candidates among the determinants of marital happines and resiliency; however, much research is needed to clarify their role in the various aspects of marital choice and maintenance. The paucity of findings and the variety of situations do not allow us to relate in a systematic way the majority of marriage failures or successes to the personality of partners.

It is probable that the quality of the relationship both reflects and buffers the impact of the couple's personality characteristics on psychosocial outcomes. The stressful events that occur during marriage and the manner in which couples cope with these difficult circumstances are no less important than the enduring personal vulnerabilities and resiliencies that spouses bring to the marriage (Karney & Bradbury, 1995). Beyond protecting the solidity of the marital union, the positivity of the relationship between partners facilitates the transition to parenthood and promotes positive parent–child relationships (Easterbrooks & Emde, 1988; Erel & Burman, 1995).

■ *Having Children.* Parenthood brings multiple challenges. Not only is there a new relationship with the child, but there are altered relations with the entire family. Parenthood changes the relationship between marital partners and their interactions with their kin. Since parenthood is generally a choice made by the couple, this myriad of effects further testifies to the influence of personal choice processes in psychosocial development.

The way in which emotions are recognized and expressed between the spouses and between parents and children are likely to exert a great influence on the marital union as well as on child development. As noted by Dix (1991), parenting is an emotional experience "that involves more joy, affection, anger and worry than do most other endeavors" (p. 3). Whereas positive affects promote intimacy and moderate stress, negative affects fuel conflict and amplify the negative effects of strain.

Regarding child care, evidence noted above indicates that the child's relationships with both parents contributes to his or her emotional and cognitive development. Another question, though, is whether particular styles of parenting are systematically related to child outcomes. This question is of broad social interest. Issues such as the disciplinary impact of firm parental supervision, of rewards and punishments contingent on behavior, and of physical punishment remain points of debate (McCord, 1995, 1997; Socolar, 1997).

Various investigators have proposed typologies of parenting styles (see, e.g., Parke & Buriel, 1998). Styles generally are differentiated according to two factors: (1) the degree of control parents exert; and (2) the parents' affective style, which may primarily be accepting and responsive or rejecting and unresponsive to children (Maccoby & Martin, 1983). Among the most influential contributions, Baumrind (1971) has distinguished three parenting types. *Authoritarian* parents exert control through a set of absolute standards. They emphasize respect for authority, preservation of order, and parent-child distance. *Authoritative* parents maintain firm rules, standards, and sanctions but communicate more openly with children. They recognize children's rights and seek to promote their individuality and sense of responsibility. *Permissive* parents maintain affectionate relationships with children but do not maintain strict and consistent disciplinary standards. Evidence suggests that an authoritative setting of limits and an age-appropriate structuring of situations to enhance the development of prosocial abilities promote social competence and adjustment (Baumrind, 1991, 1997). Authoritative parenting enhances children's sense of personal efficacy and accountability in cognitive and affective domains.

Maccoby and Martin (1983) have extended Baumrind's scheme into a fourfold model of parenting styles and have related parental control and affect to children's moral development, aggression, prosocial behavior, and adjustment. This work reveals that parenting involves more than a set of attitudes and behaviors. The effectivenes of parental care also reflects the affective development of parents. As in marital relationships, in parental relationships emotional instability and negative affectivity are frequently associated with poor relationship quality (Belsky & Pensky, 1988).

Effective parental discipline requires that parents believe that they are capable of exerting influence on the child without jeopardizing the relationship. Efficacy beliefs regarding one's capacity to meet marital and parental obligations are of paramount importance (Bandura, 1997). Children must believe that they can disclose personal feelings without risking loss of parental acceptance and sup-

port. Thus, both marital and parental efficacy beliefs play a significant role in curtailing family interactions that may eventually crystallize into stable tendencies toward depression and hostility. These considerations again highlight the fact that family members dynamically influence one another, both as elicitors of others' responses and as role models. Family member's beliefs in their ability to support one another in the pursuit of common goals may contribute to the sense of family cohesion that can contribute so strongly to individual adjustment and well-being (Cashwell & Vacc, 1996; Farrell, Barnes, & Banerjee, 1995; Fisher & Feldman, 1998).

The content of children-parent relationships changes over time. Different periods pose different child-rearing tasks (Parke, 1988). Newborns mostly need caring, and parents, too, benefit from the caring provided by spousal support (Parke, 1988). Soon, instilling norms becomes as important as caring in the socialization of children, who must acquire the self-regulatory capacities needed to interact effectively with others. Open communication and clarity and consistency in setting rules can promote autonomy and competence. In adolescence, parental control declines. Parents are more able to spend time together, in independent social activities, or in their own careers. Parental guidance mostly involves advice, and filial emotional support becomes more important for parents. In most families, conflicts are more frequent in early adolescence (see chapter 6), although conflicts tend to decrease over time as children mature and parents recognize their adulthood. The more adolescence is prolonged, as frequently happens in Western countries, the more adolescents are young adults who participate in family decision making, emotionally support the parents, and contribute economically (Scabini, 1995).

Throughout adolescence, the relationships between parents and children are continuously renegotiated along the two main axes of affect and control, with "optimal development taking place where there is a good stage-environment fit between the needs of developing individuals and the opportunities afforded them by their social environments" (Eccles et al., 1993, p. 98). The constructive negotiation of good matches rests not only on a consideration of perceived needs but also on perceived self-efficacy. Parents and adolescents must feel capable of communicating with one another. Parents must remain confident in their ability to combine discipline with interpersonal acceptance, whereas adolescents should benefit from confidence in their ability to resist peer pressures and to disclose their experiences to the parents. Among parents of younger children, mastery modeling of parenting skills builds parental self-efficacy and reduces family stress (Gross, Fogg, & Tucker, 1995). Similarly efficacy-building programs may benefit the parenting of adolescents, which may in turn affect the entire family system. Positive self-assessments tend to reinforce one another, whereas self-doubts may spread from person to person. Shared beliefs in family efficacy should serve to protect adolescents from negative peer influences, parents from feelings of inadequacy, and both from despondency and hostility.

The literature on adolescence and family interactions does not allow any firm conclusion about normative or desirable family styles. Variations among ethnic groups, social strata, and historical periods preclude generalizations about natural patterns. At the turn of the century, most children started work before puberty. Today, such employment commonly is illegal. Nowadays young people generally marry later. In some countries, they commonly live in their parents' homes until their 30s. Changing demographic patterns and employment opportunities may contribute to changes in parent and child attitudes about the point in life at which the young adult should establish an independent living. In particular, when unemployment rates are high (as in southern Europe as compared with the United States and northern Europe), the belief that a long educational path is necessary to achieve autonomy delays leaving home, as young adults pursue higher education (Cherlyn et al., 1997).

Intuitively, it seems that changing work and family-demographic patterns should have profound implications for family life. Although these links have remained relatively unexplored, some evidence suggests that negative work conditions (e.g., job instability) lower parental efficacy, with different paths of influence being found in nuclear versus single-parent families (Elder and Ardelt, 1992; cited in Bandura, 1997). Family relationships may be affected not only by parental occupational issues but by adolescents being income providers via part-time jobs, family enterprises, or permanent occupations outside the family.

New demands on parents derive from the phenomenon (more prevalent in Europe than in the United States) of young, educated adults remaining at home, in financial dependence on the parents. This social change may reorient the role of father and mother, interactions between husband and wife, and relationships of the family with the outer world. The "prolonged family" in which young adults extend their cohabitation with parents probably corresponds to a new stage of the family life cycle. Nevertheless, it is difficult to determine whether this stage is transitory and what its distinctive features are. Equally difficult is providing an account of subsequent stages of the family life cycle, because of the paucity of research on aging families and because changes in family structure make some existing research out of date.

Grandparenthood is another important turning point in the life of family members. In some families grandparents are proximal agents of socialization for children and adolescents as well as a source of support for parents. In others, they are distant figures, who are unfamiliar to children and who may impose severe emotional tolls when illness, poverty, and widowhood accompany old age. Although grandparenthood has been the subject of little research attention, King and Elder (1998) have found that grandparents' belief in their self-efficacy for contributing to their grandchildren's lives is enhanced by their own positive memories of grandparent interactions. Grandparents with higher efficacy beliefs become more actively involved in their grandchildren's daily activities.

In addressing the tasks of the family along its life cycle, we have focused on decisions involving marriage, having children, and family cohabitation. Though we highlighted intrafamily dynamics, one should not overlook the role of social acceptance of family structures. Cultures differentially accept various nuclear family arrangements, single parenthood, and stepparent families. Future work in Western and non-Western cultures should illuminate the interacting roles of family and social influences on parent and child personality development.

### Facing Adversities and Change

Some families face unusual adversities that interrupt the normative life cycle and that may jeopardize the development of family members. Any given adversity may have direct and indirect effects on multiple individuals. The death of an adult may mean the loss of a partner, provider, and parent. The birth of a handicapped child is a strain for parents, which unavoidably affects their relationships with their other children. Similarly, illness, job loss, migration, and other events may impose unexpected changes that affect the development of children and adolescents. Social factors such as kin networks, community involvement, and national support policies may moderate the psychological impact of such adversities.

A major adversity is economic hardship. Economic problems may trigger interpersonal conflicts, which amplify the economic effects. Whereas economic hardship has been endemic to the disadvantaged and low-salary social strata, prolonged illness, unemployment, and job loss can jeopardize middle-class living standards. Such threats are particularly large today in many nations. Cyclical economic crises, reallocation and reorganization of labor as a result of technological innovations and globalization of markets, and revisions in welfare and medical policies contribute to the threat. Since such conditions vary across nations, significant variations should be found in the effects of hardship on personal and family development.

In general, family life may be negatively affected by extreme parental work absorption, occupational precariousness, and job loss. However, these effects may differentially influence different family members and may be moderated by demographic factors, personality influences, and sociohistorical factors. Elder's (1974, 1999) seminal work (see chapter 4) shows how economic hardship interacts with family and personality in amplifying or mitigating individual liabilities. Parents' and children's personalities (particularly emotional instability in fathers), in conjunction with economic privations, are significantly associated with later marital discord and problematic behaviors in children (Elder, Caspi, and Downey, Elder, Caspi & van Nguyen, 1986; Elder, van Nguyen, & Caspi, 1985). Other longitudinal and cross-sectional research similarly illustrates the role of parent and child individual differences in resilience in response to adversity (Block, 1971; Schneewind, Beckman, & Engfer, 1983; Werner & Smith, 1982).

■ *Divorce.* Findings on the effects of divorce leave no doubt that the breakup of parents can have long-lasting consequences for children. The nature of the effects is not simple, however. Sex, age, peer influences, individual differences of the parents and of the children, and the subsequent marital status of the divorced parents are all moderating factors (Amato & Keith, 1991; Buchanam, Maccoby & Dornbush, 1991; Cherlyn et al., 1991; Emery, 1988; Guttman, 1993; Hetherington, 1988). For example, although adolescents and young adults with divorced parents are about three times as likely as those with nondivorced parents to experience psychosocial adjustment problems, the risks are lower among offspring who have mature, well-adjusted friends (Hartup & Stevens, 1999). Regarding sex differences, divorce often has a stronger negative impact on boys than girls. Boys' poor psychosocial outcomes may be magnified in cases in which the mother retains custody and does not remarry, yet boys may be somewhat better off than girls when a stepfather enters the family (Hetherington, 1988; also see Golombok & Fivush, 1994). Divorce also can have a particularly powerful impact on children who are of a young age that requires much parental investment.

The long-term health effects of parental divorce are documented in the 70-year Terman life cycle study, the well-known study of gifted children begun in 1921. Children who experienced parental divorce prior to age 21 are more prone to experience divorce themselves and have a 4-year lower than expected life-span (Schwartz et al., 1995; Tucker et al., 1997).

Extant findings do not provide utterly firm grounds for generalization. Most studies have been conducted in the United States, where divorce is more frequent than elsewhere. Studies other than the Terman project often examine limited spans of life and thereby may fail to capture long-term consequences of divorce (see Hess, 1995). A further consideration when weighing the impact of divorce is that strains on parent and child development also occur when marital partners are in frequent conflict but remain married.

The effects of divorce are both interpersonal and fiscal. Mothers who retain child custody must increase their work to maintain their previous standards of living, which adds a dramatic new burden (McLanahan & Garfinkel, 1986). These fiscal factors surely contribute to the fact that growing up with a single parent is associated with multiple negative outcomes, such as poor achievement, unwanted pregnancy, and unemployment (Hess, 1995; McLanahan & Sandefur, 1994). The negative effects of divorce may be reduced by the familial network. Other family members may play a parental role, especially when children are of a young age that particularly requires adult care.

Sociodemographic figures allow little optimism regarding a potential lowering of divorce rates. One ironically beneficial effect of demographic trends is that high divorce rates in society may cause children of divorced parents to be less stigmatized than in the past, which may benefit their social adjustment. Optimism about child outcomes does derive from children's frequent resilience in overcoming adversities such as parental conflict and divorce. Understanding the mechanisms that protect children against adversities is critical to orienting social programs designed to enable families to perform the magic feat of which they alone are capable: "making and keeping human beings human" (Bronfenbrenner, 1986, p. 738).

## THE SOCIAL DEVELOPMENT OF GENDER

Physical differences between the male and female sexes are determined biologically. Psychological differences between the male and female genders are constructed socially. This chapter now addresses the social contexts that influence the development of gender identity and that enable or constrain men's and women's efforts to develop their potentials. We explore how people influence the course of their development and thereby may overcome constraints imposed by traditional views of nature and nurture. The discussion in this chapter of the social construction of gender roles complements our earlier coverage of biological sex differences. Although we report these areas separately, one must remember that biological and social factors are generally intertwined and mutually influential.

It is beyond our scope to provide a comprehensive review of the extensive literature in this area. Fortunately, readers requiring more detailed coverage have access to a number of valuable, detailed reviews written from various theoretical perspectives (e.g. Ashmore, 1990; Beall & Sternberg, 1993; Bem, 1985; Bussey & Bandura, 1999; Deaux, 1984; Eagly, 1987; Golombok & Fivush, 1994; Huston, 1983; Labouvie-Vief, 1994; Lips, 1988; Maccoby, 1990, 1998; Ruble & Martin, 1998; Spence, 1985).

## Sex and Gender

The terms sex and gender commonly are used interchangeably. Scientific discourse, however, requires a distinction. *Sex* refers to biological properties involving chromosomes, gonads, hormones, and external morphology. *Gender,* which entered the scientific lexicon in the mid-1950s, refers to properties of masculinity and femininity that reflect processes of socialization and psychological development (Money, Hampson, & Hampson, 1955).

Some years after the introduction of the term gender, Rhoda Unger (1979) urged the adoption of a more precise definition of terms. She referred to sex as a person's biological maleness or femaleness. Gender signified cultural expectations for femininity and masculinity. Since then, the term gender has largely replaced what previously was called sex in the discourse of most psychologists, although this usage is not completely universal.

In the study of gender differences, one must severely caution against the tendency to draw broad generalizations from particular studies. Differences may reflect the particularities of the population that was studied and the cultural setting and historical era in which they were observed. A number of lessons should be borne in mind in reviewing this area. First, one easily can find evidence to support either of two views: that men and women are more similar or more different than one's preconceptions would suggest. Second, when looking for empirical findings, one learns that they are limited in that they so heavily involve a small corner of the world (middle-class Western whites).

A third lesson is that focusing on what is typical of men and women is an insufficient view, in that it fails to appreciate that typical characteristics may mask a range of potentialities that are suppressed or limited by sociocultural and economic circumstances that do not enable the genders to realize all aspects of their potential.

A fourth lesson is that changes in the social constructions of masculinity and femininity happen so fast, are so continuous, and so directly affect the way research is conceived

and pursued that one cannot confidently rely on findings from past decades for understanding what is going on today. Relatedly, research at no time can avoid the influence of ideological frameworks. These influences simply happen to be more salient when we reflect on some research paradigms of the past.

A fifth lesson is that reifying observed gender differences is often an obstacle to progress. Time and again, a psychological difference between the genders proves not to be a reflection of men's and women's essential qualities but a product, at least in part, of society's gender conceptions at a particular point in time and the associated opportunities made available to men and women.

## History and Change

The idea that women are in some way inferior to men can be traced back for centuries in the history of Western civilizations and non-Western cultures, in which men traditionally were granted higher status. This general trend is tempered somewhat by notable exceptions, in which women held exceptional spiritual or political roles (e.g., women in the Greek Olympus, the role of mothers in the Roman culture, the Virgin Mary in Christianity, the lady in the Middle Ages and the Renaissance, and queens from the 17th century onward).

Views of female inferiority infected personality psychology in its founding era. Simplistic interpretations of Freudian psychology provide one example of the tendency to view male psychology as a benchmark against which to compare the somewhat inferior psyche of women.

In recent decades, Western society's treatment of women has changed dramatically. The broad feminization (or demasculinization) of Western society is indicated by the massive entrance of women into the labor force and their increasing achievement of positions of power that were almost unthinkable until very recently. Surely men remain overrepresented in upper-echelon positions in business and politics, and the degree of gains made by women varies across nations. Yet the proportion of women in, for example, the legal and medical professions and the sciences is growing in most countries. Females' school achievement and attainment has surpassed that of males in many countries. The average income of women is still far behind that of men, this disparity reflecting institutional policies more than personality characteristics. Since women deliver children, are the main caregivers of children, and are the preferred custodial parent in case of divorce, they experience additional costs within work organizations, interrupt more frequently their professional career, and are more exposed to economic hardship when protective social policies are lacking.

These profound changes in women's lives have been accompanied by changing roles for men. As men provide greater child care in the contemporary family, they must exhibit traditionally "feminine" qualities such as tenderness and warmth.

In assimilating these changes, findings of previous research are valuable for orienting our efforts toward promising directions for current research. Therefore, we first review established findings on similarities and diversities between males and females in different domains of individual functioning. Then we address a number of recent theoretical developments and research directions on the developmental trajectories of men and women.

## GENDER DIFFERENCES IN COGNITIVE ABILITIES, SOCIAL BEHAVIOR, AND TRAITS

Research on gender similarities and differences offers a classic case of a swinging pendulum of opinion. Research from different historical eras appears to differentially emphasize similarities versus differences, making it difficult to reach ultimate conclusions on these questions at any point in time.

Many gender differences that had been taken for granted were seemingly eliminated by the publication of one landmark volume, Maccoby and Jacklin's (1975) volume on male–female differences. Maccoby and Jacklin's

encyclopedic literature review led them to reject as unfounded many common beliefs about gender differences, such as those involving the sociability, empathy, and suggestibility of girls and the analytical abilities and achievement orientation of boys. Even purported differences in activity levels, competitiveness, anxiety, dominance, and nurturance were judged to be equivocal. Well-established differences were few and far between, being confined primarily to male tendencies toward aggression and toward somewhat superior mathematical, visual, and spatial abilities and female superiority on measures of verbal ability (Maccoby & Jacklin, 1974).

The volume's conclusions were soon challenged. Jeanne Block (1976) critically evaluated the text on theoretical grounds and with respect to the representativeness and comprehensiveness of the literature it examined. Nonetheless, Maccoby and Jacklin's text inspired an era in which investigators primarily sought and found minimal sex differences.

In the 1980s, the so-called meta-analytic revolution ushered in statistical techniques that proved to be an important supplement to the previous narrative methods of drawing conclusions from research. Meta-analysis enabled quantitative estimates of male–female differences (e.g., Eagly & Crowley, 1986). This era further eroded traditional stereotypical beliefs about psychological distinctions between the sexes (Eagly, 1987; Rosenthal, 1991). With respect to cognitive abilities, no differences in general intelligence and only modest differences in perceptual and cognitive abilities were found. Whereas females outperformed males in perceptual speed and accuracy, showing more sensitivity to touch in their fingers and hands and to changes of sound intensity, males were more sensitive to the intensity of visual stimuli under lighted conditions and outperformed females in visual-spatial tasks (Lips, 1988; Burnett, 1986). Previous beliefs about males' superiority in mathematics and females' in verbal abilities were seriously challenged by meta-analyses reporting modest effects or no effects in the expected directions (Hyde, Fennema, & Lamon, 1990; Hyde & Linn, 1988). Gender differences in cognitive abilities as measured by the standardized psychometric tests appear to have declined or disappeared in recent decades (Feingold, 1988).

## Gender Differences in Aggression

With respect to social behavior, meta-analytic reviews suggest that males are more aggressive than females (Eagly & Steffen, 1986) and that females may be more easily influenced and more empathic than males (Eagly & Carli, 1981; also see Eisenberg & Lennon, 1983). However, as with cognitive abilities, the variance accounted for by gender was moderate at best (below 5%) and the exact findings may not fully generalize, since most studies were conducted in only one nation (the United States) and with college students or other select subgroups. A further limitation is the difficulty of determining whether different studies in a meta-analysis actually employed comparable definitions of theoretical constructs and empirical procedures. The case of aggression is paradigmatic of the variety of theoretical and methodological challenges.

At the theoretical level, defining aggression as a unitary phenomenon traceable back to an instinct, a trait, or a unique causal antecedent such as frustration unavoidably has led to different operationalizations and conclusions than has work addressing the distinctive determinants and the regulatory mechanisms of different types of aggression. Although physical assault, child abuse, rape, verbal derogation, and terrorism are hardly reducible to a common set of features and sources, most research on aggression has been conceived in the realm of the impulsive aggression model focusing primarily on the excitatory and involuntary processes instigating aggression (Berkowitz, 1962, 1993). The animal aggression paradigm has exerted a notable influence in spite of being fully inadequate for explaining most human aggression. Humans are the only species that evaluates their acts symbolically. One cannot disregard the role of norms, values, and personal standards in promoting aggression as a more or less adequate strategy to cope with reality (Caprara, Barbaranelli, & Zimbardo, 1996).

Methodologically, different assumptions lead to different operationalizations, which in turn contribute to different results. Using a well established experimental paradigm for studying the frustration-aggression hypothesis, Caprara and colleagues have repeatedly found that males deliver more shocks to an innocent confederate than do females, in spite of having the same elicitor and facilitator. Both males and females selected higher levels of shock after being exposed to a mild frustration (failure in a learning task) and after aggression-eliciting cues or strenuous physical exercise were interpolated between the frustration and the aggressive response (Caprara, Renzi, Alcini, D'Imperio & Travaglia, 1983; Caprara, Renzi, Amolini, D'Imperio, & Travaglia, 1984a; Caprara et al., 1984b). However, the nature of the gender differences varied when instead of failure, the frustration was a mild provocation and when participants had the opportunity not only to deliver shocks, in one condition, but to withdraw rewards by negatively evaluating their provoker's suitability for a desirable position, in another. Provoked males delivered more shocks but expressed more benevolent recommendations than females. Men and women withdrew rewards equally. In both males and females the reward-withholding procedure showed higher coherence and convergency among measures than the shock delivery procedure (Caprara, Passerini, Pastorelli, Renzi & Zelli, 1986). Physical aggression was a relatively rare phenomenon, people generally expressing hostility through more subtle means. These findings suggest that in the case of impulsive aggression the same mechanism operates in females and males; and that females, although more reluctant than males to resort to physical aggression, are ready to respond to provocation when more socially convenient ways of expressing their own hostility are made available. Further research should explore whether similar mechanisms underlie men's and women's proactive, premeditated forms of aggression.

A meta-analytic review is consistent with the findings just reviewed. The type of provocation markedly moderates gender differences. Appraisal of provocation, fear of danger from retaliation, and other contextual factors (e.g., type of target and form of aggression made available) also moderate gender differences in aggression (Bettencourt & Miller, 1996).

Women often employ indirect forms of aggression such as social manipulation and circuitous derogation (Bjorkvist, Osterman & Lagerspetz, 1994; Osterman et al., 1997). Gender differences in chosen forms of behavioral aggression may primarily reflect social role expectations that constrain certain type of acts in girls and women (Bussey & Bandura, 1999). Boys' aggressive acts are more socially tolerated, and boys are more facile in disengaging moral self-sanction of injurious conduct (Bandura, 1965; Bandura et al., 1996b). Girls exhibit a higher sense of efficacy in resisting peer pressure to engage in outward aggressive conduct (Caprara et al., 1998; Pastorelli et al. in press).

Most societal aggression does not involve impulsive reactions. Aggression commonly occurs without any immediate provocation. Instead, people selectively disengage moral sanctions against aggression (Bandura, 1991a). They label harmful acts as moral ones that serve worthy objectives. They obscure their own causal role in aggression by diffusing responsibility or displacing it onto others. They vilify and dehumanize their victims. Such moral disengagement may provide a better explanation for gender differences in aggression than hypothetical differences in aggressive drives or dispositions and may valuably indicate how aggression can be prevented and controlled. For example, since society trains men to be aggressive more than it trains women (e.g., through athletics or military training), moral disengagement may be a more accessible strategy for men than for women.

**Gender and Personality Traits**

One question in the study of gender and personality traits is whether masculinity and femininity can be treated as poles of one dimension, and thus constitute a single traditional bipolar personality factor or trait (Comrey, 1970; Terman & Miles, 1936; Gough, 1957; Guilford & Zimmerman, 1956). This view has been severely questioned by Constantinople (1973), who reviewed major tests of masculinity and femininity and concluded that "available data clearly point to multidimensionality" (p. 405). Evidence suggested separate masculinity and femininity dimensions. Constantinople, then, questioned whether generalized masculinity-femininity constructs, which had guided research for over a quarter of a century, could adequately capture an individual's psychological maleness or femaleness.

Another question is whether variations in masculinity and femininity correlate with other personality traits. Here one must immediately warn against any premature conclusions about essential differences between males and females. Correlations are confounded by the fact that similar test items appear on gender scales and other tests, such as measures of self-esteem (Nicholls, Licht, & Pearl, 1982).

With regard to other personality traits, the male–female comparison is confounded in that men and women differ not only on sex-linked biological and gender conceptions, but in a range of social and economic factors that vary by gender. Perhaps any subgroups that differ systematically in economic opportunities, social roles, etc., might differ on some personality characteristics. Bearing these considerations in mind, we note that significant mean differences have been found on some factors of the Multidimensional Personality Questionnaire (MPQ; Tellegen, 1982). Men score higher on social potency, alienation, and aggression. Women score higher on social closeness, stress reaction, harm avoidance, absorption, and constraint (McGue, Bacon & Lykken, 1993). A meta-analysis has revealed higher male scores on assertiveness and self-esteem and higher female scores on anxiety, trust, extraversion, and tender-mindedness or nurturance (Feingold, 1994). Kling, Hyde,

Showers, and Buswell (1999) similarly find statistically reliable, yet small gender differences in self-esteem. Men also score somewhat higher on measures of risk taking than do women, although the magnitude of the difference varies across age and social context (Byrnes, Miller, & Schaffer, 1999).

Research on the five-factor model finds higher adult female scores on friendliness and emotional instability in Germany, Italy, Spain, and the United States (Caprara et al., in press). These results should be cautiously interpreted as descriptive rather than explanatory. In addition to the points noted above, the scales on the various instruments may assess somewhat different constructs, making it difficult to aggregate findings meaningfully. For example, the Big Five Questionnaire (Caprara et al., 1993) and the NEO PI-R (Costa & McCrae, 1992), although highly correlated, may be differentially sensitive to gender differences in different contexts. Finally, social desirability, halo effects, or other response sets may impinge differently on male and female test responses. People who endorse particular gender-role beliefs may present themselves differently in personality self-reports.

Personality does not consist only of phenotypic traits. Negligible differences between males and females at a surface level do not exclude significant differences in underlying mechanisms (Eagly, 1995). Moving toward understanding processes underlying dispositions appears to be a promising avenue to capture the multidimensionality of what it means to be a male or a female at a given social latitude in a certain time. This leads beyond consideration of traits as static entities or habitual behaviors to investigation of how others' and one's own expectations, attributions, and evaluations become crystallized into personal beliefs and styles to relate to others and to the world. It suggests examining how gender identity functions as part of one's overall self-system and how gender-linked self-perceptions in turn influence behavioral strategies, aspirations, and social experiences.

## Gender Differences in Developmental Continuities, Self-Construals, and Vulnerabilities

Most societies have different expectations about the traits, abilities, and prospective achievements of men and women. Societies vary, however, in the degree to which they enforce homogenous gender conceptions. Some tolerate little variation, whereas others value diversity and allow for much variability.

Expectations about the genders are but one factor in a network of processes that can sustain gender differences in psychosocial outcomes. Expectations influence attributions about the causes of social actions. People might, for example, make different attributions about men and women who are pursuing identical career paths. These social-cognitive processes, in turn, may influence social evaluations and rewards. This social feedback inevitably shapes one's own self-referent beliefs and aspirations. With such processes in mind, we now consider gender differences that must be understood as arising from complex chains of causation that involve an interplay of individual proclivities and social expectations.

As we have noted, early differences in temperament have much predictive power. Impulsivity in 3- to 4-year-old boys, for example, predicts later antisocial and delinquent behavior (Kagan and Zentner, 1996). Temperament factors and interactions between temperament and the social environment may contribute to adult gender differences; specifically, because of different social conditions, a given temperament quality may differentially predict adult outcomes for men versus women. While studying continuities from childhood temperamental qualities to young adults' personality traits, Caspi and Silva (1995) and Caspi (1998) observed gender differences in their temperament groups (including undercontrolled, inhibited, confident, reserved, and well-adjusted temperaments). Newman, Caspi, and Moffitt (1997) reassessed these same subjects in early adulthood across four social contexts: in social networks, at home, in romantic relationships, and at work.

Both gender differences and gender–temperament interactions were found. Childhood temperament predicted indices of agency and communality among women but not men. Conversely, temperament factors predicted social maladjustment among men, but not women.

Rothbart and Bates (1998) have reviewed further evidence suggesting that temperament, gender, and their treatment by society interact to influence developmental outcomes. The social environment may be differentially accepting of the same temperament quality in males and females. Shyness, for example, may be more accepted in girls than boys (Rothbart & Bates, 1998). As a result, girls and boys who are similarly shy may experience different developmental pathways.

Individual differences in the capacity to regulate emotions may differentially contribute to long-term adjustment in males and females. In a Finnish longitudinal study of males and females assessed at ages 8, 14, 20, and 33 (Pulkinnen, 1996), early lack of self-control predicted later anxiety, pessimism, and depression in women and problems involving socially unconventional behaviors in men. Women and men adjusted to problems of emotion regulation in different ways. Women commonly pursued one of two distinct paths, involving acceptance of traditional feminine roles or a separation from conventional role expectations through assertiveness and intellectual commitment. Men adjusted primarily through activity, submission, or compliance.

■ *Continuities in Ego Functioning.* Gender differences in patterns of adjustment also are revealed by Block and colleagues' work on ego functioning (Block, 1993; Block & Block, 1980). In this extensive program of longitudinal research, more than 100 individuals were observed from nursery school through young adulthood. A variety of observer ratings and behavioral measures assessed two aspects of ego functioning: ego control, or the person's overall degree of control over impulses, and ego resilience, or the ability to modify levels of ego control to meet varying demands.

Overall, findings reveal considerable continuity in ego functioning across time. However, levels of continuity vary by gender. Although Q-sort ratings of males' ego control and ego resiliency obtained at widely different time points commonly are correlated in the .4 to .6 range, the correlations for females are much lower. There is, then, less continuity in ego resilience in girls' transition to womanhood than in boys' transition to manhood. Relatedly, childhood measures of ego functioning differentially predict adult depression for the two sexes (Block, Gjerde, & Block, 1991). Sex differences emerge gradually over time (Block, 1993), being greater at age 7 than in the preschool years.

Gender differences are also found with respect to the impact of parental practices on ego control (see chapter 4). Girls who experienced parental practices involving the constraint of emotional impulses developed into young women with high amounts of ego control. These parental practices appeared less influential in the development of young men, whose young adult characteristics were more strongly linked to aspects of their childhood personality (Kremen & Block, 1998). Commendably, this work examined the links from parenting styles to young adult personality after controlling for the effects of early childhood personality, which, of course, can partially determine parenting styles.

Gender differences also are found with respect to the outcomes of ego resiliency. In conjunction with other characteristics such as IQ, ego resiliency appears to foster different outcomes for males and females. For women, high ego resiliency may compensate for IQ. For men, high IQ may compensate for low ego resiliency (Block & Kremen, 1996). The different gender role expectations and associated social demands faced by males and females may contribute to these differential relations.

■ *Interpersonal and Family Relations.* Theorists often contend that women are more relational than men (Gilligan, 1982; Miller, 1985). Studies generally support this view, showing that women value marriage and family relations more strongly than do men, who place greater value on vocational success (Helson, Pals, & Solomon, 1997). Various theoretical explanations for these gender differences have been offered. Although theories differ in the details, most agree that social structures and norms play a significant role in dictating appropriate male and female behavior. (The notable exceptions are sociobiological and evolutionary-psychological theories, reviewed below, in which social norms are not determinative but are merely by-products of innately specified psychological mechanisms.) Helson et al. (1984) employ a "social clock" framework to interpret women's and men's preferences about alternative life paths. Society conveys expectations about the appropriate time at which men and women should marry, begin raising children, begin and end their participation in the work force, etc. The settings of this social clock may vary across subcultures or historical periods. If they do, then individual preferences and the nature of gender differences may change, too. A comparison of longitudinal studies in the United States that were conducted during different eras supports this view (Helson et al., 1997). Particularly strong family interests and weak vocational interests were shown by a cohort of women raised during the depression of the 1930s, a time during which differential gender roles were enforced particularly strongly. During periods in which social roles were less based on gender, gender differences in interests and personality were less pronounced. The magnitude of gender differences also narrowed over time within cohorts. Women tended to become more independent and assertive with age, and men become more affiliative. For example, in the Terman study of individuals with high IQ, the percentage of men who held positive attitudes about emotional expression in the home and who held personal goals involving family life increased considerably as men aged from 30 to 70 (Holahan, 1984; reviewed in Helson et al., 1997); these findings contribute to evidence that personal characteristics may change significantly during adult development.

Cross and Madson's (1997) literature review provides detailed evidence of gender difference in relational characteristics. In self-reports, women appear more interdependent, or connected with others, whereas men see themselves as more independent and self-sufficient. Women and men differ in how they reveal information and express emotions in interpersonal relationships. Differences accord with traditional stereotypes. Women closely attend to and remember information about others and seek harmonious close relationships. Women seem relatively more skilled in communicative activities that involve emotional life and help to establish intimacy with others (Cross & Madson, 1997).

Cross and Madson (1997) suggest that a fundamental factor here is that the genders differ in self-construals. Women see themselves as more interdependent, men more independent. Of course, self-construals and gender differences are both socioculturally constructed, and in this process, it is difficult to establish the degree to which one conception is constitutive of the other. The interrelations among self-construals and gender beliefs may vary widely across cultures, since cultures differ in the latitude they give individuals to construe the nature of their gender and their overall sense of self. Issues of gender differences, in other words, are closely related to the more general questions of culture and self-construal cited in other parts of this volume.

■ *Psychological and Physical Health.* Further gender differences that are unlikely to be interpretable as exclusive products of biological sex are revealed in epidemiological studies. In developed countries, women experience depression about twice as frequently as men (Culbertson, 1997; Frombonne, 1995). However, it is doubtful that one can treat this finding as a general rule that is applicable to all human societies. Ratios may vary because of cultural variations in women's likelihood to report their depression and in the frequency with which the diagnostic category of depression is invoked. Further, differences in social-cognitive functioning contribute to gender differences in depression (Nolen-Hoeksema &

Larson, in press). Similar cognitive–personality factors are differentially linked to depression in adolescent males and females. Low social self-efficacy contributes more strongly to depression among girls than among boys (Bandura et al., 1999; Block, Gjerde & Block, 1991). Girls become depressed about academic achievement despite attaining higher levels of academic achievement than boys. Gender differences also are found in affect regulation (Caprara et al., 1999), with perceived inefficacy for managing emotions being linked more strongly to depression among girls than among boys. Cultural meaning systems may influence women's proneness to adopt the beliefs and cognitive processing styles that make one vulnerable to depressive symptomatology. These considerations extend to other disease syndromes. Although many diseases are, of course, unambiguously rooted in biological dysfunctions, various affective and stress-related disorders have a clear cognitive component. Gender differences in the experience of these disorders, then, may reflect differences not only in biology but also in psychology.

Men and women differ greatly in the frequency with which they engage in antisocial conduct. Interestingly, although men engage in such conduct more frequently, once females transgress they are at higher risk of negative psychosocial outcomes (Loeber & Loeber, 1998). Although somewhat paradoxical (see Loeber & Keenan, 1994), one may conjecture that women overcome more social resistance in entering a deviant career. Once entered, it is more difficult for females than for males to desist from it. Further, women's transgressions, being rare, may be more salient and thus more stigmatizing.

## GENDER DEVELOPMENT: THEORIES AND RESEARCH PARADIGMS

Personality psychology has witnessed a range of theories about the mechanisms through which people develop a sense of being male or female, with all the social expectations and obligations that the genders imply. Since these approaches have been detailed many times, from different perspectives and with different emphases (see Ashmore, 1990; Bussey & Bandura, 1999; Huston, 1983; Ruble & Martin, 1998), we will confine ourselves here to reviewing theories and contemporary research trends that have been particularly influential at various points in the field's history.

### Psychoanalytic, Social Learning, and Early Cognitive Approaches

In psychoanalytic theory, sex typing is the fulfillment of a natural destiny resulting from the child's identification with the same-sex parent. The phallic stage, during which genitalia are the primary source of libidinal gratification, is seen as the key developmental period. The discovery of anatomical differences combines with feelings of attachment to the opposite-sex parent and jealousy and fear toward the same-sex parent, to trigger castration anxiety in males and penis envy in females. The child resolves psychological conflict by identifying with the same-sex parent. Identification here goes beyond sex typing to include a general internalization of parental moral standards and social demands, resulting in the formation of the superego. Gender role development and moral development thus are closely linked (Freud, 1933). This theory gained popularity among the general public, despite lack of empirical evidence and its being controversial within the psychoanalytical movement (Ruitenbeck, 1967). The male bias of the theory was quickly recognized, and the difficulty of demonstrating that the oedipal processes outlined by Freud were universal presented a further obstacle.

Over time, the limitations of Freudian theory of gender development became apparent. The theory of drives collapsed, to be replaced by object relations theory, in which early interpersonal relationships rather than drives are key to the development of personality and gender identification. This theme is seen in the world of Chodorow (1978). She posits that both boys and girls first assume a female identity due to their identification with the mother. Over time, boys differentiate from the mother and form a separate male identity, whereas girls remain psychologically merged with her. Because females' self-concept is more closely related to that of the mother, women, in this view, are more inclined to serve as caregivers than are men. Women are seen by Chodorow as being naturally oriented not only toward motherhood but toward general themes of relatedness and mutuality. Men, by contrast, are inclined toward individuality and autonomy. These early gender orientations are further reinforced by socialization practices, with girls being raised to be cooperative and empathic and boys to be assertive and independent.

Chodorow's thinking underpinned Gilligan's (1982) well-known analysis of moral reasoning. To Gilligan, women's reasoning about moral dilemmas is more relational than men's. Women tend to weigh interpersonal factors more heavily than abstract principles of justice (Gilligan, 1982). Research documents gender differences in moral reasoning and suggests that these differences do not involve differential capacities but differential preferences. Women are capable of contemplating abstract principles, but their preferred style of reasoning weighs interpersonal factors heavily (Golombok & Fivush, 1994).

In the early 1960s social learning theory provided an alternative conceptual frame, which was grounded in empirical research. It highlighted the influence of parents on children's adoption of expected gender roles. Modeling and social reinforcement were the basic mechanisms leading males and females to learn and enact behaviors and to internalize normative social values (Bandura & Walters, 1963; Mischel, 1966).

In the mid-1960s the advent of cognitivism led investigators to explore the active role the individual plays in construing the world, including the world's genders. Kohlberg (1966) drew on Piagetian thought in viewing sex typing as part of children's more general cognitive organization to the physical and social world. In contrast to psychoanalytic

and social learning theory, Kohlberg viewed sexual attitudes as determined neither by biological instincts nor arbitrary cultural norms. Instead, they were seen as internally organized by relational schemata that reflect universal ways of cognizing events. Sex role concepts, then, were not products of passive learning but of active structuring of experience. Parental attitudes were relevant in that they stimulated or retarded the development of sex role attitudes rather than teaching attitudes directly through reinforcement or identification.

In Kohlberg's view, the first of three steps in gender identity is the recognition that males are different from females. A variety of cues (size, strength, genitalia) prompt the acquisition of gender constancy by the age of 3. Stabilized gender identity is but one aspect of the general acquisition of constancy of physical objects taking place between ages 3 and 7. The other steps involve explicit recognition of biological differences and the creation of broader stereotypic beliefs. There is "the development of awareness of genital differences, and [then] the development of diffuse masculine-feminine stereotypes based largely on the connotation of nongenital body imagery" (Kohlberg, 1966, p. 107).

Once children begin to organize social information according to gender, they incorporate gender-linked beliefs, stereotypes, and values. In gathering information from multiple social sources, they actively shape their own gender identity. Children pass from stages in which they mostly conform to societal values to subsequent stages in which they aim "to structure and adapt oneself to physical-social reality, and to preserve a stable and positive self-image" (Kohlberg, 1966, p. 166).

Block (1973) proposed a developmental sequence in the acquisition of sex role identity. Her conceptualization drew on Loevinger's ego development theory (1966) (see chapter 5). Masculinity and femininity were expressions of the two "fundamental modalities" that characterize all living forms, agency and communion (Bakan, 1966). Agency manifests itself in self-protection, self-assertion, and self-expansion, whereas communion concerns the achievement of harmony with others.

According to Block, both sexes move from a primarily agentic stage (the presocial, impulse-ridden, and self-protective stages of Loevinger) to one in which conformity with social pressures and expectations prevails (the conformity and conscientious stages of Loevinger). Finally, masculine and feminine elements of the self may become integrated in an androgynous stage (corresponding to Loevinger's autonomous and integrated milestones of ego development). Genders thus move from being undifferentiated to strong conformity with societal gender conceptions to a final stage in which individuality prevails and gender identity takes forms that may differ greatly from traditional stereotypes.

Agency fosters competition and achievement in men. Communion may induce female docility and nurturance. Block suggests that both sexes benefit from recognizing the complementarity of reason and passion and of paternal and maternal styles. The ultimate goal in development of sexual identity thus cannot be achievement of masculinity or femininity as popularly conceived. Rather, it is desirable to develop a sense of self "in which there is recognition of gender secure enough to permit the individual to manifest human qualities our society, until now, has labeled as unmanly or unwomanly" (Block, 1973, p. 512). Thus, a full achievement of personal maturity involves an androgenous integration of agency and communion within one's personality.

Socialization in Western societies has traditionally emphasized agency in males and communion in females. Boys enjoy greater freedom to explore and develop their curiosity and independence. Girls have relatively greater access to affective expression and are encouraged to engage in interpersonal relations. Any theory of gender development must recognize that this differential socialization can impose significant burdens on both genders. Men may be excluded from tenderness, women from status. Men may feel ashamed about expressing emotional needs, and women may feel guilty for their achievement aspirations.

## The Centrality of Gender: Masculinity, Femininity, and Androgyny

In the 1970s, the feminist movement gave greater voice to women's issues. This voice was heard not only in politics and business but in the scientific literature. Past research efforts had tended to amplify sex differences and to underestimate women's capabilities, creating a scientific rhetoric that fostered sexual exclusion. Work in the 1970s emphasized that sex differences are relatively minimal. Investigators searched for ideal representations of gender that went beyond traditional myths and prototypes.

The debate on masculinity and femininity was spurred by research on androgyny, particularly that of Bem and of Spence (Bem 1974; 1977, 1981, 1985; Spence, 1985; Spence & Stapp, 1974; Spence, Helmreich & Stapp, 1975). They both treated masculinity and femininity as independent dimensions rather than as bipolar, and provided assessment tools congruent with this view (the Bem Sex Inventory, BSRI, and the Personal Attributes Questionnaire, PAQ). They both recognized the genders as social constructions rather than as essentialistic temperaments.

■ *Bem.* A central thesis of Bem (1974) was that previous bipolar conceptualizations of gender obscured two possibilities: "that many individuals might be 'androgynous,' that is, might be both masculine and feminine, both assertive and yielding, both instrumental and expressive, depending on the situational appropriateness of these various behaviors; and conversely, that strongly sex-typed individuals might be seriously limited as they move from situation to situation" (p. 155). Androgyny was proposed as an ideal amalgam of the desirable attributes of masculinity and femininity, which was suitable for both sexes.

Androgyny "swept the field like a fire on dry prairie" (Huston, 1983, p. 395). The fire, as Huston (1983) noted, was fueled by both the strength of Bem's conceptions and the sterility and the biased values of previous conceptions, which tended to promote differences between the genders. Androgyny, as Deaux (1984) noted, "became a code word for an egalitarian gender-free society, and disciples . . . advocated androgynous therapy, androgynous curricula for school children, and androgynous criteria for professional positions" (1984, p.109).

The claim of positive relations among androgyny, maturity, and psychological adjustment, however, did not find strong support in empirical findings. In part, this is because the assessment of androgyny proved not to be optimal, and therefore it failed to meet all expectations and to capture the subtle implications associated with the construct. With the passing of time, a greater awareness of the limitations of instruments such as the BSRI and the PAQ and a major concern over the unintended consequences of reifying ways of being male and female led to further conceptual revisions (Ashmore, 1990).

Bem (1981, 1985) proposed *gender schema* as hypothetical cognitive constructs underlying gender-consistent thoughts and actions. As with other cognitive schema (see chapter 9), gender schema function to filter information and organize knowledge. These cognitive generalizations about gender are constructed from the knowledge provided by one's society and culture. In Bem's view, then, gender schema were not a product of a built-in readiness for gender identity, as in Kohlberg's theory. Rather, gender was conceived of as a learned social category. Social contexts associate psychological attributes with particular genders and determine the value and significance of these attributes. Social institutions maintain these gender-linked beliefs. This network of preconceptions and expectations is assimilated into the individual's gender schema, which in turn foster gender-consistent experiences and behaviors (Bem, 1985). In this view, investigators have the responsibility not only to describe existing sex differences, but to foster social institutions that do not diminish the full range of individual differences that would otherwise exist within each sex (Bem, 1985, p.180). Some cultures' views of masculine and feminine qualities may, in other words, be incompatible with the full expression of human potentialities.

■ *Spence.* Spence viewed masculinity and femininity as separate phenomena, which parallel the dimorphism of biological sex. These gender identities were seen as a fundamental property of the individual's self-concept; all men and women possess a sense of their masculinity or femininity that is central to their identity and is important to preserve (Spence, 1985). Masculinity and femininity, then, refer to a "fundamental existential sense of one's maleness or femaleness" (Spence, 1985, p. 79). This view naturally moves one away from simple unidimensional or bidimensional models to a more complex, multidimensional view. Multiple dispositional, motivational, and behavioral factors differentiate the genders and contribute to the idiosyncrasies of individuals' gender identity. "Even among men and women who are perceived as normal representatives of their gender there is heterogeneity in the patterns of role-associated qualities and behaviors they exhibit" (Spence, 1985, p.77). Individual views often violate and transcend parental and societal expectations.

Gender identity is acquired early in life. In principle, then, it can be regarded as a forerunner of sex role identity discussed by Bem. Spence, however, questions whether sex role identifications validly capture the heterogeneity and idiosyncrasy of the characteristics individuals associate with gender. Children are exposed to multiple exemplars of maleness and femaleness that combine to create potentially unique, emergent conceptions of gender that make up a part of the individual's identity.

As Spence emphasizes, people act to maintain their gender identity. People are inclined to adhere to social pressures and models that confirm their sense of masculinity and femininity and to discount those that are incongruent. They use those gender-appropriate behaviors and characteristics they happen to possess for confirming their gender identity while they attempt to dismiss other aspects of their makeup as unimportant.

Spence's conceptions contributed greatly to changes in the field in the 1980s and 1990s. Investigators devoted increasing attention to the specific psychological processes involved in the formation of gender identity and to the possibility that these processes will give rise to somewhat idiosyncratic conceptions of what constitutes maleness or femaleness.

Ultimately, after feminists had voiced the pride of diversity (Gilligan, 1982), following too much emphasis on similarity among men and women, scientists gradually have come to acknowledge the limitation of focusing on nature and nurture, underestimating the role individuals play in shaping their gender and gender relationships.

## Contemporary Frameworks: Evolutionary Psychology, Sex Role Theory, and Social Cognitive Theory

In recent years, research on sex and gender has seen a broadening of theoretical perspectives and greater awareness of the complexity of the phenomena under investigations. Work has benefited from integrating insights from biological, anthropological, and sociological analyses into psychological models. Among the influential contemporary paradigms in the study of gender are evolutionary psychology, sex role theory, and social cognitive theory.

Evolutionary psychology, as we described earlier, understands human functioning in terms of psychological mechanisms that have evolved as a result of their success in solving recurring adaptive problems over the history of the species (Buss, 1995b, 1997a, 1999a). Men and women have faced somewhat different problems owing to their different roles in reproduction and parenting. Thus, it is plausible that the sexes have evolved somewhat different psychological mechanisms. This analysis suggests a radically different view of gender. Gender is no longer a social construction that develops during the course of ontogenesis and that is shaped by interactions with one's culture. Instead, gender differences reflect an unfolding of wired-in biological

mechanisms that have evolved through the eons. Social experiences may trigger these mechanisms and alter the thresholds at which they come into play (Buss, 1991), but they do not in any fundamental sense alter the basic biological hardware or the psychological tendencies to which it gives rise.

An evolutionary analysis suggests that men and women should exhibit different mating preferences in prospective short- and long-term relationships. Men should prefer prompt sexual availability in short-term partners but sexual exclusivity in long-term mates. Women should seek tangible resources in the context of short-term mating but value possible future resources in long-term mates. Empirical findings do suggest that women have higher thresholds for opportunistic copulation (Symons, 1979) and less permissive premarital sexual standards (Hendrick, Hendrick, Slapion-Foote, & Foote, 1985; Oliver & Hyde, 1993). Men more often seek short-term mating (Buss & Schmitt, 1993), have different mate preferences (Kenrick & Keefe, 1992), and endorse different mating tactics and strategies (Buss, 1988).

These findings must be understood as suggestive rather than definitive. It is undoubtedly true that mental mechanisms have evolved biologically, that the sexes differ in reproductive behavior, and that, at one level of analysis, biological mechanisms underlie these behavioral differences. However, this does not imply that people possess distinct brain mechanisms that are dedicated to specific tasks of mate attraction and parenting (Turkheimer, 1998). Since mating serves multiple functions beyond copulation – friendship, social status, etc. – multiple biological systems undoubtedly contribute to any particular aspect of human mating behavior. Further, at present one cannot assess the activity of the hypothesized biological mechanisms in a manner that is independent of the behaviors they are meant to explain. We only know that a particular parenting mechanism is active when we see a person engage in parenting. These considerations make it quite difficult to test evolutionary predictions in a meaningful manner in the context of the complex, multidetermined actions that make up one's day-to-day life (Cervone, 2000). Furthermore, it is difficult to link evolved strategies from the past to current contingencies with certainty. The function and meaning of particular strategies may change dramatically with the changing social context. Variability across cultures in the meanings that people assign to actions provides a considerable challenge to evolutionary analyses. Finally, evidence that individuals' experiences influence their biological makeup (Gottlieb, 1998) runs counter to the evolutionary psychologists' presupposition that brain mechanisms simply unfold during the course of development in an essentially predetermined manner.

Not surprisingly, then, psychologists who are more attuned to social and cultural considerations have offered alternative views of gender development and the transmission of gender roles. These alternatives recognize that social and technological changes have altered mating choices and reproductive functions. As we have noted, contraception disjoins sexual activity and reproduction. Abortion availability, DNA analysis, and surgical change of biological sex are further innovations that influence sex, mating, and reproduction. These developments challenge the contemporary relevance of views centered entirely on issues of resource provision and paternal certainty as they played themselves out in the hunter-gatherer societies of the past.

Sex role theory addresses more proximal determinants of behavior than does the evolutionary analysis. It explores how the organization of societal roles and functions influences gender conceptions and does so while capitalizing on both sociological inquiry and the social cognitive psychology literature (Eagly, 1987). The basic assumptions are that in Western societies men have been assigned primary responsibility for their society's political and economic institutions and women primary responsibility for nurturing children and caring for the family dwelling. Division of labor and social status assignment, distribu-

tion of power and responsibilities within the family, and differential socialization practices assign different roles to men and women. "The distinctive communal content of the female stereotype is assumed to derive primarily from the domestic role . . . the distinctive agentic content of the male stereotype is assumed to derive from men's typical roles in the society and economy," as Eagly explains (1987, p. 19). These roles crystallize into different gender stereotypes in which men are agentic and women communal. Men and women traditionally have been preordained for instrumental and expressive functions, respectively. Changes in the genders' social roles then can be seen to drive contemporary changes in how men and women view themselves.

Sex role theory succeeds in capturing gender differences that have prevailed in the past and the changes that have occurred in the present. However, it does not fully capture exceptions found in the extraordinary accomplishments of individual women of the past who prevailed over difficult times and adverse conditions. These exceptions attest to people's potential to overcome, and eventually alter, the constraints of socially proscribed stereotypes. Gender differences have declined over time in conjunction with reduced social constraints that permit women much greater freedom in interests, aspirations, and skills development.

It thus becomes critical for psychologists to explain, at a more proximal level, how the organization of a society gets reproduced in its individuals and how individuals may creatively and agentically develop the capacity to alter social systems. Masculinity and femininity are defined in interactions formed by cultural values, social norms, and reciprocal expectations. Both sexes contribute to the other's latitude of expression and their recognition of their distinctiveness. This consideration leads one to address the social and interpersonal settings where these processes take place and the psychological mechanisms through which interpersonal experiences create stable cognitive structures. It leads one to

view gender as a psychosocial cognitive construction that interlocks personality and society, neither of which can be reduced to the
other. Society provides the conditions and the
models to express one's own masculinity and
femininity. Individuals negotiate and actively
shape their own gender identities as part of
their personality.

Social cognitive theory views gender conceptions and styles as the product of a broad
network of social influences operating inter-
dependently within societal subsystems.
Social structures do not independently produce gender-linked behavior; they act through
self-processes. In some social systems "social
roles, life-style patterns, and opportunity
structures are rigidly prescribed" and account
for much of the variability in behavior,
whereas "in egalitarian social systems, personal factors serve as major influences in the
self regulation of developmental paths"
(Bussey & Bandura, 1999, p. 685). In the
social cognitive view, gender differences cannot be explained in terms of a single mechanism (whether it be an evolved adaptive
mechanism or a single socially learned gender
schema). Instead, modeling and enactive
experiences shape a gamut of competencies,
self-evaluative standards, and self-referent
beliefs, each of which contributes to gender-
linked conduct (Bussey & Bandura, 1999) and
which themselves interact as coherent psychological systems (Bandura, 1999). Families,
teachers, peers, and the media provide models
of gender-linked behavior and rewards for
gender-linked conduct. In interaction with
these social systems, individuals develop personal beliefs and competencies, through
which they adapt to and influence the environment in a way that may serve to maintain or to
change traditional roles. Although parental
influence on gender conceptions predominates at first, eventually siblings, peers, teachers, professional colleagues, and the media
play important roles.

The social cognitive analysis is consistent
with multiple findings on social factors that
sustain gender roles (Bussey & Bandura, 1999).
Parental influences include differential gender

socialization through toys, dressing, discipline,
and parental communication. Peers exert pressures for preferences consistent with one's sex.
Teachers and counselors provide differential
treatment and advice to boys and girls, especially with respect to prospective occupational
pursuits. The media, of course, provide a range
of gender-linked expectations. These factors
are understood in social cognitive theory as
subsystems that interact and operate in concert
in conveying what being male or female might
mean to an individual.

People vary in their ability to overcome or
alter gender-linked constraints. Rather than
focusing on social proscriptions, future
research would profit from greater attention
to how gender functions as a challenge and
how people can develop competencies to navigate sociostructural opportunities and overcome impediments.

## SOCIAL VALUES AND THE SYMBOLIC ENVIRONMENT

It is unusual these days to find a separate discussion of values in personality textbooks. The
contemporary field devotes far more attention
to value-free dispositions than to questions of
values and character. This is unfortunate. It
leaves the discipline less able to address a
topic that has attracted intellectual speculation for over four millennia and that is of a
particular concern today in view of contemporary criticisms that our postmodern society is
threatened by its loss of a firm, shared value
base. We bring our coverage of personality
development to a close by providing here a
brief overview of the study of values and the
processes through which social values are
transmitted to the developing individual.

When contemporary personality psychologists do study values, they tend to explore the
impact of values on other phenomena of interest, such as motivation, decision making, and
affect. The subjective value people attach to an
outcome is found, for example, to partly determine their level of motivation to achieve that
outcome and their emotional reaction to envi-

ronmental feedback (see chapters 10 and 12). Although work in these areas is highly valuable, it does not address important questions about the origin or structure of human values. Such questions have, however, received intense investigation in other disciplines. Philosophers, theologians, and legal scholars have long addressed the role of individual values in moral behavior and the maintenance of social order. Scientific investigation promises to bring a level of objectivity to the topic that is not found in these other disciplines. However, scientists share with investigators in other areas the problem that their own values may conflict with those of the people being investigated. Researchers therefore must be aware of their own world views and remain committed to fairness and openness. Objectivity in the study of values is facilitated by a clear definition of the term.

At an individual level, values concern the criteria, or standards, that people use to evaluate the actions of themselves and others (e.g., Rokeach, 1973; Schwartz, 1992). At this level of analysis, then, the notion of values overlaps with the construct of standards for performance, which receives much discussion in the next section of this volume. Key questions that arise at the individual level of analysis are whether there is a universal structure of human values and how different values are dynamically related to one another.

At a societal level, values correspond to the principles that determine rights and duties among citizens. Social values reflect the history of a society, and different societies can be characterized by their predominant, unique values; Western societies, for example, particularly value individual freedom, equality, and personal mastery of the environment. Societies maintain social orders partly by reproducing, from generation to generation, societal values in the minds of individuals.

Putting the two levels of analysis together, values can be seen to reflect the common societal endowment that is conveyed to all individuals by multiple socialization agencies and, at the level of the individual, the beliefs and standards that generally constitute a personal philosophy of life (Brewster-Smith, 1968).

Before taking up these two levels of analysis in more detail, we must note a theoretical perspective that speaks simultaneously to both of them. In sociobiological accounts (Wilson, 1975), values, morals, and ethics are not constructed in society. Instead, they are determined by our genes. Organisms act to reproduce their genetic material. Any "ethical sense" that the organism may have is merely an evolved adaptation whose ultimate function is to aid biological reproduction. In the years since the sociobiological thesis was first presented, investigators in multiple disciplines have come to recognize that it is too reductionistic to capture the complexity of human value systems and their development within cultures. Rolston (1999) provides a particularly detailed critique. As he explains, human value systems involve biology, but far more than biology. The cultural embeddedness of human value systems makes them dramatically more complex than sociobiological accounts suggest. This complexity yields emergent properties that cannot be reduced to simple biological components. In particular, people develop a "cultural self" that "comes to transcend, even to replace, in part, the biological self" (Rolston, 1999, p. 281). People become invested not only in the survival of their genetic material but in the survival of their ideas and values. Acts taken to promote virtuous ideas (e.g., the actions of religious and philosophical figures such as Jesus, Socrates, or the Buddha) can no more be explained "by asking . . . about their results in offspring . . . [than] by asking about biochemical movements in which electrons are transferred from this atom to that" (Rolston, 1999, p. 282).

### The Structure of Values

A basic question in the study of values at the level of the individual is whether there exists a set of values that is recognized universally. Can one identify a small yet comprehensive set of values that has fidelity across individuals and across cultures? A significant step in meeting this challenge is the work of Schwartz (1992), who has conducted multinational surveys of the values that people believe to be guiding principles in their lives.

In this work, individuals rate the degree to which each of a large number of values is important to them. Multidimensional scaling techniques are used to obtain a representation of the psychological space of values. The results indicate that ten distinct values (or categorical types of values) are recognized cross-culturally (Schwartz, 1992). These include the valuing of achievement, power, security, conformity, tradition, benevolence (toward people with whom one is in close contact), universalism (or concern with individuals outside one's in-group), self-direction, stimulation (i.e., the valuing of arousal and variety), and hedonism. Although different cultures, of course, differ in the degree to which they emphasize one versus another of these values, each seems to be recognized and to play a significant social role in all cultures surveyed.

The set of ten values can be represented within a two-dimensional space (Schwartz, 1992), the dimensions being openness to change versus conservation of the status quo, and self-enhancement versus self-transcendence (the latter of which combines universalist and benevolent values). This two-dimensional representation illuminates the dynamic relation among values. It is relatively easy to pursue simultaneously values that lie close together in the two-dimensional space (e.g., power and achievement, which both involve high levels of self-enhancement). Conversely, it is difficult to pursue values that are bipolar opposites (e.g., stimulation and conformity).

Schwartz' theoretical framework and associated survey instruments provide a valuable basis for research on values and individual decision making and action. Feather (1995), for example, has used the framework to study the relation between values and the attractiveness of behavioral alternatives. He presented participants with each of a series of scenarios containing behavioral options that tapped into different personal values; for example, a scenario might involve the choice of studying by oneself (to promote achievement) or with someone else who might benefit from a study group (a choice that embodies the virtue of benevolence). The subjective attractiveness of the alternative behaviors was found to be systematically related to assessments of the ten values identified by Schwartz (Feather, 1995).

## The Media and the Social Transmission of Values

Earlier sections of this chapter have discussed the role of peers and parents in transmitting values and beliefs. Here, we consider a socialization influence that has gained increasing influence in recent decades, namely, the electronic media and the symbolic environments that they present.

A key feature of the media as a socialization agent is that their influences may bear little relation to the individual's surrounding sociocultural context. Media influences combine with factors such as the mobility of people and capital to create social norms and social relations, which exist apart from their local contexts (Giddens, 1990; Halpern, 1995).

Broadcasting systems model ideas, social practices, and values (Bandura, 1986). In so doing, they contribute to an international homogenization of knowledge and preferences. For better or worse, television brings together previously separate cultures, exposing people to "foreign" modes of thought and behavior that were previously inconceivable.

Even if television is not intrinsically more powerful as a socialization agent than are other factors, its effects are particularly large for the simple reason that people spend so much of their day watching it. By the 1970s, on average Americans and Europeans were watching 3 to 4 hours of television per day (Liebert & Sprafkin, 1988), which is an amount that exceeds virtually any other waking activity. The pervasiveness of television, of course, continues to the present. Perhaps the most marked change in recent years is the greater diversity of material available through cable channels, satellite systems, and videotapes. Such diversity enhances the role of personal choice; although television programming shapes thought and behavior, people play a causal role by choosing the programs they watch (Bandura, 1986). The fact that people select programs that are congenial to their own personalities can be seen by the preference of aggressive youth for aggressive television programs (Bushman, 1995).

In this regard, the potential social effects of television viewing have been most extensively studied in the area of aggression. A vast literature has documented the fact that exposure to media violence can increase individual and social levels of aggression; although the effects are reliable, they are generally modest in size and are most apparent among people who already are predisposed to aggression (Huesmann & Eron, 1986; Liebert & Sprafkin, 1988; Paik & Comstock, 1994; Singer & Singer, 1986). Less evidence is available concerning the potential influence of the media on other problem behavior, such as suicide, eating disorders, sexual abuse, and alcohol and drug use (Strasburger, 1995; Wartella, 1995).

However, the traditional focus on antisocial effects of the media should not distract attention from its potential role in the development of prosocial values and behavior. Bandura (1986, 1997) summarizes instances in which media entertainments were systematically employed to attain socially positive outcomes on values and behavior. In Mexico, soap operas were constructed so as to provide valuable knowledge and skills about family planning and the reduction of illiteracy. In Tanzania, AIDS prevention was successfully addressed through a radio dramatic series.

The electronic media, then, may play a key role in meeting the challenging social task of providing individuals with the competencies required to cope with the rapidly changing contingencies of the modern world. We close by briefly considering the impact of such changes on individual and social value systems.

## Social Change and Materialistic and Postmaterialistic Values

Some today warn of a decay in the moral fabric of modern society. Selfish, materialistic concerns threaten to jeopardize any sense of solidarity, and a plurality of the world views makes all beliefs and ethical standards so highly relative that individuals may experience a loss of personal meanings (see Halpern, 1995). Before personality psychologists or any other social scientists investigate this purported decay, they should bear in mind a number of phenomena that suggest that certain core values have been maintained. Many people continue to volunteer in nonprofit organizations. Efforts to improve the conditions of life of the disadvantaged are increasing in most countries. Honesty, tolerance, and respect for others are held in high esteem at all ages in most countries. Confidence in democratic institutions, awareness of the environment, and pervasive norms of equity and fairness further attest to the fact that it may be premature to subscribe to the thesis of a moral decline.

It is difficult to establish the extent to which selfish, materialistic values directly compete with altruistic ones. Inglehart (1990, 1996) has proposed that societies' values reflect the availability of resources to satisfy the needs of people. He posits that economic hardship makes materialistic values salient, whereas economic plenty gives priority to postmaterialistic values such as affect, esteem, and self-realization. One caution here is that the distinction between materialistic and postmaterialistic values may not be clearcut. This distinction does not seem adequate to capture the rapid changes evident in many regions of Asia, which have experienced rapid economic growth and associated growth in materialistic values, while, in most views, simultaneously maintaining a collectivist approach that is more oriented to the needs of others than is the individualistic viewpoint of the West (see chapter 2).

In studying the impact of social changes on individual values, it is important for social scientists to recognize a point that we have raised at a number of junctures. People are not passive recipients of social influences. Instead, they actively choose and partly shape the social factors that affect them. We hope that future years will see greater attention given to the role of personality factors in the development of values and a sense of personal meaning in life, and also that investigators will explore the ways in which people contribute proactively to the acquisition of the personal values that constitute such an essential component of their personalities.

## SUMMING UP

A full understanding of personality development requires that one consider the sociopolitical and institutional systems that determine the conditions in which individuals develop, and the socialization agencies that sustain and orient individual's personal growth. An array of work in the social sciences suggests that the production and distribution of wealth and the organization of labor partly determine the beliefs and aspirations of individuals. The overall organization of society greatly influences the educational and family systems in which individuals are socialized. Social systems determine the meaning that people assign to maleness and femaleness and thus influence the nature of gender roles and the differences between men and women. The construction of personal identity and the life paths one pursues are decisively influenced by early life experiences in family and in the schools.

As many parts of our world achieve greater economic stability and political freedom, people have more opportunities than ever to determine the course of their life. The lessening of social constraints increases the impact of personal knowledge, skills, and self-directedness on the development of the individual. These critical cognitive and motivational dynamics are the focus of the next section of our text.

# PART FOUR

# The Dynamics of Personality

# INTRODUCTION

Scholars have provided an endless stream of metaphors to describe human nature. Some prove to have little value, whereas others are useful heuristics. One valuable metaphor of 20th century science is the person as information processor (e.g., Newell & Simon, 1972). A person is "a dynamic information processor whose unique memories and perceptual structures lead to a unique cognitive, affective, and behavioral signature" (Revelle, 1995, p. 318). The information processing metaphor stimulated many of psychology's advances in the latter third of the century.

Despite its value, the information processing metaphor cannot be pushed too far. It possesses four limitations as a framework for the study of personality. First, it presents an incomplete portrait of the influence of social experience on mental structures. As Edelman (1992) emphasizes, information processing systems experience a change in software but not hardware as a function of experience. One's computer does not develop a more or less elaborate circuitry based on the programs one runs. In contrast, the hardware of the brain does change as a function of experience. The nervous system itself develops "through interactions with the world" (Edelman, 1992, p. 226; also see Kolb & Whishaw, 1998). A second limitation is that the original information processing model depicted a serial processor with a central executive, which handled bits of information one at a time. In contrast, it is widely recognized that brains process multiple streams of information simultaneously or in parallel. Applied to the study of personality, this suggests that personality functioning involves organized systems of multiple processes mutually influencing one another (Shoda, 1999). Third, the information processing metaphor implies a "cold" symbolic system, whereas much of personality functioning is "hot" (cf. Metcalfe & Mischel, 1999). Cognitive and affective processes are so tightly interconnected that in some ways they are inseparable. Both psychological (Schwarz & Clore, 1996) and physiological (Damasio, 1994) analyses indicate that affective experience plays a direct informational role in reasoning and decision processes. Finally, information processing systems are not self-reflective and agentic. Your computer does not become bored and seek a new owner if you only run mundane word processing packages. The information processing metaphor thus may deflect attention from agentic properties that are so central to human personality functioning. Bruner (1990) has noted that cognitive science remains "chary of a concept of agency" (p. 204).

These shortcomings can be overcoming by conceptualizing personality as a cognitive–affective system (Mischel & Shoda, 1995, 1998). The personality system develops, functions, and modifies itself proactively through self-reflection and reciprocal interactions with the environment (Bandura, 1999). Part 4 of our text explores the cognitive and affective systems that are the basis of personality dynamics. We consider the processes involved in people's assignment of meaning to events (chapter 9), emotional reactions (chapter 10), and motivation (chapter 12). Some of these processes involve conscious self-reflection, whereas others occur outside of awareness, as we discuss at various junctures and particularly in chapter 11.

## PROCESSING DYNAMICS AND THE STRUCTURE OF PERSONALITY

There are three different ways to interpret the material that makes up this part of the text. Although all three readings recognize that the topics are critical to the study of personality and individual differences, they differ significantly.

One view is that the study of cognitive and affective processing systems illuminates the mechanisms through which traits influence behavior. Trait dimensions identified in the study of individual differences in the population may be construed as the structure of personality. Social-cognitive and affective mechanisms can then be seen as processes through which trait structures manifest themselves in behavior. From this perspective, traits shape social-cognitive mechanisms which, in turn, mediate overt behavior (McCrae & Costa, 1996). This suggests a direct integration of dispositional approaches and dynamic processing models.

A second view is that personality traits and dynamic processing mechanisms represent different levels of analysis of the person. It is possible that these levels coexist yet cannot easily be integrated. Persons can be construed in terms of both decontextualized traits and contextualized belief systems, but there may be no one-to-one mapping between these two levels of personality structure (McAdams, 1996).

The third view is that stable cognitive–affective systems constitute the structure of personality. In other words, rather than these systems being construed as mediators of personality structures or as one of a number of levels of personality structure, some contend that the structure of personality is the enduring, relatively stable organization of cognitive and affective systems that make up the individual (e.g., Mischel & Shoda, 1995, 1998). In this view, traits are no longer structures within the person; they are outputs of the cognitive–affective system and its interactions with the environment. Although this perspective may strike some as a radical view, it is noteworthy that almost all the major theories in the history of the discipline have been theories of processing dynamics in which cognitive–affective structures constitute the basic structure of personality.

Whatever one's reading, personality psychology is a place where the study of knowledge representation, conscious and unconscious thought, emotion, and motivation can come together to provide an integrated portrait of individuals and the ways they differ from one another.

# CHAPTER NINE

# Knowledge Structures and Interpretive Processes

Life would be easier if events came with labels that explained their meaning. Did that person's glance in your direction mean he is interested in meeting you? Did the handshake at the end of an interview mean that you're going to get the job? Did a professor's detailed critique of your paper mean that you are an academic failure – or that your work is so good that she was willing to devote extra time to you? Simple signals that reduce the ambiguity of events would eliminate much of the stress of social life. The absence of such signals forces people to interpret an ambiguous social world.

The meanings people assign to events pervasively influence psychological experience. Emotional reactions depend on whether events are interpreted as relevant to one's goals and as potentially controllable (Lazarus, 1991). Decisions are affected by whether prospects are interpreted in terms of gains or losses (Kahneman & Tversky, 1984; Mellers, Schwartz, & Cooke, 1998). Motivational states depend on whether activities are interpreted as personal challenges or externally imposed burdens (Deci & Ryan, 1991). Personality functioning is primarily an adaptation not to events themselves but to the meaning one assigns to them. Many theorists contend that processes of knowledge and interpretation are at the heart of personality and psychological experience (e.g., Cantor & Kihlstrom, 1987; Heider, 1958; Higgins, 1999; Kelly, 1955; Kreitler & Kreitler, 1992; Ross & Nisbett, 1991).

## GENERAL CONSIDERATIONS

Study of the processes through which people assign meaning to events contributes directly to our understanding of two classic concerns of the personality psychologist, namely, individual differences and intraindividual personality coherence. Individuals often differ, of course, in their interpretations of the same event. One person's challenge is another's burden. One's opportunity is another's threat. Many of the individual differences in emotion,

thought, and action that we judge to be most revealing of personality derive from the characteristic ways in which people interpret the events of their lives (Higgins, 1999). Furthermore, stable, organized cognitive structures underlie people's stable, coherent sense of self. Even when people face novel events, unexpected outcomes, and major life transitions, their enduring personal memories and belief systems generally foster a continuous sense of identity.

Of all the things we know about and interpret, none is more important than the self. People develop stable beliefs about their own attributes. These beliefs serve multiple functions (e.g., Baumeister, 1998). People attend to information that is pertinent to their self-concept. They act to confirm self-conceptions. They use knowledge of their strengths and weaknesses to set goals and plan for the future. In addition, they develop detailed personal autobiographies and reinterpret episodes from the past in light of current beliefs and concerns (McAdams, 1996; Ross, 1989; Ross & Newby-Clark, 1998). This process generally yields a coherent personal narrative, or a set of personal narratives, which are crucial components of one's sense of identity (Harré, 1998).

This chapter examines the psychological mechanisms through which people interpret the world and themselves. We focus on how meaning arises from the interaction between information in the environment and personal knowledge that people bring into situations. Our review encompasses a number of different aspects of personality functioning: how people's beliefs about themselves influence their interpretations of others; how subjective beliefs about the world and others contribute to individual differences in emotional distress, antisocial behavior, and interpersonal relationships; and how narrative processes contribute to the individual's sense of identity. The material covered here serves as a background to subsequent chapters of the text in that knowledge structures and interpretive processes are central elements of emotional and motivational systems.

We begin with a brief historical survey of psychological research on knowledge and meaning. Turning to the present, we review factors that influence which cognitive category, or construct, people use to interpret a given event. We then consider how personality functioning is guided by complex cognitive structures, or *schemas*, including schemas about the self. Subsequent sections of the chapter explore the role of knowledge structures in emotional experience and interpersonal behavior and the more general question of how different aspects of self-knowledge function as coherent, integrated personality systems. Our coverage of narrative processes concludes the chapter.

## Recurring Themes

Research findings on knowledge structures and processes of meaning construction have two broad implications for personality psychology. These two themes are heard repeatedly throughout this chapter. One theme is that knowledge structures are contextualized. People hold beliefs that are relevant to some social contexts but irrelevant to others. One social setting may activate beliefs that are dormant in another. The cognitive structures and thinking strategies that differentiate people from one another cannot adequately be captured by global cognitive style variables. The broader implication for analyses of personality functioning is obvious. To the extent that cognitive structures contribute to social behavior, the behavioral tendencies of the individual also cannot be fully captured by global dispositional variables.

A second theme is that the common practice of ranking individuals along individual-difference dimensions may misrepresent the underlying psychology of the individual. Findings repeatedly indicate that people who possess the same standing on a global individual-difference dimension possess different underlying cognitive structures. This point holds whether one is describing individuals who fall in the middle or at the extreme ends of individual-difference dimensions. People may fall in the middle range of a linear ranking of individuals either because they hold few

beliefs about the psychological tendency under study, and hence do not achieve an extreme high or low score, or because they hold many beliefs about the psychological tendency under study, but the beliefs conflict (e.g., Cyranowski & Andersen, 1998, reviewed below). Aggregating the diverse beliefs yields an average score, which misrepresents the cognitively complex individual and erroneously equates individuals who differ in fundamental ways. Furthermore, different people who possess equally extreme scores also may differ in the degree of knowledge they possess about the psychological attribute under study, and these differences have profound implications. The study of self-schemas, reviewed in detail below, rests heavily on a research methodology that differentiates between people who possess similar high or low scores on an individual-difference dimension but who differ in how central that dimension is to their self-concept.

In combination, these points argue against a commonly held perspective on the relation between trait-dispositional and social-cognitive research in personality psychology. This perspective suggests that social-cognitive processes mediate the influence of broad personality dimensions on social behavior. A proposed goal for research, then, is to identify the social-cognitive mechanisms associated with each of a series of trait dimensions. Hypothetically, one might identify the belief structures that characterize the moderately agreeable person or the individual who is low on conscientiousness. Although this proposal is popular among dispositional theorists (McCrae & Costa, 1996), it generally is rejected by investigators who actually study these belief structures (Cervone & Shoda, 1999c). If social-cognitive structures are contextualized and if different people with the same standing on a given personality dimension can possess different cognitive–personality structures, then research in social cognition does not explain how an individual's standing on a trait dimension influences his or her behavior. Instead, it calls into question the very notion that the trait dimension can adequately describe the individual in the first place.

## The Relation Between Personality and Social Psychology

Much of the research reviewed in this chapter was contributed by social psychologists. Questions about person perception and meaning construction dominated inquiry in this discipline throughout the second half of the 20th century. It would be a mistake, however, to view these contributions as peripheral to the concerns of the personality psychologist. The view that social and personality psychology address fundamentally different issues – the former discipline examining situational influences on behavior, and the latter examining person-based sources of variance – is an outmoded one that misstates the relation between the disciplines and underestimates their complementarity.

The idea that people respond to the subjective meaning they assign to events is emphasized in almost every major theory in the history of personality psychology. This is true even among theories that are not obviously cognitive in nature. Allport's classic definition of a personality trait inherently raises questions about knowledge and interpretive processes, since psychological systems that "render many stimuli functionally equivalent" (Allport, 1937, p. 295) of necessity must be systems that are involved in meaning and categorization. The study of knowledge and meaning processes, then, has a foundational quality in personality psychology (Higgins, 1999), just as it does in social psychology (Newman, in press). If people respond emotionally and behaviorally to the meanings they assign to social events, then a complete explanation of dispositional tendencies and personality functioning indisputably requires an analysis of knowledge structures, cognitive processes, and meaning assignment.

This does not imply that personality psychology is just an application of social psychological principles. The personality psychologist must confront problems that commonly receive little attention in the neighboring discipline. These include questions of how multiple affective and social-cognitive processes work in concert as personality systems, and how individuals develop distinctive bodies of social knowledge and self-knowledge that distinguish them from one another. Findings in social cognition, then, do not solve all the problems of the personality psychologist, but they do constitute a necessary ingredient in their solution.

## HISTORICAL BACKGROUND

The psychological study of knowledge and meaning processes has a long and distinguished history. Frederick Bartlett (1932) demonstrated that human learning and memory are not passive processes in which the mind merely records environmental information. Instead, preexisting knowledge structures, or *schemas*, dynamically influence knowledge acquisition. Schemas structure and reorganize environmental inputs. The meanings people derive from events, then, partially reflect their own prior knowledge and beliefs (Bartlett, 1932; also see Neisser, 1967). Bartlett's work foreshadowed cognitive psychology's study of top-down information processing (e.g., Rumelhart, 1975), that is, processing in which abstract, high-level knowledge is used to interpret specific situational inputs.

Jerome Bruner's analysis of *perceptual readiness* (Bruner, 1957a) was another critical precursor to contemporary research. Bruner investigated processes through which people categorize ambiguous or fragmentary information. He recognized that features of the stimulus only partly determine how it is categorized. Personal factors influence the "accessibility" of alternative categories, that is, the ease or speed with which particular categories come to mind and "capture" (Bruner, 1957b, p. 132) the environmental input. Knowledge accessibility has become a major focus of study in contemporary personality research (Higgins, 1990, 1999).

The personality theorist who placed greatest emphasis on personal knowledge and meaning processes was George Kelly (1955). In his personal construct theory, Kelly proposed that psychological experience is guided by the way people anticipate events. These subjective expectations are formed through the application of personal constructs, that is, beliefs or cognitive frameworks that function to categorize some things as being alike and as different from others. The personal construct systems, of individuals, then, are relatively enduring personality structures, which guide personality processes by shaping people's understanding of and expectations about themselves and the social world.

Two features of Kelly's work are particularly relevant to the contemporary field. First, Kelly recognized that construct systems are open to change: "No one needs to paint himself into a corner; no one needs to be completely hemmed in by circumstances; no one needs to be the victim of his biography" (Kelly, 1955, p. 15). People have the capacity to test alternative construals and thereby to enlarge and fundamentally alter their construct systems. This principle of *constructive alternativism* expands the scope of the psychology of personality. Construct systems are not static qualities that merely describe the things that people generally tend to do. They are dynamic structures that underlie people's potential for adaptability and psychological growth. In Kelly's system, then, the study of personality inherently incorporates both tendencies and potentials. In this regard, Kelly anticipated subsequent developments in the field. Work on social intelligence and cognitive expertise has revealed how cognitive systems give people the potential to cope with novel circumstances (Cantor & Kihlstrom, 1987). Cognitive-behavioral therapies show that psychological distress can be relieved by altering the beliefs people apply in interpreting life events (Beck, Rush, Shaw, & Emery, 1979), thus validating Kelly's beliefs about the malleability of construct systems and their role in mental health. Work on people's capacity to adopt alternative positions within internal dialogues about the self dovetails with Kelly's ideas about constructive alternativism (Hermans, 1996).

A second feature of enduring importance is that Kelly promoted a mix of idiographic and nomothetic research strategies. The general processes through which construct systems develop, change, and function can be studied nomothetically. However, the content of any individual's construct system must be investigated idiographically. Rather than fitting the individual into a preexisting taxonomy of individual differences, Kelly was interested in the unique personal taxonomies through which people themselves categorize events (Kelly, 1955). He developed a Role Construct Repertory (or "Rep") Test to assess the potentially idiosyncratic set of constructs employed by the unique individual. In this method, participants list individuals who fill each of a variety of social roles and then indicate how pairs of these individuals are similar to each other and different from a third person. As this assessment device reveals the respondent's construals for making sense of others, it discloses the way in which the individual organizes his or her own personal experiences. Kelly's assessment strategy foreshadowed more recently developed techniques for representing self- and interpersonal knowledge (Ogilvie, Fleming, & Pennell, 1998).

Kelly's work, then, was ahead of its time. He developed a cognitive-phenomenological theory while behaviorism dominated academy and psychoanalysis dominated the clinic. In retrospect, this timing handicapped his work. Kelly did not have access to a highly developed cognitive psychology, which could have provided a foundation for his analyses of cognition and personality. The intervening decades, of course, have witnessed enormous growth in this area. The themes developed by Kelly live on in the work of numerous investigators exploring the cognitive (e.g., Kreitler & Kreitler, 1992) and social-cognitive (reviewed in Cervone & Shoda, 1999b) foundations of personality functioning.

## THE CONTEMPORARY FIELD: ALTERNATIVE MODELS OF KNOWLEDGE REPRESENTATION

For our purposes, it is pointless to continue a history of work on knowledge and interpretive processes in personalty functioning beyond the pioneering efforts of Bartlett, Bruner, and Kelly. Developments beginning in the late 1950s and early 1960s are both too numerous to review and too familiar to require review. Psychology's "cognitive revolution" spread rapidly, with investigators in almost all subspecialties turning their attention to questions of mental representation and the use of stored knowledge.

Readers should bear in mind that the cognitive revolution has not left us with a single monolithic portrait of the mind. There exist different models with different implications. The most basic distinction differentiates cognitive architectures that view knowledge as being stored in a relatively static form in memory from those that conceive of knowledge as a construction involving multiple cognitive units, no one of which independently represents a fact about the world (see Smith, 1998). The former models are symbol-based systems. The basic units of analysis in the study of information processing are symbols stored in memory. These symbols may consist of associated constructs, exemplars, schemas, or generalized theories. The question is to understand exactly how people represent and draw on stored knowledge. In this chapter, we commonly employ the notion that knowledge consists of stored representations. The latter models are *parallel distributed processing*, or *connectionist*, models (Rumelhart et al., 1986; Read & Miller, 1998). Here, knowledge is represented as a pattern of activation that is spread across a large number of processing units. Each processing unit is extremely simple. No individual unit stores a piece of knowledge. Instead, knowledge is constructed through a pattern of activation among an organized set of units. Multiple patterns of activation may form at the same time, or in parallel. The task for the connectionist researcher is to determine whether these models can account for important phenomena that otherwise might be explained by reference to symbolic systems (Smith, 1998). Parallel-distributed processing models are important to personality psychology if only because they provide a foundation for under-

standing puzzling phenomena such as dissociations between streams of thought (Kihlstrom, 1990; see chapter 11). Such dissociations can be understood as a natural consequence of mental systems that process more than one stream of information at a time. More generally, parallel distributed processing models illustrate how information systems can perform complex tasks in the absence of high-level, executive units that control the flow of information processing. They thus illustrate a bottom-up strategy of explanation, as discussed in earlier chapters.

For our present purposes, we freely speak of knowledge as being stored in enduring mental representations, although recognizing that many of the phenomena we discuss might, in principle, be modeled by connectionist systems that do not assume the storage of static symbols.

## KNOWLEDGE ACTIVATION: TEMPORARY AND CHRONIC SOURCES OF ACCESSIBILITY

The meaning of some events is clear. Everyone recognizes that a grade of 28% correct is a failure and that a curse and vulgar gesture from a motorist constitute an insult. Such clear-cut cases, however, are relatively uncommon. We generally must assign meaning to stimuli that are inherently ambiguous. People generally resolve ambiguities not only by considering information in the situation but also by drawing on their own preexisting knowledge. Our interpretations of the world thus reflect not only the world, but ourselves.

Any given situation can, of course, be interpreted by a range of different constructs. A friend who turns down an invitation to join a study group could be seen as arrogant, shy, lazy, or independent. The particular construct that comes to mind in such circumstances is determined by both transient situational factors and enduring personal characteristics of the perceiver (Higgins, 1996a). In the following, we first review transient sources of construct accessibility, that is, factors that temporarily influence the likelihood that a given construct will be used to interpret an event. We then examine chronically accessible constructs, that is, constructs that enduringly come to mind for an individual. Chronically accessible constructs can be understood as enduring personality structures that contribute to stable patterns of individual experience and to differences among individuals.

## Temporary Sources of Construct Accessibility

Constructs can become temporarily accessible as a result of social cues that prompt people to contemplate a particular concept. These cues "prime" constructs, that is, they raise a construct's activation level (Higgins & King, 1981), making it more likely that the construct subsequently will be used to interpret a stimulus. Priming can qualitatively shift one's interpretation of events. Higgins, Rholes, and Jones (1977) primed trait constructs by asking individuals to hold a trait term in mind while they read other material. Participants then participated in a seemingly unrelated study in which they read essays describing the actions of a target person. The actions were inherently ambiguous; for example, a target's statement about his or her exceptional abilities could be a self-confident or conceited act. Participants' interpretations of the target were influenced by the construct primed in the seemingly unrelated prior experiment. People who previously had been exposed to the word "conceited," for example, tended to interpret the target as conceited and to evaluate the person negatively.

The likelihood that a construct will be used to encode a stimulus increases when it has been activated more recently and more frequently in the past (Srull & Wyer, 1979). Importantly, such priming effects are not a product of the perceiver's conscious, deliberate effort to use a primed construct. Instead, they reflect nonconscious cognitive processes. Priming effects are stronger when individuals are *not* consciously aware of a link between the prime and the target information (Lombardi, Higgins, & Bargh, 1987). Even

subliminally primed material influences social perception (Bargh & Pietromonaco, 1982). Conscious awareness of the prime may lead to contrast effects rather than the standard assimilation findings (Newman & Uleman, 1990), because people may overcorrect for the perceived influence of the cognitive prime.

In addition to the recency and frequency of priming, another factor that determines whether a construct will be used in the construction of meaning is the relation, or fit, between the construct and a given stimulus. This is referred to as the *applicability* of a construct (Higgins, 1996a). A construct is more likely to be applied to a stimulus if the features of the stimulus overlap with elements of the construct. Thus, we might think of someone as being aggressive not only if notions of aggression have recently been primed, but if features of the person (e.g., being dressed in menacing leather clothing) overlap with our beliefs about aggressive individuals.

## Chronically Accessible Constructs

Although situational cues can determine whether a given construct is used to interpret an event, the assignment of meaning to events should not be viewed as primarily a situation-driven process. Personal influences determine which features of a situation are noticed and how they are interpreted. Individual's preexisting knowledge guides encoding of events. Two types of knowledge-based individual differences can be distinguished (Higgins, 1996a, 1999). First, people differ in the constructs that are available to them. Constructs that are present in the cognitive system of one person may not be part of the mental makeup of another. Some, for example, may interpret another's good fortune as a reflection of good karma from a past life, whereas others may not even be familiar with the concept of karma. Second, among persons who all have stored a given construct in memory, there are substantial individual differences in chronic construct accessibility, that is, in the ease or readiness with which the construct typically comes to mind. Higgins, King, & Mavin (1982) provided a seminal contribution to the study of individual differences in the constructs that are chronically accessible to people.

Higgins et al. (1982) hypothesized that an individual's memories and impressions of other persons are guided by preexisting, highly accessible cognitive constructs. To test this, they first identified constructs that were relatively accessible and inaccessible for each participant in their study. Participants listed traits describing each of a series of individuals (themselves, a person they liked, a person they did not like, etc.). The traits that came to mind first in the listings were designated as accessible for the individual. One week later, subjects participated in a seemingly unrelated study in which they read an essay describing a series of actions performed by a target person. Essays were idiographically tailored to each participant. Some of the actions depicted were applicable to the participant's chronically accessible constructs (e.g., the construct "friendly" might be matched to the action "spontaneously strikes up conversations"), whereas others were linked to relatively less accessible constructs. After reading the essay, subjects described the target person and attempted to reproduce the essay. As predicted, chronically accessible constructs shaped participants' impressions and memories of the target. The targets were seen to be exemplifications of the participant's own cognitive categories. Participants tended to forget material about the target if it related to personal constructs of theirs that were relatively low in accessibility.

As it turned out, the decision to employ idiographic assessment procedures was critical to the success of this research. There proved to be little person-to-person overlap in the content of chronically accessible constructs (Higgins et al., 1982). Indeed, the majority of constructs generated were listed by only one research participant. It is noteworthy that this diversity of constructs was found despite the use of a relatively homogeneous group of research participants, namely, undergraduates enrolled at the same university. The use of a more demographically diverse group would likely accentuate the

need for idiographic assessment. The content of individual's beliefs about themselves cannot be well captured by forcing the individual into any simple, universal taxonomy of cognitive constructs.

Temporary and chronic sources of construct accessibility appear to function through common processes. Temporary variations in construct accessibility guide impression formation in the same manner as do enduring individual differences in construct accessibility. One obtains similar impression formation results if one substitutes chronically accessible constructs for constructs that are frequently primed, but not chronically accessible (Bargh, Lombardi, & Higgins, 1988). Cognitive priming thus can be seen to produce temporary individual differences (Higgins, 1999).

The effects of temporary and chronic accessibility are additive. People are most likely to use a construct if it is chronically accessible for them and if it also is primed (Bargh, Bond, Lombardi, & Tota, 1986). The combination of contextual priming and chronic accessibility can so strongly activate a construct that it may be used even when people interpret vague stimuli that seem to bear little relation to the construct (Higgins & Brendl, 1995). People who chronically interpret actions in terms of moralistic religious beliefs and who have just attended church, for example, might be prone to apply these beliefs in the interpretation of acts that others would see as completely unrelated to moral worth.

This full set of findings yields a clear understanding of the mechanisms of knowledge activation. A given construct (e.g., "intellectual snob") is more likely to be used in the interpretation of a target if the construct has recently been primed (e.g., one recently has been in a situation that contained one or more intellectual snobs), if the target exhibits features that overlap with the construct (e.g., the person ostentatiously discusses obscure avant-garde art), or if the construct chronically has a high activation level for the perceiver (the perceiver, for whatever reason, frequently contemplates the construct "intellectual snob").

Construct activation, then, is a common mechanism through which both social and personal factors influence the meaning that people assign to events. This simple conclusion has a significant implication. Instead of employing the psychologist's traditional strategy of analyzing person and situation factors through separate principles, principles of knowledge activation provide a common conceptual framework for analyzing both persons and situations. They provide, in other words, a "general principles" approach to personal and situational determinants (Higgins, 1999). To illustrate, consider a phenomenon that has been well studied by social psychologists, namely, the helping of strangers who are in need. In a traditional approach, social psychologists would propose one set of principles to explain how situations influence behavior. The number of bystanders present, for example, might determine levels of helping (Darley and Latané, 1968). Personality psychologists would propose a second set of principles to explain individual differences in helping within any given situation. Hypothetically, agreeableness might influence helping. This split strategy has serious shortcomings. The conceptual languages of "bystanders" and "agreeableness" cannot easily be reconciled. One therefore obtains no overall, generalized understanding of the common processes that might mediate both the situational and the person factors. In contrast, the analysis of construct activation yields such an understanding. The presence of few versus many bystanders may differentially activate cognitive constructs having to do with "personal responsibility." Individuals may differ in the degree to which these same constructs are chronically accessible for them. Situational and personal factors, then, are simply alternative sources of variance in the common process of knowledge activation (Higgins, 1999).

## Spontaneous Trait Inference

The work reviewed thus far examined people's interpretations and impressions under a certain set of conditions, namely, conditions in which participants are explicitly asked to give their impression of target persons. These exact conditions are relatively uncommon. In the flow of naturally occurring events, people rarely are explicitly instructed to deliberate on others' motives and attributes. Even if they were so instructed, the need to respond rapidly to situational demands may leave little time for deliberation. Rapid, spontaneous judgments characterize much of social life. An important question, then, is whether individuals differ predictably in the inferences they make quickly, or "automatically" (Bargh, 1989, 1994).

Much evidence indicates that social inferences commonly are made spontaneously, that is, in the absence of a conscious intention or awareness of forming an impression of others (Uleman, 1989; Uleman, Newman, & Moskowitz, 1996). Uleman and colleagues' cued-recall paradigm (Winter & Uleman, 1984; Winter, Uleman, & Cunniff, 1985) illustrates this phenomenon. Participants read depictions of social behaviors (e.g., "The electrician gets a promotion and raise") and subsequently try to recall the material while being prompted by alternative cues. Recall cues are either personality trait terms that are implied by the depicted actions (e.g., "good worker") or words that are semantically linked to the material (e.g., "wires"). Memory for the sentences is facilitated by trait cues as strongly as by semantic cues (Winter & Uleman, 1984). Since recall cues are beneficial to the extent that they correspond to the initial encoding of material (Tulving & Thomson, 1973), these results (also see Bassili, 1989; Newman & Uleman, 1990, 1993; Uleman et al., 1996) suggest that observers spontaneously encode the depicted action in terms of personality dispositions of the actors. Reaction time (Newman, 1991) and savings effect (Carlston & Skowronski, 1994) paradigms provide additional evidence that perceivers spontaneously draw inferences about actors' traits when observing their behavior.

The traits that people spontaneously attribute to others can influence cognitive processes even after the traits themselves can no longer be recalled (Greenwald & Banaji, 1995; Schacter, 1987). Previously inferred traits that cannot be recalled nonetheless are relearned more quickly (Carlston, Skowronski, & Sparks, 1995). Prior trait inferences thus may influence social thinking through processes that lie outside conscious awareness.

Not all people are equally prone to infer traits spontaneously when observing others' actions. Trait inferences are more common among people who believe that dispositional information is particularly useful for predicting others' behavior (Newman, 1991) and within cultures that conceive of actions in terms of individuals' personal dispositions and motives (Duff & Newman, 1997; Newman, 1993).

Spontaneous trait inference paradigms have proved to be a valuable method for detecting individual differences in personality-related beliefs. People's beliefs are revealed in the content of the social inferences that immediately "spring to mind."

Uleman, Winborne, Winter, & Shechter (1986) examined the link between the content of spontaneous inferences and individual differences in authoritarian beliefs (Adorno, Frenkel-Brunswick, Levinson, & Sanford, 1950), which involve the condemnation of people who violate moral codes and the perception of others in terms of power and toughness. In a cued-recall paradigm, individuals expressing low versus high degrees of authoritarian beliefs (Christie, 1991) differed in their degree of recall when presented with cues representing the interpretive tendencies of low-authoritarianism and high-authoritarianism persons.

Zelli and colleagues (Zelli, Cervone, & Huesmann, 1996; Zelli, Huesmann, & Cervone, 1995) explored relations between individual differences in experience with aggression and spontaneous trait inference. Chronic exposure to aggression, they reasoned, should foster highly accessible knowledge structures that predispose people spontaneously to interpret ambiguous acts as being hostile. These act categorizations should, correspondingly, affect trait inferences about the actors (Jones &

Davis, 1965; Gilbert, 1989; Trope, 1986). Zelli and associates hypothesized that these inferential tendencies would be *more* apparent when social inferences were made spontaneously than when people consciously deliberated on an encounter, because deliberation may cause people to adjust their initial inferences in a way that masks spontaneously occurring individual differences. College students reporting low versus high frequencies of aggressive experience read sentences that were open to either hostile or nonhostile interpretations. For example, "The policeman pushes Dave out of the way" could be interpreted as an aggressive or an alert act. In spontaneous inference conditions, subjects simply memorized the sentences. In deliberate inference conditions, they memorized them while considering why the actors had behaved as they did. Participants subsequently attempted to recall the sentences after receiving hostile and nonhostile recall cues. In the deliberate inference conditions, hostile and nonhostile cues were about equally effective in prompting recall among high- and low-aggressive persons. In contrast, in spontaneous inference conditions, hostile trait cues were more effective for aggressive subjects but not for nonaggressive persons (Zelli et al., 1996). This implies that aggressive individuals spontaneously inferred that the ambiguous actions were aggressive (also see Zelli et al., 1995). Explicit requests to deliberate on encounters appeared to prompt people to consider interpretations of the actor's behavior that they otherwise would not have contemplated. The content of inferences made spontaneously, then, was more revealing of underlying individual differences.

Such findings (Zelli et al., 1995, 1996) highlight the pervasive influence of highly accessible knowledge. Knowledge arising from one's past experience may influence social inferences even in situations that are relatively unrelated to the original contexts in which the experiences occurred. In work on cognitive biases among aggressive persons (Dodge, 1993; Zelli & Dodge, 1999; also reviewed below), the individual difference measures tap aggressive behavior exhibited in reaction to threats in hostile environments. These individuals' inferential biases, however, are detected in relatively sterile laboratory settings, which are completely lacking in threats or physical challenges. Even relatively benign situational inputs in the laboratory trigger the individual's chronic inferential tendencies. As Bargh et al. (1986) suggest, the influence of chronically accessible constructs may be observed "across situations, contexts, and interaction partners" (p. 877).

## Individual Differences in the Associations Among Concepts

People differ not only in the degree to which particular constructs are cognitively accessible but in the ways in which different constructs are linked in memory. Concepts that are strongly interrelated for one person may be unrelated for another. Research by Bargh, Raymond, Pryor, & Strack (1995) illustrates this principle in a context of considerable social importance, namely, sexual harassment and aggression.

Bargh et al. (1995) examined the possibility that, for some men, concepts of power and sexuality are so strongly linked that the activation of one concept automatically activates the other. They studied men who obtained high and low scores on self-report measures of tendencies to harass women sexually and to be attracted to aggressive sexual encounters. In one study, they subliminally primed concepts related to power. Among men who reported a preference for sexually aggressive stimuli and men who reported being relatively likely to harass, the subliminal priming of power concepts facilitated responding to sexual stimuli. Exposure to power concepts, in other words, caused men to respond more quickly to sexual material. In contrast, among men who reported being relatively unlikely to harass and who expressed lesser preference for sexual aggression, concepts of power and sex did not appear to be linked. A second study revealed that among men who are prone to harassment, power primes can heighten the perceived attractiveness of women (Bargh et al., 1995).

As Bargh et al. (1995) discuss, the automaticity of these power–sex links may cause some men to be unaware of their own harassing tendencies, for the following reason. Primes are particularly effective when people are not aware of their presence and influence (Lombardi et al., 1987). When constructs are primed outside of awareness, the primed construct comes to mind automatically when a relevant stimulus is presented. When people automatically encode the stimulus in terms of the given construct, the encoding seems true (Gilbert, 1991); people are far less likely to question their inferences when categorizations are made automatically than when they are based on the deliberate weighing of evidence. In the case of power–sexuality links, if being in power primes thoughts of sexuality for a man, he may *mis*interpret a woman's friendly but professional demeanor as evidence of her attraction to him and fail even to question this erroneous inference or the appropriateness of his subsequent inappropriate behavior. This, of course, does not imply that men in this position bear lesser responsibility for their inappropriate behavior. Even if one's actions may not have been fully, consciously controllable in a particular setting, people may still be seen to bear responsibility for their conduct in that they should have gained greater knowledge of how circumstances may lead them astray and have developed strong internal prohibitions against making sexual advances in circumstances involving unequal power (see Dennett, 1984).

## SCHEMATIC KNOWLEDGE STRUCTURES AND SELF-SCHEMAS

Some aspects of knowledge are not only accessible but are highly elaborated and organized. People gradually build complex cognitive structures as they experience the world and reflect on their experiences. These knowledge structures serve not only to disambiguate information but also to guide which information we attend to and how we will fill in the gaps when only partial, incomplete information is available to us. These organized, active cognitive structures are referred to as *schemas,* a term with origins in Kant's (1781) analyses of knowledge acquisition and, in psychology, in Bartlett's (1932) studies of memory (see Gardner, 1985, for a detailed historical overview).

A schema is more than just a list of information or facts. Schemas are interconnected, organized networks of knowledge (Fiske & Taylor, 1991; Singer & Salovey, 1991; Smith, 1998). The richness and complexity of these knowledge structures is so great that we often may be incapable of articulating all of our schematic knowledge of a type of person or event. Our schema for visits to a dentist's office, for example, may include not only obvious facts, such as the fact that we will sit in a special dentist's chair, but subtle details about the setting, such as details about the expected interpersonal demeanor of the dentist (Abelson, 1981). In many cases, these subtle features are ones that we would not even think to enumerate if someone were to ask us about the topic. They only become apparent to us if our schema is violated, for example, if our dentist yawns, laughs, or looks anxious during a dental procedure.

Cognitive schemas pervasively influence our thoughts and actions. When observing events, we do not passively record information but actively embed it into preexisting mental frameworks, which guide our subsequent inferences, expectations, and actions (Neisser, 1976). Schemas guide thoughts about both persons and situations. If a new acquaintance discusses fine wines and contemporary culinary trends, we interpret these facts in terms of preexisting knowledge about gourmets or, more broadly, cultured persons. Our expectations about the person are then based in part on the content of these generic person categories (Cantor & Mischel, 1979). If a social gathering features beer, spiked punch, and loud music, we recognize it as an informal party (Cantor, Mischel, & Schwartz, 1982), and our expectations about the event are driven by general beliefs about the types of behavior that are expected and appropriate in

this setting. Finally, schemas influence not only interpretations but actions. For example, self-schemas about prosocial behavior influence level of donations to others, particularly when individuals are self-aware (Froming, Nasby, & McManus, 1998). Schemas can influence behavior not only directly but through their influence on appraisal processes that regulate motivation (Cervone, 1997).

In schema-driven information processing, then, we routinely go "beyond the information given" (Bruner, 1957a). We add knowledge stored in memory to information presented in the environment to construct understandings about the social world. The application of preexisting knowledge is generally beneficial, enabling rapid judgments about complex settings. This cognitive economy, however, comes at a cost. The application of schemas that are not fully appropriate to the situation at hand can foster erroneous social judgments (Nisbett & Ross, 1981; Wilson & Brekke, 1994).

Many of our schemas are universal, at least among members of the same culture. Knowledge of cultural rituals, social institutions, and traditional patterns of interpersonal interaction are so highly shared that we may give little thought to the complex set of knowledge that facilitates smooth social functioning. Other schemas, however, may be more "particularistic" (Markus, Hamill, & Sentis, 1987), that is, they may be possessed by some individuals but not others. Even within the same cultural and social context, there is considerable individual variation in the degree to which people develop knowledge of particular aspects of social life. Political knowledge illustrates this principle (Fiske, Lau, & Smith, 1990; Krosnick, 1990). Although some people develop relatively little knowledge of the political processes, others possess elaborate schemas related to politics. People who are schematic for politics are capable of accurately identifying the ideological stands of politicians and are better able to recall political events (Fiske et al., 1990). Note that one may be schematic for politics while having attitudes anywhere on the political spectrum.

There are schematic political conservatives, moderates, and liberals.

## Schemas: Three Features

The example of political schemas introduces three aspects of schematic knowledge structures that readers should bear in mind as we consider research on schematic processing in more detail below. The first is the distinction between one's standing on an individual-difference dimension and whether one is schematic for the attribute tapped by that dimension. Level and schematicity are distinct in two respects. First, one can possess a schema for an attribute while having either a high or a low score on an associated individual-difference dimension. Just as both liberals and conservatives may possess elaborate schemas about politics, people who score at either the high or the low end of a personality trait dimension may possess elaborate schemas regarding the trait. Second, one can score at an extreme high or low end of a dimension and yet not possess a schema for the given attribute. People might see themselves as staunch conservatives while possessing relatively little knowledge about politics. Schema assessments, then, may add information about personality structure that is not provided by traditional assessments of a person's level on a trait.

A second point is that schematic knowledge is contextualized. People rarely possess "schemas in general." Instead, schematic knowledge structures develop in and pertain to particular aspects of a person's life. A person who has well-developed knowledge about interpersonal relationships among coworkers may lack an analogous understanding of interpersonal relations among family members. The person thus might be more effective at resolving interpersonal conflicts at work than at home. Schemas, then, are enduring cognitive structures, which may contribute to variation in behavior from one context to another. One exception to this rule is that people may possess some "abstract" schemas (Ohlsson, 1998), which contain knowledge that can be generalized from one situation to

another. For example, Darwinian principles of natural selection may be represented as an abstract schema that people can apply to a variety of issues involving competition for resources.

The third point concerns the cognitive and behavioral implications of possessing schematic knowledge. Schemas enable people to respond quickly and flexibly to environmental demands. People who possess a large amount of knowledge in a domain can interpret new stimuli quickly, are able to question interpretations that seem erroneous, and can generate and assess multiple coping strategies. Schemas, then, expand people's cognitive and behavioral repertoire (Cantor & Kihlstrom, 1987), giving them greater potential for action.

A general theme that emerges from these three points is that schemas are enduring structures of personality that do not function in the manner of personality traits. Trait constructs generally correspond to the mean levels of performance that people typically exhibit. Schemas, in contrast, may underlie both average response tendencies and variations in behavior across contexts, and they contribute not only to typical dispositional tendencies, but to potentialities for action that rarely manifest themselves. For example, people may vary in whether they possess schemas that contain knowledge of how to establish new personal relationships. These variations may have no effect on everyday social behavior when people are living in familiar circumstances. However, they may foster marked individual differences when people are forced to deal with unfamiliar settings, as when people move from one area to another (Cantor & Harlow, 1994). Possessing the schema gives people a greater potential for coping with the new circumstance.

## Self-Schemas

If asked, people can describe themselves with respect to a wide variety of personality attributes. Respondents' ability to complete all the items of comprehensive personality inventories attests to this fact. If not asked, however, many of these attributes rarely come to mind. From the perspective of the individual, then, all personality attributes are not alike. Some characteristics are central to our sense of self, whereas other characteristics are so peripheral that we may never think of them unless a psychologist asks.

People tend to develop relatively elaborate bodies of knowledge about these central personality characteristics. These knowledge structures are referred to as *self-schemas*. Self-schemas, then, are "cognitive generalizations about the self, derived from past experience, that organize and guide the processing of self-related information" (Markus, 1977, p. 64). Self-schemas are dynamic knowledge structures that influence the acquisition and interpretation of new information about oneself and others.

Markus's (1977) research on self-schemas proved paradigmatic in this area. She employed a dual criterion to identify individuals' schematic attributes. Participants rated themselves on a set of bipolar trait dimensions and also indicated the personal importance of each dimension. People who were categorized as schematic for a given attribute were those who had both a relatively extreme (high or low) self-rating on the dimension and identified the attribute as being highly important. This approach thus can differentiate between people who have a similar standing on a trait dimension but judge the attribute to be differentially important to their self-concept. In the research, three groups of women varying in schematicity for independence were identified: independent schematics (people for whom the dimension was personally important and who rated themselves as independent), dependent schematics (people for whom the dimension was personally important and who rated themselves as dependent), and aschematics (people who rated themselves near the middle of the bipolar dimension and indicated that independence–dependence was not important to them).

The dynamic nature of self-schemas was revealed in subsequent information-processing tasks. When judging the self-relevance of a series of trait adjectives, independent-schematic subjects endorsed independent adjectives more quickly than dependent adjectives, whereas dependent-schematic persons identified dependent adjectives faster than independent traits. Aschematic subjects, in contrast, did not differ in reaction time to dependent versus independent terms, and the schema groups did not differ on adjectives unrelated to independence. When asked to supply behavioral exemplars of traits, independent and dependent subjects were able to supply more independence- and dependence-related behavioral evidence, respectively. When predicting the likelihood of their engaging in independent and dependent actions, schematic subjects differed in their predictions for these act categories, whereas aschematic subjects did not differ in their subjective likelihood of engaging in one versus the other type of behavior. When given false test feedback that was incongruent with their self-image, schematic subjects were more likely than aschematic persons to reject the information (Markus, 1977).

Markus's (1977) use of reaction time measures was an extremely valuable addition to the personality literature. Reaction time measures enable the investigator not only to tap people's beliefs but to evaluate the rapidity or ease with which these beliefs come to mind. This is important in that whatever their content, beliefs that rarely come to mind are likely to play little role in day-to-day personality functioning. Reaction time measures also have the advantage of not being subject to conscious control. One cannot simply decide to speed up one's mental processing. The measures are thus less subject to response biases such as the desire to present oneself in a positive light. Finally, the use of reaction time techniques is based on well-established principles of mental chronometry in experimental psychology (Posner, 1978). Markus's research thus contributed to bridging work in personality and cognitive psychology.

Given these benefits, it is not surprising that much subsequent work used response time measures to explore cognitive structures of personality. Many findings confirmed that people who perceive themselves as having an extreme standing on a personality dimension respond more quickly to trait terms linked to this attribute. People respond more quickly to adjectives that are extremely like or unlike the self than to moderately self-descriptive traits (Kuiper, 1981). Individuals who rate themselves as high in femininity and low in masculinity (Markus, Crane, Bernstein, & Siladi, 1982) or are identified as feminine sex-typed via adjective check lists (Mills, 1983) respond more quickly when endorsing feminine trait adjectives. Women who are schematic for body weight are faster to endorse the self-relevance of trait adjectives relating to obesity and body silhouettes depicting prototypically heavy versus thin individuals (Markus, Hamill, & Sentis, 1987). Relatedly, Kendzierski and Whitaker (1997) have linked dieting schemas to weight loss efforts.

Differential response latencies are found not only in the rating of trait terms but in the endorsement of personality questionnaire items that are designed as indicators of a given trait. On self-report measures of both normal personality variations and psychopathology, people with higher scores on individual-difference scales endorse scale items that are consistent with the given trait more rapidly (Fekken & Holden, 1992). Response latency measures also have discriminant validity. Latencies in responding to items on a test correlate more highly with corresponding test scores than with scores on other scales that do not correspond to the response time items (Holden & Fekken, 1993). Measures of people's speed in responding to test items also demonstrate significant test–retest reliability, although such reliabilities have been found to vary across different individual-difference dimensions and to be lower than the reliabilities of the scale scores themselves (Fekken & Holden, 1992).

Response time analyses have proved useful in understanding the relation between self-views and others' views of one's personality. Work by Fuhrman and Funder (1995) suggests that the schemas people develop about themselves significantly overlap with the schematic knowledge other people have about them. The extremity of persons' self-ratings predicted not only their own reaction times for self-judgments but the speed with which well-acquainted peers make judgments about them.

In reaction time studies, investigators commonly have categorized people as schematic based solely on their having an extreme high or low self-rating on an attribute rather than on the dual criterion of extremity and self-rated importance suggested by Markus (1977) (see also Burke, Kraut, & Dworkin, 1984; Nystedt, Smari, & Boman, 1989). The studies still yield positive findings because extremity and self-rated importance generally are related; "although schema presence and trait extremity do not necessarily covary, they ordinarily do" (Fekken and Holden, 1992, p. 117). People generally develop schematic self-knowledge in domains in which they are distinctive as compared with those around them. Attributes that differ from the norm tend to be noticed and to be seen as informative about a person (McGuire & McGuire, 1988; Nelson & Miller, 1995). Research tapping people's spontaneous self-descriptions reveals that distinctive qualities tend to become more salient in the self-concept. Children tend to think of themselves in terms of a physical attribute if they have a relatively extreme standing on that attribute (McGuire & Padawar-Singer, 1976). Ethnicity is more salient when one's ethnic group is in the minority (McGuire, McGuire, Child, & Fujioka, 1978). Gender is more salient in self-concept when members of the opposite sex are a majority in one's household (McGuire, McGuire, & Winton, 1979). Self-schemas, then, reflect one's surrounding social context (Markus & Cross, 1990), and indeed, broader cultural factors also shape aspects of self-concept (Markus & Kitayama, 1994; Triandis, 1990). In Japanese culture, which stresses social roles and obligations more than personal attributes, people exhibit slower response times than Americans when characterizing themselves, particularly with respect to positive attributes (Markus & Kitayama, 1994).

Before turning to other issues in the study of self-knowledge, we note that reaction time methods are not the only technique for determining whether people possess a self-schema with respect to a given personality attribute. Another method is to assess memory performance. If after being exposed to a large list of personality descriptors, people recall relatively more terms related to a particular attribute, it can be inferred that they possess relatively elaborate schematic knowledge with respect to that attribute (Froming et al., 1998; Rogers, Kuiper, & Kirker, 1977).

■ *Self-Schemas, Processing Information About Others, and Information Processing Expertise.* Self-schemas influence not only information processing about the self but the acquisition and interpretation of information about others. When asked to evaluate others, people tend to inquire about dimensions for which they themselves are schematic and to be more confident in assessing targets on these dimensions (Fong & Markus, 1982). Personality dimensions on which people have a particularly positive view of themselves are more central to their evaluations of others (Lewicki, 1983). Knowledge related to these dimensions is more accessible when judgments about others' personality are made (Lewicki, 1984). Note, however, that the degree to which self-views shape perceptions of others varies across social contexts. Schema-driven processing is more apparent on inferential tasks that inherently encourage perceivers to draw on personal knowledge, as when perceivers' goal is to evaluate others rather than merely to recall information (Catrambone & Markus, 1987).

Self-schemas provide domain-specific social expertise that is akin to the problem-solving expertise exhibited by experts in cognitive domains such as chess (DeGroot, 1965). On problem-solving tasks, experts tend to organize material into larger meaningful units than do novices, while also having the capacity to vary their information processing strategy depending on task demands (Chase & Simon, 1973). Experts thus exhibit more efficient and flexible cognitive functioning.

Similarly, in interpersonal tasks, schemas provide expertise that facilitates more efficient and flexible personality functioning. When viewing a schema-relevant action sequence consisting of a series of stereotypically masculine behaviors, males who were schematic for masculinity organized the information into larger action units (Markus, Smith, & Moreland, 1985), which indicates that they recognized higher-order meaning in the action sequences (Newtson, 1973). When instructed to concentrate on details, however, schematics were capable of recognizing more significant lower-level actions than aschematics (Markus et al., 1985). Similarly, experts at clinical judgment organize behavioral observations into broader organizing categories than do novices and appear better able to draw on alternative explanatory theories when the behaviors they observe violate their expectations (Dawson, Zeitz, & Wright, 1989). These abilities are critical to coping effectively with interpersonal tasks that are novel or that contain unexpected features.

Research on knowledge and information processing expertise raises a critical issue in the analysis of individual differences, which we raised earlier in this text. People differ not only in abstract personal tendencies (McCrae & Costa, 1996) but in specific capabilities (Bandura & Walters, 1963; Mischel, 1973; Wallace, 1966, 1967). Observed differences in personality functioning often reflect differences in people's abilities to interpret and flexibly respond to the environment. People with rich, developed knowledge in a social domain are better able to adapt their cognitive strategies to fit the situation at hand (Cantor & Harlow, 1994; Cantor & Kihlstrom, 1987). Research on individual differences in discriminative facility, that is, the ability to detect social cues indicating the meanings of social situations, illustrates this point (Chiu, Hong, Mischel, & Shoda, 1995). Discriminative facility was assessed by measuring the degree to which individuals encoded passages from short stories in terms of complex conditional relations among actors' internal psychological states, antecedent interpersonal settings, and overt behavior. People who were capable of more complex encodings were found to have more fulfilling social interactions in their daily lives (Chiu et al., 1995).

■ *Valence in Self-Schemas.* The self-schema research reviewed thus far has contrasted individuals who either do or do not possess schematic knowledge structures in a domain. Other important contrasts, however, involve not just the presence or absence of self-schemas but their valence. Schemas may include primarily positive or negative information about the self. In some important domains, people may develop both positive and negative schematic self-knowledge. The work of Andersen and Cyranowski (1994) and Cyranowski and Andersen (1998) on women's self-schemas for sexuality illustrates this point.

Andersen and Cyranowski (1994) used a self-report index of women's cognitive generalizations about their sexual self to identify four subgroups. Positive schematics were women who had strong, consistent views of their willingness to engage in sexual experiences and their ability to experience sexual passion. Negative schematics held beliefs centering on sexual conservatism or embarrassment. "Co-schematics" strongly endorsed both positive and negative self-aspects, whereas aschematics endorsed neither. These schema groups differ in a variety of ways. As might be expected, positive schematics report more lifetime sexual partners and current sexual activities than negative schematics. Perhaps more importantly, aschematics and co-schematics differ. Co-schematics report higher levels of love and romantic involvement with previous sexual partners (Andersen & Cyranowski, 1994) and higher levels of sexual anxiety (Cyranowski & Andersen, 1998). Importantly, the groups do *not* differ on global self-reports of past sexual activity. Their behavioral histories, then, are "deceptively similar" (Cyranowski & Andersen, 1998, p. 1375). Aschematics experience moderate levels of sexual activity due to moderate levels of motivation for romantic relationships. Co-schematics experience moderate levels of sexual activity because of conflicts between high levels of desire for intimacy and of anxiety

stemming from their negative self-views. As we have emphasized repeatedly, it is impossible to identify psychological determinants from the top down (see chapter 3). The same global, surface-level tendencies have different underlying determinants for different people. Another implication of these findings is that the differences between women's self-views about sexuality cannot be captured adequately by a single linear dimension. A simple positive–negative dimension might equate aschematics and co-schematics. They both might be ranked in the middle of the scale, although they differ fundamentally.

Positive and negative self-schemas may differ not only in valence, but in their overall structure. Malle and Horowitz (1995) suggest that the network of information that constitutes negative self-schemas may, in general, be more highly interassociated than positive self-views. People with negative schemas display greater consistency in self-views across different self-report instruments than do positive schematics (Malle & Horowitz, 1995).

The study of alternative positively and negatively valenced self-schemas reinforces the point that self-concept is multifaceted (e.g., Cantor & Kihlstrom, 1987; Kihlstrom & Klein, 1994; Markus & Wurf, 1987). There are many different aspects to self-knowledge, of which some may be congruent with one another and others may conflict. We consider the coherence among aspects of the self in a subsequent section of this chapter.

### Relational Schemas

People's salient schemas do not only involve knowledge about themselves or other persons in isolation. As we described in our discussion of attachment processes in chapter 7, people also develop schemas about interpersonal interactions. Information about interpersonal relationships may be integrated with knowledge about oneself and others into a "relational schema" (Baldwin, 1992, 1999). Internalized representations of recurring interpersonal relationships guide people's expectations about, interpretations of, and emotional reactions to social encounters (Baldwin, Fehr,

Keedian, Seidel, & Thompson, 1993; Collins, 1996; Horowitz, 1991b).

Downey and Feldman (1996) provide a related analysis of cognitive processes and interpersonal relations. Their research investigates rejection sensitivity, the tendency to expect and to react strongly to the possibility of rejection from individuals with whom one might establish an intimate relationship. Downey and Feldman construe rejection sensitivity as a contextualized information-processing disposition. Some adults, perhaps because of attachment experiences in childhood (Bowlby, 1980), develop expectations of interpersonal rejection. Later in life, these thoughts are triggered by particular contexts, such as situations involving conflicts or arguments with one's relationship partner. Downey and Feldman identify rejection-sensitive persons through self-report. These individuals are found to be particularly prone to feelings of rejection when exposed to ambiguous interpersonal behavior by a stranger (Downey & Feldman, 1996, study 2). In their established intimate relationships, both rejection-sensitive individuals and their partners experience relatively less satisfaction with their relationship (Downey & Feldman, 1996, study 4). Longitudinal research reveals that the relationships of rejection-sensitive individuals are more likely to break up than are those of people who are less sensitive to the possibility of rejection (Downey, Freitas, Michaelis, & Khouri, 1998). It is noteworthy that rejection-sensitive individuals exhibit not a generalized tendency to experience negative affect but a specific vulnerability to anxious feelings of rejection in interpersonal relationships. The cognitive structures that underlie rejection sensitivity trigger context-specific emotional experiences, not global negative mood.

## KNOWLEDGE STRUCTURES, PERSONAL STANDARDS, AND EMOTIONAL EXPERIENCE

We use our personal knowledge of the social world to determine not only what events mean but what they mean for us. We interpret not only the properties of persons, situations, and actions but their implications for our personal well-being. People often assess the personal significance of events by comparing them with knowledge about the type of outcome that would be desirable or acceptable in a given setting. These criteria for evaluating the goodness of events are referred to as *standards*. Although standards sometimes are cognitively constructed by using information in the immediate environment (Miller & Prentice, 1996), we often compare events with internalized personal standards that constitute enduring structures of personality.

### Internalized Standards

Internalized standards have figured prominently in conceptions of personality throughout the field's history. Freud's (1923) analyses of the superego, Adler's (1927) and Horney's (1950) analyses of social strivings and idealized self-images (see Hall & Lindzey, 1978), and Rogers' (1959) phenomenological analysis of the actual and ideal self all recognized the impact of internalized personal standards on psychological adjustment. Lewin's (1935) field theory and Rotter's (1954) social learning approach highlighted the role of internalized aspiration levels in motivation, performance, and clinical behavior change. In the contemporary field, psychological standards are key mechanisms in the analysis of self-regulation and goal-directed action (Bandura, 1986, 1999; Carver & Scheier, 1998; Karoly, 1993b). The role of internalized standards in motivation, performance, and behavioral change is reviewed in chapter 12. Here we consider the impact of personal standards on emotional experience.

### Standards, Discrepancies, and Vulnerability to Distinct Emotional States

The emotional impact of events is not determined by the events themselves. Their impact depends on our interpretation of their personal significance and implications. A poor score on a college entrance examination could engender disappointment, embarrassment, anxiety, anger, or even relief from knowledge that one no longer has to worry about being admitted to a competitive school. These different emotional reactions largely derive from different types of knowledge that come to mind as people evaluate an event. The personal criteria, or standards, against which outcomes are compared determine many aspects of our emotional experience.

Higgins (1987, 1990) has provided a particularly valuable taxonomy of psychological standards and an analysis of the factors that determine which personal standards come to mind in a given situation. Higgins distinguishes among qualitatively different types of standards. *Factuals* are beliefs about the actual attributes of people or groups in society. *Possibilities* represent attributes one may have at some point in the future. Of particular importance in determining the immediate psychological impact of events are *guides*, which are criteria that currently are seen as valued or desirable standards for an individual (Higgins, 1990). Much research reveals that different emotional experiences ensue when people experience discrepancies between an actual state of affairs and alternative self-guides (Higgins, 1987).

Higgins, Bond, Klein, and Strauman (1986) posited two dimensions that differentiate alternative self-representations and guides. One, referred to as *domains* of the self, differentiates among attributes that one actually possesses (the *actual* self), attributes that are hoped for or wished for (the *ideal* self), and attributes that represent duties or obligations (the *ought* self). A second dimension, *standpoints* of the self, differentiates alternative viewpoints from which a person may be evaluated: the person's own standpoint and the standpoint of a significant other. Combining these dimensions yields a taxonomy that includes two views of one's current self (actual/own and actual/other) and four types of self-guides (ideal/own, ideal/other, ought/own, ought/other).

Within this taxonomy, Higgins et al. (1986) focused on discrepancies between one's actual self and ideal versus ought standards. They reasoned that actual-ideal and actual-ought discrepancies would foster qualitatively different types of emotional discomfort. If circumstances are construed as discrepant with ideal standards, the perceived failure to obtain an idealized, desired positive outcome should trigger feelings of sadness or dejection. If circumstances are construed as discrepant with ought standards, in contrast, they appear to constitute a failure to meet one's duties and obligations. The threat of negative outcomes that is associated with not meeting obligations should trigger agitation and anxiety (Higgins et al., 1986; cf. Lazarus, 1991). The same objective circumstances, then, should lead to different emotional experiences depending on whether ideal or ought standards are most accessible.

Before detailing the specific empirical strategies adopted by Higgins et al. (1986), it is instructive to consider a strategy they chose not to adopt. Although they posited two dimensions (domains and standpoints) that differentiate alternative mental representations of the self, they did not propose that individual persons could be described by locating them at a single point within a corresponding two-dimensional space. Higgins et al. (1986) and Higgins (1990) presented a taxonomy of social standards, not a taxonomy of persons. Locating people at a single point within a nomothetic dimensional system may not be an adequate strategy for capturing either the content of an individual's construct system or individual differences in self-knowledge. Some people may have chronically accessible self-discrepancies of more than one type. For example, a person may experience discrepancies involving both other/own and other/ideal standards. Placing such a person at the midpoint of an own–ideal continuum clearly would fail to capture the complexity of his or her construct system. Another person, in contrast, may not have internalized either other/own or other/ideal standards; knowledge related to these criteria may not be cognitively available for this person (Higgins, 1990), for whom placement anywhere on an other/own–other/ideal continuum may be inappropriate. Rather than searching for a nomothetic taxonomy of persons, Higgins analyzes the content of self-knowledge idiographically and combines idiographic assessments with nomothetic principles involving potential types of self-representations, the processes that influence their accessibility, and the links between accessible knowledge and emotion (Higgins, 1990).

To assess individual differences in the chronic accessibility of discrepancies between the actual self and alternative self-guides, Higgins et al. (1986) employed an open-ended assessment procedure. Participants were asked to list attributes (1) that they believed they actually possessed, (2) that they ideally would like to possess, and (3) that they believed they should, or ought to, possess. To quantify discrepancies between the actual self and each of the two self-guides, attributes in the actual-self listing were matched to ideal- and ought-self listings. The number of attribute matches was subtracted from the number of mismatches to yield actual–ideal and actual–ought discrepancy scores. Through this procedure, groups of individuals who primarily exhibited actual–ideal discrepancies and actual–ought discrepancies were identified. These subjects participated in a subsequent session, in which their affective reactions were assessed as they envisioned themselves experiencing a negative life event.

Although all participants envisioned the same event, they experienced different emotional reactions. As predicted, people with actual–ideal discrepancies became dejected but not agitated when considering the negative outcome. People with highly accessible actual–ought discrepancies became agitated but not dejected. The groups did not differ when they envisioned a positive event. Self-discrepancies, then, create specific vulnerabilities to different types of emotional distress when one is faced with setbacks.

A second study that experimentally manipulated self-discrepancies yielded converging evidence in support of self-discrepancy theory (Higgins et al. 1986). Recall that priming cues can temporarily alter the accessibility of constructs. Drawing on this fact, Higgins et al. (1986) randomly assigned persons who possessed both actual–ideal and actual–ought self-discrepancies to conditions that primed either ideal or ought standards. Priming alternative standards fostered different emotional reactions. When ideal self-discrepancies were primed, participants felt dejected. When ought standards were primed, subjects felt agitated (Table 9-1). Importantly, these emotional effects were not a necessary result of priming manipulation itself. Among a second group who possessed neither actual–ideal nor actual–ought self-discrepancies, the same priming cues had no emotional impact (Higgins et al., 1986).

---

TABLE 9-1 **Mean Change in Dejection Emotions and Agitation Emotions as a Function of Level of Self-Discrepancies and Type of Priming**

|  | Ideal priming | | Ought priming | |
| --- | --- | --- | --- | --- |
| Level of self-discrepancies | Dejection emotions | Agitation emotions | Dejection emotions | Agitation emotions |
| High actual:ideal and actual: ought discrepancies | 3.2 | –0.8 | 0.9 | 5.1 |
| Low actual:ideal and actual: ought discrepancies | –1.2 | 0.9 | 0.3 | –2.6 |

*Note:* Each of eight dejection emotions and eight agitation emotions was measured on a 6-point scale from *not at all* to *a great deal*. The more positive the number, the greater the increase in discomfort.
From Higgins et al., 1986, Study 2.

Highly accessible self-discrepancies have been linked not only to momentary shifts in emotion but to chronic emotional distress. People with predominantly actual–ideal discrepancies are prone to experience dejection, whereas those with discrepancies between their actual self-concept and ought standards are prone to experience fear and agitation (Strauman & Higgins, 1988; Straumann, 1992). Social phobics and clinically depressed patients exhibit predominantly actual–ought and actual–ideal discrepancies, respectively (Strauman, 1989). Also, Q-sort indices of incongruence between real and ought self-descriptions predict higher levels of neuroticism and lower levels of subjective well-being (Pavot, Fujita, & Diener, 1997). Self-discrepancies predict emotional experiences among parents after the birth of their children (Alexander & Higgins, 1993). Prebirth actual–ideal discrepancies foster postbirth dejection, which may result from the fact that parenting interferes with the attainment of hopes and wishes that are unrelated to family matters. Interestingly, parents with predominant actual–ought discrepancies experience less emotional agitation after the birth of their children (Alexander & Higgins, 1993). The demands of parenting appear to shift attention away from other duties and obligations that previously created distress.

The chronic experience of discrepancies between actual self-concept and valued standards also can impair physical health. People who see themselves falling short of their potential capabilities and who view these potentials as future states that others believe they should attain report greater physical distress, including headache, poor appetite, and digestive problems (Higgins, Vookles, & Tykocinski, 1992). Experimental evidence indicates that the priming of self-discrepancies can influence immune system functioning. Strauman, Lemieux, and Coe (1993) primed self-discrepancies with an idiographically tailored writing task and assessed subsequent natural killer cell activity, which is affected by levels of psychological stress. Priming induced negative affectivity and lowered natural killer cell activ-

ity (Strauman et al., 1993). Self-discrepancies also have been linked to disordered eating patterns. Among undergraduate women, actual–ideal discrepancies predict dissatisfaction with one's body, whereas actual–ought discrepancies are correlated with attitudes and behaviors characteristic of anorexia, which tends to be associated with anxiety and concern about others' demands (Strauman, Vookles, Berenstein, Chaiken, & Higgins, 1991). In work by Szymanski and Cach (1995), however, actual and ideal discrepancies did not discriminantly predict alternative forms of emotional distress associated with body image.

Despite the generally positive results, some question has been raised about whether the assessment techniques developed by Higgins and associates are adequate to identify distinct forms of self-discrepancy. In a sample studied by Tangney, Niedenthal, Covert, and Barlow (1998), different types of self-discrepancy were highly intercorrelated when assessed via Higgins' attribute listing technique. As a result, different self-discrepancies failed to predict differential emotional experiences. The study of personal constructs, standards, and emotional experience may be a domain in which theory has outstripped method at present. More sensitive tests of the theoretical ideas may require improved assessment techniques. The meanings people assign to personality attributes (Hayes & Dunning, 1997), even attributes that they believe to be uniquely self-descriptive (Cervone, 1997), can be highly variable from one person to another and may even vary within-person in different contexts. To assess self-beliefs accurately, then, the psychologist may need to do more than obtain a listing of isolated attributes. Assessment may benefit from assessing the idiosyncratic ways in which people link a particular attribute to particular social settings and interpersonal relationships. Techniques for assessing self-knowledge and belief systems are discussed in later sections of this chapter.

■ *Self-referent Constructs as Integrated Structures.* Knowledge of one's actual self and of standards representing a self-guide can become so highly interrelated that they constitute an integrated cognitive structure. Activation of any one element of this structure can activate the entire structure and trigger associated emotional states. This may occur even when the cue that initially activates the structure is linked only indirectly to one's self-concept.

Strauman & Higgins (1987) asked individuals with predominant actual–ideal discrepancies, actual–ought discrepancies, or no self-discrepancies to complete a series of sentence fragments that purportedly described other people. The sentences were idiographically tailored so that the other person's attributes matched elements of the subject's own chronic self-discrepancies. Self-report, physiological, and behavioral indices revealed that this unobtrusive priming of self-relevant attributes induced agitation and dejection in subjects with actual–ought and actual–ideal discrepancies, respectively (Strauman & Higgins, 1987). Self-discrepancy–based emotions, then, were triggered even though subjects were instructed to think about *other* people. The overlap between others' attributes and self-views activated the integrated structure of beliefs that constitutes a chronic self-discrepancy.

■ *Developmental Precursors.* Self-discrepancy theory (Higgins, 1987) suggests that both social experiences and temperamental factors may contribute to the development of stable social-cognitive structures. Until recently, however, investigators had failed to directly investigate developmental precursors of salient ideal and ought standards; instead, only indirect evidence was available. For example, recall cues linked to current self-guides were found to strongly facilitate the retrieval of childhood memories, which suggests that the self-guides are internalized representations of salient or recurrent developmental experiences (Strauman, 1992). Research on birth order (see chapter 7) reveals that discrepancies between the actual self and standards representing the standpoint of others (ideal/other and ought/other standards) predict emotional distress more

strongly among firstborn than later-born children (Newman, Higgins, & Vookles, 1992), which is consistent with the possibility that firstborn children experience greater parental socialization pressures and as a result more strongly internalize others' standards for evaluating their behavior (Higgins, 1989).

More direct evidence of early developmental contributors to adult self-regulatory standards comes from Manian, Strauman, and Denney (1998). In a retrospective design, participants reported both current self-discrepancies and their recollections of the parenting styles they had experienced in their youth. People whose current self-concepts primarily involved ideal standards reported emotionally warm parenting styles, whereas people whose self-regulatory styles involved ought standards recalled more parental rejection. Furthermore, adult self-discrepancies were meaningfully related to temperament measures of positive and negative affect; greater ideal versus ought self-discrepancies were associated, respectively, with higher levels of positive and negative affectivity (Manian et al., 1998).

Future research clearly would benefit from prospective designs. Further, it would be informative to distinguish among temperament characteristics in a finer-grained way (see Kagan, 1998a); measures of global negative affectivity are not sensitive to the possibility that different inherited temperament profiles involving anxiety versus sadness (both of which are negative) might differentially predict the development of ideal versus ought self-regulatory standards. Nonetheless, this work (Manian et al., 1998) constitutes a promising first step in addressing one of the great challenges to research on cognitive structures and personality, namely, to understand the role of inherited affective factors in the development of stable social-cognitive structures, or as Mischel puts it, to understand how biochemical and somatic factors function as *"Pre*dispositions" (Mischel, 1999b), that is, factors that predispose individuals to develop particular cognitive-affective structures, which in turn underlie enduring behavioral dispositions. Finally, it would be informative to plot self-discrepancies at multiple points in the course of development to determine the impact of family and contextual factors on the developing self-system. Harter (1998) reviews evidence that from ages 6 through 12 children increasingly develop discrepancies between their self-views and internalized perceptions of what their parents expect of them (e.g., Oosterwegel & Oppenheimer, 1993). This occurs as children increasingly acquire the ability to take their parents' perspective (Harter, 1998).

## KNOWLEDGE, ENCODING, AND INDIVIDUAL DIFFERENCES IN AGGRESSIVE BEHAVIOR

The profound personal and social costs of aggressive behavior have motivated many investigators to examine how social-cognitive mechanisms contribute to the initiation and maintenance of aggression and antisocial conduct (e.g., Bandura, 1973, 1986; Caprara, 1996a; Crick & Dodge, 1994; Dodge, 1993; Huesmann, 1988; Huesmann, 1997). A number of distinct mechanisms underlie individuals' tendencies to behave aggressively toward others and to make light of or rationalize their destructive acts (e.g., Bandura et al. 1996b; Caprara, Barbaranelli, & Zimbardo, 1996). Here, we focus on one particular mechanism, namely, the tendency to encode ambiguous situations as hostile confrontations that require an aggressive response.

A particularly detailed analysis of social-cognitive mechanisms in aggressive behavior is provided by Crick and Dodge (1994). They propose that memory for aggressive episodes one has experienced becomes integrated into aggressive schemas that guide social information processing. Highly accessible aggressive schemas may prompt individuals to encode benign situations as hostile. These interpretations may prompt them to act aggressively under circumstances in which prosocial behavior would have been fully appropriate. For example, "reliance on an aggressive schema to interpret a rough-and-tumble play

situation with a peer may lead a child to ignore cues that reveal that the situation calls for play fighting rather than retaliatory aggression" (Crick & Dodge, 1994, p. 83).

Much research documents the fact that people who are prone to aggression mistakenly attribute hostility to others more frequently and across more social situations than do their nonaggressive counterparts (reviewed in Dodge, 1986, 1993). These hostile biases are evident in ambiguous and relatively unambiguous cues (Nasby, Hayden, & DePaulo, 1980; Slaby and Guerra, 1988), when actions are directed toward subjects themselves rather than toward others (Dodge & Frame, 1982; Dodge & Somberg, 1987; Sancilio, Plumert, & Hartup, 1989), and when aggressive actions are experienced repeatedly (Waas, 1988). Aggressive persons' inaccurate interpretations of social settings result at least partly from their tendency to interpret others' behavior by reference to their own self-schemas. Rather than engaging in a careful analysis of social cues, aggressive individuals appear to rely on self-referent information to disambiguate others' actions (Dodge & Tomlin, 1987). As noted earlier, aggressive schemas can become so highly accessible that individuals who frequently experience aggression infer hostility spontaneously, that is, even when they have no conscious intention of drawing inferences about actors and their intentions (Zelli et al. 1995, 1996).

Hostile inferences have behavioral implications. Children who infer that others harbor hostile intentions toward them are more likely to respond aggressively (Dodge, 1993). Two aspects of the link from hostile inference to aggressive action are of particular note. The first is that aggressive children do not infer hostility in a consistent, generalized manner across all potentially threatening settings. Instead, children infer hostility within specific dyadic encounters. When aggressive behavior in dyads is directly observed, children's beliefs that a particular peer harbors hostile intent toward them predicts greater levels of aggression toward that peer (Hubbard et al., 1998; cited in Zelli & Dodge,

1999). Dyad-specific interpretive biases predict level of aggression within the dyad even after controlling for an actor's general attributional tendencies, the actor's typical level of behavioral aggressiveness, or the victim's typical level of victimization (Hubbard et al., 1998). This context specificity of aggressive cognition and behavior is consistent with idiographic analyses of aggression, which reveal that aggressive children display idiosyncratic patterns of high and low aggressiveness across different contexts (Shoda, Mischel, & Wright, 1994). It is consistent, more generally, with the finding that the attributions people tend to make for life events vary considerably across different domains (Cutrona, Russell, & Jones, 1985).

A second key finding from research on encoding mechanisms and aggression is that hostile interpretive biases do not predict all forms of aggression. People who tend to infer that others are acting in a hostile manner are prone to *reactive aggression*, that is, aggressive retaliations to perceived threats or provocations (Dodge & Coie, 1987; Hubbard et al., 1996). Hostile biases do not predict the performance of aggressive acts that are planned ahead of time, or are proactive. *Proactive aggression* is, instead, predicted by the belief that aggression will have positive social outcomes (Crick & Dodge, 1996; Hubbard et al., 1998). An interesting implication is that the same aggressive act, for example, a child punching a peer, may arise from different underlying cognitive mechanisms in different social contexts. If the child previously had been provoked by that peer, the behavior may reflect the child's inference that he is being threatened. If the child previously had bullied the peer, it may reflect his belief in the rewarding consequences of aggression toward this person. This research illustrates a point we emphasized in earlier chapters of this text, namely, that it is often problematic to analyze personality functioning by tracing a given surface-level dispositional tendency to an underlying cause. Different people may engage in the same act for very different reasons. Bottom-up explanations of the development

of aggression (Zelli & Dodge, 1999) avoid this problem by first specifying cognitive and affective processes that may give rise to aggression and then linking these processes to specific types of aggressive behavior.

## COHERENT SYSTEMS OF SELF-KNOWLEDGE

As we have seen, social knowledge and self-knowledge consist not of a list of isolated facts but of interconnected networks of knowledge. Further, the scope of research on social cognition and personality is not confined to narrow responses elicited in a laboratory, as the stereotype used to suggest, but includes broad, enduring cognitive structures of great significance to the person's interpersonal and social life. Contemporary work thus is beginning to fulfill Kelly's (1955) promise that an analysis of cognitive systems can provide a basis for analyzing personality structure and differences among individuals.

Nonetheless, the work we have reviewed thus far is limited in that individual studies generally have addressed only one domain of social knowledge or one aspect of person's lives. What is needed are investigations that capture the overall structure of the individual's cognitive system of personality: the most important themes in the person's belief system, the coherent interconnections among disparate bodies of knowledge, and the subjective differentiations among seemingly similar persons, places, and challenges. Theoretical analyses of the overall cognitive personality system are available. Cantor & Kihlstrom (1987), for example, suggest that social knowledge and self-knowledge consist of highly interrelated bodies of declarative and procedural knowledge; that individuals tend to develop elaborate knowledge structures in particular domains of their lives – in other words, they possess domain-specific social intelligence (cf. Markus & Wurf, 1987); and that the overall structure of knowledge varies so idiosyncratically from person to person that the content of belief systems must be assessed idiographically, even though common psychological processes may underlie its development and functioning (cf. Higgins, 1999). Putting these theoretical principles into practice, however, is quite a challenge. The difficulty lies not just in the sheer amount of information that comprises personal and social knowledge. Two further challenges are, first, that some of this knowledge is represented implicitly, rather than explicitly. Self-report measures thus may fail to tap cognitive structures of great importance (Greenwald & Banaji, 1995; Westen, 1991). Second, accessing beliefs and memories is not like taking books off a shelf. Knowledge structures are not just accessed but are dynamically constructed and reconstructed. Beliefs and narratives about the self thus may change in their telling and retelling (Hermans, 1992).

Fortunately, these challenges have not caused investigators to lose heart. A number of efforts have moved the field far beyond the analysis of isolated aspects of knowledge and toward an understanding of how coherence in cognitive systems contributes to coherence and continuity in personality functioning. We consider three research strategies here: (1) the study of the overall complexity of the person's construct system; (2) idiographic techniques for representing the structure of self-knowledge; and (3) the study of personal narratives, which often serve the function of coherently relating the diverse aspects of one's life.

## Multiple Self-Aspects and Self-Complexity

One approach to capturing the overall structure of the cognitive system is to search for dimensions along which people's belief systems differ. Although self-referent beliefs may vary idiosyncratically, there may exist common dimensions along which different individuals' construct systems can be compared.

Partly inspired by the work of Kelly (1955), investigators have examined individual differences in the complexity of people's construct systems. Some people may use a relatively simple set of attributes to categorize any of a wide variety of stimuli, whereas others may employ a rich, differentiated set of beliefs. In a classic investigation, Bieri (1955) found that people with more complex construct systems were better able to predict the social behavior of others. People with less complex systems were prone to what later became known as the false consensus effect, that is, the tendency to overestimate the likelihood that others would act in the same way as oneself (Ross, Greene, & House, 1977).

Linville (1985, 1987) has suggested that people differ in self-complexity, that is, the overall complexity of their beliefs about their personal attributes. Some people may see themselves as possessing a small number of important attributes, each of which is relevant to a large slice of their social lives. Others may perceive themselves in terms of a large number of qualities, which are differentially relevant to different domains. Greater cognitive complexity is expected to "buffer" individuals against the deleterious effects of stressful life events (Linville, 1985, 1987; cf. Steele, 1988). For persons high in self-complexity, for example, it is relatively unlikely that any single event will impinge on their diverse set of personal beliefs and goals. Linville has assessed self-complexity by having participants categorize a set of personality attributes (i.e., individual trait terms) into as many subgroups as were meaningful to them. An index of the dimensionality of their self-representations was computed (Scott, 1969). People higher in cognitive complexity were found to have less variable affective experiences in reaction to performance feedback (Linville, 1985) and to experience fewer physical and psychological symptoms during stressful periods of their lives (Linville, 1987).

Subsequent work has extended Linville's original hypothesis. Showers and Kling (1996) have found that people who tend to compartmentalize their self-beliefs into separate positively and negatively valenced categories are more vulnerable to extreme, prolonged reactions to negative events (also see Showers, Abramson, & Hogan, 1998). Niedenthal, Sutterlund, and Wherry (1992) added a temporal dimension to self-complexity research by relating cognitive complexity regarding actual versus possible selves to affective reactions on tasks relating to current versus future goals.

Subsequent work, however, has suggested that the relations between self-complexity and psychological experience are themselves more complex than first thought. In an extensive series of investigations, Woolfolk, Novalany, Gara, Allen, and Polino (1995) found that self-complexity was not a unitary construct. People differ in the complexity of their beliefs about positive versus negative aspects of the self. Measures of positive and negative self-complexity are only moderately correlated, have different psychometric properties, and differentially relate to concurrent measures of psychological distress. People with greater complexity in their negative self-views were more, rather than less, prone to depression. Woolfolk et al. (1995) found no evidence for the proposed stress-buffering effects of self-complexity.

Work by Donohue, Robins, Roberts, and John (1993) also highlights the costs rather than the benefits of a highly differentiated self-concept. Using an index of the degree to which people's views of their personal attributes were integrated versus differentiated across social roles, they found that a differentiated self-concept predicted higher levels of depression and lower levels of self-esteem and interpersonal adjustment. Rather than possessing flexible, resilient self-views, people who held differentiated views of their self-concept appeared to have a fragmented sense of self.

It is difficult to resolve the inconsistencies in the self-complexity literature. It may be that there is no direct, unchanging functional relation between overall complexity or differentiation in the self-concept and psychological experience. This could reflect a number of factors. People may differ in their interpretation of apparent inconsistencies in self-views. Kitayama and Markus (1999), for example, point out that Asian self-views are not oriented toward internal consistency but toward a balance among potentially incompatible self-aspects. Differentiation in the self-concept should have different implications in this world view than among people who are consistency seekers. Second, variables that are not generally considered in this research area may mediate the impact of self-representations on affective experience. People's sense of their efficacy in managing multiple self-referent roles and responsibilities is an obvious possibility here. Finally, there simply may be too much complexity and idiosyncrasy in self-concept to represent people's self-views in terms of one or two individual-difference dimensions (such as complexity or positive and negative complexity). Much information about the individual is lost when his or her complex, multidomain, multifaceted belief system is described in terms of simple individual-difference dimensions. This consideration has led some investigators to explore personal and social knowledge at the level of the individual case.

## Idiographic Representations of Self and Social Knowledge

Rather than searching for nomothetic dimensions along which people's cognitive systems can be compared, some investigators explore personal and social knowledge at the level of the individual case. Open-ended narratives (Horowitz, 1991a) or the rating of multiple, idiographically relevant targets (Kelly, 1955; Kihlstrom & Cunningham, 1991) provide a database for analyzing the interrelations among an individual's beliefs (also see Cantor & Kihlstrom, 1987; Singer & Salovey, 1991). Multidimensional statistical techniques such as cluster analysis (Tunis, Fridhandler, & Horowitz, 1990) or multidimensional scaling (Merluzzi, 1991) are employed to represent the pattern of interconnections in the individual's belief system. An interesting feature of such methods is that the individual providing the ratings may not be explicitly aware of these patterns until they are revealed by the multidimensional technique. Research reveals that representations obtained by using different sources of data, such as spontaneous descriptions versus more structured techniques, converge (Hart, Stinson, Field, Ewert, & Horowitz, 1995), supporting the reliability of multidimensional idiographic methods.

Mental representations of the self inherently are linked with representations of the individuals who make up one's day-to-day life. "Self-with-other" representations contribute to within-person consistency and variability in personality functioning (Ogilvie & Ashmore, 1991; Ogilvie, Fleming, & Pennell, 1998; Rosenberg, 1988). To study this process, investigators examine people's beliefs about the personal attributes they exhibit as they interact with significant individuals in their lives. Tunis et al. (1990), for example, used hierarchical cluster analyses to identify substantial overlap in a woman's self-views across different contexts that involved different individuals (her husband, father, therapist, etc.).

One promising method for representing the content of individual's belief systems is the HICLAS procedure of De Boeck and Rosenberg (1988). This is a hierarchical classification procedure (hence the name), which identifies groupings or "families" of self-with-other representations. For example, the procedure might identify a subgroup of persons (e.g., boss, old boyfriend, favorite uncle) with whom one exhibits similar personality characteristics (e.g., self-conscious, perfectionistic). In the typical procedure (see, e.g., Ogilvie et al., 1998), participants first generate sets of "targets" (usually significant others), who are important in their lives and a set of "features" (personal characteristics) that characterize themselves. They then are presented with their list of targets and are asked to indicate which features characterize their behavior toward each target. The HICLAS algorithm identifies significant target–feature clusters. Ogilvie et al. (1998), for example, report a case in which the HICLAS algorithm revealed that a particular individual's self-with-other representations were organized in two primary clusters, which represented themes involving a "weak-inadequate self" and a "powerful-strong" self, the different themes manifesting themselves in relations with different targets (Figure 5).

Multidimensional idiographic methods deserve further development. For example, it would be valuable to relate idiographic representations based on self-report to representations obtained using other sources of data. Nonetheless, even at their current stage of development, these techniques provide a valuable lesson for the study of cognition and personality.

## BEYOND DISCRETE ATTRIBUTES: NARRATIVE AND DIALOGUE

Much of the work we have reviewed indicates that self-concept consists of a collection of beliefs about one's attributes. Multiple "facts" about the self are interconnected in an overall system of self-knowledge (Markus & Wurf, 1987). The metaphor of self as an organization of knowledge (Pratkanis & Greenwald, 1985) has greatly contributed to our understanding of the dynamics of personality functioning, as we have seen already and will continue to see in subsequent chapters.

Nonetheless, this perspective on the self is not complete, in at least two respects. First, people possess not only discrete facts about the self but also personal stories or narratives that tie together the different elements of their lives. Second, people engage in internal dialogues, that is, intrapsychic conversations (Harré, 1998) or "voicings" (Hermans, 1996) through which they construct and modify these narratives. Narrative and dialogue processes are critical to maintaining a coherent sense of personal identity. Even if we could enumerate a multitude of personal attributes, life would be an existential nightmare if we could not also tell a coherent story about our past.

### Narrative

Cognitive psychologists have long noted the difference between memory for discrete facts and memory for personal experiences, or between semantic and episodic memory (Tulving, 1972). Unlike the storage and retrieval of facts in semantic memory, mem-

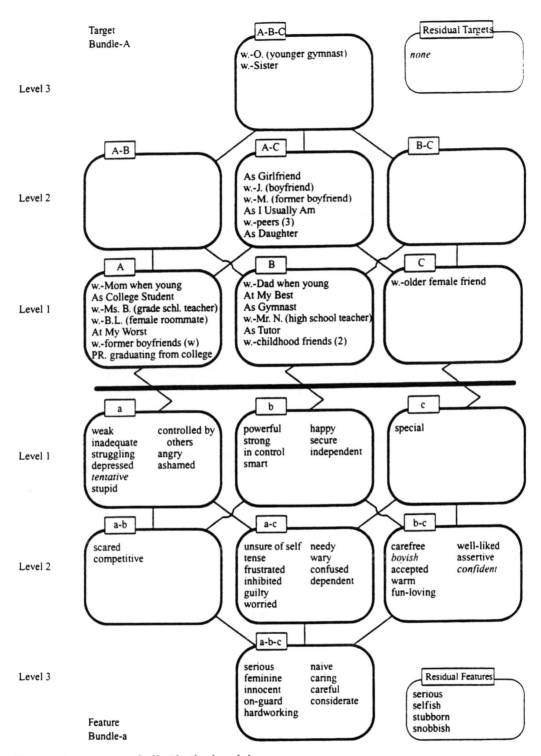

Figure 5. Representation of self-with-other knowledge yielded by the HICLAS algorithm. The HICLAS representation reveals that this individual possessed two primary belief clusters that are expressed with different individuals; one centered on weaknesses and inadequacies, the other on personal strengths. From Ogilvie et al., 1998.

ory for the episodes of one's life has a strict temporal order (one event leads to another) and a first-person perspective (the rememberer is part of the episode, which he or she views from a given location). The first-person nature of episodic memory naturally lends much greater emotional impact to episodic memories than to semantic recall. We may coolly recall the fact that we are clumsy but be flooded with feelings of embarrassment when narrating – to others or to ourselves – a particular episode in which our clumsiness was on public display.

Bruner (1986) judged the role of narrative to be so basic to mental life that he proposed two modes of thinking, paradigmatic and narrative. In the paradigmatic, or logicoscientific mode of thought, logical rules of argumentation are the guiding principle. These rules enable one to draw conclusions that are true within the overall logical framework. In contrast, the narrative mode of thought does not seek truth but "lifelikeness" (Bruner, 1986, p. 11). One tries to construct coherent, realistic stories about an event or sequence of events. Narration, then, is viewed as a fundamental class of thinking, which differs qualitatively from logical reasoning about propositional knowledge. Bruner (1990) has lamented that cognitive psychology has devoted such a large share of its efforts to the study of propositional knowledge while neglecting the contextualized narrative processes through which people attain a meaningful sense of self (also see Gergen, 1993; Sarbin, 1986).

Neuropsychological evidence supports the distinction between memory for facts and memory for autobiographical episodes. Schacter (1996), for example, describes the case of a motorcycle accident victim who sustained damage to his frontal lobes, temporal lobes, and left hippocampus. This person could perform daily activities, could recall isolated facts about his past (e.g., the name of a school he attended, some objects that he owned), and could describe the execution of complex activities in which he was skilled (e.g., changing a flat tire). Despite the intactness of these memories, Schacter reports that

the individual had no episodic memory whatsoever. He could recall no first-person autobiographical experiences. This clearly suggests that episodic memory is not merely a subsection of one's overall cognitive store but that there are distinct mental mechanisms devoted to the retrieval of autobiographical experiences.

Narrative analyses in personality psychology have evoked only sporadic interest. Murray (1938) was interested in the possibility that storytelling would reveal underlying personality structure and therefore developed the Thematic Apperception Test (TAT), a narrative psychological assessment tool. Although the TAT, of course, received widespread use (see Cramer, 1996), personality psychologists otherwise devoted relatively little attention to narrative processes during the 1940s through the 1970s. An exception to this generalization, at the end of the 1970s, was Tomkins (1979). He presented a broad-based analysis of personality functioning known as *script theory*. Tomkins, who himself considered pursuing a career as a playwright (see Tomkins, 1981), suggested that people organize their experience as a series of scenes, or memories of specific episodes. Scenes, in turn, are interpreted according to scripts, a script being a rule for assigning meaning to a set of scenes. For example, a commitment script might tie together a variety of scenes having to do with the long-term pursuit of an emotionally rewarding goal. A nuclear script is one involving strong positive emotion that is mixed with, or threatened by, emotionally negative elements. In Tomkins' theory, memories of scenes are primarily related to one another through their affective content. Scenes with a particular affective tone may trigger the recall of scenes with similar tone, creating themes in autobiographical memory.

In the 1980s and 1990s, larger numbers of personality and social psychologists turned their attention to the analysis of narratives. Work by Ross (1989), and Ross and Newby-Clark (1998) highlighted the reconstructive nature of autobiographical memory. Even when people are striving accurately to recall past experiences, their memory may be inaccurate because of implicit theories that bias the recall process. These implicit theories vary across domains, with the result that people display different autobiographical biases in different areas of their lives. For example, in the domain of attitudes and personal tendencies, people tend implicitly to believe that their attributes do not change very much. When their tendencies actually do change, their memories of their original tendencies may become inaccurate because they assimilate their original tendencies to their current dispositions. In contrast, in a domain such as skill acquisition, people implicitly expect their attributes to change significantly. Even if no change has occurred, they may perceive that there was change by distorting their recall of their original capabilities. When implicit theories lead people to distort their recall of their original abilities in a negative direction, they may conclude that their skills increased significantly when in fact little or no change occurred (Ross, 1989). These autobiographical biases can occur as a result of relatively "cold" cognitive processing. Ross and Newby-Clark (1998) emphasize that personal motives also may distort recall. When people believe that a particular personality attribute is highly desirable, they more frequently and more quickly recall engaging in behaviors that are manifestations of that attribute (Santioso, Kunda, & Fong, 1990). When people contemplate both their past and their potential future, they tend to view their past somewhat critically but are optimistic about future events (Ross & Newby-Clark, 1998).

The role of narrative processes in personality functioning and clinical change has been analyzed by Singer & Salovey (1993). They highlight the role of "self-defining memories," or vivid, affectively laden memories that reflect a person's enduring motives and goals. Their analysis, then, is similar to that of Tomkins, although Singer and Salovey place greater faith than Tomkins in people's ability to be consciously aware of how particular memories influence their personal functioning (Singer & Salovey, 1993).

A particularly extensive analysis of autobiographical memory in personality functioning is found in the work of McAdams (1993, 1994a, 1996). McAdams (1996) suggests that a complete analysis of personality functioning would include three levels: a trait level with decontextualized constructs such as the Big Five; a level of contextualized goals, expectations, and skills; and a narrative level consisting of the stories people construct to attain and maintain a stable sense of identity. McAdams sees these levels as quite distinct. He argues, for example, that the language of decontextualized traits may provide little insight into the psychological functioning at the other levels. These arguments are so convincing that it is somewhat difficult to understand why, in McAdams' model, decontextualized traits are even construed as a level of the individual's personality, as opposed to their being a language for discussing variations in populations (also see McAdams, 1994b and part 2 of our text).

In analyzing the narrative level, McAdams proposes a "life story" model of identity (McAdams, 1996). A life story is a socioculturally constructed narrative that is part of one's self-concept (or the Jamesian "me"). The life story model is a model of identity because people's personal stories lend meaning to experience and serve uniquely to define the self. Life stories integrate diverse episodes from one's life into a coherent pattern. The coherence of one's life story makes personal events far more meaningful than they otherwise would be.

Based on the analysis of a large number of life story interviews, McAdams (1996) identified a number of features that distinguish life stories from one another. Stories differ in their tone (optimism vs. pessimism), in the imagery they employ, in their goal-based themes, and in their moral stance. Some stories may be "nuclear" episodes, which are critical turning points in one's life. All stories contain imagoes, or idealized versions of the self, which exist as characters in the constructed narrative. McAdams, Diamond, St. Aubin, and Mansfield (1997) also have emphasized the role of "commitment" themes in life stories and how such themes relate to so-called generative life-styles. People often gain meaning in life by pursuing achievements that will live beyond them. Generativity, then, is the striving to nurture and care for people and things that will endure into future generations (Erikson, 1963). When McAdams et al. (1997) interviewed individuals about their lives, they found that particularly generative individuals (people who, by their actions and self-reported beliefs were particularly concerned with leaving a lasting legacy to the world) tended to interpret their lives according to a theme of commitment. The commitment theme manifested itself in a cluster of ideas including the beliefs that one has somehow been chosen to help others, that others are less fortunate and in need of help, and that one is therefore compelled to take action to assist others for the benefit of humanity despite any obstacles or personal sufferings.

### Internal Dialogue

Psychology's cognitive revolution directed attention to mental processes that could be simulated by computers. Investigators explored the storage, organization, and retrieval of knowledge. Although these information mechanisms obviously are critical to personal functioning, they are not a complete depiction of the psyche. The computer metaphor often fails to illuminate what may be the single most salient feature of mental life: People engage in internal dialogues. They converse within themselves as they contemplate their pasts and futures. People relive past conversations and "rehearse their lines" for upcoming scenes.

Hermans (1996) presents an analysis of internal dialogues that is inspired by the work of the literary theorist Bakhtin, who recognized that a novelist may not necessarily write in a single narrative voice and that, instead, a novel may be polyphonic. A writer may adopt a multiplicity of different voices, represented by different characters, each of whom presents a unique perspective in an overall dialogue. Hermans (1996) and Hermans, Kempen, and van Loon (1992), by extension,

view the self as a "dynamic multiplicity of relatively autonomous $I$ positions in an imaginal landscape" (Hermans, 1996, p. 33). People adopt the perspective of themselves and imaginary others in their internal mental dialogues. Mental life thus contains a number of distinct voices, each of which may elaborate a unique story about any given concern or event.

Internal dialogues serve a valuable function (Hermans, 1996). People have the capacity to engage not only in passive rehearsal of information but in active reflections on and reorganizations of cognitive material. This active reprocessing of information can yield greater self-understanding (cf. the constructive alternativism of Kelly, 1955). In contrast, passive rumination on negative events is of little benefit and actually can prolong depressed mood (Nolen-Hoeksema & Larson, 1999, Nolen-Hoeksema, Parker, & Larson, 1994). To Hermans (1996), then, the study of dialogue and voicing is valuable both for understanding self-referent processes and for fostering clinical change. Hermans laments that empirical research in psychology has devoted little attention to the functioning of internal voicing and dialogue, despite the fact that narrative analyses and some aspects of computer science seem capable of providing a firm theoretical foundation for research.

Harré (1998) analyzes mental processes through what he calls a discursive psychology. Most significant psychological events, he reasons, involve a mental discourse or conversation. People converse with themselves when making decisions, when trying to remember events and judging the accuracy of their memory, when reasoning about potential courses of actions, or when telling stories about their lives. People engaging in discourse, then, becomes the fundamental unit of analysis for understanding psychological functioning.

Conversations between people are guided by normative rules. People attempt to move a conversation forward while adhering to implicit rules of public conversation and social relations. In some conversations, people carefully monitor their actions in order to advance their personal goals while simultaneously adhering to conversational norms. Conversation, then, is a public performance that is constrained by social norms. In Harré's (1998) discursive psychology, interpersonal conversation is a metaphor for understanding internal psychological processes: "Every psychological process or phenomenon is a skilled performance . . . [that] is normatively constrained" (p. 45). To understand interpersonal conversations, one cannot analyze an individual in isolation, but most consider the relation among people, the setting they are in, and the meaning systems that they share. By extension, the discursive analysis of psychological processes directs attention away from the study of isolated mental entities and toward the analysis of social conditions in which an action is taken and evaluated.

Internal conversations contribute to a unitary sense of self. One aspect of self is people's collection of beliefs about their attributes and their lives. Harré (1998) emphasizes that these beliefs are developed and manifested through the stories one constructs about oneself. Thus, the development of a stable sense of identity rests on the human capability to engage in dialogue and construct coherent narratives. The dialogues, like all conversations, are socioculturally situated. Thus, the self inevitably is a historically situated sociocultural construction. Bruner (1990) similarly emphasizes that "Selves . . . take meaning . . . from the historical circumstances that gave shape to the culture of which they are an expression" (p. 138).

## The Narrative Turn: Expansion of or Challenge to Psychology's Analysis of Knowledge and Meaning?

Psychologists, as we have just seen, have devoted greater attention to narrative processes in recent years. This is not an isolated development. It is part of a broader trend in the humanities and social sciences. Polkinghorne (1988) has provided a particularly valuable review of these developments. Investigators in a discipline such as history, for example, came to question whether the cause-and-effect models of the sciences were

appropriate to their discipline. Rather than searching for scientific laws, history can be seen to provide coherent narrative understandings of events. The historian seeks to construct a meaningful story about past lives – lives that "have already been lived as stories" (Polkinghorne, 1988, p. 69) by the historical persons.

Polkinghorne (1988) suggests that all analyses of human affairs should be based on such narrative analyses. People live their lives in a "realm of meaning" (Polkinghorne, 1988, p. 4), in which they perform and interpret actions in time and engage in narrative modes of thinking to assigning meaning to their experiences. This perspective leads Polkinghorne to reject approaches to psychology that neglect the world of narrative and instead merely measure isolated personal attributes. In his view, the "traditional research implements designed by formal science to locate and measure objects and things" treat individuals as "static thing[s]" (Polkinghorne, 1988, p. 150) and thereby fail to do justice to the constructive, dynamic, lifelong processes of narrative construction through which people maintain a sense of self.

The implications of the narrative turn in the humanities and social sciences for the study of personality, then, can be read in one of two ways. One reading sees it as an expansion of the field's traditional focus. Rather than focusing exclusively on people's beliefs about discrete personal attributes, narrative analyses force one to attend to the active inter- and intrapersonal processes through which people construct a broad storylike understanding of their lives. This expansion undoubtedly is good for the field. If the proverbial visitor from another planet (endowed with mind-reading abilities) observed human beings, the most salient feature of human mental life would be the tendency to engage in internal dialogues. In this light, it is remarkable that the nature and functioning of internal dialogues has received so little attention by psychologists.

The second reading, though, is not merely an expansion but a direct challenge to psychology's traditional ways of thinking. As we saw, Polkinghorne (1988) has directly challenged the usefulness of conceptualizing a person as a collection of variables that can be measured and located through procedures borrowed from the physical sciences. Gergen (1993) has long voiced similar criticisms of the psychological enterprise. Bruner (1990) promotes a cultural psychology that is far more sensitive to contextualized processes of meaning construction than is the traditional information-processing approach. These writers see much of psychology as being too essentialistic. They criticize the tendency to infer and then attempt to measure static elements in the person that are responsible for a pattern of behavior. This way of thinking, they contend, deflects attention from the dynamic, contextualized processes of mental life. Harré (1998) perhaps states this position most forcefully: "Attempting to explain the sense of self by borrowing from the hypothetico-deductive methods from the physical sciences and postulating unobservable entities, be it the ego or be it generic traits, just populates the ontology of psychology with a class of redundant and mythical beings" (p. 178). He illustrates his argument by considering the concept of self-esteem. Generally, self-esteem researchers ask people to respond to a series of statements that measure how much self-esteem exists in the person. Self-esteem, then, is an inferred entity that accounts for a tendency to answer questions in a high or low direction. Harré (1998) suggest an alternative interpretation of this process that does not infer a construct of self-esteem. When presented with self-esteem items, people construct a narrative about their tendencies and attributes. This narrative conforms to various social conventions about displaying aspects of one's personhood. Since a good narrative is internally coherent, answers to the self-esteem items are, on psychometric grounds, internally reliable. Thus, the assessment enterprise is a success. However, the narrative viewpoint raises the question: "How do we know that the property [self-esteem] exists indepen-

dently of the 'conversational situation' set up in the 'experiment'?" (Harré, 1998, p. 131).

This question is not without answers. Ideally, the personality psychologist does not rest inferences about a psychological attribute on questionnaire responses alone. One also examines actions, experiences, and physiological reactions that, on theoretical grounds, should be related to the personality construct in question. We are more sanguine about the use of questionnaire measures than are critics such as Harré. We also are more optimistic about the ability of cognitively based analyses to provide causal explanations of how enduring personal qualities, including people's "powers, capabilities, liabilities, vulnerabilities, skills and abilities" (Harré, 1998, p. 54), contribute to enduring psychological dispositions. Still, the challenges to the field's standard operating procedures that narrative analyses present should not be ignored. They vividly remind us of the conceptual pitfalls inherent in reifying abstract psychological measures into purportedly concrete psychological entities. The study of personal narratives, from whatever perspective, convincingly makes the case that the coherence of personal experience cannot be understood merely by viewing the individual as a collection of static essential qualities.

## SUMMING UP

Philosophers and social scientists long have recognized that processes of meaning construction are at the core of human individuality. As we have seen in this chapter, contemporary psychology provides a relatively detailed understanding of the processes through which people assign meaning to events and of the individual differences in social and self-knowledge that underlie people's differential experience of objectively similar circumstances. The field has explored interrelated systems of self-knowledge that distinguish individuals and has devoted much attention to the process of constructing autobiographical stories that contribute to a coherent sense of identity.

The work reviewed in this chapter is necessary but clearly not sufficient for a thorough understanding of personality functioning. We must explore not only how people go about assigning meaning to events, but the functions served by these cognitive processes. Enduring knowledge structures underlie the individual's chronic emotional experiences, motivational states, and sense of self. Salient personal knowledge shapes conscious experiences, yet also contributes to personality processes that occur outside of conscious awareness. Social and self-knowledge enable people to plan courses of action and regulate their behavior. As we explore these phenomena in subsequent chapters, we frequently will draw on the principles discussed in this one.

# CHAPTER TEN

# Affective Experience

## *Emotions and Mood*

To understand individuals, we need to know not only their thoughts and actions but their feelings. Knowledge of a person's emotional experience is critical to our believing that we know who that person really is (Andersen & Ross, 1984). Emotional reactions reveal an individual's values and goals. They reflect basic biological tendencies as well as socially learned beliefs about the world and oneself. They reveal aspects of personality that people may wish to hide from others. Understanding emotions is key to understanding personality.

The study of emotional experience presents special challenges to the personality psychologist. Emotions are multifaceted phenomena that must be understood through multiple levels of analysis (e.g., Gross, 1999; Rosenberg & Fredrickson, 1998). Evolutionarily derived biological mechanisms foster universal tendencies in emotional response (Ekman & Oster, 1979; Izard, 1977; Plutchik, 1984; Tooby & Cosmides, 1990a). Inherited qualities contribute to differences in affective experience (Kagan, 1998a; Rothbart & Bates, 1998; see chapter 5). Specific brain circuits (Cacioppo, Bernston, & Crites, 1996; Davidson, 1992; Gray, 1991; LeDoux, 1996) and biochemical mechanisms (Zillman & Zillman, 1996; Zuckerman, 1995) mediate different aspects of emotional experience. Personal goals, standards, control beliefs, and views of self shape our emotional reactions (Bandura, 1997;

Epstein, 1998; Higgins, 1987; Lazarus, 1991; Scherer, 1984). Cultural systems teach people how to interpret their feelings and determine the types of emotional reaction elicited by particular objects and events (Kitayama & Markus, 1994; Mesquita & Frijda, 1992; Scherer, 1997; Shweder, 1993). The personality psychologist must consider each of these levels of analysis to achieve a full understanding of personality differences and intraindividual variation and coherence in affective experience.

Challenging though it may be, the study of emotional experience is required for a complete psychology of personality. The control of emotional reactions is a basic task of personality development (Freud, 1923; Metcalfe & Mischel, 1999); indeed, people's social and interpersonal skills are most clearly revealed when they attempt to manage their behavior in the face of emotionally stressful or threatening experiences (Wright & Mischel, 1987). Variations in emotional systems are seen as core elements of individual differences in extroversion and neuroticism (Ahadi & Rothbart, 1994; Watson, 2000). The study of emotions contributes to our understanding of intraindividual coherence in personality functioning, in that emotional processing can be seen as a paradigm case in which distinct physiological and cognitive mechanisms reciprocally interact with one another and thus come to function as coherent, integrated personality systems (Izard, 1994; Lewis, 1996). Finally, research on emotions informs our understanding not only of normal personality functioning but of psychological disorders (Greenberg & Safran, 1989; Scott & Ingram, 1998). To some, emotion systems are of such importance to person-environment transactions that the development of these systems is "the cornerstone of personality development" (Izard, 1994, p. 356).

Studying the emotions literature is valuable to the personality psychologist for yet another reason. The personality theorist and the emotions theorist face some similar conceptual problems (see, e.g., Smith & Pope, 1992). Two problems, in particular, are central

to both areas. One is the issue of identifying optimal units of analysis with which to conceptualize the discipline's core phenomena. In the emotions literature, some investigators study "basic" emotions. Particular categories of emotional response are seen as universal, essential categories of emotion. It generally is thought that each basic emotion is the product of a corresponding biological system that itself is a product of human evolutionary history (Izard, 1977; Plutchik, 1980). A research task, then, is to identify the basic emotions; as we will see, there is no universal agreement on which particular set of emotions is basic. The question of units of analysis arises in that other investigators, rather than asking which emotions are basic, question whether the very notion of basic emotions is an adequate foundation for a theory of emotional experience (Ortony & Turner, 1990). Emotional experience might be understood in terms of a set of physiological or cognitive systems that give rise to a continuously varying range of emotional responses. The emotions literature contains sophisticated discussions of the criteria through which one may establish basic units of analysis for the discipline (Averill, 1997; Ekman, 1992b; Izard, 1992; Ortony & Turner, 1990; Panksepp, 1992).

A second shared issue, mentioned briefly above, is the study of coherence among separate psychological mechanisms. The personality psychologist seeks not only to delineate distinct personality structures and processes but also to understand how these mechanisms develop into integrated personality systems (Caprara, 1996a, 1999). Similarly, the emotions researcher not only must characterize the distinct physiological, expressive, behavioral, and experiential aspects of emotions but also must explain how these separate processes function together as coherent response systems. Theoretical and methodological innovations in the study of coherence in emotion systems (Rosenberg & Ekman, 1994) thus address a core concern of personality psychology.

After a brief historical overview, this chapter surveys contemporary knowledge regarding the structure and function of affective experience. We review each of a series of components of emotional response. In doing so, we note that individual differences may be found within each emotion component. We then examine how the distinct physiological and psychological mechanisms involved in emotional response function together as coherent, integrated systems.

## HISTORICAL AND CONTEMPORARY ANALYSES OF EMOTIONAL EXPERIENCE

Scholars throughout the ages have recognized the centrality of emotional experience to human nature. Plato viewed emotions as one of the three essential elements of the human soul, in conjunction with reason and the basic bodily appetites. Aristotle discussed basic biological tendencies in emotional experience (Averill & More, 1993) and analyzed the relation between beliefs and emotion in a manner that foreshadowed current theorizing (Lazarus, 1999). Not only the ancients but also contemporary philosophical analyses examine the nature of emotional experience and related affective states (Rorty, 1980).

Highly detailed analyses of the variety of human emotions are found not only in Western but also in non-Western traditions. The Hindu text the *Rasādhyāya* differentiates nine basic emotions, some of which, such as feelings of awe and of heroism, have received relatively little attention in contemporary Western psychology (Shweder, 1993). The Tibetan Buddhist *Abhidharma* delineates six negative basic emotions, some of which are basic to Western psychology (e.g., anger) but others of which are not (e.g., arrogance, lack of intrinsic awareness) (Guenther & Kawamura, 1975).

The emotions theorist Robert Plutchik (1984) suggests that contemporary emotions research can be traced to four traditions founded during the late 19th and early 20th century. Each of these traditions anticipated a distinct aspect of contemporary research. In his *Expression of Emotions in Man and Animals*

(1872), Charles Darwin established an evolutionary approach to the study of emotions. Darwin catalogued the numerous similarities between human and animal emotional expression (e.g., the angry wolf's bared fangs and the angry human's sneer). From this evidence, he concluded that emotional expression reflects innate biological mechanisms that evolved through natural selection. James (1884, 1890) and Lange (1885) highlighted the role of physiological processes in emotional experience. They suggested that emotional experience is based in the perception of bodily states, with different emotions arising from our perception of different patterns of change in musculature and peripheral nervous system activity. Walter Cannon (1929) presented a different position. Rather than focusing on the periphery, Cannon argued that central nervous system processes are at the heart of emotional experience. Finally, Freud's (1900) psychoanalytic theory uncovered the potentially vast discrepancies between inner emotional life and external emotional expression. As Freud recognized, emotions may be repressed and distorted, with consequences for emotional and physical health. Contemporary research on the universality of emotional experience and expression (Ekman & Oster, 1979; Mesquita & Frijda, 1992), distinct patterns of physiology associated with discrete emotional states (Levensen, 1994), specific cortical regions underlying the generation of different emotions (LeDoux, 1996; Pankseep, 1994), and individual differences in the tendency to express or repress one's feelings (Block & Block, 1980; Egloff & Krohne, 1996; Weinberger & Schwartz, 1990) have greatly enriched the four traditions established long ago.

Finally, any historical overview of emotions research should note the contributions of Silvan Tomkins (1962, 1963), who intensively analyzed emotional experience during an era in which this topic received far too little attention from academic psychologists. Tomkins' analysis of emotions as innate mechanisms that motivate distinct forms of action and that are expressed in biologically determined patterns of facial expression greatly influenced subsequent generations of researchers, whose work is reviewed throughout this chapter.

## THE VARIETIES OF AFFECTIVE EXPERIENCE

There are many different types of feeling states, some of which clearly do not qualify as emotions. These include feelings triggered by specific internal tissue deficits, such as hunger or thirst, or the pain experienced in response to a physical injury. Of greater importance to the analysis of affect and personality are the psychological states referred to as emotions and moods.

### Moods Versus Emotions

Emotions and moods can be differentiated via a number of criteria (Ekman & Davidson, 1994). Moods generally are of longer duration than emotions. Sadness and anger, for example, may last only a few seconds or minutes, whereas moods of depression or irritability may last hours, days, or longer. Moods and emotions have different antecedent conditions. Emotions arise from evaluations of a particular encounter (Lazarus, 1991; Scherer, 1984), whereas moods often can not be traced to a particular cause. Unlike moods, then, emotions have the quality of intentionality – in other words, "they are *about* something" (Averill, 1997, p. 514). Moods can arise from changes in neurochemistry, whereas changes in internal biochemistry alone generally would not trigger specific emotions such as jealousy or pride. Moods and emotions have a distinct functional relation, in that moods predispose people to experience specific emotions. An irritable mood, for example, may predispose one to anger. Finally, moods and emotions may serve distinct organismic functions. Davidson (1994) suggests that emotions primarily influence action, biasing the organism toward particular adaptive reactions to an encounter, whereas moods primarily influence cognition, shifting our attentional and evaluative processing of stimuli.

## The Structure of the Emotion Domain

Having distinguished emotions from moods and other affective experiences, a second question arises: What is the structure of the emotion domain? What, in other words, are the different emotions, and how do they relate to one another? Despite much progress, the field lacks consensus on this question. Indeed, the structure of affective experience has been analyzed through two rather different approaches: dimensional and categorical models.

Dimensional models posit sets of factors that provide a framework for describing any and all emotional experiences. These factors jointly define a universal affective space. Specific emotional reactions are located within this universal space. In contrast to categorical models, dimensional models have the advantage of directly addressing the degree of similarity of different emotions. The relative similarity of emotions is indicated by their relative proximity within the affective space.

Most dimensional models posit two primary factors of emotional experience (Feldman, Barrett, & Russell, 1999). Investigators do not agree, however, on the exact placement and labeling of these dimensions. In one approach, emotional states are characterized according to their valence (positivity versus negativity) and degree of arousal (aroused versus unaroused). For example, Russell (1979) asked undergraduates to describe their emotional state on 11 affect scales. After correcting for response biases that can influence the affect structure one obtains (also see Green, Goldman, & Salovey, 1993, Feldman, Barrett, & Russell, 1998; Russell & Carroll, 1999), he found clear evidence that the bipolar dimensions of pleasure–displeasure and aroused–sleepy capture variations in affect.

An alternative approach rotates these two axes. Rotating the valence and arousal dimensions by 45 degrees yields the independent dimensions of aroused positive affect and aroused negative affect (Watson & Tellegen, 1985). This alternative highlights the interesting possibility that individuals' tendencies to experience positive and negative affect vary independently. We consider this possibility in detail below when discussing individual differences in subjective emotional experience.

Although dimensional models are highly useful for describing variations in affective experience, most investigators agree that they are not an adequate foundation for a theory of emotion. Dimensional models fail to capture what may be fundamental, qualitative differences between different discrete emotional states. As Averill (1997) notes by way of analogy, one could develop a dimensional taxonomy of animals (with organisms varying in size or ferociousness, for example), but the dimensions would obscure fundamental differences between species that are captured by a categorical taxonomy. Many investigators, then, pursue categorical models of emotion.

Categorical models are based on the assumption that different emotional states are qualitatively distinct phenomena. These models posit a number of discrete emotion categories, where each category may be viewed as an "emotion family" (Ekman, 1994), that is, a set of highly related states that share a large number of characteristics. Although there may be differences in our feelings of pride in our own accomplishments versus pride in the accomplishments of a family member, for example, the experiences share many features and thus can be seen as exemplars of the common emotion category "pride."

There are at least two types of categorical models. In one, investigators analyze the natural language to identify basic-level emotion categories. Like other objects (Lakoff, 1987), emotions may be categorized at various hierarchical levels. A "negative experience" may also be an instance of "righteous anger." Within such hierarchies one generally can identify an intermediate or basic level (Rosch, 1978) that is the most natural means of classifying an emotional experience. Shaver, Schwartz, Kirson, and O'Conner (1987) studied the structure of emotion knowledge by asking subjects to group a large number of emotion terms into categories. Cluster analyses revealed a hierarchy of emotion knowledge that included a basic level consisting of

five emotions, namely, anger, fear, joy, love, and sadness. People's knowledge of emotions, then, appears to be organized around this small set of generic representations of emotion types.

The study of emotion concepts is appealing because people's intuitive categories may correspond to emotions that are biologically basic. Folk categories sometimes do correspond to divisions in nature. In folk biology, the basic level categories for plant names correspond well, at the genus level, to scientific taxonomies (Lakoff, 1987). However, such correspondence can not be assumed. As recognized by investigators who study emotion concepts (Shaver et al., 1987), the structure of the layperson's intuitive emotion categories may not correspond to emotion categories in nature. Intuition may fail to cut nature at its joints. Consider our mental representation of birds. Intuitively, robins are more birdlike than penguins. In scientific taxonomies, however, both have equal bird status (Averill, 1994). Cross-cultural variations in emotion categories (Shweder, 1993) also argue against the possibility that natural-language categories map onto biologically basic emotions, at least if one assumes the existence of universal biological emotion mechanisms (also see Kitayama & Markus, 1994).

Rather than focusing on emotion categories in the lexicon, an alternative approach is to seek emotion categories that are biologically basic. Different emotion categories would correspond to distinct biological mechanisms, particularly subcortical neural circuits shared by humans and other mammals (Pankseep, 1994). Since these emotion-specific neural circuits would have evolved as an evolutionary adaptation to recurring environmental circumstances faced by the human species (Ekman, 1994), the emotion circuitry would be universal. This view, then, is immediately compatible with evidence that the facial expression of a number of discrete emotions is universally recognized across cultures (Ekman, 1993; Ekman & Oster, 1979; Ekman & Rosenberg, 1997). The view that evolution has yielded a number of universal, discrete emotions that are biologically basic is shared by many contemporary emotions theorists and guides much of the work reviewed in this chapter.

Despite the appeal of this approach, it suffers from a major limitation. There is little agreement as to the exact nature, number, and identity of the biologically basic emotions. As reviewed by Ortony and Turner (1990), some theorists posit as few as two basic states, for example, happiness and sadness (Weiner & Graham, 1984), whereas others see nine or more specific emotions as basic; Tomkins (1984), for example, suggests anger, interest, contempt, disgust, distress, fear, joy, shame, and surprise. Furthermore, although many investigators posit that specific emotions are basic, others believe that what is biologically basic are response systems, in which a given system might be associated with more than one type of emotional response. For example, Gray (1991) views the flight–fight mechanism as a hard-wired emotion system; this system is not associated with a single emotional state, but with the opposing emotions of rage and terror (Ortony & Turner, 1990). Although the concept of biologically basic emotions is supported by much evidence and is vigorously defended (Ekman, 1992a, b; Izard, 1992; Panksepp, 1992), the fact remains that the field lacks consensus on key questions about the exact number and nature of the basic emotions.

Partly motivated by this lack of consensus, some investigators reject the concept of basic emotions altogether (e.g., Averill, 1994; Shweder, 1994). These investigators do not, of course, deny that people experience coherent affective states that serve critical intra- and interpersonal functions. They simply question whether positing basic emotions is the best way of understanding this phenomenon. Ortony and Turner (1990), for example, suggest that what are basic are not molar emotions but specific subcomponents of emotional response and the linkages between these subcomponents and appraisals of the environment. There may be a basic link between perceiving an obstacle to one's goals

and frowning (see Smith, 1989) and between high levels of concentration and a furrowed brow. Appraisals that circumstances require a vigorous fight-or-flight response may be linked to heightened physiological arousal. Beliefs that an agent has caused one harm may trigger motivational tendencies to attack that agent. The biologically basic aspects of emotional response, in this view, are the emotion subcomponents consisting of specific elements of facial expression, physiological activation, and motivational tendencies. These components frequently coalesce into a prototypic emotion, not because the molar emotion is biologically basic but because of recurrent correlations between the environmental features that trigger each subcomponent. Circumstances involving an agent that has caused one harm, for example, also tend to be circumstances that involve goal blockage, require concentration, and necessitate flight or fight. The co-occurrences of the associated subcomponents, then, "are due not to hard-wired connections among subcomponents but to connections external to the feeling person" (Ortony & Turner, 1990, p. 323). Scherer (1994) similarly argues that the distinct elements of emotional response are basic and that common patterns of cooccurrence in these elements reflect common patterns of environmental appraisal.

Kagan (1988, 1996, 1998b) articulates a further drawback to postulating basic emotion categories. When positing basic emotions, we tend to discuss emotional states in the abstract. In other words, we discuss an emotion as if it had a basic essence that transcended person and place. The fear of a rat confronted with a stimulus that has been paired with shock, an infant who has been separated from her mother, and an agoraphobic who reports anxiety at the thought of going shopping may all be treated as instantiations of the same, highly generalized psychological process. The problem is that these intuitively equivalent states may involve fundamentally different underlying mechanisms. As reviewed by Kagan (1998a), different brain mechanisms mediate seemingly similar states of fear that are elicited by different contexts (painful stimuli, separation, threat signals). Further, different measurement techniques (e.g., physiological recording vs. self-report) may yield conflicting information about a person's emotional state. To understand the varieties and the causes of emotional experience, then, it may be best *not* to posit a small number of emotion categories whose essential form remains relatively invariant across context and that can be indexed by any of a variety of measures. Instead, Kagan (1998b) suggests a more contextualized strategy. Investigators might posit relatively narrower patterns of reactivity that are specific to particular types of environmental conditions.

## THE COMPONENTS AND FUNCTIONS OF EMOTIONAL EXPERIENCE

Emotions are complex, organized patterns of response, which have evolved to aid the organism's adaptation to the environment (Ekman, 1992b; Tomkins, 1962; Plutchik, 1984). They involve an integration of psychological and physiological systems, which are activated when individuals perceive that events in the environment are relevant to themselves and their goals (Frijda, 1988; Lazarus, 1991).

Virtually all emotions theorists recognize that complex emotional response involves a number of distinct components that serve different functions (e.g., Levenson, 1994; Scherer, 1984). One analytic strategy for bringing order to the complexity of emotion systems, then, is to analyze separately each of the components of emotional response. Four emotion components can be differentiated. Three of these are systems that become active during an emotional experience. These are physiological mechanisms that mediate and support emotional response, behavioral expressions that signal one's emotional state, and the subjective feelings that accompany emotional reactions. A fourth system is a critical antecedent of emotion; this system comprises the cognitive appraisal mechanisms that trigger emotional response. In the follow-

ing sections of the text, we discuss appraisal mechanisms and then examine the other three facets of emotional response. We subsequently consider how the different components of emotion are functionally related to one another, focusing particularly on the relation between external emotional expression and internal emotional experience.

As we begin this review, the reader should note that the delineation of distinct facets of emotional response has important implications for how one thinks about personality differences in emotional experience. Interindividual differences (as well as intraindividual variations) may be found with regard to each distinct component of emotional response. People may differ in the way they appraise the environment, in their physiological reactions to a given appraisal, in their tendency to express or suppress an emotional reaction once it has begun, and in their subjective experience of affective states. As Davidson (1994) explains, "the importance of recognizing the multi-componential nature of emotion for the study of individual differences is the likelihood that individuals may differ in certain emotion processes and not others" (p. 322).

### Cognitive Appraisal and Emotional Experience

Changes in affective experience arise from many sources. Biochemical factors affect how energetic or sluggish one feels. Smells and tastes induce pleasant feelings or feelings of revulsion. Music can make one feel aroused or melancholy. Some of these affective experiences occur relatively automatically, that is, with little or no explicit evaluation of the stimuli that have affected our mood (Zajonc, 1980). However, the more complex, multicomponent patternings of response that are the human emotions arise from evaluations of the environment. Complex emotions, in other words, require cognition. Emotions results from appraisal of external stimuli and internal feelings and thoughts.

■ *Appraisal Models.* A number of emotion theorists have provided detailed models of the processes through which people appraise events and the links from particular patterns of appraisal to specific emotions (Lazarus, 1991; Lazarus & Smith, 1990; Ortony, Clore, & Collins, 1988; Roseman, 1984; Scherer, 1984, 1997; Smith & Ellsworth, 1985). Although these models differ in their particulars, they converge on a number of fundamental points. First, emotions are triggered not by external events themselves, but by the subjective meaning people assign to events. A basic "law of emotion" is that "emotions arise in response to the meaning structures of given situations" (Frijda, 1988, p. 349). Different meanings trigger different emotions. A second point of agreement is that appraisals are "relational" (Lazarus, 1991). The cognitions that are critical to emotional response are not evaluations of features of the environment in isolation. They are, instead, evaluations of the meaning of events for one's personal well-being. It is the perceived relation between environmental events and personal goals, capabilities, and norms for behavior that triggers and shapes emotional experience (Frijda, 1988; Lazarus, 1991; Scherer, 1984).

Some authors have focused on the role of expectations and attributions in emotional experience. They emphasize the influence of perceived controllability on social emotions such as anger, pity, guilt, and shame and the implication of emotional attributions in motivation and interpersonal behavior (Weiner, 1986, 1992). Attribution of failure to uncontrollable causes may lead to resignation, pity, and sympathy, whereas attribution to controllable causes may lead to self-devaluation, anger, and blame. Attribution of one's own success to others' actions raises gratitude and compliance, whereas it raises pride and self-confidence when attributed to one's own ability.

A particularly detailed analysis of the appraisal process is provided by Lazarus and Smith (Lazarus, 1991; Lazarus & Smith, 1988; Smith and Lazarus, 1990). To capture the variability in people's evaluations of events, they propose six appraisal dimensions, that is, six components of cognitive appraisal. Two of these appraisals are primary, in that they involve the basic question of whether an event is important to one's well-being. These are appraisals of an event's motivational relevance (whether it bears on one's personal concerns) and motivational congruence (whether it is consistent or inconsistent with one's goals). These two appraisals determine the valence of emotional states (see also Ortony et al., 1988). The four secondary appraisals concern the individual's capabilities and options for coping with events. These are appraisals of (1) problem-focused coping potential (i.e., whether one can change circumstances to make them congruent with one's goals); (2) emotion-focused coping potential (i.e., whether one can adapt to events by altering one's own experiences and goals); (3) accountability, (i.e., who – oneself vs. others – is responsible for events); and (4) future expectancy (i.e., an expectancy of whether circumstances will change for any reason). Specific patterns of appraisal trigger particular emotions. For example, anger arises when events are appraised as motivationally relevant and motivationally incongruent and others are seen as responsible. In contrast, guilt arises when one sees oneself as accountable for motivationally relevant and incongruent events (Smith & Lazarus, 1990). Lazarus (1991) analyzes a wide spectrum of emotional experiences in this manner. Note that Lazarus's secondary appraisal constructs are closely related to expectancies and agency beliefs that are central to the analysis of behavioral self-regulation (see chapter 12).

Interestingly, cognitive appraisals also can be conceptualized at a more molar level of analysis. Multiple appraisal dimensions combine into "core relational themes" (Lazarus, 1991; Smith & Lazarus, 1990). These themes embody different types of personal meaning, which foster distinct emotional reactions. For example, the appraisal components for anger and guilt, described above, correspond respectively to the themes of other blame and self-blame for a transgression. Appraisals of motivational relevance, incongruence, low coping potential, and low expectancy of change combine into the relational theme of

**TABLE 10-1. Emotions Analyzed by Appraisal Components and Core Relational Themes**

| Emotion | Proposed adaptive function | Core relational theme | Important appraisal components |
|---------|---------------------------|-----------------------|-------------------------------|
| Anger | Remove source of harm from environment and undo harm | Other-blame | 1. Motivationally relevant<br>2. Motivationally incongruent<br>3. Other-accountability |
| Guilt | Make reparation for harm to others/motivate socially responsible behavior | Self-blame | 1. Motivationally relevant<br>2. Motivationally incongruent<br>3. Self-accountability |
| Anxiety | Avoid potential harm | Ambiguous danger/threat | 1. Motivationally relevant<br>2. Motivationally incongruent<br>3. Low/uncertain (emotion-focused) coping potential |
| Sadness | Get help and support in the face of harm/disengage from a lost commitment | Irrevocable loss | 1. Motivationally relevant<br>2. Motivationally incongruent<br>3. Low (problem-focused) coping potential<br>4. Low future expectancy |
| Hope | Sustain commitment and coping | Possibility of amelioration/success | 1. Motivationally relevant<br>2. Motivationally incongruent<br>3. High future expectancy |

From Smith & Lazarus, 1990.

irrevocable loss, which triggers sadness (see Table 10-1).

Two features of appraisal models (Lazarus, 1991) are of note. First, the links from particular appraisals to particular emotions are seen to be universal. Anyone who appraises a personally relevant and incongruent event as involving irrevocable loss will feel sad (Lazarus, 1991). However, the links from particular stimuli to particular appraisal may be highly idiosyncratic. There is considerable individual and cultural variation in the way particular stimuli are appraised. Even emotions with obvious biological significance and evolutionary origins, such as disgust, are shaped by beliefs that vary substantially across cultures (Rozin & Fallon, 1987).

A transnational survey of emotional response by Scherer and colleagues (Scherer, 1997; Scherer & Wallbott, 1994) provides detailed information about cross-cultural vari-

ability in appraisal processes. In this work, respondents from 37 countries were asked to recall situations in which they had experienced each of seven discrete emotions (joy, anger, sadness, fear, disgust, shame, and guilt). They indicated how they had appraised each situation via numerical ratings on each of nine appraisal dimensions. Two basic findings speak to the utility of appraisal theories for illuminating both universals and cultural variations in emotion. First, for any given emotion, the general pattern of appraisals was quite similar from one country and region of the world to another. Whether one is in Africa, Europe, Asia, or the Americas, joyful events are those episodes that are unexpected and interpreted as consistent with one's internal standards. Guilt- and shame-provoking circumstances are those that are appraised as internally caused and in violation of moral standards. Second, although overall patterns of appraisal were similar for each emotion across nations, individuals from different regions of the world showed significantly different mean levels of cognitive appraisal on some dimensions. As compared with Europeans, Americans, and Asians, African citizens were more likely to judge the recalled events as immoral, unfair, or externally caused, and citizens of Latin American countries less frequently judged situations to be immoral. Scherer (1997) suggests that, among other factors, relative degrees of urbanization may contribute to these differences. The less urban societies of Africa may be more likely to appraise events in terms of moral standards that reflect traditional cultural norms, whereas the more urban societies of Latin America may experience a greater mix of cultural influences and therefore adopt more secular standpoints of evaluation. As Scherer (1997) himself notes, cultural variations may be underestimated in this research. A fixed set of emotion categories and appraisal dimensions was imposed on all participants, which eliminates the possibility of discovering emotion and appraisal constructs that may be unique to a culture.

A second important aspect of cognitive appraisals is that, despite the connotation that the word appraisal may carry, they are not necessarily slow, deliberate cognitive processes. People continuously appraise the environment. Appraisals thus are well-practiced cognitions that can occur extremely quickly and outside of conscious awareness (Lazarus, 1991). Appraisal models thus are consistent with the observation that emotional reactions occur quickly, seemingly before one has even thought about an event. As with many cognitive events (Greenwald & Banaji, 1995), appraisals can occur and trigger emotions without individuals becoming consciously aware of their own appraisal processes. Recognizing the speed of this cognitive process helps to resolve earlier debates about whether cognition is necessary for emotion to occur (cf. Zajonc, 1980; Lazarus, 1982). This emphasis on rapid, nonconscious cognitive processes, it should be noted, is central both to appraisal models and to other emotion theories. For example, in

Epstein's (1998) cognitive-experiential self-theory, emotional reactions are determined by automatic cognitions about responses that are desired in a given situation.

■ *Knowledge and Appraisal.* The six appraisal dimensions delineated above are not the only aspects of cognition that shape emotional experience. Emotions are affected by people's beliefs about the world and themselves (Beck, 1976), causal attributions for events (Weiner, 1986), agency beliefs (Bandura, 1997; Lazarus, 1991), and, as reviewed in chapter 9, personal standards through which events are evaluated (Higgins, 1987). Appraisal models (e.g., Lazarus & Folkman, 1984; Lazarus & Smith, 1988) do not deny the influence of these knowledge structures. Instead, they account for them within an appraisal-theory framework by distinguishing between knowledge and appraisal (Lazarus & Smith, 1988). This distinction is a useful heuristic for understanding cognition–emotion relations and both enduring interindividual differences and intraindividual variations in emotional experience. As argued elsewhere (Cervone, 1997), this distinction also is a useful tool for understanding how cognitively based models can account for cross-situational coherence in personality functioning.

Appraisals are evaluations of particular encounters. Specifically, they are evaluations of the relevance of encounters to one's personal well-being. Knowledge, in contrast, refers to beliefs about ourselves and the world. Knowledge encompasses people's representation of the facts regarding a situation at hand, as well as more generalized self-referent and social beliefs. Although knowledge is important to emotional experience, it is not seen as sufficient to cause an emotional response (Smith, Haynes, Lazarus, & Pope, 1993). Cold facts do not elicit emotion. People respond emotionally to the appraisal of facts for their own personal well-being. Appraisals, in other words, are the "hot cognitions" (Smith et al., 1993) that function as immediate causal antecedents of emotional response. They are evaluative cognitions that are influenced by general knowledge that people bring with them into situations. Thus, appraisal theory predicts that appraisals should mediate any influence of knowledge structures on emotional reactions.

Support for this hypothesis comes from research assessing people's retrospective thoughts about emotional experiences (Smith et al., 1993). Subjects envisioned positive and negative incidents that they had experienced. They then completed assessments of two types of cognition regarding these experiences, namely, causal attributions and cognitive appraisals. To assess attributions, subjects indicated their beliefs about the causes of the events via both categorical and dimensional measures. To assess appraisals of the incidents, subjects completed measures of the six appraisal dimensions outlined above, as well as six core relational themes. Finally, subjects' emotional state during the incidents was assessed through the rating of emotional adjectives. The findings indicated that appraisals were more strongly linked to emotional experiences than were attributions. Even after statistically controlling for the influence of causal attributions on emotional experience, cognitive appraisals significantly added to the prediction of emotional response. In contrast, after accounting for the effect of appraisals, the attribution measures were only weakly related to emotion (Smith et al., 1993).

There are, at present, limitations to appraisal theory as an all-encompassing model of the generation of emotional experience. The retrospective methodology used in many studies (e.g., Smith & Ellsworth, 1985; Smith et al., 1993) is not ideal. Indices of current appraisals of ongoing events clearly would be preferable. Appraisal theories provide a less detailed account of variations in positive emotions than in negative emotions. It thus is not clear how they would account for subtle variations in positive affect of the sort recognized in non-Western emotion taxonomies (Shweder, 1993). As noted by Ellsworth (1994), appraisal theories have difficulty accounting for phenomena such as the emotional impact of music, which may elicit

rich emotional experiences in the absence of an appraisal of the relational significance of the music itself, or opponent process in emotional response (Mauro, 1988; Solomon, 1980), in which the cessation of one emotional state (e.g., fear) seems to elicit an opposing state (e.g., relief) in the absence of corresponding appraisals.

Nonetheless, appraisal theories provide great insight into the generation of emotional experience. In so doing, they speak directly to concerns of the personality psychologist. As Smith and Pope (1992) note, appraisal theories provide the sort of interactional model of personality processes that is explicitly sought by many personality psychologists (e.g., Magnusson & Stattin, 1998). Their basic unit of analysis, cognitive appraisal, is explicitly interactional. Appraisals are not properties of the person in isolation from the environment or properties of the environment conceptualized independently of persons. Cognitive appraisals are person-in-situation units, which directly capture relations between persons and the environment.

The distinction between knowledge and appraisal (Lazarus & Smith, 1988) also suggests promising strategies for explaining interindividual differences and intraindividual coherence. Knowledge structures are enduring personality characteristics. These include "goal hierarchies and beliefs about self and world" (Lazarus, 1994, p. 336), which determine how the individual characteristically appraises events. For example, people with high goal commitments are prone to perceive events as motivationally relevant, whereas people with salient beliefs regarding incompetence are prone to low coping appraisals (Smith & Pope, 1992). Cognitive appraisals, in turn, directly contribute to emotional experience. A system of knowledge structures and appraisal tendencies thus may account for the characteristics of affective dispositions. These dispositional qualities would include not only mean-level affective tendencies (e.g., a generalized tendency to experience anger or guilt) but distinctive variations in emotional experience from one situation to another. A person's characteristic beliefs and appraisals may vary substantially across circumstances (Lazarus, 1991, 1994) and thus may give rise to distinctive high and low patterns of emotional response (cf. Shoda, 1999). Cognitive appraisal models of emotion, then, explain patterns of intraindividual coherence and interindividual difference in much the same manner as do the social-cognitive models of personality discussed previously (see chapter 3).

## Physiological Substrates of Emotional Experience

Emotions involve not just the mind but the body. Emotional states are marked by physiological arousal, which if noticed, signals to us that we have become emotionally involved in an event. Recent years have seen much progress in the analysis of physiological mechanisms in emotional experience and individual difference in emotion-related physiology. Much of this work seeks to identify distinct physiological mechanisms and processes that subserve different emotional states.

In the past, similar patterns of physiology were thought to underlie different discrete emotions. Schachter and Singer's (1962) influential model suggested that emotion involves the cognitive labeling of diffuse autonomic arousal. Similar physiogical arousal, then, was seen to underlie different emotional states. Much work, however, contradicts this thesis. Distinct physiological patterns are associated with different emotions (Leventhal & Tomarken, 1986). Specific physiological mechanisms in the peripheral nervous system, in lower brain regions such as the limbic system, and in higher-level cortical function have been linked to distinct emotional experiences (Damasio, 1994; Davidson, 1992; Ledoux, 1996; Levenson, 1994). Although the physiological differences that are found when people experience different emotional states are sometimes not large, they are large enough to reject the "null hypothesis" that all emotions are subserved by a common pattern of diffuse arousal. ˙

In one sense, the contention that different emotions are mediated by different physiological systems is banal. Emotional reactions are, like other psychological phenomena, products of the activity of the nervous system. Different emotional states of necessity must involve different physiological activation of some sort. The challenge is to determine the exact nature and function of physiological systems in different emotions and to identify individual differences in physiology that contribute to difference in emotional experience.

Diverse lines of research on physiological mechanisms in emotion generally proceed from a common set of premises. Emotional response is seen to involve multiple physiological mechanisms; emotions are "multisystem events" (Cacioppo et al., 1992, p. 126). Investigators thus no longer seek to identify a single mechanism that is independently responsible for all emotional experience (cf. MacLean, 1949). Indeed, they do not even posit "a single, nonspecific construct of `emotion in general'" (Gray, 1994, p. 244). Instead, researchers recognize that different emotions arise from different brain systems (e.g., LeDoux, 1996). This fact has important implications for conceptualizations of the emotional reactivity of individuals. Since there is no single neural system of emotion, there can be no single brain system corresponding to individual differences in generalized, overall emotion.

The search for emotion-specific physiology has examined various physiological systems, including the autonomic nervous system and its influence on peripheral physiology; lower-level regions of the central nervous system, particularly the limbic system; and high-level, cortical brain activity.

■ *Autonomic Arousal.* Emotional experiences are arousing. We vividly feel the changes in heart rate, blood pressure, and sweat gland activity that indicate that we have become emotionally aroused. These changes in peripheral physiology are brought about by the autonomic nervous system. The sympathetic branch of the autonomic nervous system prepares the organism for vigorous behavior by activating physiological mechanisms that support potential action (Levenson, 1992). Since different emotions predispose one to different types of action, patterns of peripheral physiology may be emotion-specific. Since anger, for example, predisposes one to attack, it may be linked to peripheral arousal that specifically supports aggressive, attacking behavior. Thus, one potential source of emotion-specific physiology is emotion-specific patterns of arousal in physiological mechanisms controlled by the autonomic nervous system.

Evidence that different emotions are accompanied by distinct patterns of autonomic arousal primarily comes from two experimental paradigms (Levenson, 1992). In one, participants are asked to recall episodes in which they experienced a particular emotional state and to relive the emotional experience (Schwartz, Weinberger, & Singer, 1981). In another, subjects assume specific facial expressions that typically accompany a given emotion (Ekman, Levenson, & Friesen, 1983); the logic here is that posing the expressions will trigger emotion-specific affect programs in the central nervous system, which in turn will activate associated autonomic nervous system activity. These paradigms reveal a number of reliable autonomic nervous system differences between emotions (Levenson, 1992). For example, Ekman et al. (1983) instructed trained actors to move facial muscles into patterns that corresponded to the emotions of anger, fear, sadness, happiness, disgust, and surprise. In a second task, the actors were asked to relive a past episode in which they experienced each of these emotions. These tasks produced meaningful, reliable differences in autonomic nervous system activation. The posing of anger and fear raised heart rate in comparison with happiness, sadness, and disgust. This is understandable in that both the fight reactions of anger and the flight reactions of fear require the mobilization of energy, which in turn requires higher heart rate. Although associated with similar heart rate, anger and fear could be differentiated on other autonomic nervous system measures. Skin temperature (recorded at the

finger) was higher for anger than for fear, which is understandable in that in fear, blood may be directed from the periphery to the large muscles that support the locomotion needed to escape situations. Peripheral skin temperature, then, would not rise despite higher heart rate (Levenson, 1992). This general pattern of results has been replicated with nonactors (Levenson Ekman, & Friesen, 1990) and in a non-Western culture, the Minangkabau of West Sumatra (Levenson, 1992). It should be noted, however, that autonomic nervous system differences were stronger with the facial posing task than with the relived emotions procedure (Ekman et al 1983). In addition to the findings for anger and fear, sadness also has been associated with heart rate acceleration (Ekman, et al 1983; Schwartz et al., 1981), which suggests that sadness is a stressful state of high arousal. In contrast, a different negative emotion, disgust, is associated with lower heart rates (Levenson, 1992).

Although some states can be differentiated in terms of peripheral physiology, not all emotions can be differentiated in this manner. Indeed, the obtained autonomic nervous system findings are not particularly strong. Activation of the autonomic nervous system clearly does not fully determine one's emotional experience. Indeed, since the autonomic nervous system is concerned with the supply of bodily energy and different emotions may have similar energy requirements, patterns of autonomic nervous system arousal may not be the ideal place to look for emotion-specific physiology (Gray, 1994). Stronger evidence of distinct biological mechanisms subserving distinct emotions derives from research on central nervous system functioning.

■ *Central Nervous System Physiology and Emotion.* Historically, investigators studying central nervous system physiology and emotion have focused on primitive brain regions such as the limbic system. In particular, the amygdala, a nucleus of cells in the temporal lobe, has long been implicated in emotional response (Thompson, 1985; Whalen, 1998). As reviewed by Ledoux (1995, 1996), animal research indicated that lesions of the amygdala cause a loss of sensitivity to the emotional features of stimuli, even while memory of perceptual features is retained. Neuroimaging studies implicate the amygdala in affective information processing in humans (Whalen, 1998). The amygdala is involved both in the appraisal of emotion-evoking stimuli and in the activation of muscular, autonomic, and endocrine systems involved in emotional response (Ledoux, 1995). This, however, does not mean that the amygdala is a single, unitary mechanism, which independently produces emotional response. On the contrary, the activation of different emotional states involves different amygdaloid nuclei. Furthermore, the amygdala is interconnected with numerous other brain regions that are intimately involved in emotional response (Ledoux, 1995, 1996).

Although the amygdala is involved in multiple aspects of emotional experience, an analysis of amygdala functioning cannot account for all aspects of human emotional experience. Most of the research on amygdaloid functioning in emotion has involved animal models and simple "hard-wired" emotions such as fear (LeDoux, 1996). Complex human emotional responses undoubtedly involve higher-level brain regions. The neuroscientist Antonio Damasio, for example, argues that "structures in the limbic system are not sufficient to support" (1994, p. 134) the complex range of human emotions that are evoked by both actual and imagined situations. Let us consider, then, advances in the analysis of cortical regions in emotional behavior.

Investigators studying cortical involvement in emotional response have relied on electroencephalographic (EEG) recordings of brain activity. In electroencephalography, wires are attached to the scalp to record the electrical activity of underlying brain regions. Electroencephalographic records are rather gross indices of brain activity, in as much as any given electrode records the activity of large numbers of neurons, many of which may be functionally distinct (Thompson,

1974); nonetheless EEG recordings have proved extremely valuable in determining which general regions of the cortex are involved in different affective experiences.

Electroencephalographic recordings of cortical activity during emotional experience reveal a basic finding of fundamental interest. Frontal regions of the right and left hemispheres are differentially involved in different affective states. The right and left hemispheres are more active during positive–approach and negative–avoidance affective states, respectively (Davidson, 1992; Heller, Nitschke, & Miller, 1998). Converging sources of evidence support the conclusion that anterior regions of the right hemisphere are primarily activated during withdrawal-related negative emotional states, whereas left hemisphere activation predominates during approach-related positive emotions. When brain activity was recorded while subjects displayed happy versus disgusted facial expressions in response to films depicting amusing and repugnant material, greater right hemisphere activation was found during disgust experiences. Strikingly, all research participants exhibited this hemispheric asymmetry (Davidson, Ekman, Saron, Senulis, & Friesen, 1990). Additional evidence comes from research relying on the distinction between two types of smiles: (1) true smiles, or Duchenne smiles (Ekman, Davidson, & Friesen, 1990), which involve both raised corners of the mouth and contractions of muscles near the eye that cause the skin wrinkling known as crow's feet; and (2) smiles that do not include crow's feet, which might arise, for example, when social conventions compel one to smile in the absence of true positive affect. Measures of anterior cortical activity reveal greater left hemisphere activity only during Duchenne smiles (Ekman et al., 1990); thus, left hemisphere dominance is associated not merely with the muscle movements of smiling but also with positive affect. Studies of brain lesions and affective symptoms converge with these findings. Left hemisphere lesions are linked to depressive symptomatology (Davidson, 1992). Such converging evidence is critical to linking brain regions to psychological functions (Sarter, Berntson, & Cacioppo, 1996).

Although this body of findings leaves no doubt that the hemispheres are differentially involved in different emotions, a significant question remains. Does hemispheric asymmetry relate most strongly to the positivity versus negativity of emotional states, or is some other dimension that is correlated with positivity–negativity, such as approach–avoidance (Gray, 1987; Harmon-Jones & Allen, 1998), more closely related to hemispheric specialization? Work relating EEG asymmetry to chronic individual differences in affective experience bears upon this question.

■ *Individual Differences in Hemispheric Asymmetry.* The finding that the hemispheres are differentially involved in different transient emotional states suggest the possibility that stable individual differences in hemispheric activity may underlie chronic affective tendencies. Various findings link individual differences in hemispheric asymmetry to chronic tendencies to experience positive versus negative affect. First, as would be required to establish that hemispheric asymmetry is a stable individual difference, asymmetry measures have acceptable psychometric properties. Tomarken, Davidson, Wheeler, and Kinney (1992) obtained measures of activity in midfrontal and anterior regions of the cerebral cortex across a series of eight resting baseline sessions. In data analyses, they treated these eight physiological measures as akin to eight items on a test and computed the internal reliability of the overall index of hemispheric asymmetry. Resting midfrontal and anterior asymmetry demonstrated excellent internal reliability, with coefficient *a*'s in the .80 to .95 range (Tomarken et al., 1992). To assess temporal stability, these measures were taken at experimental sessions 3 weeks apart. Degrees of left versus right hemisphere activation demonstrated significant temporal consistency, although consistency correlations generally were only in the .40 to .70 range, which suggests that "resting EEG asymmetry may reflect the joint contribution of both sta-

ble individual differences and more situational state-like factors" (Tomarken et al., 1992, p. 589).

In addition to having good psychometric properties, EEG measures of hemispheric asymmetry predict individual differences in emotional experience. Subgroups of individuals with extreme, temporally stable left hemisphere dominance report greater positive and lesser negative affective experience on self-report indices of chronic affective states (Tomarken, Davidson, Wheeler, & Doss, 1992). Greater left frontal activation predicts heightened positive affect in response to amusing film clips. Greater right frontal activation, in contrast, predicts greater negative affect in response to films of fear-provoking and disgusting stimuli (Wheeler, Davidson, & Tomarken, 1993). In infants, greater right frontal activation predicts greater distress in response to maternal separation (Davidson, 1994). Such asymmetries, then, may be an early marker of later temperamental tendencies (Fox, 1991).

Although these findings indicate that individual differences in hemispheric asymmetries predict affective personality traits, they do not establish that positive and negative affectivity are the surface-level traits that are most strongly linked to the underlying physiology. Harmon-Jones and Allen (1998) stress that most research has confounded affective valence (positivity–negativity) with a conceptually distinct factor, motivational direction (i.e., approach vs. withdrawal). Most negative emotions involve withdrawal, whereas most positive emotions involve approach. One way of differentiating between the two dimensions is to study anger, a negative–approach emotion. As it turns out, people who report greater dispositional tendencies to experience anger show relatively greater activity in the *left* frontal hemishere, which previously had been linked to positive affective experience. This result suggests that anterior asymmetry is linked more closely to approach versus avoidance motivation than to positive–negative affectivity. Research (Sutton & Davidson, 1997) relating hemispheric asymmetry to individual differences in self-report measures of behavioral approach versus inhibition (Carver & White, 1994; cf. Gray, 1987) is consistent with this conclusion. A more general lesson here is that in striving to relate phenotypic tendencies to underlying physiology, identifying the appropriate phenotypic tendency is often as difficult as identifying the physiology.

## The Behavioral Expression of Emotional States

We can recognize people's emotions. Different states of emotion are associated with distinct emotional expressions, which reveal the actor's affective state (Ekman & Rosenberg, 1997). Wide eyes, raised eyebrows, and a tense, stretched lower lip indicate fear. Wide eyes accompanied by a furrowed brow and frown signal anger. We recognize emotions not only from these static features but also from dynamic changes in facial expression over time (Bassili, 1978). People are able to detect rapid, subtle variations in facial expression, particularly in the early moments of the display of an emotion (Edwards, 1998). In addition to facial expression, bodily posture and vocal tone convey information about another's emotional experience.

The expressive component of emotion serves important interpersonal functions (Keltner, Kring, & Bonanno, 1999; Levenson, 1994). The fact that facial expressions instantly communicate an actor's emotional state and potential behavioral tendencies to others has important survival value. For example, rather than becoming involved in surprising conflicts, people can read feelings of anger in other' facial expressions and choose to avoid further hostility. Emotional expression can also mobilize others to take action. Expressions of panic alert others of danger and motivate protective behaviors.

The study of facial expression has yielded one of the most striking findings in the study of emotion. Facial expressions are recognized cross-culturally. There are, in other words, universals in facial expression (Ekman & Oster, 1979; Ekman, 1994). Despite the considerable cultural variability in the nature of emotional experience (Kitayama & Markus, 1994), people from widely different cultural groups readily and accurately recognize the emotion display in each other's facial expressions. Relatively consistent results are found for six emotions: anger, disgust, happiness, sadness, fear, and surprise (Ekman & Oster, 1979). Of particular note is that preliterate groups who have not been exposed to Western media recognize emotions posed by Westerners.

Emotional states involve not only behavioral expressions of one's emotion, but motivation to take distinct forms of action (Lazarus, 1991; Tomkins, 1962; Weiner, 1992). Anger impels people to attack; disgust motivates the expulsion of offensive objects; fear drives the escape or avoidance of threats; compassion leads people to relieve others' misfortune; and shame causes people to withdraw from others. In interpersonal settings, feelings of jealousy motivate diverse acts designed to "get even" with a partner (Bryson, 1991), whereas guilt motivates affection and explicit attention to a partner, which may serve to strengthen relationships (Baumeister, Stillwell, & Heatherton, 1994).

In addition to motivating distinct forms of action, emotional arousal also can amplify existing motivational tendencies. Residual arousal from a prior emotional experience can transfer to new contexts and heighten people's level of aggressiveness toward someone who had provoked them (Zillman, 1978). In addition, as discussed in detail in chapter 12 of this text, affective states can influence motivation indirectly by influencing cognitive processes involved in the regulation of behavior (Cervone, Kopp, Schaumann, & Scott, 1994; Martin et al., 1993).

■ *Individual Differences in Expressivity.* Although emotional states are associated with expressive and motivational tendencies, emotions do not compel one to act in any particular manner. People may suppress the behavioral reactions that normally accompany a given emotional state (Gross & John, in press; Levenson, 1994). We normally laugh when something strikes us as funny, but we may suppress this reaction if the funny incident was an inadvertently humorous action by a professor or job supervisor. Social settings and transient impression management goals, then, partially determine whether we express our emotional impulses. However, enduring personal characteristics may create chronic tendencies to express or suppress emotions. People who are ambivalent about emotional expression, recognizing both the costs and benefits of revealing their inner feelings, are judged by peers as being less expressive (King & Emmons, 1990) and are relatively poor at reading the emotional expressions of others (King, 1998). Self-reported conflict over expressing one's emotions predicts psychological distress (King & Emmons, 1990, 1991)

Research by Gross and John (1997) reveals that there are multiple facets to individual differences in emotional expressivity. Factor analyses of a brief self-report measure of expressive tendencies revealed three such facets: the strength of people's internal emotional reactions, the degree to which they habitually express positive emotion, and the degree to which they habitually express negative emotion (Gross & John, 1997). Self-reports of these response tendencies predicted behavior in a laboratory setting. Subjects were observed as they viewed films designed to elicit both sadness and amusement. Self-reported tendencies to express negative emotion predicted facial expressiveness and crying in response to the sad film but did not predict responses to the amusement film. Conversely, tendencies to express positive affect predicted behavioral expression in reaction to the amusement film but were unrelated to expressions of sadness. Individuals differences, then, were specifically linked to relevant situational contexts. It is particularly noteworthy that self-reported expressivity predicted behavioral response after statistically controlling for subjects' physiological arousal during the films (Gross and John, 1997). The self-report measure of expressivity, then, did not merely tap overall levels of positive and negative affective tendencies but instead measured people's tendencies to regulate the expression

of affective states once an emotional response has begun.

■ *Facial Expression and Psychosocial Adjustment.* An intriguing possibility in the study of facial expression is that the face may serve as a "window" to a person's inner psychological life (Keltner et al., 1999). Facial expressiveness may relate systematically to people's typical emotional experiences and their levels of psychosocial adjustment to life events. Research studying people's adjustment to the death of a spouse supports this possibility (Bonanno & Keltner, 1997). Those who displayed more negative facial expressions when talking about their deceased spouse one-half year after the person's death were found to be less well adjusted, on a measure of grief severity, 1 to 2 years after the spousal loss.

Facial expressiveness also has been related to adolescent psychopathology (Keltner, Moffit, & Stouthamer-Loeber, 1995). Facial expressions were recorded as boys worked on a brief IQ test. Boys who were the most prone to antisocial behavior showed more signs of anger and fewer signs of embarrassment during the test than did others; the latter result is consistent with the possibility that embarrassment functions to motivate normative social behavior (Keltner & Buswell, 1997). Although more work involving prospective research designs is needed in this area, the present findings suggest that brief measures of facial expressiveness may be valid markers of individuals' typical affective tendencies and psychosocial adjustment.

### Subjective Emotional Experience

The fourth component of emotional response is "the richest aspect of emotions" (Epstein, 1983, p. 104), namely, subjective feeling states. Intense emotions involve powerful feelings that can overwhelm other aspects of conscious experience. These phenomenological experiences serve an important function. They lead people to focus and reflect on the source of their affect, enabling one to learn from emotional experiences (Scherer, 1984). Through emotion-induced self-reflection and forethought, people can avoid emotionally aversive situations and control the circumstances they encounter (Bandura, 1986; Damasio, 1994). Subjective affective experiences also provide informative feedback on the nature of one's circumstances (Clore, 1994; Schwarz, 1990).

Our intuitions tell us that people differ greatly in the type of emotions that they typically experience. Some people chronically seem to be in a good or a bad mood. Others seem prone to experience specific emotions, such as outbursts of anger or feelings of guilt. Although some people are even-tempered, others exhibit mood swings. Identifying and explaining these individual differences and intraindividual variations in subjective emotional experience is an important task for the personality psychologist.

Despite the clarity of our intuitions and the importance of the task, the question of exactly how one should assess subjective emotional experience is a difficult one. Clearly, self-report methods are most appropriate. If we are interested in the individual's subjective experiences, the best way of learning about them is by directly asking (Epstein, 1983; Kelly, 1955). The difficult question is what to ask. What emotions should one assess? Should one, in fact, assess discrete emotions, or instead focus on broad mood states? Which specific emotions or dimensions of mood should be assessed? What is the basic structure of affective experience? Can one assume that this structure is the same from one person to the next? Although investigators have made considerable progress in answering these questions, some fundamental issues remain unresolved. In the following, we review alternative approaches to assessing subjective emotional experience. In doing so, we highlight the common findings that emerge across these diverse perspectives.

■ *Discrete Emotions.* One approach to assessing subjective emotional experience is to assess individual differences in the tendency to experience various discrete emotional states. Drawing on categorical emotion taxonomies, discussed above, one might develop measures of people's tendency to experience each of a

series of discrete emotions. Although this is a reasonable strategy, one obstacle is immediately apparent. There is no agreement on the question of which are the basic emotions. With no taxonomic consensus, emotion theory provides no clear guidelines regarding which emotional states one should assess. This lack of theoretical consensus is evident in the variety of self-report emotion instruments currently available. Izard's Differential Emotions Scale (DES) assesses 12 different emotional states (Izard, Libero, Putnam, & Haynes, 1993), Zuckerman and Lubin's (1965) Multiple Affect Adjective Check List (MAACL) assesses 5; the Profile of Mood States (POMS) of McNair et al. measures 6 emotions; and Watson and Clark's (1997b) PANAS-X assesses 11. As Watson and Clark note, it is difficult to choose among these instruments in the absence of a clear, consensually agreed structural theory of the emotions.

A further problem is that self-report measures of seemingly distinct emotional experiences often lack discriminant validity. Measures of anxiety, depression, and hostility (Zuckerman & Lubin, 1965) vividly illustrate this problem. Although these clearly are different affective states, individual difference assessments of these states often correlate in the .7 to .9 range (Gotlib & Meyer, 1986). As a result, it is difficult, if not impossible, to use these measures to study a particular emotional state of interest. Imagine two investigators, one of whom is interested in studying cognitive correlates of individual differences in anxiety whereas the other is interested in studying cognitive correlates of depression. They each might select subjects using a self-report measure of their selected affective state. They might find interesting differences between subjects who do and do not suffer from their selected negative emotion. The problem is that the information they obtain may not be specific to anxiety or depression per se. Self-report measures of anxiety and depression may be so highly correlated that reportedly depressed and anxious subjects selected in this manner are essentially the same people (Gotlib, 1984). Both measures appear to tap into a general tendency to experience negative affect (Watson & Clark, 1992).

Despite these measurement problems, research has succeeded in demonstrating that the tendency to experience particular discrete emotions is a temporally stable personal characteristic, which is meaningfully related to personality trait measures. For example, Izard et al. (1993) studied the emotional experiences of mothers who, at the outset of their study, recently had given birth. Each of 11 discrete emotions was assessed at 2.5, 4.5, 6, and 36 months after childbirth. Mean levels of emotion changed over time in this population. Mothers experienced greater disgust, contempt, shyness, and shame soon after childbirth than later, perhaps because of the hormonal changes or life-style disruptions that follow childbirth. Mother's relative tendency to experience different emotional states, however, was highly stable. For each of the discrete emotions, women who tended to experience the emotional state soon after pregnancy continued to exhibit this tendency 6 months and 3 years after giving birth. Tendencies to experience discrete emotions also were meaningfully related to broad personality trait dimensions. The mothers who experienced greater interest and lesser shyness were more extroverted, as assessed by the Eysenck Personality Questionnaire, whereas those who experienced greater sadness, contempt, and shame were more neurotic (Izard et al., 1993).

■ *The Structure of Mood: Individual Differences in Affective Experience.* Most research on individual differences in affect has not investigated discrete emotions. Investigators instead have examined broad dimensions of affective experience, which are better characterized as mood factors than emotions. The emphasis on mood partly reflects the pragmatic difficulty of measuring emotions validly. However, there also are substantive reasons for focusing on mood experience. Intense emotional states are relatively brief and rare events. More of our experience involves low-level moods than specific intense emotions (Watson, 2000; Watson & Clark, 1994). Indeed, moods may be "always present," providing an "affec-

tive background . . . to all that we do" (Davidson, 1994, p. 52).

If asked to consider variations among mood states, most people would note that moods vary in valence. Moods are characterized as good or bad. A bipolar dimension of positivity versus negativity, then, would seem essential to describe variations in affect. As noted earlier, this bipolar dimension emerges commonly in studies of affective structure (Green et al., 1993; Russell, 1979). A second dimension of affective space captures variations in arousal that accompany different affective states (Russell, 1979). Arousal differences distinguish among both negative (e.g., annoyance vs. rage) and positive (pleased vs. ecstatic) affects. Many investigators, then, recognize these two bipolar dimensions – positivity versus negativity and arousal versus lack of arousal – as independent dimensions that define the structure of affect. Specific emotional experiences can be described by ordering them along a circle formed by the two orthogonal dimensions; in this circumplex structure, the relative placement of emotion terms indicates the degree to which they are correlated with each other (Russell, 1980).

Although this bipolar model is appealing intuitively, it conflicts with a nonintuitive empirical finding. In self-reports of emotional states, words of opposite valence often are not strongly correlated. Self-ratings of positive and negative affect, in other words, fail to show the strong negative correlations that one would expect from a bipolar modal. Although tall people can not also be short (height being an unambiguously bipolar dimension), people who experience a great deal of positive affect also may, in fact, experience a great deal of negative affect. Positive and negative affect, in other words, may be independent factors rather than opposite poles of the same dimension. The statistical independence of positive and negative affect first was found in studies of subjective well-being (Bradburn, 1969). Subsequent idiographic analyses by Zevon and Tellegen (1982) found a similar structure. Using a 60-item mood adjective checklist, subjects described their mood for 90 consecutive days; P-factor analysis, which identifies dimensions in matrices of within-person correlations, was then used to analyze each person's self-reports. For 21 of 23 subjects, variations in affective experience were well described by two independent dimensions of positive affect and negative affect (Zevon & Tellegen, 1982). Analyses involving diverse self-report instruments have since revealed a similar two-factor structure (Mayer & Gaschke, 1988; Watson & Clark, 1997; Watson & Tellegen, 1985). Although the positivity versus negativity of one's mood may be inversely related at any given point in time, independence characterizes long-term mean levels of affective experience (Diener and Emmons, 1984). This independence of positive and negative affect may partly derive from individual differences in affect intensity, that is, the intensity with which people experience emotional states of any sort (Larsen & Diener, 1987). If some people tend to experience both strong positive and strong negative affect, their response pattern would reduce or eliminate bipolarity in affect structure (Diener, Larsen, Levine, & Emmons, 1985).

Despite much supportive evidence, the conclusion that tendencies to experience positive versus negative affect vary independently has not gone unchallenged. Green et al. (1993) argue that measurement error can mask the true bipolarity of affect structure. When mood is assessed via a single self-report method, response biases introduce random error that obscures bipolarity. A respondent who tends to acquiesce, responding yes to many items, may erroneously appear to experience high degrees of both happy and sad mood. This response bias would reduce what actually might be a strong negative correlation between happiness and sadness. After correcting for such measurement errors, Green et al. (1993) obtained extremely strong negative correlations (averaging about −.85) between happy and sad moods, suggesting that affective experience indeed is bipolar (Russell, 1979).

Responses to Green at al. (1993) suggested an intermediate position. This work recog-nized that the particular emotion adjectives one selects for study influence the correlation between positive and negative affect that one obtains (Watson & Clark, 1997b). When emotion terms are sampled systematically, positive and negative affect are correlated moderately (Diener, Smith, & Fujita, 1995). This suggests that factors of positive and negative affect are not orthogonal but are "separable" (Diener et al., 1995, p. 132). Two separate dimensions, in other words, account for significantly greater variability in affective experience than does any single factor.

The work of Feldman Barrett and Russell (1998) further illustrates how the particular choice of adjectives that constitute one's self-report instrument can influence the structure of affect one obtains. They note that the items on scales that have yielded statistically independent dimensions of positive affectivity (PA) and negative affectivity (NA) (Watson and Tellegen, 1985) tend to omit major aspects of affective experience. These scales include terms connoting high arousal or activation (e.g., enthusiastic, afraid) but omit terms referring to states of low activation (serene, depressed). When a more complete comprehensive set of adjectives is included, two independent dimensions are obtained: activation and pleasantness (Feldman Barrett & Russell, 1998). In this structure, pleasant and unpleasant emotions are bipolar opposites, as suggested by Green et al., 1993). The PA and NA scales (Watson & Tellegen, 1985) remain independent, not bipolar; the key to understanding this seemingly incongruous fact is that Watson and Tellegen's "PA is not the same as positive affect" and "NA is not the same as negative affect" (Feldman Barrett & Russell, 1998, p. 979). Instead, the constructs PA and NA capture only a subset of the overall range of affective experience, specifically, subset of emotional experiences that involve high degrees of activation. On the other hand, Russell and Carroll (1999) outline a range of methodological considerations that when taken into account, suggest that positive and negative affectivity are not independent dimensions but bipolar opposites.

In sum, despite points of disagreement, a significant degree of consensus can be found in work on the structure of affective experience (Feldman Barrett & Russell, 1999). Findings repeatedly demonstrate that two dimensions are necessary and reasonably sufficient to describe individual differences in affect. Any single dimension misses much important variation, whereas dimensions beyond two generally add relatively little to prediction. A full sampling of emotion terms is beginning to yield consistent support for a two-dimensional model, with dimensions of valence (positive versus negative) and activation (high versus low). It remains difficult to integrate fully these psychometric findings with research on the neurophysiology of emotion (see Cacioppo, Gardner, & Bernston, 1997); the integration of physiological and psychometric findings is a challenge for future research.

Consistent findings also are found with regard to other issues in the study of affective experience. As we saw earlier when discussing the subjective experience of discrete emotions (Izard et al., 1993), individual differences in subjective mood are temporally stable. Stability may be found over very long time spans. When tendencies to experience positive and negative affect were assessed when participants were undergraduates and then, again, 6 to 7 years later, rank order stability correlations in the .36 to .46 range were obtained (Watson and Walker, 1996). Of course, these correlations are only moderate, which indicates that individuals of this age group may change substantially over this period of time. Affective tendencies are more stable over shorter periods (e.g., Diener & Larsen, 1984).

Individual differences in the subjective experience of positive and negative affect are consistent not only across time, but across situational contexts. When people rate their feelings across large numbers of naturally occurring situations, significant, but highly varying, degrees of cross-situational consistency are found (Diener and Larsen, 1984). As with objectively coded behaviors (Mischel & Peake, 1982), little consistency in subjective affect is found across single occasions. For example, for positive affect, the average correlation across single work versus recreational settings was .11. Aggregation across occasions, however, boosted consistency correlations (also see Epstein, 1979; Mischel & Peake, 1982), at least for some indices of subjective experience. After correcting for unreliability of measures, aggregate tendencies to experience positive and negative affect in work versus recreational settings showed correlations of .77 and .81, respectively. Aggregated tendencies to feel sociable across these settings, however, correlated only .01 (Diener & Larsen, 1984).

Data also link internal subjective feeling states to external criteria, including ratings by peers and other informants (Watson & Clark, 1997b). For example, ratings of college students' affective tendencies made by the students' peers and family members are highly correlated with the students' own self-ratings (Diener et al., 1995). The convergence of self-ratings and informant ratings is somewhat lower for negative emotionality than for positive emotionality (Funder & Dobroth, 1987; Harkness, Tellegen, & Waller, 1995).

Finally, as we have noted elsewhere, affect dimensions consistently have been linked to broad individual difference dimensions (Watson, 2000). Positive affectivity is a core element of extroversion (Watson & Clark, 1997a). Negative affect is a hallmark of neuroticism (Watson & Clark, 1984).

In summary, then, the structure of self-reported affective experience can be described fairly well by conceptual maps consisting of two orthogonal dimensions. Individual differences along these dimensions are highly stable over time, somewhat consistent across situations, and significantly correlated with both peer reports and personality trait dimensions. The exact nature and best verbal labeling of the dimensions remains a matter of some disagreement. The further issue to be resolved involves underlying mechanisms.

■ *Subjective Well-Being.* An aspect of subjective experience that is closely related to emotional experience is "subjective well-being," which is generally construed as people's evaluations of how happy or satisfied they are with their lives (Diener, 1998). The most common method for studying subjective well-being is to administer brief self-report inventories in which respondents are asked to indicate how happy or satisfied they are with their lives. Research employing such methods yields a finding that is somewhat surprising. People's subjective well-being appears to reflect their stable personality characteristics more than the circumstances of their lives (Diener, 1998).

Much evidence on this point comes from the contributions of Diener and colleagues. They find that extroverts experience greater subjective well-being than introverts across a wide range of social circumstances (Diener, Sandvik, Pavot, & Fujita, 1992; Pavot, Diener, & Fujita, 1990). Even when one does identify a situational factor that influences self-rated well-being, one may observe a stable main effect for introversion–extroversion across situations. For example, Larsen and Kasimatis (1990) found that in a sample of American college students, well-being ratings were more positive on Friday and Saturday than on other days of the week. Introversion–extroversion differences, however, were stable, with extroverts reporting greater well-being on each day.

More recent work on subjective well-being has suggested a more dynamic role for cultural and contextual factors. For example, the nature of people's experience of subjective well-being is found to vary somewhat across cultures. Suh, Diener, Oishi, and Triandis (1998) explored the degree to which subjective well-being reflects people's inner emotional experiences or their culture's norms about the desirability of life satisfaction and found that emotional experiences were more strongly linked to subjective well-being in individualistic cultures than in collectivist nations. Other work highlights the importance of marital relationships for well-being and affective experience. In a large, statistically representative sample of Americans, the experience of negative affect declined with age among married men aged 25 through 74, but no such decline was found among unmarried men (Mroczek & Kolarz, 1998).

Other work on subjective well-being draws a conclusion that has broad implications for the assessment of personality and individual differences. Simple well-being measures overlap substantially with other individual-difference constructs, particularly self-esteem. Lucas, Diener, & Suh (1996) found that measures of well-being and self-esteem were closely related, especially in informant reports rather than self-reports. Diener (1998) suggests that self-esteem measures may "primarily identify individuals who feel positive about the world in general rather than just about themselves" (p. 327).

As investigators in this area realize, the study of subjective well-being may benefit from the use of a wider variety of research tools. For example, implicit measures of well-being may differ from the explicit measures typically employed, especially within cultures that contain strong norms either toward or against the expression of positive self-views. Another consideration is that subgroups of repressors (see chapter 11) may inflate correlations between subjective well-being and other indices by adopting a positive response style across individual-difference measures. Furthermore, it may sometimes be difficult to evaluate the relation between well-being and personality measures because semantically similar items appear on measures of both constructs, thus confounding the comparisons. For example, self-ratings of happiness may appear in both well-being inventories (e.g., Diener, & Diener, 1995) and measures of extroversion (Costa & McCrae, 1992). Nicholls, Licht, and Pearl (1982) have explained how item overlap can invalidate tests of the relations between personality constructs. Additionally, the psychological literature should attend somewhat more closely to the possibility that the equation of well-being and happiness is not as universal as it might seem to the Western eye (cf. Suh et al., 1998). Some cultures and individuals may primarily value a sense of purpose or meaning in life rather than high self-esteem or the frequent experience of happiness. If so, happiness and subjective well-being may be related only weakly (cf. McGregor & Little, 1998). Finally, investigators studying personality and well-being must continue to explore the remarkably resilient qualities of personality. Despite the hardships of life, people commonly exhibit the capacity to experience positive emotion and maintain relatively high levels of subjective well being (Avia, 1997). Life may not be as grim as psychological theory sometimes makes it seem.

■ *The Structure of Mood: Idiographic Analyses.* Most of the work on the structure of subjective affective experience that we have just reviewed has examined individual differences in the population. Much of the interesting variation in affect, however, is not variation between persons but within-person. Everyone's moods and emotions change significantly across time and social context. Thus, rather than merely plotting average differences between people, many investigators have examined affective experience idiographically. These investigators recognize that idiographic and nomothetic analyses of variability in mood provide different types of information about persons and that idiographic and nomothetic structures may not converge (Epstein, 1983).

As noted above, Zevon and Tellegen's (1982) idiographic analyses of self-rated mood suggested that the structure of affective experience is similar across individuals. Subsequent analyses suggest otherwise. Epstein (1983) conducted both inter- and intraindividual factor analyses of subjective feeling states. Although two dimensions were adequate to capture differences between persons, intraindividual variations were characterized by a three- factor structure including positive affect, self-esteem, and sociability. Within-person variations in subjective affect, then, were "more differentiated" (Epstein, 1983, p. 138) than between-person differences. The relations among discrete emotions also differed in within- versus between-subject analyses. For example, between subjects, anger and sadness were highly correlated, $r = .58$ (Epstein, 1983), as would be expected

from analyses of negative affectivity (Watson & Tellegen, 1985). Within subjects, however, the correlation between sadness and anger was not even statistically significant. Epstein's (1983) findings, then, vividly illustrate the differences that can emerge in within-subject versus between-subject analyses. Between subjects, people who tended to experience anger also tended to experience sadness. Within subjects, feelings of sadness were not systematically related to anger. Watson and Clark (1997b) similarly find that the orthogonality of positive and negative affect is more apparent in between-subject than within-subject analyses.

Even if a common set of dimensions can be applied across individuals, people may differ in the degree to which one versus another dimension predominates in their subjective experience of affect. People, in other words, may differ in whether they tend to focus on one versus another aspect of emotional experience (Feldman, 1995). Some may attend primarily to valence, with the positivity versus negativity of experiences dominating their subjective experience. Others may be particularly attuned to their own physiological activation and thereby focus primarily on affective arousal. If so, the circumplex structure formed by the dimensions of valence and arousal (Russell, 1979) may vary from one person to the next. This is precisely what Feldman (1995) found in an idiographic longitudinal study of affective experience. Valence was the primary dimension of affective experience for some individuals, whereas arousal predominated for others. Thus, differentially shaped affect circumplexes characterized different people.

As Feldman (1995) notes, individual variations in the affect circumplex have major implications for a key question in emotions research, namely, whether different emotional states covary or are independent. Consider anxiety and depression. Traditionally, investigators have examined the relation between these states nomothetically. In between-person analyses, variations in anxious and depressed mood are correlated quite highly

(Gotlib, 1984). Anxiety and depression, then, appear not to be independent. However, this nomothetic approach only tells us that covariation exists *across* persons in the tendency to experience anxiety and depression. That is, people who, compared with others, say they are anxious also report that they are depressed. It does not tell us whether anxiety and depression covary for all, or any, individuals. Feldman's (1995) idiographic analyses revealed that the degree of covariation between anxious and depressed mood differs from one person to the next. Some people tend to become anxious and depressed at the same times; within-person correlations between anxiety and depression were as high as .90. For others, these affective experiences are independent; within-person correlations were as low as .16. The covariation of positive and negative affectivity similarly differed across persons, with idiographic positive–negative correlations ranging from –.72 to .21 (Feldman, 1995).

These results (Epstein, 1983; Feldman, 1995) speak powerfully to the question of personality structure, particularly in light of the established connections between affective tendencies and individual-difference dimensions. If the term personality structure refers to the structural relation among psychological features of the individual, then these findings indicate that analyses of differences between individuals can not definitely answer questions about personality structure. Personality tendencies that covary in individual difference analyses may be independent for particular individuals. Independent population factors may covary strongly within persons. Understanding the structure of personality requires that one study individual persons.

People differ not only in the types of affect they typically experience but in the way in which their moods vary over time. Patterns of change over time are a stable personal characteristic (Larsen, 1989). Larsen (1987) collected daily reports of affective experience among groups of undergraduates over periods of 2 to 3 months. Idiographic time-series analyses revealed that individuals differed in the fre-

quency with which their mood shifted over time. A combination of idiographic and nomothetic techniques showed that people who report experiencing relatively intense affective states also experience relatively more rapid changes in daily mood. Larsen (1990) argues forcefully that personality psychology should place greater focus, not on static, mean-level differences between people, but on those dynamic patterns of change over time that distinguish individuals from one another.

To conclude, we note that although two-dimensional affect structures capture much of the variation in individual differences in mood, individuals nonetheless may exhibit variations in emotional experience that cannot be adequately described by any universal two-dimensional scheme. The field thus faces two significant challenges. One is to develop descriptions of affect variability that are applicable at the level of the individual person. The other is to identify the underlying biological mechanisms, social experiences, cognitive appraisals, and interactions among these factors that contribute to the observeed tendencies.

## Coherence Among the Components of Emotional Response

Although emotions involve multiple components that are functionally distinct, the hallmark of emotional response is the coming together of these components in an integrated, coherent manner. As Tomkins (1962) suggested, the characteristic feature of an emotional response is that it "(captures) such widely distributed organs as the face, the heart, and the endocrines and (imposes) on them specific patterns of correlated responses" (pp. 243 to 244). An important task, then, is to determine how and when different aspects of emotional response cohere and whether individuals differ in the ways in which emotional response systems interrelate.

It is difficult to obtain firm evidence of the coherence among different components of emotional response. Emotions do not last long. People may feel intensely angry, elated, or disgusted for only a matter of seconds. It is necessary, then, to employ measures of multiple response systems that are targeted to these brief windows of time. Developing such measures of subjective emotional experience is a particular challenge, since asking people to report on their subjective state may disrupt the natural flow of emotional experience. One method of circumventing these difficulties has been developed by Rosenberg and Ekman (1994).

In their technique (Rosenberg and Ekman, 1994), facial expressions are videorecorded while subjects watch an emotion-provoking film. Facial expressions subsequently are categorized by use of the Facial Action Coding System (FACS) (Ekman & Friesen, 1987; Ekman & Rosenberg, 1997), a reliable method of categorizing distinct facial muscle movements into emotion categories. After this initial viewing, subjects review the film and indicate the exact emotions they were feeling at each moment of the depicted episode. Mapping the temporal links between subjective experience and videotaped facial expressions enables one to gauge the relation between the two response modes. Rosenberg and Ekman's (1994) detailed analysis yielded firm evidence of moment-by-moment coherence among response systems. Facial expressions, as categorized by the FACS, corresponded in time to reports of subjective experiences. Facial expression and subjective experience were linked particularly strongly during more intense emotional states (Rosenberg & Ekman, 1994).

Much other work in this area has examined the relation between "external" and "internal" emotion response systems. Does the suppression of overt expressions of emotion (e.g., facial expression) reduce internal response (e.g., visceral arousal)? Or does the suppression of overt expression of emotion "backfire," causing internal arousal to increase?

Both of these ideas about the relation between external emotional expression and internal sympathetic nervous system activity have been advanced in the literature (Cacioppo et al., 1992). One view is that both internal and external response systems are driven by gener-

alized physiological arousal. Arousal should affect diverse systems in a similar manner. As a result, levels of external and internal activation should be correlated positively. Someone who expresses emotions more strongly also should experience greater levels of internal sympathetic activity. The second view is exactly the opposite. Psychodynamic theory (Freud, 1923) suggests that the functional relation between systems involves the discharge of emotional energy. If energy is discharged primarily through emotional expression, relatively little is left to drive visceral arousal. In contrast, if emotional expression is suppressed, energy should discharge itself through internal physiological activity. This discharge perspective, then, predicts that emotional expressivity and internal activation should be correlated negatively, with the inhibition of emotional expression causing greater arousal. People who intentionally inhibit emotional expression, people labeled "internalizers" by Jones (1935) (cited in Cacioppo et al., 1992), thus should inadvertently raise their internal physiological distress. "Externalizers," who express their emotions, should experience less arousal.

The psychodynamic discharge model is contradicted by evidence from research that manipulates facial expression while assessing autonomic arousal (e.g., Levenson et al., 1990). Lanzetta, Cartwright-Smith, and Kleck (1976) instructed subjects either to suppress or to exaggerate their emotional expression while being exposed to painful electric shocks. When asked to inhibit the external expression of pain, subjects experienced *lower* levels of autonomic arousal, as indexed by skin conductance levels. External expression and sympathetic activity, in other words, were correlated positively (Lanzetta et al., 1976). This finding, then, would seem to support the existence of a generalized arousal mechanism. However, the arousal-based argument, too, is contradicted by empirical evidence. Studies assessing individual differences in autonomic activity and facial expressiveness often find these response systems to be correlated negatively (Cacioppo et al., 1992). For example, Notarius and Levenson (1979) identified groups of male undergraduates who tended to exhibit either great or minimal facial expressiveness in emotion-provoking situations. These two groups were then exposed to a stressful stimulus. After having physiological recording devices attached, they were led to believe that an equipment malfunction might cause them to receive a dangerous shock. Measures of heart rate and respiration indicated that people who exhibited lower facial expressiveness displayed *higher* levels of physiological activity, as would be predicted by a psychodynamic discharge formulation.

Fortunately, these contradictory findings can be resolved. Their resolution provides an important lesson both in the analysis of correlational data and in the usefulness of studying individual differences not merely by charting dispositional tendencies but by analyzing underlying mechanisms that produce variation and coherence in psychological response. Regarding the interpretation of data, careful reviews of the literature reveal that different research strategies yield different results (Buck, 1980). In between-subject research (e.g., Notarius and Levenson, 1979), less expressive individuals were found to be more internally reactive. This negative correlation in the population, however, does *not* establish that when individuals inhibit their emotional expression, they simultaneously tend to raise their autonomic reactivity. The between-subject result does not provide any information about functional relations between external and internal response systems at the level of the individual. As it turns out, within-subject designs (e.g., Lanzetta et al., 1976) indicate that activation in external and internal response systems is correlated positively (Cacioppo et al., 1992).

A simple example illustrates how positive correlations at the level of the individual can exist alongside negative correlations in the population. For most individuals, numbers of hours at work and annual income are related positively. Working more hours directly increases income for an hourly employee and

may boost performance and subsequent pay raises for a salaried worker. In the population, however, hours at work and annual income may be related negatively. Low-income persons may need a second job to make ends meet. Extremely wealthy individuals may have the luxury of being able to work relatively few hours per week.

In addition to resolving the findings at a statistical level, one also would hope to identify the underlying mechanisms responsible for the observed relations between levels of internal and external emotional response. Are there generalized arousal mechanisms or psychodynamic discharge mechanisms? Cacioppo et al. (1992) reject both of these possibilities. They posit that relations between facial expressiveness and sympathetic activation can be understood by analyzing naturally occurring individual differences in the multiple biological systems that underlie distinct aspects of emotional response. As Cacioppo et al. explain, just as there are natural individual differences in physiological structures, such as eye color or arm length, there also are likely to be individual differences in the many somatic and sympathetic systems involved in emotional expression and sympathetic arousal. Cacioppo et al. (1992) highlight a specific physiological individual difference, namely, the degree to which physiological systems react to a given input, or system "gain." Some people may have relatively large gain in nerves controlling motor output but small gain in nerves of the sympathetic system. These people would exhibit relatively greater emotional expression than internal arousal. Phenotypically, then, they might be labeled externalizers. Others, in contrast, may have high sympathetic gain and relatively low somatic gain; the resulting combination of high arousal and low expressiveness would cause them to be seen as internalizers. For any individual, stronger stimuli would tend to produce stronger external and internal responses. Thus, at the individual level, internal and external activation would be correlated positively. If system gain is distributed in the population in a nonnormal manner (a distinct possibility; see, e.g., Kagan, 1998a), individual differences in characteristic internal and external activation levels could be correlated negatively; this could occur even if large numbers of people are neither externalizers nor internalizers, that is, even if many people have similar gain in both physiological response modes (Cacioppo et al., 1992). In this model, then, expressivity and arousal are not related causally. The phenotypic label externalizer or internalizer does not map directly onto a single underlying causal mechanism. Phenotypic tendencies simply reflect variations in distinct underlying response systems.

The model of Cacioppo et al. (1992) clearly requires greater empirical support. One requires more direct indices of system gain. In contrast to their model, some evidence of functional relations between the suppression of emotional expression and sympathetic arousal has been found, at least with regard to some emotions and some physiological indices (Gross & Levenson, 1993, 1997). Nonetheless, the work of Cacioppo et al. illustrates the utility of analyzing individual differences in emotional experience by examining specific mechanisms that underlie distinct aspects of emotional response. Rather than reifying the descriptive constructs externalizer and internalizer, Cacioppo et al. suggest that these phenotypic variations in emotional tendencies can be understood through interactions among multiple causal mechanisms that give rise to the dispositional tendencies (Cacioppo et al., 1992; also see Cacioppo et al., 1996).

## SUMMING UP

Our field's understanding of psychological and physiological mechanisms in emotional response has grown enormously in recent years. Findings speak directly to the personality psychologist's goals of understanding how distinct psychological processes function as integrated systems, which give rise to both individual differences and intraindividual variation and coherence in personality functioning. Cognitive appraisal processes, physiological mechanisms that mediate the organism's response to environmental threats, mechanisms of emotional expression that signal one's intentions to others, and the subjective experience of emotional states are interacting systems of personality. Each of these systems may contribute to individual differences in emotional experience and variations in a given person's affective experience from one circumstance to the next.

The role of affective states in personality functioning extends beyond the issues discussed in this chapter. Affective states influence cognitive processes such as decision making, recall, and the evaluation of events. Emotional states play a key role in motivation and self-regulation, especially since many self-regulatory efforts are attempts to maintain or avoid particular emotional states. Emotional states may be so aversive that people exclude them from their conscious experiences. Emotional experience thus continues to figure in our discussions as we turn to questions of conscious and unconscious processes and then to issues of motivation and self-regulation.

# CHAPTER ELEVEN

# Unconscious Processes and Conscious Experience

To many observers, the study of unconscious psychological processes is personality psychology's greatest contribution to scientific knowledge. Advances in science usually involve increments in the understanding of well-known phenomena (Kuhn, 1962). Discovering entirely new phenomena is rare. Unearthing new phenomena of importance to society at large is rarer still. Evidence that psychological experience can be shaped by forces of which we are unaware (e.g., Janet, 1889; Freud, 1900) was that rarest of cases in which the field produced startling findings that altered society's view of human nature.

Evidence of unconscious influences was surprising, of course, because of the obvious importance of conscious self-reflection in human affairs. The ability to reflect on the world, ourselves, and our very capacity for self-reflection is our species' most distinguishing characteristic. The obviousness of self-reflective capabilities should not cause the personality psychologist to neglect a careful analysis of conscious experience. Subjective, private experience (Singer & Kolligian, 1987) is a critical phenomenon unto itself, and is a human capability that enables people to shape the nature of their life circumstances and to influence the course of their personal development (Bandura, 1997; Rychlak, 1997).

This chapter reviews developments in the study of unconscious processes and conscious experience. After a brief historical overview, we outline important conceptual distinctions among conscious and unconscious phenomena. We then focus on unconscious processes in personality functioning. As we will see, some unconscious processes involve motivated states of psychological defense. People strive to protect themselves from full awareness of information that is threatening to the self. Other unconscious processes, however, have nothing to do with motivation or defense of the ego. In *implicit cognition*, thinking occurs outside of conscious awareness for reasons that simply reflect the overall architecture of the human mind–brain. After this discussion of unconscious processes, we turn to the study of conscious experience. We consider individual differences in the tendency to reflect on oneself, implications of these differences for physical and mental health, and the general question of why it is so difficult to control the flow of consciousness.

## THE ELUSIVE UNCONSCIOUS AND SELF-EVIDENT CONSCIOUSNESS – OR VICE VERSA?

Psychology's views of conscious and unconscious processes have changed dramatically during the past century. Psychological labora-tories of the late 19th century studied conscious experience. "Unconscious mentation" was virtually an oxymoron. Investigators of the late 20th century, in contrast, provide convincing evidence that significant mental phenomena occur outside of conscious awareness. They struggle, however, to define consciousness, assess variations in conscious states, and explain how brain processes give rise to phenomenal experience.

## Unconscious Processes

Psychological interest in the unconscious predates the landmark analyses of Freud (1900). Two centuries earlier, Leibniz contended that our experience is influenced by perceptions that occur outside of awareness (see Merikle & Reingold, 1992). Nineteenth-century writers prior to Freud suggested that sexual impulses of which patients are unaware contribute to neuroses (Ellenberger, 1970; Perry & Laurence, 1984). Janet's (1889) analysis of how ideas and emotions can split off from consciousness and operate outside of awareness were developed somewhat before Freud's hydraulic model of unconscious processing. Nonetheless, Freud's contributions remain of everlasting value. He uncovered phenomena of fundamental importance, developed a theory to explain them, and indirectly inspired alternative theories of dynamic mental functioning. Although elements of psychoanalytic theory fare poorly in the light of contemporary knowledge, others' basic psychoanalytic postulates either have received support or continue to suggest promising research directions that may be overlooked from other theoretical perspectives (Westen, 1991, 1998). As we discussed in chapter 2, personality psychology is forever indebted to psychoanalysis for identifying fundamental scientific problems that previously had been overlooked.

Psychoanalysts' theories of unconscious process were met with skepticism in academia. It proved difficult to document the existence of unconscious phenomena in the laboratory. Researchers thus questioned whether significant psychological phenomena occur outside of awareness. A series of intellectual movements after World War II, however, gradually rekindled scientific interest in the unconscious. The New Look research program of Bruner and Postman (1947) promoted a constructivist view of perceptual processes and thereby fostered the systematic analysis of defensive processes in perception (Bruner, 1992). In the 1970's and 1980's, Erdelyi (1974, 1985) and others (Bowers & Meichenbaum, 1984; Shevrin & Dickman, 1980) reconciled traditional psychodynamic concepts of unconscious influences with information-processing theory. This alerted cognitive psychologists to the possibility of exploring unconscious processes without adopting untenable aspects of psychoanalytic theory, and cognitive-behavioral therapists to the possibility of understanding unconscious clinical phenomena within a cognitive framework (Meichenbaum & Gilmore, 1984). Greenwald (1992) suggests that the 1990s witnessed a third generation of research – a New Look 3. To Greenwald, this era firmly established the existence of unconscious cognition, reconciled unconscious phenomena with contemporary connectionist models of thought, but also suggested that unconscious cognition differs somewhat from traditional psychoanalytic accounts. Unconscious processes appear to be relatively simple and unsophisticated in comparison with the complex unconscious of psychoanalysis (Greenwald, 1992).

Psychology's renewed interest in unconscious processes also has been spurred by findings from neuropsychology. Skepticism about the existence of unconscious cognitive processes crumbles in the face of neuropsychological evidence that patients who are utterly lacking in conscious awareness of a stimulus nonetheless can be affected by that stimulus. For example, in the phenomenon of blind sight, individuals with damage to the visual cortex report no sensation of objects in their visual field. However, if asked to guess about the nature of such objects, their performance reveals implicit knowledge of the stimuli (Humphrey, 1984). Blind sight can be understood by reference to the neural pathways extending from the retina. Information from the retina projects to multiple brain sites

in addition to the primary visual cortex, thus enabling visual discriminations in the absence of conscious awareness (Weiskrantz, 1995).

The question, then, no longer is whether significant cognitive activity can occur outside of awareness. Instead, critical questions concern the range of phenomena that can occur unconsciously, the functions they serve, and the nature of interactions among unconscious processes and conscious experience.

**Conscious Experience**

As with the unconscious, interest in the study of consciousness also has fluctuated over the years. A century ago, psychology was equated with the study of consciousness (Wundt, 1902). James' (1890) detailed analysis of the stream of conscious experience influenced not only psychologists but also novelists who aimed to capture the flow of phenomenal experience. A few decades later, things had changed. Psychoanalysis shifted people's attention to unconscious dynamics and mechanisms. Behaviorism threw doubt on the validity of introspective data. By the time Allport wrote his classic text, he lamented that the study of consciousness had fully gone out of fashion (Allport, 1937, chapter 6).

Consciousness, too, managed a postwar comeback in personality psychology. Humanistic and phenomenological theories (e.g., Rogers, 1959) highlighted the role of conscious experience in personality functioning. However, whatever their other merits, the phenomenological theories of personality did not provide detailed analyses of the basic mechanisms underlying conscious experience. They were not theories of consciousness but theories of personal development and psychological change that placed conscious experience at center stage.

In the past decade, the study of consciousness has blossomed in disciplines outside of psychology. Philosophers, biological scientists, and physical scientists (e.g., Chalmers, 1995; Crick, 1994; Damasio, 1999; Dennett, 1991; Edelman, 1992; Humphrey, 1992) have confronted one of the great challenges to contemporary science, namely, explaining how the physicochemical mechanisms of the nervous system give rise to phenomenal experience. The analytical skills of philosophers such as Ned Block (1995) yield valuable schemes for differentiating among the varieties of conscious experience. Anthropologists and archeologists contribute to our understanding of how the capacity for conscious thought evolved in humans (Mithen, 1996). Personality and social psychologists have been a bit slower to take up questions about the origins and functions of consciousness (but see Sedikedes & Skowronski, 1997); a challenge for those who confront these issues is fully to draw on the advances already made in these other disciplines.

Other disciplines, then, seemed for a time to have usurped psychology's traditional dominance of the study of consciousness. Advances in social and cognitive psychology, however, have begun to reveal how the methodological tools of the psychologist can uniquely add to our understanding of subjective experience (Cohen & Schooler, 1997). As we saw in chapter 8, much research in social-cognitive psychology illuminates aspects of conscious experience and the relations between conscious and unconscious processes. Indeed, the study of "mental control" (Wegner & Wenzlaff, 1996), that is, the regulation of the content of one's conscious experiences, is a major theme in contemporary social psychology. Although cognitive psychology had for many years overlooked the study of subjective experience, work in this subdiscipline, too, has begun to reveal how conscious processes guide information processing and individuals' planning for action (Mandler, 1997; Schneider & Pimm-Smith, 1997).

The study of consciousness, then, is an apt context for restating a theme we developed at the outset of this text, namely, that personality psychologists must take a broad, interdisciplinary approach to their problems of interest. The role of consciousness in personality functioning and the possibility of systematic individual differences in conscious experience are best approached through an integrative perspective that incorporates other disciplines' advances in understanding the origins, nature, and functions of consciousness.

Despite some advances, science lacks a convincing answer to the most basic of questions: How is it that consciousness occurs in the first place? How, in other words, do brain systems give rise to subjective awareness of the world, i.e., to phenomenal experience? Even the impressive progress of the neurosciences fails to explain why particular brain states correspond to a particular subjective feeling (Chalmers, 1995; Papineau, 1996). Linking brain activity to conscious feeling states remains the "hard question" (Chalmers, 1995) of contemporary cognitive science. Progress on this question has been so slow that Pinker (1997) concludes his wide-ranging and otherwise optimistic survey of mental functioning by suggesting that the human brain simply "lacks the cognitive equipment" (p. 561) to solve the problem of how neural events create conscious experience, much as the brain of the chimpanzee lacks the cognitive equipment to solve arithmetic problems.

In the past hundred years, then, conscious and unconscious processes have effectively reversed roles. A century ago, researchers confidently gathered data on conscious experience, but unconscious processes were shrouded in mystery. Nowadays, the existence of unconscious phenomena is well established and moderately well understood, but identifying the mechanisms that give rise to phenomenal, conscious experience remains a challenge.

## Paradigm Shifts in Psychology's Understanding of Conscious and Unconscious Processes

These changing views of conscious and unconscious processes reflect broader changes in psychology's understanding of mental functioning. If one equates thinking with consciousness, the existence of conscious thought requires little explanation. A century ago, then, the question was whether, and why, significant cognitive events could occur *un*consciously. Freud provided an answer. Segregating emotionally charged ideas in a psychological system that was not available to awareness enabled individuals to protect themselves from painful intrapsychic conflict (Freud, 1911).

Thanks largely to the development of cognitive psychology, our field now has a very different view of unconscious mechanisms. As reviewed by Kihlstrom (1990), developments in this field indicated ever larger roles for unconscious processes in mental life. In the multistore information-processing models of the 1960s (Atkinson & Shiffrin, 1971), nonconscious processes were limited in scope to preattentional processing of stimuli of the sort identified in dichotic listening paradigms (Treisman, 1967). Subsequent information-processing architectures (e.g., Anderson, 1983) suggested that people may lack conscious access to a vast range of procedural knowledge. Work on modular mental mechanisms has begun to indicate that a vast range of complex skills can be performed in the absence of conscious, verbally reportable knowledge of one's activities. For example, Karmiloff-Smith (1994) posits that expertise in a domain develops as people represent and re-represent knowledge. She posits four levels of mental representation; skilled action is possible at each level, but the ability to consciously, verbally reflect on one's skills is only possible if one achieves the final, most advanced representation level. Relatedly, Mithen's (1996) analysis of the evolution of mind suggests that our ancestors were able to perform complex skills that are difficult for modern humans (e.g., the construction of stone hand axes) while lacking the ability to consciously reflect on these skills. The lack of reflective capabilities prevented them from optimally adapting their skills to changing environmental challenges (Mithen, 1996).

The recognition that much complex thought can occur outside of conscious awareness naturally changes the questions one asks. The current zeitgeist makes unconscious cognition an obvious fact of life and forces questions about the evolution, mechanisms, and functions of consciousness.

## DIFFERENTIATING AMONG CONSCIOUS AND UNCONSCIOUS PHENOMENA

It is necessary but not sufficient to distinguish between the unconscious and consciousness. This distinction is insufficient because these terms do not refer to two unitary systems; instead, each refers to a variety of distinct phenomena. Useful taxonomies of unconscious and conscious states have been based on psychoanalytic theory (Freud, 1900), information-processing analyses (e.g., Kihlstrom, 1984; Erdelyi, 1985), and connectionist models of cognition, the last of which have the advantage of easily capturing the fact that independent streams of conscious and unconscious cognition can occur in parallel (Greenwald, 1992). In the following, we draw on these various perspectives while considering distinctions that are of particular importance to the personality psychologist.

The term *unconscious* can refer either to a quality of an idea, a region of the mind in which ideas are stored, or a mode of mental functioning. The term, in other words, has more than one meaning. This reflects the influence of Freud, who used the term somewhat differently at different times (Erdelyi, 1985). In his early accounts, Freud (1900) distinguished among aspects of mental life according to a quality that ideas possess, namely, their degree of accessibility to consciousness. His topographic model divided mental life into regions – the conscious, preconscious, and unconscious – within which ideas were differentially accessible. His later model (Freud, 1923) organized the psyche according to systems that carried out different functions and that worked according to different modes of mental processing. The id, then, was an unconscious system that functioned according to rules (primary process thought) unlike those through which people consciously deliberated on the world of reality.

More generally, as a quality of mental events, "unconsciousness" refers to the fact that material is not available to awareness. A wide variety of psychological functions can operate outside of awareness, or unconsciously. Consciousness, then, "is an experiential quality that may accompany (psychological) functions," such as perception or memory, that otherwise "can proceed outside of awareness" (Kihlstrom, 1990, p. 457). As a region, the unconscious is a place in the psyche that stores ideas that cannot, under normal circumstances, be brought into consciousness. The system *Ucs* in Freud's (1900) topographic model, which stores ideas that are kept out of consciousness to protect the psyche against mental conflict, is the paradigm case.

It is important to bear in mind that storage in an inaccessible region of mind is not the only reason why mental contents may be unavailable to consciousness. Some contents are unavailable because they are represented in a form that can not easily be articulated. Material such as grammatical rules or procedures for executing motor behaviors is inaccessible because it is not stored in declarative form (Anderson, 1983). Similarly, people may be unaware of heuristic processes that underlie social judgment (Nisbett & Wilson, 1977); this lack of awareness can cause people to give erroneous reports of their own mental states, particularly when asked about material that is no longer in working memory (Ericsson & Simon, 1980). In these instances, mental contents have the quality of being unconscious, but clearly are not part of the Freudian system *Ucs*, since they lack the emotional, conflictual features that cause ideas to become repressed in the Freudian model.

Like the unconscious, *consciousness* does not refer to a single phenomenon (Kagan, 1998b); it is not a unitary entity (Block, 1995). Indeed, we are conscious of such a wide variety of phenomena – objects that we see, feelings of cold and warmth, emotional states, internally generated mental images, etc. – that it is reasonable to ask whether states of such diversity "share any scientifically significant property" (Papineau, 1996, p. 4). The numerous subtle variations in consciousness recog-

nized in meditative practice (Goleman, 1988) only accentuate this concern.

In distinguishing among the varieties of conscious phenomena, one first must differentiate our awareness of sensations (e.g., sounds, pain) from our capacity for introspective self-reflection on these sensations and other mental states (Humphrey, 1984; Mithen, 1996). Edelman (1992), for example, distinguishes "primary consciousness" (simple awareness of things in the world) from "higher-order consciousness" (which involves a sense of self). N. Block (1995) distinguishes phenomenal from access consciousness. "Phenomenal consciousness" is the experience of sensations, perceptions, feelings, and desires; it is "consciousness *of*" (Block, 1995, p. 232) something. "Access consciousness" enables us to subject something to deliberate reasoning. It involves the representation of information that can be used in reasoning, language, and the deliberate control of behavior.

In addition to phenomenal and access consciousness, Block distinguishes two further mental states. "Monitoring consciousness" does not involve sensations and feelings but the higher-order thought that one is experiencing those feelings. Finally, "self-consciousness" involves having a mental representation of the self and using this knowledge to reason about oneself.

Kagan (1998b) also suggests that the natural-language term *consciousness* incorporates at least four phenomena. He suggests the terms "sensory awareness" to refer to phenomenal awareness of sensations (taste, pain, etc.) and "cognitive awareness" to refer to people's meaningful reflection on either sensations or internal symbols ("that tastes good," "that hurts," "this plan won't work"). "Awareness of control" refers to the people's ability to be cognizant of alternative courses of action and to choose (or inhibit) a particular behavioral response. Finally, Kagan uses the term "awareness of one's features" to capture the aspects of consciousness that are tapped by awareness of one's social attributes and one's status as social object. Kagan (1998b) supports these distinctions in part by noting that the different forms of consciousness emerge at different points in the course of child development.

Kagan does not explicitly distinguish awareness of one's social features versus awareness that *someone else* is reflecting on one's own social features. This distinction would add a fifth category to the suggested taxonomy of conscious experiences.

Future years should expand and solidify our understanding of the various phenomena that involve consciousness. A greater appreciation of the multifaceted nature of consciousness should prompt analyses of individual differences in conscious experience that go beyond the one or two individual-difference dimensions that traditionally have been explored (e.g., Fenigstein, Scheier, & Buss, 1975).

Multiple processes, or modes, of thought may exist along with different regions of mind. Different mental systems may operate according to different principles. As discussed in chapter 2, psychoanalytic theory differentiated primary process thought, a mode of thinking that violates logical principles of thought and in which reality and products of fantasy are indistinguishable, from secondary process thought, through which realistic plans for satisfying needs are logically formulated. Contemporary personality psychologists have offered alternatives to the traditional psychoanalytic formulation.

Epstein (1994) criticizes the psychoanalytic view on the grounds that a mental mechanism that can not distinguish fantasy from reality is so maladaptive that evolution is unlikely to have selected for it. He instead distinguishes (1) an "experiential" cognitive system, which is holistic, processes information rapidly, and is oriented toward simple pleasure–pain distinctions, from (2) a "rational" system, which processes complex symbolic information in a logical manner. Epstein and colleagues provide a "rational-experiential inventory," which taps self-reports of individual differences in the tendency to rely on intuitive versus analytic cognition (see Pacini, Muir, & Epstein, 1998).

Epstein (1994) supports the distinction between experiential and rational processes by reviewing a multiplicity of theoretical models that differentiate alternative modes of processing. These include distinctions between verbal and nonverbal mental codes (Paivio, 1969), deliberate and automatic processing (Schneider & Shiffrin, 1977), and systematic and heuristic reasoning (Chaiken, 1980). Each of these distinctions indeed suggests that the mind does not operate according to a single processing principle (see also Zajonc, 1980; Brewin, 1989). In this respect, then, these studies support Epstein's claim that cognitive processing is not a unitary phenomenon. However, it is somewhat difficult to see how these diverse cognitive and social psychological treatments map onto and thereby truly support the specific distinction between experiential and rational processes that Epstein suggests. For example, analyses of automaticity in social-cognitive processes (Bargh, 1994) indicate that there are varying *degrees* of automaticity, rather than a clear dichotomous distinction between automatic and controlled processes. More generally, given the potential diversity of modular mental systems (Fodor, 1983; Karmiloff-Smith, 1992), it is not clear why theorists would limit themselves, a priori, to positing no more than two processing modes. Harré, Clarke, and De Carlo (1985), for example, suggest three levels of mental functioning: conscious intentional thought; automatic, nonconscious procedures that are recruited in the service of conscious intentions; and a "deep structure" of mind consisting of emotions and implicit motives that partly regulate the contents of consciousness.

Neuropsychological evidence also reveals the existence of more than one mode of processing. Damasio (1994) and colleagues conclude that decision making under risk involves "two largely parallel but interacting" (Bechara, Damasio, Tranel, & Damasio, 1997, p. 1294) information pathways. One involves high-level cognitive processes, whereas the other includes peripheral physiological mechanisms that underlie intuitive, "gut" reactions. This notion receives support from a rather startling set of results. When choosing between options, people are found to make good choices and to exhibit physiological stress reactions to poor choices before they have acquired any explicit conceptual knowledge of the fact that one decision option actually is better than another (Bechara et al., 1997). Brain-damaged patients who lack emotional input into their decision processes are found to make poor choices even when they *do* have accurate conceptual knowledge of how best to proceed (Bechara et al., 1997).

LeDoux's (1996) work on the functioning of the amygdala in fear response also uncovers a physiological underpinning for multiple processing modes. In one pathway for the activation of fear, signals travel from the thalamus to high-level cortical areas and then to the amygdala. In another, information travels from the thalamus to the amygdala directly. The latter route bypasses the cortex and thus enables a rapid fear response that is not consciously mediated (LeDoux, 1996).

## DEFENSIVE PROCESSING

Even if one rejects Freud's theoretical explanation of unconscious processing, his identification of the psychological phenomena to be explained is compelling. People often find it impossible to confront emotionally painful material. Despite the long-term benefits of directly coming to terms with one's problems, people defend themselves from conflict and anxiety by banishing traumatic material from consciousness.

Starting with the work of Breuer and Freud, psychoanalysis provided psychology's first detailed account of psychological mechanisms through which people defend themselves from anxiety (Breuer & Freud, 1895; Freud, 1900; A. Freud, 1936). Freud observed that his patients resisted therapeutic progress when an important breakthrough seemed imminent. He interpreted this resistance as evidence that patients were defending themselves against the return of anxiety-provoking material to consciousness. By extension, he reasoned that defensive processing was responsible for the material becoming unavailable to consciousness in the first place. The apparent changes in personality that

resulted when clients did consciously recall and work through such material provided vivid testimony to the enduring influence of psychological content that had been repressed.

The psychodynamic analysis of defense mechanisms provides important insights to both the therapist and the personality theorist. Continuities in personality from childhood to adulthood can be understood in terms of styles of defense that develop relatively early in life and remain stable through the life course (Block & Block, 1980). The coherence among seemingly diverse acts can be understood by reference to unconscious motives that express themselves in a myriad of different ways, depending on the countervailing forces of ego defense processes (e.g., both an unwanted sexual advance and a creative work of art could be products of repressed sexual desire against which the ego is defending). Psychoanalysis, then, shows how the stability, variability, and coherence of psychological experience can be understood by reference to interactions among multiple underlying processes, including emotional drives and ego mechanisms that defend against them. In this regard, psychodynamic theory resembles social-cognitive theory (Westen, 1991). Both approaches embrace a strategy of explanation in which the coherence of social behavior is explained in terms of multiple underlying causal mechanisms, which may give rise both to general personality patterns and to idiosyncratic personal tendencies.

### Repression and Repressive Coping Style

■ *Clinical Evidence.* Clinical cases, which were the primary database for psychoanalytic theory, provide evidence of defensive processing that is compelling but not ultimately convincing. When a client reports having recalled traumatic material that seemingly had long been forgotten, this indeed may be a return of repressed memory. There are other possibilities, however. Rather than having surmounted an unconscious motive to repress the material, the client simply may have overcome the normal difficulty associated with accessing long forgotten material. Material from one's past that is rarely accessed has low associative strength. Recalling such material may require the prolonged periods of relatively undistracted, effortful concentration that are afforded by the clinical setting.

Unlike mundane information, the recall of traumatic material that seemingly has been repressed evokes intense emotional arousal. The presence of arousal, however, does not force one to conclude that a motive to avoid aversive emotions was responsible for the difficulty in recalling the material. Recall may involve "cold" retrieval processes. Once recalled, reflection on the past trauma could trigger the emotional response.

Freud recognized this interpretive difficulty. His inferences about repression were not based merely on clients' failure to recall material but on their tendency to resist the progress of therapy just as material was being recovered. This resistance indicated that clients were motivated to protect themselves from unconscious material, specifically, from the conflict between wishes represented in the unconscious and the demands of reality. Even compelling clinical reports of resistance and repression, however, provide only equivocal evidence that material has been repressed. Clinical reports raise three difficulties of interpretation. First, it often is unclear whether clients have overcome a resistance against admitting material to themselves or to their therapist. Clients may be reporting information that previously was accessible to them but was deemed too traumatic or embarrassing to report (Erdelyi, 1985). Research employing signal detection techniques indicates that many apparent cases of the recovery of repressed memories actually involve shifts in the decision to report material that, in fact, had previously been accessible (Erdelyi, 1985).

A second problem is the difficulty of distinguishing true from false memories. The client may not be recalling a long-buried memory but merely constructing a mental image that only appears to be a record of his or her past. This possibility is heightened by the finding that false memories can be created merely by social cues that merely suggest to individuals that a particular episode had occurred to them in their distant past (Loftus, 2000). The third and perhaps most obvious limitation is that evidence from case reports rests heavily on subjective interpretations by the clinician. Clinical cases generally provide no independent measure of the working of a particular defense mechanism. Although defense mechanisms may best be construed as hypothetical constructs whose functioning can only be inferred indirectly (Smith and Hentschel (1993), it remains that objective indices of some sort are required to convince the skeptic that defensive processing – and not simple forgetting, report bias, or false memory construction – is actually at work.

Recognizing these difficulties, psychologists since Jung (1918) have pursued experimental evidence of repression and other defense mechanisms. As we review some of this work, the reader should bear in mind that laboratory evidence and traditional analytic formulations are only tenuously connected. Psychoanalysis addresses the recovery of long-buried emotional material of enormous personal significance. Laboratory studies are brief encounters, which can not possibly evoke such significant material. Any failure to uncover defensive processes in the laboratory thus may reflect a limitation of laboratory methods. Conversely, when positive laboratory evidence is obtained, the results may relate only indirectly to psychodynamic theory. As we will see, laboratory research provides abundant evidence of unconscious processing but relatively little direct support for traditional psychoanalytic accounts.

■ *Laboratory Evidence.* For much of this century, laboratory evidence for the existence of repression was weak. Promising studies often were found to suffer from methodological flaws. Holmes (1974) revealed such problems in his review of research on memory and ego threat. He identified processes other than threat-induced repression that could account for the available findings. Rather than evoking repression, ego threat could impair memory simply by functioning as a distractor. People's relatively slow response to threatening material on word association tasks could reflect the relatively lower associative strength of the ego-threatening words (Holmes, 1974). In light of these confusing results, Holmes concluded that there was "no research evidence to support . . . the theory of repression" (1974, p. 649).

During the past quarter of a century, things have changed. "Repression has returned" (Egloff & Krohne, 1996, p. 1318). Well-controlled laboratory research reveals that people's psychological experiences indeed are affected by material that they banish from awareness to protect their self-image. Actually, findings suggest that *some* people's experiences are affected in this manner. Much research veers away from traditional psychoanalytic theory, which posits that all individuals are likely to engage in some degree of repression as a result of universal mental mechanisms and psychological experiences. Instead, many contemporary investigators focus on a subset of persons who are particularly prone to repress threatening material or who exhibit a "repressive coping style."

■ *Individual Differences and Repressive Coping Style.* People cope with anxiety in different ways. Some dwell on their feelings and openly discuss their personal concerns. Others may not admit feelings of anxiety to others or even to themselves. Since suppressed thoughts may periodically reenter consciousness and create emotional distress (Wegner & Wenzlaff, 1996), those who try to repress anxiety-provoking content may in the long run heighten their own psychological and physical distress (Davison and Pennebaker, 1996).

Personality psychologists seek to assess individual differences in people's sensitization to, versus repression of, anxiety-provoking material. One strategy is to measure the degree to which people experience anxiety through self-report (e.g., Byrne, 1964). People who report that they experience little anxiety and are not bothered by everyday stress could be seen to be repressing negative emotions. Although of some value, the strategy of

directly assessing repression versus sensitization has a significant limitation. Self-reports of repression–sensitization are not psychometrically distinct from self-reports of anxiety proneness or neuroticism (Abbott, 1972). People who score as repressors, then, may be repressing anxious material or simply may be experiencing little anxiety in their day-to-day lives.

Weinberger, Schwartz, and Davidson (1979) suggested an alternative scheme for identifying individuals who chronically repress stressful emotional experiences. To distinguish repressive tendencies from low levels of anxiety, they employed both an anxiety measure (Bendig, 1956; Taylor, 1953) and the Marlowe-Crowne Social Desirability Scale (Crowne & Marlowe, 1964), which taps people's tendency to respond defensively to threats to their self-image. People who reported experiencing little anxiety and did not show defensive tendencies on the Marlowe-Crowne were labeled low anxious. In contrast, people who obtained equivalent anxiety scores but high defensive scores on the Marlowe-Crowne were labeled repressors. Finally, a high anxious group consisted of individuals who rated themselves as anxious and were not defensive. These three groups participated in an experimental task designed to detect dissociations between consciously controllable and uncontrollable measures of anxiety. They completed a phrase association task containing neutral, aggressive, and sexual content. Their speed in completing the phrases and level of autonomic arousal during the task were recorded. Weinberger at al. (1979) found that repressors and low anxious individuals – groups with equivalent scores on self-report measures of anxiety – differed significantly in anxious arousal during the task. Repressors experienced greater autonomic arousal than the other groups and also took longer to complete the phrases. Although they described themselves as calm, repressors were shown to be particularly prone to anxiety under conditions of threat.

Much subsequent work has employed the assessment strategy proposed by Weinberger et al. (1979). Repressors commonly are found to dissociate physiological arousal from conscious self-perception. Their underlying anxiety is revealed, for example, in electrodermal responses (Gudjonsson, 1981) and facial muscle movements indicative of anxiety (Asendorf & Scherer, 1983).

Repressors' tendency to dissociate verbal reports and physiological arousal varies across social contexts. These variations can provide insight into repressors' motives for denying their anxious tendencies. Newton and Contrada (1992) asked undergraduate women to give a speech describing an undesirable personality characteristic of theirs. Speeches were given in either a private setting, in which only the experimenter was present, or a public situation, which involved a small audience of observers. Measures included cardiovascular activity during the speech and self-reports of emotional experience before and after the task. The private versus public manipulation influenced degrees of dissociation between physiological and verbal responses only among the repressors. When facing an audience, repressors' heart rate increased but their self-reported emotional experience did not. In the private setting, repressors did not experience a dissociation between physiology and self-reports. Unlike the repressors, people who described themselves as high in anxiety reported significant increases in negative affect after giving the speech in either the public or the private context (Newton & Contrada, 1992). Repressors, then, may primarily be motivated to project a calm self-image to others.

Work by Baumeister and Cairns (1992) also highlights the self-presentational concerns of repressors. They studied how repressors cope with negative personal feedback. When both they themselves and others were aware of the negative feedback, repressors spent more time attending to the information than did nonrepressors. When the negative feedback was available only to themselves, the reading times of repressors and nonrepressors did not differ (Baumeister & Cairns, 1992). Individuals categorized as repressors, then, appear to have the goal of protecting themselves from negative social evaluation rather than merely protecting themselves from conscious awareness of their weaknesses.

Repressors' tendency to avoid the conscious experience of threatening material is evident not only in dissociations between verbal reports and physiology but also in their memory for personal emotional experiences. When asked to recall childhood memories, repressors recalled fewer negative experiences than truly low anxious individuals and slightly fewer negative experiences than people who reported being high in anxiety (Davis & Schwartz, 1987). Repressors, then, seem to keep negative experiences out of conscious memory, as psychoanalytic theory would expect. However, repressors also had poorer memory for positive emotional experiences (Davis & Schwartz, 1987), which suggests that the repressive coping style is associated with a more general suppression of emotional life. Research measuring participants' latency to recall emotional experiences provides converging evidence that repressors avoid emotional material (Davis, 1987).

Why do repressors have difficulty recalling emotional experiences? The answer may lie not in retrieval processes but in the way repressors initially encode emotional encounters. Repressors may not encode emotional experiences as elaborately as nonrepressors (Hansen & Hansen, 1988). They may encode an event in terms of a single dominant emotion, whereas nonrepressors may be more sensitive to the rich array of emotions evoked by an encounter. When asked to recall episodes associated with the emotions of anger, sadness, fear, and embarrassment and to rate the degree to which they experienced each of a series of 10 discrete emotions in the recalled episode (cf. Smith & Ellsworth, 1985), repressors reported experiencing similar levels of the dominant emotion but lower levels of the nondominant affects (Hansen & Hansen, 1988). When asked to appraise the emotional content of facial expressions, repressors recognized the dominant emotion that was displayed but tended not to infer the presence of secondary emotions for example, they saw an angry face as being angry, but did not also detect traces of sadness or fear (Hansen, Hansen, & Shantz, 1992). When given negative performance feedback, repressors experienced a strong dominant emotion but lower levels of nondominant emotions (Egloff & Krohne, 1996). Shimmack & Hartmann (1997) have found that repressors differ significantly from nonrepressors in their encoding of unpleasant experiences and that encoding differences largely explain later differences in the recall of unpleasant experiences. Repressors' failure to recall negative events, then, may result not from a repression of memories but from the fact that they are less likely to encode events as negative and therefore less likely to experience negative emotions in the first place.

Repressors engage in additional cognitive strategies that make them relatively unaware of their own negative emotions. Repressors tend to distract themselves from negative emotions by dwelling on positive material; this coping strategy tends to isolate the negative in memory (Boden & Baumeister, 1997). Repressors respond more slowly than individuals who are low in anxiety to ambiguous material that is potentially threatening, which suggests that they exert effort to distract themselves from or to reinterpret negative material (Hock, Krohne, & Kaiser, 1996).

In summary, a large body of work indicates that individuals who are categorized as repressors tend to experience higher levels of anxiety than they admit to others and to engage in cognitive strategies that make them less aware of their own negative emotions. This research constitutes an important advance in the study of defensive processing. Yet it still leaves some fundamental questions unanswered. We know more about what repressors tend to do than about who they are. Existing work can be seen as "atheoretical (in that) there is no explanation of the difference in underlying motivation of repressors and nonrepressors" (Mendolia, Moore, & Tesser, 1996, p. 856)." Taking this point further, there is no empirical support for the premise that one should search for "the difference" between repressors and nonrepressors in the first place. Although extant research describes the average response tendencies of the class of persons labeled as repressors, it does not tell us why this group can be treated as an equivalence class in the first place (see Bem, 1983). The population currently classified as repressors may actually be a diverse group characterized by multiple motives, goals, and affective predispositions. Rather than merely charting the average tendencies of this group, it also might be valuable to examine cognitive and motivational mechanisms that contribute to dissociations between physiology and self-report for all individuals under certain stressful circumstances. A process-based approach might provide insight not only into average individual differences but also into intraindividual variation in the tendency to avoid versus attend to unpleasant events (cf. Chiu, Hong, Mischel, & Shoda, 1995).

## Development of Defense Mechanisms

Different defense mechanisms may vary in their importance for the individual at different stages of life. Early in life, children may rely on relatively simple strategies of psychological defense, such as the denial of unacceptable impulses or threats to self-image. Later in life, people may defend the self through more complex strategies, such as sublimation, that foster socially useful goals. Different defenses, then, are seen to vary along a developmental continuum, with some defensive strategies, (e.g., sublimation) being seen as more mature than others (e.g., denial) (Cramer, 1991; Cramer & Block, 1998; Vaillant, 1992).

Cross-sectional and longitudinal data provide converging evidence of developmental trends in the use of defense mechanisms. Cross-sectionally, preschoolers are found to use denial more often than children of elementary school age or adolescents. Compared with preschoolers, older children rely more heavily on projection and identification (Cramer, 1997). Stronger evidence of developmental shifts derives from longitudinal research. In a 2-year longitudinal study of children ranging from 6.5 to 9.5 years of age, a measure of defenses was based on stories children told in response to Thematic Apperception Test cards (Cramer, 1997). From ages 6 to 9, story content indicative of both projection and identification increased, whereas story content indicative of denial decreased. It should be noted, however, that it is difficult to determine in these paradigms whether developmental changes reflect shifts in the use of defenses per se or changes in overall intellectual capacities.

The tendency to use immature defensive strategies in adulthood is somewhat predictable from defensive tendencies in childhood, although the longitudinal relations vary by gender (Cramer & Block, 1998). Participants were studied at ages 3 to 4 and at age 23 as part of the Block and Block (1980) longitudinal study of ego development. Childhood psychological disturbance (as measured via Q-sort ratings made by nursery school teachers) predicted the use of denial in young adulthood (as indexed by Thematic Apperception Test stories) among males, but child and adult personality characteristics were unrelated among females.

Historically, reseach on the development of defense mechanisms has tended to employ correlational methods that relate defensive tendencies in childhood or adulthood to other psychosocial variables. An interesting recent development in the study of psychological defense is the application of theoretical models and associated experimental methods from the study of social cognition to the problem of defensive information processing.

## Social-Cognitive Bases of Defense: Transference and Projection

Researchers in social cognition suggest that psychodynamic phenomena can be "demystified" (Andersen, Glassman, Chen, & Cole, 1995, p. 42) if they can be analyzed as a product of well-understood information-processing mechanisms. Research on the defensive phenomena of transference and of projection illustrate the value of such an approach.

Andersen and colleagues (e.g., Chen & Andersen, 1999) posit that transference can be understood as a product of basic social-cognitive principles of knowledge activation (Higgins, 1996a). In transference, aspects of a significant individual from one's past are applied to, or "transferred" to, a new person. Rather than attributing this phenomenon to drive reduction processes, Andersen and colleagues posit that mental representations of significant others constitute chronically accessible knowledge that guides perceptions of, and memory for, newly encountered persons (Andersen et al. 1995). As with other forms of highly accessible knowledge (see chapter 8), people tend to "go beyond the information given" (Bruner, 1957b). They infer that the new individuals possess characteristics of prior persons, whose features are cognitively activated in the new encounter.

Andersen and colleagues combine idiographic and nomothetic research procedures in their investigations of the social-cognitive underpinnings of transference. In an initial experimental session, participants generate sentences that describe a significant other, plus a nonsignificant acquaintance who serves as an experimental control. In a subsequent session, participants are exposed to written descriptions of target persons. These descriptions include an idiographically crafted depiction of an individual who is designed to resemble in some manner the significant other. Participants then complete a recognition memory test, which is analyzed for false positivity, that is, the tendency to infer that the novel target person possesses features that actually are characteristics of the significant other.

Andersen and colleagues find that people are prone to false positives when target persons resemble significant others but not when they resemble less significant acquaintances (Andersen & Cole, 1990). Priming knowledge of the significant others heightens the tendency to falsely infer their characteristics in others; knowledge of significant others, however, is so chronically accessible that false positives are found even in the absence of primes (Andersen et al., 1995). People transfer onto newly encountered individuals characteristics of both liked and disliked significant others. Feelings about their significant others shape people's emotional reactions to, and desire for emotional closeness with, new acquaintances (Andersen & Baum, 1994; Andersen, Reznik, & Manzella, 1996). Recent findings indicate that idiographically identified stimuli can trigger transference processes without conscious awareness (Glassman & Andersen, 1999).

Mental representations of significant others and of the self are linked in memory (e.g., Baldwin, 1992, 1999). Features of a newly encountered person that activate thoughts about a significant other thus may activate thoughts about the self. In this way, the presence of others may momentarily alter our self-image, or the contents of our "working self-concept" (Markus & Wurf, 1987). Hinkley and Andersen (1996) tested these ideas by having participants describe liked and disliked significant others, as well as their own behavioral tendencies when with these people. In a later session, participants read about novel target persons who resembled either the liked or disliked other. Participants then described themselves. The characteristics of the novel target influenced participants' own self-concept. Participants' self-descriptions tended to overlap with the behavioral tendencies that they typically display when in the presence of the liked or disliked significant other who happened to resemble the novel target person (Hinkley & Andersen, 1996).

The work of Andersen and colleagues, then, provides experimental corroboration for the general notion that people transfer onto new acquaintances thoughts and feelings about people who previously played significant roles in their life (Freud, 1912; Sullivan, 1953). However, rather than merely corroborating previous clinical intuitions, Andersen's work suggests that transference is a more widespread phenomenon than psychoanalytic accounts suggest. Transference is not limited to the therapeutic setting but instead includes features in everyday social interaction. People

commonly mistakenly attribute psychological characteristics possessed by one person to another. For example, when perceivers are informed by a communicator of the personality traits of a third individual, at a later time they may infer that the communicator him- or herself possesses the given traits (Skowronski, Carlston, Mae, & Crawford, 1998).

A similar approach to the analysis of defensive information processing is adopted by Newman, Duff, and Baumeister (1997), who analyze social-cognitive processes underlying the phenomenon of projection. In projection, people perceive that others possess characteristics that they wish to deny in themselves. Newman et al. suggest that the tendency to project one's own undesired characteristics onto others reflects the chronic accessibility (Higgins & King, 1981) of the undesired feature. Specifically, when people happen to be reminded of an undesirable characteristic of theirs, they may try to suppress thoughts about the attribute. As we discuss in detail later in this chapter, such thought suppression often fails and ironically ends up raising the cognitive accessibility of the attribute in memory (Wegner & Wenzlaff, 1996). The highly accessible attribute then naturally comes to mind as people interpret the actions of others. People tend to assimilate others' actions to the highly accessible undesired construct, resulting in the phenomenon we know as projection.

Data from individual-difference and experimental paradigms provide converging evidence for this model (Newman et al., 1997). Individual differences were examined by comparing nonrepressors with repressors, who should be particularly likely to attempt thought suppression and thus should be prone to projection. A preliminary session identified idiographically relevant threatening characteristics for each participant by asking participants to list personality attributes that they strongly wished not to possess. In a subsequent session, participants were exposed to written descriptions of ambiguous behaviors that could be interpreted in terms either of one of their threatening traits or of a more positive personality characteristic. When the ambiguous behaviors potentially represented a threatening trait, repressors were more likely than nonrepressors to judge that others' behavior in fact did reflect the undesired attribute. The undesired self-feature, in other words, guided repressors' interpretations of others' actions. Repressors did not always make negative interpretations of others, however. They interpreted others' behavior in a relatively charitable manner when their actions were not relevant to a personality characteristic that was personally threatening (Newman et al., 1997).

In an experimental test, Newman et al. (1997) exposed research participants to false negative feedback on two personality attributes. They then asked participants to try to suppress thoughts about one of the two attributes while they discussed the other trait dimension. Subsequently, participants viewed a videotape that depicted a somewhat anxious-looking individual, whom they rated on a series of trait dimensions. Participants were found to project the suppressed trait onto the target person. Although they did not rate the target more negatively on other trait dimensions, they did judge that the target possessed the personally relevant negative characteristic that they had tried to suppress. No differences between repressors and nonrepressors were found here. The instructions to suppress thoughts, then, temporarily turned everyone into a repressor, that is, both groups engaged in projection (Newman et al., 1997).

The work of Andersen, Newman, and colleagues provides a valuable general lesson for those who wish to study unconscious processes and psychological defense. Rather than focusing exclusively on individual-difference tendencies (cf. Weinberger et al., 1979), these investigators build their work on underlying causal models of general psychological processes that give rise to a given defensive phenomenon. These theoretical efforts have two major benefits. First, the theoretical models indicate how defensive tendencies can be manipulated experimentally. One thus can obtain experimental support for one's theory.

Second, they enable one to address not only individual differences but also intraindividual variations in defensive processing via a common theoretical language (also see Higgins, 1999). Variations in the tendency to engage in a given defensive process at a given point in time can reflect either the individual's chronically accessible knowledge or situational activation of knowledge (see chapter 9).

## Inhibition, Expression, and Health

*I was angry with my friend:*
*I told my wrath, my wrath did end.*
*I was angry with my foe:*
*I told it not. My wrath did grow.*

– Blake

Contemporary research confirms the intuitions of the poet William Blake. Upsetting ideas that we keep to ourselves tend to endure in the psyche. Emotional experiences that we discuss with others plague us less in the long run (Pennebaker, 1997; Smyth, 1998).

Evidence that the expression of emotional experiences reduces long-term stress derives from a research paradigm developed by Pennebaker (1989, 1997). Individuals compose narratives in which they discuss emotional issues of great personal importance. Participants often are directed to write about experiences that were traumatic and that they have not discussed with others. It is hypothesized that "confessing" these experiences (Pennebaker, 1989) will improve mental and physical health.

Pennebaker & Beall (1986) asked college students to write about a traumatic incident on each of four consecutive days, with writing sessions held in a solitary setting that encouraged participants to confront the traumatic experience in detail. Their dependent measure was an index of physical health, namely, the frequency of their visits to an on-campus health clinic. In this study, the investigators varied the level and type of personal disclosure that students included in their essays. Whereas some participants described both the facts of the trauma and their own emotional experiences during the episode, others described merely the facts of the events or only their emotional reactions. In a control condition, participants narrated a trivial event from their past. Discussing the combination of facts and feelings associated with a pent-up trauma improved health. Unlike all other conditions, participants who wrote about the facts plus the feelings associated with a previously undisclosed trauma experienced fewer health center visits in the months following the writing of their narratives (Pennebaker & Beall, 1986; also see Pennebaker, Colder, & Sharp, 1990).

Discussing emotional experiences has been shown to influence not only the frequency of physician visits but also physiological processes that directly contribute to health (Pennebaker, 1997). People who disclose deeply personal information exhibit lower skin conductance levels while talking about their experiences than do those who fail to disclose such material (Pennebaker, Hughes, & O'Heeron, 1987). The disclosure of personal information can enhance immune system functioning, as evidenced by lower levels of viral activity found among individuals who cognitively confront stressful events (Esterling et al., 1994). Further evidence derives from work that directly taps immune system functioning by taking blood samples and assessing circulating lymphocyte levels. Writing about emotional material increased lymphocyte levels. In contrast, instructions to suppress autobiographical material lowered some lymphocyte counts; somewhat surprisingly, this occurred whether people were suppressing thoughts of traumatic or of relatively trivial material (Petrie, Booth, & Pennebaker, 1998).

Writing about stressful experiences also has been shown to improve symptoms of asthma and rheumatoid arthritis (Smyth, Stone, Hurewitz, & Kaell, 1999). As compared with individuals who wrote about emotionally neutral issues, asthma and arthritis patients who were asked to write about the most stressful experience of their lives improved, respectively, on measures of lung functioning and self-reports of arthritic disease severity.

Although the link from expressing experiences to improving health is relatively well established, the mental mechanisms responsible for this phenomenon are not well understood. Pennebaker (1989) originally proposed that inhibiting the negative emotions associated with a traumatic experience takes effort that puts a strain on physiological systems. Confessing a personal trauma, then, should reduce the need for inhibition and thereby reduce stress. Unfortunately, this hypothesis is contradicted by the findings that confessing a personal trauma has health benefits even when individuals have discussed the experience with others previously (Greenberg & Stone, 1992), and when they write about imaginary traumas that they have never experienced (Greenberg, Wortman, & Stone, 1996). The assumption that the disinhibition of negative emotion is the critical factor in improved health is contradicted by the finding that participants who write about the *positive* aspects of personal trauma and loss may experience the same health benefits as those who write about the emotionally negative aspects of such experiences (King & Miner, 2000). Furthermore, people who ruminate excessively on their problems sometimes experience greater, not lesser, distress (Nolen-Hoeksema, McBride, & Larson, 1997).

The results force one to consider various alternatives to the original hypothesis about the link from writing to improved health. One possibility is that the writing task, by repeatedly exposing people to a past trauma, simply serves to extinguish negative emotional response (Bootzin, 1997). Another is that writing improves health by increasing people's understanding of traumatic events they have experienced. By expressing a traumatic episode in language, people may achieve a coherent understanding of the causes and consequences of an experience that previously was not well understood (Pennebaker, 1997). They may find meaning in the event, which can improve coping (Taylor, 1983). Finally, the writing experience may boost people's perceived self-efficacy for controlling their emotions, which may prompt greater efforts to self-regulate affect and subsequent health benefits (see Greenberg et al., 1996; King & Miner, 2000). This last possibility is promising in that the effects of perceived self-efficacy on immune system functioning are established (Wiedenfeld et al., 1990).

Whatever the precise mechanisms, research in this area speaks to people's potential to control their physical and emotional well-being. The effects of trauma are not immutable. People can agentically reduce the aftermath of trauma by engaging in activities that give them a deeper understanding of their emotional experiences.

## Defensive Processing: Summary

In evaluating contemporary work on unconscious defensive processes, three questions may be asked: Is there unequivocal evidence of their existence? Are the mechanisms underlying them understood? Does the evidence support the psychoanalytic model of defensive processing that launched this field of study? The answers appear to be yes, somewhat, and no.

Regarding the "yes," the well-controlled research paradigms we have reviewed, plus others that we have not had space to cover (e.g., Sackheim & Gur, 1985), establish that personally significant material is kept out of consciousness because people are motivated to avoid conflict and emotional upset and to maintain a consistent self-image. Regarding underlying mechanisms, we say they are somewhat understood for two reasons. On the positive side, the field is beginning to see process models of defensive processing (e.g., Newman et al., 1997), which firmly integrate this area of investigation with psychology's broader understanding of cognitive structures and processes and the motivated nature of social thinking (Kruglanski, 1989; Kunda, 1990). On the other hand, the processes underlying some of the best known phenomena in the field – confession versus inhibition of emotional experiences, individual differences in repressive coping style – remain poorly understood. Finally, we evaluate psychoanalytic theory negatively

primarily because of a lack of evidence. Investigators have not disproved psychoanalysis so much as they have disregarded it. With rare exceptions (e.g., Silverman, Bronstein, & Mendelsohn, 1976), researchers have not employed experimental stimuli that contain the sort of conflictual sexual and aggressive content that psychoanalysis sees people as defending against. Of course, even in the absence of such content, one finds evidence of defensive processing. Psychological defense, then, does not require direct activation of the sexual and aggressive motives and mechanisms posited by psychoanalysis. As is often the case in personality theory, the major empirical problem for psychoanalysis is not that it makes specific predictions that are contradicted by research findings but that research findings reveal important phenomena that would not have been uncovered had one adhered to the traditional analytic model.

One need not explain defensive processing by invoking a set of psychological mechanisms that is exclusively dedicated to protecting the ego against the release into consciousness of unacceptable emotional feelings. Instead, defensive processing can be understood in terms of general psychological principles. The work we have reviewed suggests that basic interactions among affective processes and cognitive strategies give rise to the phenomena that we label "mechanisms of defense." Lewis's (1997) theoretical analysis of psychological defense illustrates this point. In his view, defensive processing involves self-organizing cognitive-affective structures. Reciprocal interactions among negative emotional states, appraisals of emotional arousal, and alternative defensive appraisals coalesce into cognitive structures. Through repeated use, these structures become automatized. (In the language of dynamical systems theory, defensive appraisals become an "attractor.") A defense mechanism, then, is an emergent property of bottom-up reciprocal interactions over time among basic cognitive and affective processes (Lewis, 1997).

## IMPLICIT COGNITION

Of the many mental events that occur outside of awareness, only a fraction are unconscious because they elicit painful emotions. Most unconscious processes have little to do with emotion, trauma, conflict, and defense. A wide range of ordinary psychological processes can be dissociated from the stream of conscious thought and efficiently conducted outside of consciousness. These processes enable "implicit" influences on experience and action; in other words, through these processes, people's thoughts, feelings, and behaviors can be influenced by events of which people have no explicit conscious recollection (Schacter, 1987, 1996). These collections of implicit processes constitutes a "psychological unconscious – complex mental structures and processes that influence experience, thought, and action, but that are nevertheless inaccessible to phenomenal awareness" (Kihlstrom, 1990, p. 448).

### The Reality and Variety of Implicit Cognition

As we noted earlier in this chapter, much of the initial evidence for implicit cognition was derived from the study of brain-damaged individuals. It was found that their thoughts and actions could be influenced by stimuli of which they had no explicit recollection. For example, amnesia patients can learn novel motor skills while having no explicit knowledge of the information they have learned. Positron emission tomography scans document that different regions of brain are active in the execution of motor procedures versus the access of declarative information about the motor tasks (Schacter, 1996).

Although evidence involving such patients is of great interest, the personality psychologist may question whether one can generalize from these results to the personality functioning of the normal individual. Critical findings would document that the ordinary person's everyday psychological experiences can be influenced by events of which they are unaware. Research on this problem has a long history, with a rocky beginning. Work on subliminal perception conducted in the middle of the 20th century came under such forceful attack (Erikson, 1960) that most investigators abandoned the topic for years (cf. Dixon, 1971). Of the difficulties involved, a particularly thorny one was demonstrating that seemingly implicit stimuli were not, in fact, consciously noticed by any research participants. If they were, then responses that were attributed to the psychological unconscious may instead have been consciously mediated.

A number of contemporary research paradigms have directly confronted these problems and provided firm evidence of the reality of implicit cognition. One strategy for demonstrating that unconscious mechanisms, as opposed to conscious processes, mediate behavior is to devise paradigms in which unconscious and conscious have opposite effects. Jaccoby and colleagues have adopted such a strategy (Jacoby, Toth, Lindsay, & Debner, 1992). In their experimental task (Jaccoby, Woloshyn, & Kelley, 1989), participants are asked to judge whether a list of names includes those of people who are famous. Prior to evaluating the names, participants were exposed to a list of nonfamous names. In one condition, they read the nonfamous names while performing a distracting cognitive task that prevented them from processing the material deeply enough for it to be consciously accessible at a later time. A second condition provided no such distraction. Participants then received the main list of names. They were informed that if they explicitly recognized a name as having been presented previously, then the name was not famous. Within this paradigm, conscious and unconscious processes would have opposite effects. If people consciously recognize that they have seen a name previously, then they would accurately judge that it is not famous. If people recognize the name only at an implicit, unconscious level, then they would tend to judge inaccurately that it is famous, since impressions of fame would be biased by subjective familiarity. Jaccoby et al. 1989 found that nonfamous names that appeared on the preliminary list indeed were judged as famous, but only by participants in the divided-attention condition, that is, the condition in which it was more difficult to access the names consciously. This clearly suggests that judgments of fame were influenced by unconscious mechanisms rather than conscious awareness. Jaccoby et al.'s (1989) findings are consistent with research on the mere exposure effect (Zajonc, 1968, 1998), which also reveals that stimuli of which people are not consciously aware may be more impactful than stimuli that are consciously recognized (Bornstein, 1992).

Greenwald, Draine, and Abrams' (1996) "response window" paradigm provides compelling evidence of the reality of subliminal semantic activation, while simultaneously documenting severe limitations on subliminal effects. Participants make semantic judgments about a target word (e.g., they judge whether a name is male or female) during a brief "window" of time from approximately 400 to 500 msec after the presentation of the word. Before the target word is presented, participants are exposed to subliminal cognitive primes. Primes are presented very briefly (50 msec) and are visually masked to ensure that they can not be consciously attended. There are two findings of note. First, subliminal primes do influence subsequent judgments. When the semantic content of the prime and the target are congruent, participants categorize target words more accurately. Second, subliminal effects are very short-lived. If the target word occurs more than 100 msec after the prime, little or no semantic priming is found (Greenwald et al., 1996). These results suggest that subliminal perception is a real effect but a highly limited one. Claims that complex information can be learned subliminally are unwarranted (Greenwald, Spangenberg, Pratkanis, & Eskenazi, 1991).

Contemporary work not only establishes that implicit cognition exists, but reveals that a wide variety of psychological functions can occur unconsciously. In addition to perception and memory, learning and problem solving can occur outside of awareness (Kihlstrom,

1999). Stereotypes can influence social judgment without a person's conscious awareness (Greenwald & Banaji, 1995). Age stereotypes can influence motor performance (Bargh, Chen, & Burrows, 1996). Environmental cues can activate implicit goals that guide behavior in the absence of conscious mediation (Bargh, 1997; Bargh & Gollwitzer, 1994; Dijksterhuis et al., 1998).

### Implicit Individual-Difference Measures

Self-report measures of individual differences rely on explicit self-knowledge. People are asked to report directly on their tendencies, preferences, and experiences. An obvious implication of implicit cognition research is that traditional self-report strategies are limited. People may hold personal beliefs of which they are not explicitly aware. Assessing these beliefs requires indirect measures of individual differences.

Two forms of implicit individual-difference measures have received much use (Greenwald & Banaji, 1995). The first are projective tests. Although projective tests originally were based on the psychodynamic model of unconscious mental energy, their general logic dovetails with that of contemporary work on implicit cognition. Implicit beliefs may be revealed in people's construction of narratives about an ambiguous stimulus. An interesting feature of projective measures is that when used to assess motives, they may yield different results than are yielded by explicit self-report methods, probably because they tap different processes. Indeed, projective measures of motivation have proved to have significant predictive value in the domain of achievement motivation (Atkinson, 1981; McClelland, Koestner, & Weinberger, 1989). This is particularly noteworthy in view of the frequent criticisms of projective techniques (e.g., Dawes, 1994; Rorer, 1990).

A second set of techniques employs reaction-time measures (see chapter 7). These techniques are not designed to tap the contents of the free flow of thoughts as are the projective measures. Instead, they are more focused. Reaction-time techniques gauge the degree to which a particular concept (e.g., a belief about the self, another person, or a social group) is implicitly associated with another concept or is implicitly associated with positive versus negative attitudes. Semantic priming methods are a main assessment tool. A person's attitudes about a given object are revealed by the degree to which presentation of the object primes positive versus negative cognitions. Among people who holds positive attitudes toward a target, presentation of the target speeds the subsequent cognitive processing of positively valenced adjectives (Fazio et al., 1986).

An alternative procedure for measuring implicit individual differences is the implicit association test of Greenwald, McGhee, and Schwartz (1998). This technique assesses the degree to which a person implicitly associates a given attribute with one versus another concept. For example, one might be interested in whether a person associates affective pleasantness with one versus another ethnic group or associates notions of goodness with oneself versus others. To measure these associations implicitly, reaction times are measured as participants perform discrimination tasks that involve varying combinations of attributes and concepts. A discrimination task should be easier (as reflected in faster reaction times) when it combines attributes and concepts that already are associated in one's personal belief system. If, hypothetically, one likes Italians and dislikes Americans, one should be able to respond more quickly to discrimination tasks that pair Italian names (Claudio, Concetta) with positive words (cheer, honor) than discrimination tasks that pair American names (Bill, Julie) with positive words.

Findings indicate that reaction times on the implicit association test are not only a sensitive index of people's associations of attributes and concepts but are more sensitive than explicit attitude measures (Greenwald et al., 1998). In a study of white Americans' implicit attitudes toward white and black racial groups, the implicit association test detected racial bias more strongly than did explicit self-reports of race-linked beliefs. Similarly, in a comparison of Korean-American and Japanese-American students' attitudes toward these two ethnic groups, the implicit measure discriminated between the groups more strongly than did explicit self-reports. The advantage of the implicit measures surely reflects, at least in part, the fact that it is far less subject to self-presentational biases than are explicit techniques.

As Greenwald et al. (1998) note, the implicit association test is a flexible tool, which, in principle, could be used to assess any of a wide variety of beliefs about the self. Efforts of this sort could rectify social-cognitive psychology's overreliance on explicit, consciously mediated measures of cognitive content (cf. Westen, 1991).

## CONSCIOUS PROCESSES

So much complex cognitive activity can occur outside of awareness that the reader might be wondering why we have consciousness. What is the function of conscious experience? Why did consciousness evolve? What adaptive function did it serve?

Explaining the evolution of a psychological mechanism by searching for its past adaptive function is risky. The given mechanism might have evolved, not because it conferred a unique selective advantage but merely because it is a by-product of *other* mechanisms that themselves were adaptive (Gould, & Lewontin 1979). In principle, reflective consciousness could be an emergent property of interactions among other psychological processes (memory, attention, etc.), which themselves were evolutionarily advantageous. This argument, however, loses force in the present context because the functional advantage of consciousness is so compelling. Consciousness yields prediction and control. Rather than being buffeted by environmental stimuli that trigger unconscious cognitive routines, consciousness enables people to contemplate and predict the behavior of others and themselves. It allows people to plan courses of action and gauge their capacity to act. Consciousness solves the "meta-problem of what to think about next" (Dennett, 1991, p. 222). People often face novel challenges that might, in principle, be solved if one could optimally orchestrate one's skills. The organism "may have resources in it that would be very valuable in the circumstances *if only it could find them and put them to use in time!*" (Dennett, 1991, p. 222). Conscious reasoning about a problem enables people to anticipate challenges and to maximize their personal resources and chances for success.

Consciousness also enables us to have a sense of self. The ability to explicitly deliberate about the world enables us to separate "me" from "not me." Reflective self-consciousness gives people the capacity to bring knowledge about personal and social preferences, goals, and obligations to bear on their choices and actions (e.g., Edelman, 1992). Conscious self-awareness has two aspects. Objective self-awareness, which many organisms have, involves an ability to distinguish oneself from objects in the world. Subjective self-awareness involves knowledge of oneself as a goal-directed agent and emotional investment in one's goals (e.g., Hart & Karmel, 1996).

Both psychologists and nonpsychologists have grappled with the difficult problem of ascertaining the mechanisms of consciousness, that is, identifying the neural and psychological processes that are responsible for conscious experience (e.g., Damasio, 1999). At least two types of models of consciousness can be identified. In one, consciousness is equated with working memory. Consciousness is the executive in a multicomponent information-processing system. When the activation of a piece of information exceeds a certain threshold, it enters working memory and we are consciously aware of it.

In a second type of model, there is no central executive. Consciousness is not equated with a single, distinct psychological mechanism. Instead, multiple cognitive processes jointly give rise to variations in consciousness. Dennett (1991), for example, posits a model of consciousness in which there is no single threshold separating conscious and unconscious processes and no single mechanism in which all conscious experiences converge; there is, in other words, no "cartesian theater." Edelman (1992) proposes a multiprocess theory in which symbolic, especially linguistic, capabilities enable personal information to be connected to awareness of events in the world. These interconnections yield higher-order, self-reflective consciousness.

With some important exceptions, recent work in personality psychology has not addressed the problem of identifying the mechanisms that give rise to conscious experience. Instead, investigators have turned their attention to a series of issues involving subjective experience and personality functioning. It is to these topics that we now turn.

## CONSCIOUS PROCESSES AND PERSONALITY FUNCTIONING

### Individual Differences: Public and Private Self-Consciousness

As with any other psychological characteristic, the tendency to reflect on oneself and one's experiences may vary from one person to the next. There are, of course, large situational determinants of self-reflective tendencies. Being stared at by a stranger makes everyone self-conscious. Being in a crowd of cheering fans at a sporting event reduces everyone's self-consciousness. Still, there may be systematic variation in individuals' chronic, average tendency to reflect on themselves.

One strategy for assessing these individual differences is to ask people directly to report on their tendencies to consciously deliberate upon themselves. Factor analyses of individual differences in such self-reports yield two dimensions (Fenigstein et al., 1975). *Private self-consciousness* refers to awareness of one's inner thoughts and feelings. This dimension is tapped by items such as "I reflect about myself a lot." *Public self-consciousness* is awareness of oneself as a social object to which others are attending. It is tapped by items such as "I usually worry about making a good impression" (Fenigstein et al., 1975). People who score high on public self-consciousness are somewhat likely to engage in paranoid thoughts and actions (Fenigstein & Vanable, 1992). Individual differences in self-consciousness and experimental manipulations of self-consciousness (e.g., with people being made more self-aware by having a mirror placed in front of them) often yield parallel cognitive and behavioral effects (Carver & Scheier, 1990; Fenigstein & Vanable, 1992).

The distinction between private and public self-awareness is valuable. Indeed, a similar distinction is found in work on personal intelligence, in which Gardner (1983, 1993) distinguishes understanding of one's own inner feelings from awareness of other people's motives and desires and one's capacity to influence others. The self-report methodology used to assess tendencies to self-reflect, however, raises questions. People generally see themselves as high or low on a personality dimension by comparing themselves with relevant others. Since others' tendencies to self-reflect are not observable, respondents may be forced to simply guess at the degree to which they are relatively prone to self-reflect. Further, interpreting the self-reports of people low in private self-consciousness raises a logical quandary. People are being asked to report on their typical thinking patterns. How, then, should one interpret the responses of people who, according to one's assessment device, are relatively unaware of their inner thoughts? Such people, by definition, should be relatively incapable of completing the self-report accurately.

**Rumination and Coping**

Differences between individuals often are most apparent at times of stress. Progress in the study of individual differences in conscious experiences has been made by studying people's thinking patterns in response to stressful life events (Carver & Scheier, 1990; Martin & Tesser, 1996).

Earlier in this chapter, we saw that the tendency to suppress thoughts about stressful life events can deleteriously affect mental and physical health (Pennebaker, 1997).

Work by Nolen-Hoeksema and colleagues points to what, at least at first glance, appears to be an opposite possibility. People who ruminate excessively on stress or loss may prolong their periods of depression. In this research program, rumination is conceived as a passive, repetitive dwelling on one's emotional distress (Nolen-Hoeksema, 1991). Ruminative thoughts, then, are not an active attempt to solve one's problems but a relatively inactive dwelling on one's depression and lack of motivation. Individual differences in the tendency to ruminate about distress are relatively stable over time and are only moderately related to other individual-difference tendencies, such as private self-consciousness and neuroticism (Nolen-Hoeksema, Parker, & Larson, 1994). Inducing dysphoric individuals to ruminate on themselves and their feelings tends to make them less willing to engage in pleasant activities, less able to generate solutions to interpersonal problems, and more pessimistic about the future (Lyubomirsky & Nolen-Hoeksema, 1993, 1995). Furthermore, this work indicates that when dysphorics are distracted from ruminative cognition, their thinking resembles that of nondysphorics; dysphorics, then, clearly have the cognitive potential to engage in constructive patterns of thoughts that might help to alleviate their depression. In addition to its influence on depressed mood, rumination can intensify feelings of anger when people envision situations involving unfair treatment of themselves or others (Rusting & Nolen-Hoeksema, 1998).

Naturalistic longitudinal studies also support the link from ruminative cognition to depressed mood, although some empirical inconsistencies are found. Nolen-Hoeksema et al. (1994) assessed ruminative tendencies among individuals who recently had experienced the death of a family member. Specifically, participants completed a self-report questionnaire measuring their tendency to dwell on psychological distress and difficulties in day-to-day functioning. People who tended to ruminate were more depressed at a 6-month follow-up evaluation;

after controlling for initial levels of depression, rumination a month after the death predicted 8% of the variance in depression 6 months later (Nolen-Hoeksema et al., 1994). Work employing an alternative measure of ruminative tendencies, however, yielded somewhat inconsistent results. Nolen-Hoeksema, McBride, and Larson (1997) analyzed interviews in a longitudinal study of bereavement and coping (Folkman, 1997) of men whose partners had died of the acquired immunodeficiency syndrome (AIDS). Here, rumination was assessed through the coding of free-response narratives. In contrast to the earlier result, men who tended to ruminate on negative emotions and regrets about interactions with their deceased partner were not more depressed at a 12-month follow-up evaluation after controlling for their initial depression levels (Nolen-Hoeksema et al., 1997). However, more ruminative men did report lower levels of morale at the follow-up interview after controlling for initial morale levels. Also, when the narratives were coded for tendencies to self-analyze, that is, to describe oneself and what one has learned from the experience of living through the death of a partner, people with strong tendencies to self-analyze were more depressed a year after their partner's death (Nolen-Hoeksema et al., 1997).

The finding that people who engaged in less self-analysis became less depressed (Nolen-Hoeksema et al., 1997) contrasts, of course, with expectations derived from the work of Pennebaker (1997), reviewed earlier. When Pennebaker, Mayne, and Francis (1997) analyzed responses from the same population of subjects, they failed to find that expressing negative emotion had health benefits. Instead, at least among this particular population, thoughts about positive features of the relationship with the deceased partner predicted lower levels of depression (Stein, Folkman, Trabasso, & Richards, 1997).

It would be unwise at this point in our field's knowledge to draw firm conclusions about the relations between ruminative tendencies and mental and physical health. The difficulty of reconciling findings that use different measures of cognitive tendencies suggests that further methodological work is needed on this important topic. Robust results also may require more refined distinctions among different types of ruminative tendencies and different types of psychological distress. Extant findings lead us to note that rumination that is compulsive and repetitive is different from self-reflective processes aimed at thoughtful mastery of distressful experiences. The seriousness of the events being contemplated and how they are cognitively framed undoubtedly influences their short- and long-term effects on mood and health. Furthermore, one must recognize that relations between any self-conscious tendencies and subsequent health outcomes may not be linear; it indeed may be "maladaptive to think either too much or too little about a trauma and one's emotional reactions to it" (Nolen-Hoeksema et al., 1997, p. 861). Finally, future investigations might benefit from combining assessments of inhibition and rumination with assessments of other processes known to influence stress and coping, such as perceived self-efficacy (Bandura, 1997). Beliefs in coping efficacy might affect the degree and type of one's rumination (cf. Kent & Gibbons, 1987), and efficacy beliefs might moderate relations between inhibition–rumination and coping outcomes. People who dwell on setbacks but feel efficacious to change them should experience very different outcomes from those experienced by people who believe that circumstances are beyond their control.

## States of Flow and the Experience Sampling Method

In addition to assessing individual differences in chronic cognitive tendencies, another challenge for research on conscious experience is to assess variations in experience across time and context. Retrospective self-report generally is not a good method here. Retrospective reports on one's conscious experiences may reflect not only the experience, but theories about the nature of the experience that people draw on when trying to reconstruct their past (Ericsson & Simon, 1980). A superior technique is to ask people to describe the contents of their conscious experiences as they are occurring.

Cognitive psychologists commonly use think-aloud techniques to assess the conscious contents of thought (Ericsson & Simon, 1980). Verbal protocols are analyzed to discover the strategies people use to solve a problem. Think-aloud procedures also have been employed to assess people's self-reflective thoughts as they work on challenging tasks (Elliott & Dweck, 1988; Haaga & Stewart, 1992). A drawback of think-aloud procedures, however, is that they can not be used in most naturally occurring social settings (at least not without drawing a lot of attention to the research participant).

An alternative method of assessing conscious experience while individuals are engaged in everyday activities is the experience-sampling method (e.g., Csikzentmihalyi, Larson, & Prescott, 1977; Csikzentmihalyi & LeFevre, 1989). Research participants carry an electronic paging device throughout the course of a study (typically one or more weeks). Participants are signaled at random intervals. When signaled, they complete self-reports of their current thoughts and feelings. The temporal proximity between self-report and the experience on which people are reporting lessens the chances that people will inadvertently distort reports of their subjective experiences.

Csikzentmihalyi and colleagues have employed the experience-sampling method to test his theory of order, or "flow," in conscious experience (Csikzentmihalyi, 1990). Flow is a state of sustained attention to a goal-directed activity. When deeply engaged in a task, people are posited to experience a focused, ordered, pleasurable state of consciousness. According to the theory, such flow states are fostered by tasks that challenge but do not exceed people's skills and by clear task goals and feedback.

Csikzentmihalyi and LeFevre (1989) sampled people's subjective experiences as they engaged in normally occurring work and leisure activities that varied in levels of challenge and feedback. People felt more positively aroused – more active, potent, alert, and strong – when working on challenging tasks for which they perceived themselves to have requisite skills than when they were engaged in tasks that lacked challenge or for which they felt their skills were inadequate (Csikzentmihalyi & LeFevre, 1989). Interestingly, the combination of challenge and perceived skill fostered states of flow whether people were at work or at leisure. Further, flow conditions were far more likely to occur at work. In our modern society, people spend much of their leisure time on activities that lack challenge (e.g., television viewing) and that thus are not ultimately rewarding.

Two features of Csikzentmihalyi (1990) and colleagues' analysis of conscious experience are of particular note. First, the conditions of flow identified in work on consciousness – challenging goals, clear feedback, and the perception that one can meet the challenges – coincide perfectly with the conditions of maximal motivation and performance that are identified in work on goal setting and self-regulation (see chapter 12; also see Bandura, 1997; Cervone, 1993; Locke & Latham, 1990). If people perceive themselves as efficacious, difficult task goals are not aversive burdens but uplifting and rewarding challenges. Second, Csikzentmihalyi and LeFevre's (1989) findings speak to issues in the study of cross-situational coherence in personality tendencies. Csikzentmihalyi and LeFevre identify psychological ingredients that cut across superficially distinct social situations. Subjective experience can not be predicted from the knowledge that people are at work versus at leisure, but from knowing the level of challenge they experience, no matter where they are. Quite similarly, Shoda, Mischel, and Wright (1994) find that personality consistency is predictable across social situations that share a common psychological ingredient even if this ingredient occurs in different environmental contexts.

The experience sampling method also has been used extensively in research on motivation to examine how individuals' goals shape the contents of their conscious experiences (e.g., Klinger et al., 1980), as we discuss in chapter 12.

## The Control of Consciousness

Research on flow highlights one of the most fundamental feature of human consciousness – it is difficult to control. Concentrated flow experiences are relatively rare. They generally require a supportive environment that helps to structure one's experience. Achieving personal control over conscious states in the absence of environmental structures can be a lifelong task for those engaged in meditative practice (Goleman, 1988). For most people most of the time, consciousness consists of a series of remarkably fleeting thoughts and images, many of which spring to mind unintended and interfere with activities on which they had hoped to concentrate.

Why is consciousness so difficult to control? There are at least two explanations (Wegner & Wenzlaff, 1996). One is that our intentional efforts to bring order to consciousness are, at best, only partially successful. Thoughts about innumerable goals and desires are in a state of chronic activation, vying for their place in conscious awareness. Consciousness, in this view, would be a chaotic world lacking in concentrated attention were it not for intentional control mechanisms. Another possibility is the opposite. Rather than facilitating sustained attention to a task, intentional control mechanisms may make matters worse. Attempts to concentrate on one topic by banishing competing thoughts from consciousness may, ironically, cause those competing thoughts to spring to mind (Wegner, & Wenzlaff, 1996).

Research by Daniel Wegner and colleagues illustrates this phenomenon. They instruct people to banish from consciousness thoughts of a particular stimulus and measure the success of these mental control efforts and the physiological effects of attempted thought suppression. Their research reveals a number of interesting findings. First, people's attempts to control their thoughts frequently fail. When

people are asked not to think of a concrete stimulus (a white bear) but to indicate when the stimulus comes to mind by ringing a bell, people's frequent bell rings, especially during the first few minutes of this task, reveal that completely eliminating a thought from consciousness is nearly impossible (Wegner, Schneider, Carter, & White, 1987). Second, when people attempt to control emotionally exciting thoughts, failures of control increase physiological arousal. Wegner, Shortt, Blake, and Page (1990, experiment 3) asked participants not to think of sex during a 30-minute period during which they were asked to verbalize their thoughts. Skin conductance measures were taken throughout the period. Intrusions of thoughts about sex were found to be correlated with increased levels of physiological activity, but only when participants were trying to suppress these thoughts. When participants were explicitly asked to think about sex, sexual thoughts did not activate physiological arousal (Wegner et al., 1990). Third, attempts to control one's thoughts not only fail but backfire, especially when people are engaged in competing cognitive tasks that make it difficult for them to devote full attention to controlling their conscious states (or when they are "cognitively busy" [Gilbert et al., 1988]). Wegner, Erber, and Zanakos (1993, experiment 2) asked participants either to think about or not to think about a recent personal success or failure. A Stroop color-naming paradigm was used to measure the accessibility of thoughts that participants were trying not to think about. When participants simultaneously had to complete a challenging computer task, attempts to avoid thinking about the personal experience not only failed, but backfired. Stroop results indicated that when participants were cognitively busy, thoughts about the personal success or failure were *more* accessible when people were trying *not* to think about the events.

People's attempts to control their emotional states may fail for similar reasons. Wegner et al. (1993) found that, when cognitively busy, people who attempt to control their emotions experience mood states that are opposite to the moods they are trying to achieve.

Wegner (1994, 1997) suggests that "consciousness can control itself" but that "our attempts to control it" cause our thoughts to wander (Wegner, 1997, p. 298). Specifically, he posits the existence of two mental control systems. One searches for mental contents consistent with our intended thoughts. The other detects unwanted thoughts, that is, competing ideas that would interfere with our attempts to concentrate on the intended topic. By continually searching for thoughts that would constitute a failure of mental control, the latter system actually raises the cognitive accessibility of the undesired ideas. As a result, under some conditions the undesired thoughts are more likely to come to mind. Attempts to control the normal stream of conscious activity thus backfire.

## Affective States and Conscious Thought

Wegner's research on thought suppression and affect begins to provide an understanding of how variations in conscious experience influence emotional states. The field has achieved even greater understanding of the opposite relation, namely, how emotional states influence the contents of consciousness. Stimulated by the seminal contributions of Isen, Shalker, Clark, and Karp (1978) and Bower (1981), psychologists have made much progress in the past two decades in explaining how emotional states influence our thoughts.

A sign of progress in this area is that investigators recognize the complexity of affect–cognition relations. Emotions can influence thinking through multiple pathways. A multiprocess framework is required for understanding how moods influence thought (Forgas, 1995). One can delineate at least five ways in which mood states can influence cognitive processes and the contents of conscious experience. We will mention four of these briefly and then spend more time on the fifth, because of its relevance to understanding conscious experience.

First, moods can prime information in memory that is congruent with one's affective state. Because of priming, people in a positive mood (for example) are more likely to attend to positively valenced material and to recall positive episodes from memory (reviewed in Blaney, 1986; Bower, 1981; Singer & Salovey, 1988). Second, mood can influence strategies of cognitive processing. Negative affect, which generally signals the existence of threats in the environment, can cause people to process information more systematically (Schwarz, Bless, & Bohner, 1991; Sinclair & Mark, 1992). Third, mood states can motivate people to take action to regulate their conscious experience. People may engage in thinking patterns or behavioral activities designed to "repair" their negative mood (Clark & Isen, 1982). Fourth, mood may induce self-focused attention. Both positive and negative moods can increase people's tendency to direct their attention to themselves (Salovey, 1992).

The fifth pathway is particularly intriguing. Affective states can unintentionally serve as sources of input to conscious reasoning processes. Affect, in other words, functions as information (Schwarz, 1990). This influence of affect on conscious thought is particularly apparent when we are evaluating a person or object. Schwarz and colleagues' affect-as-information model (Schwarz, 1990; Schwarz & Clore, 1983, 1996) suggests that people make evaluative judgments by asking themselves how they feel about a prospect. Under such circumstances, it is difficult to distinguish affective responses to the prospect being judged (how one feels about it) from preexisting mood that is logically irrelevant to one's judgment (how one feels in general, at that particular moment). Preexisting moods thus bias social judgment. Transient affect-inducing variables, such as finding a dime on a copy machine (Schwarz, 1990) or evaluating one's life on sunny versus rainy days (Schwarz & Clore, 1983), have been shown to influence judgments of satisfaction with one's life.

Transient mood does not always serve as a source of information in social judgment. If people are cognizant of the source of their mood and recognize its potential biasing influence on their thinking, they can correct for this bias. Experimental manipulations that draw people's attention to the source of transient emotional states often eliminate the impact of mood on cognition (Schwarz & Clore, 1983; Scott & Cervone, 2000). The influence of such manipulations, though, may depend on people's chronic affective tendencies and the match between chronic tendencies and current experiences. When people's current emotional state matches their chronic tendencies, they may disregard the possibility that their current mood was influenced by transient factors. People who chronically experience anxiety are found to rely on transient feelings of anxiety as a cue in social judgment, even when made aware of the possibility that these transient feelings may have been induced by irrelevant external factors (Gasper & Clore, 1998). The self-judgments of dysphoric individuals suggest that they disregard attributional cues that suggest an external explanation for their current sad mood (Tillema, Cervone, & Scott, in press). As a more general point, the affect-as-information model indicates that people have the potential to gain greater control over their conscious judgments by reflecting on the many external factors that may influence their feelings and thoughts. In the absence of such self-reflection, feeling states can powerfully bias our subjective opinions of the world and ourselves.

## SUMMING UP

A primary benefit of reflective self-consciousness is that it enables us to gain control over, or to self-regulate, our actions and psychological experiences. The capacity to reflect on oneself and the situational factors that activate self-reflective processes play central roles in the self-regulation of action (Bandura, 1997; Carver & Scheier, 1998; Cervone, 1993). Our discussion of the functions of conscious experience continues, then, in chapter 12, which explores motivation, self-regulation, and goal-directed action.

# CHAPTER TWELVE

# Motivation and Self-Regulation

What motivates human action? This question has been central to personality psychology since the field's inception. At their core, most of the classic theories of personality primarily are theories of motivation. Psychoanalysis is a drive theory in which people are motivated to reduce aversive states of tension (Freud, 1923). Lewin's (1935) field theory saw motivation as arising from tension among regions of the life space. Humanistic theories claim that people are inherently motivated toward psychological growth and maturity (Allport, 1950; Maslow, 1954; Rogers, 1961).

Personality psychology's past, then, has seen a diversity of motivation theories. Its present, in contrast, features much consensus. Most investigators share basic beliefs about the psychological mechanisms underlying people's selection of activities, regulation of their effort, and decisions about whether to persist or to abandon endeavors. Contemporary research programs thus are complementary. Investigators capitalize on each other's theories and findings. As a result, psychologists can claim to have made genuine progress in understanding the determinants of motivation (Caprara, 1996a; Locke & Latham, 1984).

We begin this chapter by reviewing the basis for this consensus and progress. Much research reveals that action is motivated, to a substantial degree, by beliefs and feelings about the self. Self-referent processes function as personal determinants of motivation. Through their capacity to set goals, develop strategies, reflect on themselves, and evaluate their performance, people are able to self-regulate their behavior and emotional states (e.g., Baltes et al., 1998; Bandura, 1986, 1999; Carver & Scheier, 1998; Deci & Ryan, 1985; Karoly, 1993b; Mischel, Cantor, & Feldman, 1996; Schunk & Zimmerman, 1998). We outline the nature of the self-regulatory system, or self-system, below.

After this overview of the self-system, we review the history of personality psychology's study of motivation and present the major theoretical frameworks that have guided research in the field. Next, we address the central role of control beliefs and perceptions of self-efficacy in goal-directed action. The remainder of the chapter is devoted to three broad classes of phenomena: (1) goals and self-motivation, where our coverage includes questions of how people pursue challenging courses of action even in the absence of tangible incentives for doing so and how goal systems contribute to personality coherence and psychological well-being; (2) avoidance of distraction, or the question of how people can shield their attention from events that interfere with the execution of intended goal pursuit (e.g., Gollwitzer, 1993, 1996; Kuhl, 1984); and (3) impulse control, or the curbing of affectively based tendencies to act when the inhibition of action may serve one's long-term interests (e.g., Metcalfe & Mischel, 1999).

## MOTIVATION, COGNITION, AND THE SELF-REGULATORY SYSTEM

During the early parts of the 20th century, psychologists explained motivational states primarily by reference to physiological needs, instincts, or drives. Today, most investigators explain human motivation by reference to human thought processes. People's reflections on their past actions, their future prospects, and their personal qualities underlie interindividual differences and intraindividual coherence in motivated action.

The field's cognitive turn did not yield a cold, affect-free psychology of motivation (see, e.g., Martin & Tesser, 1996). As we will see, affective processes are found to contribute directly to motivational states. Affect also influences the cognitive processes that people rely upon in regulating their behavior. Cognitive processing, in turn, triggers emotional reactions to feedback on one's performance (e.g., Weiner, 1986).

Accompanying the cognitive analysis of motivation was a parallel development, namely, motivational analyses of cognition. Much thinking is motivated (Kruglanski, 1989, 1996; Kunda, 1987). People's goals partly determine how they seek out and assess information. This recognition has begun to yield an integrated psychology of motivation and social cognition (e.g., Gollwitzer & Bargh, 1996).

In this chapter, then, we focus on cognitive processes in human motivation. One should recall, however, that not all determinants of motivation are cognitive in origin. Organisms experience deficits in basic bodily needs that motivate them to reduce discomfort. Perceived threats and opportunities in the environment activate biological approach and avoidance systems (chapter 3). Research on lower organisms illuminates the functioning of these systems (e.g., Gray, 1991). Whatever the value of this work, however, it cannot yield a complete, or even a nearly complete, portrait of the motivational processes underlying human action and differences among individuals in motivational functioning. On questions of motivation, two factors make humans utterly unique. These are the capacities to evaluate actions against standards of worth and to reflect on one's capacity to execute courses of action. These self-referent processes function together as part of a cognitive and affective system through which people regulate their experiences and actions. We now review this system, focusing on its four main elements, namely, standards for performance, affective self-evaluation, self-efficacy perceptions, and goals.

### Standards and Affective Self-Evaluation

A primary personal determinant of action is the human propensity to evaluate behaviors according to criteria of worth. People do not observe the actions of themselves and others in a passive, detached manner. Instead, they judge whether actions are appropriate, commendable, and praiseworthy. They make these judgments by comparing actions to internal criteria that represent acceptable or unacceptable performance. These criteria are referred to as *standards* for performance. Standards have a motivational effect by serving as guides for action. People often adjust their efforts until they judge that their behavior has met their personal standard for performance. Virtually all students of motivation and per-

sonality posit that personal performance standards are a central mechanism of human motivation (e.g., Bandura, 1986; Carver & Scheier, 1999; Heckhausen, 1991; Higgins, 1999; Karoly, 1993b).

The role of personal standards in motivation has a major implication for how we conceptualize human nature. Contrary to the suggestions of some past theories in the social sciences, people are not primarily gluttonous, self-indulgent beings, who are bent on maximizing pleasure, reward, and sensuous gratification. Instead, people seem at least equally inclined to deny rewards to themselves until their behavior meets self-imposed standards of adequacy (Bandura, 1991b; Kagan, 1998b; see chapter 5). The capacity to acquire standards for performance is evident early in life. In an illustrative study, nursery school children played a game in which they could observe their own level of achievement and then could reward themselves to whatever degree they saw fit. Some children first viewed a model who rewarded himself only if he achieved a particularly high score on the game. Although all children were free to reward any of their accomplishments to any degree that they wished, those who had observed the model readily imposed stringent standards on themselves. They withheld self-rewards unless they attained particularly high scores in the game (Bandura & Kupers, 1964).

Standards are cognitive. They are mental representations of the criteria that define desirable or undesirable outcomes. The influence of standards on motivation, however, involves both cognitive and affective processes. Put simply, people feel good (or badly) about themselves when their behavior does (or does not) live up to their standards. They make positive feelings about the self contingent on their attaining superior levels of performance and take action that is designed to bring about positive self-feelings and avoid negative self-reactions. Affective *self-evaluative reactions* thus constitute a second important personal source of motivation (Bandura, 1977b, 1991b; Bandura & Cervone, 1983; Cervone, 1993).

Motivation, then, is guided in part by efforts to obtain positive feelings *about* oneself *from* oneself. People pursue challenges that they anticipate will bring self-satisfaction. Kagan (1998b) captures the notion perfectly: "When a person consciously selects one act over another . . . the desired state [the person seeks] is a conceptual consonance between an idea, called a standard, and the chosen action. When that consonance occurs, the person momentarily experiences a pleasant feeling because his behavior is in accord with a standard he has categorized as good" (p. 151). Kagan suggests that the process of seeking this feeling of personal pride or virtue[1] is so important that it may constitute "the most potent condition sculpting each person's traits over their lifetime" (Kagan, 1998b, p. 157).

Many of the standards against which we evaluate our actions involve rules of appropriate social conduct toward others – and the world at large. In other words, people hold ethical and moral standards. The development of an ethical sense, the nature of virtue, and the ways in which successful self-regulation of action contribute to the achievement of a virtuous life have been addressed in Western philosophy since the time of Socrates and Plato. In the contemporary philosophical literature, Nozick (1981) provides a particularly useful analysis of how ethical standards exert a "push" and "pull" on behavior. Our recognition of the types of behavior that should flow from ourselves as virtuous persons pushes us toward ethical action. Recognition of the value of other persons constrains our actions toward them and pulls our actions in an ethical direction.

Philosophical and psychological discourse have largely proceeded along separate tracks. Lakoff and Johnson (1999), however, recently have brought them together by exploring the implications of findings in cognitive science for our understanding of morality and ethics. They note that most of our moral reasoning is metaphorical. Furthermore, the metaphors we use commonly reflect the "embodied" nature of the mind, that is, the fact that thinking is shaped by anatomical features of the human body. For example, a well-functioning body is strong and is able to stand upright. A common metaphor for understanding morality, then, is the notion of moral strength (Lakoff & Johnson, 1999). Good people are upstanding and upright. The evil fall from grace. When we violate a personal norm, we slip. The metaphor of moral strength is so intuitively compelling that some have even drawn on it when constructing formal scientific theories of self-regulation, with metaphorical strength being reified and treated as an entity within the person (Baumeister & Heatherton, 1996).

An implication of Lakoff and Johnson's analysis of metaphors in moral reasoning is that moral reasoning is not a separate mental faculty. "There are few, if any, 'purely ethical' concepts" (Lakoff & Johnson, 1999, p. 333). Instead, the structure of moral reasoning is based on reasoning in other domains that have little inherently to do with morality and ethics. This point would seem to have considerable implications for the study of moral development, in which moral reasoning commonly is treated as a distinct form or stage of thinking (chapter 5).

### Self-Efficacy Beliefs and Perceived Control

Personal standards and self-evaluative reactions tell only part of the story of motivation. Even when people judge that courses of action will bring positive self-evaluations, as well as regard from others and tangible rewards, they generally fail to undertake these actions if they believe that high-quality performance is out of their reach. Motivation is strongly regulated by people's subjective assessments of whether outcomes are controllable and whether they can execute the courses of action required to control events.

---

[1] Kagan (1998b) notes that "curiously, no word in English names this feeling with precision; virtue comes close" (p. 151). We use the general term "self-evaluative reactions" (or "affective self-evaluations") to capture the class of self-referent feelings that includes pride, virtue, and self-satisfaction, as well as dissatisfaction with oneself, guilt, and shame.

There are many different aspects to the psychology of control. Different control-related cognitions, in other words, contribute to motivation. These include reflections on the controllability of the causes of past events (Peterson & Park, 1998; Weiner, 1986) and expectations about whether future rewards will be controlled by personal actions or external forces (Rotter, 1966). A paramount element of perceived control is people's appraisals of their capability to execute courses of action, or *self-efficacy* appraisals (Bandura, 1997).

Self-efficacy beliefs are of particular importance to the psychology of motivation for three reasons. First, self-efficacy perceptions directly contribute to decisions, actions, and experiences. People who doubt their efficacy for performance tend to avoid challenges, to abandon activities when faced with setbacks, and to experience debilitating anxiety (Bandura, 1997). Second, self-efficacy beliefs influence other cognitive and emotional factors that, in turn, contribute to performance. Self-efficacy perceptions influence outcome expectations and goal setting. People with higher efficacy beliefs tend to set higher goals and to remain committed to these aims (Locke & Latham, 1990). Efficacy perceptions influence causal attributions. People with a high sense of self-efficacy tend to attribute outcomes to stable and controllable factors (McAuley, Duncan, & McElroy, 1989). When people receive feedback that is inconsistent with their sense of self-efficacy, they tend to attribute it to external rather than personal causes (Alden, 1986; cf. Swann, 1983). Efficacy beliefs also influence levels of anxiety, and experiences of anxiety in turn can interfere with performance on cognitively complex tasks (Cervone, Jiwani, & Wood, 1991; Wood & Bandura, 1989). A third consideration is that self-efficacy perceptions may moderate the impact of other variables that have the potential to enhance achievement. The acquisition of skills and knowledge enhances achievement, but not if people so doubt their capabilities that they fail to put their knowledge into practice.

## Goals and the Self-Regulatory System

Personal standards, self-evaluative reactions, and self-efficacy perceptions do not function in isolation from one another. Instead, they are elements of an integrated self-regulatory system. It is easiest to understand the integration among aspects of the self-system if we first introduce one additional personal determinant of motivation, namely, goals.

A *goal* is a mental representation of the aim of a course of action (e.g., Kruglanski, 1996; Locke & Latham, 1990). Through their capacity for forethought, people are able to envision prospective accomplishments and to direct their action toward reaching these ends. The mental representation of a future accomplishment generally is termed a goal only if there is at least a minimal degree of commitment to achieving the accomplishment. Though we may daydream of being movie stars or Olympic heroes, these flights of fancy are not considered goals unless we direct, or intend to direct, some amount of planning and effort to their achievement. The motivational implications of realistic versus fantasy-based cognition (Oettingen, 1996) are discussed below.

■ *System-Level Functioning.* The four self-regulatory mechanisms we have introduced – standards, affective self-evaluations, self-efficacy perceptions, and goals – are functionally interrelated. As a result, they do not operate as independent influences on behavior but as parts of a coherent psychological system. A large number of functional interrelations among self-regulatory mechanisms can be identified. As we just noted, self-efficacy beliefs influence goals and affective arousal. Goals, in turn, commonly provide the criteria or standards against which people evaluate their performance. Indeed, the relation between the constructs *goals* and *standards* is so close that the terms commonly are used interchangeably (as we sometimes do in this chapter). However, the constructs are distinct because a person's standards and goals on an activity can differ under some circumstances. Consider a case in which performance feedback lowers self-efficacy perceptions. A student with high efficacy beliefs may aim to earn an A in a class (her goal) and may judge that only A-level performance is personally acceptable (her standard). A poor examination grade, however, may lower her sense of efficacy, causing her to abandon her goal and to reduce her effort in the class. However, in principle, she may continue to judge that only A-level work constitutes a worthy level of performance and may evaluate herself negatively because she has failed to live up to this standard.

Coherence in the self-regulatory system also derives from the fact that different goals are associatively linked to one another in memory. In Kruglanski's (2000) recent goal systems theory, goals are cognitively associated not only to one another, but to means for accomplishing their attainment. These cognitive links among goals and means are basic underlying mechanisms that explain a variety of overt motivational phenomena (also see Kruglanski, 1996).

Reciprocal links between cognition and affect further contribute to coherence in the self-regulatory system. The level and type of standard one adopts on a task partly determine one's affective experiences (cf. Carver & Scheier, 1990; Higgins, 1987; see chapter 9). Self-referent feelings, conversely, may feed back into the cognitive self-regulatory system. Dissatisfaction with oneself may trigger a more widespread negative mood. The experience of negative mood, in turn, can lead people to adopt higher, or more perfectionistic standards on tasks (Cervone, Kopp, Schaumann, & Scott, 1994; Tillema, Cervone, Scott, & in press); negative mood can make any given prospective outcome appear less satisfactory, which, in turn, drives higher standards for performance. Negative mood also may lower self-efficacy perceptions (Forgas, Bower, & Moylan, 1990; Kavanagh & Bower, 1985; Salovey & Birnbaum, 1989).

The cognitive and affective processes that come into play as people regulate their actions, then, constitute an interacting system. Different psychological processes influence one another and jointly contribute to people's efforts to gain control over their actions and experiences. Investigators increasingly view self-regulatory mechanisms as a dynamic system and apply the metatheory of nonlinear dynamic systems analysis to the study of self-regulatory processes (Carver & Scheier, 1998; Nowak & Vallacher, 1998).

■ *Differential Activation of the Self-System.* People do not spend their days continuously obsessing about their goals, ruminating on their capabilities, and evaluating the worth of each of their actions. Much of the time we focus our attention on the substance of what we are doing. Alternatively, some activities require so little conscious attention that we can devote our conscious thought to topics that have nothing whatsoever to do with our overt behavior.

We make these points here because of their bearing on the self-regulatory mechanisms we have just discussed. The self-regulatory processes we outlined above primarily involve conscious self-reflection. These deliberate self-reflections do not occur continuously but only part of the time. Phrased more formally, the self-system is differentially engaged in the regulation of action (Bandura & Cervone, 1983). Some situations cause us to dwell on ourselves, the adequacy of our past actions, and our prospects for the future. People are prone to evaluate their actions when behavior is disrupted (Vallacher & Wegner, 1987), when they receive explicit feedback on the quality of their efforts (Bandura, 1986; Cervone, 1993), or when social cues that are unrelated to the quality of one's performance happen to call attention to the self (Carver & Scheier, 1981). In many other contexts, however, action can proceed with little conscious monitoring. On highly practiced activities, action can be executed automatically, in accordance with internalized scripts for behavior (Bargh, 1997; Langer, Blank, & Chanowitz, 1978). On novel tasks, people are less inclined to engage in self-evaluation when they believe that their performance is not a reflection of their personal qualities (Dweck & Leggett, 1988) or when they do not receive explicit information about the quality of their performance (Cervone, 1993; Cervone et al., 1991). In interpersonal settings involving moral standards, people may disregard moral constraints by constructing justifications for their actions or by disparaging the people whom they harm (Bandura, 1973). Adolescents who disengage personal standards in this manner are prone to aggressive and delinquent behavior (Bandura et al., 1996b).

The activation of self-regulatory processes often involves interpersonal processes. Significant others often embody the moral or professional standards against which one compares one's action. Baldwin and colleagues find that the subtle cognitive priming of thoughts of such other persons (e.g., the pope) enhances self-criticism (Baldwin, Carrell, & Lopez, 1990).

The fact that self-regulatory processes are differentially activated in the self-regulation of behavior is an important point to consider when weighing the role of conscious versus nonconscious processes in the regulation of action. Conscious, self-reactive influences are important, not because they are continuously activated but because they come into play at critical junctures in the regulation of action. It is when people choose whether to undertake significant activities, receive feedback on the success of their undertakings, and decide whether to continue with pursuits that prove more challenging than they expected that conscious reflections on oneself and one's future prospects govern motivation.

## Temporal and Cross-Situational Coherence in the Self-System

The self-regulatory processes we have discussed can come into play as a person engages in any of a variety of individual activities. Personality psychology's study of motivation, however, must encompass not only motivation on individual, isolated tasks but also enduring motivational tendencies that are evident across multiple circumstances and activities.

As we have discussed previously, there is more than one way of accounting for broad, cross-situational patterns in personality functioning. One approach is to posit global variables that directly correspond to a broad pattern of response. In a top-down strategy of explanation (see chapter 4), one might seek to establish a universal taxonomy of global, high-level variables and to explain the behavior of the individual by fitting the person into the high-level system. In the study of motivation, this would imply seeking a universal taxonomy of global motives (e.g., a motive to succeed or a motive to self-actualize) and explaining individual action by positing that each person possess more or less of each motive.

The shortcomings of this strategy for building a motivational psychology have become increasingly apparent in recent years. Carver and Scheier (1998) articulate the problem: "To say that motives underlie behavior says nothing about the processes referenced by (or following from) the term *motive*. It implies only that some such processes exist, somewhere, in some form" (p. 2). A failure to identify underlying processes not only leaves one with little scientific understanding, but it also hinders applications. Applied efforts to help individuals to motivate themselves, regulate their emotions, and thereby realize their potentials require an understanding of specific psychological mechanisms that influence personal success and that can serve as targets of an intervention.

An alternative, bottom-up strategy would be to ask about the potential multiplicity of social and psychological mechanisms that might cause the self-system variables described above to cohere across time and place. What might cause people's goals and standards to be meaningfully interconnected from one social circumstance to another? What processes might cause people to judge themselves as having high or low efficacy for performance across multiple tasks? What might cause some people chronically to experience positive or negative self-evaluative reactions in response to feedback on their behavior?

Much progress has been made in answering these questions. Answers come in a variety of forms. Numerous processes, in other words, contribute to coherence in the self-system and in resulting motivational tendencies. Multiple task goals and performance standards may be meaningfully interrelated because they are linked hierarchically to the same long-term aim (Emmons, 1989; Carver & Scheier, 1981, 1998). A long-term aim such as earning a Ph.D. may organize a cluster of more proximal goals and standards (study for classes, establish a good relationship with one's academic advisor, make friends with highly intelligent colleagues). Self-efficacy perceptions in different situations may be meaningfully interrelated when a single, cognitively salient personal attribute is seen to bear on behavioral success in the different circumstances (Cervone, 1997, 1999). A salient belief that one tends to "get nervous in front of crowds" might contribute, in a consistent manner, to self-efficacy beliefs in diverse professional and social settings involving large groups. Self-evaluations in different circumstances may cohere because they are shaped by implicit theories about the self. For example, the belief that personal attributes are fixed versus malleable fosters different self-evaluative standards and goals. These goals, in turn, foster coherent patterns of affect and action by influencing people's interpretations of social cues and of their own actions (Grant & Dweck, 1999).

Biological and social factors that vary across the life course further contribute to coherence in the self-regulatory system. People of different ages share normative concerns and life challenges that organize multiple goals, actions, and experiences (e.g., Cantor & Kihlstrom, 1987; Sanderson & Cantor, 1999; also see chapter 5). For example, late in life people become increasingly aware of the fact that their time is ultimately limited. This causes them to reprioritize their goals. Goals involving emotional experience rather than knowledge acquisition become salient (Carstensen, Isaacowitz, & Charles, 1999). The perception of gains and losses in personal competencies across the life-span similarly organizes people's experiences. As life progresses and people face personal setbacks and declines, they must balance attempts to control the environment with efforts to manage internal psychological resources (Heckhausen & Schulz, 1995, 1998).

## Personal Agency

Our outline of the self-regulatory system raises a point that has been voiced often in previous chapters. People have the capacity for personal agency. The ability to anticipate the future and regulate actions in the service of personal goals gives people the capacity to influence the nature of their experiences, actions, and personal development.

Personal agency can not be established by fiat. Harré (1984) provides philosophical justification for a concept of agency. In his analysis, agency derives from one's sense of self. Possessing a "theory that I am a unified being . . . enables me to understand that I am the recipient both of exhortations . . . and shoves, that I can exhort and shove others and, finally, putting this together, that I can so treat myself" (p. 193). Acts of will, or volition, then, are "self-commands" that rest on a system of beliefs about one's capacity and responsibility for action. "There is no more (and no less) mystery in coming to understand how I can obey myself than in coming to understand how I can obey you" (Harré, 1984, p. 195). Just as one may motivate others through statements designed to bolster their confidence, remind them of opportunities, or induce guilt, so may one motivate oneself.

Johnson-Laird (1988) provides a rationale for the concept of agency that is grounded in principles from cognitive science. He notes that cognitive processing is often guided by mental models, that is, symbolic representations of an entity and its functioning. Thanks to the human capacity for self-reflection, people are able to construct mental models not only of the external world but of themselves. Our self-referent mental models include knowledge of our own thinking processes, or "meta-cognitive" knowledge. People can gain personal control over events by using this metacognitive knowledge to select *how* they go about making choices. They can reflect on, and choose among, alternative procedures for making decisions (e.g. think more, act now, consult with others, flip a coin), "We are free . . . because our models of ourselves enable us to choose how to choose" (Johnson-Laird, 1988, pp. 364–365).

In various past eras, psychologists have questioned people's capacity for causal agency. Behaviorists viewed self-control as an illusion. People thought they had self-control when they did not happen to be cognizant of the external determinants of their actions (Skinner, 1971). To Skinner, our decisions to enroll in a psychology course and to stop at a traffic light are similar in that both are controlled by the environment. We believe that we made a choice in the former circumstance but not the latter only because we are unaware of the complex, temporally extended array of external determinants of our behavior.

Skinner's provocative argument was compelling in its day. However, careful psychological (Bandura, 1974) and philosophical (Dennett, 1984) analyses revealed its shortcomings. Experimental research illuminated people's capacity to overcome environmental constraints (e.g., Mischel, 1974). These efforts, combined with the growth of cognitive psychology, virtually eliminated the influence of the Skinnerian model and helped to establish contemporary psychology's recognition of people's capacity for self-regulation.

More recently, the concept of self-control has again come under attack (e.g., Wegner & Wheatley, 1999). A variety of findings reveal limitations to people's ability successfully to control their actions and life outcomes. People sometimes engage in patterns of behavior that are self-defeating and thereby undermine well-intentioned efforts at control (Baumeister & Scher, 1988). Attempts to control thinking processes sometimes backfire, leading people to do exactly those things that they had been trying to avoid (Wegner & Wenzlaff, 1996). Situational factors may activate mental representations of goals and trigger goal-directed action without the individual's conscious awareness (Bargh, 1997; Bargh & Chartrand, 1999; Gollwitzer & Schaal, 1998). Attributional processes may create overconfidence in one's ability to solve problems, which in turn leads people to halt problem-solving efforts prematurely and thereby to perform suboptimally (Metcalfe, 1998). These important findings reveal signifi-

cant constraints on the controllability of action. However, they do not eliminate, and should not distract from, the vast range of instances in which people have the capacity to regulate their action by setting goals, selecting the environments they experience, monitoring their behavior, and employing cognitive strategies to cope with emotional distress. We return to these topics, including the role of nonconscious goal processes (Bargh, 1997), later in this chapter.

Conceptions of personal agency vary across cultures (Kitayama & Markus, 1999; Markus, Kitayama, & Heiman, 1996). People in European and American societies appear more oriented toward self-enhancement, personal achievement, and personal control than people in Asian cultures, for whom social obligations and group-level accomplishments are more salient. This, however, does not imply that people in Eastern cultures have little capacity for personal agency, but merely that the aims of their actions and the role of specific self-referent beliefs in motivation may vary from one culture to another. People with communal goals may exert much self-control in an effort to reach these aims. Indeed, Eastern cultures traditionally provide us with some of the most striking examples of the human capacity for self-direction in the absence of tangible external supports for behavior. The Buddhist monk who devotes himself to a hermetic life of meditative practice provides a remarkable example of human willpower. His agentic self-direction, however, is in the service of communal goals, in that the meditative practice is designed ultimately to enhance the well-being of others.

## HISTORICAL AND CONTEMPORARY THEORETICAL FRAMEWORKS

### Instinct, Drive, Need, and Motive Theories

The systematic study of human motivation predates the efforts of psychologists of the past hundred years. Scholars throughout the ages have addressed questions of human motivation. Many of these efforts have been attempts to identify fundamental instinctual tendencies that characterize human nature. The 20th-century notions that people are utility maximizers (Savage, 1954) or instinctually aggressive (Lorenz, 1966), for example, can be traced to earlier positions expressed by writers such as Thomas Hobbes and Adam Smith.

With the origins of contemporary psychology in the late 19th century, a primary construct used to explain motivated action was that of instinct. James (1890) propagated this view, suggesting that much of behavior could be explained by instinctual impulses to engage in particular forms of action. He eschewed broad, abstract constructs (e.g., a self-preservation instinct) and instead suggested a relatively large number of narrower instinctual tendencies (e.g., instincts for sucking, biting, crying, ferocity, fear, play, constructiveness). Subsequently, McDougall (1908) presented an analysis that differed somewhat from that of James. James believed that instincts operated in a relatively reflexive manner, whereas McDougall stressed that instincts are purposive. The various instincts are distinguished by the purpose at which they aim. McDougall also took on the task of developing a taxonomy of the instincts.

Some contemporary developments seem consistent with these early notions of instinct, whereas others do not. Evolutionary psychology (Barkow et al., 1992; Buss, 1997b, 1999a,b) is consistent with the view of James that a large number of human instincts exist. As we have noted, evolutionary psychology explains behavior by positing a large number of domain-specific mental modules. Since each module has evolved to solve a particular adaptive problem, each yields a distinct motive, that is, a distinct strategic tendency. This view severely challenges efforts to explain diverse social acts in terms of a small number of overarching motives (cf. Buss, 1997a,b; Pyszczynski, Greenberg, & Solomon, 1997). On the other hand, cultural psychology reveals striking cross-cultural variation in motivational processes (Kitayama & Markus, 1999). The seemingly universal motive to enhance self-esteem seems far less universal when considered in the light of Asian cultures that emphasize self-criticism rather than esteem enhancement as a mechanism for self-development (Heine et al., 1999; Kitayama et al., 1997). The seemingly universal link between the provision of personal choice and "intrinsic motivation" (e.g., Deci & Ryan, 1985) seems less universal in light of the finding that people from Asian cultures are more intrinsically motivated when choices are made by authorities or trusted peers than by oneself (Iyengar & Lepper, 1999). Such variability calls into question the entire enterprise of developing a universal taxonomy of human instincts.

A further limitation of universal instinct theories is that, without further augmentation, they bypass a central question of personality psychology, interindividual differences and intra-individual variation in motivational tendencies. Instincts are stable features of the organism, but individuals' action tendencies vary from moment to moment, from situation to situation, and from one segment of life to another. Instincts are common across individuals, but variations in action tendencies often appear to be idiosyncratic. The psychology of personality and motivation needs, at the very least, something more than a taxonomy of basic instinctual needs.

■ *Drive and Need Theories.* In subsequent eras, psychologists embraced drive theories. Perspectives as varied as psychoanalysis (Freud, 1923) and Hullian (1943) behavior theory understood motivation in terms of drives. To Hull, drives were nonspecific energizers of action; they provided energy but not direction for behavior. The direction of behavior derived from habits, which reflected the organism's history of associative learning. Behavior, then, was a multiplicative function of drive and habit. Note that Hull's notion of drive was more flexible than that of instinct, in that a drive can power a variety of behaviors depending on the organism's habit structure.

Drive theories such as that of Hull (1943) were enormously influential in psychology during the middle portions of the 20th century. However, they eventually ran into conceptual difficulties and fell out of favor. As with attempts to identify basic instincts, efforts to explain the spectrum of human motivations in terms of a small number of basic drives stretched credulity. The biologically based drives posited earlier by Freud were criticized as being insufficient for a psychology of personality and motivation in that they neglected the possibility of motives that were fundamentally social in origin and nature. Subsequent theorists posited a wider array of motivational forces. Of particular note is the work of Henry Murray (1938), who explained motivation through the construct of psychological *needs*.

To Murray (1938), a need was a psychological force that produces organized activity. When activated, a need causes the organism to seek out and attend to certain types of situations. Needs tend to endure, and thus they contribute to the individual's enduring motivational tendencies. The construct of need differs from that of drive in that needs, unlike drives, do not always impel the organism in the direction of tension reduction. In Murray's need theory, a person may allow tension to build up rather than seeking its immediate reduction, in order to increase the pleasures of subsequent tension reduction; Hall et al. (1998) note the example of sexual foreplay in this regard.

Any need theory raises the question: What are the basic needs? Murray faced this head-on by presenting a need taxonomy. It included primary needs corresponding to physical necessities (for air, water, food, sex, pain avoidance, etc.) and secondary needs related to conditions of the social world (e.g., for affiliation, autonomy, dominance, order, and of particular relevance to this chapter, achievement).

Murray's taxonomy comes under a criticism that inevitably confronts any rationally constructed taxonomy of needs. Why are the particular needs on Murray's list "basic"? What about needs not on the list? For exam-

ple, is the need for sleep not a primary need? Should needs for attachment or for novelty not be included among the secondary needs? The concern here is not the presence or absence of a particular need but the lack of an objective criterion for deciding which needs to include and exclude. A further problem is the difficulty of explaining overt action in terms of the overarching taxonomy of needs. The link from acts to needs is commonly ambiguous. A given act, for example competing in a sporting contest, could, in principle, be motivated by a variety of needs (achievement, affiliation, dominance, etc.). We note that this problem is common to many theories that posit a universal system of needs, motives, or tendencies but fail to specify the processes that link elements of the system to particular acts or to provide methodological tools for unambiguously verifying the links.

Rather than constructing a list of needs, a more powerful theoretical step would be to establish an integrated need system that explains how different needs are related to one another. Abraham Maslow (1954) provided psychology's most influential model of this sort. In his hierarchical model, higher-level needs could be pursued only after lower-level needs were fulfilled. Starting at the bottom, the individual progressively may move from concern with physiological needs (e.g., food, sleep) to needs for safety, love and social belonging, and self-esteem. Finally, individuals who reach the top of the hierarchy are driven by a need for self-actualization, that is, a need to fulfill oneself and actualize one's potentiality (Maslow, 1954).

Maslow's theory proved to have considerable practical value. Educators and managers, for example, used the model to organize educational and work settings so that students' and employees' activities served growth motives rather than merely lower-level needs. However, like other need theories, Maslow's model is not an adequate foundation for the contemporary analysis of personality variables in motivation. The processes and mechanisms related to each of the needs are poorly specified. Further, it is difficult to reconcile the model with cases in which individuals seem simultaneously to be pursuing both higher- and lower-level motives. History's many examples of people pursuing reprehensible acts in the name of higher-level purposes such as religion or nationalism provide cases in point.

■ *McClelland and Atkinson.* Historically, the limitation of need-based theories prompted conceptual alternatives. Major advances were provided in the mid-20th century by David McClelland and John Atkinson. Moving forward from Murray's analysis of achievement need, McClelland initially explored achievement motivation, both as it can be measured in the lab and as it expresses itself, at a global level, in the economic well being of nations (McClelland, 1961). In his late work, McClelland posited a theory featuring three basic motives, namely, motives for achievement, affiliation, and power (McClelland, 1985). Each motive encompasses opposing desires and fears. Achievement involves a desire for success and a fear of failure. Affiliation needs combine desire for protection and fear of rejection by others. Power needs encompass both a desire for dominance and a fear of dependency. Individuals differ in their relative strength of each motivational orientation, and situations vary in the degree to which they tap into one versus another motive. McClelland's theoretical system thus could address both individual differences and within-person variations in cognition and behavior. To McClelland, motives are learned, primarily as the result of early experiences and socialization processes (McClelland, 1985).

McClelland devoted particular empirical attention to the motive to achieve. He used the Thematic Apperception Test to tap fantasies and free associations that reflect the individual's underlying achievement orientation. A particularly interesting feature of McClelland's work was his recognition of both individual differences and cultural variations in achievement needs. A culture's socialization processes and educational practices instill a greater or lesser inclination to achieve in its members. Societies that encourage autonomy and per-

sonal achievement may achieve more rapid economic growth. McClelland examined this possibility by comparing economic development in countries where a Protestant work ethic prevailed to development in Catholic countries, which may be somewhat more inclined to endorse family- and group-related motives. In historical retrospect, these expectations about cultural norms, achievement motives, and economic development seem highly questionable. Despite its Protestant work ethic and achievement orientation, the U.S. economy declined in the 1970s and 1980s. The economies of Japan and other southeast Asian countries expanded during this period despite their collectivistic norms, contrary to what McClelland's analysis might have predicted. McClelland himself came to realize (1985) that variations such as those between Protestant and Catholic populations were far less significant than was first thought, if they existed at all.

A related approach to achievement motives was pursued by John Atkinson, who added two crucial pieces to the analysis of motivation. First, reflecting earlier work (Lewin, 1935; Tolman, 1932), he embraced an expectancy – value framework: People act when they expect that they might be able to achieve ends that are subjectively valuable to them. Atkinson thus explicitly introduced subjective thinking, rather than objective probabilities and utilities, into the psychology of motivated choice. In contrast to the drive theories, his expectancy – value framework successfully captured the purposive, future-oriented nature of human motivation. Second, Atkinson recognized that action often reflects a tradeoff between positive and negative incentives and expectations. Risk-taking entails prospective success and failure. Achievement motivation, then, reflects a combination of (1) a motive to succeed and a subjective probability of success and (2) a motive to avoid failure and a subjective probability of failure (Atkinson, 1964). Importantly, in this model Atkinson distinguished between *motivation* and *motive*. Atkinson captured the dynamics of motivation through a mathematical model in which the overall tendency to approach or avoid an achievement activity was an arithmetic function of the strength of the tendency to approach the task minus the strength of the tendency to avoid it; both approach and avoidance tendencies were themselves multiplicative functions of motive strengths, subjective probabilities, and incentive values of success and failure. Motivation is the state that results from the joint influence of incentives associated with success and with failure and the expectation that each will occur. A motive is a disposition to desire certain classes of positive and negative incentives.

Atkinson posited a mathematical model of motivation. The total strength of the tendency to approach or avoid an achievement-oriented activity was posited to be a multiplicative function of motive strength, expected probability of success, and incentive value. Incentive value, however, did not figure prominently as a separate determinant for Atkinson because value was assumed to be an inverse function of the probability of success, that is, people particularly value success on difficult tasks. Although an inverse relation between probability and value was a mathematically parsimonious assumption, in retrospect it deflected attention from unique questions about subjective values in motivation (Eccles, Wigfield, & Schiefele, 1998). Subsequent work in the expectancy – value tradition by Eccles et al. (1998) and Feather and Newton (1982) expanded the role of values in achievement theory.

Despite this limitation, Atkinson's theory received much empirical support, particularly regarding its prediction that individuals of differing motive strengths would differentially prefer moderately challenging versus easy or extremely challenging tasks (Weiner, 1992). His model dominated research throughout the 1960s. The distinction between success- and failure- related motives was a precursor to many contemporary developments in the field, such as the analysis of performance goals and self-regulatory processes associated with personal success versus the avoidance of harm or embarrassment (Grant & Dweck,

1999; Elliot & Harackiewicz, 1996; Elliot & Church, 1997; Elliot & Sheldon, 1998; Higgins, 1997, 1999).

Despite their virtues, expectancy – value theories proved insufficient as a basis for analyzing human motivation. One concern is the difficulty of reconciling the multiplicative mathematical model of choice behavior with findings in the cognitive psychology of decision making. People's limited information-processing capacities make it difficult if not impossible for them to engage in the complex utility maximization suggested by Atkinson's model. Rather than maximization of utilities, the classic contributions of Simon (e.g., 1983) indicate that rationale choice involves subjective processes such as "satisficing," or reaching a decision that is merely satisfactory under the current circumstances. The seminal work of Tversky and Kahneman (1982) reveals that people's decisions often violate basic mathematical axioms of choice. People respond differentially to objectively equivalent gains versus losses and respond erratically to extremely high and low probabilities (Kahneman & Tversky, 1979). Many contemporary investigators would judge the multiplicative choice model of achievement theory to be a mathematical abstraction, which fails to capture the decision-making processes of real individuals who must make decisions quickly, under stress, and within the cognitive constraints of limited working memory capacity.

Empirical data also question the assumptions of a universal expectancy – value system. Shah & Higgins (1997) have examined both naturally occurring and experimentally induced individual differences in people's construal of achievement tasks. When people construed tasks in terms of prospective accomplishments, expectancy – value theory was a good predictor of choice behavior. However, when people viewed the same tasks in terms of risks that they needed to avoid (e.g., risks of professional rejection that might follow poor performance), expectancy – value predictions no longer held (Shah & Higgins, 1997). When risks are involved, people appear to feel that they must attain a goal at any cost. Expectancy considerations, then, are less important determinants of behavior, and expectancy – value formulations no longer hold (Higgins, 1997). Kuhl (1986) similarly reports idiosyncratic variations in people's tendency to regulate their action according to expectancy-related versus value-related information; as he points out, these variations violate the assumption of expectancy – value models that a single rule for combining expectancy and value information can be applied to all persons.

More generally, the classic expectancy – value frameworks suffered from a limitation that became more apparent and more significant with the passing years. Atkinson's (1964) theory and other expectancy – value frameworks of this era (e.g., Heckhausen, 1967), were cognitive theories in that they examined subjective beliefs and dynamic mental processes. However, they generally did not provide analyses of the exact information-processing mechanisms through which expectancies are formed and modified. The theories simply were not informed by the contemporary cognitive psychology of mental representation, reasoning, and inference. Theorists of the day are not to be blamed for this limitation since, of course, most of the critical developments in cognitive psychology occurred after they had formulated their theories.

Finally, expectancy – value frameworks can be faulted for emphasizing expectations about the environment at the cost of giving insufficient attention to beliefs about the self. Self-referent beliefs are important in this context not only because they contribute to behavior but also because they influence the outcome expectancies analyzed in expectancy – value theories (Bandura, 1991b). People's expectations about the environmental consequences they are likely to experience are heavily determined by their beliefs about whether they can achieve performances that are worthy of reward. Contemporary approaches to personality and motivation have tended to place greater emphasis on the self.

## Contemporary Cognitive Frameworks

As we noted at the outset of this chapter, cognitive analyses of motivation gained ascendancy in the field. These frameworks had the great advantage of capitalizing on advances in the understanding of thinking processes coming from cognitive psychology and the study of social cognition. We consider here three cognitively based theoretical frameworks that have strongly influenced research on personality factors in motivation and self-regulation. The reader should understand that this is not an exhaustive review of cognitively based motivation theories. We merely address three approaches that are distinguished by their ability to analyze motivation within more comprehensive theoretical frameworks and that also illuminate issues of personality functioning, individual differences, and psychological disorders.

■ *Attribution Theory.* The way people explain their past successes and failures heavily bears on their future motivational states. Weiner (1985, 1986, 1992; Anderson & Weiner, 1992) has provided the most detailed analysis of the way in which attributional processes govern motivation and emotion. In beginning his work, Weiner expanded and reformulated the expectancy – value approach of Atkinson. Rather than explaining action in terms of affectively based motives, he viewed subjective judgments about the causes of action as a driving force. Outcomes prompt a search for their causes (Heider, 1958). Judgments about the causes of events determine affective and motivational reactions.

One's achievements can be attributed to any of an enormous variety of factors ranging from genes to astrological signs. Weiner (1996) brings order to this diversity by providing a taxonomic scheme for organizing judgments of responsibility. Perceived causes of events vary along dimensions including locus (Is the cause internal or external to the self?), controllability (Can the actor alter the cause?), and globality and stability (Does the cause generalize across situations and time?). Variations along these attribution dimensions predict aspects of social behavior. For example, people treat others more leniently when their shortcomings are attributed to uncontrollable causes (Weiner, 1996).

Attributional tendencies may be stable over time and thus constitute enduring personality variables. People develop characteristic "attributional styles," some of which may make one vulnerable to psychological distress (Peterson & Seligman, 1984). The hopelessness model of depression (Abramson, Metalsky, & Alloy, 1989), for example, posits that an attributional style involving stable, global attributions for negative life events predisposes one to experience a particular subtype of depression. Rotter's construct of locus of control (1966), which has received extensive empirical attention (e.g., Lefcourt, 1976), also is an attributional style variable, in that locus of control refers to stable, generalized expectancies about the causes of environmental outcomes.

Although attributional style variables have much appeal, as explanatory constructs they have many of the same limitations as other global, decontextualized personality variables. Characterizing people as possessing one versus another attributional style is valuable to the degree that there exists broad cross-situational consistency in attributional tendencies. Cutrona, Russell, and Jones (1985) employed the attributional style questionnaire (Peterson et al., 1982) to assess people's beliefs about the causes of six different negative events. They found "only weak evidence of a cross-situationally consistent attributional style" (Cutrona et al., 1985, p. 1043) among the population at large, and no support for the possibility that a particular subset of the population consistently engages in one versus another style of explaining events across contexts. Even if statistically significant cross-situational consistency in attributional style is observed, characterizing individuals solely in terms of an average style sacrifices potentially valuable information about how their style of explaining events may vary systematically from one social context to another (cf. Mischel & Shoda, 1995; Shoda, 1999). Zelli and Dodge (1999), for example, report that

adolescents' attributions about peers' behavior can not be captured by any global attributional variable. Instead, people's attributional "style" varies as they contemplate the actions of one versus another peer. Rather than positing global style variables, people's characteristic attributional tendencies might best be understood by examining the knowledge structures that underlie judgments of causality and the potentially idiosyncratic ways in which people link causal beliefs to particular persons, social interactions, and life outcomes of importance to them.

Attribution theory sheds much light on people's psychological experiences in both achievement and interpersonal settings. However, as Weiner (1996) himself recognizes, it can not stand alone as a comprehensive model of motivation and self-regulation. One limitation of attribution theory is its relative emphasis on retrospective judgments as opposed to people's aims and thoughts about the future. Deci (1996) contends that this feature makes attribution theory "more akin to drive theories of motivation (e.g., Hull, 1943) than to cognitive theories" (p. 221). Empirical findings suggest that future-oriented cognition rather than retrospective judgments of responsibility are the proximal causes of many achievement behaviors (Raynor, 1982). For example, Covington and Omelich (1979) find that people's perceptions of their capabilities for the future, not their beliefs about causes in the past, mediate achievement behavior. Research on attributions, cognitive appraisals, and emotions leads to similar conclusions about the relative importance of future-oriented cognition (Smith et al., 1993) (see chapter 10).

The other two theoretical frameworks we now consider place greater emphasis on psychological processes that come into play as people contemplate the future and regulate their ongoing goal-directed efforts.

■ *Control Theory.* Cybernetic, or control theory, models of self-regulation provide a comprehensive framework within which to view motivational processes (Carver & Scheier, 1981, 1998, 1999; Powers, 1973; cf. Miller,

Galanter, & Pribram, 1960). Rather than focusing on individuals' retrospective judgments about the causes of events, control theories primarily address information-processing mechanisms through which people regulate their ongoing actions. Control theory likens self-regulation to the functioning of a feedback system such as a thermostat. Feedback systems minimize discrepancies between current states and standards that represent desired states of affairs. Just as the thermostat minimizes discrepancies between desired and current temperature, a feedback system for behavioral self-regulation minimizes discrepancies between a personal standard for performance and current attainments.

Feedback systems consists of four linked elements (Carver & Scheier, 1998). An *input function* senses information in the environment. A *comparator* compares these inputs with internalized standards, or *reference values*. Depending on the match between inputs and standards, an *output function* generates behavioral output. When the comparator detects discrepancies between inputs and standards, the output function changes its behavior. The comparator is thought to become activated, or engaged, under conditions that heighten self-focused attention (Carver & Scheier, 1981). Environmental stimuli that direct people's attention to themselves lead them to compare their behavior with internalized standards (Scheier & Carver, 1983) and prompt closer matches between standards and behavior (Carver, 1974).

Control theory recognizes two types of feedback loops (Carver & Scheier, 1998). Negative feedback loops minimize discrepancies between inputs and standards, whereas positive feedback loops seek to maximize discrepancies. In positive loops, then, standards represent outcomes one wishes to avoid. One may seek to maximize the discrepancy between one's current behavior and standards representing a lazy or obnoxious self.

Control theorists acknowledge that hypothesized feedback systems are not sufficient to account for human self-regulation. Unlike thermostats, people reflect on their capabilities and give up if they expect that their efforts to reduce discrepancies will fail. Expectations about one's ability to achieve outcomes thus figure into the self-regulation of behavior (Carver & Scheier, 1998). As is consistent with control theory's emphasis on self-focused attention in behavioral regulation, expectations are found to be particularly influential in regulating behavioral persistence when people focus on the self (Carver, Blaney, & Scheier, 1979).

A strength of control theories is their ability to capture hierarchical relations among standards and goals for performance. Not only do people have goals such as "prepare dinner" and "be a better person," but their goals may be linked hierarchically. Preparing dinner may be a way of making life easier for one's spouse, which in turn is a way of being a better person (e.g., Carver & Scheier, 1998; Emmons, 1997). These relations among goals can be represented by positing feedback loops that are nested hierarchically (Carver & Scheier, 1982). Research on action identification processes (Vallacher & Wegner, 1986) indicates that people's subjective construal of their action shifts to lower levels of such hierarchies when difficulties are encountered. When scientists' lives are going well, they may regulate their actions according to standards such as "advance knowledge" or "promote my career." When they run into obstacles in their work, they may no longer construe activities in terms of these high-level classifications. Instead, their self-regulatory standards may involve lower-level construals such as "figure out principal components analysis" or "run more subjects."

Despite their obvious value, control theories have come under criticism on a number of grounds. Some contend that feedback systems are overly mechanistic and thus underestimate people's capacity for willful choice (Locke & Latham, 1990). This criticism is not surprising in light of control theorists' suggestion that robots are a valuable metaphor for understanding human self-regulation (Carver & Scheier, 1996, 1998). Some believe that control models underestimate people's capacity to contribute creatively to their personal development (Bandura, 1991b, 1997). People's tendency to set novel challenges for themselves, even when they do not receive explicit performance feedback (e.g., Bandura & Cervone, 1983), seems difficult to reconcile with the action of cybernetic systems that merely regulate action with respect to existing standards. Control theorists counter that many goals change over time, which makes control models sufficiently dynamic to account for human creativity (Carver & Scheier, 1998). Indeed, Carver & Scheier (1998) recently have indicated how nonlinear dynamic-system models can shed light on people's sudden shifts from task engagement to disengagement or from one task to another (cf. Vallacher & Nowak, 1997).

Finally, control theories may be criticized for underestimating the role of emotion in self-regulation. To be clear, control theory does address the genesis of emotion. Carver and Scheier (1990, 1998) propose that the self-regulatory system monitors not only the reduction of discrepancies but (at a "meta" level of functioning) how rapidly discrepancies are being reduced. People feel positive (or negative) affect when their rate of discrepancy reduction does (or does not) meet their standards for an acceptable rate of reduction. Although this model accounts for the generation of feelings, the resulting affective states play little role in the self-regulation of behavior. Carver and Scheier (1996), for example, suggest that it is not necessary to include affective self-reactions among the personal determinants of behavior. Some empirical findings appear inconsistent with this contention. Research on goal setting and self-regulation indicates that people's affective reactions to their own performance can contribute to behavior independently of the affects of standards and performance expectations (Bandura & Jourdan, 1991; Cervone et al., 1991; Cervone & Wood, 1995). Other findings suggest that affective states can directly influence the standards people adopt (Cervone et al., 1994; Scott & Cervone, 2000; Tillema, Cervone, & Scott, in press). Such results sug-

gest that even the comprehensive framework of Carver and Scheier (1998) may insufficiently attend to some determinants of self-regulated motivation.

■ *Social-Cognitive Theories.* Another perspective in the field is one that explores the social-cognitive processes and structures that underlie people's capacity for self-regulation. Much work has revealed how social knowledge structures and social inference processes contribute to goal-directed action (e.g., Cervone & Shoda, 1999b; Gollwitzer & Bargh, 1996; Higgins & Sorrentino, 1990; Karniol & Ross, 1996; Mischel et al., 1996). In some respects, this work follows upon the long-established tradition of linking motivation to attribution processes (Weiner, 1985). Recent efforts, however, differ from attributional approaches by placing greater emphasis on people's thoughts about the future rather than their reflections on past outcomes (see Karniol & Ross, 1996). Mental representations of future states, including visions of future desired and undesired selves (Markus & Nurius, 1986; Ogilvie 1987), prove to have great motivational force.

A particularly comprehensive analysis of social-cognitive mechanisms and self-regulation is the social cognitive theory of Bandura (1986). Since this perspective has been outlined previously (see chapter 4), and since it formed a primary basis for the review of the self-system with which we began the present chapter, we merely provide a brief overview of the sociocognitive analysis of motivation here.

Social cognitive theory explains motivational tendencies primarily in terms of the human capacity for forethought. Beliefs about the future guide behavior in the here and now. Social cognitive theory differentiates among a number of forethought-based motivational mechanisms (Bandura, 1991b). Outcome expectations involve assessments of the consequences that will follow upon alternative courses of action. Self-efficacy perceptions, in contrast, refer to people's beliefs about whether they can perform the actions in the first place. Goals and standards for performance provide a third cognitively based source of motivation by specifying the desired aims of action. Finally, affective self-reactions are a fourth self-influence. People motivate themselves through criticism of their own past efforts and by making self-satisfaction contingent on improved performance (Bandura & Cervone, 1983, 1986).

Other theoretical formulations share social-cognitive theory's interest in the role of control beliefs, expectations, and personal standards in motivation. Deci and Ryan's (1985) cognitive evaluation theory proposes that feelings of challenge and personal competence foster intrinsic interest in tasks. This approach differs from social-cognitive theory primarily by positing that feelings of self-determination are a basic human need. In contrast, in social-cognitive theory, perceived self-efficacy is not a motive or need but a cognitive appraisal. People do not seek either accurate or high self-efficacy appraisal as an end in itself. Rather, people act to attain external rewards or feelings of pride in their accomplishments, and self-efficacy appraisal is a mechanism for regulating one's efforts toward these ends (Bandura, 1997). Perceived self-efficacy, then, is a belief system that regulates action toward ends.

Another theory that bears affinity to the social-cognitive approach is the theory of planned behavior (Ajzen, 1988, 1996), in which behavioral intentions are governed by three factors: a person's attitude about performing the behavior; his or her perception of social pressure to perform the behavior (or not); and perceived behavioral control, defined as the person's perception of how easy or difficult it is to perform the behavior. Intentions, in turn, govern behavior. The theory also recognizes that control perceptions may exert a direct influence on behavior, that is, an influence that is not mediated by behavioral intentions (Ajzen, 1988). The differences between the theory of planned behavior and social-cognitive theory are threefold. First, social cognitive theory explicitly recognizes self-evaluative reactions as a unique motivational mechanism. Second, the theory of planned behavior adopts a multiplicative

(expectancy times value) model of motivation, whereas the social-cognitive approach does not assume that human thought and action can be adequately captured by such mathematical formalisms, for reasons discussed earlier. Finally, the theories differ somewhat in their treatment of control beliefs. Social-cognitive theory objects to defining control beliefs in terms of perceived difficulty because perceptions of difficulty are driven by people's appraisal of their efficacy for performance. To the extent that difficulty and efficacy beliefs diverge, self-efficacy perceptions are likely to be a stronger determinant of performance. Experts in a domain commonly display persistent effort because they judge themselves to be highly efficacious in performing tasks that they also may recognize to be difficult ones.

The approach to motivation that is perhaps closest in orientation to social-cognitive theory is the goal theory of Locke and Latham (1990). As will be reviewed in a subsequent section of this chapter, Locke and Latham identify a set of dimensions of goal setting, that is, ways in which performance goals may vary from one another. Their extensive research documents the powerful effects of variations in goal setting on motivation and achievement.

Bandura's social-cognitive theory and related goal conceptions (e.g., Locke & Latham, 1990) have come under some criticism. Some see the approach as capturing the mechanisms through which people direct their action but as failing to answer the question of "why outcomes or goals are motivating" (Deci, 1992, p. 169) or what might be termed questions of "the energization of behavior" (Deci, 1992, p. 169). This view might suggest that one should posit a system of basic needs that provide the energy for action, such as needs for competence and autonomy (Deci & Ryan, 1985). However, as noted earlier, such "basic need" taxonomies run into conceptual problems, especially in light of findings from both cultural and evolutionary psychology. As Kelly (1955) suggested long ago, it might be profitable for psychology simply to assume that human beings are active organisms and to explore the cognitive mechanisms that mobilize and organize their activity.

A second criticism is that social-cognitive theory may overemphasize rational, self-reflective processes in self-regulation. Although Bandura (1991) and many other social-cognitive theorists acknowledge that cognitive processes may become automated and occur outside of awareness, some evidence (noted above, and reviewed in more detail below) suggests that environmental factors can influence action through nonconscious psychological mechanisms that are not well specified in social-cognitive theory (Bargh, 1997).

## CONTROL BELIEFS AND PERCEPTIONS OF SELF-EFFICACY

A psychological mechanism that is utterly critical to human motivation is people's beliefs in their ability to control the events of their lives. No matter what the stakes, people are unlikely to take action if they believe that they are powerless to control a course of events. A perceived loss of control can profoundly impair mental and physical health (Seligman, 1975). A robust sense of being able to control events can have significant health benefits, even when these control beliefs are unrealistically optimistic (Taylor & Brown, 1988). Each of the cognitive frameworks we have just reviewed highlights the role of control beliefs. The perceived controllability of causes is central to attribution theory (Weiner, 1985). Self-efficacy perceptions, of course, are central to social-cognitive theory (Bandura, 1997). Even control theories, which are built on a machine-system metaphor that appears to discount the human capacity for self-reflection, posit that feelings of confidence play a role in whether people disengage from goal pursuits; Carver and Scheier (1998) provide an apt quote from Henry Ford: "Whether you think you can or think you can't, you're right" (p. 171).

Perceptions of control are so critical that behavioral and physiological responses can be affected by factors that alter perceived control while having no effect on the actual controllability of events. Geen, Davison, & Gatchel (1970) led participants to believe that the occurrence of electric shocks was either controllable or was contingent on their own task performance. In reality, participants could not control the shocks. Nonetheless, the perception of controllability reduced autonomic reactivity. Langer and Rodin (1976) exposed residents of a nursing home to living arrangements that varied their degree of control and responsibility over their day-to-day affairs. Enhanced responsibility and control improved participants' well-being and mental alertness (Langer & Rodin, 1976). Follow-up data suggested that maximizing psychological control may increase the longevity of life (Rodin & Langer, 1977).

Although people differ stably from one another in their control beliefs, it is important to bear in mind that control perceptions can be powerfully altered by even subtle contextual cues. When outcomes are determined entirely by chance, as in a lottery, the presence of factors that merely resemble those found in nonchance settings (e.g., allowing people to choose their own lottery ticket) can create an illusory sense of being able to control outcomes (Langer, 1975; Langer & Roth, 1975). When success requires personal effort, control beliefs can be lowered and motivation reduced by chance factors that have no bearing on one's actual capabilities, such as exposure to a randomly assigned social label that connotes inferiority (Langer & Benevento, 1978). Similarly, exposure to random numbers that represent high or low levels of performance can influence self-efficacy beliefs and behavior (Cervone & Peake, 1986).

### Distinguishing Among Control Beliefs

Perceived control is not a unitary psychological mechanism. As has been recognized (e.g., Rodin, 1990), there are many different aspects to perceived control. Not surprisingly, then, the psychological literature contains a large number of control constructs. A critical first step in understanding the role of control beliefs in personality functioning is to distinguish clearly among alternative aspects of perceived control and to differentiate among the sometimes confusing array of control-related personality variables in the literature. As a step in this direction, we consider two related conceptual schemes for distinguishing among control beliefs.

■ *Outcome Versus Efficacy Beliefs.* A basic distinction in the psychology of control distinguishes outcome expectations from self-efficacy perceptions. Historically, expectancy–value theories focused on expectations about outcomes, that is, whether a given response would be followed by a rewarding or punishing consequence. In his self-efficacy theory, Bandura (1977a) distinguished these expectation from logically prior ones, namely, expectations that one can perform the behavior in the first place (Figure 6). Self-efficacy perceptions, then, are people's judgments about their capabilities to execute courses of actions, not expectations about whether the actions will bring rewarding consequences.

The distinction between efficacy and outcome beliefs has been recognized, under alternative labels, by a number of writers (e.g., Abramson, Seligman, & Teasdale, 1978; Heckhausen, 1991). Ellen Skinner (1996) has presented a valuable taxonomic organization of these and other control constructs. Skinner distinguishes among *agents* (the person or group taking action to control events), *means* (the actions through which control may be achieved), and *ends* (desired and undesired to

outcomes). Agent–means relations, then, are similar to perceptions of self-efficacy and means–ends beliefs are similar to outcome expectations in Bandura's (1977a, 1997) formulation.[2] According to Skinner, the third relation, agent–ends beliefs, correspond to the person's overall sense of being able to control events.

Since one should not complicate psychological models with unnecessary constructs, the question arises as to whether the theoretical distinction between self-efficacy judgment and outcome expectations (Bandura, 1977a; Skinner, 1996) is necessary for understanding motivation. Findings from a variety of paradigms, conducted in a wide variety of settings, answer this question in the affirmative. Many investigators have assessed naturally occurring levels of perceived self-efficacy and expected outcomes as individuals engage in challenging or aversive tasks. Self-efficacy perceptions uniquely add to the prediction of approach behavior toward feared stimuli (Lee, 1984b), assertive interpersonal behavior (Lee, 1984a), athletic performance (Barling & Abel, 1983), mathematical problem solving (Sexton & Tuckman, 1991), pain tolerance (Baker & Kirsch, 1991; Manning & Wright, 1983; Williams & Kinney, 1991) and the use of coping strategies for chronic pain (Jensen, Turner, & Romano, 1991). Other studies experimentally manipulate outcome expectations and perceived self-efficacy. Efficacy judg-

[2] Bandura (1997, chapter 1) notes distinctions between his formulation and that of Skinner and colleagues. For the present purposes, we simply wish to emphasize a commonality of the frameworks, namely, the distinction between beliefs about one's capabilities for action and beliefs about how the environment will respond to one's action.

Figure 6. Distinction between outcome expectations and self-efficacy perceptions. From Bandura, 1997.

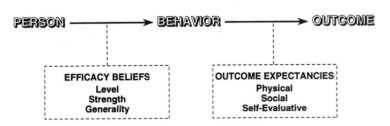

ments uniquely predict cognitive performance (Davis & Yates, 1982) and predict interpersonal behavioral intentions after controlling for both outcome expectations and outcome value (Maddux, Norton, & Stoltenberg, 1986).

Not only do self-efficacy perceptions have unique predictive value, but they commonly predict behavior more strongly than do outcome expectations. Williams and colleagues have assessed efficacy and outcome beliefs among phobics as they confront feared activities. Self-efficacy judgments commonly predict a substantial percentage of the variance in behavior after statistically controlling for the effects of outcome beliefs, whereas outcome expectations have little influence after controlling for the effects of perceived self-efficacy (see Williams, 1995; Williams & Cervone, 1998). Longitudinal investigations of cognitive performance and educational attainments point to similar conclusions. Agency–means beliefs predict school grades and performance on tests of cognitive skill, whereas means–ends beliefs do not (Chapman, Skinner, & Baltes, 1990; Little, Oettingen, Stetsenko, & Baltes, 1995).

Control beliefs and their impact on behavior may vary cross-culturally. Little et al. (1995) studied control beliefs and academic performance among middle-class and lower middle class school children in four different sociocultural settings: East Berlin, West Berlin, Moscow, and Los Angeles. Both agency–means and means–ends beliefs were used to predict grade attainment in the respective school systems (Figure 7). Two findings are of note. First, agency–means, or self-efficacy-related beliefs, were linked to attainments more strongly in the European cultures than in the United States. Little et al. (1995) surmise that the American sociocultural practice of raising expectations and feelings of self-esteem so enhances self-perceptions that they commonly deviate from students' actual capabilities and thus are relatively poorly related to school achievements. Control beliefs indeed were higher among American than among European schoolchildren. Second, agency beliefs predicted perfor-

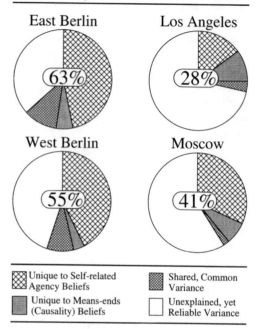

Figure 7. Predictors of academic performance among American, German, and Russian children. From Little et al., 1995.

mance more strongly than did expectations about the links between behaviors and outcomes. Even in the American sample, the predictive value of agency beliefs exceeded the unique predictive strength of means–ends cognitions.

The contention that efficacy- and outcome-based cognitions are conceptually distinct does not mean that they are empirically unrelated. Self-efficacy beliefs partly determine which prospective outcomes people dwell on (Borden, Clum, & Salmon, 1991; Kent & Gibbons, 1987). People with a low sense of efficacy are more likely to contemplate negative outcomes. Conversely, outcome beliefs may sometimes influence efficacy appraisals. The health action process approach of Schwarzer and Fuchs (1995) posits that in the domain of risk perception and health behavior, thoughts about risks and prospective outcomes may influence cognitions about self-efficacy. When people recognize that prospective outcomes have potentially great value for them, they may be more confident in their ability to muster a high degree of effort.

■ *Alternative Targets of Control Efforts.* In addition to distinctions among subjective beliefs, it also is valuable to distinguish between different types of outcomes that people may be trying to control. Care is required here because the term *control* has been used to refer both to subjective perceptions and to the targets of self-regulatory efforts (see Skinner, 1996).

In studying the targets of control, that is, the types of outcomes that people are trying to attain through their self-control efforts, it is valuable to distinguish between primary and secondary control (Heckhausen & Schutz, 1995; Rothbaum, Weisz, & Synder, 1982). Primary control attempts are efforts to alter one's environment. Secondary control attempts to modify one's internal psychological state. Heckhausen and Schultz (1995, 1998) have analyzed how people's efforts at primary versus secondary control change over the life course. In old age, biological declines force individuals increasingly to rely on secondary control strategies. Rather than exclusively trying to alter environmental circumstances, adaptive strategies for the elderly include the realistic adjustment of personal aspirations, selective social comparison, and cognitive reappraisals that help them to accept physiological decline (Heckhausen & Schutz, 1995). As we noted in chapter 4, these strategies in old age may meet the requirement of optimization through selection and compensation.

A similar distinction is found in the literature on stress and coping. Lazarus and Folkman (1984) distinguish between problem-focused and emotion-focused coping. Problem-focused coping is an attempt to alter the source of one's stress in the environment. Emotion-focused coping is an effort to reduce one's internal psychic distress, which may be accomplished by reappraising one's circumstances rather than changing them. People who doubt their efficacy to control external events tend to rely on emotion-focused strategies.

■ *Control Beliefs Versus Fantasies.* Control beliefs are thoughts about what is likely to happen in the future. They are assessments of the relations between oneself, potential actions, and prospective outcomes. Of course, control beliefs are not necessarily "cold" calculations. Much work in social cognition (Fiske & Taylor, 1991) suggests that control judgments, like any other judgments, may be affected by motivational influences that cause individuals to over- or underestimate their degree of control. Nonetheless, control judgments are attempts to accurately appraise future possibilities.

Motivational processes also may be influenced by another aspect of mental activity, namely, fantasies. Much of mental life consists of internally generated images, daydreams, and fantasies (e.g., Singer & Bonanno, 1990), whose content may bear no relation to either objective or subjective beliefs about the likelihood of events. We can happily fantasize about having won the lottery while simultaneously recognizing that our chances of winning are impossibly remote. Research by Oettingen (1996) suggests that fantasies and rational expectancies are differentially related to motivation. Optimistic expectancies are generally advantageous (Avia & Vazquez, 1998; Seligman, 1991; Taylor, 1989; Taylor & Brown, 1988), but optimistic flights of fantasy are not. Highly optimistic fantasies, Oettingen suggests, may lead people to underestimate the effort required for achievement. In a study of women participating in a weight loss program, Oettingen and Wadden (1991) assessed both expectations about weight loss and weight-related fantasies, the latter measure being a rating of the positivity of fantasies produced when participants were asked to envision their future selves after the weight loss program. Both after the program and at a one-year follow-up evaluation, expectancies and fantasies both predicted success in the program but in opposite directions. People with highly positive expectancies lost more weight, whereas those who had engaged in highly positive fantasies lost less. Analogous findings are found in studies of health behavior, interpersonal relationships, and professional achievement (Oettingen, 1996).

Having distinguished among control constructs and differentiated them from alternative variables in the psychology of motivation, we now turn to three critical questions about control beliefs and personality functioning: (1) Do a person's perceptions of control generalize from one context to another? (2) Through what mechanisms do control beliefs influence social behavior? (3) And what are the sources of high versus low control beliefs; more specifically, how can one instill the robust sense of personal control that is so often required to cope with life's challenges? We address these questions by focusing on the literature on perceived self-efficacy, because this construct is firmly embedded in a broad theory of personality (Bandura, 1986) and because it has received an extraordinary degree of empirical attention.

## Perceived Self-Efficacy

As noted above, perceived self-efficacy refers to people's judgments of their abilities to execute courses of action in designed settings. Two elements of this definition are of note. The first is that perceived self-efficacy is defined contextually, that is, with respect to the particular challenge that the individual is confronting. This definition has important implications for psychological assessment. Rather than constructing a generic assessment device, most investigators craft self-efficacy scales that are designed to tap self-assessments in a particular domain of functioning. This strategy is illustrated in measures designed to assess people's perceptions of their capability to perform socially skilled behaviors with members of the opposite sex (Hill, 1989); to avoid overeating (Glynn & Ruderman, 1986) or smoking (DiClemente, Prochaska, & Gilbertini, 1985) when feeling tense or depressed; to perform well academically (Bandura et al., 1996a); to resist peer pressure for transgressive behavior (Bandura et al., 1996; Caprara et al., 1998); to manage positive and negative emotions (Caprara, et al., 1999) to engage in normal

work or sexual activities after an abortion (Major et al., 1990); or to practice safe sex by consistently using condoms (Dilorio, Maibach, O'Leary, & Sanderson, 1997).

A second feature of the definition of perceived self-efficacy is that the construct refers to judgments of the behaviors one can perform, independently of the value one attaches to the given acts. One may, for example, have a high sense of self-efficacy for performing job duties but draw little self-worth from this if one's job is perceived to lack value or challenge.

Combining these two points illustrates the distinction between perceived self-efficacy and self-esteem. Self-esteem is a global sense of self-worth (e.g., Coopersmith, 1967); perceived self-efficacy is neither global nor an evaluation of self-worth. The differences here are far more than semantic. Perceived self-efficacy commonly is a strong predictor of behavior, whereas self-esteem measures predict behavioral acts rather weakly, leading even self-esteem researchers to question the construct's value as an explanation of social behavior (Leary, 1995).

The self-efficacy theory strategy of assessing beliefs contextually, that is, with respect to designated circumstances and acts, has great practical predictive value. As we have just noted, global assessments of self-concept are notoriously poor predictors of behavior. In contrast, contextualized self-efficacy assessments commonly predict remarkably well.

Research on the role of self-efficacy perception in phobic behavior provides striking examples of the predictive power of self-efficacy beliefs. Phobic people's self-assessments of their efficacy for performance routinely predict their subsequent behavior at correlational levels of .7 to .9 (e.g., Bandura, Adams, & Beyer, 1977; reviewed in Williams, 1995). Further, self-efficacy assessments predict not only overall levels of attainment but behavioral success and failure at the level of individual acts (Cervone, 1985). In other words, suppose that two people who are facing the same set of activities judge that they perform equal numbers of tasks but differ in the specific acts that they judge they can manage. Self-efficacy assessments commonly predict not only their overall, aggregate level of performance but the specific behaviors that they do and do not accomplish. Accurate behavioral prediction of this sort, at the level of both interindividual differences and intraindividual variation in behavior, is exceedingly rare.

Self-efficacy measures commonly predict behavior more accurately than do global trait measures and often statistically mediate the relations that are found between global dispositional variables and performance. For example, in the study of academic achievement, peer acceptance, and the occurrence of problem behavior, self-efficacy measures subsume most of the variance accounted for by Big Five scores and have predictive value beyond that of the five factors (Caprara, Barbaranelli, Pastorelli, & Cervone, 2000). In work on stress and coping, self-efficacy beliefs statistically mediate the relation between global dispositional variables (e.g., optimism, self-esteem) and adjustment to stressful events (Cozzarelli, 1993; also see Major et al., 1998).

Powerful evidence of the predictive utility of self-efficacy measures comes from a meta-analysis by Stajkovic and Luthans (1998). These investigators synthesized the results of 114 studies relating contextualized self-efficacy assessments to work performance. The overall meta-analytically derived correlation between self-efficacy perception and performance was .38. This figure is based on both laboratory and field studies, including examination of highly complex tasks on which performance is multidetermined and many factors may obscure the strength of efficacy–behavior relations. On tasks of lower complexity, the mean correlation between self-efficacy and performance was even higher, in the .5 range. As the authors note, this predictive strength contrasts sharply with the typical results of studies that attempt to link work performance to global personality trait constructs: "There still does not appear to be clear, systematic evidence indicating that self-report trait measures predict specific behavioral outcomes at levels approaching those

found in this meta-analysis" (Stajkovic & Luthans, 1998, p. 253). They also note that the obtained results likely underestimate the actual behavioral impact of self-efficacy beliefs because a major self-efficacy effect is not included in the analysis. Low efficacy perceptions not only impair performance but lead people to completely avoid activities. People who avoid work activities because of low perceived efficacy essentially select themselves out of the studies that constitute the meta-analysis. Despite this restriction of range, the obtained efficacy–behavior links are quite robust (Stajkovic and Luthans, 1998).

### Behavioral, Cognitive, and Affective Consequences of Efficacy Beliefs

Having established that self-efficacy perceptions and performance outcomes are often correlated, another question is *how* efficacy beliefs influence performance. Knowing only that people with a high sense of efficacy tend to do better on tasks is only partially informative. It leaves unanswered questions about the processes through which control beliefs influence behavioral success. Ideally, one would identify specific behavioral, cognitive, and affective mechanisms through which efficacy beliefs influence personal functioning.

Bandura (1997) identifies four processes through which efficacy beliefs influence behavioral outcomes. Each has received substantial empirical support. First, self-efficacy perceptions influence decisions about which activities to pursue. People undertake tasks for which they judge themselves efficacious and avoid pursuits that they judge they cannot handle. Research on self-efficacy determinants of career decision making illustrates this point. Even among samples of men and women of equal intellectual ability, women tend to have lower perceptions of self-efficacy for completing educational programs that require mathematical and technical proficiency. As a result, they less frequently choose course work in mathematics and sciences or consider these fields as career options (Betz & Hackett, 1981; Hackett & Betz, 1995). The effects of such decisional processes compound over time. When people avoid situations that they potentially could have handled, they forfeit opportunities to acquire valuable new skills. The lack of skills becomes a further impediment to success.

Once one undertakes an activity, self-efficacy perceptions affect effort and task persistence. Decisions about how long to persevere are based partly on self-reflections about one's capabilities. Those who doubt their efficacy tend to slacken their efforts and give up, whereas those with a strong sense of self-efficacy persevere (e.g., Cervone & Peake, 1986). The implications of this link between subjective self-perceptions and behavioral persistence are considerable, since most achievements in life require sustained, persistent effort.

Self-efficacy appraisals also influence affective responses. People with a high sense of efficacy experience less anxiety about potentially threatening events (e.g., Bandura, Cioffi, Taylor, & Brouillard, 1988; Bandura, Taylor, Williams, Mefford, & Barchas, 1985). Low self-efficacy for accomplishing important life tasks engenders depression (Cutrona & Troutman, 1986). Low academic and social self-efficacy fosters depression in young adolescents (Bandura, Pastorelli, Barbaranelli, & Caprara, 1999).

Finally, efficacy beliefs influence the quality of complex cognitive performance. On complex activities that require the acquisition of task knowledge and formulation of strategies, people with a higher sense of efficacy develop and test strategies more analytically (Cervone, 1993; Wood & Bandura, 1989). Robust efficacy perceptions also enhance performance on stressful memory tasks (Berry, West, & Dennehey, 1989); memory efficacy beliefs are particularly important among the elderly, who may reappraise their cognitive capabilities in light of possible age-related declines (Berry, 1989). The impact of self-efficacy appraisals on cognitive performance is partly mediated by cognitive interference (Sarason, Pierce, & Sarason, 1996). A low sense of efficacy may lead people to dwell not only on the task but on themselves (e.g., Elliot & Dweck, 1988).

Distraction from the task at hand interferes with performance.

By affecting people's acceptance of challenges, persistence despite setbacks, execution of complex cognitive strategies, and anxiety versus calmness in the face of threat, higher efficacy perceptions generally promote superior achievement. However, in some exceptional cases, extremely high efficacy perceptions may be dysfunctional. Highly self-efficacious persons may, for example, be overly persistent in unsolvable tasks (Janoff-Bullman & Brickman, 1982) and may engage in risky actions that they should avoid (Haaga & Stewart, 1992b; also see Baumeister & Scher, 1988).

■ *Control Beliefs as Proximal Determinants of Behavior.* A key question in the study of cognition and motivation is whether a given cognitive mechanism causally contributes to behavior or is merely epiphenomenal. A cognitive process may be correlated with other factors (third variables) that are the true causes of behavioral success. In the case of perceived self-efficacy, an obvious third variable is skill. People with more knowledge and skills do tend to have a higher sense of their capabilities. Objective skill differences might, in principle, account for correlations between subjective efficacy beliefs and performance.

Much research has addressed this issue and has substantiated the causal links from self-efficacy judgment to behavior (see Bandura, 1997; Cervone & Scott, 1995). Particularly convincing evidence comes from work that experimentally manipulates efficacy judgments while holding others factors constant. This can be done through subtle contextual cues that bias the formation of self-efficacy judgments. Cervone & Peake (1986) manipulated efficacy judgments through the use of anchoring cues (Tversky & Kahneman, 1974). A cognitive anchor is a conceptual starting point in an inference task, that is, an initial guess that people may adjust to yield a final estimate of a quantity. Final estimates tend to be biased in the direction of the anchor, even if the anchor value itself provides no information about the target of judgment (Tversky & Kahneman, 1974). Prior to performing a cognitive task, participants were asked to indicate whether they thought they could solve more or less than $X$ of the upcoming problems, the value of $X$ apparently being a random number, although the value actually was preselected to be particularly high or low. High and low anchors, respectively, raised and lowered self-efficacy perceptions. The altered self-appraisals correspondingly influenced subsequent task persistence (Cervone & Peake, 1986). Thus, self-efficacy perceptions contributed to behavior even when efficacy beliefs were altered in a manner that could not have provided any differential skills or information about the task. Variations in the order in which people consider hypothetical levels of future performance similarly influence efficacy judgment and behavior (Berry, West, & Dennehey, 1989; Peake & Cervone, 1989). Anchoring cues can affect performance by altering not only efficacy beliefs but also self-set goals (Hinsz, Kalnbach, & Lorentz, 1997).

Efficacy judgments also can be influenced by the brief contemplation of positive or negative performance-related factors. Dwelling on personal strengths versus weaknesses makes different information salient, or cognitively available, when people appraise their efficacy for performance. People who recently have contemplated their personal weaknesses display lower self-efficacy appraisals and motivation (Cervone, 1989).

These results strongly suggest that people's self-appraisals of their performance capabilities contribute causally to their levels of motivation. This conclusion is bolstered by the results of studies that manipulate self-efficacy beliefs through false performance feedback (e.g., Holroyd et al., 1984; Litt, 1988; Weinberg, Gould, & Jackson, 1979). Further evidence of the causal influence of efficacy beliefs comes from numerous studies showing that self-efficacy perceptions predict future performance after statistically controlling for the impact of past performance (reviewed in Bandura, 1997).

■ *Generalization in Self-Efficacy Perception.* People's perceptions of their capabilities may vary enormously from one circumstance to

another. All people can identify some activities that they have mastered and others that fill them with self-doubt. Despite this, it is also the case that self-efficacy beliefs may generalize substantially across settings. Circumstances that seem superficially dissimilar may be significantly interrelated in the mind of the individual contemplating his or her capacity to cope with them.

If cross-situational coherence could be identified in self-efficacy perception, this would be important not only for questions of motivation and perceived control but also for the study of personality coherence more generally. Given the well-documented influence of self-efficacy appraisal on behavior, understanding cross-situational coherence in self-efficacy judgment could be seen as a central route to understanding the coherence of personality functioning in general.

One approach to the question of generalization is to posit the existence of a broad personality factor such as generalized self-efficacy (e.g., Schwarzer, Baessler, Kwiatek, & Schroeder, 1997; Sherer et al., 1982). The attempt here is to identify individual differences in people's global tendency to be confident of their capabilities for performance. Although people clearly differ in self-perceptions, the generalized self-efficacy strategy is quite limited as a route of understanding these differences. One limitation is that it begs the question of whether there is enough consistency in self-appraisal that each individual can be meaningfully represented by a single global score in the first place. A second problem is that it sheds no light on the psychological or social mechanisms that might cause efficacy appraisals to become generalized.

An alternative approach is to explore specific psychological structures and processes that might cause people to develop a sense of personal capability or incapability across a broad range of activities. A key possibility is that particularly salient, chronically accessible aspects of self-knowledge (see chapter 9) will come to mind as individuals appraise their efficacy for performance in any of a variety of situations. Cross-situational generalization in self-efficacy appraisal, in other words, may derive from the effects of self-schemas (Markus, 1977). A given self-schema may come to mind in numerous settings and foster relatively broad patterns of cross-situational coherence in self-efficacy appraisal. If, for example, a student has developed a schema regarding his or her tendency to be anxious, this self-knowledge might come to mind and lower self-efficacy appraisals across social tasks as diverse as taking an examination asking for a date, or interviewing for a job.

Evidence that self-schemas and associated situational beliefs give rise to cross-situational coherence in self-efficacy beliefs comes from work by Cervone (1997, 1999), noted also in chapter 4. Participants took part in two assessment sessions designed to identify (1) schematic personality attributes, that is, personal attributes that were particularly salient for the given individual; and (2) situational beliefs, specifically, the way the in which individuals related any given schematic attribute to any of a wide variety of acts and social circumstances. Assessments of self-schemas and situational construals were used to identify clusters of situations across which partici-

pants were predicted to have a high versus low sense of their coping capabilities. Specifically, high and low self-efficacy perceptions were anticipated across situations that were perceived to be relevant to positively and negatively valenced schematic attributes, respectively. In a third session, people completed a self-efficacy instrument in which they indicated their confidence in executing specific behaviors in designated social contexts.

Findings revealed that efficacy beliefs do generalize across settings (Figure 8). People's relatively high versus low beliefs in their capabilities across situations were related to positive versus negative schematic attributes. In contrast, their efficacy perceptions regarding situations that related to positive and negative attributes for which they were *not* schematic did not differ. Importantly, the particular situations in which consistent patterns of self-appraisal were found varied idiosyncratically from one person to the next and rarely corresponded to traditional individual-differences categories (Cervone, 1997, 1999). These findings clearly argue against the practice of describing people as globally high or low in perceived self-efficacy, in as much as in this research, consistent patterns of both high and low efficacy belief were identified for each person. Instead, generalization in efficacy beliefs can be explained through a system of social and self-referent knowledge mechanisms that

Figure 8. Mean strength of perceived self-efficacy as a function of situation categorizations for schematic and experimenter-provided personality attributes. From Cervone, 1997.

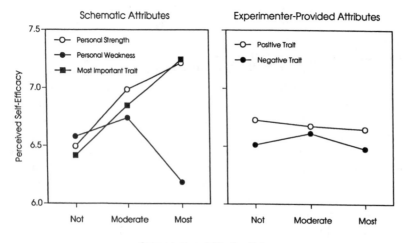

Categorization of Situation Relevance

causes self-appraisals to cohere across contexts. Marsh and Yeung (1998) have provided an analysis of global and domain-specific self-views that reaches analogous conclusions about the utility of generalized measures of self-concept.

## Boosting Efficacy Beliefs

Personality psychology should explore not only the impact of control beliefs but also the processes through which people can enhance their sense of control. How can one build a sense of efficacy among those who doubt their capability to meet life's challenges?

There is no simple path to instilling a durable sense of personal efficacy. A "pep talk" may encourage people to feel better about their abilities, but its effects are likely to be temporary if their efforts do not quickly meet with success. The most reliable way of instilling self-confidence is through first-hand success experiences (Bandura, 1997; Williams, 1995). The personal experience of mastery is difficult to deny, even among individuals who typically doubt their performance capabilities. This point is illustrated in research on phobias.

Extensive lines of research document that enactive mastery experiences are the most powerful means of boosting the self-efficacy beliefs of phobic individuals and thereby leading them to overcome their debilitating fears. Mastery treatments boost self-referent beliefs and eradicate avoidant behavior more rapidly and powerfully than do nonenactive treatments such as exposure therapies and systematic desensitization (Williams, 1990, 1995; Williams & Cervone, 1998). Behavioral success does not automatically instill a sense of confidence. In mastery-based treatments, therapists must ensure that people attribute their success to their own effort and skills. This is done by gradually reducing external aids to performance, so people can see themselves succeeding on their own (Williams, 1990). Mastery-based treatments often promote substantial amounts of behavioral change. Research on both simple phobias (Bandura et al., 1977) and agoraphobia

(Williams, Dooseman, & Kleifield, 1984) reveals that mastery-based treatments may enable clients to perform the vast majority of behavioral acts that they originally had been incapable of performing.

A robust sense of self-efficacy is particularly important to the question of how people motivate themselves to pursue personal goals whose rewards may only lie far in the future. We turn to this question now.

## GOALS AND SELF-MOTIVATION

Some circumstances compel us to act. The scrutiny of a job supervisor, a cry for help, or an impending physical danger move us to action. Such situations, however, are relatively rare. External incentives for action commonly lie far in the future, not in the immediate environment. Students must motivate themselves to study for examinations that lie months in the future. People of middle age must maintain physical fitness when many significant health risks are unlikely to occur until later in life. The challenge such people face is one of self-motivation, that is, initiating and maintaining courses of action in the absence of immediate, external incentives.

A central psychological determinant of successful versus unsuccessful self-motivation is goal setting. The way people set goals for performance and monitor their progress strongly determines the eventual success of their efforts (Locke & Latham, 1990). A basic task for the psychology of motivation, then, is to explore variations in goal systems and the way that different goals influence motivation, performance, and psychological well being.

## Variations Among Goals and Goal Systems

In the current psychological literature, the term *goal* is used in a very broad manner. Aims ranging from getting a cup of coffee to earning an A on the next day's test to avoiding a life of loneliness might be referred to as goals in the current field. As a result, the literature on goals and motivation is potentially unwieldy. Order can be brought to the field by bearing in mind three ways in which goals differ from one another.

First, goals differ quantitatively. One can identify a series of dimensions along which goals vary (Locke & Latham, 1990). Goals, for example, vary in difficulty or level of challenge. One may aspire to run a 10-kilometer race in 25 minutes or in 1 hour or to earn a passing grade or an A in academic courses. Second, goals differ qualitatively. Different goals may possess distinctly different meaning for the individual (e.g., Grant & Dweck, 1999; Higgins, 1997). For example, some goals involve the attainment of rewards and others the avoidance of loss. Some involve the cultivation of skills and others the display of skills one has cultivated. Third, goals differ in breadth. Some represent long-term aims that encompass a wide range of activities (e.g., caring for one's family, contributing to one's profession, enhancing the well-being of one's community or nation). Others specify narrower aims that can be reached via the execution of a small number of actions (e.g., completing the 10-km race, finishing reading assignments before class). Narrow and broad goals may be linked hierarchically (Emmons, 1989; Carver & Scheier, 1982, 1999). Specific task goals (e.g., getting a tan) are ways of attaining higher-level aims (e.g., making a good impression on an upcoming first date), which in turn serve broader aims (e.g., improving one's social life, getting married).

In the following, we first review how goal dimensions relate to motivation and performance and how self-regulatory processes mediate the behavioral effects of goal setting.

## Task Goal Dimensions and Self-Regulatory Processes

Different people may undertake the same task with different goals in mind. Investigators have identified a number of dimensions along which goals differ and have linked these quantitative goal dimensions to motivation and achievement (Locke & Latham, 1990). Perhaps the most important dimension of goal setting is goal level, that is the level of

challenge that people adopt as their aim on a task. Different students may strive merely to pass a class or to get an A. Workers may aim to meet productivity standards or exceed them. Scores of studies, in both laboratory and applied settings, document a strong positive relation between level of goal challenge and level of performance success (Locke & Latham, 1990; Mento, Steel, & Karren, 1987; Tubbs, 1986). As long as people remain committed to their aims, more challenging goals foster higher levels of achievement. Although this finding is not surprising, it is noteworthy that it is so robust. The performance impact of challenging goals versus either easy goals or no goals is one of the most reliable findings in the literature on human motivation (Locke & Latham, 1990).

A second, and somewhat more subtle, aspect of goal setting is goal specificity. Goals differ in the degree to which they specify an exact criterion to be achieved. Some social and professional activities involve goals that are extremely challenging yet vague. The first-year graduate student whose task is to begin a programmatic line of research faces such aims. Numerous studies have compared specific goals to nonspecific aims such as to do one's best. In the overwhelming percentage of cases, specific goals prove superior in boosting performance (Locke, Shaw, Saari, & Latham, 1981).

Goals also differ in proximity. Graduating 3 years hence with a 3.8 grade-point average and earning a 3.8 grade-point average in the current semester are both challenging and specific aims. Their differences in proximity, however, may have significant motivational implications. Proximal goals, or the combination of proximal and distal aims, generally enhance motivation more than do distal goals alone (Bandura & Schunk, 1981; Stock & Cervone, 1990). Bandura and Schunk (1981) provide evidence on this point while cleverly solving a methodological challenge in this area, namely, that people assigned to distal goal conditions in research commonly subdivide a task and set proximal goals for themselves. They studied children who were poor at arithmetic and were enrolled in a multipart arithmetic skills training program. In a distal goal condition, children were instructed to complete a 42-page workbook during the course of seven meetings. In a proximal goal condition, children were assigned the goal of completing six pages of material each day. Because of their young age and arithmetic deficiencies, children in the distal goal group were literally unable to divide the task into specific subgoals. Proximal subgoals enhanced children's self-efficacy, interest, and achievement in mathematics (Bandura & Schunk, 1981).

Two caveats are, first, that it may be burdensome to monitor one's behavior in relation to a large number of proximal aims. Overly rigid planning can cause people to become frustrated and to experience self-regulatory failure (Kirschenbaum, 1985, 1987). Second, when people initially have high levels of interest in an activity, interest may be better enhanced by distal goals than by the imposition of proximal aims (Manderlink & Harackiewicz, 1984). Nonetheless, proximal goal setting commonly aids self-regulation, if only because goals that are set far in the future provide little direction for current action.

The benefits of proximal goal setting of course require that people not lose sight of the long-term aims that are the ultimate reasons for action. People differ in their tendency to focus on such future contingencies (Karniol & Ross, 1996). As compared with those who report that they tend to neglect the future, those who tend to reflect on long-term consequences also report that they tend to engage in acts with long-term rewards, such as actions that promote personal health or an improved natural environment (Strathman, Gleicher, Boninger, & Edwards, 1994).

Goal dimensions do not translate directly into performance success. Goal effects can be understood at two different levels of explanation; in other words, two types of mediators of goal effects can be identified. The first are behavioral mechanisms through which goals of varying challenge, specificity, and proximity

affect performance (Locke & Latham, 1990). Goal setting enhances task effort and persistence (Earley, Wojnaroski, & Prest, 1987; Huber & Neale, 1987) and tends to direct people's attention to aspects of an activity that are important to behavioral success (Rothkopf & Billington, 1975). A second level of explanation explores self-referent cognitive and affective processes that mediate goal effects; we consider these below, after first addressing factors that moderate the relation between goal setting and performance.

## Moderators of Goal-Setting Effects: Feedback and Task Complexity

Challenging goals do not always boost performance. Two factors moderate the behavioral impact of goal setting. One is the cognitive complexity of tasks (Wood, Mento, & Locke, 1987). On simple activities, goals enhance effort, which in turn boosts performance. On complex tasks, effort is not enough. Success may, for example, require the development and testing of novel task strategies. Goal systems do not influence performance as reliably on complex activities (Locke & Latham, 1990; Wood et al., 1987). On complex tasks, people with challenging goals may exert a lot of effort but fail to adopt the calm, analytical frame of mind necessary for success (e.g., Cervone et al., 1991).

A second moderating factor is performance feedback. Challenging goals enhance motivation as long as people monitor their actions in response to feedback on their degree of progress. Two types of factors may interfere with such monitoring. The first is that social contexts often do not provide one with sufficient information. The aforementioned graduate student seeking to begin a programmatic line of research, for example, may be burdened not only by ambiguous aims but by a lack of faculty feedback on his or her progress toward this goal. In the absence of feedback, the assignment of challenging task goals does not reliably enhance performance. This conclusion derives from research in a wide variety of domains – for example, cognitive performance (Kazdin, 1974; Strang, Lawrence, &

Fowler, 1978), physical effort expenditure (Bandura & Cervone, 1983), and pain tolerance (Stevenson, Kanfer, & Higgins, 1984) – in which the specificity of feedback is manipulated experimentally.

A second factor is that people simply may fail to attend to feedback that is available. Research guided by control theory speaks to this point (Carver & Scheier, 1981, 1998, 1999). Control theory views motivation and self-regulation primarily as a process of feedback control. The "comparator" of the feedback loop (see outline of control theory, above) computes the relation between information about the effects of one's actions and internal standards for performance. Investigators have explored how the comparator is differentially engaged by variations in self-focused attention. More simply, people tend to seek feedback on their behavior and to compare this feedback to a performance standard when attention is directed to aspects of the self. Findings indicate that people devote more effort to evaluating their behavior when they are in the presence of a stimulus (e.g., a mirror) that calls attention to the self, and that those who are dispositionally high in self-focused attention evaluate the adequacy of their behavior more frequently than others (Scheier & Carver, 1983). By activating this comparison process, increases in self-focused attention cause people to bring their behavior into greater conformity with internal standards (Carver & Scheier, 1998, 1999). Self-focus enhances the regulation not only of behavior but of cognition. In the presence of a mirror, people are more likely to suppress socially inappropriate stereotypic thoughts (Macrae, Bodenhausen, & Milne, 1998).

The ability to compare feedback on one's actions with clear goals for performance is important not only to achievement but to the enjoyment of pursuits. Research described earlier by Csikszentmihalyi (1990) highlights the role of goal and feedback processes in psychological well-being. People feel more alert, happy, and satisfied with their activities when they are engaged in challenging tasks that provide clear feedback and when they perceive that they have the skills to meet the challenges (Csikszentmihalyi & Lefevre, 1989). Ironically, people invest much of their leisure time in passive pursuits (e.g., television watching), which lack challenge and therefore are not ultimately satisfying (Csikszentmihalyi, 1990).

## Self-Referent Cognition and Affect as Mediators of Goal-Setting Effects

As noted above, one way of explaining why goal setting boosts performance is to explore the behavioral processes that are affected by goal systems and that in turn foster success. A second level of analysis would identify the psychological mechanisms that mediate the effects of goal setting on the behaviors. Why do people with clear goals and feedback tend to exert greater effort and persistence on tasks?

The motivational effects of goal setting can be understood in terms of the self-regulatory system outlined at the beginning of this chapter. Each element of the self-system is more likely to come into play in self-regulation when people have clear goals and receive explicit performance feedback. When people receive explicit feedback on well-defined aims, they react self-evaluatively to their attainments, reflect on their efficacy for performance, and set specific goals and standards for themselves. Each of these self-processes contributes to subsequent motivation (Bandura, 1991b; Cervone 1993).

Evidence of the impact of self-regulatory processes on goal-directed motivation comes from research that assesses the self-processes, via self-report, between trials of multitrial tasks. This enables one to relate self-regulatory mechanisms to future performance while controlling for the effects of past performance. Findings reveal that self-regulatory processes explain a large portion of the variability in goal-directed motivation. On tasks involving both simple effort expenditure (Bandura & Cervone, 1983, 1986) and complex cognition (Bandura & Jourdan, 1991; Cervone, Jiwani, & Wood, 1991; Cervone & Wood, 1995), people's appraisals of self-efficacy, personal goals for performance, and self-evaluative reactions each contribute to behavioral success. Cervone & Wood (1995), for example, found that self-efficacy perceptions and personal goal setting accounted for nearly half (49%) of the variance in changes in performance from one trial to the next on a cognitively complex task. Self-evaluative reactions predicted unique variance beyond the effects of goals and efficacy beliefs. Challenging, specific goals, then, influence motivation in large part through their influence on the self-regulatory system.

Self-regulatory mechanisms can explain the behavioral effects not only of goal difficulty and goal specificity but of goal proximity. Setting proximal subgoals has two different effects on the self-system (Stock & Cervone, 1990). First, it boosts initial perceived self-efficacy. Even before people begin working on a task, mentally breaking down the activity into smaller subtasks can make it appear more manageable. Second, subgoals enhance perceived self-efficacy and self-evaluative reactions by providing markers of progress. Intermediate attainments toward a distal goal may appear insignificant in the absence of proximal goal setting. When these same activities constitute the achievement of a well-specified proximal aim, they take on much greater personal significance. Even among people who have achieved exactly the same objective goals, those with proximal subgoals may experience more positive efficacy beliefs and self-evaluative reactions (Stock & Cervone, 1990).

Research linking self-regulatory mechanisms to goal-directed behavior speaks to two other issues raised earlier. One is the differential activation of the self-system. On both simple and complex tasks, self-referent processes are more strongly linked to performance when people received clear feedback toward well-defined goals than when goals are ill-defined and feedback is lacking (e.g., Bandura & Cervone, 1983; Cervone et al., 1991). Vague goals, then, tend not to enlist the self-reactive influences through which people motivate their actions. As a result, they have less of a motivational effect than specific aims.

The second issue is the moderating effect of task complexity, that is, the fact that goal systems influence performance less strongly on complex tasks than on simple activities. On both simple and complex tasks, discrepancies between goals and performance feedback trigger negative self-evaluative reactions. People become dissatisfied with themselves and the prospect of continued inferior performance. On both simple and complex tasks, self-dissatisfaction increases effort. People take quick action to reduce dissatisfying goal–feedback discrepancies. Increased effort, however, can differentially affect performance on simple versus complex activities. Greater effort directly boosts performance on simple tasks, so people who negatively self-evaluate their performance tend to improve (Bandura & Cervone, 1983, 1986). In contrast, simple effort expenditure may not pay off, and may even backfire, on cognitively complex activities. People who became highly self-dissatisfied with their performance on a complex decision-making task tended to try a large number of different task strategies in a somewhat frantic effort to improve. In so doing, they created a decision environment that was so complex that it became unmanageable. Greater self-dissatisfaction thus led to *inferior* performance on this complex task (Cervone et al., 1991; Cervone & Wood, 1995), precisely the opposite of the result obtained on simple activities.

### Nonconscious Goal Mechanisms

Our discussion of self-motivation has highlighted self-reflective processes. People dwell on themselves and their relation to the environment as they set goals, adjust their goal-directed efforts, and contemplate their past accomplishments. However, not all motivational mechanisms involve conscious mediation. Work by Bargh and colleagues (Bargh, 1997; Bargh & Barndollar, 1996; Bargh & Gollwitzer, 1994) indicates that goals sometimes can become active and govern through nonconscious, automatic cognitive processes.

Evidence of nonconscious goal processes derives from research that cognitively primes one versus another motive prior to task performance. In one study, participants initially completed a word puzzle that happened to contain terms relating to either achievement or affiliation goals. They subsequently worked on a task with confederates who exhibited poor abilities; high personal achievement by the participant, then, might hurt the feelings of the confederate. As predicted, the priming of affiliation goals led participants to solve fewer problems than did the priming of achievement goals; importantly, participants reported no awareness of the influence of the prime (Bargh & Barndollar, 1996; also see Bargh, Chen, & Burrows, 1996; Carver, Ganellen, Froming, & Chambers, 1983; Chen & Bargh, 1997).

Interestingly, when people are primed with an exemplar of a category rather than merely the category itself, behavioral contrast effects may result. Although priming the category "elderly" can lead people to walk more slowly (Bargh et al., 1996), priming this category and presenting the image of a particular elderly individual can cause people to walk faster (Dijksterhuis et al., 1998). Priming an extreme exemplar of a category may induce people to make internal comparisons that foster the contrast effects. Priming of an image of Albert Einstein (1) heightened the accessibility not only of terms related to intelligence but of terms related to stupidity (presumably because participants viewed themselves as relatively stupid in comparison with Einstein); and (2) led participants to perform somewhat more poorly on a test of general knowledge (Dijksterhuis et al., 1998).

Findings that beliefs and goals activated outside of awareness can influence people's aims and overt behaviors are important as a kind of "existence proof." They show that environmental influences can alter behavior through psychological mechanisms that function outside of awareness. There exists, then, a nonconscious pathway from situational influence to action. Given the diversity of psychological processes that can occur outside of awareness (chapters 9 and 11), plus the intuitive observation that we sometimes find ourselves in the midst of an action sequence yet are somehow unable to remember what we intended to be doing, these nonconscious influences are perhaps not surprising. Nonetheless, they importantly remind one that not all goal-directed actions involve deliberate cognitive processing or consciously accessed mental representations of the goal of action.

Despite the importance of these findings, they should not cause the field to return to a kind of Skinnerism in which the environment is seen to control personality functioning (see Bargh, 1997; Wegner & Wheatley, 1999). Laboratory research on nonconscious goal mechanisms generally has involved relatively mundane activities (e.g., speed of walking down a hallway) that have no bearing on one's long-term well-being. When people confront challenging activities of personal significance, they devote conscious cognitive resources to assessing their future prospects. Clear goals and robust beliefs in one's capabilities are critical to the sustained self-regulatory efforts needed to meet significant challenges in life. The existence of nonconscious goal mechanisms should not distract us from the importance of conscious self-reflection to personal development.

A topic deserving greater attention is the interplay of conscious and nonconscious processes in self-regulation. Nonconsciousness processes can influence conscious goals and beliefs that, in turn, regulate behavior. For example, in a study noted earlier, the order in which people completed items on a preexperimental questionnaire influenced their subsequent task persistence (Peake & Cervone, 1989). Participants appeared not to be consciously aware of this influence (cf. Nisbett & Wilson, 1977); indeed, when debriefed about the possibility that questionnaire item order would influence their behavior, most participants were incredulous. It would be a mistake, however, to attribute these effects solely to nonconscious mechanisms. Questionnaire item order influenced conscious reflections. People who first answered questions about prospective superior performance had higher judgments of self-efficacy. Efficacy beliefs, in turn, mediated task persistence (Peake & Cervone, 1989). People generally may be unaware of the full range of contextual factors that influence the contents of consciousness. Nonetheless, their conscious thoughts may be the primary determinant of the courses of action they pursue.

## Qualitative Variations in Goals and Personal Standards

As we have seen, an analysis of goal dimensions reveals how variations in goal specificity, challenge, and proximity influence motivation through their effects on the self-system. A similar conclusion derives from research on goals that differ qualitatively. Different types of goals have different meanings for the actor, and thereby trigger different patterns of self-referent cognition, affect, and action.

■ *Judgment Versus Development Goals.* Sometimes the ultimate aim of an action is to gain a positive evaluation of one's current personal qualities. On a job interview or a first meeting with the parents of a boyfriend or girlfriend, one's primary concern is to display one's personal qualities and to have them judged positively. At other times, one's goals are more future-oriented. When pursuing a hobby, exercise program, or an educational course of study, one may be seeking to cultivate a personal characteristic or skill.

To capture this distinction, Dweck and colleagues differentiate between *judgment* and *development* goals (e.g., Grant and Dweck, 1999). Judgment goals involve the aim of testing or validating a personal characteristic. People with development goals, in contrast, seek to acquire or enhance a personal attribute. In the context of achievement motivation, these different aims often are expressed as learning versus performance goals (Dweck & Leggett, 1988; Elliot & Dweck, 1988; cf. Nicholls, 1984; Ames, 1992). People with learning goals seek to acquire knowledge and skills in an achievement domain, whereas those with performance goals strive to gain positive evaluations of their achievements from others.

Learning versus performance goals influence people's reaction to failure. When trying to maximize the evaluation of one's perfor-

mance, failure has significant implications for the self. Setbacks imply that one lacks a valuable personal quality. When one merely is trying to learn, setbacks are benign. They imply merely that one has not yet sufficiently mastered material. Elliott and Dweck (1988) induced learning versus performance goals among grade school students performing a cognitive task. Participants were told either that they were performing a task that would sharpen their mental skills (the learning goal condition) or that their performance would be evaluated by experts (the performance goal condition). Participants' beliefs in their ability on the task were also manipulated through provision of false feedback on a prior activity. The combination of performance goals and low ability beliefs impaired performance. Further, this combination of goals and beliefs influenced people's feelings and self-evaluations. In this study, participants were asked to think out loud while performing the cognitive task. Performance goals combined with low ability beliefs caused people to think not only about the task but about themselves. Participants became concerned with the causes of their performance ("I'm not very good at this") and their current feelings ("My stomach hurts") (Elliot & Dweck, 1988, p. 10). Students who had an equally low sense of their abilities but who had learning goals on the task rarely made such statements.

Goals orientations are important not only to achievement behavior but to interpersonal tasks. Erdley, Cain, Loomis, Dumas-Hines, and Dweck (1997) manipulated judgment versus development goals among children participating in a "pen-pal tryout." Children received negative feedback on an initial letter they had written, and then were given the opportunity to write a second one. As compared to children with a development goal, those who believed that the letter-writing tasks assessed their basic ability at making friends tended to withdraw effort from the task, produce poorer letters, and make internal attributions for their initial poor performance.

People's construal of tasks as involving improvement versus evaluation has implications not only for motivational states but for long-term psychological health. Dykman (1998) finds that people who are oriented toward the goal of validating their self-worth are more prone to depression after negative events than are individuals whose primary goal is self-improvement.

■ *Approach Versus Avoidance Goals.* A second distinction among goal types is that of approach versus avoidance goals. People may strive not only to attain aims but also to avoid outcomes. For example, one person may enter a social activity with the goal of pursuing friendship, whereas another is striving to avoid loneliness (Emmons, 1996). The distinction between approach and avoidance goals is partly inspired by an earlier distinction between a motive to achieve success versus to avoid failure (Atkinson, 1964). It is captured in control theory by the distinction between negative feedback loops, in which a system tries to align its behavior with a standard, and discrepancy-enlarging loops, which act to create divergences between behavior and a reference value (Carver & Scheier, 1998).

The question of approach versus avoidance goals can be examined not only at the level of the individual task but at that of the self-system as a whole. Different people may possess a preponderance of either approach or avoidance aims. Research generally highlights the detrimental consequences of an avoidance orientation. When open-ended listings of personal goals were coded for the presence of avoidance versus approach aims, adults who possessed relatively larger numbers of avoidance goals also reported less positive affect, less satisfaction with life, and somewhat higher levels of physical distress (Emmons and Kaiser, 1996). Students who report a relatively large proportion of avoidance goals also report lower life satisfaction and subjective well-being (Elliot & Sheldon, 1997) and more illness-related symptomatology, even after one controls for the effects of neuroticism (Elliot & Sheldon, 1998). Particularly low levels of well-being are expressed by people who see themselves as not making progress toward daily goals that are linked to distal feared out-comes that they hope to avoid (King, Richards, & Stemmerich, 1998). Relatedly, avoidance goals tend to undermine people's intrinsic motivation for task performance (Elliot and Harackiewicz, 1996).

Rather than having a direct effect on well-being, avoidance versus approach goals may exert their influence through mediating mechanisms involving the self-system. Path analyses suggest that people who are pursuing avoidance goals feel less competent in their ability to meet the goal and that the goal choice is less under their personal control; feelings of competence and control, in turn, predict physical well-being (Elliot & Sheldon, 1998). This conclusion is consistent, of course, with our earlier analysis of self-regulatory mechanisms and goal dimensions, which suggested that the motivational effects of goals derives not from the goals themselves but from the influence of mediating self-processes.

One caveat to these established relations between avoidance goals and well-being is that the research primarily involves American college students, who live in a culture that values bold independent action, are relatively unencumbered by responsibilities for the welfare of others, live in a social and educational context that encourages and supports personal achievement, and are of an age at which risk taking has lesser costs than it does later in life, since alternative professional and personal pathways can be pursued in the future. In this setting, focusing on personal achievement goals, as opposed to avoidance goals, is adaptive. This motivational focus may have different implications in other cultures and contexts. Avoidance orientations might be more adaptive at later ages. Approach goals might be less adaptive in Eastern cultures, where pursuing personal achievement is viewed as a source of suffering (Kitayama & Markus, 1999).

Another concern is that the common research practice of dichotomously categorizing each of a person's goals as either approach or avoidance pursuits may fail to capture the complex, multifaceted ways in which people actually think about their most valued aims in life. Many complex undertakings have both approach and avoidance elements. Elliot and Sheldon (1998) report that, not infrequently, individuals list goals that include "both approach and avoidance components" (p. 1287). Rather than assuming that each of a person's aims can be accurately classified into one versus another category, future work could explore the cognitive structure of people's beliefs about their personal aims (cf. Kruglanski, 2000) in a manner that is sensitive to the possibility that any single goal may have both approach and avoidance elements.

■ *Regulatory Focus: Promotion Versus Prevention.* Historically, the psychology of motivation has tended to divide motivational determinants into two categories. People seek pleasure and avoid pain. In the language of goal orientations, they hold approach goals or avoidance aims. Higgins (1997, 1999) has suggested that the pleasure–pain distinction is necessary but not sufficient for the psychology of motivation. It is insufficient because of self-regulatory mechanisms that cut across the traditional pleasure–pain distinction.

Higgins differentiates three aspects of self-regulation: regulatory anticipation, regulatory reference, and regulatory focus. The construct of regulatory anticipation captures the common distinction between pleasurable and painful outcomes. When regulating their action, people may focus on either their desires or their fears. Regulatory reference distinguishes self-regulation with respect to desired versus undesired end states. Desired versus undesired is not the same as pain versus pleasure because desired states, for example, include both the achievement of pleasure and the avoidance of pain. Finally, regulatory focus involves the question of regulating one's actions with regard to the acquisition of positive outcomes or the avoidance of negative ones. This distinction differs from the earlier two. A positive regulatory focus, or a "promotion" focus, can encompass both the attainment of positive outcomes and their loss. A negative, or "prevention," focus involves sensitivity to the presence of negative outcomes and their absence. Regulatory focus, then, cuts across the traditional pleasure–pain dis-

tinction. Note that Higgins's (1987) distinction between ideal and ought standards (see chapter 9) is incorporated in this more general differentiation between promotion and prevention foci. Ideals and oughts are examples of promotion-related and prevention-related standards, respectively.

Different forms of self-regulatory focus are found to sensitize people to information about approach versus avoidance. Higgins, Roney, Crowe, and Hymes (1994) induced one versus another focus by asking people to describe either their hopes or their obligations. Participants then read passages in which actors either approached personal desires (e.g., the actor was a student who woke up early to prepare for class) or avoided a mismatch to desires (e.g., the actor took steps to avoid a conflict in class scheduling). The participants' later recall of the material was assessed. People with a promotion focus were found to have greater memory for actors' approach strategies than for their avoidant acts (Higgins et al., 1994).

The value of distinguishing promotive from preventive self-regulation is also seen in a study cited earlier in this chapter. Predictions of expectancy–value theory hold when people are promotion-focused but not when they are prevention-focused (Shah & Higgins, 1997).

Note that regulatory focus can be studied as both an individual-difference variable and a psychological state that varies as a function of situational conditions. Some people may tend to focus on prevention (or promotion) more than others. As in his work on knowledge and interpretive processes (chapter 9), Higgins' analysis of motivation succeeds in identifying a general principle through which one can account for both between-person and within-person variability in experience and action (see Higgins, 1999).

## COHERENCE IN GOAL SYSTEMS

Many of our daily goals are interconnected. They are part of an organized system of knowledge about personal aims, hopes, and fears. Personality psychologists have devoted much attention to the psychological mechanisms that contribute to coherence in goal systems and to the ways that goal systems, in turn, contribute to coherence in personality functioning.

Two knowledge mechanisms contribute heavily to coherence in personal goal systems. Implicit theories about oneself and the social world guide interpretations of events and the goals one adopts. Broad, enduring aspirations in life organize multiple task-specific goals, each of which contributes to the attainment of the broader aim. We now consider these mechanisms in turn.

**Implicit Theories**

The goals individuals adopt on tasks commonly reflect deeply held beliefs about the self and others. Although many of these beliefs are explicit, some involve abstract, implicitly held conceptions about the self.

Dweck and colleagues (Dweck, 1996; Dweck & Leggett, 1988; Grant & Dweck, 1999) have extensively analyzed how implicit beliefs influence goal orientations. They focus on beliefs about the malleability of personal attributes, for example, intelligence. Some people implicitly view intelligence as a fixed quality that individuals possess to a greater or lesser degree. Others conceive of intelligence as a quality that can be increased incrementally. These *entity* versus *incremental* beliefs are predicted to influence the meanings people assign to tasks and the goals they pursue. If one believes that ability is a fixed property, then tasks function as a way of testing one's ability. In contrast, if one believes that personal attributes are malleable, activities may be seen as a forum for developing one's skills. Entity versus incremental beliefs, then, should foster performance versus learning goals.

In their research, Dweck and colleagues assess beliefs through self-report measures that inquire about the perceived malleability of personal qualities (Dweck, 1996). Rather than assuming that these beliefs generalize across all domains of a persons's life, they assess beliefs contextually – specifically, with

respect to a particular domain of functioning such as intelligence or moral character (Dweck, 1996). As predicted, beliefs about ability in these domains shape the goals people pursue. In achievement domains, people who believe that intelligence is a fixed quality tend to pursue goals that will make them look good in the eyes of others. People with incremental beliefs about intelligence, in contrast, pursue challenging tasks from which they can learn (Dweck & Leggett, 1988). In interpersonal and social settings, people who believe that relevant attributes are fixed entities tend to adopt the goal of categorizing and labeling others. This is evident in their relatively greater tendency to make trait inferences and to base behavioral predictions on trait-based information (Chiu, Hong, & Dweck, 1997), to make stereotypical judgments about ethnic groups (Levy, Stroessner, & Dweck, 1998), and to endorse punishment versus rehabilitation for criminals (Grant & Dweck, 1999).

Dweck's analysis of theories, goals, and behavior is another illustration of the type of bottom-up analysis of personality coherence that we have advocated at various points in this book. Coherent motivational tendencies are not explained by reference to a fixed taxonomy of needs or motives. Instead, they arise from interactions among a complex system of social-cognitive and affective mechanisms. People's enduring belief about themselves, goals for achievement and interpersonal behavior, and appraisals of their capabilities account for within-person coherence and intraindividual differences in motivational functioning.

**Middle-Level Goal Units**

Seemingly independent task goals become meaningfully interrelated when they serve a common purpose. A high school student may have the goals of earning an A in calculus, becoming president of a student organization, and developing good personal relationships with teachers. Although these goals encompass different tasks and require different skills, they may cohere psychologically for the student who sees them all as contributing to the goal of getting into college. Coherence in goal systems, then, can be understood by considering broad and enduring goals that bear on a variety of daily activities.

These higher-level aims have come to be known as *middle-level* goals units. Middle-level goals are more contextualized than global motives, yet broader and more inclusive than specific task goals. Aims such as developing a romantic relationship, coping with an illness, obtaining good grades at school, improving one's friendships, making oneself more attractive, improving parenting skills, or saving money for retirement (cf. Emmons, 1997) would constitute middle-level goals. The term middle-level implies a hierarchical system of goals. If specific task goals (e.g., pay for dinner) and abstract aspirations (e.g., have a happy life) are viewed as the bottom and top of a hierarchy of aspirations, then the aims being analyzed here (e.g., develop a romantic relationship) are in the middle.

Numerous research programs have explored the role of middle-level goals in personality functioning. These include Cantor and colleagues' analysis of "life tasks" (Cantor & Kihlstrom, 1987; Sanderson & Cantor, 1999), Emmons' work on "personal strivings" (Emmons, 1989, 1996), Klinger's (1975) analysis of "current concerns," and Little's (1989, 1999) "personal projects" approach. Read and Miller's (1989) analysis of interpersonal goal structures similarly identifies middle-level aims that foster coherence in personality functioning. Although these research programs and associated theoretical systems differ from one another in certain respects, their commonalities are important. They all suggest that middle-level goals foster coherent, enduring patterns of experience and action. People's aims shape the content of their day-to-day thoughts (Klinger, Barta, & Maxeiner, 1980), the situations in which they spend their time (Emmons, Diener, & Larsen, 1986), and the elements of situations to which they attend most carefully (Mueller & Dweck, 1998). Goal systems can also enhance one's sense of meaning in life. People who rate themselves as highly committed to goals that are consistent

with their personal values also report a somewhat clearer sense of purpose in life (McGregor & Little, 1998).

Middle-level goals may vary idiosyncratically from one person to another. Thus, investigators commonly assess goals via open-ended, idiographic procedures (e.g., Emmons, 1989; King, Richards, & Stemmerich, in press; Read & Miller, 1989). This idiographic focus, however, does not rule out the possibility that commonalities among individuals may be found. Common social norms, environmental settings, or biological constraints may cause individuals within a group to share a set of goals (e.g., Helson, Mitchell, & Moane, 1984). Students making the transition to college, for example, commonly share life tasks such as getting good grades and establishing new personal relationships (Cantor et al., 1991).

The structure of one's middle-level goal system has implications for one's well-being. A key consideration here is conflict among goals. Some aims are complementary (e.g., an individual may see the goals of getting good grades and making friends as jointly contributing to a successful college experience), whereas others conflict (e.g., parents' tradeoff between parenting and professional demands). People who report large amounts of goal conflict experience more symptoms of physical distress and more frequently seek health care (Emmons and King, 1988). Conflict over expressing emotion may cause people to inhibit emotional expression, which can contribute to enduring psychological distress (King & Emmons, 1990).

The relation, or fit, between goals and the social environment also affects well-being. The timing of goal pursuit is one important consideration. Goals are more stressful when they are pursued outside of society's traditional timing for a given activity (Helson et al., 1984). Such stress might be experienced by individuals who become parents particularly early or late in life or by individuals who choose to complete higher education later in life.

The distinctive strategies of goal pursuit must be included, along with the goals themselves, in a complete analysis of goal systems and personality functioning. Different individuals may pursue different paths to the same goal. That is, people may pursue different strategies, where strategies are cognitive structures of personality through which people attempt to gain control over the environment and to achieve their goals (Hettema, 1979, 1993).

As a number of writers emphasize (e.g., Cantor & Kihlstrom, 1987; Hettema, 1979), the personality construct *strategies* has the advantage of directly capturing a dynamic relationship between the actor and the social environment. Rather than creating a false separation of person and situation factors, the analysis of strategies enables one to confront the dynamic interrelations among personal resources and environmental demands.

People's strategies for goal pursuit reflect the declarative and procedural knowledge that they can bring to bear in solving problems. This knowledge gives people *social intelligence* (Cantor & Kihlstrom, 1987). Much insight into social intelligence and strategies of goal pursuit derives from the work of Nancy Cantor and colleagues. They distinguish two strategic patterns, which they refer to as *optimism* and *defensive pessimism* (Cantor & Kihlstrom, 1987; Cantor & Fleeson, 1994; Norem, 1989; Sanderson & Cantor, 1999). People who adopt an optimistic strategy of goal pursuit hold relatively positive expectations for their performance and experience little preperformance anxiety. Defensive pessimists, in contrast, express low expectations, even after previous success, and experience anxiety prior to task performance.

An interesting feature of defensive pessimists is that the negative thoughts and affect they experience may not necessarily undermine their performance. Instead, their worries may motivate them to attain superior levels of performance. In a longitudinal study of students making the transition from high school to a challenging residential college, Cantor, Norem, Neidenthal, Langston, and Brower (1987) assessed optimistic versus pessimistic strategies through self-report. They also assessed students' appraisals of upcoming academic and social challenges and their plans for meeting them. In the domain of academics, optimists and pessimists did equally well. However, they traversed different paths to success. Among students who reported optimistic strategies, superior grades were achieved by those who at the beginning of the school year expected to do well and who did not experience substantial discrepancies between their actual and ideal self-concept (Higgins, 1987). For optimists, then, positive thinking predicted success. This was not the case among pessimists. Defensive pessimists' expectations about academic performance were unrelated to subsequent achievement. Among pessimists, larger actual–ideal self-discrepancies predicted higher, not lower, academic attainment (Cantor et al., 1987). Positive versus negative thoughts, then, appeared to have very different motivational functions for the different groups.

The notion of optimists and pessimists raises the classic question of cross-situational coherence in personality functioning. Do people adopt optimistic versus pessimistic strategies in a uniform manner across domains? Or do strategies vary significantly from one life task to another? Cantor et al. (1987) identified groups of academic pessimists and optimists (i.e., people who adopted different strategies within the academic domain) and assessed their appraisals of two life tasks, getting good grades and making friends. For both tasks, they measured a range of appraisal dimensions such as the perceived difficulty, controllability, and stress of the given task. On the task of getting good grades, the appraisals of academic optimists versus defensive pessimists differed significantly on virtually every appraisal dimension. On the task of making friends, however, these same individuals did not differ on any dimension (Cantor et al., 1987). In other words, there was little evidence of task-to-task generality. People significantly discriminate between life tasks, and their strategies and beliefs may vary substantially from one domain to another.

Although academic and social tasks are distinct, experiences in one domain may spill over to another. Harlow and Cantor (1994) found that some students did link tasks across domains. Their satisfaction with their social life was partly contingent on their level of academic success. Students who allowed academic worries to spill over into their social experiences tended to be less satisfied with their social life.

The life task perspective provides an interesting perspective on questions of personality coherence and stability. Life tasks such as attaining professional success or developing rewarding personal relationships endure over time. A person's predominant goals, then, are enduring personality structures. However, stable goals may not necessarily express themselves as stable patterns of behavior. If people's circumstances change while their goals endure, the novel circumstances may require a change in behavioral strategies. Sanderson and Cantor (1999) note by way of example that the goal of developing intimacy requires different behavioral strategies for high school students than for divorced adults. Although stable affective and behavioral tendencies are the field's traditional markers of continuity in personality, it is at least as reasonable to focus on stability in goal systems, which under some circumstances may be more stable than overt actions.

## A Methodological Caveat: Do People Know What They're Doing?

We close this discussion of goal systems with a methodological caveat. Much of the work we have reviewed has assessed people's goals via self-report methods. Individuals commonly are asked to list activities that are current concerns of theirs. These procedures have much merit. The relatively unstructured techniques are sensitive to the sometimes idiosyncratic goal structures that both reflect and organize the life of the individual. However, these methods also suffer from a limitation. They may overlook important personal aims that people are either reluctant to report or are incapable of reporting.

People may sometimes be incapable of explicitly articulating a goal that, in reality, organizes many of their activities. Adolescents may engage in multiple activities whose overarching aim is to affirm their developing manhood or womanhood. However, they may not report things in this manner if you ask them. As Westen (1991) has emphasized, emotionally and sexually charged beliefs and goals are particularly unlikely to be identified by standard self-report techniques. The field may benefit, then, from expanding strategies of goal assessment beyond the traditional approach of explicitly asking people to enumerate their aims in life.

## DISTRACTION AND THE CHALLENGE OF CARRYING OUT INTENTIONS

An analysis of goals and self-referent beliefs is necessary but not sufficient to explain motivated action. The insufficiency derives from the fact that people frequently fail to enact behaviors that they value, that they are sure they can perform, and that they intend to practice. People simply become distracted by competing activities and fail to act on their good intentions.

In this regard, a distinction made by Heckhausen is quite useful. He distinguished the decision to act from the regulation of action once a decision has been taken. His "Rubicon" model of cognition and action differentiated the cognitive activities involved in deciding whether to act (e.g., Caesar's decision whether to cross the Rubican River) from those involved in implementing and pursuing that action until a goal is achieved (Heckhausen, 1991). Decisional processes govern the formation of intentions, whereas volitional processes govern the regulation of action.

This distinction is further elaborated in work that identifies four distinct stages of the action sequence (Gollwitzer, 1996; Heckhausen & Gollwitzer, 1987). People must choose one versus another goal on which to work. They then must develop plans for how to achieve the goal they have chosen. When they try to enact these plans, they must evaluate their ongoing actions and adjust their efforts and strategies as needed. Finally, as we discuss in detail immediately below, people must avoid becoming distracted by alternative activities that interfere with goal attainment (Kuhl, 1984). Gollwitzer (1996) suggests that the stage of choosing a goal toward which to work invokes a *deliberative mind set*, in which people reflect on the desirability and feasibility of alternative aims, whereas the task of pursuing a goal involves an *implemental mind set*, in which people focus on strategies and plans for reaching their objectives.

## Action and State Orientations

Kuhl (1984, 1994; Kuhl & Goschke, 1994) has comprehensively analyzed factors that interfere with the execution of intentions. He differentiates between two cognitive orientations, that is, two distinct modes of cognitive processing that may be elicited by challenges. In an *action orientation*, individuals dwell on the steps required to achieve a current intention. In a *state orientation*, people are preoccupied with thoughts that may interfere with the intention to act, including thoughts about the self or about topics that are simply irrelevant to one's action (e.g., thoughts about an alternative activity). State-oriented thinking can interfere with the execution of one's intentions, even when the intended acts are valued and potentially under one's control.

A strength of Kuhl's work is that he conceptualizes action versus state orientation as both a person variable and a process variable. Task orientation can be assessed as an individual-difference variable or manipulated experimentally. Research on the role of cognitive orientations in *learned helplessness* (Seligman, 1975) illustrates the approach.

In learned helplessness, failure on one task impairs performance on another. This can occur even when the two tasks appear quite distinct. This phenomenon generally is explained in motivational terms. Failure produces low performance expectations, which

generalize from one task to another. Low expectations reduce effort on the second activity (Seligman, 1975). However, as Kuhl (1984) notes, this explanation conflicts with the fact that expectations are generally quite task-specific. Experiences tend to produce idiosyncratic patterns of generalization (Williams, Kinney, & Falbo, 1989), not the global beliefs implied in the traditional explanation. Rather than creating generalized expectations, failure may induce state orientation (Kuhl, 1984). Poor performance on one task may induce anxiety and negative self-referent thinking, which interferes with performance on other tasks, even tasks that one expects to be able to achieve. Converging correlational and experimental data support this account. When individual differences in action versus state orientation were assessed via a face-valid self-report questionnaire, state-oriented but not action-oriented participants exhibited performance decrements after an uncontrollable event. When state orientation was induced by asking some participants to focus on their thoughts and feelings during an activity, people performed more poorly after an initial failure; people who did not receive this instruction did not show performance decrements (Kuhl, 1984).

Kuhl's analysis may help to illuminate the striking stereotype-induced failure uncovered by Steele and colleagues (Steele, 1997; Steele & Aronson, 1995). Black American college students who perform as well as white students on a cognitive task are found to perform less well than whites when the task is described as an intelligence test. The intelligence test label interferes with blacks' performance even though it does not lower their performance expectations. The label, then, can be seen to induce a state orientation. Black students, even those with high ability and high expectations for performance, become concerned about the possibility of confirming a negative stereotype about their racial group by performing poorly. These thoughts interfere with cognitive performance.

Sustained performance commonly requires that one shield one's intentions against distractions in the environment. Doing so is often difficult. Events in the environment commonly distract one's attention from a task at hand. People who possess explicit self-instructional strategies for dealing with distractions are more likely to stay on task. Patterson and Mischel's (1976) classic "clown box" study illustrates the beneficial effects of cognitive self-instruction. Children performed a task while seated near the clown box, a gaily painted box the size of a coffee table that featured a clown's face, two windows with prizes that children might receive, and a speaker that emitted distracting vocalizations. Some children received instructions to tell themselves that "I'm not going to look at Mr. Clown box." Others received either no instructions or instructions merely to remind themselves to stay on task. Children who possessed the cognitive strategy of telling themselves that they "won't look" were more able to stay on task than others.

## Initiating Goal-Directed Action

In addition to the problem of staying on task once goal-directed efforts have begun, another self-control challenge is initiating action in the first place. People often fail to "get around to" activities that potentially would be personally fulfilling.

Gollwitzer and colleagues (Gollwitzer, 1999; Gollwitzer & Brandstatter, 1997) suggest that people are more likely to initiate behavior when they have an implementation intention, that is, a specific commitment to take action when a particular circumstance is encountered. Merely being committed to a long-term goal (e.g., "I'm going to get more exercise") may fail to move one to action. However, combining this goal with an implementation intention (e.g., "I'm going to run 2 miles immediately after getting home from work on Mondays, Wednesdays, and Fridays) commits one to take action at a particular time and place. Students with specific implementation intentions for studying during a vacation period have been found to be significantly more likely to achieve their academic goals (Gollwitzer and Brandstätter, 1997).

## CONTROLLING IMPULSES

We conclude this chapter by addressing one additional feature of self-control, namely, the ability to control unwanted impulses. Impulse control differs significantly from the phenomena discussed previously. In self-motivation and the carrying out of intentions, the challenge is to initiate and maintain courses of actions that are valuable in the long run but that may bring few immediate emotional rewards. Impulse control poses an opposite challenge. Affective systems impel us to act now, but inaction may be better in the long term.

Impulse control is a central task of the psychological system that we call personality. It is so important that, to Freud, personality development could be viewed as the progressive growth of mental structures that curb biologically based drives. Further, civilization could be viewed as a set of social structures designed to curb the unacceptable impulses of the individual. We may no longer embrace Freud's explanatory system. However, he did succeed in identifying key phenomena. To function effectively in society and to maintain personal well-being, people must regulate affectively based tendencies to aggress, consume food and drink, make sexual advances, etc. Psychotherapists recognize that enhancing self-control skills is a central therapeutic task (Marlatt & Gordon, 1985).

### Ego Dimensions

Freud, of course, conceived of impulse control as a task of the ego. This insight is retained in the work of Block and Block (1980). They view the ego as a system of "structures (mechanisms, routines, frames) [that] are interrelated and are invoked sequentially" (Block & Block, 1980, p. 41) in attempts to control impulses. Two dimensions of ego functioning are identified, ego control and ego resilience (also see chapters 5 and 8). Ego control captures individual differences in the overall degree of control an individual achieves over impulses. People who are over- versus under controlled differ in whether they tend to inhibit actions, suppress impulses, and delay gratification. Ego resilience captures the ability to modify levels of ego control to meet varying demands. People at extremes of this dimension display adaptive flexibility versus rigid inflexibility that leaves them relatively unable to cope with change.

As we noted earlier, ego functioning is assessed through a combination of measures; the Blocks have emphasized the need to aggregate across multiple measures to obtain a valid index of the individual's standing on the dimensions (also see Epstein, 1979). Taking these measures at multiple points across the life-span enables one to chart the developmental trajectory of ego functioning. Findings reveal that interindividual differences in ego functioning are highly stable over time, particularly among men (see chapter 8).

As reviewed by Shiner (1998), ego control and resiliency generally are positively related to achievement and social adjustment outcomes. There are gender differences here, with ego resiliency having different implications for men than for women and interacting differently with intelligence for the two sexes (Block & Kremen, 1996).

Although research on ego control and ego resilience has contributed much to our understanding of continuities and gender differences in development (see chapters 5 and 8), as an analysis of psychological determinants of people's ability to control impulses, there are some things that this program of research does not tell us. One limitation is the difficulty of linking the ego variables to specific psychological mechanisms. It is hard to know whether any single psychological agency actually is responsible for the broad range of phenomena that are attributed to the ego (also see Shiner, 1998). A second limitation is the absence of experimental evidence. The Blocks' data sets are remarkable for their detail and for the long time periods across which individuals are studied. Ideally, one might complement the correlational data resulting from this approach with experimental evidence that manipulates psychological mechanisms posited to influence self-control abilities (if

they can be identified). This could yield more convincing evidence of how a specifiable psychological mechanism causally contributes to self-control success. We turn now to a program of research that marshalls this sort of evidence.

### Mischel's Delay of Gratification Paradigm

Mischel and colleagues (Mischel, 1974; Mischel, Shoda, & Rodriguez, 1989; Metcalfe & Mischel, 1999) adopt a strategy for investigating personal determinants of self-control that differs from that of the Blocks. Rather than identifying broad individual-difference dimensions, Mischel first sought to identify one or more specific cognitive processes that may facilitate impulse control. An understanding of individual differences could then be built on this analysis of underlying mechanisms. By specifying the exact psychological processes involved in self-control, Mischel has been able to bring both correlational and experimental evidence to bear on questions of self-control.

This program of research explores delay of gratification, that is, people's ability to forestall the consumption of rewards that are immediately available in order to obtain better outcomes in the future. An experimental paradigm presents children with the possibility of earning one of two rewards. One can be obtained immediately. This immediate reward generally consists of a small consumable item (e.g., a pretzel). A second reward can only be obtained if the child is able to wait for a period of time; this delayed reward is a larger item (e.g., a few pretzels) that is clearly preferable to the immediate reward. Children are taught a contingency in which they can obtain the immediate reward by ringing a bell, whereupon someone will respond to their call and give them the small, immediate reward. If the child can wait until the person returns spontaneously, they receive the larger reward. The dependent measure is how long children wait before ringing the bell.

Within this setting, Mischel experimentally manipulated factors that are designed to influence cognitive mechanisms which, in turn, are believed to govern people's ability to delay gratification. Specifically, he manipulated whether or not the rewards were visible to children during the delay period. This simple manipulation yielded powerful results. In the experimental condition in which children can see both rewards during the delay period, they are not better at delay of gratification but worse. Children who view the rewards appear to become frustrated at having to wait. They quickly ring the bell to obtain the small, immediate reward. When the rewards are placed out of sight, children do much better. Conditions in which no rewards are visible yield delay scores nearly 10 times longer than those obtained when both rewards are in view (Mischel, 1974).

The critical determinant of delay of gratification is not the placement of objects in the external environment but the processes occurring in the child's head. Even when rewards are in full view, children are able to delay gratification if they employ cognitive strategies that distract them from the "hot," consumability related properties of the reward objects (Metcalfe & Mischel, 1999). These strategies might include focusing on non-consumability related properties of the reward (e.g., thinking of how pretzels resemble logs), conceiving of the reward as a mere photo of the object (e.g., by mentally placing a picture frame around it), or engaging in mentation that distracts one from the rewards (e.g., singing songs, thinking fun thoughts). A series of studies show that children who are taught these strategies are better able to delay gratification (Mischel & Baker, 1975; Mischel & Moore, 1973; Moore, Mischel, & Zeiss, 1976).

This research on delay of gratification, then, clarifies the causal impact of cognitive strategies on delay ability by manipulating strategies experimentally. Virtually any child who is instructed about how to cognitively transform a frustrating environment is better able to delay gratification. In this sense, then, self-control ability is malleable. People have the potential to acquire effective cognitive

strategies and thus to gain control over their emotions and actions.

A second question addressed by Mischel and colleagues is that of individual differences. In the absence of systematic instruction in self-control skills, people might display enduring individual differences in their ability to delay gratification. Longitudinal research reveals that Mischel's delay paradigm is a remarkably good indicator of stable self-control competencies. Mischel, Shoda, and Peake (1988) related delay of gratification scores obtained by nursery school children to observer ratings of these same children when they were in high school. Children who were better able to delay gratification were rated as significantly more able to control their impulses, plan courses of action, and deal with stress as adolescents. Thus, as in the research of Block and Block, there were significant continuities between early-life self-regulatory abilities and later outcomes (also see chapter 5).

Importantly, personality ratings in adolescence were linked only to delay scores obtained in the "rewards present" condition of the delay paradigm, that is, the condition in which delaying gratification was most difficult (Shoda, Mischel, & Peake, 1990). The most difficult experimental setting, then, proved most diagnostic of enduring self-control capabilities. Other research similarly indicates that challenging circumstances may be most diagnostic of individual differences. Wright and Mischel (1987) studied children's aggressive tendencies across a range of circumstances in which it was more or less difficult to control frustration and inhibit aggression. Observer ratings of children's aggressiveness strongly predicted aggressive behavior in situations in which it was particularly difficult to control aggression, but not in more benign circumstances.

Metcalfe and Mischel (1999) have presented a theoretical framework that synthesizes research on delay of gratification. In their theory, self-control is regulated by two psychological systems: a "hot" system and a "cool" system. Impulses are hot reactions that impel one to act. Cognitive strategies are contained within a cool system that can temper impulses by directing attention away from the hot properties of the environment. This model addresses both the experimental results and the individual differences that are identified. Removing rewards from sight or instructing people in cognitive strategies both serve to deflect attention away from the hot properties of the reward objects. The hot system thus is less activated and people are better able to delay gratification. The self-knowledge and cognitive processing abilities that constitute the cool system, particularly the metacognitive knowledge required to control emotional states (Mischel & Mischel, 1983), are stable individual differences. These stable cool-system differences account for the continuity between childhood and adolescent outcomes.

This hot–cool perspective may prove to be an enduringly valuable framework for understanding self-control. It places the study of basic psychological mechanisms, situational influences, enduring individual differences, and person–situation interactions under a common theoretical umbrella–a most noteworthy accomplishment. It captures dispositional differences among individuals while also revealing people's potentiality for changing their dispositional tendencies by acquiring greater self-control skills.

One important problem that is still to be solved is determining the respective contributions of the hot and cool system to any given self-regulatory outcome. For example, stable interindividual differences in self-control ability may reflect stability in the cool system, as the theory suggests. Alternatively, it may also reflect stability in the hot system. Even among people who have equivalent cool-system competencies, different levels of reactivity in the hot system (cf. Gray, 1987; Rothbart & Bates, 1998) may yield enduring individual differences in delay ability. What is needed, then, is more work that assesses specific affective and cognitive determinants of self-control and how these affective and cognitive mechanisms interact and develop over time. Advances in this promising area may soon yield a truly comprehensive set of answers to some of the field's most basic and enduring questions about personality functioning.

## SUMMING UP

A quarter of a century ago, the fields of personality, social, and clinical psychology witnessed a common trend. Questions of self-concept and self-regulation came to the fore. Personality theorists posited that problems of motivation and self-control that had been posed since the days of Freud could be solved by advances in the study of cognition and social learning (Bandura, 1977b; Mischel, 1974). Social psychologists proposed that people's beliefs about the self guide their interpretations of the social world and motivate their social behavior (Markus, 1977; also see Markus & Nurius, 1986). Clinical psychologists recognized that a central therapeutic task was not only to change behavior but also to enhance self-control skills (Bandura, 1969; Thoreson & Mahoney, 1974). The analysis of self-concept and self-regulatory processes, then, promised to enrich psychologists' understanding of both personal and situational determinants of motivation and to strengthen their ability to enhance people's capacity for self-control.

The findings reviewed in this chapter suggest that this promise has begun to be fulfilled. Research provides firm evidence of the causal contribution of self-regulatory processes to motivation and performance. Findings show how these processes function as coherent systems and how both situational and personal factors differentially activate the self-system. Research on goal mechanisms and self-efficacy beliefs shows how these motivational mechanisms contribute to psychological well-being and personality coherence. The study of people's ability to control affectively based impulses illuminates both enduring individual differences and specific psychological processes in self-control. This body of theory and research provides a firm basis for designing psychosocial interventions that help individuals to motivate themselves, regulate their psychological experiences, and thereby maximize their potentials.

The findings we have reviewed also begin to fulfill yet another promise, namely, the possibility of bottom-up explanations of personality functioning and differences among individuals (see chapter 4). Research reviewed throughout this chapter has revealed how surface-level behavioral tendencies could be explained by reference to a system of self-regulatory mechanisms. Investigators were not content merely with charting dispositional tendencies. Instead, they showed how individual differences and intraindividual coherence could be understood by reference to specific psychological systems that causally contribute to the individual's distinctive patterns of experience and action. These accomplishments have important implications for the field as a whole. They suggest that personality psychology is beginning to advance to a point at which it can function as a unified discipline that provides a synthetic account of underlying psychological dynamics and overt dispositional tendencies. We consider this promise for the future of the field in our epilogue.

# PART FIVE

# Epilogue

# Looking to the Future

## *Is Personality Psychology in Good Health?*

Our previous chapters have explored personality psychology's past and present. In this epilogue we look to its future. We consider the field's future prospects in the hope of identifying contemporary trends that will prove to be of enduring value. In so doing, we of course are interested not only in personality psychology but in persons. Any normative discussion of the field's future must be guided by convictions about the determinants of personality functioning and the nature of human tendencies and potentials.

Discussion of an academic discipline's future can lapse into idle speculation. Anyone can identify purportedly promising trends and project them ahead. Different writers are likely to identify different trends, and there is no firm basis for evaluating the accuracy or utility of different visions. Nonetheless, pondering the future of our discipline serves a useful purpose. It forces us to evaluate critically the current state of the field; specifically, it forces an evaluation on the most fundamental of criteria: Are contemporary theories and empirical results likely to contribute to a cumulative science of personality in the long run? In other words, what will people think of our current field 50 or 100 years from now? Will history view our work as the first steps in a cumulative science of the person or as a well-intentioned but misguided enterprise of little lasting value?

## REASONS FOR OPTIMISM?

In the past two decades, commentators commonly have viewed the field with optimism (e.g., Buss & Cantor, 1989; Kenrick & Dantchik, 1983). Unlike the crisis period of the 1970s, which was initiated by Mischel's (1968) critique, the 1980s and 1990s appear to have been marked by much cumulative progress. This optimism surely is not entirely misplaced. Methodological advances have put the field on a firmer footing. Investigators' greater reliance on longitudinal data sets and increased ability to study a given personality variable through a combination of correlational and experimental techniques were particularly noteworthy steps forward. Theoretical advances also are heartening. The discipline's widespread recognition that personality develops and functions through reciprocal interactions with the sociocultural environment (e.g., Bandura, 1986; Magnusson, 1988) clearly was an advance over earlier perspectives. The substantial consensus that a five-factor structure is adequate to represent phenotypic interindividual differences was perhaps the single most encouraging development to many investigators (Goldberg, 1993).

Optimism, then, has been pervasive of late. A glance further back, however, is more sobering. Throughout its history, personality psychology has had more than its fair share of crises and fads. Popular theoretical structures have crumbled in the face of empirical evidence. Programs of empirical research have often failed to address vital questions raised in the theories. Personality psychology's "history of ups and downs" (Cervone, 1991, p. 371) suggests that today's optimism is no guarantee of a happy tomorrow.

A look to the future can be sobering, too. Kagan (1998b) prognosticates that "no present concept in personality will survive the next half century" (p. 198). Contemporary constructs will succumb to empirical scrutiny, he suggests, because they are too broad. We tend to treat a concept such as "fear" as an essential quality. We ask about its physiological basis, how best to construct self-report instruments to measure it, and whether we learn it or inherit it. The problem is that there may be no "it." Although "fear" is a single word in the dictionary, it may not be a unitary essence in nature. Qualitatively different physiological profiles may each be part of the broad category "fear." Qualitatively different phenomenological experiences may each be labeled fearful, as the term currently is used in our society. Furthermore, physiological and phenomenological markers of fear may fail to converge (also see Fiske, 1978; Hettema, 1989). As we saw in chapter 9, physiological and self-report measures of anxiety fail to converge among "repressors," a term we place in quotes because it, too, may prove to be a broad category that contains qualitatively distinct types of persons. In this view, then, history will not look kindly on those who treat broad constructs such as "fear" as unitary qualities or who assess these qualities through a conglomeration of physiological and questionnaire methods.

Whatever one's appraisal of the contemporary field, its current state is such that a scholar can reasonably argue that all of its central constructs will be jettisoned within the expected life-span of students currently earning their Ph.D.'s. Such arguments could not be made in more mature sciences. Physics and biology will progress, but no one would claim that future advances will be the death knell of

concepts such as proton, radioactivity, gene, or natural selection.

Given the wealth of evidence we have reviewed in this text, one might reasonably ask how future developments could possibly dampen enthusiasm about our current constructs. Since the optimism of the past decade has centered so heavily around the five-factor model, we pose the question in this context. Has the field not demonstrated the everlasting utility of the five-factor constructs to a science of personality?

At least six sources of evidence (see chapters 3 and 6) would suggest that the answer to this question is yes.[1] (1) In various languages and cultures, the constructs can be identified reliably in factor analyses of individual differences in self- and peer reports. (2) Interindividual differences in the factors are quite stable over time. (3) Self-ratings and peer ratings on the factors converge, albeit modestly (Kenny, Albright, Malloy, & Kashy, 1994). (4) The constructs predict significant life outcomes, albeit modestly here, too (Pervin, 1994). (5) Monozygotic twin scores correspond more closely than dizygotic twin scores, which suggests that the variables have a genetic basis. (6) There exist biological markers of some of the traits, that is, people who obtain high versus low scores on questionnaire measures differ from one another physiologically. These findings certainly appear to support the reality of the factors and the conclusion that they will enduringly play a central role in a scientific theory of personality.

How can one question this conclusion? To answer this, we consider an analogy to biology. Suppose one were to survey individual differences in physical attributes. In addition to questions about qualities such as size or appearance (Are most of your acquaintances

---

[1] The analogy that is introduced, to the hypothetical biological individual-difference variable healthiness, has been discussed in Cervone (1999) and indepndtly suggested by both Kagan (1998b) and Gopnik (1999), the latter of whom suggested that the conceptual status of general intelligence is analogous to that of general healthiness.

shorter than you?; Is your hair darker than most people's?; Do friends consider you handsome?), one might ask about physical fitness (Are you generally in good health?; Do you consider yourself to be a sickly individual?; Do you feel "run down" much of the time?). In principle, these latter items might intercorrelate so highly that (1) factor analyses suggest that the items form a unique, unitary construct, one that might be labeled *healthiness*. Furthermore, (2) individual differences in healthiness might be stable over substantial periods of time, if only because of a small number of individuals with a chronic disease; (3) self-ratings and peer ratings of healthiness may converge; (4) healthiness scores might predict important life outcomes, such as health care costs and longevity; (5) monozygotic twin scores might correlate more highly than dizygotic twin scores (owing to inherited liabilities); and (6) people with low healthiness scores might differ from those who are high in healthiness on any of a variety of biological markers (oxygen-carrying capacity of the cardiovascular system, immune system functioning, percentage of body fat, genetic abnormalities, presence of gastrointestinal viruses, etc.). These findings would suggest that healthiness is a real thing with an inherited biological basis and might imply that an individual's level of healthiness causally contributes to, and thus explains, his or her health outcomes.

No matter how strong this psychometric evidence, biologists are unlikely to conclude that healthiness is an enduringly useful explanatory construct for the science of biology. The problem, of course, is that healthiness is heterogeneous. Different people who obtain exactly the same healthiness score could differ biologically in any of an enormous variety of ways. The construct thus would have little utility for those who wish to explain the functioning of biological systems and to use this knowledge to benefit the individual.

The healthiness construct might serve some practical purposes. It could function as a screening tool. Insurers might wish to reject policy applicants who score as highly

unhealthy. It might detect changes in health status. Public health officials would be interested to learn that a population's scores had changed over time. To serve such purposes, the construct would have to have predictive validity, which it might. Healthiness scores might predict a variety of outcomes such as subjective well-being, use of health care services, or longevity. However, predictive utility is no guarantee that a construct can meet the more fundamental criterion of elucidating the determinants and mechanisms that causally contribute to phenomena under study. The ancients could predict astrological events with great accuracy but had no understanding of gravity and thought that the earth was the center of the universe. If personality psychology is to continue to progress, investigators must place ever greater emphasis not only on predicting outcomes but on identifying causal mechanisms. "Bigger correlation coefficients" can no longer be "the coin of the realm" (Bem & Allen, 1974, p. 512).

Although healthiness could not function as an explanatory construct in biology, the six healthiness findings outlined above could be of scientific value under certain circumstances. Suppose science possessed no firm knowledge of biological mechanisms and that theorists therefore held a potpourri of disparate beliefs about the causes of good versus poor health. The evidence above could refute some completely erroneous beliefs (e.g., that health outcomes are governed by phases of the moon). Furthermore, it could refute the belief that people who obtain low healthiness scores do not actually differ from others physiologically but are merely hypochondriacs; in other words, the evidence would refute the belief that healthiness does not exist. Once circumstances changed and more detailed knowledge of biological mechanisms became available, however, the healthiness construct would be jettisoned from scientific explanation. In this same way, then, contemporary dispositional constructs could be seen as inadequate in the long run (Kagan, 1998b) despite the wealth of current evidence.

This analogy may seem to have pessimistic implications for personality psychology, a field that has relied so heavily on the potential explanatory value of global dispositional constructs. However, it indirectly suggests a reason for optimism about the field. Empirical advances during the past quarter of a century enable the contemporary personality psychologist (like the healthiness researcher) to refute beliefs that previously seemed plausible. Many former points of debate are now resolved. Consider the following questions. Are there significant continuities in personality from childhood to adulthood? Can psychologists reach agreement on the number of dimensions required to describe phenotypic individual differences? Do observers and targets agree when rating the personality of the target? Would identical twins raised in different households resemble one another in personality? Can people who experience adversities early in life achieve normal adjustment and well-being in later years? Are different emotional states accompanied by different patterns of neurophysiology? Do emotions influence memory and thought? Does self-referent thought causally contribute to motivation, emotion, and behavior change? Does exposure to media violence affect people's behavior and beliefs about society? Can women function as well as men in intellectually challenging professions? Is there such a thing as unconscious cognition? Once upon a time, it was possible to defend both negative and affirmative answers to all of these questions. Today, it is virtually impossible to defend a strong negative answer to any of them.

Having refuted these points, one can now move on. Our field has reached a stage of evolution at which one no longer needs to ask whether personality exists, whether it is stable, whether it is influenced by biology, whether it is influenced by the environment, or whether it is significant to individual welfare. What we now have to ask is what it *is*. The greatest challenge is to move beyond a psychology of phenotypic tendencies to explore more fully the interacting social, cognitive, and biological determinants of personality functioning. The way to beat the healthiness critique of phenotypic dispositional constructs, then, is not merely to do more work on phenotypic dispositional constructs. It is to explore the underlying psychological systems that causally contribute to the individual's tendencies and potentials.

Of course, much progress in understanding affective and social-cognitive determinants of personality functioning has already been made, as we have reviewed throughout this volume. This progress constitutes another reason for optimism. In addition to the sheer substance of theory and findings, two other positive signs can be found here. The first is that the study of social cognition and of emotion have advanced quite rapidly. Both areas of study look dramatically different today than they did a quarter of a century ago. There is little reason to expect that progress will slow as the new century begins. A second positive sign is that the role of affective and cognitive processes in personality functioning is being explored by an increasingly large and diverse mix of investigators. Researchers in biopsychology and neuroscience, cognitive science, and social psychology routinely explore questions that are the traditional province of the personality psychologist. Even if the number of people calling themselves personality psychologists is not growing rapidly, the number of people studying personality functioning and individual differences is.

Finally, even Kagan's prophecy about the demise of our current constructs can be read optimistically. His prediction implies that knowledge of personality development and functioning will increase so substantially in the next half century as to leave us with an entirely new, and improved, set of concepts. This is a sunny forecast.

## TOWARD A COMMON PARADIGM?

Even during the most optimistic eras, enthusiasm about the state of personality psychology has been tempered by the field's lack of a common theoretical paradigm. The formulation of a generally accepted theoretical framework continues to stand as a discipline's "holy grail" (also see John, 1990). Instead of a shared paradigm, personality psychology often has been divided into competing camps.

Theoretical divisions can sometimes be stimulating, and the debates they trigger can be clarifying. However, division and debate can also be costly. Theoretical squabbles can sap the energy of the field, create a poor impression of the discipline among scientists outside of it, and divert attention from important scientific questions that happen not to be current "hot topics" for debate. A shared paradigm, then, might minimize unproductive debate while lending greater organization to the field's array of research efforts. When looking to the future of the field, then, the single most compelling question may be: Is a common paradigm on the horizon? This question can be addressed at more than one level. One can ask whether a shared paradigm will emerge at the level of broad metatheoretical principles or at the level of more specific theory.

At the level of broad principles, a shared paradigm may already be among us. As we outlined in chapter 1, a large number of investigators already share a substantial number of beliefs about personality development and functioning. Two that stand out in light of the work we have now reviewed are the principles of reciprocal influence and complex systems. Few investigators would disagree with the notion that personality develops and functions through reciprocal influence processes. Reciprocity is found repeatedly in analyses of person–situation transactions, brain mechanisms and behavioral experience, and cognition and affect. Second, investigators are coming to agreement that personality must be viewed as a complex, dynamic system. The coherence of personality functioning increasingly is viewed as an emergent property of interactions among multiple elements of the psychological system. We anticipate that the influence of complex systems analyses will grow in the coming years.

These principles are abstract. One clearly needs a more specific theory. How far are we, then, from consensus at this level? Some developments suggest that we are close. In the past, more than a dozen theoretical views competed for dominance in the field (see Hall & Lindzey, 1957). Today we find a much smaller number of broad paradigms. Although one could identify significant exceptions, many contemporary developments could reasonably be classified under the theoretical umbrellas of trait/dispositional or social-cognitive theories. This shift from many theories to a small number of frameworks seems to suggest that the discipline is moving toward consensus. However, genuine consensus is difficult to achieve. Social-cognitive and trait conceptions are hard to reconcile theoretically, as we have noted. Somewhat similarly, it is difficult to reconcile the contemporary field's varied accounts of cultural diversities versus cross-cultural universals in psychological experience.

If we again contemplate the past, we will recall that psychoanalytic theory seemed to provide a consensual framework throughout much of the 20th century. Psychoanalysis integrated the study of personality dynamics, development, and therapeutic change. It explained personality functioning in terms of a complex system of interacting structures and processes. It described the individual in depth and suggested frameworks for describing individual differences. It addressed not only the individual but how persons develop and function within the broader society.

For much of the 20th century, the impact of psychoanalysis was so great that it obscured other approaches to personality. The basic tenets of psychoanalysis received wide acceptance among the general public. It was utterly unique among psychological theories in its impact on the arts and literature. However, as reviewed by us (chapter 2) and considered in greater detail by others, psychoanalysis simply did not work well enough. Its drive theory could not be assimilated to findings in the psychology of motivation, its therapeutic method did not prove to be uniquely effective, its assessment techniques were unreliable, and many of the details of its model of mind proved difficult to reconcile with growing scientific knowledge of cognitive systems.

In the search for a new common paradigm, psychoanalytic thinking remains instructive. This is not only because of the insights psychoanalysis continues to provide (Westen, 1998), but because psychoanalytic theory reminds us of the breadth of tasks that must be accomplished by any framework claiming to be a personality theory. Psychoanalytic theorists explored personality structures and dynamics; unconscious processes and conscious experience; developmental change and stability; emotional drives and the cognitive strategies that regulate them; the interpersonal world and the person's relation to the wider society. Although their research methods were wanting and their explanations are no longer viable, psychoanalysts did get the phenomena right. In this regard, they set a high standard for the field.

The remarkable advances in brain science might suggest that personality psychology's ultimate theoretical framework will be biologically based. Future years undoubtedly will yield dramatically greater understanding of the role of genetic influences and biological mechanisms in personality. However, a thoroughly biological psychology of personality strikes us as an unlikely prospect. In their day-to-day psychological functioning, people create and respond to meaning. They construct meaning out of their life events and their experiences of themselves and attempt to regulate their activities in light of the understandings they achieve. Processes of meaning construction and self-reflection must then be a central focus in a science of the person. Even the finest of neuroscientists recognizes that the self-reflective processes through which people create meaning in life are not going to be reducible to physiological subcomponents. As Roger Sperry (1982) explains, in the analysis of personal functioning "the events of inner experience, as emergent properties of brain processes, become themselves explanatory constructs in their own right" (p. 1226).

In this volume, we have reviewed a vast body of research on the role of social-cognitive structures and processes in personality functioning. Social-cognitive analyses have proved to illuminate phenomena ranging from development to dynamics to personality dispositions. As we look to the future, we are optimistic about the long-term value of social-cognitive theory. This perhaps is not surprising, in as much as we ourselves take part in research on social-cognitive processes. But there are objective reasons for optimism. One is the speed with which social-cognitive theory has advanced. Unlike psychoanalytic theory (Freud, 1900) and trait theory (Cattell, 1946; Eysenck, 1947), the social-cognitive perspective only began to take its mature form about a quarter of a century ago (e.g., Bandura, 1977b; Mischel, 1973). Despite the brevity of this history, social-cognitive theorists already have succeeded in providing an integrative framework for analyzing personality dynamics and dispositions (Mischel & Shoda, 1998) and in extending their analyses to encompass virtually the entire gamut of phenomena that are critical to a psychology of personality (see Cervone & Shoda, 1999b). Bandura (1986, 1999), in his social cognitive theory, has succeeded in providing a uniquely broad and integrative analysis of personality functioning. Indeed, in some respects Bandura's work is broader than most of the other classic theories of personality. His social cognitive theory addresses not only personality psychology's traditional topics of affect, motivation, self-concept, self-regulation, and behavioral change but also the often overlooked question of how people acquire the cognitive and behavioral competencies that enable them to function effectively.

A second reason for optimism about social-cognitive theory is that its basic tenets now receive support from many quarters of the field. The two most basic postulates of social-cognitive theory are (1) that personality functioning involves reciprocal interactions among persons, their behavior, and the sociocultural environment; and (2) that people are causal agents, at in other words, their cognitive capabilities enable them to contribute proactively to the course of their development. At one time, these tenets were points of debate (e.g., Eysenck, 1978; Phillips & Orton, 1983). Debate subsided in light of subsequent developments. As we have noted, causal reciprocity is found at many levels of analyses, including the level of genetic mechanisms (Gottlieb, 1998). The notion of personal agency is established through both philosophical and psychological analyses and now figures prominently in many conceptions of personal development (see especially chapters 5 and 12).

We certainly would not claim that the social-cognitive perspective can currently function as a complete theory of personality, but it does provide a foundation to build upon in the years ahead. Areas of expansion can easily be identified. Ideally, social-cognitive theory would attend even more closely to subjective experience and the formation of personal identity; to the ways in which inherited affective mechanisms contribute to the development of social-cognitive systems; to knowledge structures that do not center on the self but on the community in which one lives; and to the role of self-referent processes in the regulation of affect and interpersonal behavior. Some recent findings already speak to this last point. People's beliefs in their efficacy to control their emotional states have been found to influence self-efficacy beliefs for effective interpersonal conduct. People with higher interpersonal efficacy beliefs, in turn, engage in more prosocial behavior and fewer antisocial acts (Caprara et al., in press).

Finally, social-cognitive theory has a critical pragmatic advantage. Psychology is not only called on to describe and predict behavior. It also is asked to help people change. Society expects the discipline to furnish ideas and technologies that can help people to expand their skills, achieve greater emotional adjustment, and thereby realize their potentials. Theories that view personality as an immutable collection of inherited dispositions or evolved mechanisms are of little help in meeting these expectations. What is needed is a theory that sheds light on the psychological processes and social experiences that can strengthen people's capacity to adapt to our rapidly changing world. By responding to this need, social-cognitive theory has, at the very least, taken a critical step toward a common paradigm that can meet the needs of both the academy and society.

We are well aware that we have shifted the terms of debate. In weighing alternative trends, we have considered not only the field's supply of ideas but society's demand for them. This, we feel, is fully appropriate. Forecasts for the discipline must take account of the societies in which the field will develop.

When society turns to psychology for answers, its questions most commonly are those addressed by the personality psychologist. Most psychological scientists rightfully study isolated mental mechanisms and functions. But society shares the personality scientist's interest in the whole person. Society demands, and will continue to demand, a scientifically grounded theory of the person that illuminates not only psychological dispositions but human potentials. Demand often stimulates supply. These social demands, then, provide a final reason for optimism about the future of personality psychology.

# References

Aarts, H., & Dijksterhuis, A. (2000). Habits as knowledge structures: Automaticity in goal-directed behavior. *Journal of Personality and Social Psychology, 78,* 53–63.

Abbott, R. D. (1972). On the confounding of the Repression-Sensitization and Manifest Anxiety scales. *Psychological Reports, 30,* 392–394.

Abelson, R. P. (1981). The psychological status of the script concept. *American Psychologist, 36,* 715–729.

Aboud, F. (1992). Conflict and group relations. In C. Shantz & W. W. Hartup (Eds.), *Conflict in child and adolescent development* (pp. 356–379). New York: Cambridge University Press.

Abramson, L. Y., Metalsky, G. I., & Alloy, L. B. (1989). Hopelessness depression: A theory-based subtype of depression. *Psychological Review, 96,* 358–372.

Abramson, L. Y., Seligman, M. E. P., & Teasdale, J. D. (1978). Learned helplessness in humans: Critique and reformulation. *Journal of Abnormal Psychology, 87,* 49–74.

Adamson, L. (1995). *Communication development during infancy.* Boulder, CO: Westview Press.

Adler, A. (1920). *Practice and theory of individual psychology.* London: Routledge & Kegan Paul.

Adler, A. (1927). *Understanding human nature.* New York: Greenberg.

Adler, A., & Mathews, K. (1994). Health psychology: Why do some people get sick and some stay well? *Annual Review of Psychology, 45,* 229–259.

Adorno, I. W., Frenkel-Brunswick, E., Levinson, D. J., & Sanford, R. N. (1950). *The authoritarian personality.* New York: Harper & Row.

Agronick, A., & Duncan, L. E. (1998). Personality and social change: Individual differences, life path, and importance attributed to the women's movement. *Journal of Personality and Social Psychology, 74,* 1545–1555.

Ahadi, S. A., & Rothbart, M. K. (1994). Temperament, development, and the big five. In C. F. Halverson, Jr., G. A. Kohnstamm, & R. P. Martin (Eds.), *The developing structure of temperament and personality from infancy to adulthood* (pp. 189–207). Hillsdale, NJ: Lawrence Erlbaum Associates.

Ainsworth, M. D.(1967). *Infancy in Uganda.* Baltimore: Johns Hopkins Press.

Ainsworth, M. D., Bell, S. M., & Stayton, F. J. (1971). Individual differences in strange-situation behavior of one-year-olds. In H. R. Schaffer (Ed.), *The origins of human social relations* (pp. 17–57). New York: Academic Press.

Ainsworth, M. D., Blehar, M., Waters, E., & Wall. S. (1978). *Patterns of attachment.* Hillsdale, NJ: Lawrence Erlbaum Associates.

Ainsworth, M. D., & Bowlby, J. (1991). An ethnological approach to personality development. *American Psychologist, 46,* 333–341.

Ajzen, I. (1988). *Attitudes, personality, and behavior.* Chicago: Dorsey Press.

Ajzen, I. (1996). The directive influence of attitudes on behavior. In P. M. Gollwitzer & J. A. Bargh (Eds.), *The psychology of action: Linking cognition and motivation to behavior* (pp. 385–403). New York: Guilford.

Alden, L. (1986). Self-efficacy and causal attributions for social feedback. *Journal of Research in Personality, 20,* 460–473.

Alexander, M. J, & Higgins, E. T. (1993). Emotional trade-offs of becoming a parent: How social roles influence self-discrepancy effects. *Journal of Personality & Social Psychology, 65,* 1259–1269.

Alker, H. A. (1972). Is personality situationally specific or intrapsychically consistent? *Journal of Personality, 40,* 1–16.

Allport, G. W. (1937). *Personality: A psychological interpretation.* New York: Holt.

Allport, G. W. (1950). *Becoming.* New Haven: Yale University Press.

Allport, G. W. (1960). *Personality and social encounter.* Boston: Beacon Press.

Allport, G. W. (1961). *Pattern and growth in personality.* New York: Holt, Rinehart, & Winston.

Allport, G. W. (1962). The general and the unique in psychological science. *Journal of Personality, 30,* 405–422.

Allport, G. W., & Odbert, H. S. (1936). Trait names: A psycho-lexical study. *Psychological Monographs, 47* (1, Whole No. 211).

Almagor, M., Tellegen, A., & Waller N. G. (1995). The Big Seven model: A cross-cultural replication and further exploration of the basic dimensions of natural language trait descriptors. *Journal of Personality and Social Psychology, 69,* 300–307.

Amato, P., & Keith, B. (1991). Parental divorce and the well-being of children: A meta-analysis. *Psychological Bulletin, 110,* 26–46.

Amelang, M., & Borkenau, P. (1982). The factional structure and external validity of some questionnaire scales for measurement of the dimensions of extraversion and emotional lability. [German]. *Zeitschrift Fuer Differentielle und Diagnostische Psychologie, 3,* Apr-Jun 119–145.

Ames, C. (1992). Classrooms: Goals, structures, and student motivation. *Journal of Educational Psychology, 84,* 261–371.

Ammerman, A. J., & Cavalli-Sforza, L. L. (1984). *The neolithic transition and the genetics of populations in Europe.* Princeton, N. J.: Princeton University Press.

Andersen, B. L., & Cyranowski, J. M. (1994). Women's sexual self-schema. *Journal of Personality and Social Psychology, 67,* 1079–1100.

Andersen, S. M., & Baum, A. (1994). Transference in interpersonal relations: Inferences and affect based on significant-other representations. *Journal of Personality, 62,* 459–497.

Andersen, S. M., & Chen, S. (in press). Transference in everyday social relations: Theory, evidence, and new directions from an experimental social-cognitive perspective. In H. Kurtzman (Ed.), *Cognition and Psychodynamics.* New York: Oxford University Press.

Andersen, S. M., & Cole, S. W. (1990). "Do I know you?": The role of significant others in general social perception. *Journal of Personality and Social Psychology, 59,* 384–399.

Andersen, S. M., Glassman, N. S., Chen, S., & Cole, S. W. (1995). Transference in social perception: The role of chronic accessibility in significant-other representations. *Journal of Personality and Social Psychology, 69,* 41–57.

Andersen, S. M., Reznick, I., & Manzella, L. M. (1996). Eliciting facial affect, motivation, and expectancies in transference: Significant-other representations in social relations. *Journal of Personality and Social Psychology, 71,* 1108–1129.

Andersen, S., & Ross, L. (1984). Self-knowledge and social inference: I. The impact of cognitive/affective and behavioral data. *Journal of Personality and Social Psychology, 46,* 280–293.

Anderson, C., & Weiner, B. (1992). Attribution and attributional processes in personality. In G. V. Caprara & G. Van Heck (Eds.), *Modern Personality Psychology* (pp. 200–252). London: Harvester Wheatsheaf.

Anderson, J. R. (1983). *The architecture of cognition.* Cambridge, MA: Harvard University Press.

Angleitner, A., Ostendorf, F., & John, O. P. (1990). Towards a taxonomy of personality descriptors in German: A psycholexical study. *European Journal of Personality, 4,* 89–118.

Archer, J. (1990). Sex differences in social behavior. *American Psychologist, 51,* 909–917.

Argyle, M., Furnham, A., & Graham, J. A. (1981). *Social situations.* Cambridge, U. K.: Cambridge University Press.

Aries, P. (1960). *L'enfant et la famille sous l'ancien régime.* English translation: *Centuries of Childhood.* London: Random House, 1962.

Armsden, G., & Greenberg, M. (1987). The inventory of parent and peer attachment: Individual differences and their relationships to psychological well-being in adolescence. *Journal of Youth and Adolescence, 16,* 427–454.

Armstrong, J. S. (1967). Derivation of theory by means of factor analysis or Tom Swift and his electric factor analysis machine. *The American Statistician, 21,* 17–21.

Arnett, J. J. (1999). Adolescent storm and stress, reconsidered. *American Psychologist, 54,* 317–326.

Asendorpf, J. B., & Scherer, K. R. (1983). The discrepant repressor: Differentiation between low anxiety, high anxiety, and repression of anxiety by autonomic-facial-verbal patterns of behavior. *Journal of Personality and Social Psychology, 45,* 1334–1346.

Ashmore, R. (1990). Sex, gender, and the individual. In L. A. Pervin (Ed.), *Handbook of personality: Theory and research* (pp. 486–526). New York: Guilford.

Atkinson, J. W. (1964). *An introduction to motivation.* Princeton, NJ: Van Nostrand.

Atkinson, J. W. (1981). Studying personality in the context of an advanced motivational psychology. *American Psychologist, 36,* 117–128.

Atkinson, J. W., & Birch, D. (1970). *The dynamics of action.* New York: Wiley.

Atkinson, R. C., & Shiffrin, R. M. (1971). The control of short-term memory. *Scientific American, 225,* 82–90.

Averill, J. R. (1994). In the eyes of the beholder. In P. Ekman & R. J. Davidson (Eds.), *The nature of emotion: Fundamental questions* (pp. 7–14). New York: Oxford University Press.

Averill, J. R. (1997). The emotions: An integrative approach. In R. Hogan, J. Johnson, & S. Briggs (Eds.), *Handbook of personality psychology* (pp. 513–541). San Diego: Academic Press.

Averill, J. R., & More, T. A. (1993). Happiness. In M. Lewis & J. M. Haviland (Eds.), *Handbook of emotions* (pp. 617–629). New York: Guilford Press.

Avia, M. D. (1997). Personality and positive emotions. *European Journal of Personality, 11,* 33–56.

Avia, M. D., & Vázquez, C. (1998). *Optimismo Inteligente.* Madrid: Alianza Editorial.

Azmitia, M. (1996). Peer interactive minds: Developmental, theoretical and methodological issues. In P. B. Baltes & U. Staudinger (Eds.), *Interactive minds* (pp. 133–162). New York: Cambridge University Press.

Bagozzi, R. (1993). Assessing construct validity in personality research: Applications to measures of self esteem. *Journal of Research in Personality, 27,* 49–87.

Bagozzi, R. (1994). The evaluation of structural equation models and hypothesis testing. In R. Bagozzi (Ed.), *Principles of marketing research* (pp. 386–422). Cambridge, MA: Blackwell.

Bagwell, C. L., Newcomb, A. F., & Bukowski, W. M. (1998). Preadolescent friendship and peer rejection as predictors of adult adjustment. *Child Development, 69,* 140–153.

Bak, P., & Chen, K. (1991). Self-organized criticality. *Scientific American, 262,* 92–99.

Bakan, D. (1966). *The duality of human existence.* Chicago: Rand McNally.

Baker, S. L., & Kirsch, I. (1991). Cognitive mediation of pain perception and tolerance. *Journal of Personality and Social Psychology, 61,* 504–510.

Baldwin, M. W. (1992). Relational schemas and the processing of social information. *Psychological Bulletin, 112,* 461–484.

Baldwin, M. W. (1999). Relational schemas: Research into social cognitive aspects of interpersonal experience. In D. Cervone & Y. Shoda (Eds.), *The coherence of personality: Social-cognitive bases of consistency, variability, and organization* (pp. 127–154). New York: Guilford Press.

Baldwin, M. W., Carrell, S. E., & Lopez, D. F. (1990). Priming relationship schemas: My advisor and the pope are watching me from the back of my mind. *Journal of Experimental Social Psychology, 26,* 435–454.

Baldwin, M. W . & Fehr, B. (1995). On the instability of attachment style ratings. *Personal Relationships, 2,* 247–261.

Baldwin, M. W., Fehr, B., Keedian, E., Seidel, M., & Thompson, D. W. (1993). An exploration of the relational schemata underlying attachment styles: Self-report and lexical decision approaches. *Personality and Social Psychology Bulletin, 19,* 746–754.

Baldwin, M. W., Keelen, J. P. R., Fehr, B., Enns, V., & Koh-Rangarajoo, E. (1996). Social-cognitive conceptualization of attachment working models: Availability and accessibility effects. *Journal of Personality and Social Psychology, 71,* 94–109.

Baltes, P. B. (1979). Life-span developmental psychology: Some convergent observations on history and theory. In P. B. Baltes & O. G. Brim Jr. (Eds.), *Life -span development and behavior* (Vol. 2, pp. 255–279). New York: Academic Press.

Baltes, P. B. (1983). Life-span developmental psychology: Observations on history and theory revisited. In R. M. Lerner (Ed.), *Developmental psychology: Historical and philosophical perspectives* (pp. 79–111). Hillsdale, NJ: Erlbaum.

Baltes, P. B. (1987). Theoretical propositions of life-span developmental psychology: On the dynamics between growth and decline. *Developmental Psychology, 23,* 611–626.

Baltes, P. B. (1997). On the incomplete architecture of human ontogeny: Selection, optimization, compensation as foundation of developmental theory. *American Psychologist, 52,* 366–380.

Baltes, P. B., & Baltes, M. M. (1980). *Successful aging: Perspectives from the behavioral sciences.* New York: Cambridge University Press.

Baltes, P. B., & Baltes, M. M. (1990). Psychological perspectives on successful aging: The model of selective optimization with compensation. In P. B. Baltes & M. M. Baltes (Eds.), *Successful aging: Perspectives from the behavioral sciences* (pp. 1–34). New York: Cambridge University Press.

Baltes, P. B., & Freund, A. M. (1999). *The life-mastery strategy of selection, optimization, and compensation as predictor of survival (mortality) in old age.* Unpublished manuscript, Max Planck Institute for Human Development, Berlin, Germany.

Baltes, P. B., Lindenberger, U., & Staudinger, U. (1998). Life-span theory in developmental psychology. In W. Damon (Series Ed.) & R. Lerner (Vol. Ed.), *Handbook of Child Psychology* (5th Edition). Vol. 1: *Theoretical models of human development.* (pp. 1029–1144). New York: Wiley.

Baltes, P. B., & Smith, J. (1990). Toward a psychology of wisdom and its ontogenesis. In R. J. Sternberg (Eds.), *Wisdom: Its nature, origins and development* (pp. 87–120). New York: Cambridge University Press.

Baltes, P. B., & Staudinger, U. (1996). Interactive minds in a life-span perspective: Prologue. In P. B. Baltes & U. Staudinger (Eds.), *Interactive minds.* (pp. 1–32). New York: Cambridge University Press.

Baltes, P. B., & Staudinger, U. M. (2000). Wisdom: A metaheuristic (pragmatic) to orchestrate mind and virtue toward excellence. *American Psychologist,.* pp. 122–136.

Baltes, P. B., Staudinger, U. M., & Lindenberger, U. (1999). Lifespan psychology: Theory and application to intellectual functioning. *Annual Review of Psychology, 50,* 471–507.

Bandura, A. (1965). Vicarious processes: A case of no-trial learning. In L. Berkowitz (Ed.), *Advances in experimental social psychology* (Vol. 2, pp. 1–55). New York: Academic Press.

Bandura, A. (1969). *Principles of behavior modification.* New York: Holt, Rinehart & Winston.

Bandura, A. (1973). *Aggression: A social learning analysis*. Englewood Cliffs, NJ: Prentice-Hall.

Bandura, A. (1974). Behavior theory and the models of man. *American Psychologist, 29,* 859–869.

Bandura, A. (1976). *Social learning theory.* Morristown, NJ: General Learning Press.

Bandura, A. (1977a). Self-efficacy: Toward a unifying theory of behavioral change. *Psychological Review, 84,* 191–215.

Bandura, A. (1977b). *Social learning theory.* Englewood Cliffs, NJ: Prentice Hall.

Bandura, A. (1978). The self system in reciprocal determinism. *American Psychologist, 33,* 344–358.

Bandura, A. (1982). The psychology of chance encounters and life paths. *American Psychologist, 37,* 122–147.

Bandura, A. (1986). *Social foundations of thought and action.* Englewood Cliffs, NJ: Prentice Hall.

Bandura, A. (1991a). Social cognitive theory of moral thought and action. In W. M. Kurtines & J. L. Gewirtz (Eds.), *Handbook of moral behavior and development. Theory, research and applications.* (Vol. 1, pp. 71–129). Hillsdale, NJ: Erlbaum.

Bandura, A. (1991b). Self-regulation of motivation through anticipatory and self-regulatory mechanisms. In R. A. Dienstbier (Ed.), *Perspectives on motivation: Nebraska symposium on motivation.* (Vol. 38, pp. 69–164). Lincoln, NE: University of Nebraska Press.

Bandura, A. (1997). *Self-efficacy: The exercise of control.* New York: Freeman.

Bandura, A. (1999). Social cognitive theory of personality. In D. Cervone & Y. Shoda (Eds.), *The coherence of personality: Social-cognitive bases of consistency, variability, and organization* (pp. 185–241). New York: Guilford Press.

Bandura, A., Adams, N. E., & Beyer, J. (1977). Cognitive processes mediating behavior change. *Journal of Personality and Social Psychology, 35,* 125–139.

Bandura, A., Barbaranelli, C., Caprara, G. V., & Pastorelli, C. (1996a). Multifaceted impact of self-efficacy beliefs on academic functioning. *Child Development, 67,* 1206–1222.

Bandura, A., Barbaranelli, C., Caprara, G. V., & Pastorelli, C. (1996b). Mechanisms of moral disengagement in the exercise of moral agency. *Journal of Personality and Social Psychology, 71,* 364–374.

Bandura, A., Barbaranelli, C., Caprara, G. V., & Pastorelli, C. (in press). Self-efficacy beliefs as shapers of children's aspirations and career trajectories. *Child Development.*

Bandura, A., & Cervone, D. (1983). Self-evaluative and self-efficacy mechanisms governing the motivational effects of goal systems. *Journal of Personality and Social Psychology, 45,* 1017–1028.

Bandura, A., & Cervone, D. (1986). Differential engagement of self-reactive influences in cognitive motivation. *Organizational Behavior and Human Decision Processes, 38,* 92–113.

Bandura, A., Cioffi, D., Taylor, C. B., & Brouillard, M. E. (1988). Perceived self-efficacy in coping with cognitive stressors and opioid activation. *Journal of Personality & Social Psychology, 55,* 479–488.

Bandura, A., & Jourdan, F. (1991). Self-regulatory mechanisms governing the impact of social comparison on complex decision making. *Journal of Personality and Social Psychology, 60,* 941–951.

Bandura, A., & Kupers, C. J. (1964). Transmission of patterns of self-reinforcement through modeling. *Journal of Abnormal and Social Psychology, 69,* 1–9.

Bandura, A., & Mischel, W. (1965). The influence of models in modifying delay of gratification patterns. *Journal of Personality and Social Psychology, 2,* 698–705.

Bandura, A., Pastorelli, C., Barbaranelli, C., & Caprara, G. V. (1999). Self-efficacy pathways to childhood depression. *Journal of Personality and Social Psychology, 76,* 258–269.

Bandura, A., Reese, L., & Adams, N. E. (1982). Microanalysis of action and fear arousal as a function of differential levels of perceived self-efficacy. *Journal of Personality and Social Psychology, 43,* 5–21.

Bandura, A., & Schunk, D. H. (1981). Cultivating competence, self-efficacy and intrinsic interest through proximal self-motivation. *Journal of Personality and Social Psychology, 41,* 586–598.

Bandura, A., Taylor, C. B., Williams, S. L., Mefford, I. N., & Barchas, J. (1985). Catecholamine secretion as a function of perceived coping self-efficacy. *Journal of Consulting and Clinical Psychology, 53,* 406–414.

Bandura, A., & Walters, R. (1963). *Social learning and personality development.* New York: Holt, Rinehart & Winston.

Barbaranelli, C., & Caprara, G. V. (1996). How many dimensions to describe personality? A comparison of Cattell, Comrey, and the Big Five taxonomies of personality traits. *European Review of Applied Psychology, 46,* 15–24.

Barbaranelli, C., & Caprara, G. V. (2000). Measuring the Big Five in self report and other ratings: A multitrait-multimethod study. *European Journal of Psychological Assessment, 16,* 29–41.

Barbaranelli, C., Caprara, G. V., & Maslach, C. (1997). Individuation and the five factor model of personality traits. *European Journal of Psychological Assessment, 13,* 75–84.

Barbaranelli, C., Caprara, G. V., & Rabasca, A. (1998). *BFQ-C. Big Five Questionnaire Children.* Firenze: O. S., Organizzazioni Speciali.

Bargh, J. A. (1989). Conditional automaticity: Varieties of automatic influence in social perception and cognition. In J. S. Uleman & J. A. Bargh (Eds.), *Unintended thought.* New York: Guilford.

Bargh, J. A. (1994). The four horsemen of automaticity: Awareness, intention, efficiency, and control in social cognition. In R. S. Wyer & T. K. Srull (Eds.), *Handbook of Social Cognition (2nd ed.), Vol. I: Basic Processes.* Hillsdale, NJ: Erlbaum.

Bargh, J. A. (1997). The automaticity of everyday life. In R. S. Wyer, Jr. (Ed.), *Advances in social cognition* (Vol. 10, pp. 1–61). Mahwah, NJ: Erlbaum.

Bargh, J. A., & Barndollar, K. (1996). Automaticity in action: The unconscious as repository of chronic goals and motives. In P. M. Gollwitzer & J. A. Bargh (Eds.), *The psychology of action: Linking cognition and motivation to behavior* (pp. 457–481). New York: Guilford.

Bargh, J. A., Bond, R. N., Lombardi, W. J., & Tota, M. E. (1986). The additive nature of chronic and temporary sources of construct accessibility. *Journal of Personality and Social Psychology, 50,* 869–878.

Bargh, J. A., & Chartrand, T. L. (1999). The unbearable automaticity of being. *American Psychologist, 54,* 462–479.

Bargh, J. A., Chen, M., & Burrows, L. (1996). The automaticity of social behavior: Direct effects of trait concept and stereotype activation on action. *Journal of Personality and Social Psychology, 71,* 230–244.

Bargh, J. A., & Gollwitzer, P. M. (1994). Environmental control of goal-directed action: Automatic and strategic contingencies between situations and behavior. In W. D. Spaulding (Ed.), *Nebraska symposium on motivation: Vol. 41. Integrative views of motivation, cognition, and emotion* (pp. 71–124). Lincoln, NE: University of Nebraska Press.

Bargh, J. A., Lombardi, W. J., & Higgins, E. T. (1988). Automaticity of chronically accessible constructs in person × situation effects on person perception: It's just a matter of time. *Journal of Personality and Social Psychology, 55,* 599–605.

Bargh, J. A., & Pietromonaco, P. (1982). Automatic information processing and social perception: The influence of trait information presented outside of conscious awareness on impression formation. *Journal of Personality and Social Psychology, 43,* 437–449.

Bargh, J. A., Raymond, P., Pryor, J. B., & Strack, F. (1995). Attractiveness of the underling: An automatic power–sex association and its consequences for sexual harassment and aggression. *Journal of Personality and Social Psychology, 68,* 768–781.

Barker, G. (1988). Review of C. Renfrew, *Archaeology and language: The puzzle of Indo-European Origins. Current Anthropology, 29,* 448–449.

Barker, R. G. (1968). *Ecological psychology.* Stanford, CA: Stanford University Press.

Barkow, J. H., Cosmides, L., & Tooby, J. (Eds.) (1992). *The adapted mind: Evolutionary psychology and the generation of culture.* New York: Oxford University Press.

Barling, J., & Abel, M. (1983). Self-efficacy beliefs and performance. *Cognitive Therapy and Research, 7,* 265–272.

Barrick, M. R., & Mount, M. K. (1991). The Big Five personality dimensions and job performance: A meta-analysis. *Personnel Psychology, 44,* 1–26.

Bartholomew, K. (1990). Avoidance of intimacy: An attachment perspective. *Journal of Social and Personal Relationships, 7,* 147–178.

Bartholomew, K. (1993). From childhood to adult relationships: An attachment perspective. In S. W. Duck (Ed.), *Understanding relationship processes: 2. Learning about relationships* (pp. 30–62). London: Sage.

Bartholomew, K., & Horowitz, L. M. (1991). Attachment styles among young adults: A test for a four-category model. *Journal of Personality and Social Psychology, 61,* 226–244.

Bartlett, F. A. (1932). *A study in experimental and social psychology.* New York: Cambridge University Press.

Barton, S. (1994). Chaos, self-organization, and psychology. *American Psychologist, 49,* 5–14.

Bassili, J. N. (1978). Facial motion in the perception of faces and of emotional expression. *Journal of Experimental Psychology: Human Perception & Performance, 4,* 373–379.

Bassili, J. N. (1989). Trait encodings in behavior identification and dispositional inference. *Personality and Social Psychology Bulletin, 15,* 285–296.

Bates, J. E. (1989). Applications of temperament concepts. In G. A. Kohnstamm, J. E. Bates, & M. K. Rothbart (Eds.) *Temperament in childhood* (pp. 3–26). Chichester, UK: Wiley.

Bateson, G. (1972). *Steps to an ecology of mind.* Northvale, NJ: Jason Aronson.

Baumeister, R. F. (1991). *Escaping the self.* New York: Basic Books.

Baumeister, R. F. (1998). The self. In D. T. Gilbert, S. T. Fiske, & G. Lindzey (Eds.), *The handbook of social psychology* (4th ed., Vol. 1, pp. 680–740). Boston: McGraw-Hill.

Baumeister, R. F., & Cairns, K. J. (1992). Repression and self-presentation: When audiences interfere with self-deceptive strategies. *Journal of Personality and Social Psychology, 62,* 851–862.

Baumeister, R. F., & Heatherton, T. F. (1996). Self-regulation failure: An overview. *Psychological Inquiry, 7,* 1–15.

Baumeister, R. F., & Scher, S. J. (1988). Self-defeating behavior patterns among normal individuals: Review and analysis of common self-destructive tendencies. *Psychological Bulletin, 104,* 3–22.

Baumeister, R., Stillwell, A. M., & Heatherton, T. (1994). Guilt: An interpersonal approach. *Psychological Bulletin, 115,* 243–267.

Baumgarten, F. (1933). Die Charaktereigenschaften. *Beitraege zur Charackter und Persoenlich-*

*keitsforschung, 1* (whole issue). Bern, Switzerland: Francke.

Baumrind, D. (1971). Current patterns of parental authority. *Developmental Psychology Monograph, 4*(1, Pt. 2).

Baumrind, D. (1991). Parenting styles and adolescent development. In J. Brooks-Gunn, R. Lerner, & A. C. Peterson (Eds.), *The encyclopedia of adolescence* (pp. 746–758). New York: Garland.

Baumrind, D. (1997). The discipline encounter: Contemporary issues. *Aggression and Violent Behavior, 2,* 321–335.

Beall, A. E., & Sternberg, R. J. (Eds.) (1993). *The psychology of gender.* New York: Guilford Press.

Beck, A. (1976). *Cognitive therapy and the emotional disorders.* New York: International Universities Press.

Bechara, A., Damasio, H., Tranel, D., & Damasio, A. R. (1997). Deciding advantageously before knowing the advantageous strategy. *Science, 275,* 1293–1294.

Beck, A., & Emery, G. (1985). *Anxiety disorders and phobias.* New York: Basic Books.

Beck, A. T., Rush, A. J., Shaw, B. F., & Emery, G. (1979). *Cognitive therapy of depression.* New York: Guilford Press.

Bell, R. Q. (1968). A reinterpretation of the direction of effects in studies of socialization. *Psychological Review, 75,* 81–95.

Bell, R. Q., & Harper, L. V. (Eds.) (1977). *Child effects on adults.* Hillsdale, NJ: Erlbaum.

Belsky, J., & Pensky, E. (1988). Developmental history, personality and family relationships: Toward an emergent family system. In R. Hinde & J. Stevenson-Hinde (Eds.) *Relationships within families: Mutual influences* (pp. 193–217). New York: Oxford University Press.

Belsky, J., Rovine, M., & Fish, M. (1989). The developing family system. In M. R. Gunnar & E. Thelen (Eds.), *Minnesota symposium on child psychology* (Vol. 22, pp. 119–166). Hillsdale, NJ: Erlbaum.

Belsky, J., Rovine, M., & Taylor, D. (1984). The Pennsylvania infant and family development project II: Origins of individual differences in infant-mother attachment: Maternal and infant contributions. *Child Development, 55,* 706–717.

Belsky, J., Steinberg, L., & Draper, P. (1991). Childhood experience, interpersonal development, and reproductive strategy: An evolutionary theory of socialization. *Child Development, 62,* 647–670.

Bem, D. J. (1972). Self-perception theory. *Advances in Experimental Social Psychology, 6,* 1–62.

Bem, D. J. (1973). Constructing cross-situational consistencies in behavior: Some thoughts on Alker's critique of Mischel. *Journal of Personality, 40,* 17–26.

Bem, D. J. (1983). Constructing a theory of the triple typology: Some (second) thoughts on nomothetic and idiographic approaches to personality. *Journal of Personality, 51,* 566–577.

Bem, D. J., & Allen, A. (1974). Predicting some of the people some of the time: The search for cross-situational consistencies in behavior. *Psychological Review, 81,* 506–520.

Bem, D. J., & Funder, D. C. (1978). Predicting more of the people more of the time: Assessing the personality of situations. *Psychological Review, 85,* 485–501.

Bem, S. (1974). The measurement of psychological androgyny. *Journal of Consulting and Clinical Psychology, 42,* 165–172.

Bem, S. (1977). On the utility of alternative procedures for assessing psychological androgyny. *Journal of Consulting and Clinical Psychology, 25,* 196–205.

Bem, S. (1981). Gender schema theory: A cognitive account for sex typing. *Psychological Review, 88,* 354–364.

Bem, S. (1985). Androgyny and gender schema theory: A conceptual and empirical integration. In T. B. Sonderegger (Ed.), Nebraska Symposium on Motivation (Vol. 2, pp. 179–226). Lincoln: University of Nebraska Press.

Bendig, A. W. (1956). The development of a short form of the Manifest Anxiety Scale. *Journal of Consulting Psychology, 20,* 384.

Benedict, R. (1934). *Patterns of culture.* New York: Mentor.

Benet, V., & Waller, N. G. (1995). The Big Seven model of personality description: Evidence for its cross-cultural replicability in a Spanish sample. *Journal of Personality and Social Psychology, 69,* 701–718.

Benet, V., & Waller, N. G. (1997). Further evidence for the cross-cultural generality of the Big Seven factor model: Indigenous and imported Spanish personality constructs. *Journal of Personality, 65,* 567–598.

Benet-Martínez, V., & John, O. P. (1998). *Los cinco grandes* across cultures and ethnic groups: Multitrait multimethod analyses of the big five in Spanish and English. *Journal of Personality and Social Psychology, 75,* 729–750.

Benjamin, J., Li, L., Patterson, C., Greenburg, D. B., Murphy, D. L., & Hamer, D. H. (1996). Population and familial association between the D4 dopamine receptor gene and measures of novelty seeking. *Nature Genetics, 12,* 81–84.

Bentler, P. M., & Newcomb, M. D. (1978). Longitudinal study of marital success and failure. *Journal of Consulting and Clinical Psychology, 46,* 1053–1070.

Berkowitz, L. (1962). *Aggression: A social psychological analysis.* New York: McGraw-Hill.

Berkowitz, L. (1993). *Aggression*. New York: McGraw-Hill.

Berlyne, D. (1968). Behavior theory as personality. In E. Borgatta & W. Lambert (Eds.), *Handbook of personality: Theory and research*. Chicago: Rand McNally.

Bermudez, J. (1999). Personality and health-protective behaviour. *European Journal of Personality, 13*, 83–103.

Berry, J. M. (1989). Cognitive efficacy: A life span developmental perspective. (Special Issue.) *Developmental Psychology, 35*, 683–735.

Berry, J. M., West, R. L., & Dennehey, D. (1989). Reliability and validity of the memory self-efficacy questionnaire. *Developmental Psychology, 25*, 701–713.

Berry, J. W. (1969). On cross-cultural comparability. *International Journal of Psychology, 4*, 119–128.

Berry, J. W., Poortinga, Y. H., Segall, M. H., & Dasen, P. R. (1992). *Cross-cultural psychology: Research and applications*. New York: Cambridge University Press.

Bersheid, E. (1994). Interpersonal relationships. *Annual Review of Psychology, 45*, 79–129.

Bertalanffy, L. von. (1968). *General system theory*. New York: Braziller.

Bettencourt, A. B., & Miller, N. (1996). Gender differences in aggression as a function of provocation: A meta-analysis. *Psychological Bulletin, 119*, 422–447.

Betz, N. E., & Hackett, G. (1981). The relationship of career-related self-efficacy expectations to perceived career options in college women and men. *Journal of Counseling Psychology, 28*, 399–410.

Bidell, T. R., & Fischer, K. W. (1997). Between nature and nurture: The role of human agency in the epigenesis of intelligence. In R. J. Sternberg & E. Grigorenko (Eds.), *Intelligence, heredity and environment* (pp. 193–242). New York: Cambridge University Press.

Bieri, J. (1955). Cognitive complexity–simplicity and predictive behavior. *Journal of Abnormal & Social Psychology, 51*, 263–268.

Biesanz, J. C., West, S. G., & Graziano, W. G. (1998). Moderators of self-other agreement: Reconsidering temporal stability in personality. *Journal of Personality and Social Psychology, 75*, 467–477.

Birren, J., & Shaie, K. (1996). *Handbook of the psychology of aging* (3rd ed.). San Diego: Academic Press.

Bjorkqvist, K., Osterman, K., & Lagerspetz, K. M. J. (1994). Sex differences in covert aggression among adults. *Aggressive Behavior, 20*, 27–33.

Blaney, P. H. (1986). Affect and memory: A review. *Psychological Bulletin, 99*, 229–246.

Blatt, S., & Lerner, H. (1983). Investigations in the psychoanalytic theory of object relations and object representations. In J. Masling (Ed.), *Empirical studies of psychoanalytical theories* (Vol. 1, pp. 189–249). Hillsdale NJ: The Analytic Press

Block, J. (1961). *The Q-sort method in personality assessment and psychiatric research*. Springfield, IL: Charles C. Thomas Pub.

Block, J. (1971). *Lives through time*. Berkeley, CA: Bancroft Books.

Block, J. (1977). Advancing the psychology of personality: Paradigm shift or improving the quality of research. In D. Magnusson, D. & N. S. Endler (Eds.), *Personality at the crossroads: Current issues in interactional psychology* (pp. 37–63). Hillsdale, NJ: Erlbaum.

Block, J. (1993). Studying personality the long way. In D. C. Funder, R. D. Parke, C. Tomlinson-Keasey, & K. Widaman (Eds.), *Studying lives through time: Personality and development* (pp. 9–41). APA Science Volumes. Washington, DC: American Psychological Association.

Block, J. (1995). A contrarian view of the five-factor approach to personality description. *Psychological Bulletin, 117*, 187–215.

Block, J., & Block, J. H. (1980). The role of ego-control and ego resilience in the organization of behavior. In W. A. Collins (Ed.), *Minnesota symposium on child psychology. Vol. 13: Development of cognition, affect, and social relations* (pp. 39–101). Hillsdale, NJ: Erlbaum.

Block, J., Gjerde, P. F., & Block J. H. (1991). Personality antecedents of depressive tendencies in 18-years-olds: A prospective study. *Journal of Personality and Social Psychology, 60*, 726–738.

Block, J, & Kremen, A. (1996). IQ and ego resiliency. Conceptual and empirical connection and separation. *Journal of Personality and Social psychology, 70*, 349–361.

Block, J. H. (1973). Conceptions of sex role. Some cross-cultural and longitudinal perspectives. *American Psychologist, 28*, 512–526.

Block, J. H. (1976). Issues, problems, and pitfalls in assessing sex differences: A critical review of "The psychology of sex differences." *Merrill-Palmer Quarterly, 22*, 283–308.

Block, N. (1995). On a confusion about the function of consciousness. *Behavioral and Brain Sciences, 18*, 227–287.

Boden, J. M., & Baumeister, R. F. (1997). Repressive coping: Distraction using pleasant thoughts and memories. *Journal of Personality and Social Psychology, 73*, 45–62.

Bodunov, M. V. (1993). Studies on temperament in Russia: After Teplov and Nebylitsyn. *European Journal of Personality, 7*, 299–311.

Boesch, E. E. (1991). *Symbolic action theory and cultural psychology*. Heidelberg: Springer-Verlag.

Bollen, K. A. (1989). *Structural equations with latent variables*. New York: John Wiley & Sons.

Bonanno, G. A., & Keltner, D. (1997). Facial expressions of emotion and the course of conjugal bereavement. *Journal of Abnormal Psychology, 106*, 126–137.

Bootzin, R. R. (1997). Examining the theory and clinical utility of writing about emotional experiences. *Psychological Science, 8*, 167–169.

Borden, J. W., Clum, G. A., & Salmon, P. G. (1991). Mechanisms of change in the treatment of panic. *Cognitive Therapy and Research, 15*, 257–272.

Boring, E. G. (1950). *A history of experimental psychology*. New York: Appleton-Century-Crofts.

Borkenau, P. (1990). Traits as ideal-based and goal-derived social categories. *Journal of Personality and Social Psychology, 58*, 381–396.

Borkenau, P., & Ostendorf, F. (1990). Comparing exploratory and confirmatory factor analysis: A study on the 5-factor model of personality. *Personality and Individual Differences, 11*, 515–524.

Borkenau, P., & Ostendorf, F. (1998). The big five as states: How useful is the five-factor model to describe intraindividual variations over time? *Journal of Research in Personality, 32*, 202–221.

Bornstein, R. F. (1992). Subliminal mere exposure effects. In R. F. Bornstein & T. S. Pittman (Eds.), *Perception without awareness* (pp. 191–210). New York: Guilford.

Bouchard, T. J. (1992). Genetic and environmental influences on adult personality: Evaluating the evidence. In J. Hettema & I. Deary (Eds.), *Foundations of personality* (pp. 15–41). Dordrecht, The Netherlands: Kluwer Academic Publishers.

Bouchard, T. J. (1993). The genetic architecture of human intelligence. In P. A. Vernon (Ed.), *Biological approaches to the study of human intelligence* (pp. 33–93). Norwood, NJ: Ablex.

Bouchard, T. J., Lykken, D., McGue, M., Segal, N. L., & Tellegen, A. (1990). Sources of human psychological differences: The Minnesota study of twins reared apart. *Science, 250*, 223–228.

Bower, G. H. (1981). Mood and memory. *American Psychologist, 31* 129–148.

Bowers, K., & Meichenbaum, D. (Eds.) (1984). *The unconscious reconsidered*. New York: Wiley.

Bowlby, J. (1969). *Attachment and loss. Vol. 1: Attachment*, New York: Basic Books.

Bowlby, J. (1973). *Attachment and loss. Vol. 2: Separation: Anxiety and anger*. New York: Basic Books.

Bowlby, J. (1979). *The making and breaking of affectional bonds*. London: Tavistock.

Bowlby, J. (1980). *Attachment and loss: Vol. 3: Loss: Sadness and depression*. New York: Basic Books.

Bowlby, J. (1988). *A secure base*. London: Routledge.

Bowlby, J. (1990). *Charles Darwin: A biography*. London: Hutchinson.

Boykin, A. W. (1994). Harvesting talent and culture: African-American children and educational reform. In R. Rossi (Ed.), *Schools and students at risk* (pp. 116–138). New York: Teachers College Press.

Bradburn, N. M. (1969). *The structure of psychological well-being*. Chicago: Aldine.

Brandtstädter, J., Rothermund, K., & Schmitz, U. (1998). Maintaining self-integrity and efficacy through adulthood and later life: The adaptive functions of assimilative persistence and accommodative flexibility. In J. Heckhausen & C. Dweck (Eds.), *Motivation and self-regulation across the life span* (pp. 365–388). New York: Cambridge University Press.

Bray, D. W. (1982). The Assessment Center and the study of lives. *American Psychologist, 37*, 180–189.

Bray, D. W., Campbell, R., & Grant, D. L. (1974). *Formative years in business: A long term AT&T study of managerial lives*. New York: Wiley.

Brehm, S. (1992). *Intimate relationships* (2nd ed.). New York: McGraw-Hill.

Brennan, K. A., & Morris, K. A. (1997). Attachment styles, self esteem and patterns of seeking feedback from romantic partners. *Personality and Social Psychology Bulletin, 23*, 23–31.

Brennan, K. A., & Shaver, P. R. (1995). Dimensions of adult attachment, affect regulation, and romantic relationships functioning. *Personality and Social Psychology Bulletin, 21*, 267–283.

Breuer, J., & Freud, S. (1895/1955). *Studies on hysteria*. Standard Edition (Vol. 2). London: Hogarth.

Brewin, C. R. (1989). Cognitive change processes in psychotherapy. *Psychological Review, 96*, 379–394.

Brewster Smith, M. (1963). Personal values in the study of lives. In R. White (Ed.), *The study of lives* (pp. 324–347). New York: Atherton Press.

Briggs, S., & Cheek, J. (1986). The role of factor analysis in the development and evaluation of personality scales. *Journal of Personality, 54*, 106–148.

Brody, G. H. (1998). Sibling relationship quality: Its causes and consequences. *Annual Review of Psychology, 49*, 1–24.

Brody, N. (1992). *Intelligence* (2nd ed.) San Diego: Academic Press.

Brokken, F. B. (1978). *The language of personality*. Meppel, The Netherlands: Krips.

Bronfenbrenner, U. (1986). Ecology of the family as a context for human development: Research perspectives. *Developmental Psychology, 22*, 723–742.

Bronfenbrenner, U. (1992). Ecological systems theory. Annals of child development, In R. Vasta (Ed.), *Six Theories of Child Development: Revised formulations and current issues* (pp. 187–249). London: Jessica Kingsley Publishers Lt. Previously published in 1989 with same title by Greenwich, CT: JAI Press (pp. 185–246).

Bronfenbrenner, U., & Ceci, S. (1994). Nature-nurture reconceptualized in developmental perspective: A bioecological model. *Psychological Review, 101,* 568–586.

Brown, B. (1999). Optimizing expression of the common human genome for child development. *Current Directions in Psychological Science, 8,* 37–41.

Brown, D. E. (1991). *Human universals.* New York: McGraw-Hill.

Brown, J. D. (1998). *The self.* Boston: McGraw-Hill.

Bruner, J. (1957a). On perceptual readiness. *Psychological Review, 64,* 123–152.

Bruner, J. (1957b). Going beyond the information given. In H. Gruber (Ed.), *Contemporary approaches to cognition.* Cambridge, MA: Harvard University Press.

Bruner, J. (1986). *Actual minds, possible worlds.* Cambridge, MA: Harvard University Press.

Bruner, J. (1990). *Acts of meaning.* Cambridge, MA: Harvard University Press.

Bruner, J. (1992). Another look at New Look 1. *American Psychologist. 47,* 780–783.

Bruner, J. S., & Postman, L. (1947). Emotional selectivity in perception and reaction. *Journal of Personality, 16,* 69–77.

Brunswick, E. (1956). *Perception and representative design of psychological experiments.* Berkeley, CA: University of California Press.

Bryson, J. B. (1991). Modes of response to jealousy-evoking situations. In P. Salovey (Ed.), *The psychology of jealousy and envy* (pp. 178–207). New York: Guilford.

Buchanan, C. M., Eccles, J. S., & Becker, J. B. (1992). Are adolescents the victims of raging hormones: Evidence for activational effects of hormones on moods and behaviors at adolescence. *Psychological Bulletin, 111,* 62–107.

Buchanan, C. M., Maccoby, E. E., & Dornbusch, S. M. (1991). Caught between parents: Adolescents' experience in divorced homes. *Child Development, 62,* 1008–10029.

Buck, R. (1980). Nonverbal behavior and the theory of emotion: The facial feedback hypothesis. *Journal of Personality and Social Psychology, 38,* 811–824.

Bukowski, W., Newcomb, A., & Hartup, W. (1996) (Eds.), *The company they keep.* New York, Cambridge University Press.

Burke, P., Kraut, R. E., & Dworkin, R. H. (1984). Traits, consistency, and self-schemata: What do our methods measure? *Journal of Personality and Social Psychology, 47,* 568–579.

Burnett, S. (1986) Sex-related differences in spatial ability: Are they trivial? *American Psychologist, 41,* 1012–1014.

Burnham, J. P. (1968). Historical background for the study of personality. In E. Borgatta & W. Lambert (Eds.), *Handbook of personality: Theory and research* (pp. 3–81). Chicago: Rand McNally.

Burt, C. (1937). The analysis of temperament. *British Journal of Medical Psychology, 17,* 158–188.

Bushman, B. J. (1995). Moderating role of trait aggressiveness in the effects of violent media on aggression. *Journal of Personality and Social Psychology, 69,* 950–960.

Buss, A. H., & Plomin, R. (1975). *A temperament theory of personality development.* New York: Wiley

Buss, A. H., & Plomin, R. (1984). *Temperament: Early developing personality traits.* Hillsdale, NJ: Erlbaum.

Buss, D. M. (1984). Evolutionary biology and personality psychology: Toward a conception of human nature and individual differences. *American Psychologist, 39,* 1135–1147.

Buss, D. M. (1988). The evolution of human intrasexual competition: Tactics of mate attraction. *Journal of Personality and Social Psychology, 54,* 616–628.

Buss, D. M. (1989). Sex differences in human mate preferences: Evolutionary hypotheses tested in 37 cultures. *Behavioral and Brain Sciences, 12,* 1–14.

Buss, D. M. (1991). Evolutionary personality psychology. *Annual Review of Psychology, 42,* 459–491.

Buss, D. M. (1994). *The evolution of desire: Strategies of human mating.* New York: Basic Books.

Buss, D. M. (1995a). Psychological sex differences: Origins through sexual selection. *American Psychologist, 50,* 164–168.

Buss, D. M. (1995b). Evolutionary psychology: A new paradigm for psychological science. *Psychological Inquiry, 6,* 1–30.

Buss, D. M. (1996a). The evolutionary psychology of human social strategies. In E. T. Higgins & A. W. Kruglanski (Eds.), *Social psychology: Handbook of basic principles* (pp. 3–38). New York: Guilford.

Buss, D. M. (1996b). Social adaptation and five major factors of personality. In Wiggins, J. S. (Ed.), *The five-factor model of personality: Theoretical perspectives* (pp. 180–207). New York: Guilford.

Buss, D. M. (1997a) Evolutionary foundations of personality. In R. Hogan, J. Johnson & S. Briggs (Eds.), *Handbook of personality psychology.* (pp. 317–344). New York: Academic Press.

Buss, D. M. (1997b). Human social motivation in evolutionary perspective: Grounding terror management theory. *Psychological Inquiry, 8,* 22–26.

Buss, D. M. (1999a). *Evolutionary psychology: The new science of the mind.* Boston: Allyn & Bacon.

Buss, D. M. (1999b). Human nature and individual differences: The evolution of human personality. L. A. Pervin & O. P. John (Eds.), *Handbook of personality: Theory and research* (2nd ed.). New York: Guilford.

Buss, D. M., & Cantor, N. (1989). Introduction to D. M. Buss & N. Cantor (Eds.), *Personality psychology: Recent trends and emerging directions* (pp. 1–12). New York: Springer-Verlag.

Buss, D. M., & Craik, K. H. (1983). The act frequency approach to personality. *Psychological Review, 90,* 105–126.

Buss, D. M., Haselton, M. G., Shackelford, T. K., Bleske, A. L., & Wakefield, J. C. (1999). Interactionism, flexibility, and inferences about the past. *American Psychologist, 54,* 443–445.

Buss, D. M., & Kenrick, D. T. (1998). Evolutionary social psychology. In D. T. Gilbert, S. T. Fiske, & G. Lindzey (Eds.), *The handbook of social psychology* (4th ed., Vol. 1, pp. 982–1026). Boston: McGraw-Hill.

Buss, D. M., Larsen, R., Westen, D., & Semmelroth, J. (1992). Sex differences in jealousy: Evolution, physiology and psychology. *Psychological Science, 3,* 251–255.

Buss, D. M., & Schmitt, D. P. (1993). Sexual strategy theory: An evolutionary perspective in human mating. *Psychological Review, 100,* 204–232.

Bussey, K., & Bandura, A. (1999). Social cognitive theory of gender development and differentiation, *Psychological Review, 106,* 676–713.

Byrne, D. (1964). Repression-sensitization as a dimension of personality. In B. A. Maher (Ed.), *Progress in experimental personality research* (Vol. 1, pp. 169–220). New York: Academic Press.

Byrnes, J. P., Miller, D. C. & Schafer, W. D. (1999). Gender differences in risk taking: A meta-analysis. *Psychological Bulletin, 125,* 367–383.

Cacioppo, J. T., Bernston, G. G., & Crites, S. L. Jr. (1996). Social neuroscience: Principles of psychophysiological arousal and response. In E. T. Higgins & A. W. Kruglanski (Eds.), *Social psychology: Handbook of basic principles* (pp. 72–101). New York: Guilford.

Cacioppo, J. T., Gardner, W. L., & Bernston, G. C. (1997). Beyond bipolar conceptualizations and measures: The case of attitudes and evaluative space. *Personality and Social Psychology Review, 1,* 3–25.

Cacioppo, J. T., Uchino, B. N., Crites, S. L., Snydersmith, M. A., Smith, G., Berntson, G. G., & Lang, P. J. (1992). Relationship between facial expressiveness and sympathetic activation in emotion: A critical review, with emphasis on modeling underlying mechanisms and individual differences. *Journal of Personality and Social Psychology, 62,* 110–128.

Cairns, R. B (Ed.) (1979). *The analysis of social interactions: Methods, issues and illustrations.* Hillsdale, NJ: Erlbaum.

Cairns, R. B., & Cairns, B. D. (1994). *Lifelines and risks.* New York: Cambridge University Press.

Cairns, R. B., Cairns, B. D., & Neckerman, H. J. (1989). Early school drop-out: Configurations and determinants. *Child Development, 60,* 1437–1452.

Calkins, S. D., & Fox, N. A. (1992). The relations among infant temperament, security of attachment, and behavioral inhibition at twenty-four months. *Child Development, 63,* 1456–1472.

Camaioni, L. (in press). Early language. In A. Fogel & A. Bremner (Eds.), *Handbook of infant development.* Malden, MA: Blackwell.

Campbell, D. T., & Fiske, D. W. (1959). Convergent and discriminant validity by the multitrait-multimethod matrix. *Psychological Bulletin, 56,* 81–105.

Cannon, W. B. (1929). *Bodily changes in pain, hunger, fear, and rage.* New York:: Appleton.

Cantor, N., & Fleeson, W. (1994). Social intelligence and intelligent goal pursuit: A cognitive slice of motivation. In W. D. Spaulding (Ed.), *Nebraska symposium on motivation: Vol. 41. Integrative views of motivation, cognition, and emotion* (pp. 124–179). Lincoln: University of Nebraska Press.

Cantor, N., & Harlow, R. (1994). Social intelligence and personality: Flexible life-task pursuit. In R. J. Sternberg, & Ruzgis (Eds.), *Personality and intelligence* (pp. 137–168). New York: Cambridge University Press.

Cantor, N., & Kihlstrom, J. F. (1987). *Personality and social intelligence.* Englewood Cliffs, NJ: Prentice-Hall.

Cantor, N., & Mischel, W. (1979). Prototypes in person perception. In L. Berkowitz (Ed.), *Advances in experimental social psychology* (Vol. 12, pp. 3–52). New York: Academic Press.

Cantor, N., Mischel, W., & Schwartz, J. (1982). A prototype analysis of psychological situations. *Cognitive Psychology, 14,* 45–77.

Cantor, N., Norem, J., Langston, C., Zirkel, S., Fleeson, W., & Cook-Flannagan, C. (1991). Life tasks and daily life experience. *Journal of Personality, 59,* 425–451.

Cantor, N., Norem, J. K., Neidenthal, P. M., Langston, C. A., & Brower, A. M. (1987). Life tasks, self-concept ideals, and cognitive strategies in a life transition. *Journal of Personality and Social Psychology, 53,* 1178–1191.

Caporael, L. (1997). The evolution of truly social cognition: The core configurations model. *Personality and Social Psychology Review, 1,* 276–298.

Caprara, G. V. (1987). The disposition-situation debate and research on aggression. *European Journal of Personality, 1,* 1–16.

Caprara, G. V. (1992). Marginal deviations, aggregate effects, disruption of continuity, and deviation amplifying mechanisms. In J. Hettema & I. Deary (Eds.), *Foundations of Personality* (pp. 227–244). Dordrecht, The Netherlands: Kluwer Academic Publishers.

Caprara, G. V. (1996a). Structures and processes in personality psychology. *European Psychologist, 1,* 14–26.

Caprara, G. V. (1996b). *Le ragioni del successo.* Bologna: Il Mulino.

Caprara, G. V. (1999). The notion of personality: Historical and recent perspectives. *European Review, 1,* 127–137.

Caprara, G. V., Barbaranelli, C., Bermudez, J., Maslach, C., & Ruch, W. (in press, a). Cross-cultural replication and further exploration of the five factor model: A comparison of different approaches. *Journal of Cross Cultural Psychology*,

Caprara, G. V., Barbaranelli, C., & Borgogni, L. (1993). *BFQ: Big Five Questionnaire. Manuale*. Firenze, Italy: Organizzazioni Speciali.

Caprara, G. V., Barbaranelli, C., & Borgogni, L. (1994). *BFO: Big Five Observer. Manuale*. Firenze, Italy: Organizzazioni Speciali.

Caprara, G. V., Barbaranelli, C., Borgogni, L., & Perugini, M. (1993). The Big Five Questionnaire: A new questionnaire for the measurement of the five factor model. *Personality and Individual Differences, 15*, 281–288.

Caprara, G. V., Barbaranelli, C., & Incatasciato, M. (1995). Relazioni tra affetto e personalitá. Il. Multidimensional Personality Questionnaire. *Rassegna di Psicologia, 3*, 43–61.

Caprara, G. V., Barbaranelli, C., & Livi, S. (1994). Mapping personality dimensions in the Big Five model. *European Review of Applied Psychology, 44*, 9–15.

Caprara, G. V., Barbaranelli, C., & Pastorelli, C. & Cervone, D. (2000). A comparative test of the predictive power of social cognitive theory and the Big Five factors (manuscript submitted for publication).

Caprara, G. V., Barbaranelli, C., & Pastorelli, C. (in press, b). Prosocial behavior and aggression in childhood and preadolescence. In Bohart & Stipek, (Eds.), *Constructive and destructive behavior: Implications for family, school, and society*. Washington, DC: APA Books.

Caprara, G. V., Barbaranelli, C., Pastorelli, C., Bandura, A., & Zimbardo, P. (in press, c). Social foundations of academic achievement. *Psychological Science*.

Caprara, G. V., Barbaranelli, C., & Zimbardo, P. (1996). Understanding the complexity of human aggression: Affective, cognitive and social dimension of individual differences in propensity toward aggression. *European Journal of Personality, 10*, 133–155.

Caprara, G. V., Barbaranelli, C., & Zimbardo, P. G. (1997). Politicians' uniquely simple personalities. *Nature, 385*, 493.

Caprara, G. V., Barbaranelli, C., & Zimbardo, P. G. (1999). Personality profiles and political parties. *Political Psychology, 20*, 175–197.

Caprara, G. V., De Vincenti, A., & Funaro, A. (1981) Condizione lavorativa, militanza sindacale, ed atteggiamento nei confronti della famiglia: Contributo di ricerca. *Psicologia Italiana, 3*, 5–8.

Caprara, G. V., & Gennaro, A. (1994). *Psicologia della personalitá*. Bologna: Il Mulino.

Caprara, G. V., Passerini, S., Pastorelli, C., Renzi, P., & Zelli, A. (1986). Instigating and measuring interpersonal aggression and hostility: A methodological contribution. *Aggressive Behavior, 12*, 237–247.

Caprara, G. V., & Perugini, M. (1994). Personality described by adjectives: The generalizability of the Big Five to the Italian lexical context. *European Journal of Personality, 8*, 357–369.

Caprara, G. V., Renzi, P., Alcini, P., D'Imperio, G., & Travaglia, G. (1983). Instigation to aggress and escalation of aggression examined from a personological perspective: The role of irritability and emotional susceptibility. *Aggressive Behavior, 9*, 345–351.

Caprara, G. V., Renzi, P., Amolini, R., D'Imperio, G. & Travaglia, G. (1984a). The eliciting cue value of aggressive slides reconsidered in a personological perspective: the weapons effect and irritability. *European Journal of Social Psychology, 14*, 313–322.

Caprara, G. V., Renzi, P., D'Augello, D., D'Imperio, G., Rielli, & Travaglia, G. (1984b). Interpolating physical exercise between instigation and aggression: The role of irritability and emotional susceptibility, *Aggressive Behavior, 12*, 83–91.

Caprara, G. V., & Rutter, M. (1995) Individual development and social change. In M. Rutter & D. Smith (Eds.), Psychosocial disorders in young people. (pp. 35–66). Chichester, UK: Wiley.

Caprara, G. V., Scabini, E., Barbaranelli, C. Pastorelli, C., Regalia, C. & Bandura, A. (1998). Impact of adolescent's perceived self regulatory efficacy on familial communication and antisocial conduct. *European Psychologist, 3*, 125–132.

Caprara, G. V., Scabini, E., Barbaranelli, C., Pastorelli, C., & Regalia, C. (1999). Autoefficacia, percezioni familiari e adattamento psico-sociale in un campione di adolescenti. *Età Evolutiva, 62*, 25-33.

Caprara, G. V., Scabini, E., Barbaranelli, C. Pastorelli, C., Regalia, C. & Bandura, A. (1999). Autoefficacia percepita emotiva e interpersonale e buon funzionamento sociale. *Giornale Italiano di Psicologia. 26*, 769–789.

Caprara, G. V., & Van Heck, G. (1992). Personality psychology: Some epistemological assertions and historical considerations. In G. V. Caprara & G. Van Heck (Eds.), *Modern Personality Psychology* (pp. 3–26). London: Harvester Wheatsheaf.

Caprara, G. V., & Vinci, G. (1978). Militanza sindacale, alienazione e atteggiamento autoritario nei confronti della famiglia: Contributo di ricerca. *Formazione e Cambiamento, 3*, 231–249.

Caprara, G. V., & Zimbardo, P. (1996). Aggregation and amplification of marginal deviations in the social construction of personality and maladjustment. *European Journal of Personality, 10*, 79–110.

Cardon, L., & Fulker, D. (1993). Genetics of specific cognitive abilities. In R. Plomin & G. McClearn (Eds.), *Nature, nurture and psychology* (pp. 99–120). Washington, DC: American Psychological Association.

Carlson, R. (1971). Where is the person in personality research? *Psychological Bulletin, 75,* 203–219.

Carlston, D. E., & Skowronski, J. J. (1994). Savings in the relearning of trait information as evidence for spontaneous inference generation. *Journal of Personality and Social Psychology, 66,* 840–856.

Carlston, D. E., Skowronski, J. J., & Sparks, C. (1995). Savings in relearning: II. On the formation of behavior-based trait associations and inferences. *Journal of Personality and Social Psychology, 69,* 420–436.

Carstensen, L. L. (1993). Motivation for social contact across the life-span: A theory of socioemotional selectivity. *Nebraska Symposium on Motivation, 40,* 205–254.

Carstensen, L. L. (1995). Evidence for a life-span theory of socioemotional selectivity. *Current Directions in Psychological Science, 4,* 151–156.

Carstensen, L. L., Isaacowitz, D. M., & Charles, S. T. (1999). Taking time seriously: A theory of socioemotional selectivity. *American Psychologist, 54,* 165–181.

Carver, C. S. (1974). Facilitation of physical aggression through objective self-awareness. *Journal of Experimental Social Psychology, 10,* 365–370.

Carver, C. S. (1997). Adult attachment and personality: converging evidence and a new measure. *Personality and Social Psychology Bulletin, 23,* 865–883.

Carver, C. S., Blaney, P. H., & Scheier, M. F. (1979). Focus of attention, chronic expectancy, and responses to a feared stimulus. *Journal of Personality and Social Psychology, 37,* 1186–1195.

Carver, C. S., Ganellen, R. J., Froming, W. J., & Chambers, W. (1983). Modeling: An analysis in terms of category accessibility. *Journal of Experimental Social Psychology, 19,* 403–421.

Carver, C. S., Pozo, C., Harris, S. D., Noriega, V., Scheier, M. F., Robinson, D. S., Ketcham, A. S., Moffat, F. L. Jr., & Clark, K. C. (1995). How coping mediates the effect of optimism on distress: A study of women with early stage breast cancer. *Journal of Personality and Social Psychology, 65,* 375–390.

Carver, C. S., & Scheier, M. F. (1981). *Attention and self-regulation: A control-theory approach to human behavior.* New York: Springer-Verlag.

Carver, C. S., & Scheier, M. F. (1990). Origins and functions of positive and negative affect: A control-process view. *Psychological Review, 97,* 19–35.

Carver, C. S., & Scheier, M. F. (1996). *Perspectives on personality* (3rd ed.). Boston: Allyn & Bacon.

Carver, C. S., & Scheier, M. F. (1998). *On the self-regulation of behavior.* New York: Cambridge University Press.

Carver, C. S., & Scheier, M. F. (1999). Themes and issues in the self-regulation of behavior. In R. S. Wyer, Jr. (Ed.), *Advances in social cognition.* (Vol. 12, pp. 1–105). *Perspectives on behavioral self-regulation,* Mahwah, NJ: Erlbaum.

Carver, C. S., & White, T. L. (1994). Behavioral inhibition, behavioral activation, and affective responses to impending reward and punishment: The BIS/BAS scales. *Journal of Personality and Social Psychology, 67,* 319–333.

Cashwell, C. S., & Vacc, N. A. (1996). Family functioning and risk behaviors: Influences on adolescent delinquency. *School Counselor, 44,* 105–114.

Caspi, A. (1998). Personality development across the life course. In W. Damon (Series Ed.). & N. Eisenberg (Vol. Ed.) *Handbook of child development* (5th ed.). Vol. 3: *Emotional and personality development* (pp. 311–388). New York: Wiley.

Caspi, A. (2000). The child is father of the man: Personality continuities from childhood to adulthood. *Journal of Personality and Social Psychology, 78,* 158–172.

Caspi, A., Begg, D., Dickson, N., Harrington, H., Langley, J., Moffitt, T., & Silva, P. A. (1997). Personality differences predict health-risk behaviors in young adulthood: Evidence from a longitudinal study. *Journal of Personality & Social Psychology, 73,* 1052–1063.

Caspi., A., Bem, D., & Elder, G. H. Jr. (1989). Continuities and consequences of interactional styles across the life course. *Journal of Personality, 57,* 375–406.

Caspi., A., Elder, G. H. Jr., & Bem, D. (1987). Moving against the world: Life-course patterns of explosive children. *Developmental Psychology, 23,* 308–313.

Caspi, A., & Herbener, E. S. (1990). Continuity and change: Assortative marriage and the consistency of personality in adulthood. *Journal of Personality and Social Psychology, 58,* 250–258.

Caspi, A., Herbener, E. S., & Ozer, D. J. (1992). Shared experiences and the similarities of personalities: A longitudinal study of married couples. *Journal of Personality and Social Psychology, 62,* 281–291.

Caspi, A., & Silva, P. A. (1995). Temperament qualities at age 3 predict personality traits in young adulthood: Longitudinal evidence from a birth cohort. *Child Development, 66,* 486–498.

Catrambone, R., & Markus, H. (1987). The role of self-schemas in going beyond the information given. *Social Cognition, 5,* 349–368.

Cattell, R. B. (1943). The description of personality. II: Basic traits resolved into clusters. *Journal of Abnormal and Social Psychology, 38,* 476–507.

Cattell, R. B. (1945a). The description of personality: Principles and findings in a factor analysis. *American Journal of Psychology, 58,* 69–90.

Cattell, R. B. (1945b). The principal trait clusters for describing personality. *Psychological Bulletin, 42,* 129–161.

Cattell, R. B. (1946). *Description and measurement of personality.* New York: World Books.

Cattell, R. B. (1947). Confirmation and clarification of primary personality factors. *Psychometrika, 12,* 197–220.

Cattell, R. B. (1950). *Personality: A systematic, theoretical, and factual study.* New York: McGraw-Hill.

Cattell, R. B. (1957). *Personality and motivation.* New York: World Books.

Cattell, R. B. (1963). Theory of fluid and crystallized intelligence: A critical experiment. *Journal of Educational Psychology, 54,* 1–22.

Cattell, R. B. (1965). *The scientific analysis of personality.* Baltimore: Penguin.

Cattell, R. B. (1971). *Abilities: Their structure, growth and action.* Boston: Houghton Mifflin.

Cattell, R. B., Eber, H. W., & Tatsuoka, M. M. (1970). *The handbook for the Sixteen Personality Factor Questionnaire.* Champaign, III: Institute for Personality and Ability Testing.

Cattell, R. B., & Vogelmann, S. (1977). A comprehensive trial of the scree and KG criteria for determining the number of factors. *Multivariate Behavioral Research, 12,* 289–325.

Cavalli-Sforza, L. L., Menozzi, P., & Piazza, A. (1994). *The history and geography of human genes.* Princeton, NJ: Princeton University Press.

Cervone, D. (1985). Randomization tests to determine significance levels for microanalytic congruences between self-efficacy and behavior. *Cognitive Therapy and Research, 9,* 357–365.

Cervone, D. (1989). Effects of envisioning future activities on self-efficacy judgments and motivation: An availability heuristic interpretation. *Cognitive Therapy and Research, 13,* 247–261.

Cervone, D. (1991). The two disciplines of personality psychology. *Psychological Science, 2,* 371–377.

Cervone, D. (1993). The role of self-referent cognitions in goal setting, motivation, and performance. In M. Rabinowitz (Ed.), *Cognitive science foundations of instruction* (pp. 57–96). Hillsdale, NJ: Lawrence Erlbaum Associates.

Cervone, D. (1996). People who fail at self-regulation: What should we think of them – and how? *Psychological Inquiry, 7,* 40–46.

Cervone, D. (1997). Social-cognitive mechanisms and personality coherence: Self-knowledge, situational beliefs, and cross-situational coherence in perceived self-efficacy. *Psychological Science, 8,* 43–50.

Cervone, D. (1999). Bottom-up explanation in personality psychology: The case of cross-situational coherence. In D. Cervone & Y. Shoda (Eds.), *The coherence of personality: Social-cognitive bases of consistency, variability, and organization* (pp. 303–341). New York: Guilford Press.

Cervone, D. (2000). Evolutionary psychology and explanation in personality psychology: How do we know which module to invoke? *American Behavioral Scientist, 43,* 1001–1014.

Cervone, D., Jiwani, N., & Wood, R. (1991). Goal-setting and the differential influence of self-regulatory processes on complex decision-making performance. *Journal of Personality and Social Psychology, 61,* 257–266.

Cervone, D., Kopp, D. A., Schaumann, L., & Scott, W. D. (1994). Mood, self-efficacy, and performance standards: Lower moods induce higher standards for performance. *Journal of Personality and Social Psychology, 67,* 499–512.

Cervone, D., & Peake, P. K. (1986). Anchoring, efficacy, and action: The influence of judgmental heuristics on self-efficacy judgements and behavior. *Journal of Personality and Social Psychology, 50,* 492–501.

Cervone, D., & Rafaeli-Mor, N. (1999). Living in the future in the past: On the origin and expression of self-regulatory abilities. *Psychological Inquiry, 10,* 209–213.

Cervone, D., & Scott, W. D. (1995). Self-efficacy theory of behavioral change. In W. O'Donohue & L. Krasner (Eds.), *Theories of behavior therapy* (pp. 349–383). Washington, DC: American Psychological Association.

Cervone, D., & Shoda, Y. (1999a). Beyond traits in the study of personality coherence. *Current Directions in Psychological Science, 8,* 27–32.

Cervone, D., & Shoda, Y. (Eds.) (1999b). *The coherence of personality: Social-cognitive bases of consistency, variability, and organization.* New York: Guilford.

Cervone, D., & Shoda, Y. (1999c). Social-cognitive theories and the coherence of personality. In D. Cervone & Y. Shoda (Eds.), *The coherence of personality: Social-cognitive bases of consistency, variability, and organization* (pp. 3–33). New York: Guilford Press.

Cervone, D., & Williams, S. L. (1992). Social cognitive theory and personality. In G. V. Caprara & G. L. Van Heck (Eds.), *Modern personality psychology: Critical reviews and new directions* (pp. 200–252). New York: Harvester Wheatsheaf.

Cervone, D., & Wood, R. (1995). Goals, feedback, and the differential influence of self-regulatory processes on cognitively complex performance. *Cognitive Therapy and Research, 19,* 521–547.

Chaiken, S. (1980). Heuristic versus systematic information processing and the use of source versus message cues in persuasion. *Journal of Personality and Social Psychology, 39,* 752–766.

Chalmers, D. (1995). *The conscious mind: In search of a fundamental theory.* New York: Oxford University Press.

Chambless, D. L., & Gracely, E. J. (1989). Fear of fear and the anxiety disorders. *Cognitive Therapy and Research, 13,* 9–20.

Champagne, B., & Pervin, L. A. (1987). The relation of perceived situational similarity to perceived behavioral similarity: Implications for social learning theory. *European Journal of Personality, 1*, 79–92.

Chaplin, W. F., & Goldberg, L. R. (1983). A failure to replicate the Bem and Allen study of individual differences in cross-situational consistency. *Journal of Personality and Social Psychology, 47*, 1074–1090.

Chapman, M., Skinner, E. A., & Baltes, P. B. (1990). Interpreting correlations between children's perceived control and cognitive performance: Control, agency, or means–ends beliefs? *Developmental Psychology, 26*, 246–253.

Chase, W. G., & Simon, H. A. (1973). Perception in chess. *Cognitive Psychology, 4*, 55–81.

Chen, M., & Bargh, J. A. (1997). Nonconscious behavioral confirmation processes: The self-fulfilling consequences of stereotype activation. *Journal of Experimental Social Psychology, 33*, 541–560.

Chen, S., & Anderson, S. M. (1999). Relationships from the past in the present: Significant-other representations and transference in interpersonal life. In M. P. Zanna (Ed.), *Advances in experimenal social psychology* (Vol. 31, 123–190). San Diego, CA: Academic Press.

Cherlyn, A. J., Furstenberg, F., Chase-Lansdale, L., Kierna, K., Robins, P., Morrison, D., & Teitler, J. O. (1991), Longitudinal studies of effects of divorce on children in Great Britain and the United States, *Science, 252*, 1386–1389.

Cherlyn, A. J., Scabini, E., & Rossi, G. (Eds.) (1997). Still in the nest. Delayed home leaving in Europe and the United States. *Journal of Family Issues. 18*. Special Issue.

Chiu, C., Hong, Y., & Dweck, C. S. (1994). Toward an integrative model of personality and intelligence: A general framework and some preliminary steps. In R. Sternberg & P. Ruzgis (Eds.), *Personality and intelligence* (pp. 61–103). New York: Cambridge University Press.

Chiu, C., Hong, Y., & Dweck, C. S. (1997). Lay dispositionism and implicit theories of personality. *Journal of Personality and Social Psychology, 73*, 19–30.

Chiu, C., Hong, Y., Mischel, W., & Shoda, Y. (1995). Discriminative facility in social competence: Conditional versus dispositional encoding and monitoring-blunting of information. *Social Cognition, 13*, 49–70.

Chodorow, N. J. (1978). *The reproduction of mothering: Psychoanalysis and the socialization of gender.* Berkeley: University of California Press.

Choi, I., Nisbett, R. E., & Norenzayam, A. (1999). Causal attribution across cultures: Variation and universality. *Psychological Bulletin, 125*, 47–63.

Christie, R. (1991). Authoritarianism and related constructs. In J. P. Robinson, P. R. Shaver, & L. S. Wrightsman (Eds.), *Measures of personality and social psychological attitudes* (pp. 501–571). San Diego: Academic Press.

Church, A. T., & Burke, P. J. (1994). Exploratory and confirmatory tests of the big five and Tellegen's three- and four-dimensional models. *Journal of Personality and Social Psychology, 66*, 93–114.

Church, A. T., & Katigbak, M. S. (1988). The emic strategy in the identification and assessment of personality dimensions in a non-Western cultures: Rationale, steps, and a Philippine illustration. *Journal of Cross Cultural Psychology, 19*, 140–163.

Church, A. T., Katigbak, M. S., & Reyes, J. A. (1996). Toward a taxonomy of trait adjectives in Filipino: Comparing personality lexicons across cultures. *European Journal of Personality, 10*, 3–24.

Cicchetti, D., & Toth, S. L. (1998). The development of depression in children and adolescents. *American Psychologist, 53*, 221–241.

Cimino, G., & Duchesneau, F. (1997). *Vitalisms: From Haller to the cell theory.* Firenze: Leo S. Olschki.

Clark, M. S., & Isen, A. M. (1982). Toward understanding the relationship between feeling states and social behavior. In A. H. Hastorf & A. M. Isen (Eds.), *Cognitive social psychology* (pp. 73–108). New York: Elsevier.

Cloninger, C. R. (1987). A systematic method for clinical description and classification of personality variants. *Archives of General Psychiatry, 44*, 573–588.

Cloninger, C. R., Adolffson, R., Svrakic, N. M. (1996). Mapping genes for human personality. *Nature Genetics, 12*, 3–4.

Cloninger, C. R., Svrakic, D. M., & Przybeck, T. R. (1993). A psychobiological model of temperament and character. *Archives of General Psychiatry, 50*, 975–990.

Clore, G. (1994). Why emotions are felt. In P. Ekman & R. J. Davidson (Eds.), *The nature of emotion: Fundamental questions* (pp. 103-111). New York: Oxford University Press.

Cohen, J. D., & Schooler, J. W. (Eds.) (1997). *Scientific approaches to consciousness.* Mahwah, NJ: Erlbaum.

Coie, J. D., & Dodge, K. A. (1998). Aggression and antisocial behavior. In W. Damon (Series Ed.) & N. Eisenberg (Vol. Ed.), *Handbook of child psychology* (5th ed.). Vol. 3: *Social, emotional, and personality development* (pp. 779–862). New York: Wiley.

Cole, M. (1996). *Cultural psychology.* Cambridge, MA: Harvard University Press.

Coleman, P. K., & Karraker, K. H. (1997). Self-efficacy and parenting quality: Findings and future applications. *Developmental Review, 18*, 47-85.

Collins, A., & Larsen, B. (1992). Conflict and relationships during adolescence. In C. Shantz & W.

Hartup (Eds.), *Conflict in child and adolescent development.* (pp. 216–241). New York: Cambridge University Press.

Collins, N. L. (1996). Working models of attachment: Implications for explanation, emotion and behavior. *Journal of Personality and Social Psychology, 71,* 810–832.

Collins, N. L., & Read, S. J. (1994). Cognitive representations of adult attachment: The structure and function of working models. In K. Bartholomew & D. Perlman (Eds.), *Advances in personal relationships: Attachment processes in adulthood* (Vol. 5, pp. 53–90). London: Jessica-Kingsley.

Comrey, A. (1970). *Manual for the Comrey personality scales.* San Diego, CA: Educational and Industrial Testing Service.

Comrey, A. L. (1978). Common methodological problems in factor analytic studies. *Journal of Consulting and Clinical Psychology, 46,* 648–659.

Comrey, A. L. (1980). *Handbook for the interpretation of the Comrey Personality Scales.* San Diego: EdITS Publishers.

Comrey, A. L. (1988). Factor-analytic methods of scale development in personality and clinical psychology. *Journal of Consulting and Clinical Psychology, 56,* 754–761.

Comrey, A. L. (1995). *Manual and handbook of interpretations for the Comrey Personality Scales.* San Diego: EdITS Publishers.

Comrey, A. L., & Lee, H. B. (1992). *A first course in factor analysis.* Hillsdale, NJ: Erlbaum.

Conger, R. D., Conger, K. J., Elder, G. H., & Lorenz, F. O. (1992). A family process model of economic hardship and adjustment of early adolescent boys. *Child Development, 63,* 526–541.

Constantinople, A. (1973). Masculinity-femininity: An exception to a famous dictum. *Psychological Bulletin, 80,* 389–407.

Coopersmith, S. (1967). *The antecedants of self-esteem.* San Francisco: W. H. Freeman.

Cosmides, L. (1989). The logic of social exchange: Has natural selection shaped how humans reason? Studies with the Wason selection task. *Cognition, 31,* 187-276.

Costa, P. T., & McCrae, R. R. (1976). Age differences in personality structure: A cluster analytic approach. *Journal of Gerontology, 31,* 564–570.

Costa, P. T., & McCrae, R. R. (1985). *The NEO Personality Inventory Manual.* Odessa, FL: Psychological Assessment Resources.

Costa, P. T., & McCrae, R. R. (1988). From catalog to classification: Murray's needs and the five factor model. *Journal of Personality and Social Psychology, 55,* 258–265.

Costa, P. T., Jr., & McCrae, R. R. (1989). *The NEO-PI/NEO-FFI manual supplement.* Odessa, FL: Psychological Assessment Resources.

Costa, P. T., & McCrae, R. R. (1992). *Revised NEO personality inventory (NEO-PI-R) and NEO Five-*Factor Inventory (NEO-FFI) professional manual.* Odessa, FL: Psychological Assessment Resources.

Costa, P. T., & McCrae, R. R. (1994). Set like plaster? Evidence for the stability of the adult personality. In T. F. Heatheron & J. L. Weinberger (Eds.), *Can personality change?* (pp. 21–40). Washington, D. C.: American Psychological Association.

Costa, P. T., & McCrae, R. R. (1997). Longitudinal stability of adult personality. In R. Hogan, J. Johnson & S. Briggs (Eds.), *Handbook of personality psychology* (pp. 269–290). San Diego: Academic Press.

Costa, P. T., Jr., & McCrae, R. R. (1998). Trait theories of personality. D. F. Barone, M. Hersen, & V. B., Van Hasselt (Eds.), *Advanced Personality* (pp. 103–121). New York: Plenum Press.

Costa, P. T. Jr., & McCrae, R. R. (In press). A theoretical context for adult temperament. In T. D. Wachs & G. A. Kohnstamm (Eds.), *Temperament in context.* Hillsdale, NJ: Erlbaum.

Costa, P. T., & Widiger, T. A. (Eds.) (1994). *Personality disorders and the five factor model of personality.* Washington, DC: American Psychological Association.

Costa, P. T., Zondermann, A. B., McCrae, R. R., Cornoni-Huntley, J., Locke, B. Z., & Barbano, H. H. (1987). Longitudinal analyses of psychological well-being in a national sample: Stability of mean levels. *Journal of Gerontology, 42,* 50–55.

Covington, M. (1992). *Making the grade.* New York: Cambridge University Press.

Covington, M. V., & Omelich, C. L. (1979). Are causal attributions causal? A path analysis of the cognitive model of achievement motivation. *Journal of Personality and Social Psychology, 37,* 1487–1504.

Cox, M. J. M., & Paley, N. (1997). Families as systems. *Annual Review of Psychology, 48,* 243–267.

Cozzarelli, C. (1993). Personality and self-efficacy as predictors of coping with abortion. *Journal of Personality and Social Psychology, 65,* 1224–1236.

Cozzarelli, C., Sumer, N., & Major, B. (1998). Mental models of attachment and coping with abortion. *Journal of Personality and Social Psychology, 74,* 453–467.

Craik, K. (1986). Personality research methods: An historical perspective. *Journal of Personality, 54,* 18–51.

Cramer, P. (1991). *The development of defense mechanisms: Theory, research, and assessment.* New York: Springer-Verlag.

Cramer, P. (1996). *Storytelling, narrative, and the Thematic Apperception Test.* New York: Guilford.

Cramer, P. (1997). Evidence for change in children's use of defense mechanisms. *Journal of Personality, 65,* 233–247.

Cramer, P., & Block, J. (1998). Preschool antecedents of defense mechanism use in young adults: A longitudinal study. *Journal of Personality and Social Psychology, 74,* 159–169.

Crick, N. R., & Dodge, K. A. (1994). A review and reformulation of social information-processing mechanisms in children's social adjustment. *Psychological Bulletin, 115,* 74–101.

Crick, N. R., & Dodge, K. A. (1996). Social-information-processing mechanisms in reactive and proactive aggression. *Child Development, 67,* 993–1002.

Cronbach, L. J. (1957). The two disciplines of scientific psychology. *American Psychologist, 12,* 671–684.

Cronbach, L. J. (1975). Beyond the two disciplines of scientific psychology. *American Psychologist, 30,* 116–127.

Cronbach, L. J., Gleser, G. C., Nanda, H., & Rajaratnam, N. (1972). *The dependability of behavioral measurements: Theory of generalizability for scores and profiles.* New York: Wiley.

Cross, S., & Madson, L. (1997). Models of the self: Self-construals and gender. *Psychological Bulletin, 122,* 5–37.

Crowne, D. P., & Marlow, D. (1964). *The approval motive: Studies in evaluative dependence.* New York: Wiley.

Csikszentmihalyi, M. (1990). *Flow: The psychology of optimal experience.* New York: Harper & Row.

Csikzentmihalyi, M., Larson, R., & Prescott, S. (1977). The ecology of adolescent activity and experience. *Journal of Youth and Adolescence, 6,* 281-294.

Csikszentmihalyi, M., & Lefevre, J. (1990). Optimal experience in work and leisure, *Journal of Personality and Social Psychology, 56,* 815–822.

Culbertson, F. M. (1997). Depression and gender. *American Psychologist, 52,* 25–31.

Cutrona, C. E., Russell, D., & Jones, R. D. (1985). Cross-situational consistency in causal attributions: Does attributional style exist? *Journal of Personality & Social Psychology, 47,* 1043–1058.

Cutrona, C. E., & Troutman, B. R. (1986). Social support, infant temperament, and parenting self-efficacy: A mediational model of post-partum depression. *Child Development, 57,* 1507–1518.

Cyranowski, J. M., & Andersen, B. L. (1998). Schemas, sexuality, and romantic attachment. *Journal of Personality and Social Psychology, 74,* 1364–1379.

Dabbs, J. M., & Morris, B. (1990). Testosterone, social class, and antisocial behavior in a sample of 4,462 men. *Psychological Science, 1,* 209–211.

Daly, M., Wilson, M., & Weghorst, S. (1982). Male sexual jealousy. *Ethology and Sociobiology, 3,* 11–27.

Damasio, A. R. (1994). *Descartes' error: Emotion, reason, and the human brain.* New York: Grosset/Putnam.

Damasio, A. R. (1999). *The feeling of what happens: Body and emotion in the making of consciousness.* New York: Harcourt Brace.

Damon, W., & Hart, D. (1988). *Self-understanding in childhood and adolescence.* New York: Cambridge.

Darley, J. M., & Latané B. (1968). Bystander intervention in emergencies: Diffusion of responsibility. *Journal of Personality and Social Psychology, 8,* 377–383.

Daruna, J. H., Karrer, R., & Rosen, A. J. (1985). Introversion, attention and the late positive component of event-related potentials. *Biological Psychology, 20,* 249–259.

Darwin, C. (1872). *The expression of emotions in man and animals.* London: Murray.

Davidson, R. J. (1992). Emotion and affective style: Hemispheric substrates. *Psychological Science, 3*(1), 39–43.

Davidson, R. J. (1994). Honoring biology in the study of affective style. In P. Ekman & R. J. Davidson (Eds.), *The nature of emotion: Fundamental questions* (pp. 321–328). New York: Oxford University Press.

Davidson, R. J., Ekman, P., Saron, C. D., Senulis, J. A., & Friesen, W. V. (1990). Approach/withdrawal and cerebral asymmetry: Emotional expression and brain physiology, I. *Journal of Personality and Social Psychology, 58,* 330–341.

Davies, M., Stankov, L., & Roberts, R. D. (1998). Emotional intelligence: In search of an elusive construct. *Journal of Personality and Social Psychology, 75,* 989–1015.

Davila, J., Burge, D., & Hammen, C. (1997). Why does attachment style change? *Journal of Personality and Social Psychology, 73,* 826–838.

Davis, F. W., & Yates, B. T. (1982). Self-efficacy expectancies versus outcome expectancies as determinants of performance deficits and depressive affect. *Cognitive Therapy and Research, 6,* 23–25.

Davis, P. (1987). Repression and the inaccessibility of affective memories. *Journal of Personality and Social Psychology, 53,* 585–593.

Davis, P., & Schwartz, G. (1987). Repression and the inaccessibility of affective memories. *Journal of Personality and Social Psychology, 52,* 155–162.

Davison, K. P., & Pennebaker, J. W. (1996). Social psychosomatics. In E. T. Higgins & A. W. Kruglanski (Eds.), *Social psychology: Handbook of basic principles* (pp. 102–130). New York: Guilford.

Dawes, R. M. (1994). *House of cards: Psychology and psychotherapy built on myth.* New York: The Free Press.

Dawson, V. L., Zeitz, C. M., & Wright, J. C. (1989). Expert-novice differences in personal perception: Evidence of experts' sensitivities to the organization of behavior. *Social Cognition, 7,* 1–30.

Dazzi, N., & De Coro, A. (1992). Psychoanalysis as a bipersonal psychology: Implications for a theory of personality. In G. V. Caprara & G. Van Heck

(Eds.), *Modern Personality Psychology*, (pp. 133–158). London: Harvester-Weatsheaf.

Deary, I. J. (1996). A (latent) big five personality model in 1915? A reanalysis of Webb's data. *Journal of Personality and Social Psychology, 71*, 992–995.

Deary, I. J., & Caryl, P. G. (1993). Intelligence, EEG, and evoked potentials. In P. A. Vernon (Ed.) *Biological approaches to the study of human intelligence.* (259–315). Norwood, NJ: Ablex.

Deaux, K. (1984). From individual differences to social categories. *American Psychologist, 39*, 105–116.

Deaux, K., & Major, B. (1987). Putting gender into context: An interactive model of gender-related behavior. *Psychological Review, 94*, 369–389.

De Boeck, P., & Rosenberg, S. (1988). Hierarchical classes: Model and data analysis. *Psychometrika, 53*, 361–381.

De Charms, R. (1976). *Enhancing motivation: Change in the classroom.* New York: Irvington.

Deci, E. L. (1992). On the nature and functions of motivation theories. *Psychological Inquiry, 3*, 167–171.

Deci, E. L. (1996). Making room for self-regulation: Some thoughts on the link between emotion and behavior. *Psychological Inquiry, 7*, 220–223.

Deci, E., & Ryan, R. (1985). *Intrinsic motivation and self determination in human behavior.* New York: Plenum Press.

Deci, E. L., & Ryan, R. M. (1991). A motivational approach to the self: Integration in personality. In *Perspectives on motivation.* In R. Dienstbier (Ed.), *Nebraska Symposium on Motivation* (pp. 237–288). Lincoln: University of Nebraska Press.

DeGroot, A. D. (1965). *Thought and choice in chess.* The Hague: Mouton.

Dennett, D. C. (1978). *Brainstorms: Philosophic essays on mind and psychology.* Montgomery, VT: Bradford Books.

Dennett, D. C. (1984). *Elbow room: The varieties of free will worth wanting.* Cambridge, MA: MIT Press.

Dennett, D. C. (1991). *Consciousness explained.* Boston: Little Brown.

Dennett, D. C. (1996). *Darwin's dangerous idea.* New York: Simon & Schuster.

De Raad, B. (1992). The replicability of the Big Five personality dimensions in three word-classes of the Dutch language. *European Journal of Personality, 6*, 15–29.

De Raad, B. (1998). Five big, big five issues: Rationale, content, structure, status and cross-cultural assessment. *European Psychologist, 3*, 113–124.

De Raad, B., & Hoskens, M. (1990). Personality-descriptive nouns. *European Journal of Personality, 4*, 131–146.

De Raad, B., Mulder, E., Kloosterman, K., & Hofstee, W. K. B. (1988). Personality-descriptive verbs. *European Journal of Personality, 2*, 81–96.

De Raad, B., & Schouwenburg, H. (1996). Personality in learning and education: A review. *European Journal of Personality, 10*, 303–336.

Detterman, D. K., & Sternberg, R. J. (Eds.). (1993). *Transfer on trial.* Norwood, NJ: Ablex.

Deutsch, M. (1993). Educating for a peaceful world. *American Psychologist, 48*, 510–517.

De Wolff, M. S., & Van Ijzendoorn M. H. (1997). Sensitivity and attachment. A meta-analysis on parental antecedents of infant attachment. *Child Development, 68*, 571–591.

Di Blas, L., & Forzi, M. (1998). An alternative taxonomic study of personality descriptive adjectives in the Italian language. *European Journal of Personality, 12*, 75–101.

Di Blas, L., & Forzi, M. (1999). Refining a descriptive structure of personality attributes in Italian language: The abridged Big Three Circumplex structure. *Journal of Personality and Social Psychology, 76*, 451–481.

DiClemente, C. C., Prochaska, J. O., & Gilbertini, M. (1985). Self-efficacy and the stages of self-change of smoking. *Cognitive Therapy and Research, 9*, 181–200.

Diehl, M., Elnick, A. B., Bourbeau, L. S., & Labouvie-Vief, G. (1998). Adult attachment styles: Their relations to family context and personality. *Journal of Personality and Social Psychology, 74*, 1656–1669.

Diener, E. (1998). Subjective well-being and personality. In D. F. Barone, M. Hersen, & V. B. Van Hasselt (Eds.), *Advanced personality* (pp. 311–334). New York: Plenum Press.

Diener, E., & Diener, M. (1995). Cross-cultural correlates of life satisfaction and self-esteem. *Journal of Personality and Social Psychology, 68*, 653–663.

Diener, E., & Emmons, R. A. (1984). The independence of positive and negative affect. *Journal of Personality and Social Psychology, 47*, 1105-1117.

Diener, E., & Larsen, R. J. (1984). Temporal stability and cross-situational consistency of affective, behavioral, and cognitive responses. *Journal of Personality and Social Psychology, 47*(4), 971–883.

Diener, E., Larsen, R. J., Levine, S., & Emmons, R. A. (1985). Intensity and frequency: Dimensions underlying positive and negative affect. *Journal of Personality and Social Psychology, 48*, 1253–1265.

Diener, E., Sandvik, E., Pavot, W., & Fujita, F. (1992). Extraversion and subjective well being in a U.S. national probability sample. *Journal of Research in Personality, 26*, 205–215.

Diener, E., Smith, H., & Fujita, F. (1995). The personality structure of affect. *Journal of Personality and Social Psychology, 69*, 130–141.

Digman, J. M. (1990). Personality structure: Emergence of the five factor model. *Annual Review of Psychology, 41*, 417–440.

Digman, J. M. (1997). Higher-order factors of the Big Five. *Journal of Personality and Social Psychology, 73,* 1246–1256.

Dijksterhuis, A., Spears, R., Postmes, T., Stapel, D. A., Koomen, W., van Knippenberg, A., & Sheepers, D. (1998). Seeing one thing and doing another: Contrast effects in automatic behavior. *Journal of Personality and Social Psychology, 75,* 862–871.

Di Lalla L. F., & Gottesman, I. (1989). Heterogeneity of causes for delinquency and criminality: Life-span perspectives. *Development and Psychopathology, 1,* 339–349.

Dilorio, C., Mailbach, E., O'Leary, A., & Sanderson, C. A. (1997). Measurement of condom use self-efficacy and outcome expectancies in a geographically diverse group of STD patients. *AIDS Education & Prevention, 9,* 1–13.

Dix, T. (1991). The affective organization of parenting: Adaptive and maladaptive processes. *Psychological Bulletin, 110,* 3–25.

Dixon, F. (1971). *Subliminal perception: The nature of a controversy.* London: McGraw-Hill.

Dobzhansky, T. (1972). Genetics and the diversity of behavior. *American Psychologist, 27,* 523–530.

Dodge, K. A. (1986). A social information processing model of social competence in children. In M. Perlmutter (Ed.), *The Minnesota symposium on child psychology* (Vol. 18, pp. 77–125). Hillsdale, NJ: Erlbaum.

Dodge, K. A. (1993). Social-cognitive mechanisms in the development of conduct disorder and depression. *Annual Review of Psychology, 44,* 559–584.

Dodge, K. A. (1996). Biopsychosocial perspectives on the development of conduct disorder. In J. A. Linney (Ed.), *Proceedings of the fifth national prevention Research Conference.* Washington, D. C.: National Institute of Mental Health.

Dodge, K. A. (in press). Conduct disorder. In M. Lewis & A. J. Sameroff (Eds.), *Handbook of developmental psychopathology* (2nd Ed.). New York: Plenum Press.

Dodge, K. A., & Coie, J. D. (1987). Social information processing factors in reactive and proactive aggression in children's peer groups. *Journal of Personality and Social Psychology, 53,* 1146–1158.

Dodge, K.A., & Frame, C.L. (1982). Social cognitive biases and deficits in aggressive boys. *Child Development, 53,* 630–635.

Dodge, K. A., & Somberg, D. R. (1987). Hostile attributional biases among aggressive boys are exacerbated under conditions of threats to the self. *Child Development, 58,* 213–224.

Dodge, K. A., & Tomlin, A. M. (1987). Utilization of selfschemas as a mechanism of interpretational bias in aggressive children. *Social Cognition, 5,* 280–300.

Dollard, J., & Miller, N. (1950). Personality and psychotherapy: An analysis in terms of learning, thinking and culture. New York: McGraw-Hill.

Donati, P. (1998). *Manuale di sociologia della famiglia.* Roma: Laterza.

Donohue, E. M., Robins, R. W., Roberts, B. W., & John, O. P. (1993). The divided self: Concurrent and longitudinal effects of psychological adjustment and social roles on self-concept differentiation. *Journal of Personality and Social Psychology, 64,* 834–846.

Downey, G., & Feldman, S. I. (1996). Implications of rejection sensitivity for intimate relationships. *Journal of Personality and Social Psychology, 70,* 1327–1343.

Downey, G., Freitas, A. L., Michaelis, B., & Khouri, H. (1998). The self-fulfilling prophecy in close relationships: Rejection sensitivity and rejection by romantic partners. *Journal of Personality and Social Psychology, 75,* 545–560.

Duff, K. J., & Newman, L. S. (1997). Individual differences in the spontaneous construal of behavior: Idiocentrism and the automatization of the trait inference process. *Social Cognition, 15,* 217–241.

Dunn, J., & Kendrick, C. (1982). *Siblings: Love, envy and understanding.* London: Grant McIntyre.

Dunn, J., & Plomin, R. (1990). *Separate lives: Why siblings are so different.* New York: Basic Books.

Durham, W. H. (1991). *Coevolution.* Stanford, CA.: Stanford University Press.

Dweck, C. (1996). Implicit theories as organizers of goals and behavior. In P. M. Gollwitzer & J. A. Bargh (Eds.), *The psychology of action: Linking cognition and motivation to behavior* (pp. 69–90). New York: Guilford.

Dweck, C., & Elliot, E. (1983). Achievement motivation. In P. H. Mussen (Series Ed.) & E. M. M Hetherington (Vol. Ed.), *Handbook of child psychology* (4th ed.) Vol. 4: Socialization, personality and social development. (pp. 643–691). New York: Wiley.

Dweck, C., & Leggett, E. (1988). A social-cognitive approach to motivation and personality. *Psychological Review, 95,* 256–273.

Dykman, B. M. (1988). Integrating cognitive and motivational factors in depression: Initial tests of a goal-orientation approach. *Journal of Personality and Social Psychology, 74,* 139–158.

Eagle, M. (1984). *Recent developments in psychoanalysis: A critical evaluation.* New York: McGraw-Hill.

Eagly, A. (1987). *Sex differences in social behavior: A social role interpretation.* Hillsdale, NJ: Erlbaum.

Eagly, A. (1995). The science and politics of comparing women and men. *American Psychologist, 50,* 145–158.

Eagly, A., & Carli, L. (1981). Sex-typed communications as determinants of sex differences in influenceability: A meta-analysis of social influence studies. *Psychological Bulletin, 90,* 1–20.

Eagly, A., & Crowley, M. (1986). Gender and helping behavior. A meta-analytic review of the social psychological literature. *Psychological Bulletin, 100,* 283–308.

Eagly, A., & Steffen, V. (1986). Gender and aggressive behavior: A meta-analytic review. *Psychological Bulletin, 100,* 309–330.

Eagly, A. H., & Wood, W. (1999). The origins of sex differences in human behavior: Evolved dispositions versus social roles. *American Psychologist, 54,* 408–423.

Earley, P. C., Wojnarski, P., & Prest, W. (1987). Task planning and energy expended: Exploration of how goals influence performance. *Journal of Applied Psychology, 72,* 107–114.

Easterbrooks, M. A., & Emde, R. N. (1988). Marital and parent-child relationships. The role of affect in the family system. In R. A. Hinde & J. Stevenson Hinde (Eds.), *Relationships within families: Mutual Influences* (pp. 83–103). New York: Oxford University Press.

Eaves, L., Eysenck, H., & Martin, N. (1989). *Genes, Culture and Personality.* London: Academic Press.

Ebstein, R. V., Novick, O., Umansky, R., Priel, B., Osher, Y., Blaine, D., Bennett, E. R., Nemanov, L., Katz, M., & Belmaker, R. H. (1996). Dopamine D4 receptor (DRD4) exon III polymorphism associated with the human personality trait novelty-seeking. *Nature Genetics, 12,* 78–80.

Eccles, J. S., Midgley, C., Wigfield, A., Miller Buchanan C., Rennan, D., Flanagan, C., & Mac Iver, D. (1993). Development during adolescence. *American Psychologist, 48,* 90–101.

Eccles, J. S., Wigfield, A., & Schiefele, U. (1998). Motivation to succeed. In W. Damon (Series Ed.) & N. Eisenberg (Volume Ed.) *Handbook of child development* (5th edition). Vol.3: Emotional and personality development (pp. 1017-1096). New York: Wiley.

Edelman, G. M. (1987). *Neural Darwinism: The theory of neuronal group selection.* New York: Basic Books.

Edelman, G. M. (1992). *Bright air, brilliant fire: On the matter of the mind.* New York: Basic Books.

Edwards, K. (1998). The face of time: Temporal cues in the facial expressions of emotion. *Psychological Science, 9,* 270–276.

Egloff, B., & Krohne, H. W. (1996). Repressive emotional discreteness after failure. *Journal of Personality & Social Psychology, 70,* 1318–1326.

Ehrhardt, A. (1984). Gender differences: A biosocial perspective. In R. Dienstbier & T. Sonderegger (Eds.), *Psychology and gender. Nebraska symposium in motivation,* (Vol. 32. pp. 37–57). Lincoln: University of Nebraska Press.

Eisenberg, N., & Fabes, R. A. (1991). Prosocial behavior and empathy: A multimethod developmental perspective. In M. S. Clark (Ed.), *Prosocial behavior* (pp. 34–61). Newbury Park, CA: Sage.

Eisenberg, N., & Fabes, R. A. (1992). Emotion, regulation and the development of social competence.

In M. S. Clark (Ed.), *Emotion and social behavior* (Vol. 14, pp. 119–150) Newbury Park, CA : Sage.

Eisenberg, N., & Lennon, R. (1983). Sex differences in empathy and related capacities. *Psychological Bulletin, 94,* 100–131.

Eisenberg, N., & Mussen, P. (1989). *The roots of prosocial behavior in children.* Cambridge, England: Cambridge University Press.

Ekehammar, B. (1974). Interactionism in personality from a historical perspective. *Psychological Bulletin, 81,* 1026–1048.

Ekman, P. (1992a). An argument for basic emotion. *Cognition and Emotion, 6,* 169–200.

Ekman, P. (1992b). Are there basic emotions? *Psychological Review, 99,* 550–553.

Ekman, P. (1993). Facial expression and emotion. *American Psychologist, 48,* 384–392.

Ekman, P. (1994). All emotions are basic. In P. Ekman & R. J. Davidson (Eds.), *The nature of emotion: Fundamental questions* (pp. 15–19). New York: Oxford University Press.

Ekman, P., & Davidson, R. J. (Eds.). (1994). *The nature of emotion: Fundamental questions.* New York: Oxford University Press.

Ekman, P., Davidson, R. J., & Friesen, W. V. (1990). The Duchenne smile: Emotional expression and brain physiology, II. *Journal of Personality and Social Psychology, 58,* 342–353.

Ekman, P., Levenson, R. W., & Friesen, W. V. (1983). Autonomic nervous system activity distinguishes among emotions. *Science, 221,* 1208–1210.

Ekman, P., & Oster, H. (1979). Facial expressions of emotion. *Annual Review of Psychology, 30,* 527–554.

Ekman, P., & Rosenberg, E. (1997). *What the face reveals: Basic and applied studies of spontaneous expression using the Facial Action Coding System.* New York: Oxford University Press.

Elder, G. H. Jr. (1974). Children of the great depression. Chicago: University of Chicago Press.

Elder, G. H. Jr. (1981). Scarcity and prosperity in postwar childbearing: Explorations from a life course perspective. *Journal of Family History, 5,* 410–431.

Elder, G. H., Jr. (1984). Families, kin, and the life course: A sociological perspective. In R. D. Parke (Ed.), *The Family* (pp. 80–136). Chicago: University of Chicago Press.

Elder, G. H., Jr. (Ed.) (1985). *Life course dynamics: Trajectories and transitions, 1969–1980.* Ithaca, NY: Cornell University Press.

Elder, G. H., Jr. (1999). *Children of the great depression.* Boulder, CO: Westview Press.

Elder, G. H., Jr., & Ardelt, M. (1992). (March 18–20, 1992). *Families adapting to economic pressure: Some consequences for parents and adolescents.* Paper presented at the Society for Research on Adolescence, Washington, D. C.

Elder, G. H., Caspi, A., & Downey, G. (in press) Problem behavior and family relationships: A multigenerational analysis. In A. Sorrentino & F. Weinert, & L. Sherrod (Eds.), *Human development: Interdisciplinary perspectives*. Hillsdale, NJ: Erlbaum.

Elder, G. H., Caspi, A., & van Nguyen, T. (1986). Resourceful and vulnerable children: Family influences in stressful times. In R. K. Silbereisen, K. Eyferth, & G. Rudinger (Eds.), Development as action in context: Problem behavior and normal youth development (pp. 169–186). Heidelberg & New York: Springer-Verlag.

Elder, G. H., van Nguyen, T., & Caspi, A. (1985). Linking family hardship to children's lives. Child Development, 56, 361–375.

Eley, T. C., Lichtenstein, P., & Stevenson, J. (1999). Sex differences in the etiology of aggressive and nonaggressive antisocial behavior: Results from two twin studies. *Child Development, 70*, 155–168.

Ellenberger, H. F. (1970). *The discovery of the unconscious*. New York: Basic Books.

Elliot, A. J., & Church, M. A. (1997). A hierarchical model of approach and avoidance motivation. *Journal of Personality and Social Psychology, 72*, 218–232.

Elliot, A. J., & Dweck, C. S. (1988). Goals: An approach to motivation and achievement. *Journal of Personality and Social Psychology, 54*, 5–12.

Elliot, A. J., & Harackiewicz, J. (1996). Approach and avoidance achievement goals and intrinsic motivation: A mediational analysis. *Journal of Personality and Social Psychology, 70*, 968–980.

Elliot, A. J., & Sheldon, K. M. (1997). Avoidance achievement motivation: A personal goals analysis. *Journal of Personality and Social Psychology, 73*, 171–185.

Elliot, A. J., & Sheldon, K. M. (1998). Avoidance personal goals and the personality–illness relationship. *Journal of Personality and Social Psychology, 75*, 1282–1299.

Elliott, E. S., & Dweck, C. S. (1988). Goals: An approach to motivation and achievement. *Journal of Personality and Social Psychology, 54*, 5–12.

Ellsworth, P. C. (1994). Levels of thought and levels of emotion. In P. Ekman & R. J. Davidson (Eds.), *The nature of emotion: Fundamental Questions* (pp. 192–196). New York: Oxford University Press.

Emery, R. E. (1988). *Marriage, divorce and children's adjustment*. Newbury Park, CA.: Sage.

Emmons, R. A. (1989). The personal striving approach to personality. In L. A. Pervin (Ed.), *Goal constructs in personality and social psychology* (pp. 87–126). Hillsdale, NJ: Erlbaum.

Emmons, R. A. (1996). Striving and feeling: Personal goals and subjective well-being. In P. M. Gollwitzer & J. A. Bargh (Eds.), *The psychology of action: Linking cognition and motivation to behavior* (pp. 313–337). New York: Guilford.

Emmons, R. A. (1997). Motives and goals. In R. Hogan, J. Johnson, A. & S. Briggs (Eds.), *Handbook of personality psychology* (pp. 485–512). San Diego: Academic Press.

Emmons, R. A., Diener, E., & Larsen, R. J. (1986). Choice and avoidance of everyday situations and affect congruence: Two models of reciprocal interactionism. *Journal of Personality and Social Psychology, 51*, 815–826.

Emmons, R. A., & Kaiser, H. A. (1996). Goal orientation and emotional well-being: Linking goals and affect through the self. In A. Tesser & L. Martin (Eds.), *Striving and Feeling: interactions among goals, affect, and self-regulation* (pp. 79-98). Mahwah, NJ: Erlbaum.

Emmons, R. A., & King, L. A. (1988). Conflict among personal strivings: Immediate and long-term implications for psychological and physical well-being. *Journal of Personality and Social Psychology, 54*, 1040–1048.

Endler, N. S. (1984). Interactionism. In N. S. Endler & J. M. Hunt (Eds.), *Personality and the behavioral disorders* (pp. 183–217). New York: Wiley.

Endler, N. S., Edwards, J. M., Vitelli, R., & Parker, J. D. A. (1989). Assessment of state and trait anxiety: Endler multidimensional anxiety scales. *Anxiety Research: An International Journal, 2*, 1–14.

Endler, N. S., Parker, J. D. A., Bagby, R. M., & Cox, B. J. (1991). Multidimensionality of state and trait anxiety: Factor structure of the Endler Multidimensional Anxiety Scales. *Journal of Personality and Social Psychology, 60*, 919–926.

Endler, N. S., & Magnusson, D. (1976). Toward an interactional psychology of personality. *Psychological Bulletin, 83*, 956–974.

Epstein, S. (1979). The stability of behavior: On predicting most of the people much of the time. *Journal of Personality and Social Psychology, 37*, 1097–1126.

Epstein, S. (1983). A research paradigm for the study of personality and emotions. In R. A. Dienstbier & M. M. Page (Eds.), *Nebraska symposium on motivation 1982: Personality – Current Theory and Research* (pp. 91–154). Lincoln, NE: University of Nebraska Press.

Epstein, S. (1994). Integration of the cognitive and the psychodynamic unconscious. *American Psychologist, 49*, 709–724.

Epstein, S. (1998). Emotions and psychopathology from the perspective of cognitive-experiential self-theory. In W. E. Flack & J. D. Laird (Eds.), *Emotions in psychopathology, Theory and research. Series in affective science* (pp. 57–69). New York: Oxford University Press.

Erdelyi, M. (1974). A new look at the New Look: Perceptual defense and vigilance. *Psychological Review, 81*, 1–25.

Erdelyi, M. H. (1985). *Psychoanalysis: Freud's cognitive psychology*. San Francisco, CA.: Freeman.

Erdley, C. A., Cain, K. M., Loomis, C. C., Dumas-Hines, F., & Dweck, C. S. (1997). The relations among children's social goals. Implicit personality theories, and responses to social failure. *Developmental Psychology, 33,* 263–272.

Ericsson, K. A., & Simon, H. A. (1980). Verbal reports as data. *Psychological Review, 87,* 215–251.

Erel, O., & Burman, B. (1995). Interrelatedness of marital relations and parent-child relations: A meta-analytic review. *Psychological Bulletin, 118,* 108–132.

Erez, M., & Earley, P. C. (1993). *Culture, self-identity, and work.* New York: Oxford University Press.

Erikson, E. (1950). *Childhood and society.* New York: Norton.

Erikson, E. (1963). *Childhood and society.* 2nd edition. New York: Norton.

Erikson, R., & Johnson, J. (1996). *Can education be equalized?* Boulder, CO: Westview Press.

Ernst, C., & Angst, J. (1983). *Birth order: Its influence on personality.* Berlin: Springer Verlag.

Esterling, B. A., Antoni, M. H., Fletcher, M. A., Margulies, S., & Schneiderman, N. (1994). Emotional disclosure through writing or speaking moderates latent Epstein-Barr virus antibody titers. *Journal of Consulting and Clinical Psychology, 62,* 130–140.

EUROSTAT (1997). Demographic statistics. Luxembourg, Eur OP.

Everett, J. E. (1983). Factor comparability as a means of determining the number of factors and their rotation. *Multivariate Behavioral Research, 18,* 197–218.

Eysenck, H. J. (1947). *Dimensions of personality.* London: Routledge and Kegan Paul.

Eysenck, H. J. (1959). *Manual for the Maudsley Personality Inventory.* London: University of London Press.

Eysenck, H. J. (1967). *The biological bases of personality.* Springfield, IL: Charles C. Thomas.

Eysenck, H. J. (1970). *The structure of personality* (3rd edition). London: Methuen.

Eysenck, H. J. (1978). Expectations as causal elements in behavioural change. *Advances in Behavior Research and Therapy, 1,* 171–175.

Eysenck, H. J. (1982a). Development of a theory. In H. J. Eysenck (Ed.) *Personality, genetics and behavior: Selected papers* (pp. 1–48). New York: Praeger.

Eysenck, H. J. (1982b). *Personality genetics and behavior.* New York: Praeger.

Eysenck, H. J. (1990). Biological dimensions of personality. In L. A. Pervin (Ed.), *Handbook of personality: Theory and research.* (pp. 244–276). New York: Guilford.

Eysenck, H. J. (1992a). Four ways five factors are not basic. *Personality and Individual Differences, 13,* 667–673.

Eysenck, H. J. (1992b). A hundred years of personality research, from Heymans to modern times. Bohn: Stafleu Van Loghum

Eysenck, H. J. (1993). The biological basis of intelligence. In P. A. Vernon (Ed.) Biological approaches to the study of human intelligence. (1–32). Norwood, NJ: Ablex.

Eysenck, H. J. (1994). Personality and intelligence: Psychometric and experimental approaches. In R. J. Sternberg & P. Ruzgis (Eds.) *Personality and intelligence* (pp. 3–31). New York: Cambridge University Press.

Eysenck, H. J., & Eysenck, S. B. G. (1964). *Manual for the Eysenck Personality Inventory.* London: University Press.

Eysenck, H. J., & Eysenck, S. B. G. (1975). *Manual for the Eysenck Personality Questionnaire.* London: Hodder and Stoughton.

Eysenck, S. B. G., Eysenck, H. J., & Barrett P. (1985). A revised version of the psychoticism scale. *Personality and Individual Differences, 6,* 21–29.

Fairbairn, R. D. (1952). Psychoanalytic studies of the personality. London: Tavistock Publications/Routledge & Kegan Paul.

Falconer, D. S. (1989). *Introduction to quantitative genetics* (3rd ed.) New York: Wiley.

Farber, I. E. (1964). A framework for the study of personality as a behavioral science. In P. Worchel & D. Byrne (Eds.), *Personality change* (pp. 3–37). New York: Wiley.

Farrell, M., Barnes, G. M., & Banerjee, S. (1995). Family cohesion as a buffer against the effects of problemdrinking fathers on psychological distress, deviant behavior, and heavy drinking in adolescents. *Journal of Health & Social Behavior, 36,* 377-385.

Fazio, R. H., Sanbonmatsu, D. M., Powell, M. C., & Kardes, F. R. (1986). On the automatic activation of attitudes. *Journal of Personality & Social Psychology, 50,* 229-238.

Feather, N. T. (1995). Values, valences, and choice: The influence of values on the perceived attractiveness and choice of alternatives. *Journal of Personality and Social Psychology, 68,* 1135–1151.

Feather, N. T., & Newton, J. W. (1982). Values, expectations, and the prediction of social action: An expectancy-valence analysis. *Motivation & Emotion, 6,* 217–244.

Feder, H. (1984). Hormones and sexual behavior. *Annual Review of Psychology, 35,* 165–200.

Feeney, J. A., Noller, P., & Hanrahan, M. (1994): Assessing adult attachment. In M. B. Sperling & W. B. Berman (Eds.), *Attachment in adults: Clinical and developmental perspectives* (pp. 128–152). New York: Guilford.

Feingold, A. (1988). Cognitive gender differences are disappearing. *American Psychologist, 43,* 95–103.

Feingold, A. (1992). Good looking people are not what we think. *Psychological Bulletin, 111,* 304–341.

Feingold, A. (1994). Gender differences in personality: A meta-analysis, *Psychological Bulletin, 116,* 429–456.

Fekken, G. C., & Holden, R. R. (1992). Response latency evidence for viewing personality traits as schema indicators. *Journal of Research in Personality, 26*, 103–120.

Feldman, L. A. (1995). Valence focus and arousal focus: Individual differences in the structure of affective experience. *Journal of Personality and Social Psychology, 69*, 153–166.

Feldman Barrett, L., & Russell, J. A. (1998). Independence and bipolarity in the structure of current affect. *Journal of Personality and Social Psychology, 74*, 967–984.

Feldman Barrett, L., & Russell, J. A. (1999). The structure of current affect: Controversies and emerging consensus. *Contemporary Directions in Psychological Science, 8*, 10–14.

Fenigstein, A., Scheier, M. F., & Buss, A. H. (1975). Public and private self-consciousness: Assessment and theory. *Journal of Consulting and Clinical Psychology, 43*, 522–527.

Fenigstein, A., & Vanable, P. A. (1992). Paranoia and self-consciousness. *Journal of Personality and Social Psychology, 62*, 129–138.

Feyerabend, P. K. (1975). *Against method: Outline of an anarchistic theory of knowledge*. London: NLB.

Finkel, D., & McGue, M. (1997). Sex differences and nonadditivity in heritability of the Multidimensional Personality Questionnaire Scales. *Journal of Personality and Social Psychology, 72*, 929–938.

Fish, S. (1980). *Is there a text in this class?* Cambridge, MA: Harvard University Press.

Fisher, C. S., Hout, M., Jankowski, M. S., Lucas, S. R., Swindler, A., & Voss, K. (1996). *Inequality by design*. Princeton, NJ: Princeton University Press.

Fisher, L., & Feldman, S. (1998). Familiar antecedants of young adult health risk behavior: A longitudinal study. *Journal of Family Psychology, 12*, 66–80. Check before using.

Fiske, A. P. (1991). *Structures of social life: The four elementary forms of human relations*. New York: Free Press.

Fiske, A. P. (1992). The four elementary forms of sociality: Framework for a unified theory of social relations. *Psychological Review, 99*, 689–723.

Fiske, A. P., Kitayama, S., Markus, H. R., & Nisbett, R. (1998). The cultural matrix of social psychology. In D. Gilbert, S. Fiske, & G. Lindzey (Eds.), *Handbook of social psychology* (4th ed., pp. 915–981). New York: McGraw-Hill.

Fiske, D. W. (1949). Consistency of factorial structures of personality ratings from different sources. *Journal of Abnormal and Social Psychology, 44*, 329–344.

Fiske, D. W. (1978). *Strategies for personality research*. San Francisco: Jossey-Bass.

Fiske, D. W. (1987). Construct invalidity comes from method effects. *Educational and Psychological Measurement, 47*, 285–307.

Fiske, S. T., Lau, R. R., & Smith, R. A. (1990). On the varieties and utilities of political expertise. *Social Cognition, 8*, 31–48.

Fiske, S. T., & Taylor, S. E. (1991). *Social Cognition*. New York: McGraw-Hill.

Fleeson, W. (1998). Across-time within-person structures of personality: Common and individual traits. In G. V. Caprara and D. Cervone (Chairs), *Personality and social cognition*. Symposium conducted at the 9th European Conference on Personality, Guildford, U.K.

Fleeson, W., & Heckhausen, J. (1997). More or less "me" in the past, present, and future: Perceived lifetime personality during adulthood. *Psychology and Aging, 12*, 125–136.

Flett, G. L., Endler, N. S., & Fairlie, P. (1999). The interaction model of anxiety and the threat of Quebec's separation from Canada. *Journal of Personality and Social Psychology, 76*, 143–150.

Flavell, J. H. (1992). Cognitive development: Past, present and future. *Developmental Psychology, 28*, 998–1005.

Flynn, J. R. (1999). Searching for justice: The discovery of IQ gains over time. *American Psychologist, 54*, 5–20.

Fodor, J. A. (1983). *The modularity of mind*. Cambridge, MA: MIT Press.

Fogel, A. (1993). *Developing through relationships*. New York: Harvester Wheatsheaf.

Fogel, A., Lyra, M. C. D. P., & Valsiner, J. (Eds.). (1997). *Dynamics and indeterminism in developmental and social processes*. Mahwah, N. J.: Erlbaum, 1997.

Folkman, S. (1997). Introduction to the special section: use of bereavement narratives to predict well-being in gay men whose partners died of AIDS – four theoretical perspectives. *Journal of Personality and Social Psychology, 72*, 851–854.

Fong, G. T., & Markus, H. (1982). Self-schemas and judgments about others. *Social Cognition, 1*, 191–204.

Ford, D., & Lerner, R. (1992). *Developmental systems theory*. Newbury Park, CA: Sage.

Forgas, J. P. (1995). Mood and judgment: The affect infusion model (AIM). *Psychological Bulletin, 117*, 39–66.

Forgas, J. P., Bower, G. H., & Moylan, S. J. (1990). Praise or blame? Affective influences on attributions for achievement. *Journal of Personality and Social Psychology, 59*, 809–819.

Forgas, J. P., & Van Heck, G. L. (1992). The psychology of situations. In G. V. Caprara & G. L. Van Heck (Eds.), *Modern personality psychology: Critical reviews and new directions*. (pp. 418–455) New York: Harvester Wheatsheaf.

Fox, N. A. (1991). If it's not left, it's right: Electroencephalograph asymmetry and the development of emotion. *American Psychologist, 46*, 863–972.

Fox, N. A. (1995). Of the way we were: Adult memories about attachment experiences and their role in determining infant-parent relationships: A commentary on van Ijzendoorn (1995). *Psychological Bulletin, 117*, 404–410.

Fraley, R. C., Waller, N. G., & Brennan, K. A. (2000). An item response theory analysis of self-report measures of adult attachment. *Journal of Personality and Social Psychology, 78*, 350–365.

Frankenhaeuser, M. (1991). The psychophysiology of workload, stress, and health: Comparison between the sexes. *Annals of Behavioral Medicine, 13*, 197–204.

Frankenhaeuser, M. (1994). A biopsychosocial approach to stress in woman and men. In V. J. Adesso, D. M. Reddy, & R. Fleming (Eds.), *Psychological perspectives on women's health* (pp. 39–56). Philadelphia, PA: Taylor & Francis.

Freud, A. (1936). *The ego and the mechanisms of defense*. London: The Hogarth Press.

Freud, A. (1965). *Normality and pathology in childhood*. New York: International Universities Press.

Freud, S. (1900). *The interpretation of dreams*. Standard Edition, (Vol. 4, pp. 1–338; Vol. 5 pp. 339–621). London: Hogarth Press, 1953.

Freud, S. (1911). *Formulations on the two principles of mental functioning*. Standard Edition (Vol. 12, pp. 218–226). London: Hogarth Press, 1958.

Freud, S. (1915). *Instincts and their vicissitudes*. Standard Edition (Vol. 14, pp. 117–140) London: Hogarth Press, 1957.

Freud, S. (1923). *The ego and the id*. Standard Edition (Vol. 18, pp. 12–66). London: Hogarth Press, 1961.

Freud, S. (1930). *Civilization and its discontents*. Standard Edition (Vol. 21, pp. 64–145) London: Hogarth Press, 1964.

Freud, S. (1933). *New introductory lectures on psychoanalysis*. New York: Norton.

Freund, A. M., & Baltes, P. B. (1998). Selection, optimization, and compensation as strategies of life management: Correlations with subjective indicators of successful aging. *Psychology and Aging, 13*, 531–543.

Frick, W. B. (1995). *Personality: Selected readings in theory*. Itasca, IL: F. E. Peacock.

Friedman, H. S., Tucker, J. S., Schwartz, J. E., Tomlinson-Keasey, C., Martin, L. R., Wingard, D. L., & Criqui, M. H. (1995). Psychosocial and behavioral predictors of longevity. *American Psychologist, 50*, 69–78.

Frijda, N. H. (1988). The laws of emotion. *American Psychologist, 43*, 349–358.

Frombonne, E. (1995). Depressive disorders: time trends and possible explanatory mechanisms. In M. Rutter & D. Smith (Eds.), *Psychosocial disorders in young people* (pp. 544–615). Chichester, UK: John Wiley & Sons.

Frome, P. M., & Eccles, J. S. (1998). Parents' influence on children's achievement-related perceptions. *Journal of Personality and Social Psychology, 74*, 435–452.

Froming, W. J., Nasby, W., & McManus, J. (1998). Prosocial self-schemas, self-awareness, and children's prosocial behavior. *Journal of Personality and Social Psychology, 75*, 766–777.

Fromm, E. (1947). *Man for himself*. New York: Rinehart.

Fromm, E. (1955). *The sane society*. New York: Rinehart.

Fuhrman, R. W., & Funder, D. C. (1995). Convergence between self and peer in the response-time processing of trait-relevant information. *Journal of Personality and Social Psychology, 69*, 961–974.

Fulker, D. W., Cherney, S. S., & Cardon, L. R. (1993). Continuity and change in cognitive development. In R. Plomin & G. E. McClearn (Eds.), *Nature, nurture, and psychology* (pp. 77–97). Washington, D. C.: American Psychological Association.

Funder, D. C. (1991). Global traits: A neo-Allportian approach to personality. *Psychological Science, 2*, 31–39.

Funder, D. C., & Block, J. (1989). The role of ego-control, ego-resiliency, and IQ in delay of gratification in adolescents. *Journal of Personality and Social Psychology, 57*, 1041–1050.

Funder, D. C., & Dobroth, K. M. (1987). Differences between traits: Properties associated with interjudge agreement. *Journal of Personality & Social Psychology, 52*, 409–418.

Galton, F. (1869). *Hereditary genius*. London: Macmillan.

Galton, F. (1884). Measurement of character. *Fortnightly Review, 36*, 179–185.

Gangested, S., & Snyder, M. (1985). "To carve nature at its joint": On the existence of discrete classes in personality. *Psychological Review, 92*, 317–349.

Gardner, D. B., Hawkes, G. R., & Burchinal, L. G. (1961). Noncontinuous mothering in infancy and development in later childhood. *Child Development, 32*, 225–234.

Gardner, H. (1983). *Frames of mind*. New York: Basic Books

Gardner, H. (1985). *The mind's new science*. New York: Basic Books.

Gardner, H. (1993). *Multiple intelligences: The theory in practice*. New York: Basic Books.

Gardner, R., Jackson, L., & Messick, S. (1960). Personality organization in cognitive controls and intellectual abilities. *Psychological Issues, 8*. New York: International University Press.

Garmezy, M. (1991). Resilience in children's adaptation to negative life events and stressed environments. *Pediatric Annals, 20*, 459–466.

Garraghty, P. E., Churchill, J. D., & Banks, M. K. (1998). Adult neural plasticity: Similarities between two paradigms. *Contemporary Directions in Psychological Science, 7,* 87–91.

Gasper, K., & Clore, G. L. (1998). The persistent use of negative affect by anxious individuals to estimate risk. *Journal of Personality and Social Psychology, 74,* 1350–1363.

Gazzaniga, M. S. (1992). *Nature's mind: The biological roots of thinking, emotions, sexuality, language and intelligence.* New York: Basic Books.

Gecas, V. (1990). Contexts of socialization. In M. Rosenberg & T. Turner (Eds.), *Social Psychology* (pp. 165–199). New Brunswick, NJ: Transaction Publishers.

Geen, R. (1997). Psychophysiological approaches to personality. In R. Hogan, J. Johnson & S. Briggs (Eds.), *Handbook of personality psychology.* (pp. 387–414). San Diego, CA: Academic Press.

Geer, J. H., Davison, G. C., & Gatchel, R. I. (1970). Reduction of stress in humans through nonveridical perceived control of aversive stimulation. *Journal of Personality and Social Psychology, 16,* 731–738.

Geertz, C. (1973). *The interpretation of cultures.* New York: Basic Books.

Geertz, C. (1975). On the nature of anthropological understanding. *American Scientist, 63,* 47–53.

Geertz, C. (1983). *Local knowledge.* New York: Basic Books.

Geertz, C. (1996). Welt in stucken. Kultur und politik am Endo des 20. *Jahrhunderts.* Wien, Passagen Verlag.

Gell-Mann, M. (1994). *The quark and the jaguar.* New York: Freeman.

Gelman, R., & Williams, E. M. (1998). Enabling constraints for cognitive development and learning: Domain-specificity and epigenesis. In W. Damon (Series Ed.) & D. Kuhn & R. S. Siegler (Vol. Eds.), *Handbook of Child Psychology* (5th Edition). Vol. 2: Cognition, perception, and language (pp. 575–630). New York: Wiley.

George, C., Kaplan, N., & Main, M. (1985). *Adult attachment interview.* Unpublished manuscript. University of California, Berkeley.

Gergen, K. J. (1993). *Refiguring self and psychology.* Aldershot, UK: Dartmouth Publishing Company, Ltd.

Gergen, K. J. (1994). Exploring the postmodern: Perils or potentials. *American Psychologist, 49,* 412–416.

Gergen, K. J. (1994). *Toward transformation in social knowledge* (2nd ed.). London: Sage.

Geymonat, L. (1970). *Storia del pensiero filosofico e scientifico.* Milano: Garzanti

Ghiselli, E. E. (1963). Moderating effects and differential reliability and validity. *Journal of Applied Psychology, 47,* 81–86.

Gibbon, E. (1776). *The decline and fall of the Roman Empire* (Vol. 1). New York: The Modern Library.

Giddens, A. (1990). *The consequences of modernity.* Cambridge: Polity.

Giddens, A. (1991). *Modernity and self identity: Self and society in the late modern age.* Stanford, CA: Stanford University Press.

Giddens, A. (1994). *Beyond left and right.* Cambridge: Polity Press.

Gilbert, D. T. (1989). Thinking lightly about others. In J. S. Uleman & J. A. Bargh (Eds.), *Unintended thought* (pp. 189–211). New York: Guilford.

Gilbert, D. T. (1991). How mental systems believe. *American Psychologist, 46,* 107–119.

Gilbert, D., Krull, D., & Pelham, B. (1988). Of thoughts unspoken: Social inference and the self-regulation of behavior. *Journal of Personality and Social Psychology, 55,* 685–694.

Gilbert, D. T., Pelham, B. W., & Krull, D. S. (1988). On cognitive busyness: When person perceivers meet persons perceived. *Journal of Personality & Social Psychology. 54,* 733–740.

Gill, C. (1996). *Personality in Greek epic, tragedy, and philosophy.* Oxford: Clarendon Press.

Gill, M. (1967). *Collected papers of Rapaport.* New York: Basic Books.

Gill, M. M. (1994). *Psychoanalysis in transition.* Hillsdale, NJ: Analytic Press.

Gilligan, C. (1982). *In a different voice: Psychological theory and women's development.* Cambridge, MA: Harvard University Press.

Glaser, R., Kennedy, S., Lafuse, W. P., Bonneau, R. H., Speicher, C., Hillhouse, J., & Keicolt-Glaser, J. K. (1990). Psychological-stress-induced modulation of interleukin 2 receptor gene expression and interleukin 2 production in peripheral blood leukocytes. *Archives of General Psychiatry, 47,* 707–712.

Glassman, N. S., & Andersen, S. M. (1999). Activating transference without consciousness: Using significant-other representations to go beyond what is subliminally given. *Journal of Personality and Social Psychology, 77,* 1146–1162.

Gleik, J. (1987). *Chaos: Making a new science.* New York: Penguin.

Glynn, S. M., & Ruderman, A. J. (1986). The development and validation of an eating self-efficacy scale. *Cognitive Therapy and Research, 10,* 403–420.

Goldberg, L. R. (1981). Language and individual differences: The search for universals in personality lexicons. In L. Wheeler (Ed.), *Review of personality and social psychology* (Vol. 2, pp. 141–165). Beverly Hills, CA: Sage.

Goldberg, L. R. (1982). From Ace to Zombie: some explorations in the language of personality. In C. D. Spielberger & J. N. Butcher (Eds.) *Advances in personality assessment* (Vol. 1, pp. 203–234). Hillsdale, NJ: Erlbaum.

Goldberg, L. R. (1990a). The development of markers for the Big-Five factor structure. *Psychological Assessment, 4,* 26–42.

Goldberg, L. R. (1990b). An alternative "description of personality": The Big-Five factor structure. *Journal of Personality and Social Psychology, 59,* 1216–1229.

Goldberg, L. R. (1993). The structure of phenotypic personality traits. *American Psychologist, 48,* 26–34.

Goldberg, L. R. (1994). How not to whip a straw dog. *Psychological Inquiry, 5,* 128–130.

Goldberg, L. R. (1999). International personality item pool: A scientific collaboratory for the development of advanced measures of personality and other individual differences. [On line.] Available web page: Http://ipip.ori.org/ipip.

Goldberg, L. R., & Saucier, G. (1995). So what do you propose we use instead? A reply to Block. *Psychological Bulletin, 117,* 221–225.

Goldsmith, H. H., & Alansky, J. A. (1987). Maternal and infant temperamental predictors of attachment: A meta-analytic review. *Journal of Consulting and Clinical Psychology, 55,* 805–816.

Goldsmith, H. H., Buss, K. A., & Lemery, K. S. (1997). Toddler and childhood temperament: Expanded content, stronger genetic evidence, new evidence for the importance of environment. *Developmental Psychology, 33,* 891–905.

Goldsmith, H. H., Losoya, S. H., Bradshaw, D. L., & Campos, J. J. (1994). Genetics of personality: A twin study of the five factor model and parent-offspring analyses. In C. F. Halverson, G. A. Kohnstamm & R. P. Martin (Eds.), *The developing structure of temperament and personality from infancy to adulthood* (pp. 241–265). Hillsdale, NJ: Erlbaum.

Goleman, D. (1988). *The meditative mind.* New York: Tarcher/Perigee Books.

Goleman, D. (1995). *Emotional intelligence.* New York: Bantam Books.

Gollwitzer, P. M. (1993). Goal achievement: The role of intentions. In W. Stroebe & M. Hewstone (Eds.), *European Review of Social Psychology* (Vol. 4, pp. 141–185). New York: Wiley.

Gollwitzer, P. M. (1996). The volitional benefits of planning. In P. M. Gollwitzer & J. A. Bargh (Eds.), *The psychology of action: Linking cognition and motivation to behavior* (pp. 287–312). New York: Guilford.

Gollwitzer, P. M. (1999). Implementation intentions: Strong effects of simple plans. *American Psychologist, 54,* 493–503.

Gollwitzer, P. M., & Brandstätter, V. (1997). Implementation intentions and effective goal pursuit. *Journal of Personality and Social Psychology, 73,* 186–199.

Gollwitzer, P. M., & Schaal, B. (1998). Metacognition in action: The importance of implementation intentions. *Personality and Social Psychology Review, 2,* 124–136.

Golombok, S., & Fivush, R. (1994). *Gender development.* New York: Cambridge University Press.

Gopnik, A. (1999, May 6). Small wonders (Review of the book *The Disciplined Mind: What all students should understand,* by H. Gardner). *The New York Review of Books, 46,* 33–35.

Gosling, S. D., & John, O. P. (1999). Personality dimensions in nonhuman animals: A cross-species review. *Contemporary Directions in Psychological Science, 8,* 69–75.

Gotlib, J. H., & Meyer, J. P. (1986). Factor analysis of the Multiple Affect Adjective Check List: A separation of positive and negative affect. *Journal of Personality & Social Psychology, 50,* 1161–1165.

Gottlieb, G. (1991). Experiential canalization of behavioral development: Theory. *Development Psychology, 27,* 4–13.

Gottlieb, G. (1992). *Individual development and evolution.* New York: Oxford University Press.

Gottlieb, G. (1998). Normally occurring environmental and behavioral influences on gene activity: From central dogma to probabilistic epigenesis. *Psychological Review, 105,* 792–802.

Gough, H. G. (1957). *California psychological inventory.* Palo Alto, CA: Consulting Psychologists Press.

Gough, H. G. (1987). *Manual: The California Personality Inventory.* Palo Alto, CA: Consulting Psychologists Press Inc.

Gould, S. J. (1981). *The mismeasure of man.* New York: Norton.

Gould, S. J. (1987). *An urchin in the storm.* New York: Norton

Gould, S. J., & Lewontin, R. C. (1979). The spandrels of San Marco and the Panglossian paradigm: A critique of the adaptationist programme. *Proceedings of the Royal Society of London, 205,* 581–598.

Goy, R., & McEwen, B. (1980). *Sexual differentiation of the brain.* Cambridge, MA: MIT Press.

Grant, H., & Dweck, C. (1999). A goal analysis of personality and personality coherence. In D. Cervone & Y. Shoda (Eds.), *The coherence of personality: Social-cognitive bases of consistency, variability, and organization* (pp. 345–371). New York: Guilford Press.

Gray, J. A. (Ed.) (1964). *Pavlov's typology.* Oxford: Pergamon.

Gray, J. A. (1987). *The psychology of fear and stress.* New York: Cambridge University Press.

Gray, J. A. (1989). Fundamental systems of emotion in the mammalian brain. In D. Palermo (Ed.), *Coping with uncertainty: Behavioral and developmental perspectives* (pp. 173–195). Hillsdale, NJ: Lawrence Erlbaum.

Gray, J. A. (1990). Brain systems that mediate both emotion and cognition. *Cognition and Emotion, 4,* 269–288.

Gray, J. A. (1991). Neural systems, emotion and personality. In J. Madden IV (Ed.), *Neurobiology of learning, emotion and affect.* New York: Raven Press.

Gray, J. A. (1994). Three fundamental emotion systems. In P. Ekman & R. J. Davidson (Eds.), *The nature of emotion: Fundamental questions* (pp. 243–247). New York: Oxford University Press.

Graziano, W. G., & Eisenberg, N. (1997). Agreeableness: A dimension of personality. In R. Hogan, J. Johnson & S. Briggs (Eds.), *Handbook of Personality Psychology.* (pp. 795–824). San Diego, CA : Academic Press.

Green, D. P., Goldman, S. L., & Salovey, P. (1993). Measurement error masks bipolarity in affect ratings. *Journal of Personality and Social Psychology, 64,* 1029–1041.

Greenberg, J. R., & Mitchell, S. A. (1983). *Objects relations in psychoanalytic theory.* Cambridge, MA: Harvard University Press.

Greenberg, L. S., & Safran, J. D. (1989). Emotion in psychotherapy. *American Psychologist, 44*(19–29).

Greenberg, M. A., & Stone, A. A. (1992). Emotional disclosure about traumas and its reltion to health: Effects of previous disclosure and trauma severity. *Journal of Personality and Social Psychology, 63,* 75–84.

Greenberg, M. A., Wortman, C. B., & Stone, A. A. (1996). Emotional expression and physical health: Revising traumatic memories or fostering self-regulation? *Journal of Personality and Social Psychology, 71,* 588–602.

Greeno, J. G. (1998). The situativity of knowing, learning, and research. *American Psychologist, 53,* 5–26.

Greenwald, A. G. (1992). New look 3: Unconscious cognition reclaimed. *American Psychologist, 47,* 766–779.

Greenwald, A. G., & Banaji, M. R. (1995). Implicit social cognition: Attitudes, self-esteem, and stereotypes. *Psychological Review, 102,* 4–27.

Greenwald, A. G., Draine, S. C., & Abrams, R. L. (1996). Three cognitive markers of unconscious semantic activation. *Science, 273,* 1699–702.

Greenwald, A. G., McGhee, D. E., & Schwartz, J. L. K (1998). Measuring individual differences in implicit cognition: The implicit association test. *Journal of Personality and Social Psychology, 74,* 1464–1480.

Greenwald, A. G., Spangenberg, E. R., Pratkanis, A. R., & Eskenazi, J. (1991). Doubleblind tests of subliminal self-help audiotapes. *Psychological Science, 2,* 119–122.

Griffin, D. W., & Bartholomew, K. (1994). The metaphysics of measurement: The case of adult attachment. In K. Bartholomew & D. Perlman (Eds.), *Attachment processes in adulthood* (pp. 17–52). London: Jessica Kingsley.

Grigorenko, E. L., Wood, F. B., Meyer, M. S., Hart, L. A., Speed, W. C., Shuster, A., & Pauls, D. L. (1997). Susceptibility loci for distinct components of developmental dyslexia on chromosomes 6 and 15. *American Journal of Human Genetics, 60,* 27–39.

Gross, J. (1999). Emotion and emotion regulation. In L. A. Pervin & O. P. John (Eds.), *Handbook of personality: Theory and research* (2nd ed., pp. 252–552). New York: Guilford.

Gross, D., Fogg, L., & Tucker, S. (1995). The efficacy of parent training for promoting positive parent-toddler relationships. *Research in Nursing and Health, 18,* 489–499.

Gross, J. J., & John, O. P. (1997). Revealing feelings: Facets of emotional expressivity in self-reports, peer rating, and behavior. *Journal of Personality and Social Psychology, 72,* 435–448.

Gross, J. J., & Levenson, R. W. (1993). Emotional suppression: Physiology, self-report, and expressive behavior. *Journal of Personality and Social Psychology, 64,* 970–986.

Gross, J. J., & Levenson, R. W. (1997). Hiding feelings: The acute effects of inhibiting negative and positive emotion. *Journal of Abnormal Psychology, 106,* 95–103.

Grossmann, K., Grossmann, K. E., Spangler, G., Suess, G., & Uzner, L. (1985). Maternal sensitivity and newborns' orientation responses as related to quality of attachment in northern Germany. In I. Bretherton & E. Waters (Eds.), *Growing points in attachment theory and research. Monographs of the Society for Research in Child Development, 50,* 233–278.

Gruber-Baldini, A. L., Shaie, K. W., & Willis, S. L. (1996). Similarity in married couples: A longitudinal study of marital abilities and rigidity-flexibility. *Journal of Personality and Social Psychology, 69,* 191–203.

Grunbaum, A. (1984). *The foundations of psychoanalysis: A philosophical critique.* Berkeley, CA.: University of California Press.

Gruzelier, J. H., & Mecacci, L. (1992). Brain, behavior, and personality. In G. V. Caprara & G. Van Heck (Eds.), *Modern personality psychology* (pp. 371–390). London: Harvester-Wheatsheaf.

Gudjonsson, G. J. (1981). Self-reported emotional disturbance and its relation to electrodermal reactivity, defensiveness and trait anxiety. *Personality and Individual Differences, 2,* 47–52.

Guenther, H. V., & Kawamura, L. S. (1975). *Mind in Buddist Psychology.* Berkeley, CA: Dharma Press.

Guidano, V. F. (1987). *The complexity of self.* New York: Guilford.

Guidano, V. F., & Liotti, G. (1983). *Cognitive processes and emotional disorders.* New York: Guilford.

Guilford, J. P. (1940). *Manual for an inventory of factors STDCR.* Beverly Hills, CA: Sheridan Supply.

Guilford, J. P. (1959). *Personality.* New York: McGraw Hill

Guilford, J. P. (1975). Factors and factors of personality. *Psychological Bulletin, 82,* 802–814.

Guilford J. P., & Martin H. G. (1943a). *The Guilford-Martin Inventory of factors GAMIN.* Beverly Hills, CA: Sheridan Supply.

Guilford, J. P., & Martin, H. G. (1943b). *The Personnel Inventory.* Beverly Hills, CA: Sheridan Supply.

Guilford, J. P., & Zimmerman, W. S. (1949). *The Guilford-Zimmerman temperament survey: A manual.* Beverly Hills, CA: Sheridan Supply.

Guilford, J. P., & Zimmerman, W. S. (1956). Fourteen dimensions of temperament. *Psychological Monographs, 70* (10, No. 417).

Gusdford, G. (1960). *Introduction aux sciences humaines.* Paris: Les Belles Letters.

Guthrie, W. K. C. (1962). *A history of Greek philosophy.* Cambridge, UK. Cambridge University Press.

Guttmann, J. (1993). *Divorce in psychosocial perspective.* Hillsdale, NJ: Lawrence Erlbaum.

Haaga, D. A. F., & Stewart, B. L. (1992). Self-efficacy for recovery from a lapse after smoking cessation. *Journal of Consulting and Clinical Psychology, 60,* 24–28.

Hackett, G., & Betz, N. (1995). Self-efficacy and career choice and development. In J. E. Maddux (Ed.), *Self-efficacy, adaptation, and adjustment: Theory, research, and application* (pp. 249–280). New York: Plenum Press.

Hahn, D., Lee, K., & Ashton, M. C. (1999). A factor analysis of the most frequently used Korean personality trait adjectives. *European Journal of Personality, 13,* 261–282.

Hall, C. S., & Lindzey, G. (1957). *Theories of personality.* New York: Wiley.

Hall, C. S., & Lindzey, G. (1978). *Theories of personality* (3rd Edition). New York: Wiley.

Hall, C. S., & Lindzey, G., & Campbell, J. B. (1998). *Theories of personality* (4th Edition). New York: Wiley.

Hall, G. S. (1904). *Adolescence: Its psychology and its relation to physiology, anthropology, sociology, sex, crime, religion, and education* (Vols. I and II). Englewood Cliffs, NJ: Prentice-Hall.

Halpern, D. F. (1995). Values, morals and modernity: the values, constraints and norms of European youth. In M. Rutter & D. Smith (Eds.), *Psychosocial disorders in young people.* (pp. 325–387). Chichester, UK: John Wiley & Sons.

Halpern, D. (1992). *Sex differences in cognitive abilities* (2nd ed.). Hillsdale,NJ: Erlbaum.

Halverson, C. F. Jr., Kohnstamm, G. A., & Martin, R. P. (Eds.) (1994). *The developing structure of temperament and personality from infancy to adulthood.* Hillsdale, NJ: Erlbaum.

Halverson, C. F., & Wampler, K. S. (1997). Family influences on personality development. In R.

Hogan, J. Johnson, & S. Briggs (Eds.) *Handbook of personality psychology.* (pp. 241–267). San Diego, CA: Academic Press.

Hampson, S. E., John, O. P., & Goldberg, L. R. (1986). Category breadth and hierarchical structure in personality: Studies of asymmetries in judgments of trait implications. *Journal of Personality and Social Psychology, 51,* 37–54.

Hansen, C. H., Hansen, R. D., & Shantz, D. W. (1992). Repression at encoding: Discrete appraisals of emotional stimuli. *Journal of Personality and Social Psychology, 63,* 1026–1035.

Hansen, R. D., & Hansen, C. H. (1988). Repression of emotionally tagged memories: The architecture of less complex emotions. *Journal of Personality and Social Psychology, 55,* 811–818.

Hanson, N. R. (1961). *Patterns of discovery: An inquiry into the conceptual foundations of science.* Cambridge, UK: Cambridge University Press.

Harkness, A. R., Tellegen, A., & Waller, N. (1995). Differential convergence of self-report and informant data for multidimensional personality questionnaire traits: Implications for the construct of negative emotionality. *Journal of Personality Assessment, 64,* 185–204.

Harlow, R. E., & Cantor, N. (1994). Social pursuit of academics: Side effects and spillover of strategic reassurance seeking. *Journal of Personality & Social Psychology, 66,* 386–397.

Harman, H. H. (1976). *Modern factor analysis* (2nd Ed.). Chicago, IL: University of Chicago Press.

Harmon-Jones, E., & Allen, J. B. (1998). Anger and frontal brain activity: EEG asymmetry consistent with approach motivation despite negative affective valence. *Journal of Personality and Social Psychology, 74,* 1310–1316.

Harper, L. V. (1989). *The nurture of human behavior.* Norwood, NJ: Ablex.

Harré, R. (1984). *Personal being: A theory for individual psychology.* Cambridge, Mass.: Harvard University Press, 1984.

Harré, R. (1998). *The singular self: An introduction to the psychology of personhood.* London: Sage.

Harré, R., Clarke, D., & de Carlo, N. (1985). *Motives and mechanisms: An introduction to the psychology of action.* London: Methuen.

Harré, R., & Secord, P. (1972). *The explanation of social behavior.* Oxford: Blackwell.

Harrington, D., Block, J. H., & Block. J. (1987). Testing aspects of Carl Rogers' theory of creative environments: Child-rearing antecedents of creative potential in young adolescents. *Journal of Personality and Social Psychology, 52,* 851–856.

Harris, J. R. (1995). Where is the child's environment? A group socialization theory of development. *Psychological Review, 102,* 458–489.

Harris, J. R. (1998). *The nurture assumption: Why children turn out the way they do.* New York: The Free Press.

Hart, D., Hofmann, V., Edelstein, W., & Keller, M. (1997). The relation of childhood personality types to adolescent behavior and development: A longitudinal study of Icelandic children. *Developmental Psychology, 33,* 195–205.

Hart, D., & Karmel, M. P. (1996). Self-awareness and self-knowledge in humans, apes, and monkeys. In A. E. Russon & K. A. Bard (Eds.), *Reaching into thought: The minds of the great apes* (pp. 325–347). Cambridge, U.K.: Cambridge University Press.

Hart, D., Stinson, C., Field, N., Ewert, M., & Horowitz, M. (1995). A semantic space approach to representations of self and other in pathological grief. *Psychological Science, 6,* 96–100.

Hart, D., & Yates, M. (1997). The interrelation of self and identity in adolescence: A developmental account. In R. Vasta (Ed.), *Annals of Child Development: A research annual.* (Vol. 12, pp. 207–243). London: Jessica Kingsley Publishers, Ltd.

Harter, S. (1986). Processes underlying the construction, maintenance, and enhancement of the self-concept in children. In J. Suls & A. G. Greenwald (Eds.), *Psychological perspectives on the self* (Vol. 3, pp. 137–181). Hillsdale, NJ: Erlbaum.

Harter, S. (1998). The development of self-representations. In W. Damon (Series Ed.) & N. Eisenberg (Vol. Ed.), *Handbook of Child Psychology* (5th Edition). Vol. 3: Social, emotional, and personality development (pp. 553–617). New York: Wiley.

Harter, S. (1999). *The construction of the self: A developmental perspective.* New York: Guilford.

Hartmann, H. (1939). *Ego psychology and the problem of adaptation.* New York: International Universities Press.

Hartshorn, H., & May, M. A. (1928). *Studies in the nature of character. Vol. 1: Studies in deceit.* New York: Macmillan.

Hartup, W. W. (1983). Peer relations. In P. Mussen (series Ed.) & M. Hetherington (Vol. Ed.), *Handbook of child psychology.* (4th edition) Vol. 4: Socialization, personality and social development. (pp. 103–196). New York: Wiley.

Hartup, W. W. (1992). Conflict and friendship relations. In C. Shantz & W. Hartup (Eds.), *Conflict in child and adolescent development* (pp. 186–215). New York: Cambridge University Press.

Hartup, W. W. (1996). The company they keep: Friendships and their developmental significance. *Child Development, 67,* 1–13.

Hartup, W. W., & Stevens, N. (1997). Friendship and adaptation in the life course. *Psychological Bulletin, 121,* 355–370.

Hartup, W. W., & Stevens, N. (1999). Friendships and adaptation across the life span. *Current Directions in Psychological Science, 8,* 76–79.

Hartup, W. W., & van Lieshout, C. F. M. (1995). Personality development in social context. *Annual Review of Psychology, 46,* 655–687.

Hauser, S. T. (1976). Loevinger's model and measure of ego development: A critical review. *Psychological Bulletin, 83,* 928–955.

Havighurst, R. J. (1972). *Developmental tasks and education.* New York: David McKay Co.

Havighurst, R. J. (1973). History of developmental psychology: Socialization and personality development through life-span. In P. B. Baltes & K. W. Shaie (Eds.), *Life-span developmental psychology.* New York: Academic Press.

Hayes, A. F., & Dunning, D. (1997). Construal processes and trait ambiguity. *Journal of Personality and Social Psychology, 72,* 664–677.

Hazan, C., & Shaver, P. R. (1987). Romantic love conceptualized as an attachment process. *Journal of Personality and Social Psychology, 52,* 511–524.

Hazan, C., & Shaver, P. R. (1994). Attachment as an organizational framework for research on close relationships. *Psychological Inquiry, 5,* 1–22.

Hebb, D. O. (1949). *The organization of behavior.* New York: Wiley.

Hebb, D. O. (1955). Drives and the C.N.S. (conceptual nervous system). *Psychological Review, 62,* 243–254.

Heckhausen, H. (1967). *The anatomy of achievement motivation.* New York: Academic Press.

Heckhausen, H. (1991). *Motivation and action.* Berlin: Springer.

Heckhausen, H., & Gollwitzer, P. M. (1987). Thought contents and cognitive functioning in motivational versus volitional states of mind. *Motivation and Emotion, 11,* 101–120.

Heckhausen, J., & Schulz, R. (1995). A life-span theory of control. *Psychological Review, 102,* 284–304.

Heckhausen, J., & Schulz, R. (1998). Developmental regulation in adulthood: Selection and compensation via primary and secondary control. In J. Heckhausen & C. S. Dweck (Eds.), *Motivation and self-regulation across the life span.* New York: Cambridge.

Heider, F. (1958). *The psychology of interpersonal relations.* New York: Wiley.

Heine, S. J., & Lehman, D. R. (1997). Culture, dissonance, and self-affirmation. *Personality and Social Psychology Bulletin, 23,* 389–400.

Heine, S. J., Lehman, D. R., Markus, H. R., & Kitayama, S. (1999). Is there a universal need for positive self-regard? *Psychological Review, 106,* 766–794.

Heller, W., Nitschke, J. B., & Miller, G. A. (1998). Lateralization in emotion and emotional disorders. *Current Directions in Psychological Science, 7,* 26–32.

Helson, R., Mitchell, V., & Moane, G. (1984). Personality and patterns of adherence and nonadherence to the social clock. *Journal of Personality and Social Psychology, 46,* 1079–1096.

Helson, R., Pals, J., & Solomon, M. (1997). Is there adult development distinctive to women. In R. Hogan, J. Johnson, & S. Briggs (Eds.), *Handbook of Personality Psychology.* (pp. 291–314). San Diego, CA : Academic Press.

Hendrick, S. Hendrick, C., Slapion-Foote, M. J., & Foote, F. H. (1985). Gender differences in sexual attitudes. *Journal of Personality and Social Psychology, 48,* 1630–1642.

Hendriks, A. A. J., Hofstee, W. K. B., & De Raad, B. (1999). The five-factor personality inventory (FFPI). *Personality and Individual Differences, 27,* 307–325.

Hermans, H. J. M. (1992). Telling and retelling one's self-narrative: A contextual approach to life-span development. *Human Development, 35,* 361–375.

Hermans, H. J. M., & Kempen, H. J. (1998). Moving cultures: The perilous problems of cultural dichotomies in a globalizing society. *American Psychologist, 53,* 1111–1120.

Hermans, H. J. M., Kempen, H. J., & van Loon, R. J. (1992). The dialogical self. *American Psychologist, 47,* 23–33.

Hermans, H. J. M. (1996). Voicing the self: From information processing to dialogical exchange. *Psychological Bulletin, 119,* 31–50.

Herrnstein, R., & Murray, C. (1994). The Bell Curve: Intelligence and class structure in American life. New York: The Free Press.

Hess, L. (1995). Changing family patterns in Western Europe: Opportunity and risk factors for adolescent development. In M. Rutter & D. Smith (Eds.), *Psychosocial disorders in young people* (pp. 104–193). Chichester, UK: John Wiley & Sons

Hetherington, E. M. (1988). Parents, children and siblings six years after divorce. In R. A. Hinde & J. Stevenson-Hinde (Eds.), *Relationships within families: Mutual influences* (pp. 311–333). Oxford: Clarendon Press.

Hetherington, E. M., Reiss, D., & Plomin, R. (1994). *Separate social worlds of siblings: Impact of non-shared environment on development.* Hillsdale, NJ: Lawrence Erlbaum.

Hettema, P. J. (1979). *Personality and adaptation.* Amsterdam: North-Holland.

Hettema, P. J. (1989). Principles of personality assessment. In P. J. Hettema (Ed.), *Personality and Environment: Assessment of Human Adaptation* (pp. 31–45). Chichester, U. K.: Wiley.

Hettema, P. J. (1993). Adaptation: A biosocial approach to personality. In G. L. Van Heck, & P. Bonaiuto (Eds.). *Personality psychology in Europe* (Vol. 4, pp. 63–84). Tilburg, Netherlands: Tilburg University Press.

Hettema, P. J., & Kenrick, D. (1992). Models of person-situation interactions. In G. V. Caprara & G.

Van Heck (Eds). *Modern personality psychology* (pp. 393–417). London: Harvester-Weatsheaf.

Hettema, P. J., Leidelmeijer, K. C., & Geenen, R. (2000). Dimensions of information processing: Phsyiological reactions to motion pictures. *European Journal of Personality, 14,* 39–63.

Heymans, G., & Wiersma, E. (1906–1909). Beitrage zur speziellen psychologie auf grund einer masse-nuntersuchung. *Zeitschrift fur Psychologie, 42,* 81–127/258–301; 43, 321–373; 45, 1–42; 46, 321–333; 49, 414–439; 51, 1–72.

Higgins, E. T. (1987). Self-discrepancy: A theory relating self and affect. *Psychological Review, 94,* 319–340.

Higgins, E. T. (1989). Continuities and discontinuities in self-regulatory and self-evaluative processes: A developmental theory relating self and affect. *Journal of Personality, 57,* 407–444.

Higgins, E. T. (1990). Personality, social psychology, and person-situation relations: Standards and knowledge activation as a common language. In L. A. Pervin (Ed.), *Handbook of personality: Theory and Research* (pp. 301–338). New York: Guilford.

Higgins, E. T. (1996a). Knowledge activation: Accessibility, applicability, and salience. In E. T. Higgins & A. W. Kruglanski (Eds.), *Social Psychology: Handbook of basic principles* (133–168). New York: Guilford.

Higgins, E. T. (1996b). The "self-digest": Self-knowledge serving self-regulatory functions. *Journal of Personality & Social Psychology, 71,* 1062–1083.

Higgins, E. T. (1997). Beyond pleasure and pain. *American Psychologist, 52,* 1280–1300.

Higgins, E. T. (1999). Persons and situations: Unique explanatory principles or variability in general principles? In D. Cervone & Y. Shoda (Eds.), *The coherence of personality: Social-cognitive bases of consistency, variability, and organization* (pp. 61–93). New York: Guilford Press.

Higgins, E. T., Bond, R. N., Klein, R., & Strauman, T. (1986). Self-discrepancies and emotional vulnerability: How magnitude, accessibility, and type of discrepancy influence affect. *Journal of Personality and Social Psychology, 51,* 5–15.

Higgins, E. T., & Brendl, C. M. (1995). Accessibility and applicability: Some "activation rules" influencing judgment. *Journal of Experimental Social Psychology, 31,* 218–243.

Higgins, E. T., & King, G. (1981). Accessibility of social constructs: Information processing consequences of individual and contextual variability. In N. Cantor & J. Kihlstrom (Eds.), *Personality, cognition, and social interaction.* Hillsdale, NJ: Erlbaum.

Higgins, E. T., King, G. A., & Mavin, G. H. (1982). Individual construct accessibility and subjective impressions and recall. *Journal of Personality and Social Psychology, 43,* 35–47.

Higgins, E. T., Rholes, W. S., & Jones, C. R. (1977). Category accessibility and impression formation. *Journal of Experimental Social Psychology, 13,* 141–154.

Higgins, E. T., Roney, C., Crowe, E., & Hymes, C. (1994). Ideal versus ought predilections for approach versus avoidance: Distinct self-regulatory systems. *Journal of Personality and Social Psychology, 66,* 276–286.

Higgins, E. T., & Silberman, I. (1998). Development of regulatory focus: Promotion and prevention as ways of living. In J. Heckhausen & C. S. Dweck (Eds.), *Motivation and self-regulation across the life span* (pp. 78-113). New York: Cambridge University Press.

Higgins, E. T., & Sorrentino, R. M. (Eds.) (1990). *Handbook of motivation and cognition* (Vol. 2). New York: Guilford.

Higgins, E. T., Vookles, J., & Tykocinski, O. (1992). Self and health: How "patterns" of self-beliefs predict types of emotional and physical problems. *Social Cognition, 10,* 125–150.

Hilgard, E. (1980). The trilogy of mind: Cognition, affection, and conation. *Journal of the History of Behavioral Sciences, 16,* 107–117.

Hill, G. J. (1989). An unwillingness to act: Behavioral appropriateness, situational constraints, and self-efficacy in shyness. *Journal of Personality, 57,* 871–890.

Hinde, R. (1979). *Towards understanding relationships.* London: Academic Press.

Hinde, R. A. (1997). *Relationships: A dialectical perspective.* Cambridge: Psychology Press.

Hinkley, K., & Andersen, S. M. (1996). The working self-concept in transference: Significant-other activation and self change. *Journal of Personality and Social Psychology, 71,* 1279–1295.

Hinsz, V. B., Kalnbach, L. R., & Lorentz, N. R. (1997). Using judgmental anchors to establish challenging self-set goals without jeopardizing commitment. *Organizational Behavior & Human Decision Processes, 71,* 287–308.

Hock, M., Krohne, H. W., & Kaiser, J. (1996). Coping dispositions and the processing of ambiguous stimuli. *Journal of Personality and Social Psychology, 70,* 1052–1066.

Hoffman, L. (1991). The influence of the family environment on personality: Accounting for sibling differences. *Psychological Bulletin, 110,* 187–203.

Hofstadter, D. R. (1979). *Gödel, Escher, & Bach: An eternal golden braid.* New York: Basic Books.

Hofstee, W. K. B., & De Raad, B. (1992). Personality structure through traits. In G. V. Caprara & G. Van Heck (Eds.) *Modern personality psychology* (pp. 29–55). London: Harvester Wheatsheaf.

Hofstee, W. K. B., De Raad, B., & Goldberg, L. R. (1992). Integration of the Big Five and circumplex approaches to trait structure. *Journal of Personality and Social Psychology, 63,* 146–163.

Hogan, D., & Lichter, D. (1995). Children and youth: Living arrangements and welfare. In R. Farley (Ed.), *State of the Union.* (pp. 93–139). New York: Russell Sage Foundation.

Hogan, R. (1986). *Hogan Personality Inventory manual.* Minneapolis, MN: National Computer Systems.

Hogan, R., Johnson, J., & Briggs, S. (Eds.) (1997). *Handbook of personality psychology.* San Diego, CA: Academic Press.

Hogan, J., & Ones, D. S. (1997). Conscientiousness and integrity at work. In R. Hogan, J. Johnson & S. Briggs (Eds.), *Handbook of personality psychology* (pp. 849–870). San Diego, CA: Academic Press.

Holahan, C. K. (1984). Marital attitudes over 40 years: A longitudinal and cohort analysis. *Journal of Gerontology, 39,* 49–57.

Holden, R. R., & Fekken, G. C. (1993). Can personality test item response latencies have construct validity? Issues of reliability and convergent and discriminant validity. *Personality and Individual Differences, 15,* 243–248.

Holmes, D. S. (1974). Investigations of repression: Differential recall of material experimentally or naturally associated with ego threat. *Psychological Bulletin, 81,* 632–653.

Holroyd, K. A., Penzien, D. B., Hursey, K. G., Tobin, D. L., Rogers, L., Holm, J. E., Marcille, P. J., Hall, J. R., & Chila, A. G. (1984). Change mechanisms in EMG biofeedback training: Cognitive changes underlying improvements in tension headache. *Journal of Consulting and Clinical Psychology, 52,* 1039–1053.

Holt, R. (1958). Clinical and statistical prediction. *Journal of Abnormal and Social Psychology, 56,* 1–12.

Holt, R. (1962). Individuality and generalization in the psychology of personality. *Journal of Personality, 30,* 377–404.

Holt, R. (1978). *Methods in clinical psychology.* New York : Plenum

Holt, R. (1989). *Freud reappraised.* New York: Guilford.

Holtzkamp, K. (1973). *Kritische psychologie. Vorbereitende Arbeiten.* Stuttgart: Georg Thieme Verlag.

Hood, K., Draper, P., Crockett, L., & Petersen, A. (1987). The ontogeny and phylogeny of sex differences in development: A biopsychosocial synthesis. In D. Carter (Ed.), *Current conceptions of sex roles and sex typing* (pp. 49–77). New York: Praeger.

Horkeimer, M. (Ed.) (1936). *Studien über authorität und familie.* Paris: Alcan.

Horn, J. L. (1982). The theory of fluid and crystallized intelligence in relation to concepts of cognitive psychology and aging in adulthood. In F. I. M. Craik & S. Trehub (Eds.), *Aging and cognitive processes* (pp. 237–278). New York: Plenum.

Horney, K. (1939). *New ways in psychoanalysis*. New York: Norton.

Horney, K. (1950). *Neurosis and human growth*. New York: Norton.

Horowitz, M. J. (1991a). Converging several methods for inferring person schemas. In M. J. Horowitz (Ed.), *Person schemas and maladaptive interpersonal patterns* (pp. 303–310). Chicago: University of Chicago Press.

Horowitz, M. J. (1991b). Person schemas. In M. J. Horowitz (Ed.), *Person schemas and maladaptive interpersonal patterns* (pp. 13–31). Chicago: University of Chicago Press.

Hough L. M., Hanser L. M., & Eaton N. K. (1988). *Literature review: Utility of temperament, biodata and interest assessment for predicting job performance*. Alexandria: US Army, Research Institute for the Behavioral and Social Sciences (ARI research note 88–02).

House, J. (1990). Social structure and personality. In M. Rosenberg & R. Turner (Eds.), *Social Psychology* (pp. 525–561). New Brunswick, NJ: Transaction Publishers.

Houts, A., Cook, T., & Shadish, W. (1986). The person-situation debate: A critical multiplist perspective. *Journal of Personality, 54*, 52–105.

Hrebickova, M. (1995). *The structural model of personality based on the lexical analysis: A Czech replication study of the Five-Factor Model based on a comprehensive taxonomy of personality-descriptive adjectives*. Unpublished report, Institute of Psychology, Academy of Sciences of the Czech Republic, Brno.

Hubbard, J. A., Dodge, K. A., Coie, J. D., Cillessen, A. H. N., & Schwartz, D. (1998). *The dyadic nature of social-information-processing in children's reactive and proactive aggression*. Unpublished manuscript, University of Delaware.

Huber, V. L., & Neale, M. A. (1987). Effects of self- and competitor goals in performance in an interdependent bargaining task. *Journal of Applied Psychology, 72*, 197–203.

Huesmann, L. R. (1988). An information processing model for the development of aggression. *Aggressive Behavior, 14*, 13–24.

Huesmann, L. R. (1997). Observational learning of violent behavior: Social and biosocial processes. In A. Raine, D. P. Farrington, P. O. Brennen, & S. A. Mednick (Eds.), *Biosocial basis of violence* (pp. 69–88). New York: Plenum Press.

Huesmann, L. R., & Eron, L. D. (1986). *Television and the aggressive child: A cross national comparison*. Hillsdale, NJ: Lawrence Erlbaum.

Hull, C. L. (1943). *Principles of behavior: An introduction to behavior theory*. New York: Appleton.

Humphrey, N. (1984). *Consciousness regained*. Oxford: Oxford University Press.

Humphrey, N. (1992). *A history of the mind*. London: Chatto & Windus.

Hunt, E. (1983). On the nature of intelligence. *Science, 219*, 141–146.

Hunt, N. (1993). *The story of psychology*. New York : Doubleday.

Hurrelmann, K. (1988). *Social structure and personality development*. New York: Cambridge University Press.

Huston, A. (1983). Sex-Typing. In P. H. Mussen (Ed.), *Handbook of child psychology. Socialization, personality and social development*. (Vol. 4, 4th ed., pp. 387–467), New York: John Wiley & Sons.

Hyde, J., Fennema, E., & Lamon, S.(1990). Gender differences in mathematics performance: A meta-analysis. *Psychological Bulletin, 107*, 139–155.

Hyde, J., & Linn, M. (1988). Gender differences in verbal ability: A meta-analysis. *Psychological Bulletin, 104*, 53–69.

Imperato-McGinley, J., Peterson, R., Gautier, T., & Sturla, E. (1979). Androgens and the evolution of male-gender identity among male pseudohermaphrodites with 5 alpha-reductase deficiency. *New England Journal of Medicine, 300*, 1233–1237.

Inglehart, R. (1990). *Culture shift in advanced industrial society*. Princeton: Princeton University Press.

Inglehart, R. (1996). *Modernization and post-modernization: Cultural, economic, and political change in 43 societies*. Princeton, NJ: Princeton University Press.

Isabella, R. A. (1993). Origins of attachment: Maternal interactive behavior across the first year. *Child Development, 64*, 605–621.

Isen, A. M., Shalker, T., Clark, M., & Karp, L. (1978). Affect, accessibility of material in memory and behavior: A cognitive loop? *Journal of Personality and Social Psychology, 36*, 1–12.

Iyengar, S. S., & Lepper, M. R. (1999). Rethinking the value of choice: A cultural perspective on intrinsic motivation. *Journal of Personality and Social Psychology, 76*, 349–366.

Izard, C. E. (1977). *Human emotions*. New York: Plenum.

Izard, C. E. (1992). Basic emotions, relations among emotions, and emotion-cognition relations. *Psychological Review, 99*, 561–565.

Izard, C. E. (1994). Intersystem connections. In P. Ekman & R. J. Davidson (Eds.), *The nature of emotion: Fundamental questions* (pp. 356–361). New York: Oxford University Press.

Izard, C. E., Libero, D. Z., Putnam, P., & Haynes, O. M. (1993). Stability of emotion experiences and their relations to traits of personality. *Journal of Personality and Social Psychology, 64*, 847–860.

Jaccoby, L. L., Toth, J. P., Lindsay, D. S., & Debner, J. A. (1992). Lectures for a layperson: Methods for revealing unconscious process. In R. F. Bornstein & T. S. Pittman (Eds.), *Perception without awareness* (pp. 81–120). New York: Guilford.

Jaccoby, L. L., Woloshyn, V., & Kelley, C. M. (1989). Becoming famous without being recognized: Unconscious influences of memory produced by dividing attention. *Journal of Experimental Psychology: General*, 118, 115–125.

Jackson, D. N. (1984). *Personality research form manual* (3rd ed.). Port Huron, Mich: Research Psychologists Press.

Jackson, D. N., & Paunonen, S. V. (1985). Construct validity and the predictability of behavior. *Journal of Personality and Social Psychology*, 49, 554–570.

Jacob, F. (1970). *La logique du vivant. Une histoire de l'hérédité*. Paris: Gallimard.

Jahoda, G. (1993). *Crossroads between culture and mind: Continuities and change in theories of human nature*. Cambridge, MA: Harvard University Press.

James, W. (1890). *Principles of Psychology*. New York: Holt.

James, W. (1884). What is an emotion? *Mind*, 9, 188–205.

Janet, P. (1889). *L'automatisme psychologique*. Paris: Alcan.

Janet, P. (1929). *L'évolution psychologique de la personalité*. Paris: Chahine.

Jensen, A. J. (1998). *The g factor*. Praeger: New York

Jensen, M. P., Turner, J. A., & Romano, J. M. (1991). Self-efficacy and outcome expectancies: Relationship to chronic pain coping strategies and adjustment. *Pain*, 44, 263–269.

Jervis, G. (Ed) (1999). *Il Secolo della Psicoanalisi*. Torino: Bollati Boringhieri.

Jessor, R. (1998). New perspectives on adolescent risk behavior. New York: Cambridge University Press.

John, O. P. (1990). The "Big Five" factor taxonomy: Dimensions of personality in the natural language and in questionnaires. In L. A. Pervin (Ed.), *Handbook of Personality: Theory and Research* (pp. 66–100). New York: Guilford.

John, O. P., Angleitner, A., & Ostendorf, F. (1988). The lexical approach to personality: A historical review of trait taxonomic research. *European Journal of Personality*, 2, 171–203.

John, O. P., Pals, J. L., & Westenberg, P. M. (1998). Personality prototypes and ego development: Conceptual similarities and relations in adult women. *Journal of Personality and Social Psychology*, 74, 1093–1108.

John, O. P., & Srivastava, S. (1999). The big-five factor taxonomy: History, measurement, and theoretical perspectives. In L. A. Pervin & O. P. John (Eds.), *Handbook of personality: Theory and research* (pp. 102–138). New York: Guilford.

Johnson-Laird, P. N. (1988). *The computer and the mind: An introduction to cognitive science*. Cambridge, MA: Harvard University Press.

Jones, E. E., & Davis, K. E. (1965). From acts to dispositions: The attribution process in person perception. In L. Berkowitz (Ed.), *Advances in experimental social psychology (Vol 2, pp. 220–266)*. New York: Academic Press.

Jones, R. A. (1977). *Self-fulfilling prophesies. Social, psychological and physiological effects of experiences*. Hillsdale, NJ: Erlbaum.

Jung, C. G. (1917). On the psychology of the unconscious. *Collected works, Vol. 7*. Princeton, NJ: Princeton University Press, 1953.

Jung, C. G. (1918). *Studies in word-association*. London: Heinemann.

Jung, C. G. (1921). *Psychological types. Collected works, Vol. 6*. Princeton, NJ: Princeton University Press, 1971.

Jung, C. G. (1928). *On psychic energy. Collected Works, Vol. 8*. Princeton, NJ: Princeton University Press, 1960.

Jussim, L. (1991). Social perception and social reality. *Psychological Review*, 98, 54–73.

Jussim, L., & Eccles, J. S. (1995). Naturally occurring interpersonal expectancies. *Review of Personality and Social Psychology*, 15, 74–108;

Kagan, J. (1980). Perspectives on continuity. In O. G. Brim & J. Kagan (Eds.), *Constancy and change in human development* (pp. 26–74). Cambridge, MA: Harvard University Press.

Kagan, J. (1988). The meaning of personality predicates. *American Psychologist*, 43, 614–620.

Kagan, J. (1994a). Distinctions among emotions, moods, and temperamental qualities. In P. Ekman & R. J. Davidson (Eds.), *The nature of emotion: Fundamental questions* (pp. 74–78). New York: Oxford University Press.

Kagan, J. (1994b). *Galen's prophecy: Temperament in human nature*. New York: Basic Books.

Kagan, J. (1996). Three pleasing ideas. *American Psychologist*, 51, 901–908.

Kagan, J. (1998a). Biology and the child. In W. Damon (Series Ed.) & N. Eisenberg (Volume Ed.) *Handbook of child development* (5th ed.). Vol. 3: *Emotional and personality development* (pp. 177–236). New York: Wiley.

Kagan, J. (1998b). *Three seductive ideas*. Cambridge, MA: Harvard University Press.

Kagan, J., Reznick, J. S., & Snidman, N. (1988). Biological bases of childhood shyness. *Science*, 240, 167–171.

Kagan, J., & Zentner, M. (1996). Early childhood predictors of adult psychopathology. *Harvard Review of Psychiatry*, 3, 341–350.

Kahneman, D., & Tversky, A. (1979). Prospect theory: An analysis of decision under risk. *Econometrica*, 47, 263–292.

Kahneman, D., & Tversky, A. (1984). Choices, values, and frames. *American Psychologist*, 39, 341–350.

Kamin L. J. (1974). *The science and politics of I. Q.* Potomac, MD: Erlbaum.

Kant, I. (1781). *The critique of pure reason* (J. M. D. Meiklejohn, Trans.). London: Bohn.

Kant, I. (1798/1947). *Anthropology from a pragmatic point of view.* The Hague: Nijhoff.

Kardiner, A., & Linton, R. (1939). *The individual and his society.* New York: Columbia University Press.

Karli, P. (1995). *Le cerveau et la liberté.* Paris: Editions Odile Jacob.

Karli, P. (1996). The brain and socialization: A two way mediation across the life course. In D. Magnusson (Ed.), *The life span development of individuals: behavioral, neurobiological, and psychosocial perspectives* (pp. 341–356). New York: Cambridge University Press.

Karli, P. (In press/1999). On the affective nature of "human nature": A neurobiologist's reflections. In M. Haug & R. E. Whalen (Eds.), *Animal models of human emotion and cognition.* Washington, D. C.: American Psychological Association.

Karmiloff-Smith, A. (1992). *Beyond modularity: A developmental perspective on cognitive science.* Cambridge, MA: MIT Press.

Karmiloff-Smith, A. (1994). Précis of beyond modularity: A developmental perspective on cognitive science. *Behavioral and Brain Sciences, 17,* 693–745.

Karney, B. R., & Bradbury, T. N. (1995). The longitudinal course of marital quality and stability: A review of theory, method and research. *Psychological Bulletin, 118,* 3–34.

Karniol., R., & Ross, M. (1996). The motivational impact of temporal focus: Thinking about the future and the past. *Annual Review of Psychology, 47,* 593–620.

Karoly, P. (1993a). Goal systems: An organizing framework for clinical assessment and treatment planning. *Psychological Assessment, 5,* 273–280.

Karoly, P. (1993b). Mechanisms of self-regulation: A systems view. *Annual Review of Psychology, 44,* 23–52.

Katigbak, M. S., Church, A. T., & Akamine, T. X. (1996). Cross-cultural generalizability of personality dimensions: Relating indigenous and imported dimensions in two cultures. *Journal of Personality and Social Psychology, 70,* 99–144.

Kavanagh, D. J., & Bower, G. H. (1985). Mood and self-efficacy: Impact of joy and sadness on perceived capabilities. *Cognitive Therapy and Research, 9,* 507–525.

Kazdin, A. E. (1974). Reactive self-monitoring: The effects of response desirability, goal setting, and feedback. *Journal of Consulting and Clinical Psychology, 42,* 704–716.

Kelley, H. H. (1979). *Personal relationships.* Hillsdale, NJ: Erlbaum.

Kelley, H. H. (1992). Common sense psychology and scientific psychology. *Annual Review of Psychology, 43,* 1–23.

Kelley, H. H., & Thibaut, J. W. (1978). *Interpersonal relations: A theory of interdependence.* New York: Wiley

Kelly, E. L., & Conley, J. J. (1987). Personality and compatibility: A prospective analysis of marital stability and marital satisfaction. *Journal of Personality and Social Psychology, 52,* 27–40.

Kelly, G. (1955). *The psychology of personal constructs.* New York: Norton.

Kelly, J. G. (1971). The coping process in varied high school environments. In M. J. Feldman (Ed.), *Studies in psychotherapy and behavioral change: No. 2, Theory and research in community mental health* (pp. 95–166). Buffalo, NY: State University of New York at Buffalo.

Keltner, D., & Buswell, B. N. (1997). Embarrassment: Its distinct form and appeasement functions. *Psychological Bulletin, 122,* 250–270.

Keltner, D., Kring, A. M., & Bonanno, G. A. (1999). Fleeting signs of the course of life: Facial expression and personal adjustment. *Contemporary Directions in Psychological Science, 8,* 18–22.

Keltner, D., Moffit, T., & Stouthamer-Loeber, M. (1995). Facial expressions of emotion and psychopathology in adolescent boys. *Journal of Abnormal Psychology, 104,* 644–652.

Kendler, K. S., Neale, M. C., Kessler, R. C., Heath, A. C., & Eaves, L. J. (1992). Childhood parental loss and adult psychopathology in women: A twin perspective. *Archives of General Psychiatry, 49,* 109–116.

Kendzierski, D., & Whitaker, D. J. (1997). The role of self-schema in linking intentions with behavior. *Personality and Social Psychology Bulletin, 23,* 139–147.

Kenny, D. A., Albright, L., Malloy, T. E., & Kashy, D. A. (1994). Consensus in interpersonal perception: Acquaintance and the Big Five. *Psychological Bulletin, 116,* 245–258.

Kenny, D. A., & Kashy, D. A. (1992). Analysis of the multitrait-multimethod matrix by confirmatory factor analysis. *Psychological Bulletin, 112,* 165–172.

Kenrick, D. T., & Dantchik, A. (1983). Interactionism, idiographics, and the social-psychological invasion of personality. *Journal of Personality, 51,* 286–307.

Kenrick, D. T., & Funder, D. C. (1988). Profiting from controversy: Lessons from the person-situation debate. *American Psychologist, 43,* 23–34.

Kenrick, D. T., & Keefe, R. C. (1992). Age preferences in mates reflect sex differences in reproductive strategies. *Behavioral and Brain Sciences, 15,* 75–133.

Kent, G., & Gibbons, R. (1987). Self-efficacy and the control of anxious cognitions. *Journal of Behavior Therapy and Experimental Psychiatry, 18,* 33–40.

Kernberg, O. (1976). *Object relations theory and clinical psychoanalysis.* New York: Jason Aronson.

Kernberg, O. (1980). *Internal world and external reality.* New York: Jason Aronson.

Kihlstrom, J. F. (1984). Conscious, subconscious, and unconscious: A cognitive view. In K. S.

Bowers & D. Meichenbaum (Eds.), *The uncon-scious reconsidered* (pp. 149–211). New York: Wiley-interscience.

Kihlstrom, J. F. (1990). The psychological uncon-scious. In L. A. Pervin (Ed.), *Handbook of person-ality: Theory and research* (pp. 445–464). New York: Guilford.

Kihlstrom, J. F. (1999). The psychological uncon-scious. In L. A. Pervin & O. P. John (Eds.), *Handbook of personality: Theory and research* (2nd ed., pp. 424–442). New York: Guilford.

Kihlstrom, J. F., & Cunningham, R. L. (1991). Mapping interpersonal space. In M. J. Horowitz (Ed.), *Person schemas and maladaptive interper-sonal patterns* (pp. 311–336). Chicago: University of Chicago Press.

Kihlstrom, J. F., & Klein, S. B. (1994). The self as a knowledge structure. In R. S. Wyer, Jr., & T. K. Srull (Eds.), *Handbook of social cognition* (2nd ed.). *Volume I. Basic Processes* (pp. 153–208). Hillsdale, N.J: Erlbaum.

King, L. A. (1998). Ambivalence over emotional expression and reading emotions in situations and faces. *Journal of Personality and Social Psychology, 74,* 753–762.

King, L. A., & Emmons, R. A. (1990). Conflict over emotional expression: Psychological and physical correlates. *Journal of Personality and Social Psychology, 58,* 864–877.

King, L. A., & Emmons, R. A. (1991). Psychological, physical, and interpersonal correlates of emo-tional expressiveness, conflict, and control. *European Journal of Personality, 5,* 131–150.

King, L. A., & Miner, K. N. (2000). Writing about the perceived benefits of traumatic events: Implica-tions for physical health. *Personality and Social Psychology Bulletin, 26,* 220–230.

King, L. A., Richards, J. H., & Stemmerich, E. (1998). Daily goals, life goals and worst fears: Means, ends, and subjective well-being. *Journal of Personality, 66,* 713–744.

King, V., & Elder, G. H. Jr. (1998). Self-efficacy and grandparenthood. *Journals of Gerontology Series B – Psychological Sciences and Social Sciences, 53,* 249–257.

Kirkpatrick, L. A., & Hazan, C. (1994). Attachment styles and close relationships: A four-year prospec-tive study. *Personal Relationships, 1,* 123–142.

Kirschenbaum, D. S. (1985). Proximity and speci-ficity of planning: A position paper. *Cognitive Therapy and Research, 9,* 489–506.

Kirschenbaum, D. S. (1987). Self-regulatory failure: A review with clinical implications. *Clinical Psychology Review, 7,* 77–104.

Kitayama, S., & Karasawa, M. (1997). Implicit self-esteem in Japan: Name letters and birthday num-bers. *Personality and Social Psychology Bulletin, 23,* 736–742.

Kitayama, S., & Markus, H. R. (Eds.). (1994). *Emotion and culture: Empirical studies of mutual influence.* Washington, D. C.: American Psycho-logical Association.

Kitayama, S., & Markus, H. R. (1999). Yin and Yang of the Japanese self: The cultural psychology of personality coherence. In D. Cervone & Y. Shoda (Eds.), *The coherence of personality: Social-cogni-tive bases of consistency, variability, and organiza-tion* (pp 242–302). New York: Guilford.

Kitayama, S., Markus, H. R., Matsumoto, H., & Norasakkunit, V. (1997). Individual and collective processes of self-esteem management: Self-enhancement in the United States and self-depre-ciation in Japan. *Journal of Personality and Social Psychology, 72,* 1245–1267.

Kitayama, Markus, H. R., & Nisbett R. E. (1998). The cultural matrix of social psychology. In D. T. Gilbert, S. T. Fiske, & G. Lindzey (Eds.), *The hand-book of social psychology* (4th ed., Volume 2, pp. 915–981). Boston: McGraw-Hill.

Kitayama, S., & Masuda, T. (1997). [A cultural mediation model of social inference: Correspondence bias in Japan.] In K. Kashiwagi, S. Kitayama. & H. Azuma (Eds.), [*Cultural psy-chology: Theory and research*] (pp. 109–127). Tokyo: University of Tokyo Press. (In Japanese; cited in Kitayama & Markus, 1999).

Kitcher, P. (1985). Two approaches to explanation. *Journal of Philosophy, 82,* 632–639.

Klages, L. (1926). *The Science of character.* [English translation, 1932]. London: Allen & Unwin.

Klein, G. (1970). *Perception, motives and personality.* New York: Knopf.

Klein, M. (1932). *The psychoanalysis of children.* London: Hogarth Press.

Klein, M. (1957). *Envy and gratitude: A study of unconscious sources.* New York: Basic Books.

Kline, P. (1987). Factor analysis and personality theory. *European Journal of Personality, 1,* 21–36.

Kling, K. C., Hyde, J. S., Showers, C. J., & Buswell, B. N. (1999). Gender differences in self esteem: A Meta-Analysis. *Psychological Bulletin, 125,* 470–500

Klinger, E. (1975). Consequences of commitment to and disengagement from incentives. *Psychological Review, 82,* 1–25.

Klinger, E., Barta, S. G., & Maxeiner, M. E. (1980). Motivational correlates of thought content, fre-quency, and commitment. *Journal of Personality and Social Psychology, 39,* 1222–1237.

Klirs, E. G., & Revelle, W. (1986). Predicting vari-ability from perceived situational similarity. *Journal of Research in Personality, 20,* 34–50.

Klohnen, E. C., & Bera, S. (1998). Behavioral and experiential patterns of avoidantly and securely attached women across adulthood: A 31-year longitudinal perspective. *Journal of Personality and Social Psychology, 74,* 211–223.

Klohnen, E. C., & Mendelsohn G. A. (1998). Partner selection for personality characteristics. A couple centered approach. *Personality and Social Psychology Bulletin, 4,* 268–278.

Kluckhohn, C., Murray, H. A., & Schneider, D. (Eds.) (1953). *Personality in nature, society and culture.* New York: Knopf.

Kohlberg, L. (1964). Development of moral character and moral ideology. In M. Hoffman & L. W. Hoffman (Eds.), *Review of child development research,* Vol. 1. (pp. 383–431) New York: Russel Sage Foundation.

Kohlberg, L. (1966). A cognitive-developmental analysis of children's sex-role concepts and attitudes. In E. Maccoby (Ed.), *The development of sex differences.* (pp. 173). Stanford: Stanford University Press.

Kohn, M., & Schooler, C. (1983). *Work and personality.* Norwood, NY.: Alex Publishing Corporation.

Kohn, M., & Slomczynski, K. (1990). *Social structure and self-direction.* Cambridge, MA.: Basil Blackwell, Inc.

Kohnstamm, G. A., Bates, J. E., & Rothbart, M. K. (Eds.) (1989). *Temperament in childhood.* Chichester, UK: Wiley.

Kohut, H. (1971). *The analysis of the self.* New York: International Universities Press.

Kohut, H. (1977). *The restoration of the self.* New York: International Universities Press.

Kojima, H. (1986). Japanese concepts of child development from the mid-17th to mid-19th century. *International Journal of Behavioral Development, 9,* 315–329.

Kojima, H. (1998). *History of children and youth in Japan.* Paper presented at the NIAS Conference "Are we at the end of the Century of the Child?" Wassenaar, February, 1998.

Kolb, B., & Whishaw, I. Q. (1990). *Fundamentals of human neuropsychology.* New York: Freeman.

Kolb, B., & Whishaw, I. Q. (1998). Brain plasticity and behavior. *Annual Review of Psychology, 49,* 43–64.

Krahé, B. (1990). *Situation cognition and coherence in personality.* Cambridge, U. K.: Cambridge University Press.

Kreitler, S., & Kreitler, H. (1992). The cognitive view of personality: The approaches of meaning and cognitive orientation. In G. V. Caprara & G. L. Van Heck (Eds.), *Modern personality psychology: Critical reviews and new directions* (pp. 255–281). New York: Harvester Wheatsheaf.

Kremen, A. M., & Block, J. (1998). The roots of ego-control in young adulthood: Links with parenting in early childhood. *Journal of Personality and Social Psychology, 75,* 1062–1075.

Krosnick, J. A. (1990). Expertise and political psychology. *Social Cognition, 8,* 1–8.

Krueger, J., & Heckhausen, J. (1993). Personality development across the life span: Subjective conceptions versus cross-sectional contrasts. *Journal of Gerontology: Psychological Sciences, 48,* P100–P108.

Kruglanski, A. W. (1989). *Lay epistemics and human knowledge.* New York: Plenum.

Kruglanski, A. W. (1996). Goals as knowledge structures. In P. M. Gollwitzer & J. A. Bargh (Eds.), *The psychology of action: Linking cognition and motivation to behavior* (pp. 599–618). New York: Guilford.

Kruglanski, A. (2000). *Motivation as cognition: A theory of goal systems.* Paper presented at the meetings of the Society for Personality and Social Psychology, Nashville, TN.

Kuhl, J. (1984). Volitional aspects of achievement motivation and learned helplessness: Toward a comprehensive theory of action control. In B. A. Maher (Ed.), *Progress in Experimental Personality Research* (Vol. 13, pp. 99–171). New York: Academic Press.

Kuhl, J. (1986). Motivation and information processing: A new look at decision making, dynamic change, and action control. In R. M. Sorrentino & E. T. Higgins (Eds.), *Handbook of motivation and cognition: Foundations of social behavior* (pp. 404–434). New York: Wiley.

Kuhl, J. (1994). A theory of action and state orientations. In J. Kuhl & J. Beckmann (Eds.), *Volition and personality: Action versus state orientation* (pp. 9–46). Seattle: Hogrefe & Huber.

Kuhl, J. (1996). Who controls whom when "I control myself"? *Psychological Inquiry, 7,* 61–68.

Kuhl, J., & Goschke, T. (1994). A theory of action control: Mental subsystems, modes of control, and volitional conflict-resolution strategies. In J. Kuhl & J. Beckmann (Eds.), *Volition and personality: Action versus state orientation* (pp. 93–124). Seattle: Hogrefe & Huber.

Kuhn, T. S. (1962). *The structure of scientific revolutions.* Chicago, IL.: University of Chicago Press.

Kuiper, N. A. (1981). Convergent evidence for the self as a prototype: The "inverted-U RT effect" for self and other judgments. *Personality and Social Psychology Bulletin, 7,* 438–443.

Kunda, Z. (1987). Motivated inference: Self-serving generation and evaluation of causal theories. *Journal of Personality and Social Psychology, 53,* 636–647.

Kunda, Z. (1990). The case for motivated reasoning. *Psychological Bulletin, 108,* 480–498.

Kvale, S. (Ed.) (1992). *Psychology and postmodernism.* London: Sage.

Labouvie-Vief, G. (1994). *Psyche and Eros.* New York: Cambridge University Press

Laing, R. (1965). *The divided self: An existential study in sanity and madness.* Baltimore: Penguin.

Lakatos, I. (1978). *The methodology of scientific research programs.* Cambridge, MA: Cambridge University Press.

Lakoff, G. (1987). *Women, fire, and dangerous things.* Chicago: University of Chicago Press.

Lakoff, G., and Johnson. M. (1999). *Philosophy in the flesh: The embodied mind and its challenge to Western thought.* New York: Basic Books.

Lamb, M. E. (1998). *Parenting and child development in "nontraditional" families.* Mahwah, NJ: Erlbaum.

Lamb, M., & Sutton Smith, B. (1982). *Sibling relationships: Their nature and significance across the life-span.* Hillsdale, NJ: Erlbaum.

Lamiell, J. T. (1997). Individuals and the differences between them. In R. Hogan, J. Johnson, & S. Briggs (Eds.), *Handbook of personality psychology* (pp. 117–141). San Diego: Academic Press.

Lange, C. (1885). *The emotions.* (English translation published 1922) Baltimore: Williams & Wilkins.

Langer, E. J. (1975). The illusion of control. *Journal of Personality and Social Psychology, 32,* 311–328.

Langer, E. J., & Benevento, A. (1978). Self-induced dependence. *Journal of Personality and Social Psychology, 36,* 886–893.

Langer, E. J., Blank, A., & Chanowitz, B. (1978). The mindlessness of ostensibly thoughtful action: The role of "placebic" information in interpersonal interaction. *Journal of Personality and Social Psychology, 36,* 635–642.

Langer, E., & Rodin, J. (1976). The effects of choice and enhanced personal responsibility for the aged: A field experiment in an institutional setting. *Journal of Personality and Social Psychology, 34,* 191–198.

Langer, E. J., & Roth, J. (1975). Heads I win, tails it's chance: The illusion of control as a function of the sequence of outcomes in a purely chance task. *Journal of Personality and Social Psychology, 32,* 951–955.

Lanzetta, J. T., Cartwright-Smith, J., & Kleck, R. E. (1976). Effects of nonverbal dissimulation on emotional experience and autonomic arousal. *Journal of Personality and Social Psychology, 33,* 354–370.

Laplanche, J., & Pontalis, J. (1967). *Vocabulaire de la psycanalyse.* Paris: Presses Universitaires.

Larsen, R. J. (1987). The stability of mood variability: A spectral analytic approach to daily mood assessments. *Journal of Personality and Social Psychology, 52,* 1195–1204.

Larsen, R. J. (1989). A process approach to personality psychology: Utilizing time as a facet of data. In D. M. Buss & N. Cantor (Eds.), *Personality psychology: Recent trends and emerging directions* (pp. 177–193). New York: Springer-Verlag.

Larsen, R. J., & Diener, E. (1987). Affect intensity as an individual difference characteristic: A review. *Journal of Research in Personality, 21,* 1–39.

Larsen, R. J., & Kasimatis, M. (1990). Individual differences in entrainment of mood to the weekly calendar. *Journal of Personality and Social Psychology, 58,* 164–171.

Larson, R., & Ham, M. (1993). Stress and "storm and stress" in early adolescence: The relationship of negative life events with dysphoric affect. *Developmental Psychology, 29,* 130–140.

Larson, R., & Richards, M. H. (1994). *Divergent realities: The emotional lives of mothers, fathers, and adolescents.* New York: Basic Books.

Laslet, P., & Wall, L. (1972). *Household and family in past times.* Cambridge, U.K.: Cambridge University Press.

Latané, B., & L'Herrou, T. (1996). Spatial clustering in the conformity game: Dynamic social impact in electronic groups. *Journal of Personality and Social Psychology, 70,* 1218–1230.

Laudan, L. (1977). *Progress and its problems. Towards a theory of scientific growth.* Berkeley, CA.: University of California Press.

Laursen, B., Coy, K. C., & Collins, W. A. (1998). Reconsidering changes in parent-child conflict across adolescence: A meta-analysis. *Child Development, 69,* 817–832.

Laver, J. C., & Laver, R. H. (1986). *Until death do us part: A study and guide to long term marriage.* New York: Harrington Park.

Lazarus, R. S. (1982). Thoughts on the relation between emotion and cognition. *American Psychologist, 37,* 1019–1024.

Lazarus, R. S. (1991). *Emotion and adaptation.* New York: Oxford University Press.

Lazarus, R. S. (1994). Individual differences in emotion. In P. Ekman & R. J. Davidson (Eds.), *The nature of emotion: Fundamental questions* (pp. 332–336). New York: Oxford University Press.

Lazarus, R. S. (1999). The cognition-emotion debate: A bit of history. In T. Dalgleish & M. Power (Eds.), *Handbook of cognition and emotion.* (pp. 3–19). Chichester, England: Wiley.

Lazarus, R. S., & Folkman, S. (1984). *Stress, appraisal, and coping.* New York: Springer.

Lazarus, R. S., & Smith, C. A. (1988). Knowledge and appraisal in the cognition-emotion relationship. *Cognition and Emotion, 2,* 281–300.

Leary, M. R., & Downs, D. L. (1995). Interpersonal functions of the self-esteem motive: The self-esteem as sociometer. In M. H. Kernis (Ed.), *Efficacy, agency, and self-esteem* (pp. 123–144). New York: Plenum.

LeDoux, J. E. (1996). *The emotional brain.* New York: Simon & Schuster.

LeDoux, J. E. (1994). Cognitive-emotional interactions in the brain. In P. Ekman & R. J. Davidson (Eds.), *The nature of emotion: Fundamental questions* (pp. 216–223). New York: Oxford University Press.

LeDoux, J. E. (1995). Emotion: Clues from the brain. *Annual Review of Psychology, 46,* 209–235.

Lee, C. (1984a). Accuracy of efficacy and outcome expectations in predicting performance in a simulated assertiveness task. *Cognitive Therapy and Research, 8,* 37–48.

Lee, C. (1984b). Efficacy expectations and outcome expectations as predictors of performance in a snake-handling task. *Cognitive Therapy and Research, 8,* 509–516.

Lefcourt, H. M. (1976). *Locus of control: Current trends in theory and research.* New York: Wiley.

Leffert, N., & Petersen, A. (1995). Patterns of development during adolescence. In M. Rutter & D. Smith (Eds.), *Psychosocial disorders in young people.* (pp. 67–103). Chichester, UK.: John Wiley & Sons.

Leont'ev, A. N. (1959). Problemy razvitija psichiki. [Italian translation] Problemi dello sviluppo psichico, Roma: Editori Riuniti.

Leont'ev, A. N. (1975). *Activity, consciousness and personality.* Englewood Cliffs, NJ: Prentice-Hall.

Lepper, M. R., Sagotsky, G., & Mailer, J. (1975). Generalization and persistence of effects of exposure to self-reinforcement models. *Child Development, 46,* 618–630.

Lerner, R. M. (1986). *Concepts and theories of human development* (2nd ed.). New York: Random House.

Lerner, R. M. (1989). Individual development and the family system: A life-span perspective. In K. Kreppner & R. M. Lerner (Eds.), *Family systems and life-span development* (pp. 15–32). Hillsdale, NJ: Erlbaum

Lerner, R. M. (1995). The limits of biological influence: Behavioral genetics as the emperor's new clothes. *Psychological Inquiry, 6,* 145–156.

Lerner, R. M. (1998). Theories of human development: Contemporary perspectives. In W. Damon (Series Ed.) & R. M. Lerner (Vol. Ed.), *Handbook of Child Psychology* (5th Edition). Vol. 1: Theoretical models of human development (pp. 1–24). New York: Wiley.

Lerner, R. M., & Busch-Rossnagel, N. A. (1981). Individuals as producers of their development: Conceptual and empirical bases. In R. M. Lerner & N. A. Musch-Rossnagel (Eds.), *Individuals as producers of their development: A life-span perspective.* New York: Academic Press.

Lesch, K. P., Bengel, D., Heils, A., Zhang Sabol, S., Greenburg, B. D., Petri, S., Benjamin, J., Müller, C. R., Hamer, D. H., & Murphy, D. L. (1996). Association of anxiety-related traits with a polymorphism in the serotonin transporter gene regulatory region. *Science, 274,* 1527–1530.

Levenson, R. W. (1992). Autonomic nervous system differences among emotions. *Psychological Science, 3,* 23–27.

Levenson, R. W. (1994). Human emotion: A functional view. In P. Ekman & R. J. Davidson (Eds.), *The nature of emotion: Fundamental questions* (pp. 123–126). New York: Oxford University Press.

Levenson, R. W., Ekman, P., & Friesen, W. V. (1990). Voluntary facial action generates emotion-specific autonomic nervous system activity. *Psychophysiology, 27,* 363–384.

Leventhal, H., & Tomarken, A. J. (1986). Emotion: Today's problems. *Annual Review of Psychology, 37,* 565–610.

Levey, A. B., & Martin, I. (1981). Personality and conditioning. In H. J. Eysenck (Ed.), *A model for personality.* Berlin: Springer-Verlag.

Levine, J. M., Resnick, L. B., & Higgins, H. T. (1993). Social foundations of cognition. *Annual Review of Psychology, 44,* 585–612.

Levinson, D. J. (1978). *The season's of a man's life.* New York: Knopf.

Levinson, D. J. (1981). Exploration in biography: Evolution of the individual life structure in adulthood. In A. I. Rabin, J. Aronoff, A. M. Barclay & R. Zucker (Eds.), *Further explorations in personality* (pp. 44–79). New York: Wiley.

Levy, S. R., Stroessner, S. J., & Dweck, C. S. (1998). Stereotype formation and endorsement: The role of implicit theories. *Journal of Personality and Social Psychology, 74,* 1421–1436.

Lewicki, P. (1983). Self-image bias in person perception. *Journal of Personality and Social Psychology, 45,* 384–393.

Lewicki, P. (1984). Self-schema and social information processing. *Journal of Personality and Social Psychology, 48,* 463–474.

Lewin, K. (1935). *A dynamic theory of personality: Selected papers.* New York: McGraw-Hill.

Lewin, K. (1936). *Principles of topological psychology.* New York: McGraw-Hill.

Lewin, K. (1951). *Field theory in social science.* New York: Harper & Row.

Lewin, K., Dembo, T., Festinger, L., & Sears, P. S. (1944). Level of aspiration. In J. M. Hunt (Ed.), *Personality and the behavior disorders* (Vol. 1, pp. 333–388). New York: The Ronald Press.

Lewis, M. (1990). Self-knowledge and social development in early life. In L. Pervin (Ed.), *Handbook of personality: Theory and research* (pp. 277–300). New York: Guilford.

Lewis, M. (1994). Does attachment imply a relationship of multiple relationships? *Psychological Inquiry, 5,* 47–51.

Lewis, M. (1996). Self-organising cognitive appraisals. *Cognition and Emotion, 10,* 1–25.

Lewis, M. D. (1997). Personality self-organization: Cascading constraints on cognition-emotion interactions. In A. Fogel, M. C. D. P. Lyra, & J. Valsiner (Eds.), *Dynamics and indeterminism in developmental and social processes* (pp. 193–216). Mahwah, NJ: Erlbaum.

Leyens, J. P. (1983). *Sommes nous tous des psychologues?* Bruxelles: Pierre Mardaga Editeur.

Lichtenberg, J. (1989). *Psychoanalysis and motivation.* Hillsdale, NJ: The Analytic Press.

Liebert, R. M., & Sprafkin, J. (1988). *The early window: Effects of television on children and youth* (3rd ed.). New York: Pergamon Press.

Lillard, A. (1998). Ethnopsychologies: Cultural variations in theories of mind. *Psychological Bulletin, 123,* 3–32.

Lindsay, P., & Norman, D. (1972). *Human information processing.* New York: Academic Press.

Linville, P. (1985). Self-complexity and affective extremity: Don't put all your eggs in one basket. *Social Cognition, 3,* 94–120.

Linville, P. (1987). Self-complexity as a cognitive buffer against stress-related illness and depression. *Journal of Personality and Social Psychology, 52,* 663–676.

Linville, P., & Clark, L. F. (1989). Production systems and social problem-solving: Specificity, flexibility, and expertise. In R. S. Wyer & T. K. Srull (Eds.), *Advances in social cognition* (Vol. 2, pp. 123–130). Hillsdale, NJ: Erlbaum.

Lips, H. (1988). *Sex & gender.* Mountain View, CA.: Mayfield Publishing Company.

Litt, M. D. (1988). Self-efficacy and perceived control: Cognitive mediators of pain tolerance. *Journal of Personality and Social Psychology, 54,* 149–160.

Little, B. R. (1989). Personal projects analysis: Trivial pursuits, magnificent obsessions, and the search for coherence. In D. M. Buss & N. Cantor (Eds.), *Personality psychology* (pp. 15–31). New York: Springer-Verlag.

Little, B. (1999). Personality and motivation: personal action and the conative evolution. In L. A. Pervin & O. P. John (Eds.), *Handbook of personality: Theory and research* (2nd ed.; pp. 501–524). New York: Guilford.

Little, T. D., Oettingen, G., Stetsenko, A., & Baltes, P. B. (1995). Children's action control beliefs about school performance: How do American children compare with German and Russian children? *Journal of Personality and Social Psychology, 69,* 686–700.

Locke, E. A., & Latham, G. P. (1984). *Goal-setting: A motivational technique that works!* Englewood Cliffs, NJ: Prentice-Hall.

Locke, E. A., & Latham, G. P. (1990). *A theory of goal setting and task performance.* Englewood Cliffs, NJ: Prentice-Hall.

Locke, E. A., Shaw, K. N., Saari, L. M., & Latham, G. P. (1981). Goal setting and task performance: 1969–1980. *Psychological Bulletin, 90,* 125–152.

Loeber, R., & Keenan, K. (1994). The interaction between conduct disorder and its comorbid conditions: Effects of age and gender. *Clinical Psychology Review, 14,* 497–523.

Loeber, R., & Southamer Loeber, M. (1998). Development of juvenile aggression and violence. *American Psychologist, 53,* 242–259.

Loehlin, J. C. (1982). Are personality traits differentially heritable? *Behavior Genetics, 12,* 417–428.

Loehlin, J. C. (1992). *Genes and Environment in Personality Development.* Newbury Park, CA. Sage.

Loehlin. J. C. (1992). *Latent variable models.* Hillsdale, NJ: Lawrence Erlbaum.

Loehlin, J. C., & Rowe, D. C. (1992). Genes, environment, and personality. In G. V. Caprara & G. Van Heck (Eds.) *Modern personality psychology* (pp. 352–370). London: Harvester-Wheatsheaf.

Loevinger, J. (1966). The meaning and measurement of ego development. *American Psychologist, 21,* 195–266.

Loevinger, J. (1976). *Ego development: Conceptions and theories.* San Francisco: Jossey-Bass.

Loevinger, J. (1997). Stages of personality development. In R. Hogan, J. Johnson, & S. Briggs (Eds.), *Handbook of personality psychology* (pp. 199–208). San Diego, CA: Academic Press.

Loevinger, J., & Wessler, R. (1970). *Measuring ego development. 1. Construction and use of a sentence completion test.* San Francisco: Jossey-Bass.

Loftus, E. (2000). Suggestion, imagination, and the transformation of reality. In A. A. Stone & J. S. Turkkan (Eds.), *The science of self-report: Implications for research and practice* (pp. 201–210). Marwah, N.J.: Erlbaum.

Lombardi, W. J., Higgins, E. T., & Bargh. J. A. (1987). The role of consciousness in priming effects on categorization. *Personality and Social Psychology Bulletin, 13,* 411–429.

Lombardo, G. P., & Duichin, M. (1997). *Frenologia fisiognomica e psicologia delle differenze individuali in Franz Joseph Gall.* Torino: Bollati Boringhieri.

Lord, C. G. (1982). Predicting behavioral consistency from an individual's perception of situational similarities. *Journal of Personality and Social Psychology, 42,* 1076–1088.

Lorenz, K. (1966). *On aggression.* New York: Harcourt, Brace, & World.

Luborsky, L. (1984). *Principles of psychoanalytic psychotherapy.* New York: Basic Books.

Lucas, R. E., Diener, E., & Suh, E. (1996). Discriminant validity of well-being measures. *Journal of Personality and Social Psychology, 71,* 616–628.

Lykken, D. T. (1971). Multiple factor analysis and personality research. *Journal of Experimental Research in Personality, 5,* 161–170.

Lykken, D. T., McGue M., Tellegen, A., & Bouchard, T. J. (1992). Emergenesis. *American Psychologist, 47,* 1565–1577.

Lyons, M. J., True, W. R., Eisen, S. A., Goldberg, J., Meyer, J., Faraone, S. V., Eaves, L. J., & Tsuang, M. T. (1995). Differential heritability of adult and juvenile antisocial traits. *Archives of General Psychiatry, 52,* 906–915.

Lyubormirsky, S., & Nolen-Hoeksema, S. (1993). Self-perpetuating properties of dysphoric rumination. *Journal of Personality and Social Psychology, 65,* 339–349.

Lyubormirsky, S., & Nolen-Hoeksema, S. (1995). Effects of self-focused rumination on negative thinking and interpersonal problem-solving. *Journal of Personality and Social Psychology, 69,* 176–190.

Maccoby, E. E. (1990). Gender and relationships: A developmental account. *American Psychologist, 45,* 513–520.

Maccoby, E. E. (1998). *The two sexes: Growing up apart, coming together.* Cambridge, MA: Belknap Press.

Maccoby, E. E., & Jacklin, C. N. (1974). *The psychology of sex differences.* Stanford, CA: Stanford University Press.

Maccoby, E. E., & Martin, J. A. (1983). Socialization in the context of the family: Parent-child interaction. In P. Mussen (Series Ed.) & M. Hetherington (Vol. Ed.), *Handbook of Child Psychology* (4th edition). Vol. 4: *Socialization, personality and social development* (1–101). New York: Wiley.

Maccoby, J. (1980). *Social development: Psychological growth and the parent-child relationship.* New York: Harcourt Brace Jovanovich.

Maciel, A. G., Heckhausen, J., & Baltes, P. B. (1994). A life-span perspective on the interface between personality and intelligence. In R. J. Sternberg, & P. Ruzgis (Eds.), *Personality and intelligence* (pp. 61–103). New York: Cambridge University Press.

MacLean, P. D. (1949). Psychosomatic disease and the "visceral brain": Recent developments bearing on the Papez theory of emotion. *Psychosomatic Medicine, 11,* 338–353.

MacLean, P. D. (1977). On the evolution of three mentalities. In S. Arieti & G. Chrzanowski (Eds.), *New dimensions in psychiatry: A world view* (Vol. 2, pp. 306–382). New York: Wiley.

MacLean, P. D. (1990). *The triune brain in evolution: Role in paleocerebral functions.* New York: Plenum.

Macrae, C. N., Bodenhausen, G. V., & Milne, A. B. (1998). Saying no to unwanted thoughts: Self-focus and the regulation of mental life. *Journal of Personality and Social Psychology, 74,* 578–589.

Maddux, J. E., Norton, L. W., & Stoltenberg, C. D. (1986). Self-efficacy expectancy, outcome expectancy, and outcome value: Relative effects on behavioral intentions. *Journal of Personality and Social Psychology, 51,* 783–789.

Madison, L. S., Madison, J. K, & Adubato, S. A. (1986). Infant behavior and development in relation to fetal movement and habituation. *Child Development, 57,* 1475–1482.

Magnus, K., Diener, E., Fujita, F., & Pavot, W. (1993). Extraversion and neuroticism as predictors of objective life events: A longitudinal analysis. *Journal of Personality and Social Psychology, 65,* 1046–1053.

Magnusson, D. (1988). *Individual development from an interactional perspective: A longitudinal study.* Hillsdale, NJ: Erlbaum.

Magnusson, D. (1992). Individual development: A longitudinal perspective. *European Journal of Personality, 6,* 119–138.

Magnusson, D. (1998). The logic and implications of a person approach. In R. B. Cairns, L. R. Bergman, & J. Kagan (Eds.), *The individual as a focus in developmental research* (pp. 33–64) New York: Sage.

Magnusson, D. (1999). Holistic interactionism: A perspective for research on personality development. In L. A. Pervin & O. P. John (Eds.), *Handbook of Personality: Theory and Research* (2nd ed., pp. 219–247). New York: Guilford.

Magnusson, D., & Endler, N. S. (Eds.) (1977). *Personality at the crossroads: Current issues in interactional psychology.* Hillsdale, NJ: Erlbaum.

Magnusson, D., & Stattin, H. (1998). Person-context interaction theories. In W. Damon (Series Ed.) & R. M. Lerner (Vol. Ed.), *Handbook of Child Psychology* (5th edition). Vol. 1: *Theoretical models of human development* (pp. 685–760). New York: Wiley.

Magnusson, D., & Törestad, B. (1993). A holistic view of personality: A model revisited. *Annual Review of Psychology, 44,* 427–452.

Maier, S., Watkins, L., & Fleshner, M. (1994). Psychoneuroimmunology. *American Psychologist, 49,* 1004–1017.

Main, M., Kaplan, N,., & Cassidy, J. (1985). Security in infancy, childhood and adulthood: A move to the level of representation. *Monographs of the Society for Research in Child Development. 50* (1–2, Serial No. 209).

Major, B., Cozzarelli, C., Sciacchitano, A. M., Cooper, M. L., Testa., M., & Mueller, P. M. (1990). Perceived social support, self-efficacy, and adjustment to abortion. *Journal of Personality and Social Psychology, 59,* 452–463.

Major, B., Richards, C., Cooper, M. L., Cozzarelli, C., & Zubek, J. (1998). Personal resilience, cognitive appraisals, and coping: An integrative model of adjustment to abortion. *Journal of Personality & Social Psychology, 74,* 735–752.

Malle, B. F., & Horowitz, L. M. (1995). The puzzle of negative self-views: An explanation using the schema concept. *Journal of Personality and Social Psychology, 68,* 470–484.

Manderlink, G., & Harackiewicz, J. M. (1984). Proximal versus distal goal setting and intrinsic motivation. *Journal of Personality and Social Psychology, 69,* 918–928.

Mandler, G. (1997). *Human nature explored.* New York: Oxford University Press.

Mangan, G. (1982). *The biology of human conduct: East-West models of temperament and personality.* Oxford: Pergamon Press.

Manian, N., Strauman, T. J., & Denney, N. (1998). Temperament, recalled parenting styles, and self-regulation: Testing the developmental postulates of self-discrepancy theory. *Journal of Personality and Social Psychology, 75*, 1321–1332.

Manning, M. M., & Wright, T. L. (1983). Self-efficacy expectancies, outcome expectancies, and the persistence of pain control in childbirth. *Journal of Personality and Social Psychology, 45*, 421–431.

Markus, H. (1977). Self-schemata and processing information about the self. *Journal of Personality and Social Psychology, 35*, 63–78.

Markus, H., Crane, M., Bernstein, S., & Siladi, M. (1982). Self-schemas and gender. *Journal of Personality and Social Psychology, 42*(1), 38–50.

Markus, H., & Cross, S. (1990). The interpersonal self. In L. A. Pervin (Ed.), *Handbook of Personality: Theory and Research* (pp. 576–608). New York: Guilford.

Markus, H., Hamill, R., & Sentis, K. P. (1987). Thinking fat: Self-schemas for body weight and the processing of weight relevant information. *Journal of Applied Social Psychology, 17*, 50–71.

Markus, H. R., & Kitayama, S. (1994). A collective fear of the collective: Implications for selves and theories of selves. *Personality and Social Psychology Bulletin, 20*, 568–579.

Markus, H. R., Kitayama, S., & Heiman, R. J. (1996). Culture and "basic" psychological principles. In E. T. Higgins & A. Kruglanski (Eds.), *Social Psychology: Handbook of basic principles* (pp. 857–913). New York: Guilford.

Markus, H., & Nurius, P. (1986). Possible selves. *American Psychologist, 41*, 954–959.

Markus, H., Smith, J., & Moreland, R. L. (1985). Role of the self-concept in the social perception of others. *Journal of Personality and Social Psychology, 49*, 1494–1512.

Markus, H., & Wurf, E. (1987). The dynamic self-concept: A social psychological perspective. *Annual Review of Psychology, 38*, 299–337.

Marlatt, G. A., & Gordon, J. R. (Eds.) (1985). *Relapse prevention: Maintenance strategies in the treatment of addictive behaviors*. New York: Guilford.

Marsh, H. W., & Yeung, A. S. (1998). Top-down, bottom-up, and horizontal models: The direction of causality in multidimensional, hierarchical self-concept models. *Journal of Personality and Social Psychology, 75*, 509–572.

Martin, H. G. (1945). The construction of the Guilford-Martin Inventory of Factors GAMIN. *Journal of Applied Psychology, 5*, 335–350.

Martin, L. L., & Tesser, A. (Eds.) (1996). *Striving and feeling: Interactions among goals, affect, and self-regulation*. Mahwah, NJ: Erlbaum.

Martin, L. L., Ward, D. W., Achee, J. W., & Wyer, R. S., Jr. (1993). Mood as input: People have to interpret the motivational implications of their moods.

*Journal of Personality and Social Psychology, 64*, 317–326.

Marx, K. (1844). *Economic and philosophic manuscripts*. Translated by M. Miligan, Buffalo, NY: Prometheus Books. 1988.

Maslach, C. (1974). Social and personal bases of individuation. *Journal of Personality and Social Psychology, 29*, 411–425.

Maslach, C., Stapp, J., & Santee, R. T. (1985). Individuation: Conceptual analysis and assessment. *Journal of Personality and Social Psychology, 49*, 729–738.

Maslow, A. H. (1954). *Motivation and personality*. New York: Harper.

Matthews, G., & Deary, I. (1998). *Personality traits*. Cambridge UK: Cambridge University Press.

Matthews, G., & Gilliland, K. (1999). The personality theories of H. J. Eysenck and J. A. Gray: A comparative review. *Personality and Individual Differences, 26*, 583–626.

Maturana, H., & Varela, F. (1980). *Autopoiesis and cognition: The realization of the living*. Boston: D. Riedel.

Maughan, B., & Rutter, M. (1998). Continuities and discontinuities in antisocial behavior from childhood to adult life. In *Advances in Clinical Child Psychology, 20*, 1–47.

Mauro, R. (1988). Opponent process in human emotions? An experimental investigation of hedonic contrast and affective interaction. *Motivation and Emotion, 12*, 333–351.

Mayer, J. D., & Carlsmith, K. M. (1997). Eminence rankings of personality psychologists as a reflection of the field. *Personality and Social Psychology Bulletin, 23*, 707–716.

Mayer, J. D., & Gaschke, Y. N. (1988). The experience and meta-experience of mood. *Journal of Personality and Social Psychology, 35*, 102–111.

Mayr, E. (1988). *Toward a new philosophy of biology: Observations of an evolutionist*. Cambridge, MA: Harvard University Press.

McAdams, D. P. (1992). The five factor model of personality: A critical appraisal. *Journal of Personality, 60*, 329–361.

McAdams, D. P. (1993). *The stories we live by: Personal myths and the making of the self*. New York: Guilford.

McAdams, D. P. (1994a). *The person: An introduction to personality psychology*. Fort Worth, TX: Harcourt Brace.

McAdams, D. P. (1994b). A psychology of the stranger. *Psychological Inquiry, 5*, 145–148.

McAdams, D. P. (1996). Personality, modernity, and the storied self: A contemporary framework for studying persons. *Psychological Inquiry, 7*, 295–321.

McAdams, D. P. (1997). A conceptual history of personality psychology. In R. Hogan, J. Johnson, & S.

Briggs (Eds.), *Handbook of personality psychology* (pp. 3–39). San Diego, CA: Academic Press.

McAdams, D. P., Diamond, A., St. Aubin, E., & Mansfield, E. (1997). Stories of commitment: The psychosocial construction of generative lives. *Journal of Personality and Social Psychology, 72,* 678–694.

McAuley, E., Duncan, T. E., & McElroy, M. (1989). Self-efficacy cognitions and causal attributions for children's motor performance: An exploratory investigation. *The Journal of Genetic Psychology, 150,* 65–73.

McCartney, K., Harris, M. J., & Bernieri, F. (1990). Growing up and growing apart: A developmental meta-analysis of twin studies. *Psychological Bulletin, 107,* 226–237.

McClelland, D. (1961). *The achieving society.* Princeton, NJ: Van Nostrand.

McClelland, D. (1985). *Human motivation.* Glenview, IL: Scott, Foresman and Co.

McClintock & Herdt (1996). Rethinking puberty: The development of sexual attraction: *Current Directions in Psychological Science, 5,* 178–183.

McCord, J. (Ed.) (1995). *Coercion and punishment in long-term perspective.* New York: Cambridge University Press.

McCord, J. (1997). Discipline and the use of sanctions. *Aggression and Violent Behavior, 2,* 313–319.

McCrae, R. R. (1989). Why I advocate the Five Factor model: Joint analysis of the NEO-PI and other instruments. In D. M. Buss & N. Cantor (Eds.), *Personality psychology: recent trends and emerging directions* (pp. 237–245). New York: Springer Verlag.

McCrae, R. R. (1996). Social consequences of experiential openness. *Psychological Bulletin, 120,* 323–337.

McCrae, R. R., & Costa, P. T. (1985). Comparison of EPI and psychoticism scales with measures of the five factor model of personality. *Personality and Individual Differences, 6,* 587–597.

McCrae, R. R., & Costa, P. T., Jr. (1987). Validation of the five-factor model of personality across instruments and observers. *Journal of Personality and Social Psychology, 52,* 81–90.

McCrae, R. R., & Costa, P. T. (1989). Reinterpreting the Myers-Briggs Type Indicator from the perspective of the five-factor model of personality. *Journal of Personality, 57,* 17–40.

McCrae, R. R., & Costa, P. T., Jr. (1990). *Personality in adulthood.* New York: Guilford.

McCrae, R. R., & Costa, P. T. (1995). Trait explanations in personality psychology. *European Journal of Personality, 9,* 231–252.

McCrae, R. R., & Costa, P. T. (1996). Toward a new generation of personality theories: theoretical contexts for the five-factor model. In J. S. Wiggins (Ed.), *The five-factor model of personality.*

*Theoretical perspectives* (pp. 51–87). New York: Guilford.

McCrae, R. R., & Costa, P. T. (1997). Personality trait structure as a human universal. *American Psychologist, 52,* 509–516.

McCrae, R. R., & Costa, P. T. (1999). A five-factor theory of personality. In L. A. Pervin & O. P. John (Eds.), *Handbook of personality: Theory and research* (2nd ed.; pp. 139–153). New York: Guilford.

McCrae, R. R., Costa, P., De Lima, M. P., Simoes, A., Ostendorf, F., Angleitner, A., Marusic, I., Bratko, D., Caprara, G. V., Barbaranelli, C., Chae, J., Piedmont, R. L. (1999). Age differences in personality across the adult life span: Parallels in five cultures. *Developmental Psychology, 35,* 466–477.

McCrae, R. R., & John, O. P. (1992). An introduction to the Five Factor Model and its applications. *Journal of Personality, 60,* 175–215.

McCrae, R. R., Yik, S. M., Trapnell, P. D., Bond, M. H., & Paulus, D. L. (1998). Interpreting personality profiles across cultures: Bilingual, acculturation, and peer rating studies of Chinese undergraduates. *Journal of Personality and Social Psychology, 74,* 1041–1055.

McCrae, R. R., Zonderman, A. B., Costa, P. T., Bond, M. H., & Paunonen, S. V. (1996). Evaluating replicability of factors in the revised NEO Personality Inventory: Confirmatory Factor Analysis and Procrustes Rotation. *Journal of Personality and Social Psychology, 70,* 552–565.

McDougall, W. (1908). *An introduction to social psychology.* Boston: Luce.

McGregor, I., & Little, B. R. (1998). Personal projects, happiness, and meaning: On doing well and being yourself. *Journal of Personality and Social Psychology, 74,* 494–512.

McGue, M., Bacon, S., & Lykken, D. T. (1993). Personality stability and change in early adulthood. A behavior genetic analysis. *Developmental Psychology, 29,* 96–109 :

McGue, M., Bouchard, T. J. Jr. Iacono, W. G., & Lykken, D. T. (1993). Behavioral genetics of cognitive ability: A life-span perspective. In R. Plomin & G. McClearn (Eds.), *Nature, nurture and psychology* (pp. 59–67). Washington, DC: American Psychological Association.

McGue, M., & Lykken, D. T. (1991). Genetic influence on risk of divorce. *Psychological Science, 3,* 368–373.

McGuire, W. J., & McGuire, C. V. (1988). Content and process in the experience of self. In L. Berkowitz (Ed.), *Advances in Experimental Social Psychology, Vol. 21. Social psychological studies of the self: Perspectives and programs.* San Diego: Academic Press.

McGuire, W. J., McGuire, C. V., Child, P., & Fujioka, T. (1978). Salience of ethnicity in the spontaneous self-concept as a function of one's ethnic distinctiveness in the social environment. *Journal of Personality and Social Psychology, 36,* 511–520.

McGuire, W. J., McGuire, C. V., & Winton, W. (1979). Effects of household sex composition on the salience of one's gender in the spontaneous self-concept. *Journal of Experimental Social Psychology, 15,* 77–90.

McGuire, W. J., & Padawar-Singer, A. (1976). Trait salience in the spontaneous self-concept. *Journal of Personality and Social Psychology, 33,* 743–754.

McHenry, J. J., Hough, L. M., Toquam, J. L., Hanson, M. A., & Ashworth, S. (1990). Project A validity results; The relationship between predictor and criterion domains. *Personnel Psychology, 43,* 335–367.

McLanahan, S., & Casper, L. (1995): Growing diversity and inequality in the American family. In R. Farley (Ed.), *State of the Union* (Vol. 2, pp. 1–45). New York: Russell Sage Foundation.

McLanahan, S., & Garfinkel, I. (1986). Single mothers and their children: A new American dilemma. Washington, D. C.: Urban Institute Press.

McLanahan, S., & Sandefur, G. (1994). *Growing up with a single parent: What hurts, what helps.* Cambridge, MA: Harvard University Press.

Mead, G. (1934). *Mind, self and society.* Chicago, IL: University of Chicago Press.

Meadows, S. (1993). *The child as thinker.* London: Routledge.

Meehl, P. E. (1954). *Clinical versus statistical prediction.* Minneapolis: University of Minnesota Press.

Meehl, P. E. (1978). Theoretical risks and tabular asterisks: Sir Karl, Sir Ronald and the slow progress of soft psychology. *Journal of Consulting and Clinical Psychology, 46,* 806–834.

Meehl, P. E. (1992). Factors and taxa, traits and types, differences of degree and differences in kind. *Journal of Personality, 60,* 117–174.

Meichenbaum, D. (1977). *Cognitive-behavior modification: An integrative approach.* New York: Plenum.

Meichenbaum, D. (1990). Paying homage: Providing challenges. (Book review essay on Bandura's *Social Foundations of Thought and Action.) Psychological Inquiry, 1,* 96–100.

Meichenbaum, D., & Gilmore, J. B. (1984). The nature of unconscious processes: A cognitive-behavioral perspective. In K. S. Bowers & D. Meichenbaum (Eds.), *The unconscious reconsidered* (pp. 273–298). New York: Wiley-Interscience.

Mellers, B. A., Schwartz, A., & Cooke, D. J. (1998). Judgment and decision making. *Annual Review of Psychology, 49,* 447–477.

Mendolia, M., Moore, J., & Tesser, A. (1996). Dispositional and situational determinants of repression. *Journal of Personality and Social Psychology, 70,* 856–867.

Mento, A. J., Steel, R. P., Karren, R. J. (1987). A meta-analytic study of the effects of goal setting on task performance: 1966–1984. *Organizational*

*behavior and Human Decision Processes, 39,* 52–83.

Merikle, P. M., & Reingold, E. M. (1992). Measuring unconscious perceptual processes. In R. F. Bornstein & T. S. Pittman (Eds.), *Perception without awareness* (pp. 55–80). New York: Guilford.

Merluzzi, T. V. (1991). Representation of information about self and other: A multidimensional scaling analysis. In M. J. Horowitz (Ed.), *Person schemas and maladaptive interpersonal patterns* (pp. 155–166). Chicago: University of Chicago Press.

Mesquita, B., & Frijda, N. H. (1992). Cultural variations in emotions: A review. *Psychological Bulletin, 112,* 179–204.

Messick, S. (1996). Bridging cognition and personality in education: the role of style in performance and development. *European Journal of Personality, 10,* 353–376.

Metcalfe, J. (1998). Cognitive optimism: Self-deception or memory-based processing heuristics? *Personality & Social Psychology Review, 2,* 100–110.

Metcalfe, J., & Mischel, W. (1999). A hot/cool-system analysis of delay of gratification: Dynamics of willpower. *Psychological Review, 106,* 3–19.

Mickelson, K. D., Kessler, R. C., & Shaver, P. R. (1997). Adult attachment in a nationally representative sample. *Journal of Personality and Social Psychology, 73,* 1092–1106.

Mikulciner, M. (1995). Attachment styles and mental representation of the self. *Journal of Personality and Social Psychology, 36,* 951–962.

Mikulincer, M. (1997). Adult attachment style and information processing: Individual differences in curiosity and cognitive closure. *Journal of Personality and Social Psychology, 72,* 1217–1230.

Mikulincer, M. (1998a). Adult attachment style and individual differences in functional versus dysfunctional expression of anger. *Journal of Personality and Social Psychology, 74,* 513–524.

Mikulincer, M. (1998b). Adult attachment style and affect regulation: Strategic variations in Self Appraisals. *Journal of Personality and Social Psychology, 75,* 420–435.

Mikulincer, M., & Orbach, I. (1995). Attachment styles and repressive defensiveness: The accessibility and architecture of affective memories. *Journal of Personality and Social Psychology, 68,* 917–925.

Mikulincer, M., Orbach, I., & Iavnieli, D. (1998). Adult attachment style and affect regulation: Strategic variations in subjective Self-Others similarity. *Journal of Personality and Social Psychology, 75,* 436–448.

Miller, G. A., Galanter, E., & Pribram, K. H. (1960). *Plans and the structure of behavior.* New York: Holt, Rinehart & Winston.

Miller, J. G. (1984). Culture and the development of everyday social explanation. *Journal of Personality and Social Psychology, 46,* 961–978.

Miller, J. G. (1999). Cultural psychology: Implications for basic psychological theory. *Psychological Science, 10,* 85–91.

Miller, J. B. (1985). *Toward a new psychology of women.* Boston: Beacon Press.

Miller, D. T., & Prentice, D. A. (1996). The construction of social norms and standards. In E. T. Higgins & A. W. Kruglanski (Eds.), *Social Psychology: Handbook of Basic Principles* (3–38). New York: Guilford.

Miller, S. M. (1996). Monitoring and blunting of threatening information: Cognitive interference and facilitation in the coping process. In I. G. Sarason, G. R. Pierce, & B. R. Sarason (Eds.), *Cognitive interference: Theories methods and findings* (pp. 175–190). Mahwah, NJ: Erlbaum.

Mills, C. J. (1983). Sex-typing and self-schemata effects on memory and response latency. *Journal of Personality and Social Psychology, 45,* 163–172.

Minuchin, P. (1985). Families and individual development: provocation from the field of family therapy. *Child Development, 56,* 289–302.

Minuchin, P., & Shapiro, E. (1983). The school as a context for social development. In P. Mussen (series Ed.) & M. Hetherington (Vol. Ed.), Handbook of child psychology. (4th edition) Vol. 4: Socialization, personality and social development (197–274). New York: Wiley.

Minuchin, S. (1974). *Families and family therapy.* Cambridge, MA: Harvard University Press.

Mischel, W. (1966). A social-learning view of sex differences in behavior. In E. Maccoby (Ed.), *The development of sex differences* (pp. 25–81). Stanford: Stanford University Press.

Mischel, W. (1968). *Personality and assessment.* New York: Wiley.

Mischel, W. (1973). Toward a cognitive social learning reconceptualization of personality. *Psychological Review, 80,* 252–283.

Mischel, W. (1974). Processes in delay of gratification. In L. Berkowitz (Ed.), *Advances in experimental social psychology* (Vol. 7, pp. 249–292). San Diego, CA: Academic Press.

Mischel, W. (1979). On the interface of cognition and personality: Beyond the person – situation debate. *American Psychologist, 34,* 740–754.

Mischel, W. (1990). Personality dispositions revisited and revised: A view after three decades. In L. A. Pervin (Ed.), *Handbook of personality: Theory and research* (pp. 111–134). New York: Guilford.

Mischel, W. (1993). *Introduction to Personality* (5th ed.). New York: Holt, Rinehart, and Winston.

Mischel, W. (1999a). *Introduction to personality* (5th ed.). New York: Harcourt Brace.

Mischel, W. (1999b). Personality coherence and dispositions in a cognitive-affective processing system (CAPS) approach. In D. Cervone and Y. Shoda (Eds.), *The coherence of personality: Social-cognitive bases of consistency, variability, and organization* (pp. 37–60). New York: Guilford Press.

Mischel, W., & Baker, N. (1975). Cognitive transformations of reward objects through instructions. *Journal of Personality and Social Psychology, 31,* 254–261.

Mischel, W., Cantor, N., & Feldman, S. (1996). Principles of self-regulation: The nature of willpower and self-control. In E. T. Higgins & A. W. Kruglanski (Eds.), *Social psychology: Handbook of basic principles* (pp. 329–360). New York: Guilford.

Mischel, W., & Mischel, H. A. (1976). A cognitive social learning approach to morality and self-regulation. In T. Lickona (Ed.), *Moral development and behavior* (pp. 84–107). New York: Holt, Rinehart, & Winston.

Mischel, W., & Mischel, H. N. (1983). Development of children's knowledge of self-control strategies. *Child Development, 54,* 603–619.

Mischel, W., & Moore, B. (1973). Effects of attention to symbolically-presented rewards on self-control. *Journal of Personality and Social Psychology, 28,* 172–197.

Mischel, W., & Peake, P. K. (1982). Beyond déjà vu in the search for cross-situational consistency. *Psychological Review, 89,* 730–755.

Mischel, W., & Shoda, Y. (1995). A cognitive-affective system theory of personality: Reconceptualizing situations, dispositions, dynamics, and invariance in personality structure. *Psychological Review, 102,* 246–286.

Mischel, W., & Shoda, Y. (1998). Reconciling processing dynamics and personality dispositions. *Annual Review of Psychology, 49,* 229–258.

Mischel, W. & Shoda, Y. (1999). Integrating dispositions and processing dynamics within a unified theory of personality: The cognitive–affective personality system. In L. A. Pervin & O. P. John (Eds.), *Handbook of Personality: Theory and Research* (2nd ed., pp. 197–218). New York: Guilford.

Mischel, W., Shoda, Y., & Peake, P. K. (1988). The nature of adolescent competencies predicted by preschool delay of gratification. *Journal of Personality and Social Psychology, 54,* 687–696.

Mischel, W., Shoda, Y, & Rodriguez, M. L. (1989). Delay of gratification in children. *Science, 244,* 933–938.

Mithen, S. (1996). *The prehistory of the mind: The cognitive origins of art, religion and science.* London: Thames & Hudson.

Moffitt, T. (1993). Adolescence-limited and life-course-persistent antisocial behavior. *Psychological Review, 100,* 674–701.

Molfese, D. L., & Segalowitz, S. J. (Eds.) (1988) *Brain lateralization in children: Developmental implications.* New York: Guilford Press.

Money, J. (1955). Hermaphroditism, gender and precocity in hyper-adrenocorticism: psychological findings. *Bulletin of the Johns Hopkins Hospital,* 96, 253–264.

Money, J. (1987). Propaedeutics of diecious G-I/R: Theoretical foundations for understanding Dimorphic Gender-Identity/Role. In J. Machover Reinisch, L. A., Rosenblum & S. A. Sanders (Eds.), *Masculinity/Femininity* (pp. 13–28). New York: Oxford University Press.

Money, J., & Ehrhardt, A. (1972) *Man and woman, boy and girl: Differentiation and dimorphism of gender identity from conception to maturity.* Baltimore: Johns Hopkins University Press.

Money, J. Hampson, J. G., & Hampson, J. L. (1955). An examination of some basic sexual concepts: The evidence of human hermaphroditism. *Bulletin of the Johns Hopkins Hospital,* 97, 301–319.

Montagu, A. (Ed.) (1999). *Race & IQ.* New York: Oxford University Press.

Moore, B., Mischel, W., & Zeiss, A. R. (1976). Comparative effects of the reward stimlulus and its cognitive representation in voluntary delay. *Journal of Personality and Social Psychology, 34,* 419–424.

Morin, E. (1977). *La methode.* 1. Paris: Seuil.

Morin, E. (1980). *La methode.* 2. Paris: Seuil.

Morin, E. (1986). *La methode.* 3. Paris: Seuil.

Morris, M. W., & Peng, K. (1994). Culture and cause: American and Chinese attributions for social and physical events. *Journal of Personality and Social Psychology, 67,* 949–971.

Mortimore, P. (1995). The positive effects of schooling. In M. Rutter (Ed.), *Psychosocial disturbances in young people* (pp. 333–363). New York: Cambridge University Press.

Moruzzi, G., & Magoun, H. W. (1949). Brain stem reticular formation and activation of the EEG. *Electroencephalography and Clinical Neurophysiology, 1,* 455–473.

Mroczek, D. K., & Kolarz, C. M. (1998). The effect of age on positive and negative affect: A developmental perspective on happiness. *Journal of Personality and Social Psychology, 75,* 1333–1349.

Mueller, C. M., & Dweck, C. S. (1998). Praise for intelligence can undermine children's motivation and performance. *Journal of Personality and Social Psychology, 75,* 33–52.

Mueller, J. H. (1982). Self-awareness and access to material rated as self-descriptive or nondescriptive. *Bulletin of the Psychonomic Society, 19,* 323–326.

Murphy, G. (1958). *Human potentialities.* New York: Basic Books.

Murray, H. A. (1938). *Explorations in personality.* New York: Oxford University Press.

Murray, H. A. (1951). In nomine diaboli. *The New England Quarterly, 24,* 435–453.

Murphy, G. (1947). *Personality: A biosocial approach to origins and structure.* New York: Harper and Brothers.

Myers, I. B., & McCaulley, M. H. (1985). *Manual: A guide to the development and use of the Myers-Briggs type indicator.* Palo Alto, CA: Consulting Psychologists Press.

Nadel, J., & Camaioni, L. (Eds.) (1993). *New perspectives in early communicative development.* London: Routledge.

Nasby, W., Hayden, B., & DePaulo, B. M. (1980). Attributional bias among aggressive boys to interpret unambiguous social stimuli as displays of hostility. *Journal of Abnormal Psychology, 89,* 459–468.

Nebylitsyn, V. D. (1972). The problem of general and partial properties of nervous system. In V. D. Nebylitsyn & J. A. Gray (Eds.), *Biological bases of individual behavior.* (pp. 400–417). New York: Academic Press.

Neisser, U. (1967). *Cognitive psychology.* Englewood Cliffs, NJ: Prentice-Hall.

Neisser, U. (1976). *Cognition and reality.* San Francisco: Freeman.

Neisser, U., Boodoo, G., Bouchard, T. J. Jr., Boykin, A. W., Brody, N., Ceci, S. J., Halpern, D. F., Loehlin, J. C., Perloff, R., Sternberg, R. J., & Urbina, S. (1996). Intelligence: Knowns and unknowns. *American Psychologist, 51,* 77–101

Nelson, C. A. (1999). Neural plasticity and human development. *Contemporary Directions in Psychological Science, 8,* 42–45.

Nelson, L. J., & Miller, D. T. (1995). The distinctiveness effect in social categorization: You are what makes you unusual. *Psychological Science, 6,* 246–249.

Nesselroade, J. R., & Molenaar, P. C. M. (1999). Pooling lagged covariance structures based on short, multivariate time-series for dynamic factor analysis. In R. Hoyle (Ed.), *Research strategies for small samples* (pp. 223–250). Thousand Oaks, CA: Sage Publications, Inc.

Newcomb, T. M. (1929). *Consistency of certain extrovert-introvert behavior patterns in 51 problem boys.* New York: Columbia University Press, Teachers College, Bureau of Publications.

Newcomb, A. K., & Bagwell, C. L. (1995). Children's friendship relations: A meta-analytic review: *Psychological Bulletin, 117,* 306–347.

Newell, A., & Simon, H. A. (1972). *Human Problem Solving.* Englewood Cliffs, NJ: Prentice-Hall.

Newman, D. L., Caspi, A., & Moffitt, T. (1997). Antecedents of adult interpersonal functioning: Effects of individual differences in age 3 temperament. *Developmental Psychology, 33,* 206–217.

Newman, L. S. (1991). Why are traits inferred spontaneously? A developmental approach. *Social Cognition, 9,* 221–253.

Newman, L. S. (1993). How individualists interpret behavior: Idiocentrism and spontaneous trait inferences. *Social Cognition, 11,* 243–269.

Newman, L. S. (in press). A cornerstone for the science of interpersonal behavior? Person perception and person memory, past, present, and future. In G. B. Moskowitz (Ed.), *Cognitive social psychology: On the tenure and future of social cognition*. Mahwah, NJ: Erlbaum.

Newman, L. S., Duff, K. J., & Baumeister, R. F. (1997). A new look at defensive projection: Thought suppression, accessibility, and biased person perception. *Journal of Personality and Social Psychology, 72*, 980–1001.

Newman, L. S., Higgins, E. T., & Vookles, J. (1992). Self-guide strength and emotional vulnerability: Birth order as a moderator of self-affect relations. *Personality & Social Psychology Bulletin, 18*, 402–411.

Newman, L. S., & Uleman, J. S. (1990). Assimilation and contrast effects in spontaneous trait inference. *Personality and Social Psychology Bulletin, 16*, 224–240.

Newman, L. S., & Uleman, J. S. (1993). When are you what you did? behavior identification and dispositional inference in person memory, atribution, and social judgment. *Personality and Social Psychology Bulletin, 19*, 511–523.

Newton, T. L., & Contrada, R. J. (1992). Repressive coping and verbal-autonomic response dissociation: The influence of social context. *Journal of Personality and Social Psychology, 62*, 159–167.

Newtson, D. (1973). Attribution and the unit of perception of ongoing behavior. *Journal of Personality and Social Psychology, 28*, 28–38.

Nicolis, G., & Prigogine, J. (1987). *Exploring complexity: An introduction*. Munich: Piper Gmbh.

Nicholls, J. G. (1984). Achievement motivation: Conceptions of ability, subjective experience, task choice, and performance. *Psychological Review, 91*, 328–346.

Nicholls, J. G., Licht, B. G., & Pearl, R. A. (1982). Some dangers of using personality questionnaires to study personality. *Psychological Bulletin, 92*, 572–580.

Niedenthal, P. M., Setterlund, M. B., & Wherry, M. B. (1992). Possible self-complexity and affective reactions to goal-relevant evaluation. *Journal of Personality and Social Psychology, 63*, 5–16.

Nisbett, R. E., & Ross, L. (1981). *Human inference: Strategies and shortcomings of social judgment*. Englewood Cliffs, NJ: Prentice-Hall.

Nisbett, R. E., & Wilson, T. D. (1977). Telling more than we can know: Verbal reports on mental processes. *Psychological Review, 84*, 231–259.

Nolen-Hoeksema, S. (1991). Responses to depression and their effects on the duration of depressive episodes. *Journal of Abnormal Psychology, 100*, 569–582.

Nolen-Hoeksema, S., & Larson, J. (1999). *Coping with loss*. Mahwah, NJ: Erlbaum.

Nolen-Hoeksema, S., McBride, A., & Larson, J. (1997). Rumination and psychological distress among bereaved partners. *Journal of Personality and Social Psychology, 72*, 855–862.

Nolen-Hoeksema, S., Parker, L. E., & Larson, J. (1994). Ruminative coping with depressed mood following loss. *Journal of Personality and Social Psychology, 67*, 92–104.

Noller, P., Law, H., & Comrey, A. L. (1987). Cattell, Comrey and Eysenck personality factors compared: More evidence for the five robust factors? *Journal of Personality and Social Psychology, 53*, 775–782.

Norem, J. (1989). Cognitive strategies as personality: Effectiveness, specificity, flexibility, and change. D. M. Buss & N. Cantor (Eds.), *Personality psychology: Recent trends and emerging directions* (pp. 45–60). New York: Springer-Verlag.

Norman, W. T. (1963). Toward an adequate taxonomy of personality attributes: Replicated factor structure in peer nomination personality ratings. *Journal of Abnormal and Social Psychology, 66*, 574–583.

Norman, W. T. (1967). *2800 personality trait descriptors: Normative operating characteristics for a university population*. Department of Psychology, University of Michigan, Ann Arbor, MI.

Notarius, C. I., & Levenson, R. W. (1979). Expressive tendencies and physiological response to stress. *Journal of Personality and Social Psychology, 37*, 1204–1210.

Nowak, A., & Vallacher, R. R. (1998). *Dynamical social psychology*. New York: Guilford Press.

Nozick, R. (1981). *Philosophical explanations*. Cambridge, MA: Belknap Press of Harvard University Press.

Nyborg, H. (Ed.) (1997). *The scientific study of human nature*. New York: Pergamon Elsevier Science Ltd.

Nystedt, L., Smari, J., & Boman, M. (1991). Self-schemata: Ambiguous operationalizations of an important concept. *European Journal of Personality, 5*, 1–14.

Oettingen, G. (1995). Cross-cultural perspectives on self-efficacy. In Bandura, A. (Ed.), *Self-efficacy in changing societies* (pp. 149–176). New York: Cambridge University Press.

Oettingen, G. (1996). Positive fantasy and motivation. In P. M. Gollwitzer & J. A. Bargh (Eds.), *The psychology of action: Linking cognition and motivation to behavior* (pp. 236–259). New York: Guilford.

Oettingen, G., & Wadden, T. A. (1991). Expectation, fantasy, & weight loss: Is the impact of positive thinking always positive? *Cognitive Therapy and Research, 15*, 167–175.

Ogilvie, D. M. (1987). The undesired self: A neglected variable in personality research. *Journal of Personality and Social Psychology, 52*, 379–385.

Ogilvie, D. M., & Ashmore, R. D. (1991). Self-with-other representations as a unit of analysis in self-concept research. In R. A. Curtis (Ed.), *The relational self: Theoretical convergences in psycho-*

*analysis and social psychology* (pp. 282–314). New York: Guilford.

Ogilvie, D. M., Fleming, C. J., & Pennell, G. (1998). Self-with-other representations. In Barone, D. F., Hersen, M., & Van Hasselt, V. B. (Eds.), *Advanced Personality*. New York: Plenum.

Ohlsson, S. (1998). Spearman's g = Anderson's ACT?: Reflections on the locus of generality in human cognition. *The Journal of the Learning Sciences, 7*, 135–145.

Oliver, M. B., & Hyde, J. S. (1993). Gender differences in sexuality. A meta-analysis. *Psychological Bulletin, 114*, 29–51.

Olweus, D., Mattison, A., Shalling, D., & Low, H. (1988). Circulating testosterone levels and aggression in adolescent males: A causal analysis. *Psychosomatic Medicine, 50*, 261–272.

Oosterwegel, A., & Oppenheimer, L. (1993). *The self-system: Developmental changes between and within self-concepts*. Hillsdale, NJ: Erlbaum.

Ortony, A., Clore, G. L., & Collins, A. (1988). *The cognitive structure of emotions*. New York: Cambridge University Press.

Ortony, A., & Turner, T. J. (1990). What's basic about basic emotions? *Psychological Review, 97*, 315–331.

Ostendorf, F. (1990). *Sprache und Personlichkeitsstruktur: Zur validitat des Funf-Faktoren-Modells der Personlichkeit*. Regensburg, Germany: Roderer-Verlag.

Ostendorf, F., & Angleitner, A. (1992). On the generality and comprehensiveness of the five-factor model of personality: Evidence of five robust factors in questionnaire data. In G. V. Caprara & G. Van Heck (Eds.) *Modern personality psychology* (pp. 73–109). London: Harvester-Wheatsheaf.

Osterman, K., Björkqvist, K., Lagerspetz, K. M. J., Kantiainen, A., Landau S. F., Fraczek, A., & Caprara, G. V. (1998). Cross-cultural evidence of female indirect aggression. *Aggressive Behavior, 24*, 1–8.

Overton, W. (1984). World views and their influence on psychological theory and research: Kuhn-Lakatos-Laudan. In H. Reese (Ed.), *Advances in Child Development and behavior* (pp. 191–226). New York: Academic Press.

Overton, W., & Reese, H. (1973). Models of development: Methodological implications. In J. Nesselroade & H. Reese (Eds.), *Life-span developmental psychology: Methodological issues* (pp. 65–86). New York: Academic Press.

Ozer, D. J. (1989). Construct validity in personality assessment In D. M. Buss & N. Cantor (Eds.), *Personality psychology: Recent trends and emerging directions* (pp. 201–209). New York: Springer Verlag.

Pacini, R., Muir, F., & Epstein, S. (1998). Depressive realism from the perspective of cognitive-experiential self-theory. *Journal of Personality and Social Psychology, 74*, 1056–1068.

Paik, H., & Comstock, C. (1994). The effects of television violence on antisocial behavior: A meta-analysis. *Communication Research, 21*, 516–546.

Paikoff, R., & Brooks-Gunn, J. (1991). Do parent-child relationships change during puberty? *Psychological Bulletin, 110*, 47–66.

Paivio, A. (1969). Mental imagery in associative learning and memory. *Psychological Review, 76*, 241–263. 1969

Pajares, F. (1996). Self-efficacy beliefs in academic settings. *Review of Educational Research, 66*, 543–578.

Panksepp, J. (1990). Gray zones at the emotion/cognition interface: A commentary. *Cognition and Emotion, 4*, 289–392.

Panksepp, J. (1992). A critical role for "affective neuroscience" in resolving what is basic about basic emotions. *Psychological Review, 99*, 554–560.

Panksepp, J. (1994). The clearest physiological distinctions between emotions will be found among the circuits of the brain. In P. Ekman & R. J. Davidson (Eds.), *The nature of emotion: Fundamental questions* (pp. 258–262). New York: Oxford University Press.

Papineau, D. (1996, June 21). A universe of zombies?: The problem of consciousness and the temptations of dualism. *The Times Literary Supplement*, pp. 3–4.

Parke, R. D. (1988). Families in life-span perspective. A multilevel developmental approach. In M. Hetherington, R. Lerner & M. Perlmutter (Eds.), *Child development in life-span perspective* (pp. 159–190). Hillsdale, NJ: Erlbaum.

Parke, R. D. (1996). *Fatherhood*. Cambridge, MA: Harvard University Press.

Parke, R. D., & Buriel, R. (1998). Socialization in the family: Ethnic and ecological perspectives. In W. Damon (Series ed.) & N. Eisenberg (Volume ed.) *Handbook of child development* (5th edition). Vol. 3: *Emotional and personality development* (pp. 3463–552). New York: Wiley.

Parsons, J. (1980). Psychosexual neutrality: is anatomy a destiny? In J. Parsons (Ed.), *The psychobiology of sex differences and sex roles.* (pp. 3–29). New York: Hemisphere.

Pastorelli, C., Caprara, G. V., Barbaranelli, C., Rola, J., Rozsa, S., & Bandura, A. (in press). Structure of children's perceived self-efficacy: A cross-national study. *European Journal of Psychological Assessment*.

Patterson, C. J. (1997). Children of lesbian and gay parents. *Advances in Clinical Child Psychology, 19*, 235–282.

Patterson, C. J., & Mischel, W. (1976). Effects of temptation-inhibiting and task-facilitating plans on self-control. *Journal of Personality and Social Psychology, 33*, 209–217.

Patterson, G. (1982). *Coercive family process*. Eugene, OR: Castalia.

Paunonen, S. (1998). Hierarchical organization of personality and prediction of behavior. *Journal of Personality and Social Psychology, 74,* 538–556.

Pavlov, I. P. (1927). *Conditioned reflexes.* Oxford: Oxford University Press.

Pavlov, I. P. (1935). *Conditioned reflexes and psychiatry.* New York: International Publishers.

Pavlov, I. P. (1955). *General types of animal and human higher nervous activity. Selected works.* Moscow: Foreign Language Publishing House (original work published in 1935).

Pavot, W., Diener, E., & Fujita, F. (1990). Extraversion and happiness. *Personality and Individual Differences, 11,* 1299–1306.

Pavot, W., Fujita, F., & Diener, E. (1997). The relation between self-aspect congruence, personality and subjective well-being. *Personality and Individual Differences, 22,* 183–191.

Peabody, D. (1987). Selecting representative trait adjectives. *Journal of Personality and Social Psychology, 52,* 59–71.

Peabody, D., & Goldberg, L. R. (1989). Some determinants of factor structures from personality-trait descriptors. *Journal of Personality and Social Psychology, 57,* 552–567.

Peake, P. K., & Cervone, D. (1989). Sequence anchoring and self-efficacy: Primacy effects in the consideration of possibilities. *Social Cognition, 7,* 31–50.

Pelham, B. (1995). Self-investment and self-esteem: Evidence for a Jamesian model of self-worth. *Journal of Personality and Social Psychology, 69,* 1141–1150.

Peng, K., & Nisbett, R. E. (1999). Culture, dialectics, and reasoning about contradiction. *American Psychologist, 54,* 741–754.

Pennebaker, J. W. (1989). Confession, inhibition, and disease. In L. Berkowitz (Ed.), *Advances in Experimental Social Psychology* (Vol. 22, pp. 211–244). San Diego, CA: Academic Press.

Pennebaker, J. W. (1997). Writing about emotional experiences as a therapeutic process. *Psychological Science, 8,* 162–166.

Pennebaker, J. W., & Beale, S. K. (1986). Confronting a traumatic event: Toward an understanding of inhibition and disease. *Journal of Abnormal Psychology, 95,* 274–281.

Pennebaker, J. W., Colder, M., & Sharp, L. K. (1990). Accelerating the coping process. *Journal of Personality and Social Psychology, 58,* 528–537.

Pennebaker, J. W., Hughes, C. F., & O'Heeron, R. C. (1987). The psychophysiology of confession: Linking inhibitory and psychosomatic processes. *Journal of Personality and Social Psychology, 52,* 781–793.

Pennebaker, J. W., Mayne, T. J., & Francis, M. E. (1997). Linguistic predictors of adaptive bereavement. *Journal of Personality & Social Psychology, 72,* 863–871.

Perloff, L., & Fetzer, B. K. (1983). Self-other judgments and perceived vulnerability to victimization. *Journal of Personality and Social Psychology, 50,* 502–510.

Perry, C., & Laurence, J. R. (1984). Mental processing outside of awareness: The contriutions of Freud and Janet. In K. S. Bowers & D. Meichenbaum (Eds.), *The unconscious reconsidered* (pp. 9–40). New York: Wiley-Interscience.

Perry, D., Perry, L., & Kennedy, E. (1992). Conflict and the development of antisocial behavior. In C. Shantz & W. W. Hartup (Eds.), *Conflict in child adolescent development* (pp. 301–329). New York: Cambridge University Press.

Pervin, L. A. (1990a). A brief history of modern personality theory. In L. Pervin (Ed.), *Handbook of personality: Theory and research.* (pp. 3–18). New York: Guilford.

Pervin, L. A. (Ed.) (1990). *Handbook of personality: Theory and research.* New York: Guilford.

Pervin, L. A. (1994). A critical analysis of current trait theory. *Psychological Inquiry, 5,* 103–113.

Pervin, L., & John, O. P. (Eds.) (1999). *Handbook of personality: Theory and research* (2nd ed.). New York: Guilford.

Petersen, A., & Taylor, B. (1980). The biological approach to adolescence: Biological change and psychological adaptation. In J. Adelson (Ed.), *Handbook of adolescent psychology* (pp. 117–155). New York: Wiley.

Peterson, C., & Park, C. (1998). Learned helplessness and explanatory style. In D. F. Barone, M. Herson, & V. B. Van Hasselt (Eds.), *Advanced personality* (pp. 287–310). New York: Plenum.

Peterson, C., & Seligman, M. E. P. (1984). Causal explanations as a risk factor for depression: Theory and evidence. *Psychological Review, 91,* 347–374.

Peterson, D. R. (1968). *The clinical study of social behavior.* New York: Appleton.

Petrie, K. J., Booth, R. J., & Pennebaker, J. W. (1998). The immunological effects of thought suppression. *Journal of Personality and Social Psychology, 75,* 1264–1272.

Phillips, D. C., & Orton, R. (1983). The new causal principle of cognitive learning theory: Perspectives on Bandura's "reciprocal determinism". *Psychological Review, 90,* 158–165.

Piaget, J. (1932). *Le jugement moral chez l'enfant.* Paris: Presses Universitaires de France.

Piaget, J. (1947). *La psychologie de l'intelligence.* Paris: Colin.

Piaget, J. (1970). *La situation des sciences de l'homme dans le système de la recherche entredisciplinaire et mecanismes communs.* Paris: Mouton.

Pinker, S. (1997). *How the mind works.* New York: Norton.

Plomin, R. (1994). *Genetics and Experience.* Thousand Oaks, CA: Sage.

Plomin, R., & Bergeman, C. (1991). The nature of nurture genetic influence on "environmental" measures. *Behavioral and Brain Sciences, 14,* 373–427.

Plomin, R., & Caspi, A. (1998). DNA and personality. *European Journal of Personality, 12,* 387–407.

Plomin, R., & Daniels, D. (1987). Why are children in the same family so different from one another? *Behavioral and Brain Sciences, 10,,* 1–15.

Plomin, R., De Fries, J., & Loehlin, J. C. (1977). Genotype-environment interaction and correlation in the analysis of human behavior. *Psychological Bulletin, 84,* 309–322.

Plomin, R., De Fries, J., McClearn, G., & Rutter, M. (1997). *Behavioral genetics* (3rd ed.). New York: Freeman.

Plomin, R., Owen, M. J., & McGuffin, P. (1994). The genetic basis of complex human behaviors. *Science, 264,* 1733–1739.

Plutchik, R. (1980). *Emotion: A psychobioevolutionary synthesis.* New York: Harper & Row.

Plutchik, R. (1984). Emotions: A general psychoevolutionary theory. In K. R. Scherer & P. Ekman (Eds.), *Approaches to emotion* (pp. 197–219). Hillsdale, NJ: Erlbaum.

Politzer, G. (1947). *La crise de la psychologie contemporaine.* Paris: Editions Sociales.

Polkinghorne, D. (1988). *Narrative knowing and the human sciences.* Albany, NY: State University of New York Press.

Popper, K. (1959). *The logic of scientific discovery.* London: Hutchinson.

Popper, K. (1969). *Conjectures and refutations.* London: Routledge & Kegan Paul.

Posner, M. I. (1978). *Chronometric explorations of mind.* Hillsdale, NJ: Lawrence Erlbaum Associates.

Powers, W. T. (1973). *Behavior: The control of perception.* Chicago: Aldine.

Pratkanis, A. R., & Greenwald, A. G. (1985). How shall the self be conceived? *Journal for the Theory of Social Behavior, 15,* 311–329.

Pribram, K., & McGuiness, D. (1975). Arousal, activation, and effort in the control of attention. *Psychological Review, 82,* 116–149.

Pulkkinen, L. (1996). Female and male personality styles: A typological and developmental analysis. *Journal of Personality and Social Psychology, 70,* 1286–1306.

Putallaz, M., & Sheppard, B. (1992). Conflict management and social competence. In C. Shantz & W. Hartup (Eds.), *Conflict in child and adolescent development* (pp. 330–355). New York: Cambridge University Press.

Pyszczynski, T., Greenberg, J., & Solomon, S. (1997). Why do we need what we need: A terror management perspective on the roots of human social motivation. *Psychological Inquiry, 8,* 1–20.

Radke-Yarrow, M., Zahn-Waxler, C., & Chapman, M. (1983): Children's prosocial dispositions and behaviors. In P. H. Mussen (Ed.) (Series Ed.) & M. Hetherington (Vol. Ed.), *Handbook of child psychology* (4th edition). Vol. 4th: *Socialization, personality and social development.* (pp. 469–545). New York: Wiley.

Rapaport, D. (1960). *The structure of psychoanalytic theory.* New York: International Universities Press.

Raynor, J. (1982). *Motivation, career striving, and aging.* Washington, D. C.: Hemisphere.

Read, S. J., & Miller, L. C. (1989). Inter-personalism: Toward a goal-based theory of persons in relationships. In L. A. Pervin (Ed.), *Goal concepts in personality and social psychology.* Hillsdale, NJ: Erlbaum.

Read, S. J., & Miller, L. (1998) (Eds.). *Connectionist models of social reasoning and social behavior.* Mahwah, NJ: Erlbaum.

Reich, W. (1945). *Character analysis: Principles and techniques for psychoanalysis in practice and training* (3rd ed.). New York: Orgone Institute Press.

Reinert, G. (1979). Prolegomena to a history of lifespan developmental psychology. In P. B. Baltes & O. G. Brim, Jr. (Eds.)., Life-span development and behavior (Vol. 2, pp. 205–254). New York: Academic Press.

Reiss, S. (1991). Expectancy model of fear, anxiety, and panic. *Clinical Psychology Review, 11,* 141–153.

Renfrew, C. (1989). The origins of Indo-European languages. *Scientific American, 261,* 106–114.

Renfrew, C. (1992). Archaeology, genetics, and linguistic diversity. *Man, 27,* 445–478.

Resnick, S. M., Berenbaum, S. A., Gottesman, I. I., & Bouchard, T. J., Jr. (1986). Early hormonal influences on cognitive functioning in congenital adrenal hyperplasia. *Developmental Psychology, 22,* 191–198.

Revelle, W. (1995). Personality processes. *Annual Review of Psychology, 46,* 295–328.

Riemann, R., Angleitner, A., & Strelau, J. (1997). Genetic and environmental influences on personality: A study of twins reared together using the self-and peer report NEO-FFI scales. *Journal of Personality, 65,* 449–475.

Roberts, B. W. (1997). Plaster or plasticity: Are adult work experiences associated with personality change in women? *Journal of Personality, 65,* 205–232.

Robins, R. W., John, O. P., Caspi, A., Moffitt, T. E., & Stouthamer-Loeber, M. (1996). Resilient, overcontrolled, and undercontrolled boys: Three replicable personality types. *Journal of Personality and Social Psychology, 70,* 157–171.

Robins, R. W., John, O. P., & Caspi, A. (1994). Major dimensions of personality in early adolescence: The big five and beyond. In C. F. Halverson, Jr., G. A. Kohnstamm, & R. P. Martin (Eds.), *The developing structure of temperament and personality from infancy to adulthood* (pp. 267–291). Hillsdale, NJ: Erlbaum.

Robinson, R. (1995). The principles of genetics and heredity. The New Encyclopedia Britannica. Macropaedia. (Vol. 19, pp. 699–740). Chicago, IL : Encyclopedia Britannica Inc.

Rodin, J. (1990). Control by any other name: Definitions, concepts, and processes. In J. Rodin, & C. Schooler (Eds.), *Self-directedness: Cause and effects throughout the life course* (pp. 1–17). Hillsdale, N.J.: Erlbaum.

Rodin, J., & Langer, E., (1977). Long-term effects of a control-relevant intervention with the institutionalized aged. *Journal of Personality and Social Psychology, 35,* 897–902.

Rogers, C. (1959). A theory of therapy, personality, and interpersonal relations, as developed in a client-centered framework. In S. Koch (Ed.), *Psychology: A study of a science* (Vol. 3, pp. 184–256). New York: McGraw-Hill.

Rogers, C. (1961). *On becoming a person.* Boston: Houghton Mifflin.

Rogers, T. B., Kuiper, N. A., & Kirker, W. S. (1977). Self-reference and the encoding of personal information. *Journal of Personality and Social Psychology, 35,* 677–688.

Rogoff, B. (1990). *Apprenticeship in thinking: Cognitive development in social contexts.* New York: Oxford University Press.

Rogoff, B. (1998). Cognition as a collaborative process. In W. Damon (Series Ed.) & D. Kuhn & R. S. Siegler (Vol. Eds.), *Handbook of Child Psychology* (5th Edition). Vol. 2: Cognition, perception, and language (pp. 679–744). New York: Wiley.

Rohner, R. P. (1998). Father love and child development: History and current evidence. *Contemporary Directions in Psychological Science, 7,* 157–161.

Rokeach, M. (1973). *The nature of human values.* New York: The Free Press

Rolston, H., III (1999). *Genes, genesis, and God: Values and their origins in natural and human history.* Cambridge, UK: Cambridge University Press.

Rorer, L. G. (1990). Personality assessment: A conceptual survey. In L. A. Pervin (Ed.), *Handbook of personality: Theory and research* (pp. 693–720). New York: Guilford.

Rorty, A. O. (Ed.). (1980). *Explaining emotions.* Berkeley: University of California Press.

Rosch, E. (1978). Principles of categorization. In E. Rosch & B. B. Lloyd (Eds.), *Cognition and categorization* (pp. 27–48). Hillsdale, NJ: Erlbaum.

Rose, R., & Kaprio, J. (1988). Frequency of social contact and intrapair resemblance of adult monozygotic cotwins – Or does shared experience influence personality after all? *Behavior Genetics, 18,* 309–328.

Roseman, I. J. (1984). Cognitive determinants of emotion: A structural theory. In P. Shaver (Ed.), *Review of Personality and Social Psychology. Vol. 5: Emotions, relationship, and health.*

Rosenberg, E. L., & Ekman, P. (1994). Coherence between expressive and experiential systems in emotion. *Cognition and Emotion, 8,* 201–229.

Rosenberg, E. L., & Fredrickson, B. L. (1998). Overview to special issue: Understanding emotions means crossing boundaries within psychology. *Review of General Psychology, 2,* 243–246.

Rosenberg, M. (1979). *Conceiving the self.* New York: Basic Books.

Rosenberg, S. (1988). Self and others: Studies in social psychology and autobiography. In L. Berkowitz (Ed.), *Advances in experimental social psychology* (Vol. 21, pp. 57–95). New York: Academic Press.

Rosenberg, S., Nelson, C., & Vivekananthan, P. S., (1968). A multidimensional approach to the study of personality dimensions. *Journal of Personality and Social Psychology, 9,* 283–294.

Rosenthal, C. (1978). Interpersonal expectancy effects: The first 345 studies. *Behavioral and Brain Sciences, 1,* 377–415.

Rosenthal, R. (1991). *Meta-analytic procedures for social research.* Newbury Park, CA: Sage.

Rosenthal, R. (1994). On being one's own study: Experimenter effects in behavioral research 30 years later. In W. R. Shadish & S. Fuller (Eds.), *The social psychology of science* (pp. 214–279). New York: Guilford.

Rosenthal, T. L., & Zimmerman, B. J. (1978). *Social learning and cognition.* New York: Academic Press.

Rosenthal, R., & Jacobson, L. (1968). *Pygmalion in the classroom.* New York: Holt, Rinehart, & Winston.

Ross, H., & Conant, C. (1992). The social structure of early conflict: Interaction, relationships, and alliances. In C. Shantz & W. Hartup (Eds.), *Conflict in child and adolescent development* (pp. 153–185). New York: Cambridge University Press.

Ross, L. (1977). The intuitive psychologist and his shortcomings: distortions in the attribution process. In L. Berkowitz (Ed.), *Advances in experimental social psychology. (Vol. 10,* pp. 174–220). New York: Academic Press.

Ross, L., Greene, D., & House, P. (1977). The false consensus effect: An egocentric bias in social perception and attribution processes. *Journal of Experimental Social Psychology, 13,* 279–301.

Ross, L., & Nisbett, R. E. (1991). *The person and the situation.* New York: McGraw-Hill.

Ross, M. (1989). Relation of implicit theories to the construction of personal histories. *Psychological Review, 96,* 341–357.

Ross, M., & Newby-Clark, I. R. (1998). Construing the past and future. *Social Cognition, 16,* 133–150.

Rothbart, M. K. (1989) Biological processes in temperament. Temperament in childhood. In G. A.

Kohnstamm, J. E. Bates & M. K. Rothbart (Eds.) *Temperament in childhood.* (pp. 77–110), Chichester, UK: Wiley.

Rothbart, M. K. (1994). Emotional development: Changes in reactivity and self-regulation. In P. Ekman & R. J. Davidson (Eds.), *The nature of emotion: Fundamental questions* (pp. 369–375). New York: Oxford University Press.

Rothbart, M. K., Ahadi, S. A., & Hershey, K. L. (1994). Temperament and social behavior in childhood. *Merrill-Palmer Quarterly, 40,* 21–39.

Rothbart, M. K., & Bates, J. (1998) Temperament. In W. Damon (Series Ed.) & N. Eisenberg (Vol. Ed.), *Handbook of child psychology* (5th edition). Vol. 3: *Social, emotional, and personality development* (pp. 105–176). New York: Wiley.

Rothbaum, F., Weisz, J. R., & Snyder, S. S. (1982). Changing the world and changing the self: A two-process model of perceived control. *Journal of Personality and Social Psychology, 42,* 5–37.

Rothkopf, E. Z., & Billington, M. J. (1975). A two-factor model of the effect of goal descriptive directions on learning from text. *Journal of Educational Psychology, 67,* 692–704.

Rotter, J. B. (1954). *Social learning and clinical psychology.* Englewood Cliffs, NJ: Prentice-Hall.

Rotter, J. B. (1966). Generalized expectancies for internal versus external control of reinforcement. *Psychological Monographs, 80.*

Rowe, D. C. (1994). *The limits of family influence.* New York: The Guilford Press.

Rowe, D. C., Rodgers J. L., & Meseck-Bushey, S. (1992). Sibling delinquency and the family environment: Shared and unshared influences. *Child Development, 63,* 59–67.

Rozin, P., & Fallon, A. E. (1987). A perspective on disgust. *Psychological Review, 94,* 23–41.

Rubin, K. H., Hastings, P. D., Stewart, S. L., Henderson, H. A., & Chen, X. (1997). The consistency and concomitants of inhibition: Some of the children, all of the time. *Child Development, 68,* 467–483.

Ruble, D. N. (1994). A phase model of transitions: Cognitive and motivational consequences. In M. P. Zanna (Ed.), *Advances in experimental social psychology* (Vol. 26, pp. 163–214). San Diego: Academic Press.

Ruble, D. N., Fleming, A. S., Hackel, L. S., & Stangor, C. (1988). Changes in the marital relationship during the transition to first time motherhood: Effects of violated expectations concerning division of household labor. *Journal of Personality and Social Psychology, 55,* 78–87.

Ruble, D. N., & Martin, C. L. (1998). Gender development. In W. Damon (Series Ed.) & N. Eisenberg (Vol. Ed.), *Handbook of Child Psychology* (5th edition): Vol. 3: *Social, emotional and personality development* (pp. 933–1016). New York: Wiley.

Ruitenbeck, H. M. (Ed.) (1967). *Psychoanalysis and female sexuality.* New Haven, CT: College and University Press.

Rumelhart, D. (1975). Notes on a schema for stories. In D. G. Bobrow & A. M. Collins (Eds.), *Representation and understanding: Studies in cognitive science.* New York: Academic Press.

Rumelhart, D. E., McClelland, J. L., & PDP Research Group (1986). *Parallel distributed processing: Explorations in the microstructure of cognition: Vol. 1. Foundations.* Cambridge, MA: MIT Press.

Rusalov, V. M. (1979). *Biological bases of individual psychological differences.* Moskow: Nauka.

Rusalov, V. M. (1989). Object related and communicative aspects of human temperament: a new questionnaire of the structure of temperament. *Personality and Individual Differences, 10,* 817–827.

Rushton, J. P. (1995). *Race, evolution, and behavior: A life history perspective.* New Brunswick, N.J. Transaction Publishers

Russell, B. (1945). *A history of Western philosophy.* New York: Simon & Schuster.

Russell, J. A. (1979). Affective space is bipolar. *Journal of Personality and Social Psychology, 37,* 345–356.

Russell, J. A., & Carroll, J. M. (1999). On the bipolarity of positive and negative affect: Rumors of its death are greatly exaggerated. *Psychological Bulletin.*

Rusting, C. L., & Nolen-Hoeksema, S. (1998). Regulating responses to anger: Effects of rumination and distraction on angry mood. *Journal of Personality and Social Psychology, 74,* 790–803.

Rutter, M. (1987). Resilience in the face of adversity. Protective factors and resistance to psychiatric disorder. *British Journal of Psychiatry, 147,* 598–611.

Rutter, M., Dunn, J., Plomin, R., Simonoff, I, Pickles, A., Maughan, B., Ormell, J., Meyer J., & Eaves, L. (1997). Integrating nature and nurture: Implications for person-environment correlations and interactions for developmental psychopathology. *Development and Psychopathology, 9,* 335–364.

Rutter, M., & Rutter, M. (1993). *Developing minds: Challenge and continuity across the life span.* Harmondsworth, UK: Penguin.

Rychlak, J. F. (1997). *In defense of human consciousness.* Washington, D. C.: American Psychological Association.

Sackeim, H. A., & Gur, R. C. (1985). Voice recognition and the ontological status of self-deception. *Journal of Personality and Social Psychology, 48,* 1365–1368.

Salmon, W. C. (1989). Four decades of scientific explanation. In P. Kitcher & W. C. Salmon (Eds.), *Minnesota studies in the philosophy of science, Vol. XIII. Scientific Explanation.* Minneapolis: University of Minnesota Press.

Salovey, P. (1992). Mood induced self-focused attention. *Journal of Personality and Social Psychology, 62*, 699–707.

Salovey, P., & Birnbaum, D. (1989). Influence of mood on health-relevant cognitions. *Journal of Personality and Social Psychology, 57*, 539–551.

Salovey, P., Hsee, C. K., & Mayer, J. D. (1993). Emotional intelligence and the self-regulation of affect. In D. M. Wegner & J. D. Pennebaker (Eds.), *Handbook of mental control* (pp. 258–277). Englewood Cliffs, NJ: Prentice-Hall.

Salovey, P., & Mayer, J. D. (1990). Emotional intelligence. *Imagination, Cognition and Personality, 9*, 185–211.

Salovey, P., & Mayer, J. D. (1994). Some final thoughts about personality and intelligence. In R. J. Sternberg, & P. Ruzgis (Eds.), *Personality and intelligence* (pp. 303–318). New York: Cambridge University Press.

Salovey, P., Mayer, J. D., & Rosenhan, D. L. (1991). Mood and helping: Mood as a motivator of helping and helping as a regulator of mood. In M. S. Clark (Ed.), *Prosocial behavior: Review of personality and social psychology* (Vol. 12, pp. 215–237). Newbury Park, CA: Sage.

Sameroff, A. J. & Chandler, M. J. (1975). Reproductive risk and the continuum of caretaking casualty. In F. D. Horowitz, E. M. Hetherington, S. Scarr, & G. M. Siegel (Eds.) *Review of child development research* (pp. 187–244). Chicago: University of Chicago Press.

Samuels, A. (1985). *Jung and the postjungians.* London: Routledge and Kegan Paul.

Sancilio, M. F., Plumert, J. M., & Hartup, W. W. (1989). Friendship and aggressiveness as determinants of conflict outcomes in middle childhood. *Developmental Psychology, 25*, 812–819.

Sanderson, C. A., & Cantor, N. (1999). A life task perspective on personality coherence: Stability versus change in tasks, goals, strategies, and outcomes. In D. Cervone & Y. Shoda (Eds.), *The coherence of personality: Social-cognitive bases of consistency, variability, and organization* (pp. 372–392). New York: Guilford Press.

Santioso, R., Kunda, Z., & Fong, G. T. (1990). Motivated recruitment of autobiographical memories. *Journal of Personality and Social Psychology, 59*, 229–241.

Sarason, I. G., Pierce, G. R., & Sarason, B. R. (Eds.), (1996) *Cognitive interference: Theories, methods, and findings.* Mahwah, NJ: Erlbaum.

Sarason, I. G., Smith, R. E., & Diener, E. (1975). Personality research: Components of variance attributable to the person and the situation. *Journal of Personality and Social Psychology, 32*, 199–204.

Sarbin, T. R. (Ed.), (1986). *Narrative psychology: The storied nature of human conduct.* New York: Praeger.

Sarter, M., Berntson, G. G., & Cacioppo, J. T. (1996). Brain imaging and cognitive neuroscience: Toward strong inference in attributing function to structure. *American Psychologist, 51*, 13–21.

Saucier, G., & Goldberg, L. R. (1996). The language of personality: Lexical perspectives on the five-factor model. In J. Wiggins (Ed.), *The five-factor model of personality* (pp. 21–50). New York: Guilford.

Saucier, G., & Goldberg, L. R. (1998). What is beyond the big five? *Journal of Personality, 66*, 495–524.

Saudino, K. J., McGuire, S., Reiss, D., Hetherington, E. M., & Plomin, R. (1995). Parent rating of EAS temperament in twins, full siblings, half siblings and step siblings. *Journal of Personality and Social Psychology, 68*, 723–733.

Saunders, D. R. (1956). Moderator variables in prediction. *Educational Psychology Measurement, 16*, 209–222.

Savage, L. J. (1954). *The foundations of statistics.* New York: Wiley.

Scabini, E. (1995). *Psicologia sociale della famiglia.* Torino: Bollati Boringhieri.

Scarr, S. (1992). Development theories for the 1990s: Development and individual differences. *Child Development, 63*, 1–19.

Scarr, S. (1993). Biological and cultural diversity: The legacy of Darwin for development. *Child Development, 64*, 1333–1353.

Scarr, S., & McCartney, K. (1983). How people make their own environments: A theory of genotype–environment effect. *Child Development, 54*, 424–435.

Schacter, D. L. (1987). Implicit memory: History and current status. *Journal of Experimental Psychology: Learning, Memory, and Cognition, 13*, 501–518.

Schacter, D. L. (1996). *Searching for memory: The brain, the mind, and the past.* New York: Basic Books.

Schachter, S., & Singer, J. E. (1962). Cognitive, social, and physiological determinants of emotional state. *Psychological Review, 69*, 379–399.

Schank, R., & Abelson, R. (1977). *Scripts, plans, goals, and understanding.* Hillsdale, NJ: Erlbaum.

Scheier, M. F., & Carver, C. S. (1983). Self-directed attention and the comparison of self with standards. *Journal of Experimental Social Psychology, 19*, 205–222.

Schein, E. H. (1985). *Organizational culture and leadership: A dynamic view.* San Francisco: Jossey Bass.

Scherer, K. R. (1984). On the nature and function of emotion: A component process approach. In K. R. Scherer & P. Ekman (Eds.), *Approaches to emotion* (pp. 293–317). Hillsdale, NJ: Lawrence Erlbaum Associates.

Scherer, K. R. (1994). Toward a concept of "modal emotions." In P. Ekman & R. J. Davidson (Eds.),

*The nature of emotion: Fundamental questions* (pp. 25–31). New York: Oxford University Press.

Scherer, K. R. (1997). The role of culture in emotion-antecedent appraisal. *Journal of Personality and Social Psychology, 73,* 902–922.

Scherer, K. R., & Wallbott, H. G. (1994). Evidence for universality and cultural variation of differential emotion response patterning. *Journal of Personality and Social Psychology, 66*(2), 310–328.

Schmitt, M., & Borkenau, P. (1992). The consistency of personality. In G. V. Caprara & G. Van Heck (Eds.) *Modern personality psychology* (pp. 29–55). London: Harvester-Wheatsheaf

Schmitt, D. P., & Buss, D. M. (1996). Strategic self promotion and competitor derogation: Sex and context effects on the perceived effectiveness of mate attraction tactics. *Journal of Personality and Social Psychology, 70,* 1185–1204:

Schneewind, K., Beckmann, M., & Engfer, A. (1983). *Eltern und Kinder.* Stuttgart: Kohlhammer.

Schneider, W., & Pimm-Smith, M. (1997). Consciousness as a message aware control mechanism to modulate cognitive processing. In J. D. Cohen & J. W. Schooler (Eds.), *Scientific approaches to consciousness* (pp. 65–80). Mahwah, NJ: Erlbaum.

Schneider, W., & Shiffrin, R. M. (1977). Controlled and automatic human information processing. I. Detection, search, and attention. *Psychological Review, 84,* 1–66.

Schunk, D. H. (1989). Self-efficacy and cognitive skill learning. In C. Ames & R. Ames (Eds.), *Research on motivation in education. Goals and cognitions* (Vol. 3, pp. 13–44). San Diego: Academic Press.

Schunk, D. (1995). Self-efficacy and education and instruction. In J. E. Maddux (Ed.), *Self-efficacy, adaptation, and adjustment: Theory, research, and application* (pp. 281–303). New York: Plenum.

Schunk, D. H., & Zimmerman, B. J. (Eds). (1998). *Self-regulated learning: From teaching to self-reflective practice.* New York: Guilford.

Schwartz, G. E., Weinberger, D. A., & Singer, J. A. (1981). Cardiovascular differentiation of happiness, sadness, anger and fear following imagery and exercise. *Psychosomatic Medicine, 43,* 343–368.

Schwartz, J. E., Friedman, H. S., Tucker, J. S., Tomlison-Keasey, C., Wingard, D. L., & Criqui, M. H. (1995). Childhood sociodemographic and psychological factors as predictors of mortality across the life-span. *American Journal of Public Health, 85,* 1237–1245.

Schwartz, S. (1992). Universals in the content and structure of values: Theoretical advances and empirical tests in 20 countries. In M. P. Zanna (Ed.), *Advances in experimental social psychology* (Vol. 25, pp. 1–65). New York: Academic Press.

Schwarz, N. (1990). Feelings as information: Information and motivational functions of affective states. In E. T. Higgins and R. M. Sorrentino (Eds.), *Handbook of motivation and cognition:*

*Foundations of social behavior,* (Vol. 2, pp. 527–561). New York: Guilford.

Schwarz, N., Bless, H., & Bohner, G. (1991). Mood and persuasion: Affective states influence the processing of persuasive communication. In M. Zanna (Ed.), *Advances in experimental social psychology* (Vol. 24, pp. 161–199). San Diego, CA: Academic Press.

Schwarz, N., & Clore, G. L. (1983). Mood, misattribution, and judgments of well-being: Informative and directive functions of affective states. *Journal of Personality and Social Psychology, 45,* 513–523.

Schwarz, N., & Clore, G. L. (1996). Feelings and phenomenal experience. In E. T. Higgins & A. W. Kruglanski (Eds.), *Social psychology: Handbook of basic principles* (p. 433–465). New York: Guilford.

Schwarzer, R., & Fuchs, R. (1995). Changing risk behaviors and adopting health behaviors: The role of self-efficacy beliefs. In A. Bandura (Ed.), *Self-efficacy in changing societies* (pp. 259–288). New York: Cambridge University Press.

Schwarzer, R., Baessler, J., Kwiatek, P., & Schroeder, K. (1997). The assessment of optimistic self-beliefs: Comparisons of the German, Spanish, and Chinese versions of the general self-efficacy scale. *Applied Psychology: An International Review, 46,* 69–88.

Scott, W. A. (1969). Structure of natural cognitions. *Journal of Personality and Social Psychology, 12,* 261–278.

Scott, W. D., & Cervone, D. (2000). *Induced negative affect and high standards: Attribution for affect leads to a discounting effect.* Unpublished manuscript, University of Wyoming.

Scott, W. D., & Ingram, R. E. (1998). Affective influences in depression: Conceptual issues, multiple mechanisms, and cognitive consequences. In W. F. Flack & J. D. Laird (Eds.), *Emotions in psychopathology: Theory and research.* Series in affective science (pp. 200–215). New York: Oxford University Press.

Searle, J. R. (1998). *Mind, language, and society.* New York: Basic Books.

Sears, R. R. (1950). Personality. *Annual Review of Psychology, 27,* 105–118.

Sears, R. R. (1951). Social behavior and personality development. In T. Parsons & E. A. Shils (Eds.) *Toward a general theory of action* (pp. 465–478). Cambridge, MA: Harvard University Press.

Sears, R. R., Rau, L., & Alpert, R. (1965). *Identification and child rearing.* Stanford, CA: Stanford University Press

Sedikedes, C., & Skowronski, J. J. (1997). The symbolic self in evolutionary context. *Personality and Social Psychology Review, 1,* 80–102.

Segall, M. H., Lonner, W. J., & Berry, J. W. (1998). Cross-cultural psychology as a scholarly discipline: On the flowering of culture in behavioral research. *American Psychologist, 53,* 1101–1110.

Seligman, M. E. P. (1975). *Helplessness*. San Francisco: W. H. Freeman.

Seligman, M. E. P., & Csikszentmihalyi, M. (Eds.) (2000). Positive psychology [Special issue]. *American Psychologist, 55* (1).

Seligman, M. E. P. (1991). *Learned Optimisim*. New York: Alfred A. Knopf.

Séve, L. (1975). *Marxisme et théorie de la personnalité*. Paris: Editions Sociales.

Sexton, T. L., & Tuckman, B. W. (1991). Self-efficacy beliefs and behavior: The role of self-efficacy and outcome expectations over time. *Personality and Individual Differences, 12*, 725–736.

Shadel, W. G., Niaura, R., & Abrams, D. (in press). An idiographic approach to understanding personality structure and individual differences among smokers. *Cognitive Therapy and Research*.

Shaffer, D. (1996). Understanding bias in scientific practice. *Philosophy of Science, 63*, (Supplement), 89–97.

Shah, J., & Higgins, E. T. (1997). Expectancy x value effects: Regulatory focus as a determinant of magnitude *and* direction. *Journal of Personality and Social Psychology, 73*, 447–458.

Shaver, P. R., & Hazan, C. (1993). Adult romantic attachment: Theory and evidence. In D. Perlman & W. Jones (Eds.), *Advances in personal relationships* (Vol. 4, pp. 29–70). London: Jessica Kingsely Publishers.

Shaver, P., Schwartz, J., Kirson, D., & O'Connor, C. (1987). Emotion knowledge: Further explorations of a prototype approach. *Journal of Personality and Social Psychology, 52*, 1061–1086.

Shaver, P. R., & Brennan, K. A. (1992). Attachment styles and the "Big Five" personality traits: Their connections with each other and with romantic relationship outcomes. *Personality and Social Psychology Bulletin, 18*, 536–545.

Shavit, Y., & Blossfeld, H. (1993). *Persistent inequality*. Boulder, CO: Westview Press.

Sheldon, W. H., & Stevens, S. S. (1942). *The varieties of human temperament*. New York: Harper & Row.

Sherer, M., Maddux, J. E., Mercandante, B., Prentice-Dunn, B. J., & Rogers, R. W. (1982). The Self-Efficacy Scale: Construction and validation. *Psychological Reports, 51*, 663–671.

Shevrin, H. (1988). Unconscious conflict: a convergent psychodynamic and electro-physiological approach. In M. J. Horowitz (Ed.), *Psychodynamics and cognition*. Chicago, IL: University of Chicago Press.

Shevrin, H., & Dickman, S. (1980). The psychological unconscious: A necessary assumption for all psychological theory? *American Psychologist, 35*, 421–434.

Shimmack, U., & Hartmann, K. (1997). Individual differences in the memory representation of emotional episodes: Exporing the cognitive processes in repression. *Journal of Personality and Social Psychology, 73*, 1064–1079.

Shiner, R. L. (1998). How shall we speak of children's personalities in middle childhood? A preliminary taxonomy. *Psychological Bulletin, 124*, 308–332.

Shmelyov, A. G., & Pokhil'ko, V. I. (1993). A taxonomy-oriented study of Russian personality-trait names. *European Journal of Personality, 7*, 1–17.

Shoda, Y. (1999). Behavioral expressions of a personality system: Generation and perception of behavioral signatures. In D. Cervone & Y. Shoda (Eds.), *The coherence of personality: Social-cognitive bases of consistency, variability, and organization* (pp. 155–181). New York: Guilford Press.

Shoda, Y., & Mischel, W. (1998). Personality as a stable cognitive-affective activation network: Characteristic patterns of behavior variation emerge from a stable personality structure. In S. J. Read, & L. C. Miller, (Eds.). *Connectionist models of social reasoning and social behavior*. (pp. 175–208). Mahwah, NJ, USA: Lawrence Erlbaum Associates.

Shoda, Y., Mischel, W., & Peake, P. K. (1990). Predicting adolescent cognitive and self-regulatory competencies from preschool delay of gratification: Identifying diagnostic conditions. *Journal of Personality and Social Psychology, 26*, 978–986.

Shoda, Y., & Mischel, W., & Wright, J. C. (1994). Intraindividual stability in the organization and patterning of behavior: Incorporating psychological situations into the idiographic analysis of personality. *Journal of Personality and Social Psychology, 67*, 674–687.

Showers, C. (1992). Evaluatively integrative thinking about characteristics of the self. *Personality and Social Psychology Bulletin, 18*, 719–729.

Showers, C. J., Abramson, L. Y., & Hogan, M. E. (1998). The dynamic self: How the content and structure of the self-concept change with mood. *Journal of Personality and Social Psychology, 75*, 478–493.

Showers, C. J., & Kling, K. C. (1996). Organization of self-knowledge: Implications for recovery from sad mood. *Journal of Personality & Social Psychology, 70*, 578–590.

Shweder, R. A. (1991). *Thinking through cultures*. Cambridge, MA: Harvard University Press.

Shweder, R. A. (1993). The cultural psychology of the emotions. In M. Lewis & J. Haviland (Eds), *Handbook of emotions* (pp. 417–431). New York: Guilford

Shweder, R. A. (1994). "You're not sick, you're just in love": Emotion as an interpretive system. In P. Ekman & R. J. Davidson (Eds.), *The nature of emotion: Fundamental questions* (pp. 32–44). New York: Oxford University Press.

Shweder, R. A. & Sullivan, M. (1990). The semiotic subject of cultural psychology. In L. A. Pervin (Ed.) *Handbook of Personality* (pp. 399–416). New York: Guilford.

Sills, D. L. (Ed.). (1968). *International encyclopedia of the social sciences*. New York: The Macmillan Company & The Free Press.

Silverman, L. H. (1983). The subliminal psychodynamic activation method; Overview and comprehensive listing of studies. In J. Masling (Ed.) *Empirical studies of psychoanalytical theories*, (Vol. I, pp. 69–100). New York: Analytic Press.

Silverman, L. H., Bronstein, A., & Mendelsohn, E. (1976). The further use of the subliminal psychodynamic activation method for the experimental study of the clinical theory of psychoanalysis: On the specificity of the relationship between symptoms and unconscious conflicts. *Psychotherapy: Theory, Research, and Practice, 13*, 2–16.

Simon, H. A. (1983). *Reason in human affairs*. Stanford, CA: Stanford University Press.

Sinclair, R. C., & Mark, M. M. (1992). The influence of mood state on judgment and action: Effects on persuasion, categorization, social justice, person perception, and judgmental accuracy. In L. L. Martin & A. Tesseor (Eds.), *The construction of social judgment* (pp. 165–193). Hillsdale, N. J.: Erlbaum.

Singer, J. L., & Bonanno, G. (1990). Personality and private experience: Individual variations in consciousness and in attention to subjective phenomena. In L. A. Pervin (Ed.), *Handbook of Personality: Theory and Research* (pp. 419–444). New York: Guilford.

Singer, J. L., & Koligian, J. Jr. (1987). Personality: Developments in the study of private experience. *Annual Review of Psychology, 38*, 533–574.

Singer, J. L., & Salovey, P. (1988). Mood and memory: Evaluating the network theory of affect. *Clinical Psychology Review, 8*, 211–251.

Singer, J. L., & Salovey, P. (1991). Organized knowledge structures and personality: Person schemas, self schemas, prototypes, and scripts. In M. J. Horowitz (Ed.), *Person schemas and maladaptive interpersonal patterns* (pp. 13–31). Chicago: University of Chicago Press.

Singer, J. L., & Salovey, P. (1993). *The remembered self: Emotion and memory in personality*. New York: The Free Press.

Singer, J. L., & Singer, D. G. (1986). Family experience and television viewing as predictive of children's imagination, restlessness and aggression. *Journal of Social Issues, 42*, 107–124.

Skinner, B. F. (1971). *Beyond Freedom and Dignity*. New York: Knopf.

Skinner, E. A. (1995). *Perceived control, motivation, and coping*. Thousand Oaks, CA: Sage.

Skinner, E. A. (1996). A guide to constructs of control. *Journal of Personality and Social Psychology, 71*, 549–570.

Skowronski, J. J., Carlston, D. E., Mae, L., & Crawford, M. T. (1998). Spontaneous trait transference: Communicators take on the qualities they describe in others. *Journal of Personality and Social Psychology, 74*, 837–848.

Skuse, D. H., James, R. S., Bishop, D. V. M., Coppin, B., Dalton, P., Aamodt-Leeper, G., Bacouse-Hamilton, M., Creswell, C., McGurk, R., & Jacobs, P. A. (1997). Evidence from Turner's syndrome of an imprinted X-linked locus affective cognitive function. *Nature, 387*, 705–708.

Slaby, R. G., & Guerra, N. G. (1988). Cognitive mediators of aggression in adolescent offenders: I. Assessment. *Developmental Psychology, 24*, 580–588.

Smith, C. A. (1989). Dimensions of appraisal and physiological response in emotion. *Journal of Personality and Social Psychology, 56*, 339–353.

Smith, C. A., & Ellsworth, P. C. (1985). Patterns of cognitive appraisal in emotion. *Journal of Personality and Social Psychology, 48*, 813–838.

Smith, C. A., Haynes, K. N., Lazarus, R. S., & Pope, L. K. (1993). In search of the "hot" cognitions: Attributions, appraisals, and their relation to emotion. *Journal of Personality and Social Psychology, 65*, 916–929.

Smith, C. A., & Lazarus, R. S. (1990). Emotion and adaptation. In L. A. Pervin (Ed.), *Handbook of personality: Theory and research* (pp. 609–637). New York: Guilford.

Smith, C. A., & Pope, L. K. (1992). Appraisal and emotion: The interactional contribution of dispositional and situational factors. In M. S. Clark (Ed.), *Annual Review of Personality and Social Psychology, Vol. 14: Emotion and Social Behavior* (pp. 32–62). New York: Sage.

Smith, D. (1995). Living conditions in the twentieth century. In M. Rutter & D. Smith (Eds.) *Psychosocial disorders in young people* (pp. 194–295). Chichester, UK: John Wiley & Sons.

Smith, E. R. (1998). Mental representations and memory. In D. T. Gilbert, S. T. Fiske, & G. Lindzey (Eds.), *The handbook of social psychology* (4th ed., Volume 1, pp. 391–445). Boston, MA: McGraw-Hill.

Smith, G. J. W., & Hentschel, U. (1993). Percept-genetic methodology. In Hentschel, U., Smith, G. J. W., Ehlers, W., & Draguns, J. G. (Eds.), *The concept of defense mechanisms in contemporary psychology* (pp. 101–121). New York: Springer-Verlag.

Smith, M. V. (1994). Selfhood at risk: Postmodern perils and the perils of postmodernism, *American Psychologist, 49*, 405–411.

Smith, R. E, (1989). Effects of coping skills training on generalized self-efficacy and locus of control. *Journal of Personality and Social Psychology, 56*, 228–233.

Smuts, B. (1995). The evolutionary origins of patriarchy. *Human Nature, 6*, 1–32.

Smyth, J. M. (1998). Written emotional expression: Effect sizes, outcome types, and moderating variables. *Journal of Consulting and Clinical Psychology, 66*, 174–184.

Smyth, J. M., Stone, A. A., Hurewitz, A., & Kaell, A. (1999). Effects of writing about stressful experiences on symptom reduction in patients with asthma or rheumatoid arthritis: A randomized trial. *Journal of the American Medical Association, 281,* 1304–1309.

Snyder, M. (1974). The self-monitoring of expressive behavior. *Journal of Personality and Social Psychology, 30,* 526–537.

Snyder, M. (1987). *Public appearances/private realities: The psychology of self-monitoring.* New York: Freeman.

Snyder, M., & Ickes, W. (1985). Personality and social behavior. In G. Lindzey & E. Aronson (Eds.), *Handbook of Social Psychology: Vol. 2. Special fields and applications* (3rd ed., pp. 883–948). New York: Random House.

Socolar, R. R. (1997). A classification scheme for discipline: Type, mode of administration, context. *Aggression and Violent Behavior, 2,* 355–364.

Solomon, R. L. (1980). The opponent-process theory of acquired motivation: The costs of pleasure and the benefits of pain. *American Psychologist, 35,* 691–712.

Spalding, L. R., & Hardin, C. D. (1999). Unconscious unease and self-handicapping: Behavioral consequences of individual differences in implicit and explicit self-esteem. *Psychological Science, 10,* 535–539.

Spearman, C. (1927). *The abilities of man.* London: Macmillan.

Spence, J. T. (1985). Gender identity and its implications for the concepts of masculinity and femininity. In T. B. Sonderegger (Ed.), *Nebraska Symposium on Motivation* (Vol. 32, pp. 59–96). Lincoln: University of Nebraska Press.

Spence, J. T., Helmreich, R., & Stapp, J. (1975). Ratings of self and peers on sex-role attributes and their relation to self-esteem and conceptions of masculinity and femininity. *Journal of Personality and Social Psychology, 32,* 29–39.

Spence, J. T., & Stapp, J. (1974). The Personal Attributes Questionnaire: A measure of sex role stereotypes and masculinity-femininity. *JSAS: Catalog of Selected Documents in Psychology, 4,* 43. (Ms. No. 617)

Sperry, R. W. (1982). Some effects of disconnecting the cerebral hemispheres. *Science, 217,* 1223–1226.

Sperry, R. (1995). The future of psychology. *American Psychologist, 50,* 505–506.

Spitzer, S., & Parke, R. D. (1994). Family cognitive representations of social behavior and children's social competence. Paper presented at APA Meetings, Washington, D. C. (Cited in Parke & Buriel, 1998).

Sprecher, S., Sullivan, Q., & Hatfield, E. (1994). Mate selection preferences: Gender differences examined in a national sample. *Journal of Personality and Social Psychology, 66,* 1074–1080.

Sroufe, A. (1988). The role of infant-caregiver attachment in development. In J. Belsky & T. Nezworski (Eds.), *Clinical implications of attachment* (pp. 18–38). Hillsdale, NJ: Erlbaum.

Sroufe, A. (1996). *Emotional development.* New York: Cambridge University Press.

Srull, T. K., & Wyer, R. S., Jr. (1979). The role of category accessibility in the interpretation of information about persons: Some determinants and implications. *Journal of Personality and Social Psychology, 38,* 841–856.

Stallings, M. C., Hewitt, J. K., Cloninger, C. R., Heath, A. C., & Eaves, L. J. (1996). Genetic and environmental structure of the Tridimensional Personality Questionnaire: Three or four temperament dimensions. *Journal of Personality and Social Psychology, 70,* 127–140.

Stajkovic, A. D., & Luthans, F. (1998). Self-efficacy and work-related performance: A meta-analysis. *Psychological Bulletin, 124,* 240–261.

Staudinger, U., & Baltes, P. B. (1996). Interactive minds: A facilitative setting for wisdom-related performance? *Journal of Personality and Social Psychology, 71,* 746–762.

Staudinger, U. M., Marsiske, M., & Baltes, P. B. (1995). Resilience and reserve capacity in later adulthood: Potentials and limits of development across the life span. In D. Cicchetti & D. J. Cohen (Eds.), *Developmental Psychopathology, Vol. 2: Risk, disorder, and adaptation* (pp. 801–847). New York: Wiley.

Steele, C. M. (1997). A threat in the air: How stereotypes shape intellectual identity and performance. *American Psychologist, 52,* 613–629.

Steele, C. M. (1988). The psychology of self-affirmation: Sustaining the integrity of the self. In L. Berkowitz (Ed.), *Advances in experimental social psychology* (Vol. 21, pp. 261-302). New York: Academic Press.

Steele, C. M., & Aronson, J. (1995). Stereotype threat and the intellectual test performance of African-Americans. *Journal of Personality and Social Psychology, 69,* 797–811.

Stein, N., Folkman, S., Trabasso, T., & Richards, T. A. (1997). Appraisal and goal processes as predictors of psychological well-being in bereaved caregivers. *Journal of Personality & Social Psychology, 72,* 872–884.

Stelmack, R. M., & Achorn-Michaud, A. (1985). Extraversion, attention, and the habituation of the auditory evoked response. *Journal of Research in Personality, 19,* 416–428.

Stern, D. N. (1977). *The first relationships: Infant and mother.* Cambridge, MA.: Harvard University Press.

Stern, D. N. (1985). *The interpersonal world of the infant.* New York: Basic Books.

Stern, W. (1935). *Allgemeine Psychologie auf person-alisticher Grundlage*. Dordrecht, the Netherlands: Nijhoff.

Sternberg, R. J. (1985). *Beyond IQ: A triarchic theory of human intelligence*. New York: Cambridge University Press.

Sternberg, R. J. (1988). *The triarchic mind*. New York: Viking.

Sternberg, R. J. (1990). *Wisdom: Its nature, origins, and development*. New York: Cambridge University Press.

Sternberg, R. J. (1994). Thinking styles: Theory and assessment at the interface between intelligence and personality. In R. J. Sternberg & P. Ruzgis (Eds.) *Personality and intelligence* (pp. 169–187). New York: Cambridge University Press.

Sternberg, R. J. (1996). Personality, pupils, and purple cow: We have the right answers but do we have the right questions? *European Journal of Personality, 10*, 447–452.

Sternberg, R. J. (1997a). The concept of intelligence and its role in lifelong learning and success. *American Psychologist, 1030–1037.*

Sternberg, R. J. (1997b). *Thinking styles*. New York: Cambridge University Press.

Sternberg, R. J. (1999). The theory of successful intelligence. *Review of General Psychology, 3*, 292–316.

Sternberg, R. J., Conway, B. E., Keton, J. L., & Bernstein, M. (1981). People's conceptions of intelligence. *Journal of Personality & Social Psychology, 41*, 37–55.

Sternberg, R. J., & Grigorenko, E. (Eds.) (1997). *Intelligence, heredity and environment*. New York: Cambridge University Press.

Sternberg, R. J., & Ruzgis, P. (Eds.) (1994). *Personality and intelligence*. New York: Cambridge University Press.

Sternberg, R. J., & Wagner, R. K. (Eds.) (1986). *Practical intelligence: Nature and origins of competence in everyday world*. New York: Cambridge University Press.

Sternberg, R. J., & Williams, W. M. (1997). Does the Graduate Record Examination predict meaningful success in the graduate training of psychology? A case study. *American Psychologist, 52*, 630–641.

Stevenson, M. K., Kanfer, F. H., & Higgins, J. M. (1984). Effects of goal specificity and time cues on pain tolerance. *Cognitive Therapy and Research, 8*, 415–426.

Stock, J., & Cervone, D. (1990). Proximal goal-setting and self-regulatory processes. *Cognitive Therapy and Research, 14*, 483–498.

Stokols, D. (1987). Conceptual strategies of environmental psychology. In D. Stokols & I. Altman (Eds.), *Handbook of Environmental Psychology* (pp. 41–71). New York: Wiley.

Strang, H. R., Lawrence, E. C., & Fowler, P. C. (1978). Effects of assigned goal level and knowl-edge of results on arithmetic computation: A laboratory study. *Journal of Applied Psychology, 63*, 29–39.

Strasburger, V. C. (1995). *Adolescents and the media. Medical and psychological impact*. Thousand Oaks, CA: Sage.

Strathman, A., Gleicher, F., Boninger, D. S., & Edwards, C. S. (1994). The consideration of future consequences: Weighing immediate and distant outcomes of behavior. *Journal of Personality and Social Psychology, 66*, 742–752.

Strauman, T. J. (1989). Self-discrepancies in clinical depression and social phobia: Cognitive structures that underlie emotional disorders? *Journal of Abnormal Psychology, 98*, 14–22.

Strauman, T. J. (1992). Self-guides, autobiographical memory, and anxiety and dysphoria: Towards a cognitive model of vulnerability to emotional distress. *Journal of Abnormal Psychology, 101*, 87–95.

Strauman, T. J., & Higgins, E. T. (1987). Automatic activation of self-discrepancies and emotional syndromes: When cognitive structures influence affect. *Journal of Personality and Social Psychology, 53*, 1004–1014.

Strauman, T. J., & Higgins, E. T. (1988). Self-discrepancies as predictors of vulnerability to distinct syndromes of chronic emotional distress. *Journal of Personality, 56*, 685–707.

Strauman, T. J., Lemieux, A. M., & Coe, C. L. (1993). *Journal of Personality & Social Psychology, 64*, 1042–1052.

Strauman, T. J., Vookles, J., Berenstein, V., Chaiken, S., & Higgins, E. T. (1991). Self-discrepancies and vulnerability to body dissatisfaction and disordered eating. *Journal of Personality and Social Psychology, 61*, 946–956.

Strelau, J. (1983). *Temperament, personality, activity*. New York: Academic Press.

Strelau, J. (1997). The contribution of Pavlov's Typology of CNS properties to personality research. *European Psychologist, 2*, 125–138.

Strelau, J. (1998). *Temperament: A psychological perspective*. New York: Plenum.

Strelau, J., & Angleitner, A. (Eds.) (1991) *Explorations in temperament: International perspectives on theory and measurement*. New York: Plenum Press.

Strelau, J., Angleitner, A., Bantelmann, J., & Ruch, W. (1990). The Strelau Temperament Inventory-Revised (STI-R): theoretical considerations and scale development. *European Journal of Personality, 4*, 209–235.

Strelau, J., Angleitner, A., & Ruch, W. (1990). Strelau Temperament Inventory (STI); general review and studies based on German samples. In J. N. Butcher & C. D. Spielberger (Eds.), *Advances in personality assessment* (Vol. 8, pp. 187–241). Hillsdale, NJ: Erlbaum.

Strelau, J., & Plomin, R. (1992). A tale of two theories of temperament. In G. V. Caprara & G. L. Van Heck (Eds.) *Modern personality psychology* (pp. 327–351). London: Harvester Wheatsheaf.

Strelau, J., & Zawadzki, B. (1995). The formal characteristics of behaviour temperament inventory (FCB-TI): validity studies. *European Journal of Personality, 9*, 207–229.

Stromquist, V. J., & Strauman, T. J. (1991). Children's social constructs: Nature, assessment, and association with adaptive versus maladaptive behavior. *Social Cognition, 9*, 330–358.

Stryker, S. (1990). Symbolic interactionism: Themes and variations. In M. Rosenberg & R. Turner (Eds.), *Social psychology* (pp. 3–29). New Brunswick, NJ: Transactions Publishers.

Suh, E., Diener, E., Oishi, S., & Triandis, H. C. (1998). The shifting basis of life satisfaction judgments across cultures: Emotions versus norms. *Journal of Personality and Social Psychology, 74*, 482–493.

Sullivan, H. (1953). *The interpersonal theory of psychiatry.* New York: Norton.

Sulloway, F. J. (1996). *Born to rebel.* New York: Pantheon Books.

Suh, E., Diener, E., Oishi, S., & Triandis, H. C. (1998). The shifting basis of life satisfaction judgments across cultures: Emotions versus norms. *Journal of Personality and Social Psychology, 74*, 482–493.

Susman, E. J., Inoff-Germain, G., Nottelmann, E. D., Loriaux, L., Cutler, G. B., & Chrousos, G. P. (1987). Hormones, emotional dispositions, and aggressive attributes in young adolescents. *Child Development, 58*, 1114–1134.

Sutton, S. K., & Davidson, R. J. (1997). Prefrontal brain asymmetry: A biological substrate of the behavioral approach and inhibition systems. *Psychological Science, 8*, 204–210.

Swaab, D., & Fliers, E. (1985). A sexually dimorphic nucleus in the human brain. *Science, 228*, 1112–1115.

Swann, W. B. Jr. (1983). Self-verification: Bringing social reality into harmony with the self. In J. Suls & A. G. Greenwald (Eds.), *Psychological perspectives on the self* (Vol. 2, pp. 33–66). Hillsdale, NJ: Erlbaum.

Symons, D. (1979). *The evolution of human sexuality.* New York: Oxford University Press.

Szarota, P. (1996). Taxonomy of the Polish personality-descriptive adjectives of the highest frequency of use. *Polish Psychological Bulletin, 27*, 343–351.

Szirmak, Z., & De Raad, B. (1994). Taxonomy and structure of Hungarian personality traits. *European Journal of Personality, 8*, 95–117.

Szmanski, M. L., & Cach, T. F. (1995). Body-image disturbances and self-discrepancy theory: Expansion of the body-image ideals questionnaire. *Journal of Social and Clinical Psychology, 14*, 134–146.

Tangney, J. P., Niedenthal, P. M., Covert, M. V., & Barlow, D. H. (1998). Are shame and guilt related to distinct self-discrepancies? A test of Higgins's hypotheses. *Journal of Personality and Social Psychology, 75*, 256–268.

Tangey, J. P., Wagner, P. E., Fletcher, C., & Gramzow, R. (1992). Shamed into anger? The relation of shame and guilt to anger and self-reported aggression. *Journal of Personality and Social Psychology, 62*, 669–675.

Taubman, P., & Behrman, J. R. (1986). Effects of number and position of siblings on child and adult outcomes. *Social Biology, 33*, 22–34.

Taylor, J. A. (1953). A personality scale of manifest anxiety. *Journal of Abnormal & Social Psychology, 48*, 285–290.

Taylor, S. (1983). Adjustment to threatening events: A theory of cognitive adaptation. *American Psychologist, 38*, 1161–1173.

Taylor, S. (1989). *Positive Illusions.* New York: Basic Books.

Taylor, S. E., & Brown, J. D. (1988). Illusion and well-being: A social-psychological perspective on mental health. *Psychological Bulletin, 103*, 193–210.

Tellegen, A. (1982). *Brief manual for the Differential Personality Questionnaire.* Unpublished manuscript. Minneapolis: University of Minnesota

Tellegen, A. (1985). Structures of mood and personality and their relevance to assessing anxiety, with an emphasis on self-report. In A. Tuma & J. D. Maser (Eds.), *Anxiety and the anxiety disorders* (pp. 681–706). Hillsdale, NJ: Erlbaum.

Tellegen, A., Lykken, D., Bouchard, T. J., Wilcox, K. J., Segal, N., & Rich, S. (1988). Personality similarity in twins reared apart and together. *Journal of Personality and Social Psychology, 54*, 1031–1039.

Teplov, B. (1972). The problem of types of human higher nervous activity and methods of determining them. In V. Nebylitsyn & J. A. Gray (Eds.), *Biological bases of individual behavior* (pp. 1–10). New York: Academic Press.

Terman, L. M. (1938). *Psychological factors in marital happiness.* New York: McGraw-Hill.

Terman, L. M., & Miles, C. (1936). *Sex and personality.* New York: McGraw-Hill.

Terman, L. M., & Oden, M. H. (1947). *Genetic studies of genius: The gifted child grows up.* Stanford., CA: Stanford University Press.

Thagard, P. (1992). *Conceptual revolutions.* Princeton, NJ: Princeton University Press.

Thelen, E. (1992). Development as a dynamic system. *Current Directions in Psychological Science, 1*, 189–193.

Thelen, E., & Smith, L. (1994). *A Dynamic Systems approach to the development of cognition and action.* Cambridge, MA: The MIT Press.

Thomä, E., & Kächele, H. (1985). *Lehrbuch der psychoanalytischen therapie.* Berlin: Springer.

Thomas, A., & Chess, S. (1977). *Temperament and development.* New York: Bruner/Mazel.

Thomas, A., & Chess, S. (1980). *The dynamics of psychological development.* New York, Bruner/Mazel.

Thomas, A., & Chess, S. (1986). The New York longitudinal study: From infancy to early adult life. In R. Plomin and J. Dunn (Eds.) *The study of temperament changes, continuities, and challenges.* Hillsdale, NJ: Erlbaum.

Thompson, R. F. (1985). *The brain: An introduction to neuroscience.* New York: W. H. Freeman.

Thoreson, C. E., & Mahoney, M. J. (1974). *Behavioral self-control.* New York: Holt, Rinehart, & Winston.

Thornton, G., & Byham, W. (1982). *Assessment centers and managerial performance.* New York: Academic Press.

Thurstone, L. L. (1934). The vectors of mind. *Psychological Review, 41,* 1–32.

Thurstone, L. L (1935) *The vectors of mind.* London: Macmillan.

Thurstone, L. L. (1938). *Primary mental abilities.* Chicago: University of Chicago Press.

Thurstone, L. L. (1947). *Multiple factor analysis.* Chicago: University of Chicago Press.

Tice, D. M. (1989). Metatraits: Interitem variance as personality assessment. In D. M. Buss & N. Cantor (Eds.), *Personality psychology: Recent trends and emerging directions* (pp. 194–200). New York: Springer-Verlag.

Tillema, J., Cervone, D., & Scott, W. D. (in press.) Negative mood, perceived self-efficacy, and personal standards in dysphoria: The effects of contextual cues on self-defeating patterns of cognition. *Cognitive Therapy and Research.*

Tipton, R. M., & Worthington, E. L. (1984). The measurement of generalized self-efficacy: A study of construct validity. *Journal of Personality Assessment, 48,* 545–548.

Tolman, E. C. (1932). *Purposive behavior in animals and men.* New York: Appleton-Century-Crofts.

Tomarken, A. J., Davidson, R. J., Wheeler, R. E., & Doss, R. C. (1992). Individual differences in anterior brain asymmetry and fundamental dimensions of emotion. *Journal of Personality & Social Psychology, 62,* 676–687.

Tomarken, A. J., Davidson, R. J., Wheeler, R. E., & Kinney, L. (1992). Psychometric properties of resting anterior EEG asymmetry: Temporal stability and internal consistency. *Psychophysiology, 29,* 576–592.

Tomkins, S. S. (1962). *Affect, imagery, and consciousness, Vol. I. The positive affects.* New York: Springer-Verlag.

Tomkins, S. S. (1963). *Affect, imagery, and consciousness, Vol. II. The negative affects.* New York: Springer-Verlag.

Tomkins, S. S. (1979). Script theory: Differential magnification of affects. In H. E. Howe & R. A. Dienstbier (Eds.), *Nebraska symposium on motivation* (Vol. 26; pp. 201–236). Lincoln: University of Nebraska Press.

Tomkins, S. S. (1981). The quest for primary motives: Biography and autobiography of an idea. *Journal of Personality and Social Psychology, 41,* 306–329.

Tomkins, S. S. (1984). Affect theory. In K. R. Sherer & P. Ekman (Eds.), *Approaches to emotion* (pp. 163–195). Hillsdale, NJ: Erlbaum.

Tooby, J., & Cosmides, L. (1990a). The past explains the present: Emotional adaptations and the structure of ancestral environments. *Ethnology and Sociobiology, 11,* 375–424.

Tooby, J., & Cosmides, L. (1990b). On the universality of human nature and the uniqueness of the individual: The role of genetics and adaptation. *Journal of Personality, 58,* 17–67.

Tooby, J., & Cosmides, L. (1992). Psychological foundations of culture. In J. Barkow, L. Cosmides, & J. Tooby (Eds.), *The adapted mind* (pp. 19–136). New York: Oxford University Press.

Treas, J., & Torrechilha, R. (1995). The older population. In R. Farley (Ed.), *The state of the union* (pp. 47–92). New York: Russell Sage Foundation.

Treisman, A. M. (1967). Strategies and models of selective attention. *Psychological Review, 76,* 282–299.

Triandis, H. C. (1990). Cross-cultural studies of individualism and collectivism. In J. J. Berman (Ed.), *Nebraska Symposium on Motivation (Vol. 37,* pp. 41–143). Lincoln, Nebraska: University of Nebraska Press.

Triandis, H. C. (1994). Culture and social behavior. New York: McGraw-Hill.

Triandis, H. C. (1997). Cross-cultural perspectives on personality. In R. Hogan, J. Johnson, & S. Briggs (Eds.), *Handbook of personality psychology* (pp. 439–464). San Diego, CA: Academic Press.

Triandis, H. (1995). *Individualism and collectivism.* Boulder, CO: Westview Press.

Trivers, R. (1972). Parental investment and sexual selection. In B. Campbell (Ed.), *Sexual selection and the descent of man* (pp. 136–179). Chicago: Aldine.

Trope, Y. (1983). Self-assessment in achievement behavior. In J. M. Suls & A. G. Greenwald (Eds.), *Psychological perspectives on the self* (Vol. 2., pp. 93–122). Hillsdale, NJ: Erlbaum.

Trope, Y. (1986). Identification and inferential processes in dispositional attribution. *Psychological Review, 93,* 239–257.

Tubbs, M. E. (1986). Goal setting: A meta-analytic examination of the empirical evidence. *Journal of Applied Psychology, 71,* 474–483.

Tucker, J. S. Friedman, H. S., Schwartz, J. E., Criqui, M. H., Tomlinson-Keasey, C., Wingard, D. L., & Martin, L. R. (1997). Parental divorce: effects on individual behavior and longevity.

*Journal of Personality and Social psychology, 73,* 381–391.

Tulving, E. (1972). Episodic and semantic memory. In E. Tulving & W. Donaldson (Eds.), *Organization of memory.* New York: Academic Press.

Tulving, E. E., & Thomson, D. M. (1973). Encoding specificity and retrieval processes in episodic memory. *Psychological Bulletin, 76,* 105–110.

Tunis, S. L., Fridhandler, B. M., & Horowitz, M. J. (1990). Identifying schematized views of self with significant others: Convergence of quantitative and clinical methods. *Journal of Personality and Social Psychology, 59,* 1279–1286.

Tupes, E. C., & Christal, R. C. (1961). *Recurrent personality factors based on trait ratings.* Technical report, USAF, Lackland Air Force Base, TX.

Turkheimer, E. (1998). Heritability and biological explanation. *Psychological Review, 105,* 782–791.

Tversky, A., & Kahneman, D. (1974). Judgment under uncertainty: Heuristics and biases. *Science, 185,* 1124–1131.

Tversky, A., & Kahneman, D. (1982). Judgments of and by representativeness. In D. Kahneman, P. Slovic, & A. Tversky (Eds.), *Judgment under uncertainty: Heuristics and biases* (pp. 84–100). New York: Cambridge University Press.

Uleman, J. S. (1989). A framework for thinking intentionally about unintended thoughts. In J. S. Uleman & J. A. Bargh (Eds.), *Unintended thought* (pp. 425–449). New York: Guilford.

Uleman, J. S., Newman, L. S., & Moskowitz, G. B. (1996). People as flexible interpreters: Evidence and issues from spontaneous trait inference. In M. P. Zanna (Ed.), *Advances in Experimental Social Psychology, Vol. 29* (pp. 211–279). San Diego: Academic Press.

Uleman, J. S., Winborne, W. C., Winter, L., & Schecter, D. (1986). Personality differences in spontaneous personality inferences at encoding. *Journal of Personality and Social Psychology, 51,* 396–403.

Unger, R. (1979). Toward a redefinition of sex and gender. *American Psychologist, 34,* 1085–1094.

Vaillant, G. E. (1977). *Adaptation to life.* Boston, MA: Little, Brown & Co.

Vaillant, G. E. (Ed.) (1992). *Ego mechanisms of defense: A guide for clinicians and researchers.* Washington, D. C.: American Psychiatric Association.

Vaillant, G. E. (1993). *The wisdom of the ego.* Cambridge, MA: Harvard University Press.

Vallacher, R. R., & Nowak, A. (1994). *Dynamical systems in social psychology.* San Diego, CA: Academic Press.

Vallacher, R. R., & Nowak, A. (1997). The emergence of dynamical social psychology. *Psychological Inquiry, 8,* 73–99.

Vallacher, R. R., & Wegner, D. M. (1986). What do people think they're doing?: Action identification in human behavior. *Psychological Review, 94,* 3–15.

Valsiner, J. (1998). *The guided mind: A sociogenetic approach to personality.* Cambridge, MA: Harvard University Press.

Van Geert, P. (1998). A dynamic systems model of basic developmental mechanisms: Piaget, Vygotsky, and Beyond. *Psychological Review, 105,* 634–677.

Van Heck, G. L. (1984). The construction of a general taxonomy of situations. In H. Bonarius, G. L. Van Heck, & N. Smid (Eds.), *Personality psychology in Europe: Theoretical and empirical developments* (Vol. 1, pp. 149–164). Lisse, The Netherlands: Swets & Zeitlinger.

Van Heck, G. L. (1989). Situation concepts: Definitions and classification. In P. J. Hettema (Ed.), *Personality and environment* (pp. 53–69). Chichester, UK: Wiley.

Van Heck, G. L., Perugini, M., Caprara, G. V., & Froger, J. (1994) The big five as tendencies in situations. *Personality and Individual Differences, 16,* 715–731.

Van Ijzendoorn, M. (1995). Adult attachment representations, parental responsiveness, and infant attachment: A meta-analysis on the predictive validity of the adult attachment interview. *Psychological Bulletin, 117,* 387–401.

Van Ijzendoorn, M. H., & Barkemans-Kranenburg, M. (1997). Intergenerational transmission of attachment. A move to the contextual level. In L. Atkinson & K. Zucker (Eds.), Attachment and psychopathology (pp. 135–170). New York: Guilford.

Van Ijzendoorn, M. H., Juffer, F., & Duyvesteyn, M. (1995). Breaking the intergenerational cycle of insecure attachment: A review of the effects of attachment-based interventions on maternal sensitivity and infant security. *Journal of Child Psychology and Psychiatry, 36,* 225–248.

Van Ijzendoorn, M. H., & Kroonenberg, P. (1988). Cross-cultural patterns of attachment: A meta-analysis of the strange situation. *Child Development* (pp. 713–734), *59,* 147–156.

Van Ijzendoorn, M. H., & Sagi, A. (1999) Cross cultural patterns of attachment: universal and contextual dimensions. In J. Cassidy & P. Shaver (Eds.) *Handbook of attachment theory and research.* (pp 713–734) New York: Guilford.

Van Lange, P. A. M., Otten, W., De Bruin, E. M. N., & Joireman, J. A. (1997). Development of prosocial, individualistic and competitive orientation: Theory and preliminary evidence. *Journal of Personality and Social Psychology, 73,* 733–746.

Van Ryn, M., & Vinokur, A. D. (1992). How did it work? An examination of the mechanisms through which an intervention for the unemployed promoted job-search behavior. *American Journal of Community Psychology, 20,* 577–597.

Vansteelandt, K., & Mechelen, I. V. (1998). Individual differences in situation-behavior profiles: A triple typology model. *Journal of Personality and Social Psychology, 75,* 751–765.

Vernon, P. A. (1993). *Biological approaches to the study of human intelligence.* Norwood, NJ: Ablex.

Vernon, P. E. (1964). *Personality assessment: A critical survey.* New York: Wiley.

Vico, G. B. (1725). *The New Science.* English translation by T. G. Bergi & H. Fisch, Ithaca N.Y.: Cornell University Press. 1948.

Viken, R. J., Rose, R. J., Kaprio, J., & Koskenvuo, M. (1994). A developmental genetic analysis of adult personality: Extraversion and neuroticism from 18 to 59 years of age. *Journal of Personality & Social Psychology, 66,* 722–730.

Vinokur, A. D., van Ryn, M., Gramlich, E. M., & Price, R. H. (1991). Long-term follow-up and benefit-cost analysis of the Jobs Program: A preventive intervention for the unemployed. *Journal of Applied Psychology, 76,* 213–219.

Vinokur, A. D., & Schul, Y. (1997). Mastery and inoculation against setbacks as active ingredients in the JOBS intervention for the unemployed. *Journal of Consulting and Clinical Psychology, 65,* 867–877.

Vygotsky, L. (1925). Sozanie kak problema psichologii povedenija. [Italian Translation] La coscienza come problema della psicologia del comportamento, Storia e critica della psicologia, 1, 1980, pp. 268–295.

Vygotsky, L. (1929). The problem of the cultural development of the child. *Journal of Genetic Psychology, 36,* 415–434.

Vygotsky, L. (1934). *Thought and language.* English translation. Cambridge, MA: MIT Press. 1962.

Wachs, T. D., & G. A. Kohnstamm (Eds.) (In press), *Temperament in context.* Hillsdale, NJ: Erlbaum.

Wagner, R. K., & Sternberg, R. J. (1985). Practical intelligence in real-world pursuits: The role of tacit knowledge. *Journal of Personality and Social Psychology, 49,* 436–458.

Waldrop, M. M. (1992). *Complexity: The emerging science at the edge of order and chaos.* New York: Simon & Schuster.

Walker, R. E., & Foley, J. M. (1973). Social intelligence: Its history and measurement. *Psychological Reports, 33,* 839–864.

Wallace, J. (1966). An abilities conception of personality: Some implications for personality measurement. *American Psychologist, 21,* 132–138.

Wallace, J. (1967). What units shall we employ? Allport's question revisited. *Journal of Consulting Psychology, 31,* 56–64.

Waller, N., & Shaver, P. R. (1994). The importance of nongenetic influences on romantic love styles: A twin-family study. *Psychological Science, 5,* 268–274.

Wartella, E. (1995). Media and problem behaviours in young people, in M. Rutter & D. Smith (Eds.), *Psychosocial disorders in young people* (pp. 296–323). Chichester, UK: John Wiley & Sons.

Watson, D. (2000). *Mood and temperament.* New York: Guilford.

Watson, D., & Clark, L. A. (1992). Affects separable and inseparable: On the hierarchical arrangement of the negative affects. *Journal of Personality and Social Psychology, 62,* 489–505.

Watson, D., & Clark, L. A. (1994). Emotions, moods, traits, and temperaments: Conceptual distinctions and empirical findings. In In P. Ekman & R. J. Davidson (Eds.), *The nature of emotion: Fundamental questions* (pp. 89–93). New York: Oxford University Press.

Watson, D., & Clark, L. A. (1997a). Extraversion and its positive emotional core. In R. Hogan, J. Johnson & S. Briggs (Eds.), *Handbook of personality psychology.* (pp. 767–793) San Diego, CA: Academic Press.

Watson, D., & Clark, L. A. (1997b). Measurement and mismeasurement of mood. *Journal of Personality Assessment, 68,* 267–296.

Watson, D., Clark, L. A., & Tellegen, A. (1988). Development and validation of brief measures of positive and negative affect: The PANAS scales. *Journal of Personality and Social Psychology, 54,* 1063–1070.

Watson, D., & Tellegen, A. (1985). Toward a consensual structure of mood. *Psychological Bulletin, 98,* 219–235.

Watson, D., & Walker, L. M. (1996). The long-term stability and predictive validity of trait measures of affect. *Journal of Personality and Social Psychology, 70,* 567–577.

Watson, J., & Crick, F. (1953a). Molecular structure of nuclei acids. *Nature, 171,* 737–738.

Watson, J., & Crick, F. (1953b). Genetical implications of the structure of deoxyribonucleic acid. *Nature, 171,*964–967

Watzlavick, P., Bavelas, J., & Jackson, D. (1967). *Pragmatics of human communication.* New York: Norton.

Webb, E. (1915). Character and intelligence. *British Journal of Psychology Monographs,* Nos 1&3.

Wechsler, D. (1981). *Manual for the Wechsler Adult Intelligence Scale-Revised.* New York: Psychological Corporation

Wegner, D. (1997). When the antidote is the poison: Ironic mental control processes. *Psychological Science, 8,* 148–150.

Wegner, D. M. (1994). Ironic processes of mental control. *Psychological Review, 101,* 34–52.

Wegner, D. M., Erber, R., & Zanakos, S. (1993). Ironic processes in the mental control of mood and mood-related thought. *Journal of Personality and Social Psychology, 65,* 1093–1104.

Wegner, D. M., Schneider, D. J., Carter, S., III, & White, L. (1987). Paradoxical effects of thought suppression. *Journal of Personality and Social Psychology, 53,* 5–13.

Wegner, D. M., Shortt, J. W., Blake, A. W., & Page, M. S. (1990). The suppression of exciting thoughts. *Journal of Personality and Social Psychology, 58,* 409–418.

Wegner, D. M., & Wenzlaff, R. M. (1996). Mental control. In E. T. Higgins & A. W. Kruglanski (Eds.), *Social psychology: Handbook of basic principles* (pp. 466–492). New York: Guilford.

Wegner, D. M., & Wheatley, T. (1999). What cognitive mechanisms make us feel as if we are acting consciously and willfully? *American Psychologist, 54*, 480–492.

Weinberg, R. S., Gould, D., & Jackson, A. (1979). Expectations and performance: An empirical test of Bandura's self-efficacy theory. *Journal of Sport Psychology, 1*, 320–331.

Weinberger, D. A., & Schwartz, E. (1990). Distress and restraint as superordinate dimensions of self-reported adjustment: A typological perspective. *Journal of Personality, 58*, 381–417.

Weinberger, D. A., Schwartz, G., & Davidson, R. J. (1979). Low-anxious, high-anxious, and repressive coping styles: Psychometric patterns and behavioral and psychological responses to stress. *Journal of Abnormal Psychology, 88*, 369–380.

Weiner, B. (1985). An attributional theory of achievement motivations and emotion. *Psychological Review, 92*, 548–573.

Weiner, B. (1986). *An attributional theory of motivation and emotion.* New York: Springer-Verlag.

Weiner, B. (1992). *Human motivation.* Newbury Park, CA: Sage.

Weiner, B., & Graham, S. (1984). An attributional approach to emotional development. In C. E. Izard, J. Kagan, & R. B. Zajonc (Eds.), *Emotions, cognition, and behavior* (pp. 167–191). New York: Cambridge University Press.

Weinstein, N. D. (1980). Unrealistic optimism about future life events. *Journal of Personality and Social Psychology, 39*, 806–820.

Weiskrantz, L. (1995). Blindsight: Not an island unto itself. *Current Directions in Psychological Science, 4*, 146–151.

Weitlauf, J., Smith, R. E., & Cervone, D. (in press). Generalization of coping skills training: Effects of self-defense instruction on women's task-specific and generalized self-efficacy, aggressiveness, and personality. *Journal of Applied Psychology.*

Wellman, H. M., & Gelman, S. A. (1998). Knowledge acquisition in foundational domains. In Kuhn pp. 523–573.

Werner, E. E., & Smith, R. S. (1982). *Vulnerable but invincible.* New York: McGraw-Hill.

Werner, E. E., & Smith, R. S (1992). *Overcoming the odds: High risk children from birth to adulthood.* Ithaca, NY: Cornell University Press.

Westen, D. (1991). Social cognition and object relations. *Psychological Bulletin, 109*, 429–455.

Westen, D. (1998). The scientific legacy of Sigmund Freud: Toward a psychodynamically informed psychological science. *Psychological Bulletin, 124*, 333–371.

Westen, D., Klepser, J., Ruffins, S. A., Silverman, M., Lifton, N., & Boekamp, J. (1991). Object relations in childhood and adolescence: The development of working representations. *Journal of Consulting and Clinical Psychology, 59*, 400–409.

Westerlundh, B., & Sjoback, H. (1986). *Activation of intrapsychic conflict and defense: The amauroscopic technique.* In U. Hentschel, G. Smith & J. Draguns (Eds.), The roots of perception (pp. 161–216). Amsterdam: North Holland.

Westerlundh, B., & Smith, G. (1992). Psychoanalysis as a theory of personality. In G. V. Caprara & G. Van Heck (Eds.), *Modern personality psychology: Critical reviews and new directions* (pp. 113–132). London: Harvester-Weatsheaf.

Whalen, P. J. (1998). Fear, vigilance, and ambiguity: Initial neuroimaging studies of the human amygdala. *Contemporary Directions in Psychological Science, 7*, 177–188.

Wheeler, R. E., Davidson, R. J., & Tomarken, A. J. (1993). Frontal brain asymmetry and emotional reactivity: A biological substrate of affective style. *Psychophysiology, 30*, 82–89.

White, R. W. (1959). Motivation reconsidered: The concept of competence. *Psychological Review, 66*, 297–333.

White, R. W. (1981). Exploring personality the long way: The study of lives. In A. I. Rabin, J. Aronoff, A. M. Barclay & R. Zucker (Eds.), *Further explorations in personality* (pp. 3–19). New York: Wiley.

Whiting, B., & Child, I. (1953). *Child training and personality.* New Haven: Yale University Press.

WHO (1993). *Life skills education in schools.* Geneva: WHO.

Widaman, K. F. (1985). Hierarchical nested covariance structure models for multitrait-multimethod data. *Applied Psychological Measurement, 9*, 1–26.

Wiedenfeld, S. A., O'Leary, A., Bandura, A., Brown, S., Levine, S., & Raska, K. (1990). Impact of perceived self-efficacy in coping with stressors on components of the immune system. *Journal of Personality and Social Psychology, 59*, 1082–1094.

Wiggins, J. S. (1979). A psychological taxonomy of trait-descriptive terms: The interpersonal domain. *Journal of Personality and Social Psychology, 37*, 395–412.

Wiggins, J. S. (Ed.) (1996). *The five-factor model of personality: Theoretical perspectives.* New York: Guilford Press.

Wiggins, J. S. (1996). An informal history of the interpersonal circumplex tradition. *Journal of Personality Assessment, 66*, 217–233.

Wiggins, J., Steiger, J., & Gaelik, L. (1981). Evaluating circumplexity in personality data. *Multivariate Behavioral Research, 16*, 263–285.

Williams, S. L. (1990). Guided mastery treatment of agoraphobia: Beyond stimulus exposure. In M. Hersen, R. M. Eisler, & P. M. Miller (Eds.),

*Progress in Behavior Modification* (Vol. 26, pp. 89–121). Newbury Park, CA: Sage.

Williams, S. L. (1995). Self-efficacy, anxiety, and phobic disorders. In J. E. Maddux (Ed.), *Self-efficacy, adaptation, and adjustment: Theory, research, and application* (pp. 69–107). New York: Plenum.

Williams, S. L., & Cervone, D. (1998). Social cognitive theory. In D. Barone, M. Hersen, & V. B. Van Hasselt (Eds.), *Advanced personality* (pp. 173–207). New York: Plenum.

Williams, S. L., Dooseman, G., & Kleifield, E. (1984). Comparative effectiveness of guided mastery and exposure treatments for intractable phobias. *Journal of Consulting and Clinical Psychology, 52,* 505–518.

Williams, S. L., & Kinney, P. J. (1991). Performance and nonperformance strategies for coping with acute pain: The role of perceived self-efficacy, expected outcomes, and attention. *Cognitive Therapy and Research, 15,* 1–19.

Williams, S. L., & Kinney, P. J., & Falbo, J. (1989). Generalization of therapeutic changes in agoraphobia: The role of perceived self-efficacy. *Journal of Consulting and Clinical Psychology, 57,* 436–442.

Wilson, E. O. (1975). *Sociobiology: The new synthesis.* Cambridge, MA: Harvard University Press.

Wilson, G. D. (1997). Sex and personality. In H. Nyborg (Ed.), *The scientific study of human nature* (pp. 165–188). New York: Pergamon Elsevier Science Ltd.

Wilson, G. D., Barrett, P. T., & Gray, J. A. (1989). Human reactions to reward and punishment: A questionnaire examination of Gray's personality theory. *British Journal of Psychology, 80,* 509–515.

Wilson, G. D., Gray, J. A., & Barrett, P. T. (1990). A factor analysis of the Gray-Wilson personality questionnaire. *Personality and Individual Differences, 11,* 1037–1045.

Wilson, T., & Brekke, N. (1994). Mental contamination and mental correction: Unwanted influences on judgments and evaluations. *Psychological Bulletin, 116,* 117–142.

Winnicott, D. (1958). *Collected papers: Through pediatrics to psychoanalysis.* London: Tavistock Publications

Winter, L., & Uleman, J. S. (1984). When are social judgments made? Evidence for the spontaneousness of trait inferences. *Journal of Personality and Social Psychology, 47,* 237–252.

Winter, L., Uleman, J. S., & Cunniff, C. (1985). How automatic are social judgments? *Journal of Personality and Social Psychology, 49,* 904–917.

Witkin, H., & Goodenough, D. (1981). *Cognitive styles: Essence and origins. Psychological Issues, 51.* New York: International Universities Press.

Wood, J. V. (1989). Theory and research concerning social comparisons of personal attributes. *Psychological Bulletin, 106,* 231–248.

Wood, R. E., & Bandura, A. (1989). Social cognitive theory of organizational management. *Academy of Management Review, 14,* 361–384.

Wood, R. E., Mento, A. J., & Locke, E. A. (1987). Task complexity as a moderator of goal effects: A meta-analysis. *Journal of Applied Psychology, 72,* 416–425.

Woolfolk, R. L., Novalany, J., Gara, M. A., Allen, L. A., & Polino, M. (1995). Self-complexity, self-evaluation, and depression: An examination of form and content within the self-schema. *Journal of Personality and Social Psychology, 68,* 1108–1120.

Wright, J. C., & Mischel, W. (1987). A conditional approach to dispositional constructs: The local predictability of social behavior. *Journal of Personality and Social Psychology, 53,* 1159–1177.

Wundt, W. (1896). *Grundriss der Psychologie.* Leipzig: Engelmann.

Wundt, W. (1902). *Outlines of Psychology* (Translated by C. H. Judd). Leipzig: Englemann.

Wylie, A. (1995). Unification and convergence in archaeological explanation: The agricultural 'wave of advance' and the origins of Indo-European languages. *Southern Journal of Philosophy,* Supplement, *Explanation in the Human Sciences, 34,* 1–30.

Yang, K. S., & Bond, M. H. (1990). Exploring implicit personality theories with indigenous or imported constructs: The Chinese case. *Journal of Personality and Social Psychology, 58,* 1087–1095.

Youniss, J. (1980). *Parents and peers in social development.* Chicago: University of Chicago Press.

Youniss, J., & Smollar, J. (1985). *Adolescent relations with mothers, fathers, and friends.* Chicago: University of Chicago Press.

Zajonc, R. B. (1968). Attitudinal effects of mere exposure. *Journal of Personality and Social Psychology* [Monograph] 9, 1–27.

Zajonc, R. B. (1976). Family configuration and intelligence. *Science, 192,* 227–236.

Zajonc, R. B. (1980). Feeling and thinking: Preferences need no inferences. *American Psychologist, 35,* 151–175.

Zajonc, R. B. (1983). Validating the confluence model. *Psychological Bulletin, 93,* 457–480.

Zajonc, R. B. (1998). Emotions. In D. T. Gilbert, S. T. Fiske, & G. Lindzey (Eds.), *The handbook of social psychology* (4th ed., Volume 1, pp. 591–632).

Zajonc, R. B., & Mullally, P. (1997). Birth order: Reconciling conflicting effects. *American Psychologist, 52,* 685–699.

Zelli, A., Cervone, D., & Huesmann, L. R. (1996). Behavioral experience and social inference: Individual differences in aggressive experience and spontaneous versus deliberate trait inference. *Social Cognition, 14,* 165–190.

Zelli, A., & Dodge, K. A. (1999). Personality development from the bottom up. In D. Cervone & Y. Shoda (Eds.), *The coherence of personality: Social-cognitive bases of consistency, variability, and organization* (pp. 94–126). New York: Guilford Press.

Zelli, A., Huesmann, L. R., & Cervone, D. (1995). Social inference and individual differences in aggression: Evidence for spontaneous judgments of hostility. *Aggressive Behavior, 21,* 405–417.

Zevon, M., & Tellegen, A. (1982). The structure of mood change: An idiographic/nomothetic analysis. *Journal of Personality and Social Psychology, 43,* 111–122.

Zillmann, D. (1978). Attribution and misattribution of excitatory reactions. In J. H. Harvey, W. Ickes & R. F. Kidd (Eds.), *New directions in attribution research. Vol. 2.* (pp. 335–368). Hillsdale, NJ: Lawrence Erlbaum Associates.

Zillmann, D., & Zillmann, M. (1996). Psychoneuro-endocrynology of social behavior. In T. Higgins & W. Kruglanski (Eds.), *Social psychology: Handbook of basic principles* (pp. 39–71). New York: Guilford.

Zimbardo, P. G. (1999). Discontinuity theory: Cognitive and social search for rationality and normality may lead to madness. In M. Zanna (Ed.), *Advances in Experimental Social Psychology* (Vol. 31, pp. 345–486). San Diego, CA: Academic Press.

Zimmerman, B. J. (1990). Self-regulating academic learning and achievement: The emergence of a social cognitive perspective. *Educational Psychology Review, 2,* 173–201.

Zola-Morgan, S. (1995). Localization of brain functions: The legacy of Franz Joseph Gall. *Annual Review of Neurosciences, 18,* 359–383.

Zuckerman, M. (1984). Sensation seeking: A comparative approach to human traits. *Behavioral and Brain Sciences, 7,* 413–471.

Zuckerman, M. (1991). *Psychobiology of personality.* New York: Cambridge University Press.

Zuckerman, M. (1994). *Behavioral expressions of biosocial bases of sensation seeking.* New York: Cambridge University Press.

Zuckerman, M. (1995). Good and bad humours: Biochemical bases of personality and its disorders. *Psychological Science, 6,* 325–332.

Zuckerman, M., Kuhlman, D. M., Joireman, J., Teta, P., & Kraft, M. (1993). A comparison of three structural models for personality: The big three, the big five and the alternative five. *Journal of Personality and Social Psychology, 65,* 757–768.

Zuckerman, M., & Lubin, B. (1965). Normative data for the Multiple Affect Adjective Check List. *Psychological Reports, 16,* 438.

Zuckerman, M., Kuhlman, D. M., Thornquist, M., & Kiers, H. (1991). Five (or three) robust questionnaire scale factors of personality without culture. *Personality and Individual Differences, 12,* 929–941.

# Author Index

# Subject Index